Strategic Survey 2011
The Annual Review of World Affairs

published by

 Routledge
Taylor & Francis Group

for

The International Institute for Strategic Studies

The International Institute for Strategic Studies

Arundel House | 13–15 Arundel Street | Temple Place | London | WC2R 3DX | UK

Strategic Survey 2011
The Annual Review of World Affairs

First published September 2011 by **Routledge**
4 Park Square, Milton Park, Abingdon, Oxon, OX14 4RN

for **The International Institute for Strategic Studies**
Arundel House, 13–15 Arundel Street, Temple Place, London, WC2R 3DX, UK

Simultaneously published in the USA and Canada by **Routledge**
270 Madison Ave., New York, NY 10016

Routledge is an imprint of Taylor & Francis, an Informa business

This publication has been prepared by the Director-General of the Institute and his Staff, who accept full responsibility for its contents, which describe and analyse events up to 30 June 2011. These do not, and indeed cannot, represent a consensus of views among the worldwide membership of the Institute as a whole.

British Library Cataloguing in Publication Data
A catalogue record for this book is available from the British Library

Library of Congress Cataloguing in Publication Data

ISBN 978-1-85743-618-1
ISSN 0459-7230

Contents

Strategic Geography (after p. 198)

Index of Regional Maps

Events at a Glance

July 2010–June 2011

July 2010

9   **Pakistan:** Two bombs kill 105 people in the Mohmand region of northwestern Pakistan.

11 **Uganda:** Bomb attacks on a rugby club and a restaurant in Kampala kill 76 people as they watch the football World Cup final on television. Somali Islamist group al-Shabaab claims responsibility and says Uganda and Burundi must withdraw peacekeeping troops from Somalia. Three Kenyans are later charged with murder.

12 **Sudan:** International Criminal Court charges President Omar al-Bashir with genocide over the conflict in Darfur. He had already been charged with war crimes and crimes against humanity.

15 **United States:** Oil company BP succeeds in stopping the flow of oil from a spill caused by the explosion of the *Deepwater Horizon* drilling rig on 20 April.

15 **Iran:** Nuclear scientist Shahram Amiri returns to Iran from the United States, more than a year after disappearing while on a pilgrimage to Mecca, Saudi Arabia. He claims to have been kidnapped and mistreated by the US Central Intelligence Agency, but Washington says he was in the US of his own free will and was also free to leave.

21 **North Korea:** US announces financial sanctions on North Korea in response to the sinking of a South Korean naval ship in March.

22 **Kosovo:** International Court of Justice rules that Kosovo's 2008 declaration of independence 'did not violate international law'.

29 **Pakistan:** Floods caused by exceptionally heavy monsoon rains cause massive flooding across the country, killing more than 1,700 people and affecting some 20m.

August 2010

4 **Kenya:** Voters approve new constitution reducing presidential powers, establishing a Senate, and providing for land reform.

5 **Chile:** Underground collapse traps 33 miners. On 13 October, all are rescued.

15 **Russia:** A ban on grain exports from Russia is introduced following a drought, causing a surge in global prices which accelerates from 2 September when the ban is extended into 2011. A consequent 30% rise in official bread prices in Mozambique causes food riots, killing 13 people, until it is rescinded.

16 **China:** Quarterly statistics show China overtakes Japan as second-largest economy behind the US.

17 **Iraq:** Bomb kills about 60 people at army recruitment centre in Baghdad. On 25 August, 56 people are killed in a wave of attacks across the country.

21 **Australia:** General election results in hung parliament. Labor Prime Minister Julia Gillard retains office at the head of a minority government.

24 **Mexico:** Troops find bodies of 72 migrants, murdered by a drug cartel while apparently trying to reach the US. Later, two people investigating the crime are found dead.

24 **Somalia:** Insurgents attack hotel in central Mogadishu killing 30 people including six members of parliament.

31 **Iraq:** US combat mission in Iraq ends, leaving 50,000 troops to support Iraqi forces.

September 2010

2 **Israel/Palestine:** US hosts first direct peace talks between Israeli and Palestinian leaders for 20 months. A second round is held on 14 September in Egypt. No progress is made and in December the US says direct talks will not resume.

6 **Lebanon:** Prime Minister Saad Hariri recants allegation that Syria had been behind the assassination in 2005 of his father, Rafik Hariri, saying it had been a 'political accusation'.

8 **Japan/China:** A Chinese trawler captain is arrested after his boat collides with two Japanese patrol vessels close to the disputed Senkaku/Diaoyu islands. Following a diplomatic row, he is released on 24 September.

12 **Turkey:** Voters support constitutional reforms in a referendum, giving parliament more say in appointing judges to a constitutional court and removing protection from leaders of a 1980 military coup.

12 **Switzerland:** Central banks agree to impose higher minimum capital requirements on the world's banks.

13 **Cuba:** Government announces labour-force reforms expected to lead to more than 500,000 workers losing government jobs.

19 **Sweden:** Centre-right coalition retains power as minority government, but far-right Sweden Democrats win 5.7% of votes and 20 out of 349 seats in parliament.

22 **Colombia:** Victor Julio Suarez Rojas, military commander of the FARC guerrilla group, is killed by the Colombian military.

28 **Russia:** Yuri Luzhkov, mayor of Moscow since 1992, is sacked by President Dmitry Medvedev. Sergei Sobyanin, a close ally of Prime Minister Vladimir Putin, is chosen to replace him.

28 **North Korea:** Kim Jong-un, youngest son of ruler Kim Jong-il, is appointed a general and made a vice-chairman of Central Military Commission of the Workers' Party, indicating that he will succeed his father. On 10 October, he appears with his father at a military parade.

30 **Ecuador:** State of emergency is declared as police uprising leads to President Rafael Correa being tear-gassed, and then rescued by soldiers after police prevent him from leaving a hospital.

30 **Pakistan:** NATO air strike on border post kills three Pakistani troops, causing Pakistan temporarily to close NATO supply routes into Afghanistan. Supply convoys stuck in Pakistan are attacked by the Taliban.

October 2010

1 **Nigeria:** Two car bombs explode in Abuja, killing 12 people, close to a ceremony celebrating the 50th anniversary of Nigeria's independence. A rebel group in the Niger delta had threatened to attack the event.

4 **Hungary:** Reservoir holding waste at a metals plant bursts, spilling toxic red sludge through villages, killing nine people and threatening an ecological disaster as it reaches the river Danube. However, damage is contained.

4 **Pakistan:** US drone attack reportedly kills eight militants of German nationality in North Waziristan.

8 **Norway:** Nobel Peace Prize is awarded to Chinese dissident Liu Xiaobo, serving an 11-year prison sentence on subversion charges. Beijing protests strongly and places his wife under house arrest. The award ceremony takes place on 10 December with an empty chair.

14 **Netherlands:** Coalition government headed by Mark Rutte is sworn in after four months of negotiations following June elections, which followed February collapse of previous government over the issue of Dutch troops in Afghanistan. The new government has the support of the anti-Islamic Party for Freedom.

16 **France:** Wave of strikes and protests over plans to raise retirement age causes fuel shortages. On 19 October, more than a million people demonstrate against the pension changes. On 27 October, National Assembly passes them.

18 **China:** Xi Jinping is appointed a vice-chairman of the Communist Party's Central Military Commission, increasing expectations that he will become China's next president in 2012.

20 **Saudi Arabia:** Obama administration notifies Congress of plan to sell $60 billion in arms to Saudi Arabia.

20 **United Kingdom:** Government announces sharp spending cuts to reduce the budget deficit. It plans to eliminate 500,000 public-sector jobs and to cut departmental spending by an average 19% over four years, or a total of £83 billion ($130bn). Defence spending is to be reduced by 8% in the same period, with cuts in personnel and equipment. Welfare benefits are cut, value-added tax increased and planned increases in the retirement age are accelerated.

25 **Indonesia:** Earthquake and tsunami off the west coast of Sumatra kill more than 400 people.

26 **Haiti:** Outbreak of cholera in earthquake-torn Haiti reaches Port-au-Prince, the capital, after killing more than 250 people. By 20 December, it has killed more than 2,500.

27 **Argentina:** Former President Nestor Kirchner, husband of current President Cristina Fernandez, dies of a heart attack, aged 60.

29 **United Kingdom, United Arab Emirates:** Unexploded bombs are found in the cargo holds of commercial aircraft at East Midlands airport in the UK and Dubai, UAE. The bombs were hidden in printer cartridges. They had travelled on flights that originated in Yemen and the packages were addressed to synagogues in Chicago, United States. Their discovery followed a tip-off from Saudi Arabia's intelligence agency.

31 **Iraq:** Attack by al-Qaeda-linked militants on Syriac Catholic church in Baghdad leaves 52 dead after security forces try to rescue worshippers.

31 **Brazil:** Dilma Rousseff, previously a close aide to outgoing President Luis Inácio 'Lula' da Silva, is elected to succeed him, defeating Jose Serra by 56% to 44%.

November 2010

2 **United States:** Republican Party makes large gains in Congressional elections, winning control of House of Representatives. Democrats lose six Senate seats but retain majority.

2 **UK/France:** UK Prime Minister David Cameron and French President Nicolas Sarkozy sign wide-ranging defence treaty, agreeing to cooperate on a joint task force, on aircraft carriers and other equipment, and on nuclear deterrents.

3 **United States:** Federal Reserve, the central bank, announces plan to buy up to $600bn of longer-term Treasury securities, in effect printing money with the aim of boosting economic recovery.

4 **Pakistan:** Attacks on mosques in Peshawar kill 71 people.

7 **Guinea:** Alpha Condé is elected president following two years of military rule, marking first democratic transfer of power since independence in 1958.

7 **Myanmar:** Parliamentary elections are held for the first time in 20 years, but are seen internationally as flawed. The Union Solidarity and Development Party, set up by the ruling military government, wins most of the seats.

12 **South Korea:** G20 leaders, meeting in Seoul for their fifth summit, fail to solve differences on trade imbalances and exchange rates, agreeing only to establish 'indicative guidelines' that would help to identify imbalances requiring corrective action.

13 **Myanmar:** Aung San Suu Kyi, opposition leader, is released after seven years under house arrest. She has spent 15 of the last 21 years under house arrest.

14 **India:** Andimuthu Raja, telecommunications minister, resigns in corruption scandal over award of mobile phone operators' licences. Charges are later brought against him, which he denies.

17 **United States:** Ahmed Ghailani is convicted on one count of conspiracy but acquitted on 285 other charges connected with the 1998 bombings of US Embassies in Kenya and Tanzania. Evidence against the former inmate of the US prison at Guantanamo Bay was ruled inadmissible because it was obtained under coercion.

20 **North Korea:** US scientist Siegfried Hecker reports that he has been shown a uranium-enrichment facility with 2,000 centrifuges at North Korea's Yongbyon nuclear complex.

20 **Afghanistan:** NATO leaders, meeting in Portugal, agree that Afghan security forces will take responsibility for security in all areas of Afghanistan by the end of 2014, with the transition beginning in 2011.

22 **Ireland:** Government formally requests a financial rescue package from the European Union and the International Monetary Fund. Prime Minister Brian

Cowen says he will call an election in early 2011. On 24 November, government announces austerity package of spending cuts and tax rises to reduce budget deficit. On 28 November, European governments and the IMF agree to provide €67.5bn in bailout loans.

23 **South Korea:** North Korea launches artillery bombardment of South Korea's Yeonpyeong Island. South Korea raises military readiness level. On 25 November, South Korean Defence Minister Kim Tae-young resigns. On 20 December, South Korea conducts artillery drills on the island.

28 **Côte d'Ivoire:** Presidential election results in deadlock after incumbent Laurent Gbagbo refuses to accept victory of Alassane Ouattara. On 7 December, West African leaders exclude Côte d'Ivoire from the ECOWAS regional grouping and demand that Gbagbo leaves office. The African Union also suspends the country's membership. In December, UN Security Council refuses Gbagbo's demand to withdraw 9,000-strong peacekeeping force and the EU and US impose sanctions on Gbagbo.

29 **Iran:** A nuclear scientist is killed and another is injured after attackers riding motorcycles place bombs on their cars

December 2010

6 **United States:** President Obama reaches compromise with Republicans under which Bush administration tax cuts for the rich are extended in return for extension of tax cuts for less well-off and of unemployment benefits for 2m people without jobs. The $801bn tax-cut bill splits both Democrats and Republicans in Congress but is passed on 16 December.

7 **United Kingdom:** Julian Assange, the Australian head of the WikiLeaks website, is arrested in London under a warrant issued in Sweden on charges of rape and molestation. Publication by WikiLeaks of secret American diplomatic cables has embarrassed the United States and other governments. Hackers attack companies, such as Mastercard, Visa, PayPal and Amazon, which blocked services to WikiLeaks.

11 **Mexico:** UN talks in Cancun make progress towards an eventual agreement on climate change, averting the collapse of the UN process.

11 **Sweden:** Bomb attack in central Stockholm fails. Only the bomber, an Iraqi-born Swede who had lived for some years in the UK, is killed.

13 **Iran:** Foreign Minister Manouchehr Mottaki is sacked by President Mahmoud Ahmadinejad and replaced by Ali Akbar Salehi, head of the Iran Atomic Energy Organisation.

13 **United States:** Richard Holbrooke, US special envoy to Afghanistan and Pakistan and previously architect of Bosnian peace agreeement, dies after heart surgery, age 69.

14 **Iran:** Bomb attacks in southeastern city of Chabahar kill about 40 Shia Muslims. Militant Sunni group Jundullah claims responsibility.

14 **Italy:** Coalition led by Prime Minister Silvio Berlusconi defeats no-confidence vote in parliament by three votes as demonstrations in Rome against budget cuts turn into riots.

17 **Tunisia:** Mohamed Bouazizi, a fruit and vegetable seller in the town of Sidi Bouzid, sets himself alight in protest at confiscation of his produce. Protests begin and spread to other areas, including Tunis, the capital.

18 **South Korea:** Eight Chinese fishermen are detained by South Korea after a collision between their vessel and a patrol ship.

19 **Belarus:** Alexander Lukashenko is declared winner of presidential election, winning a fourth term with nearly 80% of the vote. Opposition leader Vladimir Neklyayev is injured as riot police break up protests.

21 **Iran:** US announces sanctions on Iranian shipping and gas companies and on Revolutionary Guard Corps.

21 **Iraq:** Parliament approves formation of new government headed by Prime Minister Nuri al-Maliki, ending nine months of negotiations since parliamentary elections.

22 **United States:** Senate ratifies New START arms-control treaty with Russia.

January 2011

1 **Bolivia:** President Evo Morales cancels withdrawal of fuel subsidies which had raised petrol prices by 70% and provoked protests and strikes.

1 **Egypt:** Bomb kills 21 people outside Coptic Christian church in Alexandria. The attack prompts violent protests.

3 **Algeria:** Protests against rises in food prices and unemployment break out in many Algerian towns and cities, and are suppressed by police. On 8 January, government cuts duties on sugar and cooking oil, but protests continue over coming weeks.

4 **Tunisia:** Mohamed Bouazizi dies in hospital, 18 days after immolating himself. Protests at unemployment and corruption grow into an uprising dubbed the 'Jasmine Revolution'. Security forces attempt to crack down on rioters. By 11 January the official death toll is 23. On 12 January, President Zine al-Abidine Ben Ali sacks interior minister. Curfew declared in Tunis. On 13 January, Ben Ali says he will not stand for re-election in 2014.

4 **Pakistan:** Salman Taseer, governor of Punjab province, is shot dead by a member of his security detail because of his opposition to blasphemy laws.

9 **Sudan:** Referendum begins on independence for southern Sudan.

12 **Lebanon:** National-unity government headed by Saad Hariri collapses after Hizbullah withdraws its ministers from the cabinet over expected indictments from a UN-backed special tribunal investigating the 2005 assassination of Hariri's father, former Prime Minister Rafik Hariri.

14 **Jordan:** Protests begin in Amman and other cities against rising food and fuel prices.

14 **Tunisia:** After 23 years in power, Ben Ali flees to Saudi Arabia.

18 **Iraq:** Suicide bomber kills 60 people outside police recruiting centre in Tikrit.

19 **Tunisia:** Four ministers from newly formed unity government resign as protests continue over dominance of Ben Ali's RCD party. On 19 January, 33 members of Ben Ali's family are arrested and an investigation into corruption in the previous regime is launched. Government, headed by Prime Minister Mohamed Ghannouchi, agrees to allow previously banned political parties and to give amnesty to political prisnoers. Ghannouchi and other ministers resign from RCD membership.

21 **Somalia/South Korea:** South Korean special forces free a hijacked freighter from Somali pirates in the Indian Ocean, rescuing all on board and killing eight pirates.

24 **Russia:** Bomb explosion in the international arrivals hall at Moscow's Domodedovo airport kills 35 people. The attacker is alleged to be a 20-year-old man from Ingushetia.

25 **Lebanon:** Najib Mikati, a telecommunications magnate, is appointed prime minister with the support of Hizbullah. He says he will not interfere with the UN-backed tribunal investigating the murder of Rafik Hariri. However, he is unable to form a government until 13 June.

25 **Egypt:** Thousands demonstrate against the rule of President Hosni Mubarak, in power for 29 years. Protests take place in many cities in response to calls for a 'day of wrath. Riot police use rubber bullets, batons, tear gas and water cannon as protests continue over the next two days.

27 **Pakistan:** Raymond Davis, later revealed to be contractor working for the US Central Intelligence Agency, shoots dead two motorcyclists in Lahore, one of whom allegedly brandished a pistol at him as he drove his car. A third man is killed by a US vehicle speeding to the scene. Davis is arrested and charged with murder, but the US claims he has diplomatic immunity. The incident causes a dispute between Washington and Islamabad.

27 **Yemen:** President Ali Abdullah Saleh, in power for 32 years, is the next target of protests demanding an end to his rule. Thousands demonstrate in Sana'a, following smaller protests since the ousting of the Tunisian president. On 2 February, Saleh says he will not stand for re-election at the end of his term in 2013 and will not hand power to his son. However, protests continue in the coming weeks.

28 **Egypt:** Hundreds of thousands protest on the streets after Friday prayers and violence escalates, with battles between protesters and police in Cairo, Alexandria and Suez. The headquarters of the ruling National Democratic Party is set on fire. Mubarak orders Egyptians' access to the Internet and mobile telephone networks to be barred. In the evening, the army is deployed but does not seek to suppress protests. The police withdraw from the streets. Residents form local militias to protect neighbourhoods. On 29 January, Mubarak appoints Omar Suleiman, the intelligence chief and a close loyalist, as vice-president. He sacks and replaces his cabinet. Protesters continue to occupy Cairo's Tahrir Square. On 31 January, the army says it will not use force against protesters. Foreign countries airlift their citizens out of Egypt. On 1 February, following a nationwide 'million-person march', Mubarak says he will step down in September. On 2 and 3 February, violence breaks out again as government supporters attack protesters in Tahrir Square. The attempted crackdown includes arrests of journalists and human-rights activists. On 6 February, Suleiman holds talks with opposition groups including the banned Muslim Brotherhood. On 7 February, Wael Ghonim, a Google executive who had organised a Facebook protest, is released after 11 days of detention, and gives interviews that bolster the protesters. On 10 February, army says its leadership will support the people's rights and safeguard stability. In the evening, Mubarak says on television that he will not step down until September, but has delegated powers to Suleiman. Crowds in Tahrir Square, who had expected his resignation, angrily shout 'go, go, go'. Some 300 people are estimated to have been killed in 18 days of protests.

31 **Kazakhstan:** President Nursultan Nazarbayev, in power for 20 years, drops plan to hold referendum that could have allowed him to rule until 2020, and calls early election. The election is held on 3 April and Nazarbayev wins 95% of the votes.

February 2011

1 **Jordan:** In response to continuing protests demanding political and economic reforms, King Abdullah sacks government and appoints Marouf al-Bakhit as prime minister. The new government is ordered to take steps towards political reform.

7 **Sudan:** Referendum result shows that 98.8% of voters backed independence for southern Sudan. President Omar al-Bashir accepts the outcome. The separation is set to take place on 9 July.

10 **Pakistan:** Suicide bomber kills 31 soldiers at training centre in northwest Pakistan.

11 **Egypt:** Mubarak steps down and leaves for his residence at Sharm el-Sheikh. The news is greeted by crowd celebrations in Egypt, Algeria, Jordan and Yemen. Supreme Council of the Armed Forces assumes responsibility for the transition for six months until elections, suspends the constitution and dissolves parliament. Field Marshal Hussein Tantawi, the council chairman,

will represent the country, and Egypt will keep to all international treaties. On 15 February, a committee of legal experts is appointed to propose changes to the constitution.

14 **Bahrain:** Riot police attack mostly Shia protesters with tear gas and rubber bullets as they seek to reach the Pearl roundabout in the centre of Manama on a 'day of rage'. On 15 February, a man is shot dead at the funeral of a man killed the previous day. King Hamad bin Isa al-Khalifa appoints Shia deputy prime minister to investigate the deaths. Thousands of demonstrators then occupy the Pearl roundabout, demanding political and economic reform, the release of political prisoners and the removal of Prime Minister Sheikh Khalifa bin Salman Al Khalifa, in office for 39 years. On 17 February, police launch night-time attack on demonstrators on Pearl roundabout, killing at least four people and wounding hundreds with shotgun blasts. The army is sent to patrol the streets and the roundabout is cleared of protesters. On 18 February, the army opens fire on mourners marching from a funeral towards the roundabout. King Hamad orders his son Crown Prince Salman bin Hamad Al Khalifa to open a dialogue with the demonstrators. On 19 February, the police withdraw from the streets, including Pearl roundabout, and thousands of demonstrators again occupy it. On 22 February, government says it will free political prisoners and stop the trial of 25 people accused of plotting a coup. Protests continue, with big demonstrations in coming weeks. On 3 March, clashes break out, but a political dialogue with opposition groups continues.

14 **Iran:** Thousands of people demonstrate in Tehran, Isfahan and other cities in support of Arab uprisings, defying official warnings and threats. Police use tear gas and batons against them. Opposition leaders are placed under house arrest.

15 **Sudan:** South Sudan's government reports that some 200 people, mostly civilians, were killed in fighting with rebel leader George Athor in Jonglei state.

17 **Libya:** Protests in Benghazi and elsewhere are met with arrests, firing and tear gas from security forces. On 18 February, violent clashes escalate in Benghazi and Bayda as security forces attempt to crack down on protesters demanding the removal of Muammar Gadhafi, the leader in power for 41 years. On 19 and 20 February, hundreds are killed in Benghazi when government forces reportedly fire indiscriminately on unarmed civilians with machine guns. Protests are also reported in Tripoli. By 21 February, Benghazi is under the control of anti-government residents after army units side with them. Two fighter pilots land in Malta, saying they had been ordered to bomb Benghazi. Much of eastern Libya falls into rebel hands. Some Libyan diplomats abroad resign their posts in protests against the killing of civilians. Tens of thousands of foreign residents scramble to leave the country. On 22 February, Gadhafi threatens to kill protesters 'house by house'. Loyalist militias and mercenaries are reported to have killed many people in a rampage through parts of Tripoli. On 23 February, western city of Misrata is reported to be in rebel hands. However, forces loyal to Gadhafi fight back in Misrata, Zawiya, Ajdabiya and elsewhere. Many deaths of residents are reported in Zawiya. On 25 February, pro-Gadhafi forces open fire on demonstrators in Tripoli after Friday prayers.

18 **Djibouti:** Riot police use tear gas against thousands of demonstrators demanding against the rule of President Ismail Omar Guelleh, in office for 11 years.

20 **Morocco:** Protests take place in Rabat and other cities, demanding constitutional change and other reforms.

22 **Somalia:** Pirates kill four Americans on a hijacked yacht while negotiating with US forces who subsequently board the yacht, killing some pirates and capturing 13.

22 **Iran:** Two Iranian naval vessels pass through Suez Canal for the first time since 1979. Israel calls the move a provocation.

22 **Thailand/Cambodia:** Association of South East Asian Nations agrees to send observers to the border between Thailand and Cambodia, following clashes in previous weeks.

22 **New Zealand:** Earthquake causes widespread damage to Christchurch, New Zealand's second largest city. 181 people are killed.

23 **Saudi Arabia:** King Abdullah, on return from three months' absence for medical treatment, announces 15% increase in public-sector salaries, and aid for students and unemployed.

24 **United Kingdom:** Judge rules Julian Assange, WikiLeaks chief, should be extradited to Sweden to face sex assault charges. Assange appeals against the decision.

24 **Algeria:** President Abdelaziz Bouteflika lifts state of emergency in force for 19 years, meeting a key demand of protesters. However, protests continue over following weeks.

25 **Ireland:** General election, called following collapse of coalition led by Fianna Fail party over Ireland's financial problems, results in win for Fine Gael party. Enda Kenny becomes prime minister of coalition with Labour party. Coalition agrees to stick to financial bailout agreement with EU/IMF, but will seek to renegotiate terms.

25 **Jordan:** Thousands demonstrate in Amman, demanding political reform and greater democracy.

25 **Yemen:** Largest anti-government demonstration so far takes place in cities including Sana'a and Ta'izz following a promise by President Saleh not to crack down on protesters. On 26 February, Hussein al-Ahmar, a prominent tribal leader, resigns from the ruling party and calls for an end to Saleh's regime. On 28 February, an offer by Saleh to form a national unity government is rejected by the opposition. Large protests continue across the country.

26 **Libya:** UN Security Council passes Resolution 1970, imposing sanctions on the Gadhafi regime. It orders an arms embargo and a freeze on the assets of the

Gadhafi family. It refers the situation in Libya to the International Criminal Court. US, British and German leaders call on Gadhafi to step down. On 27 February, rebel leaders in Benghazi form a Transitional National Council (TNC) to coordinate their efforts, led by Mustafa Abdul Jalil, a former justice minister. On 28 February David Cameron, UK prime minister, calls for a no-fly zone, and discussions begin among governments on military action. Russia is among those voicing opposition, and US Defense Secretary Robert Gates cautions against US military involvement in another Middle Eastern country. However, US moves naval assets towards Libya. Pro-Gadhafi forces attack rebel positions in various places, and rebel forces also make advances in the following days. More than 200,000 people are estimated to flee across the Tunisian and Egyptian borders. A civil war develops as pro-Gadhafi forces counter rebel advances and seek to keep control of Tripoli – disappearances and rapes of residents by militiamen are reported, and forces open fire on demonstrators. The fighting is most intense in the western town of Zawiya. Reports say pro-Gadhafi forces fire at residents indiscriminately, including at ambulances. On 9 March, Gadhafi's air force bombs main oil terminal. On 10 March, France recognises the TNC as Libya's legitimate government.

27 **Oman:** Sultan Qaboos, responding to several days of protests and clashes with security forces, orders the creation of 50,000 jobs and payments for the unemployed. The sultan, in power for 40 years, twice reshuffles his cabinet, removing Ahmed Makki, economy and finance minister, in response to protesters' demand.

27 **France:** Michèle Alliot-Marie loses her position as foreign minister following criticism of her contacts with the former Tunisian regime.

27 **Tunisia:** Mohamed Ghannouchi, who had continued as prime minister in an interim capacity since 14 January, steps down following large protests demanding his resignation, which resulted in several deaths. He is replaced by Beji Caid-Essebsi, 84, who reshuffles government and abolishes state security department.

March 2011

1 **Germany:** Karl-Theodor zu Guttenberg, defence minister, resigns following accusations of plagiarism in his PhD thesis.

2 **Germany:** Two American air-force personnel are killed when a gunman opens fire on a US forces bus at Frankfurt airport. A man from Kosovo is arrested.

2 **Pakistan:** Shahbaz Bhatti, the only Christian government minister, is shot dead in his car because of his opposition to Pakistan's blasphemy laws.

3 **Egypt:** Ahmed Shafiq, who was appointed prime minister during Mubarak's last days in office, is removed by ruling military council, meeting a demand of protesters. He is replaced by Essam Sharaf. He removes several Mubarak-appointed ministers from cabinet. Protesters storm several buildings of State

Security and find shredded documents. Mubarak's once-feared interior minister, Habib El-Adly, appears in court on corruption charges. Amid continuing turbulence, clashes between Christians and Muslims leave 13 people dead.

4 **Côte d'Ivoire:** Troops open fire on unarmed protesters in Abidjan, killing seven women. UNHCR estimates that 200,000 people have been displaced by fighting between forces of rivals Gbagbo and Ouattara. By 24 March, UN estimates 700,000 have left Abidjan to escape mounting violence.

7 **United States:** President Obama orders resumption of military trials at the Guantanamo Bay prison, which he had planned to close.

8 **Serbia/Kosovo:** First direct talks between Serbia and Kosovo are held under EU auspices, on technical issues.

9 **Morocco:** King Mohammed promises 'comprehensive' constitutional reform, with a referendum to be held on a draft constitution.

11 **Yemen:** Largest demonstration yet is held in Sana'a and other cities. On 12 March, clashes with security forces leave several dead.

11 **Japan:** An earthquake measuring 9.0 shakes Japan and creates a tsunami that sweeps onto the northeastern coast. Entire towns are destroyed. The death toll is later estimated at 15,000, with a further 8,000 missing. Water and electricity supplies and transport are cut off in large areas. A nuclear emergency is declared after cooling systems fail in nuclear reactors at the Fukushima No. 1 power station as a result of loss of electricity supply. Exposure of nuclear fuel rods causes apparent partial meltdowns in three of the six reactors, as well as hydrogen explosions. People living within 20km of the plant are evacuated. As workers make desperate efforts to cool the reactors, contain radiation and carry out repairs, water is repeatedly pumped and dropped into the reactors in effort to cool fuel rods. Radiation is released from the plant through a combination of uncontrolled events and controlled releases of steam to reduce pressure. Radioactivity in Tokyo drinking water for a time exceeds the safe level for infants. Some milk and vegetables from Fukushima prefecture are unfit for consumption. On 27 March, extremely high levels of radiation are reported in the plant's No. 2 reactor, and the level of radioactive iodine-131 in sea water near the plant has risen to 1,850 times the legally permissible level. On 28 March, operator says radioactive water has leaked out of reactors into a network of underground maintenance tunnels. On 31 March, operator says radiation may be flowing continuously into the sea. The leak is sealed on 6 April.

12 **Libya:** Arab League, meeting in Cairo, calls on United Nations to impose no-fly zone over Libya to prevent attacks by pro-Gadhafi forces on civilians. Rebels lose the towns of Zawiya, Ras Lanuf and later Ajdabiya as Gadhafi forces advance.

14 **Bahrain:** Saudi Arabian troops and police from United Arab Emirates enter Bahrain under a Gulf Cooperation Council agreement, following weeks of

protests and unrest. On 15 March, King Hamad declares martial law. On 16 March, security forces attack protesters at Pearl roundabout and clear it. Hospital staff accuse security forces of attacking patients and relatives. On 17 March, security forces continue attacks in Shia villages and arrest leaders of opposition groups. On 18 March, they destroy Pearl monument at centre of roundabout.

15 **Germany:** Chancellor Angela Merkel announces temporary closure of the oldest seven of Germany's nuclear power plants following the Fukushima accident. A safety review of all Germany's 17 nuclear plants is to be carried out. The decision was a reversal of policy following large demonstrations protesting against Merkel's previous move to extend Germany's nuclear programme into the 2030s. On 28 March, Merkel's CDU party loses power in state elections in Baden-Württemberg for the first time in 58 years, to an anti-nuclear Green party/Social Democrat grouping.

16 **China:** Government suspends approval of new nuclear power plants, pending safety reviews following Fukushima accident.

16 **Pakistan:** Raymond Davis, CIA officer charged with murder in Lahore, is released following weeks of negotiations between governments and agreement to pay 'blood money', reported to be $2.3m, to families of those killed.

17 **Pakistan:** US drone attack in North Waziristan kills about 40 people. Pakistan claims they included tribal elders holding a peaceful meeting and condemns the attack.

17 **Libya:** UN Security Council votes to take 'all necessary measures' to protect Libyan civilians from threat of attack. It imposes a no-fly zone and tightens sanctions on Gadhafi regime. China, Russia, Germany, India and Brazil abstain on the vote, which follows a switch in the view of the US. Gadhafi threatens to take Benghazi 'house by house, room by room'. Obama warns of military action unless Gadhafi stops all attacks and withdraws from rebel-held cities. On 19 March, following a meeting of leaders in Paris, a coalition of countries launches strikes with *Tomahawk* cruise missiles, bombers and fighter jets, directed at Libya's air defences, air force and command and control facilities, as well as at Gadhafi's forces advancing on Benghazi. Gadhafi's troops had already reached Benghazi, and fierce fighting had broken out. Strikes on a column of armoured vehicles by French jets halt the Gadhafi forces' advance. Fighting continues between Gadhafi and rebel forces in following days. While US military assets play a prominent role in the opening attacks, the US says it will cede command of the operation within days. France resists command being passed to NATO, but agreement is reached on this on 25 March. Lieutenant-General Charles Bouchard of Canada is appointed task-force commander for all aspects of the operation. While leaders of many coalition countries call on Gadhafi to quit, they also make clear that this is not the goal of the military operation, of which the purpose is to execute UNSCR 1973. However, with the help of the air attacks on Gadhafi's armoured forces, rebels advance westwards and recapture Ajdabiya, Brega and Ras Lanuf.

18 **Egypt:** Referendum backs proposed changes to constitution, with 77% of voters in support. Presidents will serve a maximum of two four-year terms, and restrictions on electoral candidates are eased. A committee of members of the next parliament will carry out a full review of the constitution. The vote, clearing the way for quick parliamentary and presidential elections, is a victory for the army and established parties and a defeat for groups of young activists which had argued for a longer transition so as to establish themselves in advance of the polls. On 28 March, military council says Mubarak and his family are under house arrest.

18 **Syria:** After weeks of relatively small protests, large demonstrations are mounted in many cities against the regime of President Bashar al-Assad. Security forces crack down with tear gas and firing. Violence is greatest in the southern town of Deraa, where schoolchildren who had painted anti-regime slogans on walls had been arrested. Protests continue for several days in the face of a heavy security presence and more than 30 deaths are reported by 24 March.

18 **Yemen:** Saleh declares state of emergency after snipers fire on protesters in Sana'a, killing 45 as tens of thousands demonstrate. Several ministers and senior officials resign in protest. On 20 March, Saleh sacks government. On 21 March, a senior general, Ali Muhsin al-Ahmar, sides with the opposition. Protests go on, with a large encampment at Sana'a University continuing to grow. On 24 March, Houthi rebel forces take control of capital of northwestern governorate of Sa'ada. Governor and top officials flee and Houthis take control of whole governorate. On 25 March, Saleh says he is willing to hand over power to 'safe hands'.

23 **Portugal:** Prime Minister José Sócrates resigns after losing parliamentary vote on austerity measures. The vote increases the chances that Portugal will need a financial rescue from eurozone countries and the IMF.

25 **Syria:** Violence escalates as troops fire on tens of thousands of demonstrators in Deraa. Protests in many other towns are also met by violent force. Unrest spreads to northern cities, including port of Latakia. On 26 March, Assad frees some political prisoners. Some offices of ruling Ba'ath Party are set on fire. In further moves to placate protesters, cabinet resigns on 29 March, and on 31 March, Assad sets up committee to review emergency laws. Protests continue, with tens of thousands demonstrating on 1 April. On 8 April, more than 20 people are reported killed in demonstrations in Deraa. Protests continue in the coming weeks in spite of a security crackdown.

28 **Yemen:** Explosion at an ammunition factory near southern town of Jaar kills 150 people. The plant was being ransacked by locals after its guards abandoned it as government forces withdrew from the area, allegedly following skirmishes with al-Qaeda-linked militants. Following the blast, hundreds of thousands demonstrate on 30 and 31 March, demanding Saleh's departure. On 4 April, security forces fire on protesters in Ta'iiz. GCC ambassadors launch a mediation effort.

29 **Libya:** Meeting of more than 40 countries in London seeks to increase pressure on Gadhafi to quit, but he remains defiant. His forces fight back, retaking several towns on 30 March. On 31 March, Musa Kusa, Gadhafi's foreign minister, defects and is flown to Britain. Ali Abdussalam Treki, UN ambassador and former foreign minister, resigns. As fighting continues in the following days, five African leaders visit Tripoli on 10 April for talks with Gadhafi but no ceasefire results as rebels reject their peace plan because it does not provide for Gadhafi's departure. As war sinks into stalemate, the UN estimates that more than half a million people have fled Libya in two months up to 10 April.

29 **Iraq:** Militants storm government office in Tikrit, killing council members and officials and taking hostages. Following security forces' assault and recapture of the building, more than 55 people are dead.

30 **Côte d'Ivoire:** Forces loyal to president-elect Ouattara enter Yamoussoukro, the administrative capital, and on 31 March enter Abidjan, the commercial hub, triggering heavy fighting with forces of incumbent president Gbagbo. On 3 April, France increases troop presence by 300 to 1,400 and takes over Abidjan's airport. On 4 April, UN helicopters fire rockets at a military base loyal to Gbagbo.

30 **Myanmar:** Thein Sein, formerly prime minister, becomes president following November 2010 elections. Than Shwe, previously head of military junta, gives up power.

31 **Kuwait:** Cabinet resigns after parliament seeks to question ministers over alleged mistakes.

April 2011

1 **Afghanistan:** Crowd attacks UN compound in Mazar-e-Sharif, killing seven UN workers and five Afghans, in protest against burning of the Koran in Florida, USA by pastor Terry Jones.

3 **Pakistan:** Bomb attacks kills 41 people at Sufi shrine in Punjab province.

3 **China:** Ai Weiwei, artist and critic of Communist rule, is arrested at Beijing airport and held until 22 June when he is released on bail on tax evasion charges.

4 **United States:** US says it will try Khaled Sheikh Mohammed, accused of being an architect of the 9/11 attacks, in a military tribunal at Guantanamo Bay, Cuba, and not in a civilian court in New York, as the administration had planned.

7 **Mexico:** Mass graves discovered in the northern state of Tamaulipas are found to contain the remains of 183 people, apparently the victims of bus hijackings by the Zetas criminal gang.

11 **France:** Ban on women wearing Islamic veil in public comes into force.

11 **Belarus:** Bomb explosion in evening rush hour kills 12 people at metro station in Minsk.

11 **Côte d'Ivoire:** Forces of president-elect Ouattara arrest Gbagbo, ending conflict in which more than 1,500 people are estimated to have been killed. Ouattara takes power.

13 **Egypt:** Prosecutor orders detention of former president Mubarak and his two sons for interrogation over corruption allegations. On 13 May, his wife Suzanne is also detained. On 24 May, it is announced that Mubarak and his sons will face criminal charges over the killing of demonstrators during the revolution.

13 **Japan:** The accident at Fukushima No. 1 plant is raised to seven, the highest level, on the International Atomic Energy Agency's scale, ranking it alongside the 1986 meltdown at Chernobyl, Ukraine. The decision by the Japanese nuclear authorities comes even though the amounts of radiation released so far are far lower than from Chernobyl.

15 **Burkina Faso:** President Blaise Compaoré, in office since 1987, sacks his government and military chiefs after months of popular unrest and an army mutiny over pay. He appoints himself defence minister in a new government.

15 **Afghanistan:** Chief of police in Kandahar province is assassinated by a suicide bomber. On 25 April, about 500 prisoners escape from Kandahar's main prison through kilometre-long tunnel dug by the Taliban from outside.

16 **Nigeria:** Goodluck Jonathan, who became president in 2010 following the death of Umaru Yar'Adua, is elected president with 59% of the vote. The result sparks protests in the north, where voters mostly backed his opponent, Muhammadu Buhari. Hundreds are reported dead.

17 **Finland:** True Finns party, which opposes bailouts of eurozone countries, wins 19% of vote in parliamentary elections and becomes third-largest party in parliament. The result throws a proposed bailout package for Portugal into question.

18 **United States:** Rating agency Standard & Poor's issues warning about triple-A status of US government debt, changing the outlook from 'stable' to 'negative'. The decision reflects US government's failure to address fiscal deficit.

19 **Libya:** UK sends ten military officers to Benghazi to give advice to rebels. France and Italy also send advisers.

21 **Haiti:** Michel Martelly, a musician, is declared the winner of the presidential election with 67% of the vote.

21 **Syria:** Emergency rule is lifted after 48 years and Supreme State Security Court is abolished. However, new regulations covering demonstrations are introduced. On 22 April, thousands demonstrate in cities across the country and more than 100 people are killed when security forces fire on crowds. On 25 April, tanks and troops move into Deraa. The move signals a stepping up of a nationwide crackdown by security forces.

25 **Sri Lanka:** UN report by panel of experts finds 'credible allegations' of war crimes committed by both government forces and Tamil Tiger rebels in final stages of civil war in 2008–2009.

27 **United States:** Wave of tornadoes across southern states kills about 350 people, many of them in Alabama.

27 **Afghanistan:** Eight US service personnel and a US contractor are killed when an Afghan air force officer opens fire during a meeting at Kabul airport.

28 **Bahrain:** Four protesters are sentenced to death for killing two policemen. On 3 May, the government says that 47 doctors and nurses who treated wounded protesters will be tried in a military court. On 8 May, 21 people alleged to be involved in a plot to overthrow the government go on trial. The king announces he will lift the state of emergency from 1 June.

28 **Morocco:** Bomb kills 16 people, mostly foreigners, in a café in Marrakesh.

28 **United States:** President Obama nominates Leon Panetta, CIA chief, to be secretary of defense on retirement of Robert Gates. General David Petraeus, commander of NATO-led force in Afghanistan, is to replace Panetta at CIA. Later, US Army General Martin Dempsey is nominated to replace Admiral Michael Mullen as chairman of the Joint Chiefs of Staff.

28 **India:** Government shortlists two European aircraft, Eurofighter *Typhoon* and *Rafale*, for an $11bn fighter contract, rejecting the US F/A-18 and F-16 as well as Russian and Swedish aircraft. Timothy Roemer, US ambassador to India, resigns.

May 2011

2 **Pakistan:** Osama bin Laden, al-Qaeda's leader, is killed in a raid by US special forces on a house in Abbottabad, Pakistan. Three other men and a woman are also killed. Bin Laden's body is buried at sea. It emerges that he had been living in the house for several years, close to Pakistan's military academy. The US did not warn Pakistan of the raid, and its armed forces apparently did not detect it. Obama says bin Laden must have had a 'support network' in Pakistan, but the US does not accuse the Pakistani government of knowledge of his location. Three wives are taken into Pakistani custody.

2 **Canada:** Conservative party headed by Prime Minister Stephen Harper wins outright majority in general election, after previously governing as a minority. New Democratic Party makes large gains to become second largest party at the expense of the Liberals, whose leader Michael Ignatieff resigns.

3 **Portugal:** Portugal announces €78bn rescue package with EU and IMF, under which it will cut spending and raise taxes in order to reduce the budget deficit. Some of the money will be used to bolster the capital of Portuguese banks.

4 **Palestine:** Hamas and Fatah, rival Palestinian political groups, sign reconciliation agreement brokered by Egypt, under which they will form a unified government and hold elections within a year.

7 **Syria:** Tanks move into town of Baniyas as crackdown by security forces continues. On 10 May EU names 13 Syrian officials who will be subject to an assets freeze and travel ban. On 11 May tanks are reported to be shelling the city of Homs. Reports say 700 people have been killed since protests broke out in March.

8 **Egypt:** Twelve people are killed in sectarian clashes between Muslims and Christians in Cairo.

14 **United States:** Dominique Strauss-Kahn, IMF managing director, is arrested in New York and charged with attempted rape of a hotel chambermaid. On 18 May, he resigns. On 28 June, Christine Lagarde, French finance minister, is appointed to replace him.

15 **Israel:** Israeli forces open fire on pro-Palestinian protesters on borders with Syria and Lebanon. At least four people are killed in the Golan Heights and at least 10 on the Lebanese border. On 5 June, Israeli soldiers again open fire, killing up to 20 people, as hundreds of protesters try to cross Syrian border into Israel in Golan Heights.

16 **Libya:** Luis Moreno-Ocampo, chief prosecutor of the International Criminal Court in The Hague, requests arrest warrants for Gadhafi, his son Saif al-Islam, and intelligence chief Abdullah al-Senussi, on grounds of crimes against humanity.

18 **Syria:** US imposes sanctions, including assets freeze and a ban on US business, on President Bashar al-Assad and other individuals and entities. It estimates that 1,000 people have died in Syrian violence.

22 **Honduras:** President Porfirio Lobo signs agreement with former president Manuel Zelaya, ousted in a 2009 coup, allowing Zelaya to return to the country safely. The Organisation of American States readmits Honduras to membership.

22 **United States:** Tornado devastates town of Joplin, Missouri, killing 151 people.

22 **Sudan:** Some 40,000 people are reported to be fleeing as the town of Abyei, claimed by both Sudan and seceding South Sudan, is engulfed in fighting between northern and southern troops.

22 **Egypt:** Saudi Arabia agrees to provide $4bn of emergency funding to Egypt.

22 **Pakistan:** Twelve naval personnel are killed in an attack on a naval air base at Karachi by six Pakistani Taliban militants who hold off security forces for 16 hours.

23   **Yemen:** Fighting breaks out in Sana'a as Hashid tribesmen loyal to Sadeq al-Ahmar attack government ministries following President Saleh's refusal to sign an agreement on transfer of power mediated by Gulf countries. On 27 May, Islamist fighters capture southern coastal city of Zinjibar. On 30 May, government forces storm a square in the city of Ta'iiz which had been occupied by protesters for months.

26   **Vietnam/China:** Chinese patrol ships cut the cables of a Vietnamese survey ship in the South China Sea, Hanoi says.

26   **Serbia:** Ratko Mladic, former Serbian general wanted for 16 years on charges of war crimes including the Srebrenica massacre, is arrested. On 31 May, he is flown to The Hague to face the International Criminal Tribunal for the Former Yugoslavia.

28   **Egypt/Palestine:** Egypt ends blockade of Gaza, opening Rafah border crossing and allowing Palestinians to enter, though still subject to some visa restrictions.

30   **Germany:** Government decides to close all 17 of the country's nuclear power plants by 2022, following Fukushima accident.

June 2011

3   **Yemen:** President Saleh is wounded by shrapnel in an attack on the mosque at his presidential palace which killed 11 people. On 5 June, he is flown to Saudi Arabia for medical treatment. The prime minister and other senior politicians and officials are also flown to Saudi Arabia for treatment. Fighting continues in many parts of the country.

5   **Peru:** Socialist candidate Ollanta Humala wins Peruvian presidential election, succeeding Alan Garcia and defeating Keiko Fujimori, daughter of imprisoned former president Alberto Fujimori.

5   **Portugal:** Social Democrats win general election, ousting Socialists from government, and Pedro Passos Coelho becomes prime minister.

6   **Syria:** Some 120 members of security forces are killed in northern town of Jisr al-Shughour. Government says they were ambushed by armed gangs, but residents say they were defecting and were shot in the back by other soldiers. Thousands flee the town to Turkey as army launches violent crackdown. Protests continue around the country.

8   **Somalia:** Fazul Abdullah Mohammed, head of al-Qaeda in East Africa and key suspect in 1998 bombings of US embassies in Kenya and Tanzania, is killed by Somali troops at a checkpoint in Mogadishu.

9   **Myanmar:** Fighting breaks out between government forces and the rebel Kachin Independence Army in northeastern Myanmar, displacing thousands.

9   **Taiwan/China/Indonesia:** About 600 people, almost all from Taiwan and China, are arrested in Indonesia, Taiwan, China, Cambodia, Malaysia and Thailand in a coordinated operation against Internet fraud.

12   **Turkey:** Ruling Justice and Development Party (AKP) wins third term in power, increasing its vote in general election.

14   **Sudan:** Tens of thousands of people are reported to have fled from the province of South Kordofan as government forces launch a bombing campaign.

15   **Greece:** Tens of thousands take part in street protests against additional austerity measures that the government proposes to enact in order to reach agreement with the EU and IMF on a second financial bailout package. On 22 June, Prime Minister George Papandreou, having reshuffled his government, wins a parliamentary vote of confidence. On 28 June, amid violent street protests, parliament approves the austerity measures.

19   **Afghanistan:** US Defense Secretary Robert Gates says there have been 'very preliminary' contacts between the Taliban and a number of countries, including the US.

19   **Morocco:** Thousands of people demonstrate against King Mohammed's plans for constitutional reform, saying they are insufficient.

20   **Sudan:** The governments of Sudan and South Sudan agree to demilitarise the disputed Abyei region and to allow a force of Ethiopian peacekeepers into the area.

22   **Bahrain:** Military court sentences eight opposition leaders to life imprisonment on charges of plotting to oust the government. Thirteen others receive shorter sentences. On 29 June, King Hamad appoints a five-person international commission to carry out an independent investigation into the country's period of unrest.

22   **Afghanistan:** President Obama, declaring that 'the tide of war is receding', announces 10,000 American troops will be withdrawn in 2011 and a further 23,000 by September 2012, reversing the surge that he announced in December 2009. The figures are higher than military commanders wanted.

27   **Libya:** International Criminal Court issues arrest warrants for Muammar Gadhafi, his son Saif al-Islam and the head of state intelligence, Abdullah al-Senussi

28   **Afghanistan:** Militants attack Intercontinental Hotel in Kabul, killing 12 people in a four-hour assault in which all nine attackers also die.

30   **Venezuela:** President Hugo Chávez announces from Cuba that he has had surgery to remove a cancerous tumour.

30   **Lebanon:** UN-backed international tribunal asks Lebanese government to arrest four people, including three Hizbullah members, over the 2005 assassination of former Prime Minister Rafik Hariri.

Chapter 1

Perspectives

This was a year in which the pace of history quickened. Revolutionary fervour suddenly seized the Arab world. Dictators were toppled by fearless and determined street protests, and more leaders were threatened with the same fate. Just as at the end of the Cold War, decades-old certainties crumbled along with corrupt regimes and their oppressive security agencies. There were no certainties at all about what would follow.

The revolutions in Tunisia and Egypt, followed by the descent of Libya, Syria and Yemen into varying degrees of civil war, were not the only momentous events of the year to mid-2011. Conflicts that had dominated the past decade seemed to move towards an end, if not a resolution. Osama bin Laden, leader of the al-Qaeda terrorist group, was killed in Pakistan by US special forces. NATO leaders agreed to end their combat mission in Afghanistan by the end of 2014, and US President Barack Obama later announced that 33,000 American troops would be withdrawn by September 2012. 'The tide of war is receding', he declared. But Pakistan continued to be severely affected by violent militancy with which its political establishment seemed unable to cope.

There were unsettling developments in northeast Asia as North Korea revealed the existence of a long-suspected uranium-enrichment programme, and its military provocations of South Korea posed a risk of war. China, which continued to build its global presence, sought to persuade the world that its military build-up was peaceful and defensive, even as it was involved in maritime scraps over various disputed territories.

In Japan, more than 15,000 people were killed by an earthquake and tsunami. Even for a stoic country in which earthquakes are a constant fact of life, the devastation was hard to take. The tsunami also caused the most serious nuclear accident since that at Chernobyl, Ukraine in 1986, prompting Germany to plan to close all its nuclear power plants.

Elsewhere, the aftermath of the 2008 financial crisis continued to endanger the global economy, as many Western governments struggled with high debts and slow economic growth. Ireland and Portugal joined Greece in receiving financial bailouts to tide them over debt problems. Greece's first rescue turned out to be inadequate, and a second emergency loan package was being organised, imposing unpopular austerity measures on Greeks, to prevent a default that could threaten the unity of the euro, the common currency of 17 countries.

Arabs inspired to rebel

The men who ran Tunisia, Egypt, Libya and Yemen had been in power for 23, 30, 42 and 33 years respectively. The Syrian president and his father had ruled for a total of 40 years. All had held on to power through a close controlling network of loyal aides and family members, and with the help of brutal security services. These ruling elites, and their weary populations, could not possibly have imagined the events that followed the self-immolation, on 17 December 2010, of a young Tunisian vegetable seller, Mohamed Bouazizi. His desperate reaction to being insulted and beaten after refusing to pay a bribe to the police inspired hundreds of thousands of Arabs to protest against the indignities inflicted upon them for decades by their governments. There were anti-government demonstrations in 19 of the 22 member countries of the Arab League.

The revolution that forced President Zine el-Abidine Ben Ali to flee Tunisia just four weeks after Bouazizi's self-sacrifice was startling enough. But it proved to be the precursor for the mass popular movement in Egypt that culminated in President Hosni Mubarak stepping down a mere 17 days after protests began on 25 January. The huge protests in Cairo's Tahrir Square and elsewhere, and the constant live coverage by global television networks – with the Qatar-based al-Jazeera channel in the lead – lent an air of seeming inevitability to the outcome. The machine of live television coverage has to be fed by new developments all the time, so that things that happen with amazing speed can seem slow to the impatient television producer, correspondent and viewer. In this environment, the government of the United States can appear behind the curve if it takes a week to abandon a leader it has closely supported for 30 years. The fevered atmosphere was one in which the elderly Mubarak, with his distant, staged, middle-of-the-night televised addresses, could not hope to regain political ground.

Yet events in other countries showed that there was no inevitability at all about the events in Tunisia and Egypt. Crucially, the success of the revolutions in those two countries depended on the forbearance of the armed forces. In both cases, the military declined to attack the protesters. Other security forces that remained loyal to the two leaders did not have the resources to deal with the sheer size of the popular protests – and in Egypt, the hated police force was actually taken off the streets. Once the presidents were gone, the military then played a key role in the transition to the future. But it was not the same story elsewhere. In Libya, rebels in the east split from the regime of Muammar Gadhafi, but by mid-2011 they had failed to dislodge him in a civil war even with the help of a NATO bombing campaign. In Yemen, President Ali Abdullah Saleh lost control of the country in the midst of mass protests, fighting, defections and factionalism, and was then taken to Saudi Arabia for medical treatment after a bomb attack. But he seemed still to be clinging to power. In Syria, President Bashar al-Assad's security forces cracked down violently on protests across the country, and the outcome was far from clear. In much smaller Bahrain, King Hamad, from the Sunni minority, ordered mostly Shia protesters to be violently suppressed, and this was done with the help of troops from Saudi Arabia and other Gulf countries. Protests in other Arab countries were contained mostly without violence, and with promises of reform. Oppositions were seemingly unwilling to try to unseat established monarchies.

Even in Egypt and Tunisia, it was not obvious that the removal of long-time leaders would bring fundamental change. Transitions were under way to elections, and everything was still to play for. Military, business and religious establishments were seeking to hold their corners in the face of younger, less-experienced activists. Continuing sporadic street protests and violence indicated that the struggle was not over. Elections would provide crucial tests, and signposts to the future. The 'Arab Awakening' – as it is termed in this book – is examined in a special chapter (pages 43–96).

Altered perspectives

The Awakening was a surprise not just in the obvious ways – its breathtaking speed, its massive mobilisation of young people, its sweeping away of old regimes. It also shattered the prism through which the Muslim world had been viewed by the West since the 9/11 terrorist attacks on the United

States. US foreign and security policy, beginning with President George W. Bush's 'global war on terror', had been crafted in large measure around the threat of Islamist terrorism. Under Bush, other countries' relations with Washington were calibrated according to the extent of their collaboration in countering that threat. Moreover, the danger to America's long-established friends in the Middle East, such as Mubarak, had been perceived to come from Islamists – a belief that suited the regimes because it further empowered their ruthless security agencies. But when the Arab Awakening began, Islamist groups played no determining role, even though their members were on the streets of Tunis and Cairo. The protests were about jobs and injustices, not about the role of Islam or the victimisation of Muslims. The Islamists' philosophy was, at least for the time being, irrelevant.

Clearly, Islamist groups – the Muslim Brotherhood in Egypt and An-Nahda in Tunisia – had the opportunity to reassert themselves. They had the benefit of decades of organisation while in suppressed opposition. But the Muslim Brotherhood's leadership seemed, even to its members, as sclerotic as the Mubarak regime, and splits were taking place. It seemed possible that parties arising out of these movements could form part of more 'normal' politics in the years to come. Some commentators pointed to the success of Turkey's ruling Justice and Development Party, which developed from Islamist roots. But at mid-2011 it was too early to tell what political forces would emerge on top in Egypt and Tunisia. At any rate, it was clear that for the West to shape its thinking about the Middle East around a perspective of Islamic fundamentalism would be short-sighted, especially in view of the new opportunities for democracy and development that now lay ahead.

If the salience of Islamism was now in question, so too were important elements of the regional balance of power. The discomfort of the Saudi Arabian and Bahraini ruling families played strongly into the hands of Iran, though the travails of Assad's Syria were less welcome in Tehran. Meanwhile, to Israel the Arab unrest seemed nothing but bad news. Like Saudi Arabia, it watched with disquiet as Washington discarded its old friend Mubarak. Israel faced uncertainty about its 32-year-old peace treaty with Egypt, which formed the bedrock of its strategic posture. While the Egyptian military, with the inducement of US military aid, seemed likely to want to adhere to the treaty, the future attitude of an Egyptian government could not be known. Meanwhile, Egypt relaxed border controls for people in Gaza.

America's role

The United States – and the West in general – was being forced into a recalibration of its relationships and policies in the region. As the Arab Awakening began, the leaders of Egypt and Tunisia were close allies of the West. Gadhafi, previously a pariah, was being embraced by Western governments and businesses after renouncing his nuclear programme. Saleh was an ally of the United States in the fight against al-Qaeda militants in his country. Assad, vilified by Washington during the Iraq War, was now being wooed because of Syria's pivotal position in the region, especially with regard to Iran. The imperatives driving US policy – the fight against terrorism, the need to contain Iran's nuclear ambitions, the desire to resolve the Israel–Palestine dispute, and the requirement for stable energy supplies – indicated that Washington needed to remain on good terms with these countries, as well as with its allies in the Gulf.

After playing for so long the role of dominant arbiter of the region's affairs, the United States now recognised that it had little ability directly to influence events on the streets of the Arab world. It was torn between its natural inclination to back democratic reform and its equally natural wish to maintain stable relationships that would support its policy goals. The Obama administration thus shaped its positions as each uprising developed. This resulted in some awkward contortions, but its approach was not as hapless as some sought to portray it. The administration was quick to grasp what was behind the upheavals. As the Tunisian protests grew, Secretary of State Hillary Clinton told a conference in Qatar that most people in the region were under 30 and 'in many places, there are simply not enough jobs'. Many people, she said, 'have grown tired of corrupt institutions and a stagnant political order. They are demanding reform to make their governments more effective, more responsive, and more open.' Addressing leaders directly, Clinton said: 'Those who cling to the status quo may be able to hold back the full impact of their countries' problems for a little while, but not forever. If leaders don't offer a positive vision and give young people meaningful ways to contribute, others will fill the vacuum.'

America, Clinton reminded her audience, could not solve the region's problems. But it did make a highly significant gesture less than three weeks later, when Obama called on Mubarak to begin an immediate and orderly transition from power. The Pentagon actively engaged Egyptian army chiefs, who receive $1.3 billion of US military aid annually, and urged them to show restraint on the streets.

While the United States embraced the Egyptian revolution, it held back from endorsing regime change elsewhere. Events dictated shifts in Washington's position: in Syria, for example, the violent crackdown by the security forces led it to move away from strategic engagement with Assad towards condemnation and sanctions. Having been very reluctant to engage in a new war in the region, it was persuaded that the humanitarian situation in Libya demanded military action. Although there was no UN mandate to remove Gadhafi, Obama then joined the British and French leaders in saying that for the Libyan leader to remain in power would be a betrayal of the Libyan people. Most awkwardly of all, having enraged Saudi Arabia's rulers by abandoning Mubarak, Washington watched uncomfortably as Saudi troops entered Bahrain, home of the US Navy's Fifth Fleet, and as the Bahraini ruling family cracked down on demonstrators, with opposition leaders, doctors and nurses put on trial. US–Saudi relations fell to a new low. Though they seemed later to be patched up, America's regional sway seemed to have suffered another blow.

This was part of a long-running global trend. After the controversial war in Iraq and the 2008 financial crisis, and amidst the quagmire of the conflict in Afghanistan, the world was becoming accustomed to the idea that the clout of the United States in world affairs was reduced, at least in relative terms. Obama himself had acknowledged this. Addressing the United Nations in 2009, he said: 'Those who used to chastise America for acting alone in the world cannot now stand by and wait for America to solve the world's problems alone.' He had repeatedly said that other countries must share the burden – in fact, this was being called the 'Obama doctrine' and it was to be seen in sharp relief in Libya.

Al-Qaeda and Afghanistan: receding tide?
Given the portrayal of America (by Obama's political opponents) as an over-cautious spectator of the Arab Awakening, and also given the irrelevance of Islamist fundamentalism to the Arab uprisings, the subsequent killing of Osama bin Laden had a symbolism well beyond its operational impact.

Bin Laden, killed by US Navy SEALs in a house in a middle-class, military neighbourhood in Pakistan, was discovered to have been living there for five years. A video found in the house showed him grey-bearded and hunched in a blanket, watching images of himself on television. Still, diminished and solitary figure that he may have been, the raid carried out by US special forces and the Central Intelligence Agency (CIA) represented a major success for the United States and for Obama. The president had taken a risk in ordering a hostile military raid deep into Pakistan, whose government was not notified in advance. The attack, though it followed an extensive covert surveillance operation, was carried out on the basis of incomplete intelligence. Obama won acclaim from all parts of the US political spectrum.

As the United States prepared to mark ten years since the 9/11 attacks masterminded by bin Laden on New York and Washington, which killed 3,000 people, it seemed arguable that al-Qaeda was a much-diminished force and that the intensive intelligence effort coordinated by the United States since 2001 had borne fruit – though such statements would always be one successful terrorist atrocity away from being invalidated (see text box, pages 33–5). Many of its senior figures had been killed by strikes from CIA unmanned aircraft in the tribal areas of Pakistan. US officials said there were very few al-Qaeda operatives left in Afghanistan, where it had had its base before 9/11. While al-Qaeda had made many attempts, it had carried out very few successful attacks in the West since then. Though terrorist violence inspired by al-Qaeda, fuelled by its narrative of Muslim victimhood at the hands of the West, still posed an international threat, the fighters for its cause seemed increasingly caught up in local conflicts, such as those in Pakistan, Somalia and Yemen. Significantly, the death of bin Laden did not provoke outrage in the Arab world, though it seriously damaged already testy US–Pakistan relations.

The success of the raid armed Obama for his bold decision to override military advice and order the withdrawal of the 33,000 'surge' troops that he had sent to Afghanistan. The manner of the decision contrasted sharply with the highly public (especially after the publication of Bob Woodward's book *Obama's Wars*) stand-off in 2009 in which military commanders forced through the troop increase over the new president's desire to consider a wider range of options. At mid-2011, the NATO-led International Security Assistance Force (ISAF) had been at its peak level of about 140,000 troops for about six months, and the size of Afghanistan's ISAF-trained army was growing. But progress towards the stable Afghanistan that NATO wanted to build was mixed at best.

Military commanders claimed that the troop surge had enabled them to make gains in the south against Taliban insurgents, and that this was building pressure on the Taliban that would be beneficial in the achievement of a political solution. But the Western appetite for the fight appeared to be steadily diminishing. After his election in 2010, David Cameron, the UK prime minister, had made clear that he wanted the combat to end by 2015. His position became formal NATO policy at the Lisbon summit in November, at which it was agreed that the Afghan government would be responsible for security in all areas of the country by the end of 2014, with the transition due to begin in 2011. In accordance with this timetable, Obama said he would withdraw 10,000 troops in 2011 and a further 23,000 by September 2012, leaving a further 68,000 troops to be pulled out later. This time there was no lengthy public agonising about Obama's decision, the process was closely held, and the decision was accompanied by the president's replacement of the top military chiefs. Both Democratic and most Republican politicians seemed to support it.

It was widely acknowledged that a political solution was needed, that the Taliban would have a role in future arrangements, and that contacts were

Al-Qaeda: ten years after 9/11

With the death of Osama bin Laden at the hands of US forces on 2 May 2011, the al-Qaeda terrorist group lost the leader who had founded it in Pakistan in the dying days of the anti-Soviet jihad. Its focus in the late 1980s was on overthrowing Arab regimes perceived as repressive and un-Islamic. Bin Laden concluded, however, that this could only be achieved if Western nations, in particular the United States, could be intimidated into withdrawing support for these regimes. His vision was the creation of a global insurgency within the Islamic world. Al-Qaeda came to global prominence in 1998 with the bombings of the US Embassies in Kenya and Tanzania, and later with the attack on the USS *Cole* in Yemen in 2000. Even then, al-Qaeda was not generally perceived as a major global threat until its attacks on the United States on 11 September 2001. On that day, nearly 3,000 people died as terrorists hijacked commercial aircraft and flew them into the Pentagon in Washington DC and the twin towers of the World Trade Center in New York. A fourth aircraft crashed in Pennsylvania.

The attacks had far-reaching consequences. They led to a US invasion of Afghanistan and the overthrow of the Taliban regime, which had hosted al-Qaeda without appreciating the risks involved. They defined the security and foreign-policy agenda of the two-term presidency of George W. Bush, obliquely influencing his decision to invade Iraq in 2003 due to the fear that transnational terrorism and weapons of mass destruction might come together in a uniquely toxic combination.

Following the overthrow of the Taliban, al-Qaeda's leadership regrouped in the tribal territories of Pakistan. Assisted by supporters such as long-time jihadist Jalaluddin Haqqani, and in collaboration with Pakistani jihadist groups such as Lashkar-e-Tayiba, al-Qaeda played an enabling role in the insurgency which developed in Afghanistan. Aspirant jihadists from abroad who had gone to training camps in Pakistan were cherry-picked and persuaded to return to their countries to undertake terrorist attacks. Few were successful: only in Madrid in 2004 and London in 2005 did al-Qaeda carry out terrorist atrocities in the West. Many plots failed, such as an attempt to blow up a Detroit-bound airliner in 2009 and to explode a car in Times Square, New York in 2010. Most were frustrated by a much-enhanced global intelligence effort orchestrated by the United States.

under way. However, it was difficult to be optimistic about the political prospects. It was not clear whether the Taliban, even if its representatives were taking part in preliminary talks, really felt an incentive to engage in meaningful bargaining – and it was far from being a unified grouping. NATO claimed to have killed many senior Taliban fighters in special-forces raids. But while the insurgents did not approach the 2011 fighting season with the zeal that NATO commanders had expected, the military situation was murky. Meanwhile, there was little sign that President Hamid Karzai was taking steps that many saw as essential to improve governance and present the government in Kabul as able to inspire the confidence of Afghans in a just, prosperous and secure future. His anti-NATO rhetoric seemed to

Al-Qaeda was, however, more successful in implementing a franchising system whereby regional groups in Southeast Asia, East Africa, the Arabian Peninsula, Iraq and North Africa all became part of its brand. Many of these groups posed a threat only in the regions in which they operated, but they were still a significant danger to Western interests. Al-Qaeda in Mesopotamia became a major part of the anti-US insurgency in Iraq by aligning with Sunni groups. In Saudi Arabia attacks by al-Qaeda in the Arabian Peninsula (AQAP) targeted Western-operated businesses and residences and came close to destroying Saudi Arabia's Abqaiq oil terminal. In Yemen, AQAP launched multiple attacks on Western diplomatic targets and attempted, so far unsuccessfully, to undertake bombings in the United States. In Algeria and the Sahel, al-Qaeda in the Islamic Maghreb was responsible for numerous kidnappings of Western travellers and forced the cancellation of the Paris–Dakar rally. In Somalia, the al-Qaeda-linked group al-Shabaab has posed a major threat to the tenuous authority of the UN-backed administration.

All the indications are that al-Qaeda has failed in its aim of sparking a global Islamic insurgency. Mainstream Islam has rejected bin Laden's nihilistic vision, aware that most of the victims of al-Qaeda's violence have been Muslims. Al-Qaeda's leadership has suffered high levels of attrition from US Central Intelligence Agency (CIA) attacks, culminating in the killing of bin Laden himself in Abbottabad, close to the Pakistani capital. Al-Qaeda, taken unawares by the Arab Awakening, has struggled to assert its continuing relevance. However, its ideology still has appeal for some young people. Its concept of transnational jihadism continues to define the security agenda in parts of the Islamic world characterised by weak governance and institutions. The problem is particularly acute in Pakistan, where a wide range of jihadist groups either enjoy a degree of state sanction or are beyond state control. While it is likely that much of the violence perpetrated by such groups will occur locally – and Pakistan has suffered in excess of 30,000 deaths from terrorism over the past decade – the fear that some of this activity might migrate overseas is real.

The threat from al-Qaeda has fundamentally altered many aspects of global security culture, in particular in areas such as air travel, mass transit and the protection of critical infrastructure. The cost in lives and money of dealing with the threat from al-Qaeda has been onerous, especially for the United States. There can be no guarantee that it will not continue to be so.

increase following further instances of civilian casualties from air strikes – which ISAF was at pains to avoid. This prompted Karl Eikenberry, the outgoing US ambassador and a former military commander in Afghanistan, to retort: 'When Americans, who are serving in your country at great cost – in terms of lives and treasure – hear themselves compared with occupiers, told that they are only here to advance their own interest, and likened to the brutal enemies of the Afghan people … they are filled with confusion and grow weary of our effort here.' Opinion polls showed that few Westerners would disagree that NATO's forces should be brought home. It was clear in any case that Obama, Cameron and other leaders had taken the fundamental decision that the costs of the combat mission in Afghanistan outweighed the possible strategic advantages that might be gained by staying, which were in any case questionable, and also outweighed the risks of leaving. While military commanders inevitably called for 'one more heave', few people were convinced that it was worth the effort.

Libya: Europe's turn

If the tide of war was indeed receding in Afghanistan, the Arab Awakening produced another surprise: a NATO-led bombing campaign in Libya. This, like previous such foreign interventions, risked turning into a long-term commitment, though the outcome was far from clear at mid-2011.

While not a large operation in military terms or in broad strategic significance, the Libyan mission was nevertheless illuminating in that it seemed to offer signposts to the future – to a world in which the Iraq and Afghanistan wars were receding into history and the balance between powers, both established and emerging, was visibly changing.

Firstly, the operation resulted from a European initiative: not from the European Union, which trailed far behind the public discourse, but specifically from the United Kingdom and France. Cameron and French President Nicolas Sarkozy personally spearheaded the move to military action as the Libyan rebels who had gained control of the eastern city of Benghazi were in danger of losing it and of suffering a massacre at the hands of Gadhafi's advancing forces. The initiative gained momentum at the UN from the 'responsibility to protect' principle adopted by the international community in an effort to prevent atrocities like that in Rwanda in 1994. Obama and US Defense Secretary Robert Gates were reluctant, not seeing Libya as of overriding importance and not wishing to get involved in another war. Yet the United States agreed to back a UN Security Council resolution on the basis that, after an initial burst of American strikes to eliminate Gadhafi's air defences, the Europeans would be in charge with the US military in support. This was a big change after a decade of American-led military intervention.

Secondly, Europe was far from united in taking on this challenge. The Libyan mission rapidly exposed the gap that existed in Europe between countries that had retained and developed capabilities for combat – and were willing to use them to deal with international crises – and those that had not. In particular, Britain and France, in spite of defence cuts, had far greater military might than other European countries, a fact that was emphasised in 2010 by their agreement of a wide-ranging bilateral defence-cooperation treaty – itself an important departure from the past. While 13 European countries took part in the Libyan operation, only a few took a prominent role in the bombing. Moreover, Germany – smarting from the UK–French bilateral move – took no part at all. The absences meant that the countries taking the lead, which were also contributing importantly to the Afghanistan campaign and had other deployments as well, would find themselves hard pressed to keep up the commitment. On a final trip to Brussels as US defense secretary, Gates delivered a lacerating speech about Europe and NATO, noting that 'while every alliance member voted for the Libya mission, less than half have participated at all, and fewer than a third have been willing to participate in strike missions'. He added: 'Frankly, many of those allies sitting on the sidelines do so not because they do not want to participate, but simply because they can't. The military capabilities simply aren't there.' However, his words found little traction as European countries continued to cut defence spending as part of budget stringency.

The lack of unity raised a third issue, about command. With the United States taking a 'back seat', there was verbal skirmishing about who should have military control. One option would have been a joint French–British command, but neither the UK nor some other allies favoured this. The choice of a NATO command, under a Canadian general, underlined the utility of the alliance's well-established structures and standards. On the other hand, it was highly unusual to have a NATO operation without the participation of key allies such as Germany and Poland. Thus, over and above Gates's demand for more capabilities, the mission raised further questions – as did the Franco-British defence treaty – about the alliance's longer-term future.

Fourthly, there was the confused nature of the mission itself. UN Security Council Resolution 1973 authorised 'all necessary measures to protect civilians and civilian-populated areas under threat of attack', but forbad ground occupation. It also ordered a no-fly zone. Quickly, the air strikes stopped the advance of Gadhafi's forces, thereby fulfilling the demand to protect civilians. But the next move was not clear. Under pressure to show progress, NATO began to target Gadhafi himself, but at mid-2011 had not succeeded in hitting him or causing his regime to fall. Cameron, Sarkozy and Obama sought to justify their interpretation of the UN mandate by writing jointly that it was 'impossible to imagine a future for Libya with Gadhafi in power'. This apparent commitment to regime change created, in the words of veteran military commentator Max Hastings, writing in the *Financial Times*, 'a yawning gap between military means and declared ends'. With the United States displaying no more enthusiasm for the operation than it had at the start, after four months the campaign seemed fraught with political risk not just for Gadhafi, but for Cameron and Sarkozy as well.

Finally, the very passing of UNSCR 1973 seemed a sign of times to come. Though there were no votes against, Germany and all four of the 'BRIC' emerging economies abstained. The five included three aspirants to permanent Security Council seats – Brazil, India and Germany – as well as two that already held them, China and Russia. The abstentions perhaps indicated that a less interventionist world could result from potential changes to international institutions to reflect the changing economic balance, though they did not vote against the intervention, and it did proceed.

Prolonged financial hangover

Governments were, in any case, under growing pressure to curb military interventionism for a more mundane reason: lack of money. The 2008 financial crisis continued to overshadow the Western world. European governments were seeking to impose fiscal discipline through spending cuts and tax increases, but the price was a slow pace of recovery from recession. The United States appeared to have no strategy to restore fiscal probity, and was also suffering from slow growth and stubbornly high unemployment. The largest emerging economies, including China, India and Brazil, continued to show rapid growth but were worried by inflation. All economies were affected by sharply rising commodity and energy prices, though inflation rates in the Western world remained quite low.

Arguments about how the industrialised West should best manage the after-effects of the financial crisis were no closer to resolution. Some economists believed strong government stimulus should be provided in order to prevent economies from slipping into a 1930s-style depression. For them, the mere absence of a strategy to bring down the US fiscal deficit was not nearly enough. At the other end of the spectrum, the shift to the right in the Republican Party brought an increased desire to curb spending, including on foreign wars, though politicians baulked at the specific measures that this would involve, such as in subsidised health care for the elderly. The argument was not helped by the vicious partisan atmosphere that persisted in US politics. But while it raged – brought into focus by the need to raise the legally enshrined allowed government debt limit – the International Monetary Fund (IMF) warned that it was critical for the United States to 'launch a deficit reduction plan that includes entitlement reform and revenue-raising tax reform'. The IMF did concede that if economic growth should falter, the pace of fiscal adjustment should be slowed, though it should be credible over the medium term. Standard and Poor's, the US credit-rating agency, warned that it would consider lowering the country's triple-A sovereign debt rating 'because the US has, relative to its AAA peers, what we consider to be very large budget deficits and rising government indebtedness, and the path to addressing these is not clear to us'. Nevertheless, it seemed unlikely that a credible medium-term strategy to address the US fiscal deficit could find agreement among the administration and Congress before the 2012 presidential election, and even after that it promised to be challenging. Meanwhile, the weak state of the banking system following its collapse in 2008 continued to limit the advancing of credit, and many people continued to be affected by fallen property prices. Unemployment hovered around 9%. Thus, the excessive government indebtedness built up under G.W. Bush, coupled with the aftermath of the financial crisis that reached a climax in his last months in office, had not yet been effectively addressed. This meant that the United States had not eliminated the risk of a repeat of the 1930s.

In Europe, the argument was different. Politicians on all sides embraced the need for fiscal discipline. But some smaller economies – Greece, Ireland and Portugal – had particularly high budget deficits that they were no longer able to finance, and so had to arrange rescues. They owed large amounts to commercial banks, which therefore were under threat of losses that they could ill afford following the 2008 trauma (see Strategic Geography, pages XVI–XVII). In normal circumstances these problems could have been dealt with the usual mixture of IMF-imposed austerity, devaluation and debt rescheduling. But the three countries were among the 17 to use the euro as a common currency, meaning that devaluation was not possible and debt rescheduling, unless handled very carefully, could have complex consequences. Therefore, Europe's main preoccupation over the year to mid-2011 was the preservation of the common currency. This effort caused severe political strains in both creditor and debtor countries. The Irish and Portuguese governments fell, while the Greek government, which had exposed the false budget figures of its predecessor but then had to introduce several rounds of unpopular measures, just hung on. Elsewhere there was resentment (especially in Germany) at taxpayers having to fund other Europeans' profligacy, and there were calls for Greece to leave the euro – a move that could well lead to the unravelling of the currency. All this made for the continuation of a long period of introversion within Europe that seemed set to continue in spite of the Libyan campaign and of the tireless efforts of France's Sarkozy, as rotating chairman of the G8 and G20, to inspire greater global activism.

Ubiquitous China

Against this pattern of introversion, slow growth and lowered ambitions in the United States and Europe, the march of China continued. Economic growth exceeded 10% in 2010 and was projected close to that level in 2011 and 2012. On a widening international stage, Beijing repeatedly displayed a degree of assertiveness – even belligerence – that it later seemed to moderate, perhaps perceiving it as counterproductive.

There was scarcely a region of the world where China's visibility was not increasing, as its leaders made frequent foreign trips to boost trade and investment links. In Latin America, which has benefited enormously from Chinese demand for raw materials, Beijing was proposing to build a rail link from Colombia's Pacific to its Caribbean coast, to rival the Panama Canal. Meanwhile, Chinese investment in Africa continued to grow, and Beijing also diversified an increasing proportion of its currency reserves out of the dollar and into the euro. This gave it a stake in the survival of the euro, and Premier Wen Jiabao pledged to make continuing investments in the government bonds of European nations. In a further example of China's spreading engagement, the People's Liberation Army carried out joint military exercises with Turkey, its first in a NATO member state.

The Chinese and American economies were bound tightly together by American demand for Chinese exports and Chinese investment in US government debt. The past year, however, saw bilateral friction on both economic and military issues. Although in both areas there was a thaw as the months passed, Washington remained concerned about the undervaluation of the Chinese currency and about the PLA's military modernisation. Beijing insisted that its programme of military renewal (see essay, pages 126–38) reflected its economic growth and that its intentions were entirely defensive and peaceful. Regional countries, however, had reason to doubt this as Chinese vessels were repeatedly involved in hostile incidents related to islands whose sovereignty was disputed with, in particular, Japan and Vietnam. The Vietnamese defence minister, speaking at the 2011 IISS Shangri-La Dialogue in Singapore, said: 'We look forward to seeing action that corresponds to China's declarations.'

China's role was pivotal in the other worrying series of events in northeast Asia, as North Korea's armed forces repeatedly tried to provoke South Korea. Its actions perhaps sprang from machinations surrounding the transition of leadership from Kim Jong-il to his youngest son, Kim Jong-un. China declined directly to blame North Korea for two attacks and also protected Pyongyang from international condemnation when it revealed to US scientists the existence of a long-suspected uranium enrichment plant, which further muddied the prospects for any agreement to end its nuclear programme.

New and old themes

The North Korean developments were a reminder that perennial themes of international affairs (and of *Strategic Survey: The Annual Review of World Affairs*) were not receding from view. The nuclear ambitions of North Korea and Iran would continue to occupy diplomats and military planners, as they threatened to create a world in which many more countries would have nuclear arsenals. Similarly, violence in – and emanating from – Pakistan underlined the enduring nature of the threats coming from that region, and of the need to find a political solution in Afghanistan that gave all regional countries of the region an incentive to contribute to stable a future. In Africa, economic advances were blighted by conflicts: Sudan, as it split into two countries, was riven by fighting that displaced tens of thousands; Côte d'Ivoire erupted into war while a leader defeated in an election refused to cede power; pirates operating off the coast of lawless Somalia showed no sign of being defeated by international efforts.

But while these dangers remained persistent, the events of the year to mid-2011 opened up new possibilities for the world. The Arab Awakening was a reminder of the futility of making forecasts in international affairs. Far from America changing the map of the Middle East as Bush-era neoconservatives had dreamed, this was a sudden and unexpected re-shaping of the Arab world by its own young people. The manner in which they mobilised for peaceful action was profoundly refreshing. They showed that they had the normal and obvious grievances of any young people anywhere, and these could be shared and communicated across borders. While the extent of the lasting changes that they would bring remained in doubt, their actions potentially provided some of the initial brush strokes of a new phase in international affairs.

This was a world in which Robert Gates, viewed by some as the best-ever US defense secretary, could say to an audience at the West Point military academy: 'In my opinion, any future defense secretary who advises the president to again send a big American land army into Asia or into the Middle East or Africa should "have his head examined," as General MacArthur so delicately put it'. The odds on America again invading, pacifying and administering a large third-world country were low, he said, though the US still needed swift-moving expeditionary forces.

While Gates would probably not relish the interpretation, his words seemed to encapsulate a new view of America of itself, less exceptionalist and, under Obama, certainly less Atlanticist. While this self-image reflected Obama's beliefs – and would be furiously rejected by some Republicans – it was in any case forced upon the United States by the chastening lessons of Iraq and Afghanistan, and by the need for financial stringency after a period of rampant excess. It did not at all mean that America had ceased to be the lynchpin of international security – indeed the tensions between Pacific nations showed how vital was America's diplomatic and military presence.

American ambitions were thus curtailed, and Europe's were stagnant, its push for closer unity having stalled. New powers were on the rise. The Arab uprisings pushed forward the global shift away from the established balances of the twentieth century. After the former era's power blocs and global confrontations, the twenty-first-century world was beginning to resemble more buccaneering times of the past. It was an age in which new spheres of influence could be built, and old-fashioned diplomacy could win an edge.

Chapter 2
The Arab Awakening

As 2010 drew to its end, there was little indication that extraordinary upheavals were about to take place in the Arab world. The region seemed frozen in its old ways, with authoritarian regimes firmly in place and tamed populations struggling to cope with economic malaise and political stagnation.

The permanent features of the region's security and political landscape – the vicissitudes of the Israeli–Arab peace track, the prospect of a protracted cold war with Iran, the relative stabilisation of Iraq and the downhill trajectory of Yemen – were disturbed only by the publication by WikiLeaks, the anti-secrecy group, of confidential US diplomatic cables. These disclosures injected awkwardness into the region's political theatrics; they also further hurt the standing of the United States as Arab leaders measured the damage done by the revelation of their private utterances. Yet the disclosures did not seem to change the region's fundamental dynamics.

By 14 January 2011, however, the ossified Arab political order was facing its biggest challenge in decades, one that came from within rather than from without. That day, Zine el-Abedine Ben Ali, Tunisia's president since 1987, fled the country after a month of spreading street protests and political contestation that followed the self-immolation of street vendor Mohamed Bouazizi after an argument with the municipal police. This was the first time that a popular uprising – rather than a military coup – had ousted a sitting Arab head of state. To many, Tunisia seemed an improbable place for such upheaval. The security state built by Ben Ali looked impregnable, its economic development surpassed that of the rest of the region and its well-educated, largely secular and apparently quiescent population seemed to be an unlikely agent of revolutionary change.

What was even more surprising was the contagion that ensued. At first, Arab officials refused to accept that this could occur. Four days after the ouster of Ben Ali, Egyptian Foreign Minister Ahmed Aboul Gheit called such a possibility 'pure nonsense'. In an interview with the *Wall Street Journal*, Syrian President Bashar al-Assad argued that he had already taken the reform path and proclaimed that his country was stable 'because you have to be very closely linked to the beliefs of the people'. Muammar Gadhafi, the Libyan leader, appeared on television after Ben Ali's fall to chide the Tunisian people and declare that Libya would see no such upheaval.

To be sure, popular discontent compounded pre-existing fractures in Arab societies along ethnic, sectarian and political lines. Such fissures and each country's unique circumstances meant that the unfolding and outcome of each revolution would necessarily differ from the others. Still, by March, five countries out of the 22 members of the Arab League – Egypt, Libya, Syria, Tunisia and Yemen – were undergoing major upheaval. Another 14 experienced more contained forms of unrest.

Of the first five, none could yet be said definitively by mid-2011 to have had a successful revolution. Tunisia and Egypt, which had deposed their leaders, were grappling with the perils and uncertainties of transition. Both had scheduled national elections but faced potential breakdowns of public order and major economic difficulties. Libya had descended into civil war; Syria and Yemen were on the verge. After a rough beginning, rebel groups in Libya, backed by NATO air power, succeeded in containing Gadhafi's forces and established a transitional council in Benghazi. However, they seemed unable to bring the conflict to a quick end without greater foreign intervention. In Yemen, third-party mediation to ensure the peaceful departure of the sitting president Ali Abdullah Saleh failed, opening the door to civil war in what was already a fragile state. Saleh was later seriously injured in a bombing and left the country for treatment without resigning, creating even more uncertainty. The Syrian protest movement, though mostly contained to the periphery of the country's two major urban centres, proved resilient to massive repression by the security forces. The regime in Damascus, facing the prospect of exhaustion and collapse, was forced to acknowledge and engage at least part of the long-suppressed opposition.

Among other countries experiencing unrest, the situation in Bahrain seemed the most serious. A peaceful uprising was followed by a failed dialogue, and was then crushed by a violent crackdown backed by troops from other Gulf states; doctors and nurses were among those subsequently put on trial. In the United Arab Emirates, five political activists were jailed following the publication of a benign but unprecedented petition demanding political reforms; protests in Iraq turned violent but failed to gather momentum due to war fatigue and a modicum of representative politics that allowed for the venting of frustrations through non-violent channels; Jordan and Morocco pre-empted massive turbulence by making timid moves towards constitutional reforms.

Shared predicament

The various uprisings, regardless of their level of success, had much in common. Many popular grievances were shared, especially the feeling of unrelenting assault on human dignity and of a denial of basic rights by Arab regimes. Everywhere, the sense was strong that the ruling elite was manipulating the state for its own benefit to the detriment of the citizens and the greater public good.

Significantly, Egypt, Libya, Tunisia, and Yemen were facing the issue of who would succeed their long-established leaders. In all four countries, ageing dictators were cultivating and positioning their sons or close relatives as political heirs. (Only Syria among Arab states had seen a successful hereditary presidential – as opposed to monarchical – succession.) The political manoeuvring undertaken to groom successors meant even greater consolidation of power; sophisticated campaigns were designed to convince the population of the merits of hereditary succession and glorify the chosen heir. Within the elite, allies were rewarded, dissenters punished. Elections were manipulated, as was the case with the November 2010 legislative poll in Egypt, and constitutional changes were made to smooth filial transitions. Egyptians and others saw these attempts at turning their countries into *'gumlukiyyas'*, a term coined by the Egyptian sociologist turned political dissident Saadeddine Ibrahim to describe the transformation of Arab republics into de facto monarchies, as yet more evidence of the enshrinement of ruling elites.

Growing inequalities accentuated the widespread perception of collusion between the political elite and the business establishment. Market-friendly reforms, often recommended by international financial organisations, led to the slashing of subsidies, a freeze in public-sector employment, privatisation and decreased state largesse in general. However, while these structural reforms and other factors led to growth in most Arab economies, the wealth created as a result did not reach the masses. Rather, it primarily enriched business figures closely aligned with the various regimes. The lack of transparency and accountability that surrounded reforms, including preferential treatment and questionable transfers of state assets and privileges to regime loyalists, only heightened popular disaffection with economic policies. These feelings peaked just as food and energy prices surged, driving ever more people into poverty and limiting the employment prospects of young people.

These trends compounded a pervasive sense of the deterioration of governance and of political malaise. Throughout the Arab world, even the most timid promises of political reform, often made to placate international and especially American pressure, were not fulfilled. Political liberalisation, from the empowerment of civil society to the opening of the public sphere to new political actors, remained a mirage. At a conference on political reform in Qatar on 11 January, US Secretary of State Hillary Clinton gave a stark and prescient warning: 'While some countries have made great strides in governance, in many others, people have grown tired of corrupt institutions and a stagnant political order. The region's foundations are sinking into the sand.' A week later, the secretary general of the Arab League, Amr Moussa, echoed this assessment by declaring in the presence of Arab leaders at an economic conference: 'the Arab soul is broken by poverty, unemployment and general recession'.

Tellingly, simmering discontent at pervasive state abuse and endemic police brutality made Bouazizi's tragedy resonate beyond Tunisia. Egyptians in particular were dismayed by similar episodes. A prominent Facebook group during Egypt's revolution was named 'We are all Khaled Said' after a young man from Alexandria who died in police hands in June 2010. In Syria, the video of the tortured body of 13-year old Hamza Khatib, caught by the security forces during a protest, galvanised the opposition.

Protesters also shared slogans and tactics. Use of social media, notably Facebook, Twitter and YouTube, for awareness and communication with the outside world was widespread (albeit not vital) to the course of the uprisings (see essay, pages 97–108). Still, authorities in every country tried to prevent use of the Internet and even engaged in online warfare and communications disruption, with mixed results as Internet activists found ways to bypass censorship and communicate with people abroad.

Another striking similarity among the various uprisings was the use and prevalence of two slogans, 'Selmiyah, Selmiyah' (peaceful, peaceful) and 'Al-sha'ab youreed iskat al-nizam' (the people want the demise of the regime). Protesters' demand for the departure of the leader was firm and absolute in Egypt, Libya, Syria, Tunisia and Yemen. Concessions from sitting rulers, including dismissal of their governments and promises not to run again, were met with uproar. Protesters had no confidence that such promises would be upheld and feared that time would allow rulers to regroup, renege and restore their rule. However, while there was a common urge to move fast and dismantle the pillars of the regimes, there was no unified vision of the kind of transition that should follow the leaders' departure.

Government responses to unrest

Taken aback by sudden popular revolts, Arab leaders struggled to respond. Invariably, the first instinct to mollify dissenters was the recourse to spending money. Since rising food and energy prices were eroding purchasing power, states increased subsidies or reversed cuts even when they could not afford to do so. Cash hand-outs were offered in Bahrain and elsewhere. Oil-rich countries such as Saudi Arabia unveiled ambitious programmes that prioritised housing, infrastructure and public-sector employment.

Political responses included the sacking of entire governments, with very different impacts in Egypt, Jordan, Oman and Syria. They were often accompanied by announcements of relaxation of stringent security measures that eroded rather strengthened the government's standing, as they were seen as admissions of weakness and evidence of previous unwarranted oppression. In Syria, the state of emergency was lifted in April after 48 years, although the crackdown continued unabated.

All governments sought to portray instability as provoked and directed from abroad, and demonstrators as doing the bidding of foreign patrons. In particular, foreign media, including the prominent Qatar-based al-Jazeera television channel but also Western networks, were accused of manipulating the news for nefarious purposes. Protesters were accused equally of being Israeli pawns, Iranian agents, Salafist activists, al-Qaeda terrorists and American puppets. In this information war, however, governments were unable to present coherent, credible narratives in spite of their control of state media.

Governments also seemed unable to take advantage of the fact that, while uprisings were fuelled by strong moral and political motivations, they were not driven by clear agendas. This reflected the fragmented nature of the opposition groups and the spontaneous, euphoric nature of the revolutions. In every case, uncertainty about cohesion, leadership and transition would therefore loom large after the revolutions, or as popular agitations continued.

Role of the security forces

The position adopted by each country's armed forces would inevitably be crucial as populations rose. Well-entrenched Arab leaders believed that they could count above all on the loyalty of their militaries – or at least, of particular units. The uprisings tested the standing, resilience and reliability of the costly security apparatuses in which every regime had heavily invested. The armed forces' conduct, largely a function of their institutional position, their composition and organisation, their degree of autonomy vis-à-vis the rulers, and their calculations about the likely outcome, proved critical in shaping the unfolding of events. When ordered to intervene, Arab militaries followed one of three courses: maintain awkward neutrality and ease the transition, side with the regime and block any change, or split and join the civil war.

In Tunisia, the Ben Ali regime favoured the police and Presidential Guard over the regular military, which was underfunded but respected among the population. As the popular wave of protest swept from inland provinces to more densely populated coastal areas, much hinged on the behaviour of the regular army. The capacity of the police to maintain control shrank considerably, with the extreme brutality that it practised only hardening the resolve of the demonstrators. The Presidential Guard, whose head, General Ali Seriati, was a close Ben Ali ally, was tasked with protecting key regime sites, including the presidential palace, while gangs of armed loyalists were deployed to break the protests. The refusal of the Tunisian army chief of staff, General Rachid Ammar, to order his troops to contain the demonstrations marked a turning point. Regular army units sided with the protesters and clashed with the Presidential Guard. This shift prompted Ben Ali, himself a former army intelligence chief, to flee the country. Afterwards, the Tunisian military resisted the temptation to oversee the transition and deferred to interim civilian authorities.

Similarly, the Egyptian regime of Hosni Mubarak, himself a former air force commander, relied chiefly on the Interior Ministry and State Security to enforce its authority. Egypt's notoriously corrupt and brutal internal security agencies were engaged as much in political monitoring and control as in countering terrorism. In comparison, the Egyptian army enjoyed popular esteem for its history as the defender of the nation and for being based on conscription.

At the start of Egypt's revolution on 25 January, the regime, concerned by the Tunisian precedent, ordered massive police deployments, supported by paid regime thugs known as *baltajiyya*. Within days, however, the extent of the popular mobilisation and the use of new tactics had overwhelmed the security forces throughout the country. The police lost battles for the control of the key bridges over the Nile and most importantly of Tahrir Square. Protesters also converged on the Interior Ministry, whose despised head Habib El-Adly became an iconic villain. Outside Cairo too, police stations came under attack from protesters.

Only after the Central Security Forces – controlled by the Interior Ministry – and the police had retreated from the central areas of Cairo did the Egyptian army deploy, including in Tahrir Square. In its statements, the army pointedly stressed its neutrality, proclaiming its wish to protect people and state. Yet behind closed doors, the military's manoeuvring to protect its own position would prove central to the demise of Mubarak. When Mubarak announced his resignation on 11 February, the Supreme Council of the Armed Forces, headed by Defence Minister Field Marshal Mohammed Hussein Tantawi, became the country's de facto ruling body. It suspended the constitution and ruled by decree, yet showed no inclination to perpetuate this situation; in fact, its refusal to transfer power to an interim civilian authority was intended to speed up the transition. Its pre-occupation – as well as to restore order – was to preserve its institutional position and privileges and to extricate itself from politics. Even as it tried to manage a transition that would pursue these interests, the army leadership, populated by aging generals, seemed confused and was at times overtaken by Egypt's rapidly changing politics. Under street pressure, several of its red lines were crossed, from the resignation of top officials to the dismantlement of the State Security apparatus and the decision to prosecute Mubarak. Its main interest was to achieve a rapid transition that would enable it to maintain its position.

In Libya, Syria and Yemen, the armed forces were designed as mere instruments of control, cultivated through special privileges and rewarded for loyalty. The Syrian army proved mostly cohesive; however, the Yemeni and Libyan militaries split.

The Libyan uprising started on 15 February with civilian demonstrations in Benghazi that were immediately repressed by the police. Within days, the movement had spread through eastern Libya and reports of the defection of army units and senior military officials emerged. A week later Gadhafi's interior minister, General Abdul Fatah Younis, joined the rebellion; he was eventually to lead its military operations. These defectors formed the core of the Free Libyan Army that fought forces loyal to Gadhafi together with unorganised rebel groups. Another blow to the Gadhafi regime was the defection of former intelligence chief Musa Kusa. Gadhafi, however, could count on special units led by his sons, most prominently Khamis, whose battlefield performance proved crucial against NATO and the rebellion.

Splits in Yemeni armed forces also occurred as Saleh sought to remain in power. Close relatives of the president held key security positions. His son, Ahmed, commanded the Republican Guard; his half-brother Mohammed the air force; his nephew Yahya the riot police; another nephew, Tariq, his personal protection unit; yet another nephew, Amar, the National Security Agency. Still, there was resentment of Saleh among the ranks of the military, exhausted by years of counter-insurgency against various domestic groups but also bitter over Saleh's nepotistic ways. The most prominent defection was that of General Ali Muhsin al-Ahmar, a relative of Saleh and a key army commander, who joined the opposition in March and ordered his troops to protect the demonstrators. This led to a stand-off between his division and forces loyal to Saleh.

In comparison, the Syrian security forces remained unified. Three months into the Syrian uprising, there was still no significant defection at the top or massive desertions. This was largely due to the presence at the top of officers picked for their loyalty to the regime, mostly from the Alawite and other minorities, and the preferential treatment granted to elite units under their command. Importantly, Maher al-Assad, the president's brother, headed the elite Fourth Division and the Republican Guard, and Asef Shawkat, his brother-in-law, was army deputy chief of staff. To quell the protests in the hotbeds of Baniyas, Deraa, Homs and Jisr al-Shughour, the regime dispatched the Alawite-dominated Fourth Armoured Division rather than rely on regular units composed of Sunni conscripts who could not be counted, on given the increasingly sectarian nature of the uprising.

Elsewhere, in Bahrain, Jordan and Oman, where lower levels of violence occurred, there were no cracks in the security services. The Bahrain Defence Force and the police include large number of foreigners from Jordan, Pakistan, Syria and Yemen whose loyalty is entirely to the ruling family, which provides the most senior commanders.

Defining moment for political Islam

If the Arab world's militaries were confronted with unfamiliar and unwelcome choices, so too were its political parties. In particular, the uprisings presented unexpected challenges for both mainstream and radical Islamist parties. The sudden opening of the political field meant that they had to adapt abruptly, with varying degrees of difficulty.

For long, mainstream Islamist movements, allowed to operate under strict constraints when not repressed, had adopted a low political profile. In Egypt, the Muslim Brotherhood, which was officially banned but tolerated, was effectively routed out of parliament in the November 2010 elections. Tunisia's outlawed An-Nahda (Renaissance) party was fiercely repressed by the Ben Ali regime. Membership in the Syrian Muslim Brotherhood still carried a death sentence. Libya's weak Islamist opposition, split between low-key moderates and radical elements affiliated with al-Qaeda, was deemed an existential threat by the Gadhafi regime.

Initially, the pace and nature of the popular protests took established Islamist parties by surprise. Having grown risk averse after years of repression, they were unwilling to challenge the state for fear of heavy reprisals in case of failure. The non-religious, diverse character of initial protests and the leading role of new, non-traditional actors – labour organisations in Tunisia, youth groups in Egypt – confused and alienated them. In Egypt, the Muslim Brotherhood resisted direct participation and even attempted to prevent, vainly, its youth from participating in the Tahrir Square demonstrations. For a time it seemed that Islamist groups had been overtaken by events.

Yet the enduring power of the Muslim Brotherhood was made amply clear two weeks after the resignation of Mubarak. In an unmistakable display of political muscle, two million people in Tahrir Square greeted Sheikh Yousef al-Qaradawi, an influential conservative preacher who lived in exile. Wael Ghonim, the young Google executive who had emerged as an icon of the youth movement, was prevented from taking the stage.

Islamist movements, better organised and with a clear leadership, were indeed best placed to advance their cause once the Ben Ali and Mubarak regimes collapsed. Realising the opportunity, the Muslim Brotherhood and An-Nahda became partners of the transitional authorities in Egypt and Tunisia respectively. In Egypt, the Brotherhood made sure not to clash with the military leadership, with which it shared the goals of rapid transition, early elections and return to order. Both the Brotherhood and the military feared that a longer transition and delayed elections could hand an advantage to newer, younger political groups. This explained the Brotherhood's support for the constitutional reforms advocated by the military leadership and its opposition to further street action, putting it at odds with the rest of the opposition.

At mid-2011, Tunisia's An-Nahda and Egypt's Muslim Brotherhood seemed well placed to win significant representation in upcoming legislative elections, which explained their apparent preference for parliamentary systems. Yet the two appeared prudent at first, mindful of the concerns of other segments of society and the international implications of a show of force. The Brotherhood leadership insisted it did not seek domination of Egypt and Tunisia's new politics but rather was willing to engage in parliamentary and coalition politics. Egypt's Muslim Brotherhood decided to present candidates in only 50% of the country's districts and, like An-Nahda, promised not to field a presidential candidate. Its newly established political wing, the Justice and Freedom party, appointed a Coptic vice-president – significant given persistent tensions between Muslims and the Copts, the Egyptian Christian community.

However, it became clear that Islamists themselves were divided over political action. In Egypt, several prominent Brothers split from the organisation. A reformist Brother, Abdel Moneim Aboul Fotouh, announced his presidential candidacy. Former members of a liberal persuasion established the Al-Wasat party. Notably, youth leaders decided to form their own party out of frustration with a leadership they deemed conservative and sclerotic.

Perhaps more worryingly, Egypt's and Tunisia's Muslim Brotherhood faced the prospect of being outflanked on their right. The emergence of Salafist movements in both countries willing to challenge the arguably uneasy consensus over secularism aroused concern about the readiness of Islamists to work within the system rather than design a new one in line with their conservative beliefs. Well funded and well organised, often suspected of ties to Saudi Arabia, Salafist factions announced their intention to contest electoral seats.

This Salafist rise contributed to a sharpening of communal tensions. Between February and May, communal clashes in Egypt between Muslims and Copts led to dozens of deaths. Several Coptic churches were torched, and a newly appointed Coptic governor was removed under pressure from Salafists. Army attempts to contain the violence suffered from the general state of disorder across the country and suspicions of an unspoken alliance between the military and the Brotherhood. In Syria, sectarian manipulation became an instrument of mobilisation for the regime. Government claims that Salafists and Muslim Brothers were directing the uprising bolstered fears among the Alawite, Christian and Druze communities, which largely rallied behind the regime. Rumours abounded that protest slogans included 'Alawites to the grave, Christians to Beirut'.

Alongside mainstream Islamist movements, radical Islamist groups, many affiliated to al-Qaeda, also faced challenges of an existential nature. If the demise or weakening of regimes backed by repressive security agencies allowed greater operational freedom, it also exposed the inability of their ideology and violent tactics to achieve results to compare with those of non-violent uprisings, including the mobilisation of large segments of society in favour of change. To remain relevant, jihadist organisations were compelled to adopt different local strategies. The outbreak of civil war in Libya provided Libyan jihadists, many of whom had engaged in global terrorism and the Iraq war after suffering heavy losses at the hands of the Gadhafi regime, with an opportunity to join the local fight. In the early days of the civil war, they often proved more battle-hardened and effective than the rag-tag rebel forces they operated alongside. But whether they could find a place in any post-Gadhafi political arrangement remained uncertain.

For al-Qaeda in the Arabian Peninsula (AQAP), which had emerged in recent years as a global as well as domestic terrorist threat in Yemen, the popular challenge to Saleh came as a respite since it diverted security resources to ensure the survival of his regime. Seizing this opportunity, AQAP moved into the southern town of Zinjibar and the province of Abyan. There was a significant risk that a prolonged security and political vacuum would allow AQAP and like-minded groups to consolidate their presence in Yemen. Meanwhile, two events served as further reminders of the enduring potency of the terrorist threat. On 28 April in the Moroccan city of Marrakesh, a bomb killed 17 people, including Western tourists. On 2 May, the US killing of Osama bin Laden exposed both the irrelevance of his ideology to the most profound dynamics shaping the future of Arab societies, and the fact that the spectre of jihadist violence and retaliation still hovered above them. Tellingly, the bin Laden killing failed to provoke any serious grassroots reaction in the Arab world.

Economic setbacks

Paradoxically, while the Arab Awakening has deep roots in economic underperformance and growing social inequalities, its unfolding and the resulting disorder only aggravated, at least for the short term, the economic, social and fiscal woes of Arab countries. While economies in the oil-rich Gulf states continued to grow as a result of high oil prices, resource-poor countries in political turmoil found themselves struggling between deteriorating economic conditions and fiscal largesse. In Egypt, Syria and Tunisia, tourism, a main source of employment, government revenue and foreign currency, was hard hit by massive cancellations and reputational damage at the peak of the season.

In all three countries, banking and finance also suffered. The Egyptian stock market was closed for two months, and Egyptian officials approached the Dubai stock market for dual listing of Egyptian stocks. Capital flight was recorded due to political uncertainty, creating pressures on currencies and foreign exchange reserves and requiring the intervention of central banks. Debt ratings were cut, making access to international financial markets more difficult and costly.

Uncertainty about the business environment deterred private investors. Businessmen accused of corruption and favouritism were hauled to jail, especially in Egypt. In Tunisia, the pervasive business interests of the family of Ben Ali were in the process of being dismantled. In many instances, assets, concessions and licenses acquired from the state were scrutinised for suspected abuse in the acquisition process. The private sector often likened this scrutiny to a witch-hunt. In parallel to political protests, labour groups organised strikes demanding higher pay, disrupting commercial and industrial activity. In Syria, the collusion between the regime and the business elite was also a source of anger among the population. For example, early in the uprising protesters torched a branch of Syriatel, Syria's main mobile operator owned by Rami Makhlouf, cousin of President Assad. In Bahrain, where the financial sector represents up to a quarter of the economy, concerns about the viability of Manama as a leading banking centre were raised.

Almost all governments responded to political unrest by pledging to increase subsidies and salaries. This created inflationary pressures and deepened fiscal problems. In general, fears increased that a populist and statist reaction would stall, delay and possibly reverse market-friendly policies and further distort Arab economies. The appointment of ministers critical of economic liberalisation as pursued in the past decade and the preference of large segments of Egyptian society for a greater regulatory role for the state seemed to validate these concerns.

The prospect that the Tunisian and Egyptian economies would shrink without outside help, jeopardising their political transition, prompted larger countries to intervene. The United States pledged in May to forgive $1 billion of Egypt's debt and offer another $1bn in economic assistance. A statement on the Arab Awakening at the May G8 summit at Deauville, France, said multilateral development banks could provide $20bn, a figure that could be increased by bilateral support. Another source of capital was the Gulf states, flush with budget surpluses due to high oil prices. Saudi Arabia and Qatar pledged $4bn and $10bn investment packages respectively for Egypt. The Gulf states also extended financial assistance to Bahrain and Oman in the form of a $10bn package for each to fund stimulus plans and housing and infrastructure projects. On the other hand, Yemen, already facing massive economic decay, an acute shortage of resources and depleted foreign currency reserves, found itself on the verge of economic collapse.

A new Arab order?

The Arab Awakening seems certain to alter the region's dynamics and alliances. As of mid-2011, however, the balance of power had not yet shifted in a clear and decisive manner.

Before the uprisings swept the region, the organising principle for the regional security architecture revolved around Iran's influence and suspected intentions. A Western-backed, US-orchestrated front composed of the Gulf states, Egypt and Jordan, as well as most North African states, confronted an Iranian-led alliance grouping Syria, Hizbullah, Hamas and powerful Iraqi factions. Egypt played a central role in this architecture by virtue of its close relations with the United States, Israel and the Gulf states. For its part, Israel calculated that an objective convergence of interests over Iran would overcome Arab frustration over its own intransigence on the Palestinian issue and the peace process. Meanwhile Turkey, capitalising on its image in the Arab street, its economic success and its global recognition, was pursuing a self-confident outreach campaign towards the Arab world.

The Arab Awakening forced a fundamental rethink of the posture of each country. When the revolutionary tide hit Egypt, a cornerstone of the old Arab order, concerns and calculations surfaced about the region's new geopolitics. During the Egyptian revolution, Emirati Foreign Minister Abdullah bin Zayed paid Mubarak a visit that was widely interpreted as showing Gulf support for his rule. Saudi officials also made clear their attachment to Mubarak as a reliable ally.

The decision by US President Barack Obama to call for Mubarak's departure led, therefore, to a deterioration of relations between Washington and its Gulf allies, who saw it as strategically dangerous and naive.

Gulf concerns about Egypt subsequently revolved around three matters: the transition and the fate of Mubarak; domestic politics and the rise of the Muslim Brotherhood; and the country's strategic orientation. On the latter, the new Egypt's more accommodating position vis-à-vis Iran raised Gulf anxieties. The decision to elevate diplomatic relations with Tehran and the permission given to two Iranian warships to transit the Suez Canal suggested to them that Cairo would distance itself from Mubarak's hardline anti-Iranian position. The Gulf states, notably Saudi Arabia, moved quickly to try to ensure that Egypt's military rulers did not deviate too much from previous policies, using capital and influence. Indirect Gulf influence was felt through the rise of the Salafist movements. An episode of this struggle for influence played out at the Arab League. An election to replace outgoing Secretary General Amr Moussa pitted Egyptian Foreign Minister Nabil Al Arabi, distrusted in Gulf capitals, against a Qatari diplomat. Ultimately, Al Arabi won the largely powerless but symbolic position only with the conditional blessing of the Gulf states.

A further key issue was the possible impact on the Israel–Palestine peace process. There was keen interest in the fate of the peace treaty signed by Egypt and Israel in 1979, which had governed the strategic posture of both countries ever since. Egypt's military, out of concern for stability but also to preserve its privileged relationship with the United States, was adamant that it would uphold the country's treaty obligations even as calls from many corners of Egyptian society demanded a revision of the peace agreement or a new approval process. Mubarak's ouster also removed a key player in the effort to contain Hamas, seal off Gaza and shore up the Palestinian Authority. Post-Mubarak, the Egyptian tone vis-à-vis Israel hardened. To Israel's dismay, the interim government proceeded to reach out to Hamas, broker reconciliation between Hamas and Fatah and open its border with Gaza.

The spread of the unrest to Syria from March threatened further to disrupt the regional order. As Iran's only Arab ally and its conduit to Hamas and Hizbullah, Syria had positioned itself in Iran's strategic orbit. Damascus banked that such a positioning would grant it a pivotal role out of proportion to its real economic, political and military strength. It was therefore ironic that, in spite of the repressive nature of the Assad regime, no major player seemed to want its downfall. This was partly because Syria, ostracised for several years for its disruptive role in Lebanon, Iraq and the Palestinian territories, had recently been the subject of intense courtship by the United States, Europe and Arab countries. Meanwhile, Iran had a paramount need for its ally; Turkey had found a junior and obedient partner; Israel had learned to live with a weak and deterrable enemy; the Gulf states were opposed to further turmoil; and Washington, with little leverage, worried about a civil war. However, the brutality of the crackdown quickly alienated the United States, Europe and, importantly, Turkey, which faced the spillover effect of the repression in the form of incoming Syrian refugees and Kurdish unrest.

Indeed, the turmoil in the Arab world tested Turkey's approach to its Middle East neighbourhood, known as its 'zero-problem' policy. Predicated on political stability, it suffered its first blow in Libya. At first, Prime Minister Recep Tayyip Erdogan opposed any foreign intervention in the face of the Gadhafi repression because of significant Turkish business interests there. Later, Turkey reversed its position and even joined the NATO effort.

Turkey faced its biggest crisis with regard to Syria. Eager to turn it into a partner, Erdogan had invested political capital and built a friendship with Assad. The two countries had lifted visa and trade restrictions and even conducted joint military exercises. Once the Syrian revolt and the repression gathered steam, Erdogan became vulnerable to accusations that he had accommodated a dictator who slaughtered Sunnis. After a few weeks of vain encouragement of reforms rather than repression, Turkey increasingly voiced condemnation of Syrian actions, with Erdogan calling them 'inhumane'. This provoked a forceful reaction in Damascus, which accused Turkey of manipulating the Muslim Brotherhood to reassert its imperial power. The split between the two countries has shattered what had been emerging as a strong regional axis that balanced America's Arab allies.

Faced with these momentous changes in the region, the conservative Gulf states, led by Saudi Arabia, became the protectors of the old order. Worried that the transformations were distracting the United States and strengthening Iran, they embarked on a regional campaign to contain the upheaval or shape its outcome. This effort, labelled by many as a counter-revolution, relied on their political but also financial power.

Nowhere was this more evident than in their response to the reform movement in Bahrain. Saudi Arabia in particular feared that the opposition, dominated by movements representing the island state's Shia majority, would win fundamental reforms including the establishment of a constitutional monarchy. This precedent would in turn embolden its own, suppressed Shia minority. After a failed attempt at dialogue, faced with the prospect of sectarian clashes and in reaction to alleged Iranian meddling, the Khalifa royal family requested the intervention of the six-member Gulf Cooperation Council (GCC), which deployed units in Bahrain under the banner of its military arm, the Peninsula Shield Force. The Gulf states also provided political cover for the crackdown in Bahrain, which the United States initially condemned. Faced with a concerted Gulf front on Bahrain and reliant on Saudi influence to manage other issues, Washington retreated after having encouraged dialogue.

The unravelling of Yemen also tested the power of the GCC. Geographical proximity, societal relations and an interest to prevent the collapse of Yemen prompted the GCC to launch a mediation plan to obtain Saleh's peaceful departure. Headed by GCC Secretary General Abdullatif Al-Zayani of Bahrain, the effort seemed on the verge of success several times, only for Saleh to renege at the last minute. This frustrated the Gulf states, especially Saudi Arabia, Saleh's increasingly ambivalent funder. The effort was suspended after Saleh sent vigilantes to the embassy of the United Arab Emirates, where the Gulf envoys were gathered. Later, Saudi Arabia took in Saleh for treatment after he was injured in an attack on his palace. The Gulf states then used that opportunity to quietly reach out to the various Yemeni parties to secure a viable transition.

The assertiveness of the GCC in its own neighbourhood in the face of both Iran and the United States, more a sign of anxiety than confidence, was accompanied by a greater effort to reach out to new security partners, especially in Asia. It also took the form of a surprise announcement that the GCC would welcome the entry of Jordan and Morocco into the organisation. This led to speculation that the potential inclusion of these two Sunni kingdoms would form a monarchical front in the region to resist the wave of change. However, the prospects for such an enlargement remained small.

Discussion on the balances of power in the Arab world could not have been expected to form a prominent part of this year's *Strategic Survey: The Annual Review of World Affairs*. Such was the truly surprising nature of the Arab Awakening. Given that the upheavals are continuing and the transitions in countries that have toppled their leaders are still in their early stages, the longer-term effects of the events of the first half of 2011 will await analysis in future years. The rest of this chapter recalls the events in each of the countries affected by the Arab Awakening. In addition, the regular sections on Iran, Iraq and Israel/Palestine appear in chapter 6 and on Turkey in chapter 5.

Tunisia: The Unrest Begins

An Arab favourite of international organisations for its economic performance and of Western states for its counter-terrorism record and secular character, Tunisia seemed at the beginning of 2011 to be an improbable catalyst for widespread political change. Its powerful security apparatus had managed to squash any meaningful opposition to President Zine el-Abidine Ben Ali's 23-year rule and to his ruling party, the Rassemblement Constitutionnel Democratique (RCD). The unrest provoked by the suicide of fruit-seller Mohamed Bouazizi therefore appeared, at first, unlikely to shake the regime or to inspire revolutionaries throughout the Arab world.

The Arab Awakening starts in Sidi Bouzid

On 17 December 2010, 26-year-old Bouazizi set himself on fire after police confiscated the cart of fruit and vegetables he was selling without a permit in the town of Sidi Bouzid. In an environment marked by growing un- and under-employment, corruption, food inflation and police brutality, Bouazizi's self-immolation – he died on 4 January – resonated nationally and regionally. Several other men committed suicide in subsequent days.

Discontent at Ben Ali's rule had been fuelled by the slowdown of the economy in recent years and by revelations about the extent of corruption among his close circle, including the publication of a US government cable by WikiLeaks shortly before the protests. In particular, the growing concentration of power and wealth by the reviled Trabelsi clan, Ben Ali's in-laws, was alienating not only Tunisian citizens but also many in the elite who felt displaced by these newcomers.

At first, protests were confined to poorer, peripheral rural areas, away from the developed urban centres on the coast. Early attempts by the government to placate demonstrators by extending largesse, and to crush the movement by force, failed. By late December, the movement reached Tunis and gained the support of Tunisia's well-organised labour unions, lawyers and other segments of society. On 28 December, Ben Ali appeared on television for the first time since the start of the unrest to condemn the protesters' violence and pledge to remain firm. At the same time, he offered minor concessions, including the dismissal of security, regional and government officials, and made economic promises.

The spread of the protests eventually attracted coverage by the international media, fed by Tunisian citizens who contributed pictures and videos through Twitter and Facebook (see pages 98–101). A broad crackdown, tight media censorship and Internet restrictions failed to block popular momentum. As demonstrations spread and escalated, the security forces resorted to deadly use of force, for example killing dozens of people in the town of Kasserine, and requested the backing of the military, which deployed in many cities but refused to engage in anti-protest operations. Tunisian Army Chief of Staff Rachid Ammar reportedly declined an order by Ben Ali to open fire. After the collapse of the riot police and domestic intelligence, Ben Ali could count only on the Republican Guard. On 13 January, the president announced in a televised address political concessions, including a promise not to seek re-election in 2014. The next day, he declared a state of emergency, dismissed his government and announced fresh legislative elections. This did little to appease the protesters, and demonstrations continued.

In still unclear circumstances, Ben Ali was persuaded on 14 January to board a plane for what he expected to be a momentary absence while the Republican Guard seized control of the situation. Denied permission to land in several European states, Ben Ali ultimately found refuge in Saudi Arabia.

Contested transition

Twenty-eight days after popular unrest had begun, Prime Minister Mohamed Ghannouchi announced that he had temporarily assumed the presidency. He announced several security and political measures, including a military curfew in the capital to restore order. But the constitutionality and unfolding of the transition remained uncertain, with many disputing Ghannouchi's self-promotion.

Indeed, the next day, the country's constitutional court ordered that the speaker of parliament, Fouad Mebazaa, should become president. He asked Ghannouchi to form a coalition government by including opposition parties, civil society, labour groups and youth movements. The line-up announced by Ghannouchi, however, kept key figures of the Ben Ali regime in place, angering the revolutionaries. To placate them, Mebazaa, Ghannouchi and several ministers resigned from the RCD.

This and other concessions announced in February failed to satisfy the activists, who mobilised again, also demanding the banning of the RCD (which was eventually suspended by the judiciary) and the prosecution of former regime officials. The concern among revolutionaries that remnants of the Ben Ali regime would manage to hijack the transition and preserve the old system was the prime motivation. A month of protests and deadly clashes followed, forcing Ghannouchi to step down on 27 February, replaced by Beji Caid el Sebsi, a former minister untainted by association with the previous regime.

The interim government of Caid el Sebsi agreed with the High Council for the Realisation of the Objectives of the Revolution, a collection of politicians, activists and prominent people, on sequencing for the transition. An election was to be held in July to form a constituent assembly, later followed by presidential and legislative elections. Though the army presented itself as the protector of the revolution, its role was considerably less central or decisive than that of Egypt's military. Rather, the transition was civilian led.

Tunisia's transition, though smoother than Egypt's, also experienced difficulties. A debate over the date of the election went sour, with parties divided over a possible delay requested by the electoral commission on organisational grounds. Tunisia's leading parties, the Islamist An-Nahda and the centre-left Parti Démocrate Progressiste (PDP), opposed a postponement, arguing that it would only prolong political uncertainty. Most other parties, however, supported the commission's recommendation to schedule the elections on 23 October. The High Council's approval of this delay and concerns that secular parties were manipulating the transition to undermine An-Nahda led to the Islamist party's withdrawal.

Indeed, the once-banned An-Nahda, an affiliate of the Muslim Brotherhood, emerged as an important player in Tunisia's post-revolutionary politics. Its exiled head, Rached Ghannouchi, returned to acclaim from the party's lower- and middle-class constituency in late January. A crucial division developed between Islamists on the one hand and the liberals and leftists on the other over the constitution and identity of Tunisia. An-Nahda, itself in the process of rebuilding after a 20-year absence, claimed that the postponement of elections and other moves by the High Council were aimed at checking its power ahead of the elections despite its stated commitment to democracy, personal freedoms, citizenship and gender rights. Among progressives, fears abounded that An-Nahda would halt, and reverse, Tunisia's liberal achievements.

Still, An-Nahda had to contend with Tunisia's lively and diverse political scene. By mid-2011, polls indicated that An-Nahda would be the largest party but would not win a majority of seats, suggesting that it would be forced to engage in coalition politics. The PDP was expected to come a close second. A myriad of liberal and leftist parties, including Congress for the Republic and the Communist Party, but also remnants of the RCD, were gearing up for the elections, all resolute in their opposition to An-Nahda.

Egypt: Mubarak Toppled

Following the rigged elections of November 2010, which saw a massive victory for the ruling National Democratic Party (NDP) and the weakening of all segments of the opposition, 2011 was widely expected to see the consolidation of the regime of Hosni Mubarak ahead of a transition that was likely to bring his son, Gamal, to power.

Yet, in 18 days, popular pressure combined with crucial intervention by the military ended Mubarak's 30-year rule, brought massive change to Egyptian politics and put the country on an uncertain, bumpy road to a more open political system. It also shook a main pillar of the Arab regional order, ensuring that Egypt's internal transformation would have considerable geopolitical implications.

Tunisia triggers activists

If the prospect of another Mubarak presidency had already motivated opposition activists, notably online opposition groups, into considering political and street action, the sudden fall of the Ben Ali regime in Tunisia provided inspiration and momentum. Activists came together to fight the nepotistic, autocratic and sclerotic nature of the Mubarak regime, the brutality and corruption of its police, growing inequalities, worsening economic and social conditions and a widespread sense of political and economic decay. Anger had been building for years, expressed mostly through small opposition gatherings and labour protests. The striking similarities with Tunisia and a sense of opportunity encouraged opposition groups, dominated by youth movements, to call for a day of mobilisation on 25 January.

On that day, tens of thousands of people took to the streets calling for an end to Mubarak's presidency. The protests flooding Cairo's huge Tahrir Square as well as the centres of Egypt's other main cities were met with brutal force from the police, who used rubber bullets, tear gas and concussion grenades to disperse the crowds. Over the next few days, both popular mobilisation and government repression escalated. The unforeseen success of the opposition convinced people who had initially been cautious, including the youth branch of the Muslim Brotherhood, to join its ranks. Predictably, the regime relied on its security forces to crush the protests. Hundreds of protesters and political activists were arrested. In the subsequent clampdown, the Egyptian government resorted to various measures (including a blockade of social-media sites such as Twitter and Facebook) in an attempt to curtail the protesters' information-sharing and organisational tools. Foreign media, accused of fomenting and facilitating unrest, were targeted; a curfew was declared; pro-Mubarak supporters were mobilised, at times to sow chaos. In parallel, Mubarak offered political concessions, from the formation of a new government to the appointment of a vice-president to the announcement of an inclusive national dialogue, and stated his desire to retire after the end of his mandate.

This strategy of minor concessions and coercion failed to mollify and divide the core opposition. Central to its resilience was the fragmented, popular nature of the protest movement in which organised, traditional parties were marginal actors; its diverse makeup along economic, political, religious, organisational and generational lines; its maximalist character, which ensured that the regime's concessions, however tangible, failed to placate popular demands; and its resistance to state violence, which galvanised rather than weakened the movement.

The inability of the Central Security and the State Security forces to break the protests or even retake the ground occupied by the protesters, most symbolically in Tahrir Square, provoked a shift in the regime's survival strategy. Mubarak asked the Egyptian military, a respected institution, for help. The army was cheered as its vehicles rolled into Tahrir Square and other centres of protest. But as civil order collapsed, the military found itself playing an uncomfortable, ambivalent role, visible and present on the streets but unwilling to break the protests and equally reluctant to force Mubarak out of power.

Ultimately, it was Mubarak's own intransigence and aloofness that precipitated his downfall. On 10 February, he delivered a speech in which he transferred power to new Vice President Omar Suleiman but also announced his intention to remain in office. The next day, popular uproar, army pressure and growing condemnation abroad led to his resignation and the transfer of power to the Supreme Council of the Armed Forces (SCAF) headed by Defence Minister Field Marshal Mohamed Hussein Tantawi.

Army-led transition
Mubarak's departure left SCAF in charge of overseeing the transition, a decisive and central role for which it seemed culturally and politically ill prepared. Tasked with protecting the nation and ensuring internal order after the battered and reviled police disappeared from the streets, it appeared equally concerned with preserving its own position and privileges and ensuring that no brutal change in Egypt's strategic orientation be made. The military dissolved parliament, suspended the constitution and formed a committee to recommend constitutional changes ahead of elections.

The transition the military envisioned was swift, smooth and benign in terms of impact on the political order. To achieve this, the military, which wanted rapidly to extricate itself from this unwanted responsibility, paradoxically chose to discard power-sharing with civilians and instead adopted a hands-on approach. It sought quick elections. Protesters, however, distrusted the military's aims. Their suspicions that it intended to preserve several pillars of the previous regime led to public confrontation. The army was forced to sanction several things that it had not intended. The prime minister, a holdover of the Mubarak era, was forced to resign and was replaced by Essam Sharaf, deemed more acceptable by the revolutionaries. Other ministers were forced out, and several were sent for trial, notably Mubarak's information and interior ministers. The revolutionaries obtained the dismantling of State Security, the domestic security branch responsible for political monitoring and repression, after storming its headquarters. Finally, under street pressure, prosecutors seized assets held by Mubarak and his family, barred them from leaving the country while being investigated for corruption, and later put them under arrest.

Nevertheless, the basic shape of the transition remained as the military intended. Constitutional amendments that it designed, limiting the powers of the presidency, were passed by an overwhelming majority of 77% in a referendum on 19 March. The revolutionaries had campaigned against these amendments, considering them too limited. They preferred the forming of a constituent assembly that would draw up a new constitution, preserve the secular character of the state and strip the presidency of much of its powers, to the benefit of the legislative and judicial branches. However, the military wanted to preserve the presidential system, from which it derived much of its institutional authority. It prevailed in the referendum largely because of popular fatigue with upheaval and an unspoken alliance between the military and the Muslim Brotherhood. The latter was engaged in a delicate game to reassure the military of its good intentions without alienating revolutionary activists.

In spite of their referendum defeat, the revolutionaries, albeit now divided over tactics and strategy and having lost the support of Islamist movements, kept up the pressure. In April and May, large demonstrations were held in Tahrir Square despite a new law banning protests and strikes. Demands ranged from a new electoral timetable to the prosecution of former officials. The military responded by addressing some grievances, including the banning of the former ruling National Democratic Party, but also arrested activists and journalists deemed to be endangering the transition or attacking the military.

However active and successful they were on the streets, the revolutionaries appeared less capable of organising themselves politically and preparing for the elections (due to be held in September for the legislature and November for the presidency). The liberal, leftist and youth groups that spearheaded the revolution were underfunded and disorganised, incapable of reaching out beyond their urban constituencies. Some, like the April 6 youth movement, opted not to transform into political parties but rather to operate as political watchdogs.

As Islamist groups gained greater sway during the transition, the key demands of revolutionary activists were for the postponement of the elections and the approval of a new constitution ahead of any election. They feared that big Islamist electoral gains would decisively shape Egypt's future. Several activist groups pledged to work together to counter the emerging nexus between the military, the Muslim Brotherhood and the remnants of the NDP. Other groups, however, including the liberal Al-Wafd, joined a Brotherhood-led slate for the elections, hoping that this alliance of convenience would help them win seats in parliament.

Another victim of the breakdown of order and the uncertain transition was Egypt's economy. Tourism, which accounts for one in eight jobs, was hardest hit, and the financial sector suffered from prolonged paralysis. Capital flight and pressures on the Egyptian pound strained foreign reserves. The transition also strained state finances, with promises of increased subsidies, salaries and state-funded projects. At the same time, labour protests and other forms of labour activism multiplied, paralysing industrial and commercial activity. Public demands for prosecution of those in the business elite who were associated with Mubarak's regime were perceived as a witch-hunt by the private sector. Leftist revolutionaries also called to stop or reverse market-friendly economic reforms. In essence, Egypt's economic woes worsened, requiring foreign assistance at a time Egyptians were less likely to respond positively to economic and political conditionality from the Western states and international organisations. Indeed, in late June, the Egyptian government decided to turn down a loan from the International Monetary Fund. However, Gulf states, seeking to maintain their influence in post-revolutionary Egypt, pledged $14bn in aid and investment.

Rise of sectarianism
In parallel to the political upheaval and a broadly shared sense of a breakdown of order, tensions between segments of the Muslim and Christian communities grew. This was occurring even before the revolution: worshippers leaving a New Year's Mass were killed in an explosion outside a Coptic church in Alexandria. The attack was later attributed to an al-Qaeda-linked, Gaza-based Palestinian militant group, though there were allegations it was orchestrated by the Mubarak regime.

Despite Coptic participation in the Egyptian revolution, which featured scenes of inter-religious solidarity, tensions between the communities escalated again after the departure of Mubarak. Muslim attackers torched several churches after deadly clashes, notably in the district of Imbeba south of Cairo. The government yielded after a demonstration by tens of thousands of Muslims asking for the rejection of the appointment of a Coptic Christian governor in the province of Qena.

The Coptic community was shaken by the emergence of hardline Salafist groups, which were more involved in sectarian violence than the Muslim Brotherhood (which called for calm) and were allegedly funded by Saudi Arabia. Christians were also concerned that Islamist electoral gains would enshrine the role of sharia law in any new constitution.

The rise of the Muslim Brotherhood

Although its role and ideology were marginal in the unfolding of Egypt's revolution, the Muslim Brotherhood seemed particularly well placed in the post-Mubarak era. It demonstrated cunning and pragmatism by partnering with the military leadership over the transition plan and desire for order, and specifically on the referendum.

Recognising that there was concern at home and abroad about its rising influence, it made a series of promises to allay such fears, including the commitment not to field a presidential candidate, not to run in more than half of the country's districts and even to form an electoral list with the liberal Wafd and other parties. It formed a new political party, called Justice and Freedom, which claimed to seek inspiration from Turkey's ruling Justice and Development Party (it even appointed a Copt as vice-president). Rather than taking power, the Muslim Brotherhood argued that it aimed to become the country's main political force and engage in parliamentary and coalition politics. In this way it sought to energise its political base.

At the same time, the Muslim Brotherhood faced considerable internal discontent. Tolerated (though officially banned) during the Mubarak era, it now faced the challenge of adapting to a more open playing field in which its tactics, methods of mobilisation and even ideology seemed out of date. Its leadership, deemed too cautious and sclerotic by some members, had originally resisted any participation in the revolution – guidance that its youth branch discarded. In the spring, leaders of the youth branch announced they would break from the organisation. A prominent liberal Brother, Abdel Moneim Aboul Fotouh, announced his candidacy for the presidency, publicly breaking with the leadership. By June, five splinter groups had emerged from the movement. The Muslim Brotherhood also faced a challenge from its right with the rise of the Salafist movement.

Egypt's upheaval shakes regional order

The end of Mubarak's regime sent tremors through the Arab world and beyond. During the uprising, torn between its old alliance with Mubarak and its democratic ideals, the United States wavered, sending mixed messages. Ultimately, when it became evident that Mubarak had been decisively weakened, Obama called for his resignation and for the military not to use force against the revolutionaries. The United States struggled to regain the favour of Egypt's new rulers. The military, keen to preserve its relations with Washington and the substantial military aid it receives, was accommodating. But protesters, resentful of US wavering, gave a cold shoulder to Clinton during her first visit to Cairo after the revolution. Still, mindful of the importance of Egypt's successful transition, the United States announced a series of measures to support its economy and civil society.

While in the long term the possible return of a strong Egypt on the regional scene could serve as a check on Iranian regional ambitions, the Gulf states worried that its immediate weakening and a possible – if improbable – strategic shift would strengthen Iran's influence. They embarked on a campaign to ensure that Egypt's strategic and political choices remained aligned with theirs.

Meanwhile, anxiety in Israel also rose. Mubarak had preserved peace with Israel, contained Hamas and taken a tough line against Iran. His removal led to a debate within Egypt about the peace treaty, an Egyptian-brokered reconciliation between Hamas and Fatah and a relative warming of ties with Tehran.

Libya: NATO Intervenes in Civil War

Colonel Muammar Gadhafi was the first leader to react publicly and vociferously to the demise of the first president swept away by the Arab Awakening, Tunisia's Ben Ali. He scolded the Tunisian revolutionaries on 16 January, saying: 'There is none better than Zine to govern Tunisia. Tunisia ... is becoming prey to hooded gangs, to thefts and fire. [The situation is one of] chaos with no end in sight.' A month later, a popular movement erupted in the eastern city of Benghazi that brought the revolution to Libya. It soon escalated into a civil war and drew foreign intervention that threatened to end Gadhafi's rule.

On 15 February, small protests against the regime took place in Cyrenaica, Libya's eastern region. Though largely uncoordinated, they were heavily suppressed, and the effect was to inflame popular opinion in eastern Libya. Peaceful demonstrations quickly escalated into full-fledged civil war. The demand for Gadhafi's ouster unified ragtag groups of revolutionaries, including Islamists previously affiliated with al-Qaeda, and encouraged the defection of regular army units. Scores of senior Libyan diplomats, security and government officials, including Gadhafi's interior minister and later his foreign minister, defected from the regime. The fighting exacerbated Libya's tribal rivalries, with prominent tribes siding with the rebels. In the first weeks of Libya's revolution, rebel groups managed to advance as far as the suburbs of Tripoli, the capital, and Sirte, Gadhafi's home town. Protests even took place in the capital. On 27 February, prominent figures established a Benghazi-based Transitional National Council to coordinate the political and military activities of the rebellion and seek foreign support, including the freezing and transfer of Gadhafi assets outside Libya. The International Criminal Court announced the launch of an investigation into war crimes.

His survival at stake and amidst rumours of his flight, Gadhafi made two rambling and thunderous televised speeches in which he promised harsh punishment for the rebels, who he claimed used drugs and were manipulated by outside forces, including al-Qaeda. 'We are ready to hand out weapons to a million, or two million or three million, and another Vietnam will begin', he declared. His son and presumed heir Saif al-Islam, once seen as a moderniser, also appeared on television to threaten the rebels. Loyalist forces, which included conventional army units and African mercenaries as well as elite units under the command of Gadhafi's sons and relatives, managed to regroup in early March following a string of defeats. Better equipped, trained and led, they began to roll back the rebels. By mid-March, they had regained most of the territory lost and were advancing towards Benghazi, the rebellion's centre. The fighting provoked a major humanitarian crisis, pushing thousands of Libyans to flee to neighbouring Tunisia and Egypt. It also forced tens of thousands of foreign workers to seek emergency departure from Libya's congested ports and airports.

The rebel cause found allies in the Arab world. Unrelenting television coverage, Gadhafi's threats and concern among many Arabs that the Arab Awakening would end on the Libyan battlefields led to broad mobilisation of support. Members of the Gulf Cooperation Council and the Arab League issued statements condemning the violence against Libyan civilians and urging a UN-enforced no-fly zone – a measure first called for on 28 February by David Cameron, the British prime minister. Other countries, like Turkey and Germany, were at first reluctant to support a foreign intervention because of business interests and the safety of their workers. Mediation efforts by the African Union, itself divided over any UN action, failed to sway Gadhafi or even to obtain rebel approval.

The prospect of mass atrocities, the rebels' military setbacks, the unprecedented Arab advocacy for an intervention and the mobilisation of Western intellectuals increased pressure on Western governments to act. A reluctant Obama, torn between advisers advocating intervention on humanitarian grounds and others urging non-intervention for lack of an obvious national-security interest, eventually sided with Cameron and French President Nicolas Sarkozy at the UN Security Council. Yet the United States made it clear its role would be limited in time and deployment and would shift the burden to its allies after the initial phase.

The NATO military campaign

On 17 March , the UN Security Council passed Resolution 1973 authorising all necessary measures – except occupation by ground forces – to protect civilians under threat of attack in Libya, and imposing a no-fly zone. By that point, the Gadhafi regime was on the verge of defeating the rebels in eastern Libya and recapturing Benghazi. It had clearly signalled its intent to exact retribution. The regime had also cleared rebels from much of western Libya. There remained a few rebel strongholds in the Jebel Nafusa south of Tripoli and the rebels were under siege in the port city of Misrata. Both enclaves seemed to have little prospect of withstanding regime attacks.

French air attacks on 19 March stopped a regime armoured column on the road to Benghazi, and US-led operations to impose a no-fly zone began shortly afterwards. A maritime force was deployed to enforce an arms embargo and support the air campaign. Within the first few days the regime's air-defence capability was neutralised. NATO, which then assumed command of the campaign under Canadian Lieutenant-General Charles Bouchard, claimed that its attacks on regime ground forces had reduced the regime's military capability by over a third and had significantly degraded regime logistics, military supplies and command and control.

Eighteen nations were taking part in the NATO-led campaign, with 15 enforcing the no-fly zone. Belgium, Canada, Denmark, Italy, France, the Netherlands, Norway, Sweden the United Arab Emirates (UAE), the United Kingdom and the United States took part in ground attacks, with Jordan, Qatar, Spain and Turkey limiting themselves to policing the no-fly zone and

flying supporting missions. Bulgaria, Greece and Romania were participating in maritime operations only. By the beginning of June, after almost
10,000 NATO air sorties, regime forces had failed to defeat the eastern rebels.
Anti-Gadhafi forces in the west had pushed back regime troops encircling
Misrata. They had sustained their position in the Jebel Nafusa, captured
the town of Wasin and opened up a land corridor to Tunisia (see Strategic
Geography, pages VI–VII). Military defeat of the rebels by regime forces had
been avoided, but Gadhafi's troops had adapted to make it much harder for
NATO to attack them from the air.

Without NATO's air attacks the regime's efforts to defeat the rebels
would probably have succeeded. However, NATO had not yet applied sufficient combat power to either decisively change the balance on the ground
or to compel Gadhafi to comply with UNSCR 1973.

The regime was attempting to both minimise further rebel gains and
maintain its hold on the population and energy resources of western Libya
by sustaining a climate of fear and repression to deter Libyan civilians from
showing anti-regime sentiment. But there was evidence of a major shortage
of fuel for civilian vehicles and economic hardship for local businesses. And
encounters between ordinary Libyans and journalists who manage to elude
their minders suggested that support for Gadhafi was far less universal than
portrayed by the regime. When the government destroyed rebel forces in
Zawiya in early March, it made an example of high-profile defector Abu
Mousa. His family was 'disappeared' and his home demolished. Yet this did
not stop a steady stream of deserters from fleeing the country, often in secret.

France and Italy recognised the Transitional National Council (TNC)
as the legitimate government of Libya, followed by Qatar, the first Arab
nation to do so, and several other countries. A number of countries supplied
'non-lethal' military equipment to the rebels, including communications
equipment and body armour. The UK, France and Italy deployed diplomatic
and military teams to Benghazi, both to better assess the situation and to
assist the TNC. There was no evidence that any foreign forces were actively
training the eastern rebels or that special forces had been deployed, although
there were persistent but unconfirmed reports that the rebels had acquired
weapons from other countries, including Qatar. In late June, France admitted it had delivered small and light weaponry to rebels.

In eastern Libya the rebels pushed the regime forces back from the edge
of Benghazi, but were unable to dislodge government troops from a strong
defensive position at Brega. There was then a relative stalemate with the
rebels adopting a defensive position around Ajdabiya.

The fighting in eastern Libya showed the rebels there to have very limited military effectiveness. Their obvious enthusiasm and their possession of large numbers of light weapons and former regime military officers seemed not to have added significant value to their capability. Experience of developing the capability of indigenous forces in Iraq and Afghanistan suggested that it would take many months for the capability of the eastern Libyan rebels to improve to the extent that they could take on regime forces on equal terms, let alone display any military advantage.

In western Libya, the combination of a tenacious rebel defence and NATO air strikes defeated regime efforts to capture the city of Misrata. The defenders were also aided by small boats conveying supplies and fighters from eastern Libya, and by delivery of humanitarian aid and evacuation of casualties and stranded migrant workers.

In May NATO sought to reduce the threat of attack by regime artillery and armour by targeting logistic facilities and vehicle depots. As Western political leaders came under pressure to show results from the campaign, it stepped up efforts to attack regime leadership, command and control and the machinery of repression. NATO was benefiting from improved intelligence and surveillance provided by defectors and the Benghazi authorities. For example, Western media showed the aftermath of NATO attacks that had revealed previously unknown underground bunkers. NATO also attacked nondescript buildings that had been identified as offices of Gadhafi's intelligence and security services. Several strikes on his compounds and key regime facilities suggested that NATO forces were attempting to eliminate Gadhafi. The deployment of drones and French and British attack helicopters in June represented a further tactical escalation. A steady stream of defections and reports of collapsing morale among Gadhafi loyalists suggested that his hold on power, though still sustained by significant financial resources, was steadily eroding.

Political management of the war

Leadership of the operation to enforce UNSCR 1973 was vested in a NATO-led coalition which, as well as NATO members, included Jordan, Qatar, Sweden and the UAE. Diplomatic and economic activity was coordinated by the Libya Contact Group, which met at the levels of foreign ministers in Paris, Rome, Doha and Abu Dhabi. Delegates of the TNC also attended for consultations. The Contact Group also created a temporary financial mechanism to allow frozen regime financial assets to be passed to the TNC which, however, complained that the release of assets is was not occurring and that foreign military and financial support was lacking. It received help from Qatar to sell oil on the international market and to restart banking activity. The TNC also urged a widening of NATO operations.

Gadhafi tried to manipulate internal NATO tensions by offering cease-fires, leveraging Russian and Chinese displeasure with the war, courting African Union mediators and sending envoys to discuss political settlements that did not include his removal from power. Even as ideas were floated for a political settlement, though, the TNC remained adamant that no negotiation should occur before Gadhafi's departure.

By mid-2011 rebel setbacks, political divisions and a general sense of stalemate had eroded hopes that the NATO intervention would be short and decisive. Yet the fierce struggle for Misrata, the killing and kidnapping of foreign journalists, reports of atrocities by Gadhafi forces and the much-publicised case of rape victim Eman Al-Obaidi maintained Western and Arab support for the war. The International Criminal Court sought the arrest of Gadhafi and his intelligence chief Abdallah Senoussi on charges of war crimes.

Risks were posed to NATO's strategy by the unpredictable dynamics of civil wars, the possibility of bombs causing civilian casualties, increasing international doubts about NATO's approach, divisions within NATO about burden-sharing and strategy, the growing refugee crisis and US reluctance to increase its involvement. These risks could be reduced by increased political efforts to persuade Gadhafi to stand down coupled with stepping up the military effort. But the latter option would pose uncomfortable political and military choices for the United States, the UK and France.

Saudi Arabia: Resisting Change

Already fending off an ideological and strategic challenge from Iran and preparing for a potentially complicated monarchical succession, Saudi Arabia found itself in the first half of 2011 facing a major upheaval in its immediate neighbourhood. The Arab Awakening swept away its most precious Arab ally, Egyptian President Mubarak, and brought demands for political change and strife to its immediate borders. Saudi Arabia reacted by extending state largesse at home, launching a regional counter-revolution and adopting a more assertive tone and posture in its foreign policy.

Concerns about the succession to King Abdullah bin Abdulaziz Al Saud brought new attention to the complex politics of the Saudi royal family. The monarch spent several months abroad for medical treatment, returning in February 2011. During his absence, he delegated the country's affairs to Crown Prince Sultan bin Abdulaziz, his equally ill half-brother. In effect, this put ailing Prince Naif bin Abdulaziz, the hardline interior minister and the apparent next-in-line for succession, in charge of the country. Much speculation focused on the next generation, with several princes – Mohammed bin Naif, Khaled al Faisal and Bandar bin Sultan – emerging as possible choices.

Rocky US relations

Relations with the United States have tended towards tension on several occasions in recent years, and Saudi Arabia has assiduously been building relations with China and other powers. On one issue, however, the two are in agreement: the threat posed by Iran. Saudi Arabia's perception of Iran as its paramount strategic threat remained the driver of its foreign policy. The depth of its anxiety over Iran's nuclear programme was exposed by US diplomatic cables released by whistleblower website WikiLeaks. An April 2008 cable revealed details of a meeting of high-level US officials with King Abdullah in which he urged the United States to 'cut off the head of the snake', a veiled reference to a preventive strike against Iranian nuclear targets. At the same meeting, Foreign Minister Prince Saud al-Faisal pressed for tougher sanctions against the Iranian regime. WikiLeaks cables quoted US Secretary of Defense Robert Gates resisting such military action on the grounds that it would delay Iran's pursuit of nuclear capabilities only by three years at most.

Against this background, the kingdom pursued its military build-up and increased defence cooperation with the United States. In late 2010, it concluded a weapons deal worth $60bn over 15 to 20 years. The arms sale, the largest ever by the United States, was to include F-15 fighter jets and *Apache* attack helicopters. Though the shopping spree was largely motivated by Saudi fears over a nuclear-armed Iran, it also included weaponry more suited for the kind of war that Saudi Arabia fought against the Houthi rebels in Yemen in 2009–10. Since for Saudi Arabia arms procurement also amounts to an insurance policy and a way to reward allies, the large purchase served to consolidate its at times rocky relationship with the United States, the kingdom's top external security provider. Explaining the rationale behind the deal, a senior US defence official commented that 'bolstering Saudi Arabia's own defence capabilities would improve US security in a vital part of the world where fears are growing over Iran's nuclear programme'.

However, just as the deal was being finalised, tensions between Riyadh and Washington rose dramatically over Saudi displeasure at the US management of the Arab Awakening. Saudi officials felt that the US decision to call for Mubarak's prompt departure was strategically misguided and increased Iran's regional power. For the Saudi regime, it raised fundamental questions about the wisdom and reliability of the United States. The quarrel peaked over the unrest in Bahrain. There, the United States was encouraging peaceful dialogue between government and protesters even as Saudi Arabia detected Iranian mischief and worried that any agreement on a constitutional monarchy would embolden its own Shia community and set a precedent for other Gulf kingdoms. Relations reached a nadir in March when up to 1,500 Saudi troops entered Bahrain as part of the GCC Peninsula Shield Force without prior US knowledge or approval. King Abdullah rebuffed a request for a meeting from Gates. However, relations were soon re-established and Gates flew to Riyadh in early April to meet the king. US National Security Adviser Tom Donilon made a similar trip and Obama pointedly failed to mention Saudi Arabia in a major address on the Arab world in May. Such courting by Washington, concerned about the implications of a breakdown for other important US interests, and a lower US profile on Bahrain seemed to satisfy Saudi rulers. Even then, questions were raised about diverging perceptions and policies in both countries.

Support for embattled leaders

As the Arab revolutions unfolded, Saudi Arabia emerged as the primary defender of the status quo. Taken by surprise by the pace of events and deeply inimical to the demand for political change, it scrambled to extend political and financial support to embattled allied rulers in Bahrain, Egypt, Jordan and Morocco. It welcomed the Tunisian president after he fled his country. After failing to save Mubarak, Riyadh worked to ensure that Egypt's new political order and strategic orientation did not contradict its interests. It did so through aggressive diplomacy, subtle outreach to Egypt's new military rulers, support for the Salafist movement and pledges of economic assistance to the country's beleaguered economy. It intervened militarily in Bahrain and lobbied within the GCC in favour of extending membership to Morocco and Jordan, two Sunni monarchies.

Saudi Arabia also responded to the crisis in the Arab world by reaching out to non-Western allies. In April Prince Bandar bin Sultan, the king's national-security chief, made a visit to Pakistan, a traditional Saudi ally and military power, and other Asian states including China. Riyadh increasingly saw diversification of strategic relations as a way to balance its security dependency on the United States. It concluded a security and intelligence-sharing agreement with Malaysia and a defence-cooperation agreement with Indonesia.

Before unrest broke out in Syria, Riyadh had been seeking to rebuild ties as part of an effort to distance Damascus from Tehran and to contain the risks of internal conflict in Lebanon. This culminated in a joint visit by King Abdullah and Syrian President Bashar al-Assad to Lebanon in July 2010. Saudi policy towards Lebanon and Syria, handled by Prince Abdulaziz bin Abdullah, the king's son, was aimed at brokering an agreement between Lebanon's various factions to mitigate the impact of expected indictments by an international tribunal of Hizbullah members over the assassination of Rafik Hariri, the former Lebanese prime minister. It failed over the reluctance of Hariri's son, serving Prime Minister Saad Hariri, to compromise. This led in January 2011 to the collapse of Hariri's government, and a move by Hizbullah and Syria to take political control of Lebanon. Saudi Arabia's restrained reaction betrayed fatigue and lack of options.

The popular unrest against the Syrian regime then placed Saudi Arabia in a complex predicament, since it pitted the Sunni majority against the ruling Assad family, which came from the Alawite majority. The Saudi sense of religious solidarity with the protesters was strong, and there would also be real political and strategic benefits in the fall of Assad, including the weakening of Iran's reach in the region. Still, the kingdom had adopted a pro-status quo stance and feared the alternative in Syria.

Protests countered

The Arab Awakening prompted the Saudi Arabian government to boost spending and to contain possible unrest among Shi'ites in the Eastern Province. In response to a planned 'Day of Rage' in March, Saudi forces deployed security personnel to secure the city of Qatif, and arrested dozens of activists. Saudi religious authorities condemned demonstrations against the Al Saud family. The country's top religious scholar, Sheikh Abdel Aziz bin Abdulla al-Sheikh, issued a fatwa outlawing protests as a violation of Islamic principles and declaring that 'Islam strictly prohibits protests in the kingdom because the ruler here rules by God's will'. On the day of the protests, only a few hundred demonstrators participated in scattered marches across several cities, amongst a tightened security presence. Activism did, however, increase online.

To pre-empt further unrest, King Abdullah enacted measures amounting to $130bn to provide economic and social benefits to Saudi citizens. These included the establishment of a monthly minimum wage of $800, increases in social and welfare benefits, and the addition of 60,000 military and security jobs. The King also announced the construction of as many as 500,000 new housing units, valued at a total of $67bn. In parallel to these moves to assuage the population, the king warned that security forces would hit whoever 'considers undermining the Kingdom's security and stability'. Further warnings against public criticism of the religious establishment followed in televised appearances.

Government reforms proved successful in warding off unrest even though, only a few days after the king's warning, small-scale protests occurred outside the Interior Ministry demanding the release of thousands of prisoners who had been held for years without trial. In the face of scattered protests around the country, the monarchy sustained its strategy of limited political concessions and a hardline security stance. Promises to combat corruption were made, and municipal elections were announced for the second time in Saudi Arabia's history, although women remained excluded from the electoral process. In the following weeks, nearly 160 protesters were arrested.

Women's rights once again moved to the forefront in Saudi Arabia as a by-product of the Arab Awakening. On 22 May, Saudi authorities briefly detained Manal al-Sherif after she launched a campaign against the ban on women drivers. The campaign included a video of her driving and called for a mass breach of the ban on 17 June. Several Saudi women responded to the call to drive, taking the authorities by surprise and attracting condemnation from the most conservative corners of Saudi society.

Bahrain: Protests Crushed

The fragile political balance maintained between Bahrain's Shia opposition and its Sunni-minority ruling Khalifa royal family gave way in 2010, as the Bahraini government pursued an increasingly hard line against dissidents.

In the weeks leading up to parliamentary elections in October 2010, authorities arrested up to 250 opposition activists. Twenty-three people were charged with implementing an Iranian-backed plot to overthrow the government. Despite the arrests and discontent over reforms passed by King Hamad bin Isa Al Khalifa in 2001, Bahrain's opposition participated in the electoral process for the second time in a decade. Al Wefaq, the Shia community's main moderate party, made sweeping gains in the elections, securing 60% of the vote but only 18 out of 40 parliamentary seats because of gerrymandering. Even then, the fact that the lower chamber lacked real powers meant the opposition lacked a venue to convey popular dissatisfaction.

The Arab Awakening provided further impetus for Bahrain's opposition to renew demands for political and constitutional reform. On 14 February 2011, youth activists declared a 'Day of Rage', which attracted thousands across Shia villages in Bahrain. Police responded by firing tear gas and rubber bullets into the crowds, killing one protester. As the death toll from protests increased, demonstrators amassed in the capital city, Manama, and camped out at the centrally located Pearl roundabout, with some calling for the downfall of the monarchy and others for constitutional reforms.

Mixed responses towards the political opposition from Bahrain's government suggested an internal rift within Bahrain's ruling family. In a pre-dawn raid on protesters at the roundabout on 17 February, security forces killed three demonstrators and subsequently deployed military assets to secure the site. The next day, Bahrain's Crown Prince Sheikh Salman bin Hamad Al Khalifa, widely viewed as a reformist, expressed his sorrow at the deaths and invited Bahrainis to engage in a national dialogue. He also ordered the immediate removal of the military from the streets. A coalition of seven opposition political societies rejected the crown prince's initial offer of dialogue, demanding fulfilment of several preconditions including the establishment of a committee to redraft the constitution. As protesters returned to the roundabout area, the government took steps to appease opposition activists, including the pardon of exiles, the release of political prisoners and a minor cabinet reshuffle. These reforms complemented hand-outs of 1,000 Bahraini dinars per family that had been made in early February.

In parallel, however, the country witnessed a rise of sectarian tensions, with Sunni leaders calling for the formation of self-defence committees. Bouts of violence threatened to escalate into communal conflict. The opposition was divided over strategy and goals, with moderates unable to steer street protesters toward dialogue and hardliners eager to escalate demands and organise disruptive action.

In this tense environment, the crown prince announced a framework for dialogue, a desperate measure to bring the opposition to the table. But in the most public indication of internal disagreement within the ruling family,

King Hamad appeared on television hours later and declared a three-month state of national emergency. He also announced the immediate entry of troops from the GCC's Peninsula Shield Force to guarantee security. The security forces once again cleared the Pearl roundabout and entered the main hospital, which the government said had become a site of abuse by protesters.

The deployment of Peninsula Shield forces suggested that hardline Saudi-backed elements in the Bahraini government had reasserted themselves, ruining prospects for a political solution. The GCC forces, composed of Saudi, Emirati and Qatari troops, were deployed around critical infrastructure. Kuwait announced the deployment of a naval patrol to assist in securing Bahrain's territorial waters, following the refusal of its parliament to authorise the deployment of ground troops. The Bahraini military sealed off access to protest sites, established military checkpoints and enforced a nationwide curfew.

In the following weeks, the military authorities took measures designed to crush the political opposition. The country's largest state-run hospital was placed under military control and the Pearl Monument – the symbolic centre of the protests – was bulldozed. Military trials for opposition leaders accused of conducting an Iranian-backed plot to overthrow the government led to eight life sentences. The resignation of 11 Al Wefaq members of parliament was also accepted by the government, which announced elections to replace them for September.

Human-rights violations included the destruction of dozens of Shia mosques, arrests and prosecutions of doctors and nurses, the dismissal of over 1,300 workers for participation in political protests, and the deaths of four individuals in custody. Bahrain's reputation as a regional hub for investment took a direct hit. This led to the cancellation of several high-profile events, including motor racing's Formula One Grand Prix. Additionally, several businesses, including investment banks and consulting firms, temporarily closed their offices in Bahrain or shifted their business to other regional offices. However, Bahrain's small size, developments in Libya and Syria, aggressive Gulf diplomacy, Western unease about how to proceed and paranoia about Iran helped explain why it avoided the degree of international opprobrium that descended on other countries.

To salvage Bahrain's battered image and economy, King Hamad announced the lifting of the state of emergency on 1 June, two weeks ahead of schedule. However, the Bahraini government requested that Peninsula

Shield forces remain in the country. The crown prince, perceived domestically and internationally as weakened, announced that the offer for dialogue would be renewed, though within narrow parameters. The opposition welcomed the declaration, but lacking guarantees and with many of its leaders in jail, it seemed unwilling to proceed at first. The formation by the king of an independent commission to investigate events and abuses that took place in February and March and composed of respected legal experts seemed, however, able to sway Al Wefaq and other moderate factions into joining the talks.

Bahraini accusations and repression, and later the entry of GCC troops, strained Bahrain's relations with Iran, whose foreign minister described the Saudi intervention as an occupation. Bahrain recalled its ambassador to Tehran, and Iran reciprocated. A Bahraini confidential report to the United Nations alleged that Hizbullah had trained Bahraini opposition figures and had subversively coordinated with the Bahraini opposition. Iran dismissed the Bahraini charges as fabrications and as a pretext for Saudi and American interference in Bahrain's internal affairs. Iranian denials failed to convince the Gulf states, who rallied behind the hardline posture preached by Saudi Arabia.

Yemen: Loss of Control

Yemen's descent into the abyss continued in the year to mid-2011. The terrorist threat increased, and internal challenges to the autocratic President Ali Abdullah Saleh gained momentum amid persistent popular protests.

Central state weakens

The government's failure to contain the activities of the al-Qaeda in the Arabian Peninsula (AQAP) terrorist group and its inability to secure a political solution to the Houthi and southern secessionist insurgencies reflected the shrinking territorial and political control of the state. The international threat posed by AQAP captured global attention when a terrorist plot originating in Yemen was foiled. Thanks to Saudi intelligence, two sophisticated explosive devices bound on separate cargo planes from Yemen to the United States through Dubai were discovered in October 2010, one in Dubai and the other at a British airport. In a statement released days later, AQAP claimed responsibility for the failed attacks.

In addition to AQAP's international activities, the organisation conducted a campaign against the Yemeni security apparatus. The Yemeni government responded by launching several large-scale security operations against the group, primarily in the southern Abyan province, an AQAP stronghold, offering rewards for information leading to the capture of leading AQAP militants, including the influential US-born jihadi preacher Anwar al-Awlaki. It also obtained a US pledge to double military aid to $250 million for the year 2011 to assist its fight against terrorism. Still, Saleh's ambiguous relations with AQAP and the absence of a comprehensive strategy to address the roots of AQAP support appeared to doom the counter-terrorism effort. Saleh faced more awkwardness and loss of credibility with his people after leaked US diplomatic cables revealed the extent of US–Yemeni coordination against terrorist targets. Saleh was quoted as having authorised secret US drone attacks that have enraged the Yemeni population, stating that 'we will continue saying the bombs are ours, not yours'.

The lack of a political strategy by the central authorities was also felt in the two rebellions that threatened Yemeni integrity. Despite deploying substantial military assets, the Yemeni authorities still had to contend with the surviving Houthi rebellion in the north. In mid-2010, clashes broke out between the Houthis and government-backed tribes, ending a fragile six-month truce. Houthi rebels subsequently captured a military post, seizing and then releasing 200 soldiers belonging to the army's Republican Guards. Dissidence in southern Yemen also grew over deep resentment of political and economic misgovernance.

The Arab Awakening reaches Yemen

Revolutionary inspiration from Egypt and Tunisia further compounded Yemen's already volatile situation. From February, thousands of Yemenis took to the streets demanding Saleh's immediate departure. Faced with his intransigence and profoundly distrustful of any settlement that would allow him to stay in office, the opposition, though weak and fragmented, came together to demand the president's resignation.

As in Egypt, youth and civil society groups spearheaded the movement, joined later by the opposition umbrella group, the Joint Meeting Parties, and the al-Ahmar family, Saleh's foremost political rivals and leader of the Hashid tribal confederation. Houthi followers and southern separatists later joined the popular movement. Members of Saleh's ruling party, ministers, parliamentarians, diplomats and security officials abandoned him. General

Ali Muhsin al-Ahmar, a top military commander and former Saleh confidant, also defected, ordering his troops to protect the demonstrators. This led to a tense armed stand-off with units loyal to Saleh.

Saleh responded by announcing concessions, including electoral reforms, a transition to a parliamentary system and a vague willingness to step down. However, thinking he could still play Yemeni politics to his advantage and counting on the support of the security forces commanded by his immediate relatives, he mobilised his supporters who organised large counter-rallies and ordered a security crackdown that escalated into bloodshed despite the peaceful nature of the opposition.

By late April, violence had spread to many cities outside the capital Sana'a, especially Ta'izz, where government forces used heavy force, including US-equipped special forces meant to combat AQAP. The death toll rose to several hundred. AQAP fighters took advantage of the distraction of Saleh's security forces to temporarily seize the town of Zinjibar and advance through the region of Abyan.

Despite the violence, protests and calls for Saleh to quit continued unabated. On 23 April, Saleh accepted a political deal brokered by the GCC. In exchange for stepping down within 30 days and transferring power to his vice-president during a transitional period, he would obtain immunity from prosecution for the deaths of many protesters and corruption. Saleh subsequently refused to sign the agreement on several occasions, resorting to constitutional arguments to stay in power until the end of his term in 2013 and accusing Qatar of conspiring against him. The GCC then suspended its mediation efforts. Saleh's scheming cost him the backing of the United States, which now supported his ouster. It also alienated his main ally, Saudi Arabia, which worried most about the consequences of a failed state at its southern border.

As a result, tribal fighters declared their support for the opposition and clashed with loyalist security forces in Sana'a and elsewhere. The fighting involved heavy artillery and mortar shelling, attacks on the house of the al-Ahmar family and retaliation against the presidential compound.

Saleh was seriously injured in a bomb attack at his palace on 3 June and flew to Saudi Arabia for treatment, transferring presidential power to his vice-president. Despite early claims that this transfer was temporary, the severity of Saleh's condition and Saudi Arabia's apparent reluctance to let him return opened the door for a settlement. Saleh could however still rely on his relatives who controlled key elite units and stood to lose power and privileges.

Oman: Sultan Responds to Protests

Two months after Oman celebrated the 40th anniversary of Sultan Qaboos bin Said's rule, its stability was called into question by growing popular demand for increased political rights, as well as by the continued absence of a succession plan.

The issue of succession in Oman is complicated by the fact that the sultan has no children. The concentration of power in his hands, including the positions of prime minister, finance minister and defence minister, creates considerable concern and uncertainty about transition. Article Five of Oman's constitution, which sets the mechanism for succession, stipulates that the Ruling Family Council shall decide on a successor to the throne within three days of the sultan's death. In the event of disagreement over a successor, the council is required to appoint the candidate recommended by the sultan, which is recorded in a secret letter sealed prior to his death.

In spite of this uncertainty, Oman seemed an unlikely candidate for political unrest, especially as Qaboos retained popular sympathy. Yet the wave of political activism sweeping through the Arab world inspired Omani activists to mobilise to demand economic and political reform. Several demonstrations took place in the cities of Muscat and Salalah, demanding the creation of additional jobs, higher wages and the resignation of several ministers accused of corruption. Protesters also demanded increased political representation through the largely toothless Shura, Oman's partially elected legislative body, which retained an advisory role to the sultan. The protesters, however, reiterated their attachment to the sultan and monarchical rule.

Following the tactics of several of its neighbours, the Omani government responded through a mix of repressive and concessionary measures. In late February, a police crackdown on a group of activists in Sohar resulted in the deaths of two protesters. Following continued demonstrations, in which protesters blocked roads to Oman's second-largest port, Qaboos announced a series of reforms including the creation of 50,000 jobs in the public sector and the introduction of unemployment benefits of over $300 per month. In subsequent days, the sultan also announced a government shakeup, the dismissal of most ministers and the transfer of some legislative and regulatory powers to the Shura. He also announced the establishment of a committee to propose amendments to the constitution and a plan to spend $2.6bn as a state grant to 'satisfy popular demands'. He received precious financial support from other Gulf states in the form of a $10bn package to fund infrastructure and job-creation projects. This mollified activists, although small-scale protests across Oman continued into April and May.

Oman also had to contend with tensions with the UAE over reports that it had dismantled an Emirati espionage ring accused of targeting the Omani government and military. This compounded existing border disputes. Regional political instability prompted a rapid reaction from other Gulf states to solve this dispute. A Kuwaiti mediation effort led by Sheikh Sabah al-Ahmad al-Jaber al-Sabah, emir of Kuwait, proved successful. Still, Oman also broke with other GCC states over Iran's alleged destabilising interference in Bahrain. Qaboos pointedly met with Iranian Foreign Minister Ali Akbar Salehi in Muscat, praising the Iranian government as an important country seeking to promote peace and security in the region.

Kuwait: Political Wrangles

The Gulf's most politically liberal state, Kuwait, continued to suffer from paralysis due to intense disputes between the parliament and the executive branch. Parliament itself reflected the profound sectarian, tribal and political divisions that afflict Kuwaiti society.

Parliamentary oversight of the government, an oddity in the Gulf, translated into debilitating, vindictive politics. Fundamental disputes, from public finances to oil policies, extended to the position of Prime Minister Sheikh Nasser Mohammed al-Ahmad al-Sabah, the emir's nephew, who had been reappointed in 2009. In December 2010, he faced intense grilling in parliament over alleged police brutality at an opposition rally. The closed-door session was his second grilling following his defeat of a vote of no confidence in December 2009.

On 31 March 2011, the Kuwaiti cabinet faced another round of questioning by parliament over renewed allegations of corruption, prompting the cabinet to submit its resignation to the emir to avoid such interrogation. The emir accepted but instructed the government to act as a caretaker pending the formation of a new cabinet. The resignation marked the sixth such episode in the five years since the embattled prime minister was first appointed. The new cabinet was presented in May 2011, headed by Sheikh Nasser and including most ministers from the previous cabinet.

Parliament was later dismissed for a month following a brawl between Sunni and Shia parliamentarians on the floor, sparked by remarks about

Guantanamo Bay prisoners. Despite the temporary recess, three Sunni opposition parliamentarians attacked the prime minister over his alleged sympathy for Iran, claiming that he opposed sending Kuwaiti troops to Bahrain. Calls for his removal once again rose, backed by demonstrations against him and his deputy over allegations of corruption and mismanagement. His deputy, a member of a rival branch of the ruling family, resigned in June, ostensibly because of parliamentary pressure but possibly over internal family disputes.

Kuwait's intense parliamentary politics insulated the country from the kind of upheaval visited on others in the region, but there too the government adopted economic measures to mollify its population. In early 2011, the National Assembly approved a decree by the emir granting each Kuwaiti citizen 1,000 dinars ($3,650). The measure was announced to coincide with the 50th anniversary of the country's independence and the 20th anniversary of its liberation from Iraqi occupation. In addition to the cash handout, the emir announced the provision of subsidised basic food supplies for the rest of the year, at a total cost of 1.4bn dinars ($5.1bn).

Despite the handouts, stateless Arabs known as *bedoon* and other activists organised demonstrations calling for basic rights and citizenship. Kuwait is believed to have 100,000 stateless persons living within its borders, denied the economic and political benefits associated with citizenship. On 19 March, a gathering of several hundred demonstrators was attacked by water cannons, a move that the government alleged was in response to violence by protesters.

As in other GCC states, Kuwait's relationship with Tehran was further strained when it expelled Iranian diplomats, including the ambassador, in April over charges of espionage. Iran responded by expelling several Kuwaiti diplomats, prompting Kuwait to recall its ambassador. Relations soured even more when a Kuwaiti court sentenced two Kuwaitis and an Iranian national to death for spying. Iran vehemently rejected the charges. While Iran announced that the countries had agreed to return ambassadors, relations remained strained.

United Arab Emirates: Reform Calls Ignored

Though insulated from political turmoil by its wealth and paternalistic system, the UAE felt mild tremors from the Arab Awakening. Economic disparities between the Emirates, a lack of transparency in public finances, questions of demography and identity and a general frustration at the lack of political development fuelled Emiratis' discontent.

The greatest expression of political activism came from 130 Emirati intellectuals, former government officials, and civil society activists who signed a petition to the president of the federation, Sheikh Khalifa bin Zayed al-Nahyan, calling for comprehensive reform of the parliamentary system and universal suffrage ahead of elections scheduled for late 2011. Members of the 40-member Federal National Council (FNC), which has an advisory role and does not hold legislative powers, are either directly appointed by the emirs or elected by a group of citizens chosen by federal decree.

The authorities responded to calls for political reform by arresting five activists, including a prominent economist and a human-rights advocate. They dissolved the boards of the UAE lawyers' and teachers' associations, replacing members with state appointees for a six-month interim period. These associations were two of four civil-society groups that had lent their support to the petition. The crackdown hurt the UAE's image as a haven for culture and education. To pre-empt further unrest, the federal authorities also announced infrastructure investments worth $1.6bn in the northern Emirates, the poorest, neglected part of the country where discontent has been rising. They also announced that the number of citizens allowed to elect FNC members would be increased from 7,000 to nearly 80,000, and that all citizens could be granted that right in 2019.

Meanwhile, the extent of Emirati anxiety about Iran was revealed in US WikiLeaks cables. The crown prince of Abu Dhabi and de facto top defence official, Sheikh Mohammed bin Zayed, emerged as deeply concerned about Iran's nuclear progress and asymmetric threat and as recommending a tough approach towards Tehran. UAE fears also translated into closer than acknowledged cooperation with Israel. In a March 2009 cable, the political adviser of the US Embassy in Tel Aviv described 'the good and personal relationship' between the UAE's Foreign Minister Abdullah Bin Zayed and his Israeli counterpart, Tzipi Livni. The adviser further noted that the two ministers would not 'do in public what they say behind closed doors'. These revelations contrasted with the public Emirati anger at the suspected January 2010 Mossad assassination in Dubai of Mahmoud al-Mabhouh, the leader of Hamas's security wing.

In an attempt to preserve its technological edge over Iran's military, the UAE pursued a rapid defence-modernisation effort. In previous years it had acquired aircraft and missile-defence technology from the United States, but it also sought to diversify its arms procurement as part of a strategy to reach out to new partners. This included talks with Brazil over a $1.6bn plan to acquire military aircraft. In February 2011, the UAE signed contracts worth $4bn with German and French defence companies. In May 2011, it was revealed that the Emirates had contracted Xe Services, the US defence contractor previously called Blackwater, to build, train and equip an 800-member battalion of mercenaries to protect critical infrastructure and oil facilities, but also as an instrument of domestic control and as a counterbalance to Iran's designs.

Qatar: Bigger Global Role

The global profile of the resource-rich state of Qatar grew significantly in the year to mid-2011, giving it influence out of proportion to its size, but alienating other Arab states. In December 2010, Qatar won the competition to host the 2022 FIFA World Cup football tournament, the first time the event was to be held in the Middle East. Notwithstanding accusations of corruption, Qatar found itself celebrated on the world stage for taking bold risks, in contrast to the usual conservatism of Arab states.

Because of its wealth, its homogeneous and quiescent population and benign leadership, Qatar did not experience any serious unrest when Arab revolts started to spread. On the contrary, Qatar became one of the few beneficiaries of the Arab Awakening, its image bolstered by the diplomatic and media role it played. The relentless coverage by Qatar-based al-Jazeera, the satellite television news channel, of every revolution from Tunisia and Egypt to Yemen and Syria played a critical role in the course of events in those countries. Al-Jazeera provided a platform for the voicing of political grievances banned from state television, and broadcast live images of state repression. Its role became the focus of anger of many Arab regimes that considered al-Jazeera a mere instrument of Qatari diplomacy. The Egyptian, Syrian, Yemeni and Libyan presidents all directly accused the network of conspiring against them. However, al-Jazeera found itself in a predicament over Bahrain: Qatar's decision to take part in the GCC force that entered Bahrain to shore up its embattled government translated into muted coverage on al-Jazeera Arabic of the reform movement there. Al-Jazeera's English-language network gained international standing for its coverage, winning the praises of Clinton and other US officials for offering 'real news'.

Qatar was also instrumental in mobilising Arab support against Muammar Gadhafi. It lobbied within the GCC and the Arab League for foreign military intervention to help the Libyan rebel movement and impose a no-fly zone over Libya, to which it contributed four *Mirage* 2000 fighter jets. In late March 2011, Qatar became the first Arab country to recognise the Libyan Transitional National Council as the 'people's legitimate representative' and hosted a meeting of the newly formed International Contact Group on Libya. As part of its strategy to support the Libyan rebels, Doha offered to market Libyan oil to help meet basic food and medicinal needs and secretly started to provide weaponry and funding.

Lebanon: Fate Tied to Syria

Lebanon reached a political crisis amidst the continuing aftermath of the 2005 assassination of former Prime Minister Rafik Hariri. The government led by his son, Saad Hariri, collapsed as a result of political manoeuvres ahead of the expected indictments of members of the Shia militant group Hizbullah by a UN-backed international tribunal investigating the murder.

The functioning and performance of the national-unity cabinet put together in 2009 by Saad Hariri were already hampered by the country's polarised politics. A Syrian–Saudi attempt to defuse tensions over the tribunal, by obtaining an undertaking from Hariri that the government would distance itself from the body, failed even after the Saudi monarch and the Syrian president made a symbolic joint visit to Beirut in July 2010. Hariri's refusal to compromise in what had become a near-existential political struggle was countered by the call by Hassan Nasrallah, leader of Hizbullah, to boycott and combat the tribunal altogether. Hizbullah and its allies, supported by Syria, launched a political and media campaign to discredit the tribunal as an American and Israeli instrument and warned of disastrous consequences for the country.

The issue came to a head in January 2011, when Walid Jumblatt, a Druze leader and former ally of Hariri, switched his allegiance to Hizbullah out of concern that he would lose out in this confrontation. This brought down the Hariri government – a setback for the Western and Saudi-backed faction and a victory for Syria and Iran. Hizbullah, Jumblatt and their allies, who now controlled a parliamentary majority, moved swiftly to have Najib Mikati, a Sunni billionaire and friend of Syrian President Bashar al-Assad, appointed as prime minister. This angered large swathes of the Sunni community that supported Hariri and felt entitled to the position. Still, Mikati was prevented from quickly forming a cabinet by sectarian Lebanese politics, by hedging among Lebanese factions as the Arab revolutionary wave hit Syria, and indecision in Damascus. Meanwhile, the UN prosecutor issued sealed indictments against suspects in the Hariri investigation. He later submitted more detailed indictments to be released publicly later in the year.

The political crisis was overshadowed by the wave of unrest elsewhere in the Arab world, but it worsened the security vacuum in the country. Estonian tourists were kidnapped in the Bekaa Valley and a bomb attack targeted UN troops. In May, as a reminder that Lebanon's security was intimately intertwined with regional dynamics, Lebanese and Palestinian protesters marched to the border with Israel, where ten of them were killed after Israeli soldiers opened fire. Many suspected Hizbullah and Syrian manipulation to divert attention from the growing protests against the Assad regime.

In June 2011, under pressure from Syria (which wanted to assert its control over Lebanon as it faced international criticism for repression of the pro-democracy movement), Mikati announced after a five-month vacuum the formation of a government that included all of Syria's allies, including Hizbullah, and excluded Hariri and his allies. Fears that Lebanon would suffer consequences from the turmoil in Syria arose as Syrian refugees sought a haven on Lebanese soil and Lebanese Sunnis and Alawites clashed in the northern Lebanese town of Tripoli.

Syria: Regime Cracks Down

Until it began violently to repress popular protests, Syria had appeared to be on track towards international respectability following years of diplomatic isolation over its destabilisation of Lebanon and Iraq. Engaged by Saudi Arabia over Lebanon and courted by the Obama administration to advance the Arab–Israeli peace process, it seemed to have regained a significant regional role by virtue of its relations with Hamas, Hizbullah and Iran. A main motivation behind the intense courtship of Syria was the hope that it would break ties with Iran despite the strength and strategic nature of their alliance.

International engagement was not, however, reciprocated with cooperation from Damascus. Instead, it led to greater Syrian confidence and intransigence. In Lebanon, Syria helped, through its allies, to bring down the government of Saad Hariri. UN reports also indicated the steady supply of weaponry to Hizbullah through Syria. There were no signs of a weakening of the relationship with Iran.

In January, as Egypt was undergoing massive upheaval, President al-Assad told the *Wall Street Journal* of his conviction that his regime would be spared a similar fate as a result of the reforms he had undertaken, his proximity with his people and the legitimacy he derived from his resistance to the United States and Israel. At first, Assad seemed poised to benefit from the Arab Awakening as it brought down Mubarak, a rival, and weakened pro-US states in the region, and because events seemed to be unfolding to Iran's advantage. The regime's strong, Alawite-dominated security apparatus, memories of the repression of the 1980s, and the co-option of urban and Sunni elites seemed enough to prevent political and economic grievances from translating into unrest.

Initial calls for democracy protests in mid-March attracted only a few hundred people. Days later, security forces arrested several children for writing anti-regime slogans in the southern city of Deraa, and killed three protesters. This inflamed the city, where popular resistance to security forces emerged and symbols of the regime, including statues of Assad's father and the local branch of Syriatel, the mobile phone operator owned by the reviled cousin of Assad, Rami Makhlouf, were destroyed. The heavy-handed security response in Deraa, led by a cousin of Assad and meant to deter further unrest, only served to alienate people in other cities.

In a defiant speech to the Syrian parliament in late March, Assad showed no willingness to introduce significant reforms. Instead, he blamed the unrest on foreign agents, criminal gangs, the Muslim Brotherhood and Salafist militants. Still, even as he escalated repression, he offered minor concessions in the hope of dividing the opposition. This included the formal lifting of the 48-year state of emergency, the release of some political prisoners and measures to appease the Sunni and Kurdish communities. Assad directed his advisers to meet with opposition leaders, though nothing tangible emerged from these contacts. He also sacked his government, a measure seen as cosmetic since the formal cabinet lacked real power and since the new line-up did not include any reformist figures. The regime also played on sectarian fears to shore up support from the Alawite, Christian and Druze minorities, by ordering the state media to portray the protesters as extremists and terrorists. However, evidence of sectarian violence remained scarce.

This strategy failed. Although the two main urban and economic centres of Aleppo and Damascus remained relatively calm, their suburbs as well as the cities of Baniyas, Deir El-Zor, Hama, Homs, Lattaqiyah and the Kurdish area in the northeast saw regular large anti-regime demonstrations by mid-April. Military units loyal to the regime were heavily mobilised, including elite troops from the Fourth Armoured Division, the Republican Guard and the Shabihha, an Alawite militia. Conventional army units, seen as less reliable, were kept away from the centres of dissent. Even so, a growing number of defections, mostly from junior officers and soldiers, were recorded, raising questions about the army's cohesiveness. Importantly, the disparate Syrian opposition gathered in Qatar and Turkey to establish a coordination committee and prepare a platform. All factions were represented, including the Muslim Brotherhood and the Kurdish parties, except for dissidents from the Assad family and regime defectors like former Vice-President Abdel Halim Khaddam.

The rising death toll and the refugee crisis that ensued drew international attention to Syria. At first the international response to the crisis in Syria was subdued. This reflected Arab unwillingness to criticise Syria, whose standing and importance remained greater than Gadhafi's Libya. The Assad regime also benefited from the aversion to further political change in the Gulf states, who extended political support for Assad in return for his endorsement of the GCC intervention in Bahrain. Western fears of a civil war and the regional instability that it could cause – combined with reluctance to launch another intervention while engaged in Libya – explained their initial reticence. The United States (which argued that its initial inaction was due to a lack of leverage) and the European Union eventually imposed sanctions on members of the Syrian security and political leadership. The United States also accused Syria of seeking Iranian help to put down the uprising. Turkey in particular found itself torn between its close ties to Syria and its professed values.

Calls for restraint and reforms from Ankara, Paris, Washington and elsewhere were, however, ignored. Rather, as Assad fought for survival, he alienated the three countries that had once been closest to him: Turkey, which his media accused of imperial ambitions; Qatar, which was blamed for supporting Sunni extremists; and France, which sought to push a sanctions resolution at the UN that failed after Russian and Chinese opposition.

In spite of international pressure, there was no sign of a let-up in the regime's ruthless response to protests. In June, its forces seized control of the northern city of Jisr al-Shughour, which had seen large anti-regime protests.

The Syrian authorities alleged that 120 members of its security forces had been slaughtered there, although other reports disputed that version, accusing loyalist troops of killing defectors and civilians. The assault on the city sent thousands of refugees across the border to Turkey. Later, security forces moved on Hama, a city still scarred by the massacre of 1982 but nonetheless a major centre of mobilisation. At the same time, Assad announced in a new speech at Damascus University his intention to conduct more reforms. He even allowed a meeting of opposition intellectuals in Damascus, which was seen by many as a ploy to divide the opposition.

Even then, the international community struggled to respond. The UN commissioner for human rights deplored the killings, UN Secretary-General Ban Ki-moon complained that Assad was not taking his telephone calls and China, Russia and other non-Western countries seemed set to block any tough resolution at the Security Council. Further international action against Syria was, however, in store: the International Atomic Energy Agency approved a report by its director-general describing the Kibar facility destroyed by the Israeli air force in September 2007 as probably a nuclear reactor and referring the case to the UN Security Council. Calls for referral of Assad to the International Criminal Court increased as well.

Jordan: Frustration with Slow Reform

In November 2010, Jordanians elected a new parliament with strongly loyalist and conservative credentials, amidst accusations of fraud and following a boycott by several parties. Jordan's reform process had proved frustratingly slow and uncertain, and the limited powers of the assembly had provoked criticism of the monarchy from Islamist, Palestinian and leftist factions in parliament. The new assembly was expected to be more docile.

Yet Jordan proved not to be immune to the Arab Awakening. Protests grew from January and attracted diverse segments of society, including some previously considered loyal to King Abdullah II. Indeed, the participation of tribal elements and military retirees signalled a deep frustration with his stewardship during his 12-year rule, as well as with corruption among the elite, the role of his wife, rising unemployment and deteriorating living conditions. In an effort to assuage his critics, the monarch announced in late January a $400m plan to raise subsidies and salaries. He dismissed Prime Minister Samir Rifai and his government of technocrats, blamed for unfair and painful economic policies. They were replaced, however, by Marouf al-Bakhit, a former officer and member of the old guard, and ministers with security and tribal backgrounds and with a questionable commitment to political and economic reform.

Protesters were not placated by these concessions. Demonstrations persisted, fuelled by online activism and the involvement of youth and civil society, which contributed to a consolidation of political demands. They were often met with violence by the police forces and government-affiliated thugs. The protests, which peaked on 24 and 25 March, never reached the level of intensity or the numbers of those in Egypt and elsewhere, but their diverse character was evidence of a turning point in Jordanian politics. In response, the government resorted to repression and intimidation of the media to contain the protests, leading to the resignation of the information minister. The regime also organised counter-rallies.

Even then however, pro-reform activists distinguished between the government and the system, calling for the fall of the former and the reform of the latter. They also distinguished between the king and the institution of the monarchy, criticising the former's performance while supporting the latter. Indeed, there were few calls for wholesale regime change, which were even rejected by the Jordanian Muslim Brotherhood affiliate, the Islamic Action Front.

On 12 June, King Abdullah announced ambitious reform plans, including the selection of future governments by the parliament and a new law on political parties, designed to liberalise political activity. However, he offered no timeline or implementation plans, leading many to doubt his intentions given that previous promises of reform had fizzled. The next day, in an unprecedented gesture of defiance, his motorcade was pelted with stones while crossing the town of Tafila. The persistence of calls for political change even after the king's televised speech suggested that the movement would not lose momentum or succumb to division.

The strategic predicament of resource-poor Jordan was also magnified during this phase of unrest. The king's choice of alignment with the West and peace with Israel came under attack from many demonstrators, even as US envoys privately pressed for more reforms for fear of popular uprising. In May, a Jordanian request for membership of the GCC was positively considered by the Gulf states, though no firm decision was made. Later, Saudi Arabia extended a $400m aid package to the kingdom. These moves increased concerns that increasing dependency on the Gulf states could slow or derail political reforms.

Algeria: Protests Contained

Proximity to Tunisia and its own history of political unrest made Algeria, a country still recovering from a bloody civil war and under quasi-military rule, an obvious candidate for upheaval. Within days of the departure of Ben Ali in January, four Algerian men set themselves on fire in gestures reminiscent of Mohamed Bouazizi's suicide. Soon after, mass demonstrations took place across the country to protest declining living conditions, rising food prices and high unemployment, all of which were spurring young men to leave the country.

Flush with reserves of $157bn thanks to rising energy prices, the Algerian government's initial response was to cut the price of basic food products, invest in housing, distribute cash hand-outs and increase public-sector salaries. It also outlawed further demonstrations. Despite the ban, the National Coordination for Change and Democracy, an umbrella group of political parties and civil-society organisations, called for a demonstration on 12 February. At the heart of their demands were political reforms, the lifting of the state of emergency in place since 1992, greater media freedoms and the liberation of political prisoners. Algeria's large and experienced security forces successfully contained the marches, causing fewer deaths than elsewhere in the Arab world and avoiding the use of live fire. The momentum for change seemed to be broken for the short term.

In late February, the government announced the lifting of the state of emergency, which had been in place since the 1990s ostensibly to combat Islamist terrorism, though it also gave the state wide and intrusive powers to control politics. Other restrictions on political activity remained in place, and were used by the government to prevent further protests.

The weakness of the protests could be explained partly by the fatigue and wariness of the Algerian population after the deeply traumatic decade of the 1990s. The bloody turn of events in Libya, Syria and Yemen served as a further deterrent among Algerians. Moreover, Algeria's weak political parties were mutually suspicious and divided: several prominent opposition factions declined to participate in the marches or to coordinate their activities, and the National Coordination for Change and Democracy was unable to consolidate demands. Various segments of the population preferred to mobilise separately to defend their own parochial interests instead of embracing a broader cause, as evidenced by the absence of youth groups and labour organisations, including the powerful General Union of Algerian Workers. Calls for regime change remained marginal in comparison with demands for specific actions. The revolutionary fever did not take hold in Algerian society.

The role of the Algerian military, from which President Abdelaziz Bouteflika came, proved decisive if obscure. Although rivalries were rife among the senior ranks of the military, the army had a paramount need to protect its institutional power and business interests.

Morocco: King Proposes Reforms

Morocco's march toward constitutional and political reform, a declared if unsustained project of King Mohammed VI since he succeeded his uncompromising, authoritarian father in 1999, benefited from the Arab Awakening. On the heels of the Tunisian and Egyptian revolutions, Moroccan democracy activists called for mass demonstrations on 20 February throughout the country. The government, which allowed the protests, was surprised by the popular response. Tens of thousands of people from all sectors of society took part in the largest demonstrations in decades, unhappy at the deteriorating economy, shrinking social services, and widespread corruption – including in the royal court – as well as at the slow pace of and many setbacks to the agenda for political reform.

The police response, limited and far less deadly than in other Arab countries, still led to clashes with protesters and rioting in many cities. The movement was, however, largely peaceful and, as elsewhere, led by youth and civil-society groups rather than political parties, many of which were already engaged in the relatively open Moroccan political space. As in Jordan, calls were made for a meaningful reform of the monarchical system and better governance rather than outright regime change, underlining the significant degree of legitimacy retained by the king. The protesters could not sustain high levels of mobilisation, and the security forces adopted less aggressive methods.

On 9 March, the king, seemingly sensitive to the seriousness of the crisis and eager to proactively respond to popular pressure, made a televised speech to lay out an ambitious reform agenda. He formed a committee to propose constitutional reforms to be put to a referendum. Protesters were sceptical about the king's commitment to reform and emboldened by the success of other revolutions. On 29 May, mass protests were met with a considerably harsher security response, which led to an escalation. In the meantime, a terrorist attack on 28 April against a cafe popular with tourists in Marrakech that left 15 dead served as reminder of the vulnerability of the country to al-Qaeda-type terrorism.

On 17 June, King Mohammed again addressed Moroccans to lay out constitutional reforms to be approved by referendum on 1 July. They included a stronger separation of powers, giving the judiciary more independence and parliament the right to pick the prime minister and approve the cabinet. The powers of the prime minister would be enhanced. Security policy would however remain the responsibility of the monarch, who would be constitutionally recognised as the highest authority in the country. The king's proposals received a mixed welcome from the leadership of the protest movement.

Conclusion

As spring turned into summer, there appeared to be no inevitability or linear trajectories in the many uprisings shaking the Arab world. Even as revolutionaries and reform activists everywhere were motivated by similar sets of grievances and aspirations, the outcomes would naturally vary from country to country, depending on the political, ethnic and sectarian make-up, the level of institutional development and political maturity, the role of security forces and other individual factors.

Two sets of what could ultimately be positive processes were in motion: the transitions in Egypt and Tunisia and the moves towards constitutional reform in Morocco and Jordan. Yet each was vulnerable to political fragmentation, domestic infighting, economic deterioration, the rise of sectarianism, and terrorist violence. These forces could eventually return some of these countries to authoritarianism if the yearning for order supplanted the hunger for change. In others, competition between Islamist and secular forces may well become the defining characteristic of the new political order.

Regional dynamics too would shape these outcomes. A war in the Levant or renewed violence in the Palestinian territories could shape or divert processes of change. Egypt's elections were to take place just as the Palestinians were to demand recognition for their state at the UN (see Israel and Palestine section, pages 267–78). Arab citizens' vociferous demands for change and dignity were not only the product of bad governance and authoritarianism; they were also due to the perception that their governments had become servile. As each country struggled to achieve an orderly transition, it was vulnerable to the efforts of other governments to influence or disrupt the process: Jordan and Egypt in particular were sensitive to competing Western and Gulf influences, the former pushing for reforms and the latter eager to maintain the status quo.

What was particularly lacking was a regional support system that could help states undergoing massive change to set clear objectives. After the end of the Cold War, Eastern European states strove to enter NATO and the European Union, and made the necessary political and economic reforms. For Arab states, there was no such motivation or path.

In some states, conflict was raging at mid-2011. The civil war in Libya and the quasi-civil wars in Syria and Yemen were in danger of escalating. As well as causing heavy bloodshed and spreading instability in their neighbour-hoods, these events had the potential to deter attempts at political change elsewhere.

Nevertheless, by removing the debilitating element of fear that charac-terised Arab societies, the Arab Awakening, singular in its suddenness and domino effect, fundamentally changed the relationship between govern-ing elites and citizens. This achievement, entirely owned by Arab citizens, proved that societal forces can cause as much strategic upheaval as tradi-tional forms of violence that have plagued the Arab world.

Chapter 2
Strategic Policy Issues

Digital Activism and the Arab Awakening

When young activists stormed the streets of Tehran in summer 2009, many observers proclaimed a 'Twitter revolution'. Though in the end no revolution occurred, the international attention that the protesters attracted by using social media resonated with activists worldwide, prompting many to adopt digital tools.

In 2011, the world watched in awe as Tunisians, and then Egyptians, rallied together against their respective governments, using social media first to spark awareness and then to capture the world's attention, as they brought down two of the Middle East's long-standing dictators within weeks.

These movements were not the first to use digital tools for activism, nor will they be the last. But the successes of online activists in Tunisia and Egypt have profound implications, both for activists and for policymakers.

A Twitter revolution?
Digital communications – mobile phones and online journalism – had played a role in Ukraine's 2004 Orange Revolution, and many analysts saw Twitter, the online social networking and microblogging site, as a catalyst in the 2009 popular uprising in Moldova after the Party of Communists won a majority of seats in that year's parliamentary election. Though some enterprising Moldovans did indeed use Twitter to draw attention to the demonstrations, later analysis found that fewer than 200 people within the country were

actually registered with the service, suggesting that the role of social media had been overstated.

Two months later, the re-election in Iran of President Mahmoud Ahmadinejad led to upheaval as young Iranians, claiming that the election had been rigged, took to the streets demanding their voices be heard. Foreign journalists quickly noticed Iranians using Twitter, the social-networking service Facebook and other tools to disseminate information about the protests and focused on this in their reporting. Iran's nearly 33m Internet users (as of 2009) had long faced pervasive Internet censorship and surveillance. Persian-language news content, human-rights organisations, 'immoral' content, and several social-networking sites were primary targets for official filtering, along with perhaps thousands of local blogs. However, despite the many barriers to free access, Iran boasts one of the largest and most active blogospheres in the world.

While Facebook and various other social networking sites were blocked prior to the start of the 2009 uprising, Twitter remained available. In addition to accessing Twitter.com directly, Iranians with mobile phones – around 60% of the population – could send messages to Twitter via SMS. The reportedly widespread use of the service, coupled with a global solidarity campaign in which supporters of the Green Movement changed their Twitter avatars green and their stated location to Tehran, led journalist Andrew Sullivan of *Atlantic* magazine to proclaim that 'the revolution will be Twittered'.

Ultimately, the role of Twitter in the protests appeared, again, to have been overstated. While its users' 140-character messages, or tweets, from inside Iran certainly drew international attention to the Green Movement's cause, Twitter was not a key mobilising factor within the country itself: with Twitter still relatively new to the social media landscape, few Iranians had adopted the tool in 2009. And while the '#iranelection' subject hashtag trended consistently, the majority of its users were found to be outside the country. Moreover, efforts by the solidarity movement to obscure the identities of those actually in Iran by changing their stated locations made it more difficult for researchers to come to solid conclusions about how many Twitter users actually tweeted from Iran, and how many were involved in protests.

Tunisia online: igniting the Arab Awakening

The self-immolation of 26-year-old fruit and vegetable seller Mohamed Bouazizi on 17 December 2010 did not seem an event likely to bring down a government. Following a public humiliation by a female police officer, Bouazizi doused himself in gasoline in the centre of the Tunisian town of

Sidi Bouzid, sparking nationwide protests that would lead to the fall of President Zine el-Abidine Ben Ali just 28 days later.

Were it not for social media, it is possible that Bouazizi's act would have been consigned to local memory. But photographs, along with videos of subsequent protests in Sidi Bouzid, were uploaded to Facebook and quickly spread amongst Tunisia's approximately 1.6 million Facebook users (about 15% of the population). The site was an obvious vehicle for Tunisians. The government's censorship apparatus had managed to block virtually every commercial video-sharing site, but Tunisians were able to use Facebook, which remained unblocked save for a brief period in 2008 before a widespread outcry led to a lifting of the ban.

Images of Bouazizi and the protests that followed eventually reached a producer at the al-Jazeera television network, and were broadcast on its Arabic-language channel, reaching Tunisians via satellite television. This was particularly important, as the majority of Tunisians still do not have access to the Internet. It was the combination of traditional media and citizen journalism via online social media that led to the upsurge of international attention.

Using a combination of tools, Tunisians worked to chronicle and sustain the protests, which quickly spread from Sidi Bouzid to the neighbouring state of Kasserine, and to the country's capital Tunis. Images and videos were captured and disseminated on Facebook and via e-mail, reaching international journalists and television networks. The world's media used these materials, as well as the social-network connections to Tunisians, to report on the ever-growing demonstrations.

As the protests turned into a large-scale uprising, the regime, recognising the value of the Internet to the opposition, stepped up its efforts to disrupt the flow of information, interfering with mobile communications and hacking e-mail and Facebook accounts. On 5 January, police arrested activist Slim Amamou, a move to which he alerted people by putting his location on Google Latitude – which allows mobile phone users to indicate where they are – as the Ministry of the Interior, where he was being held.

The loosely organised and decentralised global online collective calling itself 'Anonymous', which had become increasingly involved in political activism, engaged in collective attacks against Tunisian government websites, disabling the site of Prime Minister Mohamed Ghannouchi as well as the government's home page. Anonymous also assisted in expanding access to circumvention tools, which helped Tunisians get around Internet censorship. Ultimately, Ben Ali was faced with the dictator's dilemma: to employ greater force to quell the protests, or to offer greater openness to appease the protesters. In his final address to the nation on 13 January, one of his promises – in addition to job creation and a new cabinet – was an end to Internet censorship. It was too late; a day later he fled to Saudi Arabia.

Online activists had been busy in Tunisia well before the 2011 revolution. In 1991, Tunisia had become the first Arab country to connect to the Internet. The government was then among the first in the world to filter the Internet – that is, to block access to specified websites through Internet Service Providers (ISPs) within the country; in 1996, the Tunisian Ministry of Communications formed the Tunisian Internet Agency (ATI) to take control of the country's Internet backbone and Domain Name Services. Such centralised control made it easy for the government to filter the Internet, a practice first documented by The OpenNet Initiative (ONI), a watchdog group, in 2005.

Plans for the World Summit on the Information Society to be held in Tunis in 2005 first cast international light on the country's Internet censorship practices. Though at the time Tunisia had only 953,000 Internet users (or 9.6% of the population), the ONI found a variety of websites blocked across numerous categories, including pornography, human rights, sex education and translation. Between 2005 and 2009, online censorship increased dramatically, eventually encompassing social networking and video-sharing sites; the sites of prominent human-rights organisations such as Amnesty International, Freedom House and Reporters Without Borders; and the majority of political opposition sites. Tunisia was also able to block the intermediary 'anonymiser' and 'proxy' sites used to hide the identity or geographical location of people using the Internet, and thus to allow them to bypass censorship. Meanwhile, Internet access increased to 34% of the population in 2009, the highest on the African continent, leading to the development of a real cyber culture.

Tunisia, long accustomed to restricting press freedom, was alert to the freedom provided by the Internet. With the arrest in 2002 of Zouhair Yahyaoui, founder of the opposition website TuneZine, the government became one of the first in the world to prosecute an online journalist. Over the next nine years, the Tunisian authorities would arrest or intimidate nearly two dozen bloggers and online journalists. Yahyaoui's arrest and the widespread blocking of websites led to the establishment of an anti-censorship and open-source movement in the country, many of whose early proponents would be instrumental in the dissemination of information during the 2011 uprising.

One such outlet was the collective blog Nawaat, founded in 2004 and written by Tunisian exiles and dissidents. It played an early role in the use of the Internet as a tool for activism. In 2007, its founders garnered international attention when they posted photographs of Ben Ali's presidential plane parked at airports across Europe on dates when he was not travelling on official business. The activists mapped the aircraft's travel, posting a video to YouTube and the French site Dailymotion. Both video-sharing sites were soon blocked within Tunisia.

Encouraged by Nawaat's success, Tunisian activists turned to online tools for a variety of campaigns, innovating with techniques such as 'Google Earth bombing', in which they tagged photographs and videos of torture and pegged them on Google Earth to the presidential palace. When users of the site 'visited' the palace, they would be bombarded with the content.

In May 2010, a group of activists planned a street protest against Internet censorship. Slim Amamou, Lina Ben Mhenni and Yassine Ayari applied for permits and announced the details through online and offline channels. The protest, however, never took place. Shortly after going to a police station to apply for permits, Ayari and Amamou were detained, and forced to cancel the demonstration. Police officers demanded that Amamou (who was later appointed a minister in the post-revolutionary government) record a video telling people not to show up to the event, and required him to sign a document acknowledging that such a demonstration was 'wrong'. While the police guarded the Technology and Communication Ministry on the planned day of the protest, Tunisian dissidents and their supporters in Paris, Bonn and New York protested against the country's Internet censorship.

No clear series of events, on or off line, led to the uprising that began seven months later. What is clear, however, is that a core contingent of activists with a common enemy – censorship – had already been mobilised. It was that common cause that enabled online activists to act quickly when events suddenly accelerated.

Egypt rises up

In Egypt, opposition activists were paying close attention to events in Tunisia. On the day Ben Ali left the country, a small group protested in solidarity outside the Tunisian Embassy in Cairo. Almost immediately, activists scheduled Tuesday 25 January (just over a week hence) to be a national 'Day of Rage' to call for an end to emergency laws, an increase of the minimum wage, and the dissolution of parliament. On Twitter, activists selected the hashtag '#jan25' days in advance, enabling users to search the website for related information, while on Facebook, a popular group posted details of where demonstrations would take place. On 25 January more than 20,000 Egyptians took to the streets.

Egypt and Tunisia are similar in key respects: they have comparable rates of literacy and Internet penetration, and similar demographics in terms of urban population and a rising preponderance of young people. In contrast to Tunisia, however, the Mubarak regime had allowed a relatively free press and much greater Internet freedom. Though a few sites had sometimes been blocked, Egypt did not employ large-scale filtering against its approximately 20m Internet users.

Egyptian activists took advantage of this relative openness, using online tools to initiate various movements. One example is the anti-torture movement; with blogger Wael Abbas playing a prominent role. Egyptians have for several years used video to capture incidents of police brutality, uploading them to YouTube, Facebook and other platforms. In 2007, YouTube took down Abbas's many videos, claiming that they were in violation of their terms of service. Abbas fought back, winning the right to keep the videos up and sparking a policy change at YouTube: violent content would be allowed to stay up if context was provided and a specific human-rights element was involved. The change had a significant impact on the hundreds of YouTube users in Tunisia, Egypt, Syria and elsewhere who use the site to document atrocities.

Despite Egypt's relative openness, more than 30 bloggers and online journalists had been arrested, detained or harassed over the last decade. While most were arrested during protests, their online writings no doubt made them greater targets to a government that saw the Internet as a threat. Authorities did not discriminate ideologically; bloggers affiliated with the Muslim Brotherhood were arrested, but so was Abdul Kareem Nabeel Suleiman, or 'Kareem Amer', imprisoned for four years for criticising Islam on his blog.

Though various other groups, including the Kefaya and April 6 movements, had also used technology in their organising and outreach strategies, this had little impact beyond gaining external attention for their causes. Previous demonstrations organised online had managed to mobilise hundreds, but never thousands. But in June 2010, the death of 28-year-old computer programmer Khaled Said at the hands of police in Alexandria spurred a segment of the population into action. Said was dragged from the cyber cafe where he was sitting and beaten to death by two detectives. The detectives claimed that Said had resisted arrest and was in possession of drugs; their further claim that he had suffocated from swallowing a bag of hashish was supported by two autopsy reports. Said's family claimed that the police had targeted Said because he was in possession of a video implicating members of the police in a drug deal.

Said's family was permitted to visit his corpse in the morgue, where his brother snapped pictures using a mobile phone. The images showed Said's battered and deformed face, his jaw dislocated and nose broken, and his family released them online. International watchdog organisation Human Rights Watch stated that the image showed 'strong evidence that plainclothes security officers beat him in a vicious and public manner'.

The photographs attracted international attention, eventually leading Egyptian authorities to consent to a trial for the two detectives involved. The outcry also led a young Google marketing executive, Wael Ghonim, to start a Facebook page in Said's honour. The Facebook group grew rapidly: within a month, it had nearly 130,000 members; by January 2011 they numbered almost half a million, many of whom responded to the administrator's call to protest, echoed across other social-media platforms.

When the call for a 'Day of Rage' was issued, Egyptians were prepared. Like their Tunisian counterparts, they had developed a strong online culture, characterised by a vast, diverse and multilingual political blogosphere and a formidable anti-torture movement. And while Egypt's Internet penetration stood at around 25%, well below Tunisia's, the sheer size of the population meant that over 20m Egyptians were online compared to Tunisia's 3.5m.

On 25 January, as more than 20,000 citizens poured into the streets, the authorities – responding to the live-tweets on Twitter and live streaming video coming from Tahrir Square – blocked access to Twitter, to streaming site Bambuser, and to the site of the independent opposition newspaper *Al-Dostor*. Fearing a ban on Facebook, the members of the 'We Are All Khaled Said' Facebook group began collecting members' e-mail addresses in a Google document. Their fears were well founded: on 26 January, Facebook was blocked. The decision to block these sites marked a dramatic change in the regime's approach.

Despite the bans, protests continued unabated, and the authorities – recognising the role of the Internet in mobilising young people on to the streets – ordered ISPs to cut off access to the Internet. In doing so, they were following a precedent first set by the Maldives in 2004 amidst demonstrations, and carried on by Nepal in 2005 and Myanmar in 2007 in response to popular protests. On 28 January at 12:34 am, Egyptians found themselves disconnected from the global Internet, although the large volume of traffic between Europe and Asia that runs through Egypt was unaffected. Mobile-phone companies were also ordered to shut down voice and SMS service in some areas.

After a period of initial confusion, however, it became clear that one ISP – Noor Group, with 8% of the market – remained online, and that by sheer luck or coincidence, a number of activists remained connected through this ISP. Several set up their homes as hubs for uploading video and photos, while an emergent digital hub in Tahrir Square used wires spliced from street lights to keep their laptops and cameras charged in order to capture the essence of the protests. Over the course of two days, the group of digital activists had reportedly collected as much as one hundred gigabytes of content.

On 31 January, Noor Group was disconnected, leaving networked Egyptians entirely in the dark. That same day, American companies Google and Twitter released a new tool which they claimed had been developed over the weekend; Speak2Tweet, as it was called, allowed Egyptians to use their mobile phones – which were still connected – to call a number and leave a voicemail, which would then be 'tweeted' on the Twitter website. Realising that the majority of calls were in Arabic, a variety of outside groups–among them the American-founded 'Alive In' project–quickly mobilised to form translation teams, transcribing and translating the messages into English. On 1 February, Mona Seif, the daughter of well-known activist and professor Leila Seif, called and left a message, encouraged by family members outside the country who had learned of the service. Her message – in which she called for the Mubarak regime to 'bring it on!' – was rebroadcast by news outlets throughout the world, branding the younger Seif a voice of the revolution.

Once again, social media and traditional media became closely linked, with traditional news sources broadcasting information from social media back to viewers both inside and outside Egypt. Reporting from both local and international journalists captivated the world's attention, despite considerable attempts by Egyptian authorities to oust global news outfits. But just as in Tunisia, the information they provided contrasted sharply with that of state-run media, presenting a troubling picture to those who had previously trusted the regime.

On 2 February, possibly bowing to economic pressure (the shutdown is said to have cost Egypt $90 million) the regime resumed Internet services. Several bloggers, reconnecting after nearly a week, confirmed what many had suspected: that shutting down the Internet had in fact encouraged some to join the crowds in Tahrir Square. On 7 February, the importance of the

Internet came into sharp focus as Wael Ghonim, the previously anonymous Google executive responsible for the 'We Are All Khaled Said' Facebook page, was released from detention after having been missing for 11 days. Ghonim's tearful interviews – in which he admitted his role in creating the page and proclaimed all Egyptians as heroes – gave a public face to the young protesters, revitalising the crowds in Tahrir Square. Over the next four days, the world watched in awe as the protests built and as international television networks broadcast live from inside the square. After Mubarak's final speech on 10 February, in which it became apparent that he had no intention to resign, protesters marched toward the presidential palace. As the army let them pass without incident, it became apparent that Mubarak had already left. The next day, it was announced that he had stepped down.

External effects

What role did digital media play in the fall of the Tunisian and Egyptian regimes? While technology certainly helped politicise subsets of the population and in calling citizens to the streets, its principal role appears to have been to draw international attention. While Twitter may not have fomented Iran's Green Movement, it certainly ensured that the world was watching, and in Tunisia and Egypt, tweets from the street complemented the reporting of journalists.

A framework suggested by researchers at George Washington University (GWU) in Washington DC for analysing how new and social media affect struggles for political change sees five levels of effects:

- individual transformation (for example, politicisation)
- intergroup relations (the synergising of various groups)
- collective action (the potential for organisation via social media)
- regime policies (the response of regimes to online efforts)
- external attention (the mobilisation of media and other external bodies in response to online efforts).

In Tunisia, Egypt, Iran and Moldova, the gaining of external attention was clear: indeed, social media's most prominent function was in attracting international attention, thus bringing protests to prominence and eventually affecting the external policy of governments to one degree or another.

However, the extent to which further effects – and the ultimate success of the revolutions – within Tunisia and Egypt were attributable to use of social media is less clear. The creation of the 'We Are All Khaled Said' page may certainly have politicised a subset of the population, while the released images of Bouazizi may have spurred collective action, but it remains unclear to what extent these actions affected the broader spectrum of protests. While the Said page in Egypt invited citizens into the streets, the sheer number and variety of participants in the 25 January demonstrations and those that came after indicate other (offline) influences. Furthermore, while organising did occur online in both countries (through both public instances such as Facebook groups and more private ones, such as e-mail), the eventual number of participants in protests in both countries far exceeded the participants in those online groups.

It seems obvious that, while Internet penetration has been growing, the reach of satellite television is far greater. However, in chaotic situations such as the 2011 revolutions, television networks also rely to some extent on citizen reporting via social media, which they monitor.

Within the GWU researchers' framework, there is considerably more work to be done to understand the effects, beyond external attention, of social media. Is there evidence of large-scale individual transformation as a result of social media? And while, in Egypt, groups like Kefaya and the April 6 Movement separately used digital tools in their activism, it is not clear to what extent those same tools enabled them to work together or spurred them to collective action.

Limited role elsewhere

After Egypt's revolt, unrest broke out in several other countries, notably Bahrain, Libya, Yemen and Syria. But the role of social media in those protests appeared to be limited. Events in some of these countries have shown that opposition activists are not the only people who can use Internet tools to advance their cause. In Bahrain and Syria, for example, pro-regime forces have taken to the social networks to drown out dissent. On Twitter, automated spambots (accounts that 'tweet' automated feeds using third-party applications) target popular hashtags in an effort to drown news of protests. On Facebook, various actors – using the platform's community-reporting tools – target other groups for terms-of-service violations (such as Facebook's rule that users must use only their real, full names), in the hopes that sheer force will trigger an automated mechanism to bring a group down.

The degree of Internet access is clearly a factor: in Egypt and Tunisia, Internet users made up a quarter or more of the total population. In Syria penetration is below 20%, and in pre-war Libya it was only 5% – although in Bahrain it is 88%. There, while security forces sustained a brutal crackdown on street protesters, regime supporters took to social networks to intimidate and harass those supporting the protests. This led to an eerie quiet from a once-active blogosphere, the result of intimidation and fear.

In Syria, the government blocked many sites, including all those using Israel's '.il' Internet domain, as well as those belonging to the Muslim Brotherhood, political opposition groups and certain social networks and blogs. Bloggers had a modicum of freedom compared to their journalist counterparts, but scores were arrested for content posted online. In February 2011, just as protests began taking off on the streets of Damascus and Deraa, authorities unblocked Facebook, Blogspot and YouTube for the first time in four years. To some, this appeared a means of quelling dissent and appeasing the networked community; to others, it was apparent that the goal of the Syrian authorities was to spy on citizens. For years, Syrians had evaded the bans by using circumvention technology. The ability to obscure the IP address of the user gave a little protection to those using websites to organise protests.

The end of the Facebook ban meant that the regime could use new techniques to track down activists. Members of the country's security forces, the Mukhabarat, detained activists and demanded their Facebook passwords, threatening their families if they dared to change their password. In May 2011, it was reported that the authorities had conducted a 'man-in-the-middle' attack by presenting a fake security certificate to Syrian Facebook users who attempted to access the site via the World Wide Web. This meant that anyone who clicked past the certificate was essentially handing over their login details to the authorities.

A model for soft power?

In January 2010, US Secretary of State Hillary Clinton put forth Internet freedom as a tenet of US foreign policy, emphasising the importance of unfettered access and calling on American companies to take a principled stand against censorship.

This so-called 'net freedom agenda' was a development on programmes that the US government had already begun to promote on the use of digital media. For example, the State Department, through the Middle East Partnership Initiative (MEPI), and the US Agency for International Development (USAID) have for several years been funding the development of digital tools, such as circumvention technologies, and digital training for activists. The State Department designated $28 million in grants for 2011, chiefly to fund circumvention technologies. Additionally, government-funded organisations such as the National Democratic Institute and Freedom House offer training, for example in how to use anonymity and circumvention technology, for digital activists in many countries.

The Council of Europe has proposed a set of draft principles for Internet freedom, for example that 'Internet governance arrangements must ensure the protection of user rights and freedoms in accordance with international human rights standards and the rule of law'. Furthermore, organisations such as Hivos in the Netherlands and the Heinrich Böll Foundation in Germany provide or fund digital training in various regions, focused on similar issues to their US counterparts.

Such programmes, however, have been criticised as providing only some of the skills needed, and as not being sufficiently integrated with other government policies. For example, US support for democratic change in some countries in the Arab world only emerged once the revolutionary tide had begun to turn.

The success of online campaigns depends heavily on the knowledge and determination of the campaigners. Egyptians' online success, for example, was largely the result of years of hard work by activists with developed digital skills and training, as well as learning from the mistakes and successes in Iran and Tunisia. But it is unclear to what extent the training offered by US government agencies played a role.

Ultimately, state policies that favour free expression and an open Internet can only be considered a positive thing; and yet, accompanying policies, decisions and grant-making efforts are part of a comprehensive agenda on Internet freedom and need to be thoughtfully designed to match overarching foreign-policy goals. Moreover, while it is certain that widely available digital tools have played the role of amplifier for local voices, drawing international attention and thus having some effect – at least through solidarity with the goals of protesters – the extent to which the same tools have acted as catalysts, politicising youth and spurring them to action, or as a mechanism for organising, is less clear.

Global Agriculture and Food Security

Since the middle of the last decade the world has experienced a substantial increase in the volatility of food prices, with spikes to record levels in both 2008 and 2011. This volatility has had several consequences. It has been a major catalyst for inflation, and has disrupted trade. It has caused unease among governments, which have resorted to a range of sometimes counter-productive policy responses. And it has contributed to insecurity and unrest in numerous countries, most notably the 'Arab Awakening' revolts in the Middle East. Food-security issues relate to broader concerns about increasing resource scarcity. The political and security impacts of recent volatility and of the longer-term outlook for global agriculture – and of individual and collective governmental responses – may be profound.

What causes volatility?

Fluctuations in food prices were significantly greater over the past decade than in the previous two. Prices rose sharply in 2006 and 2007, hitting a peak in summer 2008 at the same time oil prices peaked at $147 a barrel. They then declined sharply as the financial crisis and subsequent global economic downturn exerted downward pressure on commodity prices as a whole, but increased once more from 2009 onwards. In spring 2011, the UN Food and Agriculture Organisation (FAO) Food Price Index and a range of individual commodity price indices stood at levels higher than those reached in 2008.

Monthly Real Food Price Index, 1990–2011

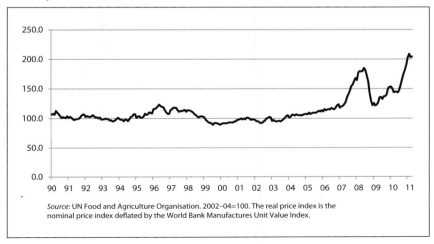

Source: UN Food and Agriculture Organisation. 2002–04=100. The real price index is the nominal price index deflated by the World Bank Manufactures Unit Value Index.

Many factors lie behind the trend towards higher and more volatile food prices, and there has been much debate over which have been most important. In broad terms, they form three principal clusters: demand factors, supply factors and 'multipliers' that amplifiy inflation and volatility.

On the demand side, three main causes stand out: population growth, income growth and demand for biofuels. Global population is rising steadily and is increasing demand for food. The world's population now stands at just under 7 billion, and new UN estimates published in 2011 show the total reaching 9.3bn in 2050 and 10.1bn in 2100 under median projections. The overall global rate of growth has slowed markedly since its peak in the 1960s (although it remains high in many low-income countries, among them some of the world's most fragile states), but the fact that the world will have nearly half again as many people to feed over the coming century is a key feature of the food-security landscape.

At the same time, the world's middle class is becoming both larger and more affluent, particularly due to rapid income growth in middle-income countries and emerging economies. In the process, more people are shifting to 'Western' diets richer in meat, dairy products and processed foods, all of which are more intensive in the use of grain, energy, water and other inputs.

Together, these drivers mean that aggregate demand for food is projected to increase by 50% by 2030, and by 70-100% by 2050. But rapidly growing demand for crops for use as feedstock in the manufacture of biofuels such as ethanol or biodiesel is an additional factor. During 2011, for example, ethanol was expected to account for up to 40% of corn (maize) production in the United States, the world's largest producer of the crop. This is a significant new variable in the pattern of demand for crops. In its 2008 *World Economic Outlook,* for example, the International Monetary Fund (IMF) noted that 'although biofuels still account for only 1.5% of the global liquid fuels supply, they accounted for almost half the increase in the consumption of major food crops in 2006–07, mostly because of corn-based ethanol produced in the United States'.

But while demand for crops is rising rapidly, there are also questions about the capacity of supply growth to keep pace. Again, a range of factors is involved. There are signs that growth in productivity (crop yield per unit area) has begun to slow. From 1970 to 1990, global aggregate yields grew at an average rate of 2.0% per year, thanks largely to the Green Revolution of new seed varieties, increased irrigation and more effective use of fertiliser. But this growth slowed to an average of 1.1% between 1990 and 2007, and is projected by the US Department of Agriculture to continue to fall over the next decade.

This slowdown in yield growth was partly due to a long-term trend of under-investment in agriculture, particularly in many developing countries. After the successes of the Green Revolution in the 1960s and 1970s, international aid donors largely forgot about agriculture as newer policy agendas diverted their attention. For example, according to Jacques Diouf, director-general of the FAO, the proportion of official development assistance allocated to agriculture fell from 17% to 3% between 1980 and 2006, while the total amount of aid spent on agriculture fell 58%.

Agricultural yields have also been impacted by extreme weather. The 2008 food spike was exacerbated by a severe drought in Australia, a major wheat exporter, for example; more recently, the drought in Russia in 2010 also led to marked price impacts. Many other countries have seen crop yields affected by extreme weather in recent years, with additional price impacts; during the first half of 2011, for example, fears about drought in China and crop forecasts in the United States drove further price rises on futures markets.

Finally, high oil prices have also exerted upward pressure on food prices. Modern agricultural production methods are highly intensive in their use of fossil fuels, not only in on-farm energy use, processing and transportation, but also because fossil fuels are directly used as feedstock for the manufacture of fertilisers. As a result, high oil prices push up input costs for agriculture, and biofuels become more attractive and competitive as prices for oil increase, exacerbating the trend. Oil prices followed a similar trajectory to food prices during the 2006–08 food-price spike, and peaked at around the same time; a similar correlation can be seen for the more recent food spike.

While demand for crops has been increasing markedly, then, supply growth has been more stuttering. The effect of this tight balance between demand and supply has been amplified in recent years by several factors rooted in how markets work and the policies applied by governments, where four drivers are particularly important to note: levels of food stocks, currency movements, financial speculation and government actions.

Global food stocks fell to historically low levels before the 2006–08 food spike. Before 2000, stocks stood at 110 days' worth of demand, but by 2004 this had fallen to just over 60 days. This was partly because the long-term slump in food prices prior to 2000, coupled with the development of just-in-time supply chains, had led many governments and companies to conclude that their stocks were an expensive encumbrance. But it was also because demand had simply outpaced supply: global use of grains and oilseeds was greater than production for seven of the eight years between 2000 and 2008. Since 2008, stock levels have increased to some extent, due to good harvests and reactions to the food spike, but the steady underlying increase in demand means that the world is in effect banking on bumper harvests every year.

Currency movements have also been a factor in rising food prices, particularly in the case of the US dollar. The fact that trade in many agricultural and other commodities is denominated in dollars means that when the US dollar depreciates, as it did from 2002 to mid-2008, prices for those commodities rise. Conversely, when the dollar appreciates, as it did from mid-2008 onwards during the global economic crisis, food prices drop. Food price volatility may also be amplified by financial speculation, although its precise impact remains contentious. While the amount of money invested in financial derivatives markets for agricultural commodities increased sharply over the last decade, analysts argue about whether or not this has been a major driver for rising prices. There is, however, an emerging consensus among international agencies that, as the FAO put it, 'increased participation by non-commercial actors such as index funds, swap dealers and money managers in financial markets probably acted to amplify short term price swings and could have contributed to the formation of price bubbles in some situations'.

Finally, and probably most fundamentally, food prices have been affected by government actions. The height of the 2006–08 food spike saw many governments lapse into panic or kneejerk reactions, including food-export restrictions (imposed by over 30 governments at the height of the spike), hoarding and panic buying (particularly evident among a number of import-dependent Middle East and North African governments in the spring of 2011, as they cast about for ways to contain domestic unrest). While some of these actions may have been rational in the short term for individual governments, all of them had the overall effect of exerting additional destabilising effects on already turbulent world markets.

The long-term outlook
At the height of the 2006–08 food-price spike, many analysts took a broadly sanguine view about long-term prospects, in effect assessing the spike as an anomaly. A report on the global agricultural outlook to 2017, published jointly by the Organisation for Economic Cooperation and Development

(OECD) and the FAO in May 2008, argued that record prices 'will not last and ... will gradually come down because of the transitory nature of some of the factors that are behind the recent hikes ... the underlying forces that drive agricultural supply (by and large productivity gains) will eventually outweigh the forces that determine stronger demand, both for food and feed as well as for industrial demand, most notably for biofuel production. Consequently, prices will resume their decline in real terms, though possibly not by quite as much as in the past.' However, this broadly upbeat assessment has been challenged by analysts who have pointed out that it takes little account of the effect of trends in resource scarcity and environmental degradation which, if fully factored into the analysis, might lead to a different conclusion. Four such trends are particularly significant: water scarcity, competition for land, high oil prices and climate change.

Demand for water has risen sharply over the last century. While in 1900 average water use per person was 350m^3, according to Earthscan's *Atlas of Water*, this had risen to 642m^3 by 2000; total global annual water withdrawal grew over the same period from 579 to 3,973 cubic kilometres. This level of water extraction is unsustainable. Many aquifers and other groundwater systems are being depleted faster than the replacement rate, and many rivers and lakes are also being used unsustainably. Climate change, moreover, will be an additional factor: water scarcity is seen by scientists as among the most significant near-term impacts of global warming. The effect of these trends is that by 2000, half a billion people lived in countries classified as chronically short of water, and by 2050 this total is projected to rise to 4bn.

Agriculture and food feature heavily in the global water outlook, in terms of both cause and effect. Agriculture accounts for around 70% of total human freshwater use, and while its proportion of human water use is in decline as cities and industry take larger shares, its absolute consumption levels are rising steadily. Highly inefficient irrigation systems, which often see up to 75% of water wasted, are a major driver. While technologies such as drip irrigation would allow water to be used far more efficiently, uptake of them remains low, in part because there are often no charges for water use. Changing dietary patterns also increase demand for water, through the much higher water intensity of meat and dairy products.

At the same time, water scarcity is poised to be a major limiting factor on agricultural production in the century ahead, as well as an increasing security issue in its own right. While conflicts for direct control of water are rare, competition for water is already recognised as a significant threat multiplier in a range of fragile states, for example in the Horn of Africa; between states, meanwhile, tension is increasing over access to shared water resources, particularly in the Nile and Indus watersheds.

Competition for land, too, is increasing due to the convergence of growth in demand for a range of key resources which depend on it. Demand is increasing for land to grow crops for human consumption, since increased acreage must fill the gap if increases in yield fail to keep pace. The global shift towards 'Western' diets creates more demand for land on which to graze livestock and grow feed for their consumption; biofuels also account for substantial land demand. On top of this are growing requirements for land for carbon sequestration, conservation, and the world's growing cities, which often encroach on the best agricultural land.

Energy security, particularly the availability of oil at affordable prices, also has an important bearing on long-term food-security prospects. The International Energy Agency has warned consistently in recent years that the amount of money currently being invested in upstream oil production is inadequate to meet projected demand, and that there is the risk of a new supply crunch as demand continues to rise. A second source of concern relates to the question of the imminence of 'peak oil', the point at which affordable global oil production reaches a plateau and then starts to decline. Although this had until relatively recently been regarded by many analysts as a 'fringe' concept, it has become more mainstream in recent years.

Finally, climate change is likely to be a key factor in the long-term global agricultural outlook (see essay, pages 119–25). While the Intergovernmental Panel on Climate Change (IPCC) projects that 'on the whole' global warming of between 1–3°C will increase food production, it also suggests that yields will decrease above this level – and also that yields will fall even within this range in lower latitudes, where most developing countries are located. And the IPCC's overall projections take no account of projected increases in the frequency and severity of extreme weather events, such as droughts, floods and heat waves, despite the fact that such factors can and do have a marked impact on crop yields (as the impact of the 2010 heat wave on Russian wheat production demonstrated).

The overall long-term outlook of increasing climate change and resource scarcity, together with structural supply and demand factors, suggest good reasons to be cautious of arguments that the 2008 food-price spike was merely a blip. As the UK government's 2011 Foresight report on *The Future of Food and Farming* concluded, 'any one of these pressures ("drivers of change") would present substantial challenges to food security; together they constitute a major threat that requires a strategic reappraisal of how the world is fed'. So while global markets are already characterised by high levels of price volatility, long-term drivers suggest that volatility will increase still further in the future, depending on the scale and effectiveness of the policy and market response to these challenges.

Impacts of volatility

By far the largest impacts of the food-price volatility of recent years have been on poor people around the world, who are most vulnerable to spikes both because they spend a high proportion of household income (often as much as 80%) on food, and because a broader lack of resilience can lead to the use of coping mechanisms with harmful long-term consequences (for example, selling productive assets such as livestock to meet immediate consumption needs).

Prior to the 2008 food-price spike, FAO estimates suggested that the global total of undernourished people stood at around 854 million, but as a result of the spike it rose in 2009 to over a billion people for the first time, before declining somewhat as the global economic downturn led to a brief decline in commodity prices. The number is likely to rise again in 2011 due to the second price spike, which exceeded 2008 levels. The impact on chil-

Global Undernourishment (millions), 1969–2010

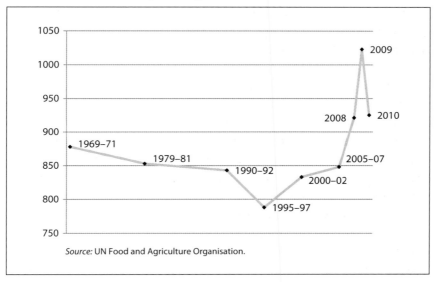

Source: UN Food and Agriculture Organisation.

dren of food-price volatility has been especially severe; malnutrition before the age of five frequently leads to stunted growth and lifelong impairment of cognitive function.

The human impact of volatile food prices has been concentrated in rural areas in developing countries, where three-quarters of the world's absolute poor (those living on less than a dollar a day) are located. While many of these people rely on farming for at least part of their income, they have tended to lose rather than benefit from food-price inflation since their yields are so low that they are net buyers of food. Political attention, however, has often focused on discontent about food (and fuel) inflation among urban consumers, particularly when this discontent spills over into unrest, protests or rioting. An analysis undertaken by the International Food Policy Research Institute found that 61 countries experienced some form of unrest during the 2006–08 food-price spike, with protests classified as 'violent' in 23 cases. (The same analysis also found that fragile states were somewhat more likely to experience unrest as a result of high food prices, and that instances of unrest in fragile states were substantially more likely to become violent.) More recently, food prices have been widely noted as one of a range of sources of discontent prefiguring the unrest of the 'Arab Awakening' in the Middle East and North Africa.

In economic terms, the main impact of the perfect storm affecting food prices was more general price inflation. In developed countries, food prices were a significant driver of rising inflation rates, while in emerging and developing countries (where food accounts for a larger share of the consumer price basket), the effect was even more pronounced. The IMF estimated in April 2008 that food prices represented 44% of global inflation in 2007, with the figure rising to as much as 67.5% in Asia. The impact of food-price inflation was magnified by the parallel fuel-price trend.

For import-dependent countries (and, above all, low-income importers), the effects of food-price inflation and volatility have been especially pronounced, leading to balance of payments problems for many. Such effects have been especially severe in fragile states with poor public financial management. In Yemen, for example, which imports 80% of its food, political unrest led in spring 2011 to Yemeni importers finding it increasingly difficult to obtain letters of credit. While the central bank supported the imports of some core commodities such as flour, rice and sugar, many businesses were believed to have stopped importing food altogether.

Another economic impact of food-price volatility was a series of trade shocks, in particular the wave of export bans that rippled around the world during summer 2008. At the peak of the 2008 food-price spike, more than 30 governments had bans or restrictions in place, with the inevitable if unintended consequence that prices elsewhere were forced still higher. At the same time, some importing governments lapsed into panic buying on international markets or hoarding food, again with the effect of driving further inflation.

Finally, fears over security of supply have led some strategically significant import-dependent countries (particularly in East Asia and the Persian Gulf) to seek to improve their access to food through long-term food or land access deals in third countries (particularly, but not exclusively, in Africa and South Asia). These sorts of deals, often referred to as 'land grabs' in the media, have raised concerns because of their potential impact on vulnerable communities, with the World Bank arguing that such investments often fail to drive improvements in productivity or poverty reduction due to weak land governance, lack of host-country capacity, or insufficiently clear investor proposals, among other factors. Land-access deals can also have direct consequences for stability and security: in Madagascar in 2009, for example, news that a South Korean investor had leased one-half of the country's arable land for 100 years, for no payment other than the putative creation of local employment opportunities, led to increased discontent and a subsequent coup.

Policy responses

As prices rose in 2007 and 2008, many governments framed the challenge primarily in terms of increasing investment in agriculture and food production to catalyse a supply-side response. The 2008 G8 summit in L'Aquila, Italy, for example, saw governments pledging $20bn over three years for rural development in developing countries, with the United States playing a particularly important role in brokering agreement and pledging funds. But many of the pledges were not fulfilled, and others proved to be re-announcements of existing funding commitments.

Private-sector investment in the agricultural sector has been more forthcoming, with many institutional and retail investors now interested in commodities as an asset class with long-term growth potential. While this has helped drive bigger harvests in the last few years, however, it is unlikely to substitute fully for public investment in areas such as research and development, particularly on crops grown primarily in developing countries, and in scaling up agricultural extension systems that can diffuse new technologies.

A second policy response has been to seek to improve access to food. Producing enough food to feed a population is no guarantee that everyone in that population will actually be fed (the world produces enough food to feed all 6.9bn inhabitants, but a billion still fail to get enough to eat). International organisations such as the World Bank and United Nations have suggested that the best option for developing countries is to invest in targeted social-protection systems that provide support to their poorest citizens, rather than spending on economy-wide subsidies (which are often fiscally crippling) or imposing price controls (which reduce incentives for producers to increase output and create other market distortions). However, while many governments agree with this advice in principle, it is often difficult for them to reform existing subsidy regimes. Pakistan, for example, has tried several times to eliminate subsidies that are manifestly unaffordable for the country, only to back down when popular discontent threatened to cause the government to collapse.

A third response has been an attempt to increase the resilience of international trade to food-price shocks. This has been a particular priority of the 2011 French presidency of the G20, which has been examining rules or codes of conduct to reduce the risk of export bans; ways to increase market transparency; possible rules to place new restrictions on commodity speculation; and a range of other measures. But many other areas remain largely unaddressed: for example, the fragmented nature of international institutions working on agriculture and food security; finding ways of making agriculture more resilient (for example to climate-change impacts) and environmentally sustainable; and ways to make small farmers in poor countries better placed to benefit from the long-term outlook for higher food prices.

Conclusion

Global food security, like security of other resources such as land, water and oil, appears to be delicately balanced between a zero-sum future involving a slide towards increasing resource nationalism, with access to food, water, energy and land becoming a source of strategic competition between states and rising instability within them; and a mutually beneficial scenario where resource pressures act as a catalyst for a shift towards increased international cooperation. In either scenario, food security and wider issues of resource security are likely to become increasingly central to politics, economics and security over the rest of the century.

Human Security and the Changing Climate

At the end of the warmest decade in history, 2010 saw global mean temperatures set new records. According to both the National Climatic Data Center of the US National Oceanic and Atmospheric Administration (NOAA), and NASA's Goddard Institute for Space Studies, 2010 was in a statistical tie with 2005 for the hottest year on record, while the Hadley Centre of the UK's Met Office ranked it second (by 0.02°C) after 1998. (The minor disagreements stem from subtle methodological differences, notably handling of regions with inadequate instrumental records and choice of baseline period.) The Northern Hemisphere set a clear record for warmth, while it was the sixth-hottest year on record in the Southern Hemisphere.

The record high temperature in 2010 was noteworthy because it came despite relatively low solar activity. A clear record high for a 12-month period set in summer 2010 was helped by a strong El Niño, with the warmest-ever March, April, May and June globally. But that record was again surpassed by the 12 months to the end of November, despite a return to cooler La Niña conditions in the second half of the year. Temperatures were particularly high in Greenland and Canada as well as the Middle East and North Africa, and were above average in southern Africa, eastern Europe, eastern Russia and southern Asia, but cooler than average in central Russia and northern Europe. In fact, the winter of 2009/10 was the coldest in Europe since 1978/79.

The world has already warmed by 0.7°C since pre-industrial times, and is bound to see at least a further 0.6°C rise simply from emissions already in the atmosphere. But in 2010, according to the International Energy Agency, energy-related greenhouse-gas emissions also hit record highs, despite the global economic slowdown, with increases in the developing world and emerging economies more than compensating for any reductions elsewhere. Overall emissions growth continued to track, roughly, the worst-case 'business as usual' scenario of the Intergovernmental Panel on Climate Change (IPCC). While the underlying dynamics in the real world differed from the IPCC scenarios, given comparable levels and sustained growth rates of emissions, there appeared to be no improvement in the prognosis for global warming, related climate change and associated human consequences. While uncertainties remained for both short- and long-term forecasts, prospects for keeping the overall rise in global average temperatures below what many see as a critical threshold of 2°C looked increasingly dim.

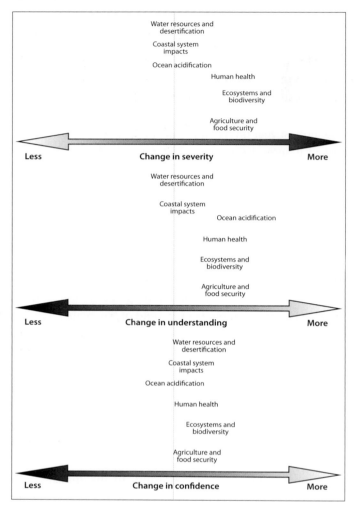

Figure 1: Change in severity, understanding and confidence in projections for post-AR4 climate impacts science (sources for figs 1–2: see page 432)

Impacts and risks

Scientific understanding and confidence with regard to most aspects of climate change and its impacts have continued to improve in the half-decade since the cut-off point for consideration in the IPCC's Fourth Assessment Report (AR4) published in 2007. Such advances have led to an increase in the expected severity of many impacts, especially on human health and food and water security (see Figure 1). This was a continuation of a trend reflected in successive IPCC reports since 1990, and most notably illustrated by an update of the 'burning embers diagram', a graphic summation of increas-

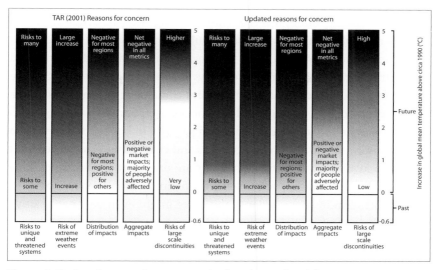

Figure 2: Updated reasons for concern: the 'burning embers' diagram

ing risk with increasing temperatures across various 'reasons for concern', which originally appeared in the IPCC's 2001 assessment report. The update was prepared for the 2007 report but omitted (despite inclusion of the textual analysis on which it was based) due to objections by China, Russia, Saudi Arabia and the United States. Viewed by the UK, Germany and several other countries as an essential diagram, it showed how the risks across all five reasons for concern were much greater than had previously been thought, and that the 2°C guardrail, thought in 2001 to allow the worst dangers to be avoided, is insufficient (see Figure 2).

There is an emerging consensus among scholars and analysts, reflected in a 2008 EU Council/Commission Report, the 2010 US Quadrennial Defense Review and the October 2010 UK Strategic Defence and Security Review that climate change stemming from global warming is a security 'threat multiplier'. Through its impacts on the availability of clean water and food, the geographical pattern of disease vectors and the stability of communities and shelter, anthropogenic climate change has the potential to exacerbate human insecurity and contribute directly or indirectly to political or violent conflict in weak and failing states. This means that the types of threats to international stability emanating from such states will be enhanced. (These issues were discussed at length in *Strategic Survey 2007: The Annual Review of World Affairs* (pages 46–68) and the final report of the IISS Transatlantic Dialogue on Climate Change and Security in January 2011.) The same dynamic applies in the case of the human security of the people who will be directly affected by global warming, but in this case climate change may be better described as a risk multiplier rather than a threat multiplier.

For example, climate change is one of four broad and interrelated trends threatening global food security (see essay, pages 109–18). The dynamics of food security are complex, but climate (or weather), as both a chronic problem and through sudden shocks, is commonly mentioned as one factor among many influencing food security in household surveys in the developing world. Falling crop yields and crop failures due to reduced rainfall or availability of irrigation water are only part of the story. Some effects of climate change, such as longer growing seasons, may be positive in the short term in some regions, and there might even be a net positive effect with modest global temperature increases. The impacts will vary from region to region, however, and for the most part the regions worst affected will also be those already experiencing high levels of food insecurity and least able to compensate or adapt. Fisheries and aquaculture will be affected by ocean warming and acidification and destruction of coral reefs, while sea-level rise can result in salinisation of coastal soils and aquifers. Crop pathogens, such as wheat stem rust, particularly the virulent Ug99 strain (first identified in Uganda in 1999) that has been damaging normally resistant wheat crops in Africa, Asia and most recently the Middle East, are spreading more widely and more quickly as winters become wetter and warmer.

Natural variability, whether daily, seasonal or from year-to-year, has been and remains much greater than the long-term warming trend since the Industrial Revolution, and it will be some years before the impact of global warming begins to be noticeable against the backdrop of extreme events such as seasonal or multi-year droughts; heat waves and cold snaps; and storms and floods. But an increase in the frequency and severity of such extreme events is expected to be an early manifestation of anthropogenic climate change, and there is evidence that it is happening already. Winter 2009/10 was unusually cold in Europe, Russia and the United States, but unusually warm in the Arctic, Canada and much of the Southern Hemisphere; the globe experienced its fourth-warmest January and sixth-warmest February, and March not only set a record but saw the third-highest deviation from the average of any month on record. The year to mid-2011 was characterised by extreme weather throughout the world (see Strategic Geography, pages XII–XIII). Millions were made homeless, thousands killed and crops and infrastructure damaged by flooding in Pakistan, China, Australia, the American Midwest and parts of Africa and South America; wildfires raged across Russia, Mexico, several southern US states and the Canadian province of Alberta; drought and heat waves damaged crops in Russia, China, western Europe and parts of Africa; chronic drought conditions continued in Brazil and Australia; major winter storms struck North America and China; and a record number of severe tornados hit the United States, including regions not normally affected. In many cases these were 'hundred-year' or even 'thousand-year events' (similarly severe events would not be expected, on average, to happen more frequently than once in the stated period). Arctic sea ice reached its lowest-ever volume in summer 2010. Other areas of the globe also experienced severe, if not so extreme, weather events of their own. But just as global warming means new extremes of both heat and cold, storm patterns are also changing. The 2010 hurricane season in the Northeast Pacific, for example, was one of the least active and produced the fewest number of named storms on record. However, Typhoon Megi, which struck the Philippines in October, was one of the strongest tropical cyclones ever recorded, and other regions experienced cyclones unusual in their timing, strength or location.

Climate is a statistical average of the weather over several decades, so the weather in a single year, let alone a single event, is not an indication of climate change. But while climate scientists are divided over how much the recent extreme weather can be attributed to global warming, few doubt that it has been a major contributor, and there is a consensus that the pattern of extremes is consistent with the projections from global climate models. Much of the extreme weather in the year to mid-2011 can be linked to short-term changes in oceanic and atmospheric circulation patterns, so the individual events are not always independent of one another, and will not necessarily persist in the next few years. But the circulation pattern and the degree of shift, while not unprecedented, were greater than would normally be expected. Moreover, where it has been possible to analyse specific events statistically in sufficient detail, such as the UK floods of 2000, the European heat wave of 2003 and the Russian heat wave of 2000, there are indications that global warming has made comparable events anywhere between twice and eight times as likely to occur in a given year. Moreover, global warming has increased the amount of water vapour in the atmosphere by about 4%, which has been a driver common to many of the recent extreme weather events. Swiss Re, the insurance firm, has estimated that global losses from natural disasters have risen more than four-fold since the 1980s. In part this is due to population increase and economic growth – there is more wealth and there are more lives to lose – but the number of climate-related disasters has more than doubled, while the number of non-climate-related disasters has remained level.

Besides a direct impact on food production and prices, climate change is already affecting human security in other ways. A World Health Organisation calculation of global disease burden and risk factors concluded that 154,000 deaths of the nearly 56m in 2000, or 0.3%, and 5.5m disability-adjusted life years (years lost to illness, disability or premature death), or 0.4% of the total, could be attributed to the climate change that had occured since the baseline period 1961–1990. According to the UN Human Development Report 2007/2008, nearly 5% of people in developing countries were affected by climate-related disasters between 2000 and 2004 (compared to less than one-tenth of 1% in the developed world, an indication of both the geographical distribution of the threat and the far greater resilience that comes with wealth). By 2009 the Geneva-based Global Humanitarian Forum reported that (with, to be sure, fairly large uncertainties and margins of error) climate change was already causing, on average, more than 300,000 deaths and economic losses of $125bn and 'seriously affecting' 325m people every year. (The definition of being 'seriously affected' includes someone in need of immediate assistance in the context of a weather-related disaster or whose livelihood is significantly compromised. This condition can be temporary, where people have lost their homes or been injured in weather-related disasters, or permanent, where people are living with severe water scarcity, are hungry or suffering from diseases such as diarrhoea and malaria.) Over the preceding half-decade, weather-related disasters had caused anywhere between $50bn and $300bn in a given year.

Social and political ramifications

The more nebulous but nevertheless real social and political impacts of climate change are also being felt. The violence in Darfur in the past decade, for example, was the largest and latest in a series of sporadic conflicts going back to the 1980s, originating in tribal competition over access to grazing land and water. Historically, agriculturalists and pastoralists coexisted without clashing, and in fact functioned symbiotically. But population growth, together with declining productivity of agricultural land due to low rainfall and increasing losses to pests, necessitated the expansion of land under cultivation. A simultaneous deterioration of pastureland meant pastoralists needed more area to support a growing animal population, and shifts in ecological zones due to changes in aridity affected the competition between pastoralism and agriculture in a given area. There was an extended period of desiccation in the Sahel from the 1960s to the 1990s, with severe drought in the early 1970s and early to mid-1980s. Darfur in particular experienced a very severe drought in 1980–84, and again in 1990. In the 1990s a trend towards wetter conditions in the Sahel began, and in 2003 there was especially abundant rainfall, causing flooding and landslides in parts of the region. Exceptionally wet conditions, with rainfall about 15% above the average of the previous 55 years, or 60% above the average for 1971–2000, occurred again in 2005. But rainfall remained below long-term norms, with 2005 a particularly bad year and 2007 the worst in over a decade. By 2007 over two million people in Darfur had been displaced, many fleeing across the border to Chad, and the number of killed and wounded has been estimated at somewhere between 200,000 and 500,000.

The Arab Awakening that began in early 2011 (see pages 43–96) offers another example. The food-price spike, in part due to the extreme global weather (see essay, pages 109–18), was an important factor behind the initial protests and uprisings in Tunisia and Egypt that set off a chain reaction throughout the Middle East and North Africa. Although World Bank President Robert Zoellick described food prices as an 'aggravating factor' in the turmoil, rather than as the principal cause, it was a vivid illustration of the way climate change acts as a risk multiplier for human insecurity both directly, through its impacts on food security, and indirectly, through the knock-on effect on political stability and the different responses of governments to the unrest. The range of outcomes, from relatively peaceful democratic transitions to autocratic repression to civil war and foreign interventions, illustrates the unpredictable nature of the risks.

China's Growing Military Power

China's expanding military capabilities have continued to provoke concern in the United States and other Western countries as well as in Asia-Pacific states. Increasingly, these capabilities threaten to undermine (though by no means eclipse) the United States' regional military superiority in the East Asia, while utterly outclassing the militaries of other states in the region. China is not only developing more capable armed forces, but also deploying military units further from home for exercises and on operational missions – notably in the Gulf of Aden since December 2008. Anxiety over the implications of China's rising defence spending and growing military clout contributes importantly to the ambivalence felt by many states regarding China's re-emergence as a major power.

China's 2010 Defence White Paper, actually released in March 2011, outlines how far the People's Liberation Army (PLA) has come in terms of both its ambition and its capabilities. The White Paper's claim that China's goal was one of 'maintaining world peace and stability' highlighted Beijing's growing confidence in its military capacity. The PLA has evolved from an internally focused force incapable of joint-service operations or of extending its reach beyond China's borders to one that now routinely deploys and exercises overseas. The Defence White Paper was released soon after the first flight of the PLA Air Force's J-20 stealth combat aircraft in January 2011, and not long before reports suggested that the PLA Navy (PLAN) was soon to begin sea trials of its first aircraft carrier. These high-profile projects, as well as publicity over events such as the PLA's parade for the People's Republic of China's 60th anniversary in October 2009 and the PLAN's 60th-anniversary fleet review in April 2010, have stimulated heightened international interest in China's military rise.

Although the international media focus on China's developing military power has come relatively suddenly, the PLA's current capabilities are the result of a decades-long process. Until the 1980s, the PLA's main focus was on internal and border issues. This seemed to be justified in 1989, when the Chinese Communist Party used the PLA to crush the student and worker revolt in Beijing, just three months after the army had suppressed riots in Tibet. These incidents reinforced the army's dominance within the PLA, with the air force, navy and Second Artillery Force (which controls the country's nuclear-armed long-range missiles) remaining secondary in status. The events of 1989, which included the Tiananmen Square massacre, could therefore have had the effect of constraining the PLA's modernisation were it not for events two years later.

The PLA was dealt a rude shock by the Gulf War in 1991, in which a US-led coalition rapidly destroyed out-dated and poorly organised Iraqi forces occupying Kuwait with joint-service operations facilitated by effective communications and information networks, total air supremacy and stand-off weaponry. It was all too obvious that, should there be a conflict in the future, the PLA would be unable to compete effectively with such overwhelmingly powerful US forces, and that previous expectations that the PLA could prevail in a war arising out of the status of Taiwan were probably unrealistic.

The effect was to reinvigorate China's military modernisation process, with a redoubling of efforts begun during the 1980s to reequip the PLA with high-technology weapon systems. Following the American belief that new computer, communications, surveillance and targeting technologies could change the nature of warfare, the 1990s saw the emergence of the 'Revolution in Military Affairs with Chinese characteristics', and the doctrine of 'winning local wars under informationised conditions'. The PLA was aware of its great shortcomings in what came to be known as network-centric warfare, and strove to correct these.

Mechanisation and combined-arms operations

The new Defence White Paper describes the PLA modernisation process as 'taking mechanisation as the foundation and informationisation as the focus'. During the 1990s, the PLA began enhancing its forces' mobility. Simultaneously, it reduced the overall personnel strength, with the land army's size declining from 2.3 million in 1990 to 1.6m in 2010.

In common with many of the world's major armies, over the last 20 years the PLA has attempted to create more powerful, deployable and operationally flexible formations with modern equipment. From the late 1990s onwards, many of the PLA's old divisions were disbanded and reformed as smaller but mechanised or motorised, all-arms brigade groups while others were transferred to the People's Armed Police in an internal security role.

A shortage of experienced officers capable of commanding the new brigades apparently halted the formation of additional modern brigades in 2003. Since then, the PLA has experimented with 'special mission battalions', usually infantry battalions from mechanised or motorised brigades, specifically trained for rapid deployment. This process has intensified since 2006, with the formation of 'combined battalions' and with battlegroups formed from company-sized units drawn from up to a dozen combat and combat-support arms.

Alongside this reorganisation, the PLA has made substantial efforts to modernise its armoured vehicles. However, the army's sheer size has hindered this process significantly, effectively forestalling any introduction of new vehicles across the board. For example, the PLA is believed to possess only enough modern Type-96 and Type-99 tanks to equip roughly one-third of its tank units. Similarly, the new Type-04 armoured infantry fighting vehicles and Type-09 armoured personnel carriers are only available in small numbers, and distributed to selected units. Most PLA tank battalions still operate old Type-59 main battle tanks, while most mechanised battalions still make do with Type-63, Type-86 and Type-92 vehicles. The PLA has never benefited from the helicopter support available to Western armies, and the number of helicopters remains low relative to the overall size of the force. However, the entry into service in 2010 of the WZ-10, China's first real attack helicopter, marked some progress towards overcoming this deficit.

Joined-up operations

The PLA has also been working hard to improve its capacity for joint operations. One of the key lessons from the 1991 Gulf War – seen again with ever-increasing sophistication in conflicts since – was the ability of the US armed forces to work together: infantry could call in precision air strikes; naval bombardment using cruise missiles was a crucial aspect of the air campaign; and artillery, armour and the air force collaborated to destroy massed formations comprehensively and rapidly.

At the time, the Chinese military's ability to mount joint-service operations was extremely limited. Recognising this shortcoming, the PLA commenced reforms aimed at coordinating the logistic and support functions of each service, including health services, fuel supply and vehicle maintenance, with a view to facilitating future joint-service operations. Joint Logistics Departments were formed in all seven military regions during 2000, while Jinan Military Region was the first to introduce a Theatre Joint Logistic Department in 2007, which differed from the Joint Logistics Department by having a headquarters staffed by personnel from all three services in dedicated logistics roles. Exercises gradually built up the PLA's experience of joint operations. In 2001, *Exercise Liberation 1* held on Dongshan Island brought the army, navy and air force together for their first-ever large-scale joint exercise.

New naval capabilities

The army's dominance continues to constrain the PLA's joint-service capabilities, but the fact that the 2010 Defence White Paper noted that the army is merely the 'first among equals' reflected the greater resources and prestige accorded to the PLA's navy and air force. Particularly since its deployment to the Gulf of Aden from December 2008, the international media has focused great attention on the PLAN. The anti-piracy mission, which involves the long-term presence of two surface combatants and a supply ship at any given time, has been the PLA's first-ever active operation beyond Asian waters.

This has drawn attention to the fact that modernisation of the navy has also been under way. Most international interest has focused on the PLAN's aircraft-carrier programme, because of the increased ability to project power that this will bring. This involves in the first instance the conversion of the Soviet-built *Varyag* into an operational vessel likely to be deployed with a complement of J-15 combat aircraft, which have reportedly been copied from the Russian Su-33. Photographs of the *Varyag* released in April 2011 suggested the vessel was nearing completion of its refurbishment, with close-in weapons systems installed and a reconstructed 'island'. Sea trials for the *Varyag* could conceivably start in 2011, although the official launch may not be until late 2012 or 2013.There has been much more, though, to China's naval modernisation than its carrier programme. The number of frigates and destroyers in the fleet expanded from 50 in 1995 to 80 in 2010. The PLAN's submarine fleet has also expanded to a current total of approximately 70 boats, with a rapid improvement in capability during the last decade. Not only has the PLAN invested in Russian-built *Kilo*-class submarines, which are stealthier than other 'hunter-killer' boats in the Chinese fleet, but it has also developed various classes of conventional submarines indigenously, notably the *Song* and *Yuan* classes.

The increase in submarine capability has led to considerable conjecture in the West that China is pursuing an anti-access or area-denial strategy in the western Pacific. Such a strategy, intended to deny use of the sea to potential adversaries rather than concentrating on the more ambitious aim of sea control, could seriously complicate the US Navy's plans for operations in the East Asian littoral, including the Taiwan Strait. China's continuing development of advanced anti-ship missiles, in particular cruise missiles, provides additional evidence that the PLAN is thinking in terms of denying the US Navy access to East Asian waters. As an example of its growing flexibility, the Navy has a 65-strong fleet of Type 022 fast attack craft, which would be able to inflict major damage on larger US vessels in hit-and-run attacks, and which are armed with the YJ-83 anti-ship cruise missile. In early 2011, China's reported development of an anti-ship ballistic missile, which could be used to deter operations by US aircraft-carrier battle groups and thus constrain US military options in the western Pacific, provided a further example of the PLA's emerging anti-access capabilities.

Not all of the navy's developments have been focused on anti-access or area denial strategies, however. Alongside the aircraft-carrier programme, new amphibious capabilities suggest a parallel interest in developing power-projection capabilities. Only a decade ago, the PLA's amphibious-assault capabilities were extremely limited, relying on a relatively small number of ageing, unreliable landing ships. In 2007, however, the first Type 071 (*Yuzhao*-class) amphibious assault ship, the *Kunlun Shan*, entered service as the navy's largest vessel at 18,500 tonnes. In November 2010, a second ship in the same class was launched. The PLAN Marine Corps has also grown in size and is benefiting from new equipment such as the ZBD 2000 amphibious armoured fighting vehicle.

Air-force modernisation
The PLA Air Force (PLAAF) is in the midst of modernising both its equipment and its doctrine, which increasingly stresses regional power projection in a joint-operational environment.The maiden flight in January 2011 of the Chengdu J-20, China's first stealth combat aircraft, highlighted the air force's rapid modernisation. While the J-20 is expected to enter service around 2018–20, the PLAAF is already bringing into service capable 'fourth-generation' combat aircraft such as the Chengdu J-10, derived from the Israeli *Lavi* project, and locally built variants of the Russian Su-27. Upgraded versions of the Su-27 and the J-10, such as the Shenyang J-11B and J-11BS, and the J-10B respectively, will provide an improved combat capability pending the arrival of the J-20 and presumably other next-generation combat aircraft designs. The PLAAF has also introduced the PL-12 active radar-guided air-to-air missile, a weapon with a greater engagement envelope than the Russian *Vympel* R-77, previously the air force's main air-to-air weapon. A new short-range air-to-air missile is also under development.

The PLAAF's strike capability relies mainly on older aircraft. China, however, has repeatedly upgraded the H-6 bomber, which was first produced under licence from the Soviet Union in the 1950s, the latest iteration being the H-6K. This appears to have new engines and to be armed with an air-launched derivative of the CJ-10 (DH-10) cruise missile. The somewhat younger JH-7 fighter-bomber, which first flew in 1988, has also been upgraded, with KD-88 air-to-surface missiles improving its tactical strike capability.

China's air force is also developing new special-missions aircraft, which will increase operational flexibility and effectiveness. Electronic-warfare variants of the JH-7 and the Y-8 transport aircraft are in the pipeline, while at least two types of airborne early warning and control aircraft are entering service. A range of unmanned systems is also under development, including medium-altitude long-endurance designs for the intelligence surveillance and reconnaissance role including the BZK-005, which may already be in limited service. Taken collectively – and correctly utilised – such capabilities would provide the PLAAF with the ability to mount a relatively sophisticated offensive air campaign at the regional level, although its ability to sustain extended-range operations remains hampered by its limited numbers of tanker aircraft. Nevertheless, the air systems under development will, if they all come to fruition, provide the PLAAF with significantly enhanced combat capabilities.

New doctrine – and old
The most important trend in the PLA over the past 30 years, and in particular since the early 1990s, has been a greater emphasis on technology over manpower. The result has been a slimmed-down and more mobile force with increased potential to project military power into China's immediate region, and to a limited extent further afield. These developments in the PLA's force structure and capabilities reflect a gradual but nevertheless fundamental doctrinal shift as the PLA has moved away from preparing for an all-out war of national survival based on territorial defence – a so-called People's War – towards the type of capabilities that would allow the PLA to wage a 'local war' (that is, a conflict in China's near-abroad, most likely in the East China Sea, Southeast Asia or within 200 miles of its land borders). Tellingly, the 2010 Defence White Paper did not mention People's War.

Nevertheless, the PLA has not totally abandoned Maoist doctrine and the concept of People's War. The 2010 White Paper noted that 'China implements the military strategy of active defence in the new era'. Active defence, much lauded by Mao Zedong, embodied the idea that for the PLA any defensive position was only temporary: it would quickly be used for offensive gain. The PLA's contemporary use of the term suggests an attempt to explain the fact that the PLA's capabilities are increasingly outwardly focused, but without unnerving competitors, emphasising as it does the defensive nature of the military.

The People's War doctrine still permeates other aspects of the PLA's mind-set and its procurement policies. The Type 022 fast attack craft provides an example of how the PLA would still rely on the 'mobile warfare' tactics espoused by the People's War doctrine: theoretically, it could be used in a form of coastal manoeuvre warfare, with the PLAN allowing an adversary to approach China's coastline before launching a rapid counter-attack with a local concentration of force.

Similarly, other aspects of the country's defence and security establishment, particularly the marshalling of the country's resources and population for military ends, reflect the continuing salience of People's War. For example, because of its insufficient transport capabilities, the PLA has increasingly integrated its logistical capabilities with those of the civilian transport sector, particularly the state-run rail network and airline companies. In its cyber-warfare efforts, the PLA is leveraging civilian capacity, with complicated clandestine links between military organisations and ideologically motivated civilian groups and 'patriotic associations'.

Problems and challenges

While developments in the PLA have been impressive, some media coverage analysing the PLA has been tinged with political bias, and has sometimes exaggerated the scale of China's military modernisation.

The PLA is still beset by a range of problems and challenges that hamper its ability to deploy rapidly, to project power beyond its borders and to fight effectively. It has inadequate air and sea transport capacity, and its army is still insufficiently mechanised. The navy and air force are only now receiving the investment necessary to adapt to the missions increasingly expected of them. More broadly, the PLA's capabilities suffer from the fact that China has not fought in a significant conflict since its war against Vietnam in 1979. While this gap has provided the PLA with a breathing space in which to concentrate on reform and capability development using its new equipment and doctrine, it also means that China's armed forces have gained no significant combat experience for more than 30 years, with the result that the PLA's current military thinking and equipment have not been tested operationally. Because the modernised PLA has not faced combat, it is unclear how it would perform when faced with a capable enemy.

A dearth of realistic exercises with other countries' armed forces exacerbates this lack of combat experience. China's combined training schedule has intensified significantly over the last decade. The PLA's first foreign army exercise was conducted in Kazakhstan in 2002, naval exercises with

India began in 2003 (followed by land exercises in 2007), and now there are also regular exercises with Russia and Pakistan. In 2007, the PLA held its first bilateral military exercise with Thailand: this focused on counter-terrorism, and in 2009 it commenced counter-terrorism drills with Singapore. During 2010, inaugural combined exercises were held with Australia (a live-fire joint naval exercise) and with Turkey (the first exercise with a NATO member state). However, such training is often small in scale and lacking in realism. For example, the army exercises held with India since 2007 have involved just a single company from each country. Even where comparative training assessment has been possible, as with the tri-service *Peace Mission* exercises held with Russia (and sometimes small contingents from other Shanghai Co-operation Organisation members), the results have been inconclusive. Overall, the PLA's exercises with foreign partners have been more valuable in defence diplomacy than in military training terms.

The lack of combat experience has also hampered the PLA by depriving it of seasoned non-commissioned officers. The NCO corps was only introduced in 1978. Given that NCOs constitute the vital link between commissioned officers and enlisted men, impart their knowledge and training to the enlisted personnel, and provide tactical leadership in combat, they form the backbone of any military organisation. China's NCOs have not benefited from the knowledge and experience that comes from being involved in combat, and so the robustness of PLA combat and support units is uncertain.

Despite the rhetorical emphasis on 'informationisation' as part of current military reform efforts, the PLA continues to suffer from C4ISR (command, control, computers, communications, intelligence, surveillance and reconnaissance) capabilities that are still insufficient to be able to launch rapid, joint-service operations with full situational awareness. This is being tackled to some extent by a busy launch schedule for dual-use satellites, seven of which were launched during 2010. These satellites included the first five operational *Beidou-2* vehicles (two earlier launches were of a test satellite and an operational satellite that failed to enter orbit), which will eventually form a 35-vehicle constellation of satellites to provide China's second-generation satellite navigation system. Designed to match the United States' Global Positioning System and Russia's GLONASS, China's Compass Navigation Satellite System has the long-term goal of providing continuous, real-time geospatial positioning and speed measurement. The military application of these satellites will allow the PLA to greatly enhance its situational awareness, improve the accuracy of its guidance systems and allow continued development of its network-centric warfare capabilities.

Continuing modernisation

After a concerted reform process lasting decades, the contemporary PLA is beginning to pose a credible military challenge to states in the Asia-Pacific region, and to complicate the United States' strategic calculations about military options in the event of major tensions or conflict in the region involving both major powers. However, continuing shortcomings in strategic transport and logistical support would probably prevent the PLA from sustaining high-tempo operations for any length of time or distance from China. Any conflict that involved supply lines stretching further than 200 miles or did not involve a contiguous land corridor would prove challenging for the PLA and would severely restrict its ability to deploy and sustain its forces. Any operation lasting more than six months and that required the sustainment of forces more substantial than a brigade in a hostile environment without continuous, land-based supply lines would likely prove impossible for the Chinese military. Command and control problems, either stemming from a lack of communications and intelligence or a dearth of joint-service experience, will also constitute a difficult challenge for the PLA to overcome.

Aware of its deficiencies, the PLA is in the throes of a three-stage modernisation programme, paralleling the three-stage economic reform process intended to lead to China becoming a developed country by 2050. According to the 2006 Defence White Paper, this process initially involved '[laying] a solid foundation by 2010, the second is to make major progress around 2020, and the third is to basically reach the strategic goal of building informationised armed forces and being capable of winning informationised wars by the mid-21st century'. According to Section XV of China's 12th five-year plan released in April 2011, the PLA's focus will be to continue its modernisation, improve the professionalism of officers and integrate its services. The army will further reduce its personnel (absorbing a disproportionate share of the overall projected cut of 500,000 from the PLA's overall strength), command and control will be a focus for investment, and the PLA's supply chain is likely to rely increasingly on civilian industry in the longer term.

The air force and navy (and to a lesser extent the Second Artillery's strategic forces) are likely to assume greater prestige, and with it funding, within the PLA, though the army may resist this. The overall goal will be to create a more balanced military, where the services are able to work together without single-service domination, and the small, more modular and more professional force is able to adapt to different situations quickly to ensure rapid, effective responses.

The PLA's equipment-procurement programme will blend the acquisition of traditional and non-traditional capabilities. On the one hand, it will acquire what might be called 'asymmetric weapons' in the form of ballistic and cruise missiles, and submarines. These would be effective against potential adversaries – notably the United States – that China currently views as militarily superior. On the other hand, it will continue to acquire 'symmetric' weapons such as larger surface combatants including aircraft carriers, more effective combat aircraft, amphibious armoured fighting vehicles and upgraded main battle tanks. These could form the basis for future offensive operations – against Taiwan, or in the South China Sea, for example.

Information technology will be an increasingly important part of the PLA's strategic thinking and development, both offensively and defensively: in May 2011 the PLA confirmed that a cyber-warfare unit had been created and a cyber drill held in Guangzhou Military Region. Improvements in C4ISR capabilities, particularly new airborne early warning and control aircraft, tactical UAVs, battle management and mobile acquisition radars and the *Beidou*-2 navigation systems, should improve the PLA's situational awareness and ability to outmanoeuvre opponents, although unit-level connectivity remains poor.

The PLA's aim is to be able to prevail in wars on China's periphery through technological strength and modern doctrine rather than primarily through military mass – to be able to, for instance, invade, occupy and control Taiwan through the use of targeted strikes, rapid, concentrated amphibious deployment and air–land–sea joint operations rather than through the attritional use of waves of amphibious assaults in small landing craft without sufficient air support or early use of missile strikes. Such a goal remains years away. Joint, networked operations involving the deployment of sustainable forces thousands of miles from home could yet be decades away. In the meantime, much could change in China that would affect the PLA's modernisation, from domestic economic, social and political upheaval, or conflict with one or more other states over territory or resources. Nonetheless, on balance, China seems to be on track to reach its goal of fielding a military capable of mounting operations enabled by modern technology in its near abroad within the next decade, and projecting this power further overseas in substantial, joint-service operations by the middle of this century.

Regional reactions
To prevent this military modernisation from causing unease in its neighbours, senior Chinese representatives have, unsurprisingly, consistently

portrayed China's international intent as peaceful. Typically, when speaking at the IISS Shangri-La Dialogue in Singapore in June 2011, Minister of National Defence General Liang Guanglie emphasised his country's 'purely defensive' defence policy, and detailed how the PLA was contributing to regional peace and stability through security cooperation with other states in the Asia-Pacific region and elsewhere. Liang enlarged upon China's engagement in international military cooperation, including 'friendly contacts' between PLA troops and those of 12 neighbouring countries along China's international borders, the exchange of nearly 400 visits and more than 40 joint exercises with foreign armed forces, defence consultations and dialogues with 22 countries, and military assistance provided without any political conditions. Furthermore, he said, cumulatively the PLA had deployed more than 20,000 troops in 20 United Nations peacekeeping operations, and had so far sent eight 'task forces' to the Gulf of Aden and Somali coast. The PLA had also deployed forces on disaster relief operations in Haiti, Indonesia, Japan and Pakistan, and during 2010 a PLAN hospital ship had visited various African states as well as Bangladesh.

However, Beijing's efforts to use defence diplomacy as a means of reassuring other states, particularly in the Asia-Pacific region, of its overriding interest in what its spokesmen refer to repeatedly as 'peace and stability' have done little – if anything - to stymie a growing perception in regional states that China's foreign and security policies resemble the proverbial iron fist in a velvet glove. There is an acute awareness throughout the region of China's rapidly increasing defence budget and the concurrent expansion of the PLA's capabilities, particularly at sea. China's maritime paramilitary forces, themselves increasingly well funded and well equipped, and apparently acting as auxiliaries to the PLAN, have taken the lead in aggressive operations to protect and advance the country's interests in the South China Sea and East China Sea. In September 2010, Japan detained a Chinese fishing boat captain accused of ramming two Japan Coast Guard vessels, provoking a diplomatic crisis. In March 2011, two Chinese surveillance ships ordered a Philippine survey craft to leave a disputed area, and threatened to ram it. In late May and early June 2011, Vietnam claimed that Chinese boats had cut cables from Vietnamese oil exploration vessels inside the country's Exclusive Economic Zone.

Although the PLAN itself was not directly involved in these incidents, China's naval power does loom increasingly large over the Asia-Pacific littoral. Major Chinese naval deployments close to Japan in April 2010 and again during June 2011 were, according to Japanese Defence Minister Toshimi

Kitazawa, part of a pattern evident since 2008 in waters off Okinawa that was causing Tokyo concern. Also in June 2011, against the backdrop of escalating tensions in the South China Sea between China on the one hand and Southeast Asian states (particularly Vietnam) on the other, an editorial in *The Global Times* – an English-language offshoot of the party-controlled *People's Daily* newspaper – warned that China needed to be ready to respond to Vietnam's 'provocation' with 'political, economic or even military coun-ter-strikes'. Specifically, the editorial cautioned that if 'Vietnam continues to provoke China ... China will first deal with it with maritime police forces, and if necessary, strike back with naval forces ... If Vietnam wants to start a war, China has the confidence to destroy invading Vietnam battleships [sic].' Notwithstanding their recognition of the economic benefits (as well as challenges) accompanying China's rise, strategic prudence has impelled many states throughout the Asia-Pacific region – including Australia, India and Japan as well as several Southeast Asian countries – to take measures aimed at balancing Beijing's evidently rapidly growing strategic will and capability. This has involved not only moves to bolster diplomatic and military cooperation with the United States, efforts to bolster defence and security collaboration among Asian states, and the engagement of China through multilateral regional structures such as the East Asia Summit and the ASEAN Defence Ministers' Meeting Plus Eight (which met for the first time in Hanoi in October 2010), but also efforts to boost national military capabilities. Indeed, it would be fair to say that China's military rise is an important contributory factor to the arms race which, some commentators argue, is increasingly apparent in the Asia-Pacific region.

Chapter 3
The Americas

United States: Broken Consensus

Michael Bloomberg, the mayor of New York, is not a thrilling speaker. As he stood in front of a microphone on Governor's Island in early August 2010, his voice struggled against the wind and the water traffic of New York Harbour. But the mayor's text was hard and clear. His short speech – answering a campaign to stop the development of a Muslim and ecumenical community centre on a site one block from the destroyed World Trade Center – contained a forceful element of New York chauvinism, and an assertion of municipal ownership over the 11 September tragedy and its meaning. 'We come here to state as strongly as ever – this is the freest city in the world', said Bloomberg. He continued for nine paragraphs to identify *New York* values of diversity and tolerance, referring only once or twice, and obliquely, to any wider American narrative. The New York narrative was hardly whitewashed: it was about a struggle for religious freedom that included seventeenth-century Dutch Governor Peter Stuyvesant's refusal to allow the building of a synagogue in lower Manhattan, and the later repression of Quaker and Catholic religious practice. The current battle over a Muslim community centre was, according to Bloomberg, as 'important a test of the separation of church and state as we may see in our lifetime'. Bloomberg's eyes teared as he remembered thousands of police and fire-fighters 'rushing into burning buildings' – and 'not one of them asked, "What God do you pray to?"'

Bloomberg was challenging a current of anti-Muslim hysteria that was both new and manifestly at odds with President George W. Bush's efforts,

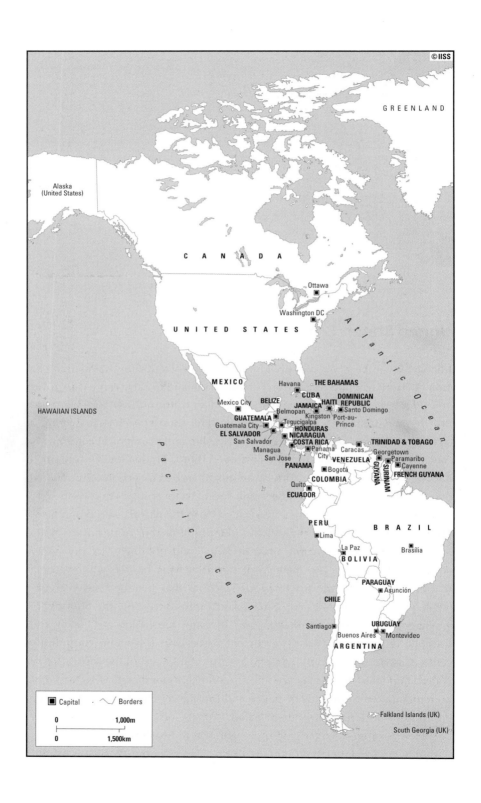

©IISS

GREENLAND

Alaska
(United States)

C A N A D A

Ottawa

U N I T E D   S T A T E S

Washington DC

HAWAIIAN ISLANDS

Atlantic Ocean

Havana
MEXICO
THE BAHAMAS
CUBA
Mexico City
BELIZE
DOMINICAN
JAMAICA
HAITI
REPUBLIC
Belmopan
Kingston
Santo Domingo
GUATEMALA
Port-au-
Guatemala City
Tegucigalpa
Prince
HONDURAS
EL SALVADOR
NICARAGUA
San Salvador
COSTA RICA
TRINIDAD & TOBAGO
Managua
Panama
Caracas
Georgetown
San Jose
City
Paramaribo
PANAMA
VENEZUELA
Cayenne
Bogotá
GUYANA
SURINAM
FRENCH GUYANA
COLOMBIA
Quito
ECUADOR

Pacific Ocean

PERU
B R A Z I L
Lima
La Paz
Brasília
BOLIVIA

PARAGUAY
CHILE
Asunción

URUGUAY
Santiago
Buenos Aires
Montevideo

A R G E N T I N A

Falkland Islands (UK)

South Georgia (UK)

■ Capital   Borders

0   1,000m

0   1,500km

nine years earlier, to discourage such a backlash. Bloomberg was also challenging the Republican Party, his former home, for moving so far and so fast to abandon the Bush rhetoric of tolerance. The media storm over the 'Ground Zero Mosque' – which was more than a mosque and not really at ground zero – had been set off by a series of Sarah Palin tweets to her followers, including 'Peaceful New Yorkers, pls refute the Ground Zero Mosque plan if you believe the catastrophic pain caused @ Twin Towers site is too raw, too real'. Former House Speaker Newt Gingrich piled on the pressure by comparing the idea of a Mosque near Ground Zero to Nazi signs at Washington DC's Holocaust Museum.

About a year later, in June 2011, Gingrich launched a bid for the Republican presidential nomination. By the time *Strategic Survey 2011: The Annual Review of World Affairs* went to press a month after that, his campaign appeared to have imploded. He could not be considered a marginal figure, however, and his rhetoric needed to be taken seriously as a manifestation of American political fever. Gingrich also joined, for example, the battle against imposition of sharia law in the United States. Though one might imagine that this spectre would rank fairly low on the list of clear and present dangers to the American republic, at least 18 states considered legislation in 2010 and 2011 to prevent judges from exercising their – so far, well concealed – plans to replace Anglo-Saxon jurisprudence with an Islamic substitute. Gingrich portrayed a titanic conflict: 'I am convinced that if we do not decisively win the struggle over the nature of America, by the time [my grandchildren are] my age they will be in a secular atheist country, potentially one dominated by radical Islamists and with no understanding of what it once meant to be an American'. Though the juxtaposition – atheist and Islamist – might seem puzzling, political blogger Matthew Yglesias observed that it made sense if one appreciated that the essential anxiety into which Gingrich was tapping consisted of white conservatives' fears about their fading ethno-cultural landscape. The 'birther' obsessions of numerous conservatives, whereby Obama had supposedly lied about his birthplace and thereby his citizenship, was also more explainable in the context of this anxiety.

This likewise is the most plausible explanation for the former House speaker's cynical embrace of a barely coded racist thesis from conservative writer Dinesh D'Souza, published by *Forbes Magazine*, and turned into a book titled *The Roots of Obama's Rage*. The essential argument was that the American president was endowed with radical, anti-American socialism by the anti-colonial rage of his Kenyan father. In truth, Obama met his father exactly one time: the president was raised by Kansans, not Kenyans. Yet, for

Gingrich, the D'Souza thesis embodied a 'stunning' and 'profound' insight. 'What if [Obama] is so outside our comprehension, that only if you understand Kenyan, anti-colonial behavior, can you begin to piece together [his actions]?' Gingrich asked. 'That is the most accurate, predictive model for his behavior.' Not long afterwards, Mike Huckabee, the former Arkansas governor who ran for president in 2008 and was leading in the Republican polls for 2012 until he decided not to run, speculated in a radio interview that Obama must have internalised a 'Mau Mau' worldview while growing up in Kenya. (Huckabee later said he misspoke and meant to say Indonesia, where Obama had indeed spent some years as a child, though how he was supposed to have adhered in Indonesia to the Mau Mau revolt in Kenya was left unexplained.) And for several years, starting well before Obama's election as president, the hugely influential right-wing radio talk-show host Rush Limbaugh incessantly warned his listeners that Obama's primary purpose in life and politics was to punish American whites for the racial sins of their forefathers. It took a former George W. Bush speechwriter, David Frum, to state the obvious: 'When last was there such a brazen outburst of race-baiting in the service of partisan politics at the national level? George Wallace took more care to sound race-neutral.'

The racial dimension to America's political polarisation was complicated, however. There is, on the one hand, no question that the twentieth-century struggle over racial segregation, and the nineteenth-century civil war over slavery, hardened sectional dividing lines that remain important in American politics. Certainly the evidence indicates that important conservative political leaders believe that stigmatising the president for his black otherness can pay political dividends. They are not likely to be completely misinformed about this: certainly a significant white minority harbours real racial resentment. And yet, for a president presiding over dire economic conditions, Obama remained remarkably popular. If the cathartic effects of his 2008 election victory had faded by 2011, the fact of his presidency nonetheless continued to demonstrate America's rather stunning social progress in the 50 years since Obama was born.

Paradoxically, however, America's acute problem of political polarisation stems systemically from its immense progress towards racial enlightenment – and not merely, or even primarily, due to the Limbaugh brand of white backlash. To understand the current systemic problem it is instructive to compare the American antagonisms of 2011 to the political and social turmoil of the 1960s. On one level, the 1960s tumult was far more dramatic. It was the decade of assassinations, southern lynchings of blacks and black riots in the north, Vietnam protests and campus unrest, and a Maoist-tinged domestic terrorism on the fringes of the American version of 1968. This decade was followed, of course, by the constitutional crisis of Watergate, into which all sorts of personal and political enmities between Richard Nixon and his enemies were poured. And yet, throughout these years it was still possible, at the level of politics, to maintain a working consensus on the purposes and operations of government. Part of the paradox, as Yglesias and others have pointed out, is that, even as the civil-rights movement advanced, the remaining structures of segregation helped that consensus function. The Democratic Party was a ramshackle coalition that included Southern segregationists and Northern and Midwestern liberals. The Republican Party included a healthy share of moderates and liberals, as well as the New Right conservatives such as Barry Goldwater. These were the variegated ideological conditions that allowed President Lyndon B. Johnson to fashion bipartisan majorities for such landmark legislation as the 1964 Civil Rights Act. But the majorities themselves were a victim of his success. Over the ensuing generation, Southern conservative Democrats moved steadily from the Democratic to Republican Party. As the Republican Party became more and more conservative, liberals and moderates found it less and less congenial.

Though Ronald Reagan has become an iconic figure on the American right, his initial package of 'supply-side' tax cuts was followed by some major tax *increases* to repair the fiscal damage. He also appointed a commission to propose reforms that would shore up the solvency of Social Security, the American state pensions system, and was able to work with the Democratic House Speaker, Thomas 'Tip' O'Neill, to get the reforms implemented. Ideological currents in both parties remained fluid enough for such cooperation to work.

It was in the 1990s under the leadership of Gingrich, however, that the modern Republican Party took shape as an extremely conservative movement dedicated above all to anti-tax zealotry. Reagan's successor, George H.W. Bush, was vilified as an apostate for violating his 'read my lips' pledge in the 1988 campaign against any new taxes. Right-wing anger at this broken promise contributed to his 1992 defeat by Bill Clinton, who returned the federal government to solvency with a combination of tax rises and budget cuts. The George W. Bush administration, moderate by the standards of today's Republicans, nonetheless reduced marginal tax rates again, ostensibly to deal with the problem of a government budget surplus. The legislation included a ten-year expiry date, at which point taxes were to revert back to

Clinton-era levels, so the cuts could be scored as more affordable. But the Republicans had always assumed and planned for their extension.

Tea and liberty

One month into Obama's presidency, CNBC Business News Editor Rick Santelli became agitated while broadcasting from the floor of the Chicago Mercantile Exchange. He was indignant about the administration's emergency plans to help refinance millions of unpayable home mortgages that were a major cause of the financial crisis. 'The government is promoting bad behaviour', Santelli yelled. 'How about this, Mr President and new administration? Why don't you put up a website to have people vote … to see if we really want to subsidise the losers' mortgages?' The Chicago traders cheered, and after comparing Obama's 'collective' plans to what Castro had accomplished in Cuba, Santelli declared, 'It's time for another tea party.'

The 'Santelli rant' became a viral sensation on the web, and within weeks the 'Tea Party' movement had become a driving engine of right-wing reaction to the Obama presidency. The movement mainly overlapped with the conservative base of the Republican Party, but whereas that base previously was preoccupied with the cultural causes of the Christian Right – especially opposition to abortion and gay marriage – Tea Partiers agitated on a more secular and libertarian front against the 'socialist' threat that Obama posed to American liberties. The Tea Partiers could appeal to a resonant historical fact: the United States had been founded, at least in part, as the consequence of a tax revolt (and the original Boston Tea Party was a rebellious ritual of throwing English tea into Boston Harbor rather than paying newly imposed duties to drink it). But that was 235 years ago. The present-day Tea Party was driven by a visceral reaction against real existing America as shaped by Franklin Roosevelt's New Deal. This reaction was not entirely new: the favoured Tea Party texts were the works of Ayn Rand, a crank novelist and philosopher who had attracted a cult following after she published her major novels, *The Fountainhead* (1943) and *Atlas Shrugged* (1957). Rand, an exile from revolutionary Russia, was in essence an inverted Marxist who argued that the true creators of value – capitalists, industrialists, artists and scientists – needed to liberate themselves from exploitation by the masses of socio-economic inferiors, Santelli's 'losers'. Rand was also a radical atheist, a fact that might cause some dissonance in Republican ranks if it were widely known. But her central argument that any kind of redistribution was not just economically inefficient, but morally abhorrent, had become the animating idea of Republican conservatism. It explained the authority of conservative political entrepreneur Grover Norquist, who, since the tax 'betrayal' of the first President Bush, had demanded a written pledge from every Republican candidate never to vote for a tax increase, or even a tax reform that increased net revenues. Astonishingly, all but a handful of House and Senate Republicans had signed the pledge.

To hold on to majorities in Congress that his party had won in 2006 and improved in 2008, President Obama would have needed substantially improved economic conditions. This did not happen. Though most economists believed that the stimulus package of his first year averted even greater disaster, it barely compensated for the spending cuts of state and local governments. On 2 November 2010, election day, the US unemployment rate was a staggering 9.8%. The Republicans won 60 seats and took control of the House of Representatives. In the Senate the Democrats lost six seats and narrowly held onto their majority.

The new power balance in Washington helped shift the debate from the current economic emergency to a potential future one. Washington was seized by the notion that the federal government's debt and deficit constituted the most urgent crisis facing the United States. This notion carried considerable ideological baggage, allowing Republicans to claim that the United States faced a fiscal emergency of such proportions that it should respond to a collapse of economic demand by cutting demand further, or must, in effect, abolish the welfare state.

Yet the United States was not insolvent in any common-sense meaning of the term. Though there were repeated warnings that bond markets might lose confidence in US Treasuries, the federal government's actual borrowing costs remained very low. Moreover, its medium-term budget deficit would be mostly erased if Washington returned to Clinton-era tax rates – as current law in fact mandated to happen at the end of Obama's first term. Letting all Bush tax cuts expire at the end of 2012 would cut $3.9 trillion off the national debt by 2020, reducing that debt to about 2.5% of GDP, meaning, under reasonable economic conditions, the debt would no longer be growing faster than the economy. Thus, the fundamental problem was political and ideological: the fact that one of the two major political parties in the United States had adopted the position that in an already historically low-taxed country, it was nonetheless a matter of unyielding dogma that taxes must always go down and never up. Operating according to such dogma could indeed bankrupt the country. But such a disaster would be caused by a somewhat surreal political refusal to pay for the basic needs of an advanced democratic society, rather than by America living beyond its means.

The United States did also face a significant long-term budget and debt problem beyond 2020. If one could erase the effects of the tax cuts, and discount the costs of two wars, there would remain genuinely difficult problem of health-care costs for the elderly, which drives most of the long-term deficit. In theory, these costs should be containable – after all, Canada and the rich European countries spend considerably less on health care with better results. In practice, given the hybrid nature of an American system that combines private insurance with a huge socialised protection for the elderly, there remained strong ideological resistance to imposing the kind of centralised cost controls that have succeeded, at least in relative terms, in Europe and Canada.

A new Republican radicalism was revealed by the party's rejection of what had been mainstream conservative positions as recently as the 2008 campaign against Obama. Senator John McCain had run for president touting a market-based 'cap and trade' scheme to curtail carbon emissions. Two years later, it was obligatory dogma for Republican presidential candidates to deny that global warming was taking place, or that humankind had anything to do with it, or – in the most moderate version – that it could be remotely worth the cost in economic liberty to do anything about it. Likewise, the Obama health-care reforms that Republicans excoriated as a dangerous encroachment on freedom were very similar – indeed, partly modelled on – the plan that Republican presidential front-runner Mitt Romney had proudly implemented in Massachusetts when he was governor there.

The sharp shift to the right did start to look potentially costly for Republicans. Wisconsin Governor Scott Walker provoked weeks of protest when he pushed through legislation to eliminate collective-bargaining rights for most state employees: the fierce reaction turned Madison, Wisconsin into the ground zero of American politics in February 2011. Soon afterwards, Congressman Paul Ryan introduced his plan to close the government's long-term spending gap by converting Medicare – the government's health-care coverage for the elderly – into voucher payments of decreasing real value to be used for private insurance. There were numerous aspects of Ryan's accounting that did not seem plausible, but it was the Medicare changes that proved most unpopular.

A plurality of Americans label themselves conservative, but on the details of government taxation and spending, polls show them siding with the Democrats. In the long run, this fact suggests that the Republican Party will need to tack back to the ideological centre. In the medium term, however, a breakdown of cross-party consensus on the operations and purposes of government raised questions of American governability. America's broken consensus on the science of climate change (which made the United States unique among capitalist democracies) left it unable to lead a global community in measures to curb global emissions; if this does not change over the next 20 years, the world could face global temperature rises and climate changes that would be potentially catastrophic and almost certainly irreversible for a span of centuries. A broken consensus on Keynesian remedies to the collapse of economic demand meant that the United States had run out of options for addressing the unemployment emergency: with private household debt – and especially mortgage debt – a continuing drag on the economy, the likely consequences would include millions of blighted lives. Meanwhile, a broken consensus on fiscal arithmetic presented the spectre of a new financial crisis.

This possibility was raised by an arcane feature of federal budgeting, whereby the Congress that appropriates spending has to hold a separate vote to authorise the debt to cover it. In the past that second vote was routine – since the debt is obviously created by the spending in excess of revenue, not the debt 'authority' – even if some legislators used it to grandstand against the causes of the debt, as indeed Obama had done when voting as a senator against raising the debt ceiling. But it was innovative for a newly elected House majority to attempt to use the debt-ceiling authority as pressure to impose its policy choices. This was precisely what the Republicans set out to do. Controlling just one house of Congress, with Democrats in charge of the Senate and the White House, they nevertheless claimed a mandate to impose their vision of how to close the budget gap. Their vision was in fact not all that specific, except in one respect: it had to include zero new revenues.

The predicted consequences of the US government defaulting on its debt, for even a day, ranged from dire to catastrophic. That debt would almost certainly be downgraded by credit-rating agencies, resulting in increased borrowing costs – already a massive share of the budget – and a return to technical recession was very possible if not extremely likely. There were fears that the global financial system would seize up as it had in 2008, and this new financial crisis was threatened at a time when several European countries were teetering on the brink of bankruptcy. Another systemic crisis was possible.

Under these circumstances of high-stakes blackmail, Obama's increasingly numerous liberal critics were astonished that he would enter into policy negotiations at all. It seemed to them a far wiser course for the president to insist that the debt ceiling was a purely technical issue, albeit an immensely grave one, which he refused to link to policy questions at all. This was the practice of the past, and it would, they argued, put the entire onus of risking US government creditworthiness on the Republicans, who would presumably want to avoid responsibility for the consequences. But it eventually became clear that Obama saw this as an opportunity to strike a 'grand bargain' to remove the long-term debt overhang. He was willing to concede a great deal of liberal spending for a pact that would make liberal governance more practical in the future. To this end he held secret talks with the Republican House speaker, John Boehner, who was also attracted to the idea, and they discussed the rough outlines of an ambitious debt reduction: roughly $4 trillion over ten years. The package was heavily skewed towards Republican preferences, about $4 in spending cuts for every $1 in increased revenue.

The negotiations collapsed after it was clear that Boehner would not be able to bring his Tea Party class of Republicans to vote for the deal. When it came to revenue increases, they told him, zero meant zero. Some Republicans also expressed doubt about predictions of default and financial crisis. By the middle of July, Boehner and his Senate counterpart, Minority Leader Mitch McConnell, were showing signs of panic: it did not appear that they could control their members. The default deadline was 2 August.

Declining power?

For the world at large, an obvious question was whether Washington's political, financial and economic dysfunction would confirm and hasten what many expected to be a steady decline in American power. In relative terms, certainly, the US share of military and economic clout seemed bound to shrink: the increasing share of global GDP claimed by China, India, Brazil and other rising powers would, almost by definition, make it impossible for America indefinitely to sustain its global strategic hegemony. Such predictions had been heard before, of course. For more than a generation there had been expectations of strategic and economic power shifts from the Euro-Atlantic arena towards the Asia-Pacific in general and China in particular. Some of this wisdom is inadequately examined – glossing over the reality that China, if and when it surpasses the United States in GDP, will remain, per capita, a poor country with huge political challenges and the demographic problem of an ageing population of equal magnitude to Europe's and considerably worse than the United States'. Still, the Great Recession and ongoing economic and financial crises in the United States and Europe have thrown the question of respective geopolitical weights into sharper perspective. China and other Asia-Pacific nations weathered the economic crisis rather well. The United States and Europe, by contrast, remained mired in it.

Moreover, the basic mechanism of US and Chinese growth for almost a generation – Chinese saving and American spending – may no longer be viable. If so, it is not clear what replaces this mechanism. What Charles de Gaulle called the 'exorbitant privilege' of the US dollar derived in large measure from the extraordinary burden that America assumed after 1945 in financing the world's – especially Europe's – post-war economic recovery, and in extending its military protection against Soviet threats. Yet the financial underpinnings of this project, which were established at Bretton Woods but survived Bretton Woods' demise, carried at least two significant long-term problems for the international system. First, the seigniorage accorded to the United States through the dollar's reserve-currency role allowed Washington to ignore fundamental strategic choices and limits. The power to print the world's currency conveyed the ability to finance a global strategic role without commensurately taxing American citizens. Arguably, the ongoing economic crisis stems from this American habit of ignoring limits: the Sino-American financial and trading relationship created a large share of the massive imbalances that helped cause the financial meltdown of 2008.

It is difficult for a superpower to retrench, however; interests and worldwide commitments cannot simply be liquidated, or ignored. In this context, the killing of Osama bin Laden on 2 May 2011, a triumph for US intelligence and special forces, as well as an undoubted political win for the American president, also fit well with an emerging Obama doctrine of muscular but more narrowly focused pursuit of American interests. While not quite constituting the elusive 'victory' in the war on terrorism, the successful operation was nonetheless an event of huge importance. It raised the hopeful possibility that Americans could now put a weakened al-Qaeda into some kind of reasonable perspective: still a serious security problem, to be sure, but not an existential challenge.

This was important for a doctrine of managed retrenchment, because an exaggerated view of the al-Qaeda threat had cost the United States dearly. Bin Laden had consciously pursued a strategy against America that he claimed to have practised against the Soviet Union. 'We, alongside the mujaheddin, bled Russia for 10 years, until it went bankrupt', bin Laden later asserted. He promised to repeat the anti-Soviet success by 'bleeding America to the point of bankruptcy'. The promise was predicated on a highly exaggerated view of American weaknesses, and it is fitting that he met his end through – and, perhaps, had a moment to comprehend –

the courage and tenacity of America's security forces. One must concede, however, that he was shrewd about the national psychology that would compel the United States to expend vast treasure and blood in reaction to the attacks of 11 September 2001. A rough reckoning of the financial costs of the Iraq War and the Afghanistan War, together with massive upgrades to general counter-terrorism and homeland security, comes to more than $5tr over the past decade. There arguably were also huge indirect costs stemming, as Ezra Klein has written, from the Federal Reserve's decision to cut interest rates to counter both a possible 'fear-induced recession' as well as high oil prices after the Iraq invasion. 'That decade of loose monetary policy may well have contributed to the credit bubble that crashed the economy in 2007 and 2008.' The American reaction to 9/11 also destroyed or blighted hundreds of thousands of lives – through war in Iraq and Afghanistan – and degraded America's moral reputation at Abu Ghraib and Guantanamo. In broader strategic terms, the United States was weakened by being drawn into land wars in the Middle East and South-Central Asia.

So bin Laden's death arguably also gave Obama a new opportunity to pursue his small-c conservatism, aimed at restoring a balance between international commitments on the one hand, and American capabilities and resources on the other. The president and his advisers took pains to emphasise the relationship between current and future resources and various kinds of deficits: a fiscal deficit and strategic over-commitment embodied in two ongoing wars; a moral deficit embodied in the Bush administration's official sanction of torture, Abu Ghraib, Guantanamo, the invasion of Iraq and close ally Israel's occupation of the West Bank; and an attention deficit caused by the United States' over-commitment in the Middle East to the detriment of other interests and concerns, especially the key strategic theatre of the Asia-Pacific.

The US defence budget, almost as large as all other countries' combined spending, had long existed in a kind of magical kingdom where the normal rules of political bargaining over finite resources did not apply. But it seemed now to be coming under real pressure. There was certainly precedent for squeezing US defence spending in real terms to the point of significant impact on the federal fiscal balance. The post-Cold War peace dividend reduced the military share of American GDP from 5.62% in fiscal year 1989 to 2.98% in FY 1999. Over the same period the fiscal deficit fell from 2.8% of GDP to zero, and the budget then went into a 1.4% surplus. Modest tax increases and strong economic growth played the largest role in this improvement, but the impact of restrained defence outlays was far from negligible. It would be difficult to argue, moreover, that the Clinton-era budgets weakened the United States militarily, for they funded the armed forces that helped topple the Taliban and then invaded Iraq. And while the military budget constitutes only 20% of the federal budget, it is a huge share of discretionary spending.

Under these circumstances, by summer 2011 the war in Afghanistan became an unavoidable subject of budget scrutiny. In FY 2011 budgeted outlays for Afghanistan were $106 billion, and this certainly understated the true cost that included such expensive commitments as long-term care for the severely wounded. 'Money is the new 800-pound gorilla', a senior Obama administration official told the *Washington Post's* Rajiv Chandrasekaran in June 2011. 'It shifts the debate from "Is the strategy working?" to "Can we afford this?" And when you view it that way, the scope of the mission that we have now is far, far less defensible.'

America was war-weary in any event. Even as US forces drew down from Iraq, the Obama-approved 'surge' of US forces into Afghanistan had pushed troop levels over the same symbolic threshold of 100,000 that President Lyndon B. Johnson crossed in the year after his November 1964 election victory. American combat fatalities in Afghanistan rose from 155 in 2008 to 317 in 2009 to 499 in 2010, the year of the surge. This was lower, but not an order of magnitude lower, than the 1,863 Americans who lost their lives in Vietnam in the year of escalation, 1965. In the Obama White House there was a vocal faction, led by Vice President Joe Biden, and including many of Obama's top political advisers, that considered the Afghan mission to be unavoidably under the shadow of Vietnam, strategically incoherent and not discernibly connected to any overriding American interest or purpose. The United States had been drawn into Afghanistan by al-Qaeda's attack on the United States, but al-Qaeda in the meantime had been driven mainly out of Afghanistan and into Pakistan, where its leadership enjoyed de facto sanctuary. Nothing that the United States could do in Afghanistan would change the reality that the military and especially intelligence leadership of a precarious Pakistan was playing a double game: fighting with considerable sacrifice against Islamist militants in tribal areas, yet at the same time hedging with continued support for the very Taliban that it had helped create in the first place. How to change Pakistan's behaviour was an excruciating problem, but banging America's head against the door in Afghanistan had little to do with solving it. The nightmare scenarios for American interests included a takeover of the state and its nuclear weapons by the Islamist militants that Pakistan had nurtured in Frankenstein style as weapons against India, or an

Indo-Pakistan nuclear war. Indeed, the former was one catastrophic avenue to the latter. Pakistan's schizoid behaviour was said to stem from its fear of being left alone with a huge and conventionally superior India. But Obama himself had observed the contradiction in arguing that America had to stay in Afghanistan to reassure Pakistan against another strategic abandonment, since the ostensible American *purpose* in Afghanistan was to strengthen the government of President Hamid Karzai, which Pakistan considered an Indian puppet, and was determined to undermine. Strengthening the Karzai government was a losing proposition in any event, according to the Biden faction. Kabul's intractable corruption and mal-governance was a primary and renewable source of Taliban strength.

By summer 2011, opinion polling showed sagging public support for the Afghanistan War. Congressional Democrats were becoming restless; in June 2011 the House of Representatives came close to passing a resolution calling for a fixed timetable for withdrawal. The vote was 204 to 215, compared to 162–260 on a similar resolution the year before. Even some Republicans started to express doubt, including Romney, who argued in a New Hampshire debate that 'it's time for us to bring our troops home as soon as we possibly can, consistent with the word that comes to our generals that we can hand the country over to the [Afghan] military in a way that they're able to defend themselves'. Romney added: 'We've learned that our troops shouldn't go off and try and fight a war of independence for another nation. Only the Afghanis can win Afghanistan's independence from the Taliban.'

To the extent that Obama's thinking about Afghanistan included political calculations, those calculations were inevitably complicated. Compared to the dismal economy, Afghanistan's impact on the president's re-election chances was likely to be marginal. It would be an excellent thing for him, no doubt, to be able to show voters that troop levels were going steadily down. Yet a resurgent Taliban, and the suggestion of an American defeat, would be irresistible banners for his Republican opponent to wave against him, and might be effective.

On 21 June 2011, Obama announced that 33,000 troops would be withdrawn from Afghanistan by September 2012, with 10,000 leaving before the end of 2011. This was at the accelerated end of the options he had been presented, and both Secretary of Defense Robert Gates, about to retire, and Afghan commander David Petraeus, about to take over as director of the CIA, had argued for a slower drawdown. But notwithstanding his 2009 decision to escalate, Obama had clearly decided that US interests, though significant, were limited. The decision seemed consonant with a rough public and elite consensus. Republican critics did accuse him of telegraphing a lack of will to the Taliban, inviting the insurgents, in effect, to wait America out. The accusation was fair, but the alternative was not so clear. And it could not be assumed that a Republican president inaugurated in 2013 or 2017 would set a fundamentally different course.

For any strategy of managed retrenchment, the administration also somehow had to reconcile its commitment not to accept a nuclear-capable Iran with its determination to avoid a third war in the greater Middle East. Here, as Obama approached the end of his third year in office, the glass was perhaps a quarter full. Earlier US offers of engagement with Iran's regime clearly had not succeeded, and despite episodic meetings in Geneva, the administration was disinclined to expect any breakthroughs. Obama aides argued, however, that their earlier overtures had been manifestly sincere, and that the United States had reaped some diplomatic benefits in terms of UN support for tougher resolutions. Over the course of 2010, meanwhile, it had become evident that the Stuxnet computer virus – perhaps created by US or Israeli saboteurs, or both – as well as other successful intelligence operations, and effective controls on technology to Iran, had imposed substantial delays on the Iranian programme. It now seemed likely that Washington's crisis point of decision – when US officials would have to choose between taking military action, sanctioning Israeli air strikes, or accepting the fact of a nuclear-capable Iran – could be put off until sometime in the next term or next administration.

This assumed that Israel could be persuaded to accept the same time-line. But while military ties between the United States and Israel were more robust than ever, political relations between the Obama administration and Benjamin Netanyahu's rightist coalition had become increasingly fraught. At the beginning of his presidency, Obama had launched a kind of moral demarche to the world's Arabs and Muslims. Heralded in his June 2009 Cairo speech, this demarche had included the overtures to Iran, the repudiation of torture, closing of Guantanamo, and Obama's demands to Israel for a settlements freeze and progress on the peace process. Yet, although torture was duly repudiated, America was denied much of the credit for that repudiation because Congress refused to grant the symbolic victory of closing Guantanamo. And hopes raised by the Cairo speech were destroyed almost immediately by the intransigence of Israel's coalition government, which refused to stop building settlements in occupied territory and thereby delivered to the president the most dramatic foreign-policy defeat of his first term in office.

Israel's defiance continued into summer 2011. By this time Netanyahu's trips to Washington were becoming regular rituals of barely disguised animosity between the prime minister and the president. A repeat performance, scheduled around Netanyahu's May 2011 visit to address the annual convention of AIPAC, the most powerful pro-Israel lobbying group in the United States, became even more fraught after Boehner invited Netanyahu also to address a joint session of Congress. Concerned that the Israeli leader would use the occasion to leverage pro-Israeli sentiment against the administration, Obama aides scheduled the president to go first with another major speech on the Middle East. Though framed mainly as an American response to the Arab Awakening, Obama also used the occasion to set out a more explicit American commitment to a two-state solution based on pre-1967 borders with land-swaps to accommodate the largest Jewish settlements. Netanyahu responded with another sharp rejection of the president's vision and policies. The 1967 borders were a complete non-starter, he said before and after his meeting in the White House, in his address to AIPAC, and his speech before Congress – which responded with 29 standing ovations.

White House aides were furious, and mystified. Though Obama had been somewhat clearer than past presidents, the 1967 parameters were the underlying policy of every administration going back to Lyndon B. Johnson immediately after the June 1967 war. The concept had been embraced by Netanyahu's defence minister, Ehud Barak, when he was Labour prime minister negotiating with Yasser Arafat, and by Netanyahu's immediate predecessor, Ehud Olmert. The current prime minister's shrill rejection of the same parameters could only suggest real doubt about the sincerity of his recent, and palpably grudging, embrace of the two-state concept.

The White House also worried that Israel was oblivious to the strategic implications of the Arab Awakening. Though the administration was committed to trying to head off a UN resolution recognising a Palestinian state, which the Palestinians planned to introduce in September, Obama also argued that the empowerment of Arab peoples could only make the Israeli occupation even less tenable. Clearly, the Israel–Palestine problem was not the driving cause that had inspired Arab populations to rise up against their rulers. Just as clearly, the arrival of real politics to Arab lands would place new pressures and obligations on Israel and its American ally.

The Arab Awakening had already underlined the sharp limits to Washington's ability to anticipate, much less control, events of seismic importance. This was an old story of an American intelligence community that could plainly see that autocratic regimes wouldn't last forever, but was helpless to predict when the fall might come. In early 2011, the Arab world was convulsed following the self-immolation of a Tunisian fruit and vegetable vendor.

Washington rightly considered Egypt, containing half of the world's Arabs, to be the strategic pivot. Egypt had also been an America ally for more than three decades, over which it had maintained a critical peace treaty with Israel. And for most of those years, Egypt had been touted as Exhibit A by those who argued that the American interest in regional stability entailed excessive moral collusion with despotic regimes.

The decision to help push President Hosni Mubarak out of office thus entailed real dilemmas for US policy – some compared it to President Jimmy Carter's abandonment of the shah of Iran in 1979 – but standing indefinitely behind the Egyptian regime was not a viable option. Obama was predictably criticised for his characteristically hedged response. It was not in his conservative nature to lean very far forward in declaiming for a democratic revolution, and he justified this caution by insisting that real empowerment of the Egyptian people required less rather than more association with American aims. However, the administration warned publicly and in strong terms against violent repression of the demonstrations, while privately employing the two countries' close military-to-military contacts to involve the Egyptian army in ending Mubarak's rule.

In the early jockeying for the next US election, right-wing presidential aspirants, including Gingrich and Minnesota Congresswoman Michele Bachman, attacked the president for abandoning an ally and opening the door for an Islamist takeover of Egypt. More importantly, however, the Republican Party's foreign policy elites – roughly speaking, the neoconservatives – recognised the cognitive dissonance in supporting democracy while fixating on a Muslim Brotherhood threat. Without precisely saying that the president had done a good job, the neoconservatives broadly supported his Egyptian policy.

Another key American ally, Saudi Arabia, was far less happy about that policy. Uninterested in American lectures about inevitable democratic change, the Saudis added to US difficulties in the region by sending troops across the causeway to support the repression of demonstrations in the adjacent Gulf kingdom of Bahrain. Bahrain was home base to the American Fifth Fleet, a key element in the US plan to contain Iran, and moving the fleet elsewhere in the Gulf was not a real option since no other Gulf Cooperation Council (GCC) state would be keen to offend the Bahrainis, or Saudis, by accepting it. GCC ruling families claimed anyway that containing Iran was very much the point of repressing the Shia protesters in Bahrain who, according to Gulf Arab leaders, were mere tools of Iranian mischief. Washington adamantly rejected that diagnosis, and warned that legitimate Shia grievances could indeed be turned into Iranian assets if Bahrain's rulers did not handle them wisely. 'The only way forward', Obama said of Bahrain in his May speech on the Middle East, 'is for the government and opposition to engage in a dialogue, and you can't have a real dialogue when parts of the peaceful opposition are in jail.' The president pointed in the same speech to Yemen, another key ally where the United States was trying to uproot an al-Qaeda presence; 'President [Ali Abdullah] Saleh', Obama said, 'needs to follow through on his commitment to transfer power'. In practice, however, US policy was devolving to what one Pentagon official called a 'bifurcated' strategy that emphasised stability in the Gulf and democracy in North Africa.

There was also, of course, a North African war – the third war in the Middle East that the Obama administration so much wanted to avoid. Libyan leader Muammar Gadhafi, having in 2003 negotiated with the United States and Britain to abandon nuclear- and chemical-weapons programmes, had been supported in a quid pro quo in his bid for international rehabilitation. That rehabilitation ended abruptly in February 2011 when the Libyan dictatorship, having fired on its own protesters, bore down on Benghazi and threatened to hunt down its rebels from house to house, 'like rats'. Within days of that statement, mere weeks after the Libyan protests and repression started, the UN Security Council authorised member states to use 'all necessary measures' to keep Gadhafi's forces from the hunt.

The resolution – its passage enabled by arguably constructive abstentions from Russia and China – was surprisingly robust, with language conforming to American preferences. It was preceded, however, by a fierce debate within the administration, one that pitted Secretary of State Hillary Clinton, who favoured an intervention, against Gates, who was far more cautious. Gates worried about being drawn into a long-term conflict with unclear aims.

It could be argued, however, that the Obama administration did not have much choice; it was going to be very difficult to stand aside as Gadhafi's troops went from house to house in Benghazi. 'It was not in our national interest to let that happen', Obama said in his 28 March speech explaining his decision. This was not some post hoc rationalisation; the obligation for humanitarian intervention had been a clear argument of his 2009 Nobel Peace Prize acceptance speech.

Obligation does not guarantee capacity, however, and since a major theme of the Obama presidency has been to remedy America's strategic over-extension, it was important that he could claim that other countries would do most of the heavy lifting. France and Britain had pushed originally and most enthusiastically for the air campaign, and if there was a clear doctrine coming out of the Obama administration's response, it had less to do with the conditions for humanitarian intervention than with a new style of American leadership. 'American leadership is not simply a matter of going it alone and bearing all of the burden ourselves', Obama said in the same speech. 'Real leadership creates the conditions and coalitions for others to step up as well; to work with allies and partners so that they bear their share of the burden and pay their share of the costs'. In a *New Yorker* article, one administration official described this as a doctrine of 'leading from behind'. It was not a very politic quote, but reasonably accurate in describing administration hopes that US alliances and partnerships could be leveraged to promote peace and stability without bankrupting the United States in the process. In the specific case of Libya, however, the success of the doctrine hinged on whether the French, British and other Europeans were up to the challenge.

Exceptional circumstances

At the outset of the 2012 presidential campaign, if there was an overarching critique from Republican contenders, it was that Obama did not believe in an innate American exceptionalism. In domestic policy, he was trying to turn America against its nature into a version of Europe. Leaving aside whether wealthy European democracies should be considered socialist dystopias, there was a real problem in claiming that the huge market failures that the president tried to fix – financial meltdown after a housing bubble, and a health-insurance market that excluded tens of millions – should really be considered the sources of American greatness. Still, the Republicans were on to an arguable idea insofar as American exceptionalism probably did have to be defined as a contrast to those societies America most resembled. And maybe the rough-and-tumble excitement of American society would be flattened if made to conform to more staid European traditions. It is just difficult to imagine the circumstances under which that would happen.

In foreign policy, the charge relied mainly on taking egregiously out of context something Obama had said in response to a question about the concept of American exceptionalism he was posed at a press conference in Strasbourg early in his administration. It could reasonably be argued that Obama was naturally more cautious about asserting American superiority to foreign audiences. But then, George W. Bush had run for president promising to present a more humble face to the world, and no one thought to thereby accuse him of being ashamed of his country.

These foreign-policy accusations had become increasingly shrill just before the moment that Obama rendered them utterly ineffective. The decision to send Navy Seals to kill Osama bin Laden was a risky one: there was only indirect evidence that he was actually in that Abbottabad compound; and if the mission had failed, with American deaths and Pakistani victims, Obama would have been pilloried as relentlessly as Jimmy Carter after an analogous failure 31 years before. But the mission did not fail.

In summer 2011, the field of Republican contenders did not look formidable. Romney, the obvious establishment choice and leading in the polls, was an accomplished governor and manager who looked the part. But he was a Mormon in a party full of evangelical Christians who considered Mormonism a non-Christian cult, and he was hobbled by a reputation for being too eager to please whatever audience he was addressing, and by the fact that his landmark achievement as governor was passage of a health-care reform that closely resembled the demonised 'Obamacare'. Palin had not ruled herself out of the race, but her star was being eclipsed by Bachman, who was more disciplined and coherent as a candidate, albeit equally extreme in her views.

Such extremism did seem to threaten the Republican prospects for posing a plausible alternative to the centrist Obama. Though Obama's job-approval ratings were marginally negative, he remained personally popular. His cautious progressivism did seem to reflect the direction of the countries. Though its election-day turnout could not be guaranteed, the country's youth was trending clearly left and Democratic. In June 2011, for example, the Republican-controlled New York State Senate narrowly passed a law to recognise same-sex marriages, and opinion surveys now showed that a majority of Americans approved such marriages. They also supported allowing gays to serve in the military, and in December 2010 the president signed a bill repealing the obscurantist policy of 'don't ask, don't tell'. Obama had managed that process cautiously, and too slowly for gay-rights activists, but he did manage to win Pentagon support for a move that the military had previously opposed.

Yet, though the Republicans seemed out of step, they could not be counted out. It is worth recalling that in 1992 – the year Bill Clinton was elected to become a very popular president – he was initially derided with his fellow Democratic contenders as having hardly a chance against the popular and – in retrospect – clearly successful President George H.W. Bush. The elder

Bush lost, moreover, even though he did not have to contend with anything like the economic emergency that still confronted Obama. If the Republican nominee finds a good way to pose the question that Reagan deployed so effectively against Carter – are you better off than you were four years ago? – it is hard to see how Obama will answer.

Latin America's Shift Towards Centrism

In a year which saw great political turmoil, major conflicts and upheavals in much of the world, Latin America was notably quiet, as countries in the region tended towards greater predictability and pragmatism.

Latin America has been shedding its reputation for sharp ideological swings and erratic politics. The results of a number of recent elections indicated that the region was settling in the centre of the left–right political continuum. While ideology still dominated the political discourse in some countries, practical approaches to economic, social and security challenges have increasingly become the norm. This helps explain the region's newfound confidence on the world stage, where various Latin American countries have become more assertive on policy questions and have adopted an independent posture by forging new alliances. In 2010, Latin America showed economic growth of nearly 6% and foreign investment in the region reached $113 billion, a 40% increase from 2009.

These impressive political and economic improvements have been in part eclipsed, however, by the deterioration of security conditions in Mexico and Central America. Although this unfortunate development can be tied to many structural problems such as police corruption or the legacies of past conflict, it is most directly attributable to the proliferation of organised crime and drug cartels seeking to take advantage of the global market for drugs. The resulting violence and spreading criminality is Latin America's most urgent problem.

Long the traditional power in the hemisphere, the United States has seen its political influence wane and its economic pre-eminence challenged by Latin America's changing profile. During US President Barack Obama's visit to the region in March 2011, he recognised Latin America's rise as a worthy 'guide for people around the world who are beginning their own journeys toward democracy'. At stops in Brazil, Chile and El Salvador, Obama attributed the region's enormous progress in recent years to the combination of sound macroeconomic performance with concern for the social agenda and a commitment to pragmatic, democratic politics.

In Brazil, Obama recognised the country's impressive ascent as an influential global player, and in a speech in Santiago he held up Chile's successful transition from military rule over the past two decades as a lesson for Egypt and other Middle Eastern countries that were seeking to move to a new, democratic order. El Salvador was added to the president's itinerary, however, in part to underscore the deep concern within the United States and throughout the hemisphere about the violence and criminal activity that has spread from Mexico into Central America, threatening to destabilise already fragile democracies.

Drug trafficking and organised crime have become a major challenge to Latin America's political and economic progress. The extreme violence fuelled by the drug trade in Mexico and Central America contrasted starkly with the accomplishments of countries like Brazil, Chile, Colombia and Peru – the different priorities of these countries illustrated that the region has in some ways become increasingly complex. Indeed, while the Andean region remained the epicentre of global coca production, it was Mexico and Central America that were particularly devastated over the past year by the brutal, far-reaching drug war. The countries of South America were able to pursue greater autonomy and expansive social agendas at the same time that the drug issue came to dominate the domestic and international concerns of Mexico and its neighbours.

Nevertheless, it was clear in 2010 that Latin America's capabilities had grown and that significant changes were under way. In Brazil's October 2010 presidential election, the policy differences between the two leading candidates – Dilma Rousseff of the Worker's Party and José Serra of the Social Democratic Party – were mostly negligible, with Rousseff favouring a continuation of Brazil's active foreign policy and assigning a somewhat more important role to the state in the management of economic affairs. Both candidates promised strikingly broad continuity with the successful policies of fiscal discipline and expanded trade pursued by outgoing president Luiz Inácio 'Lula' da Silva, for whom Rousseff had served as chief of staff. Rouseff defeated Serra, 56% to 44%, in the 31 October runoff.

In Colombia and Chile, pragmatism also defined the political agenda. A notable trend toward centrism on key public policies among politicians of varying stripes was seen in their most recent presidential elections. In Colombia, the substantive differences among the candidates vying to replace popular incumbent Alvaro Uribe in the May 2010 presidential contest were

China and Latin America

The most striking evidence of Latin America's rise is that other rising powers such as China and India have looked to increase their economic footprint in the region. This is especially true of China, which has accelerated trade throughout the region (see table, below) and loaned many billions of dollars to countries such as Peru, Argentina, Venezuela, Ecuador and Brazil for the development of new infrastructure. Overall, China contributed 9% of total foreign investment in Latin America in 2010. Chinese corporations have taken key roles helping manage operations in strategically important sectors such as telecommunications and the oil industry, but upwards of 90% of China's Latin America investments are directed towards the extraction of natural resources. The Chinese government has become both an observer at the Organisation of American States (OAS) and a member of the Inter-American Development Bank. Despite having become an extremely important economic player, the Chinese government has so far chosen not to get overtly involved in the regions' political affairs.

China's Rank as a Trading Partner for Selected Latin American Countries, 2000 and 2008

Country	Exports		Imports	
	2000	2008	2000	2008
Argentina	6	2	4	3
Bolivia	12	10	8	6
Brazil	12	1	11	2
Chile	5	1	4	2
Colombia	35	4	15	2
Costa Rica	26	2	16	3
Ecuador	13	9	10	2
El Salvador	35	16	18	5
Guatemala	30	18	15	4
Honduras	35	11	18	7
Mexico	25	5	6	3
Nicaragua	19	14	18	4
Panama	22	4	17	4
Paraguay	11	9	4	1
Peru	4	2	13	2
Uruguay	5	8	6	3
Venezuela	37	3	18	3

Source: Economic Commission for Latin America and the Caribbean.
Notes: Data for Honduras and Nicaragua are for 2007 rather than 2008. The EU is considered a single trading partner.

modest. Even in Chile, where voters elected the conservative Sebastián Piñera in 2010 after 20 years of centre-left rule, the new president essentially continued to pursue the popular social programmes of his immediate Socialist predecessors.

A controversial election in Haiti and an ideologically tinged campaign in Peru were exceptions to the trend. Singer and political novice Michel 'Sweet Micky' Martelly was overwhelmingly elected Haiti's president in the country's 20 March 2011 run-off election, defeating former First Lady Mirlande Manigat with 67.6% of the vote. Martelly, one of Haiti's best-known musicians, gained fame as an often raucous performer, but mounted a serious, if at times idiosyncratic, campaign. He ran on a platform of increasing job and educational opportunities for a population faced with almost 50% unemployment, building housing for the approximately one million Haitians still homeless after the 12 January 2010 earthquake, and restoring Haiti's armed forces to diminish the military component of the United Nations peacekeeping mission.

Three centrist candidates split the vote in Peru's April 2011 election, sending Ollanta Humala (a nationalist, leftist ex-army colonel) and Keiko Fujimori (the right-leaning daughter of imprisoned Peruvian ex-president Alberto Fujimori) to the June 2011 run-off. The results of the first round were a reminder of Peru's weak political system, which had remained fragile even as growth made the country a rising economic power in the region. The economic boom – thanks largely to trade and exports – contributed to a drop in poverty and even inequality, but high growth went hand in hand with high levels of political disaffection. Humala narrowly defeated Fujimori in the June run-off.

Although Peru was the outlier in a year of electoral continuity, the country's problems illustrated the considerable democratic deficits that still faced the entire region: weak and corrupt political institutions; inadequate judicial systems; stubbornly high levels of inequality; rampant organised crime; and citizen insecurity. The issue of security was especially worrisome for Mexico, where a cycle of warfare between the government and the cartels, and among rival cartels, caused a record number of deaths in 2010. The widening of this violence to Central America was an alarming development, and there was little progress towards the development of any regional strategy to prevent its continued spread.

There were also signs in the past year of an undercurrent of discontent with 'politics as usual'. Young voters in particular, many from the region's expanding urban middle classes, sent strong messages to the political establishment that they wanted cleaner and more open government. These concerns over cronyism and corruption played a role in recent elections, as outsider candidates in Colombia (Antanas Mockus, Green Party), Chile (Marco Enríquez-Ominami, independent socialist), Brazil (Marina Silva,

Green Party) and Haiti (Martelly) made impressive showings in part by pointedly challenging the traditional politics of their countries.

Apart from Martelly, none of these challengers were ultimately elected. But their successes indicated something beyond voter dissatisfaction: they showed that the democratic systems in many countries had matured to allow for robust debate and often even compromise in the policy arena. Pragmatic politics, strong economics and an assertive global presence all pointed towards a strong decade for the Latin American region, which appeared to be poised to control its path more directly than ever before. The diminished power of the United States, replaced by new and rapidly changing political and economic alliances, also looked to test the region's ability to fashion adequate responses to its most pressing challenges.

Mexico: Next Phase in the Drug War

On 12 January 2011, the Mexican government released its official tally of the Mexicans killed in drug-related violence since President Felipe Calderón took office in 2006: a staggering 34,612 people through the end of 2010. The government estimated that the total, which included government security

forces, local police, suspected criminals, and innocent bystanders, encompassed over 30,000 'execution-style killings' and over 3,000 deaths as a result of shootouts.

Aggressively targeting the drug cartels was a signature initiative of the Calderón administration, yet 2010 was the bloodiest in the five-year conflict, with 15,273 drug-related murders. Half of all the killings took place in the states of Chihuahua, Sinaloa and Tamaulipas, while over 3,000 people were killed in northern Ciudad Juarez alone. The violence and cartel activity were concentrated in Mexico's northern and Pacific regions where territory and proximity to United States trafficking routes was of chief value. The singular importance of access to Mexico's northern neighbour was underscored by the relatively low murder rate in other regions of the country.

More than 50,000 federal police and military troops had been deployed to fight the cartels, but Mexico remained vulnerable to violence resulting from battles between rival cartels and the security forces, which frequently harmed bystanders and rendered some areas virtual war zones. With no end in sight, the Calderón administration's war against Mexico's powerful, monied and ruthless criminal organisations remained devastatingly violent and politically unpalatable. In the past year, some observers argued that Calderón's strategy of directly attacking the cartels had failed, given that the most powerful of them appeared to control large swathes of certain states and had successfully kidnapped or killed scores of government officials, human-rights activists and law-enforcement officials.

The state of Tamaulipas, where the Zetas and the Gulf Cartel battled with each other for control of a lucrative 370km stretch of the US–Mexico border that abuts the state of Texas, provided one example of the expanding battlegrounds across the country. Dozens of mass graves containing at least 183 bodies were discovered there in April 2011, a record number for a state where the number of drug-related killings jumped from 90 in 2009 to more than 1,200 in 2010. Organisations that track security issues in Mexico have classified large parts of Tamaulipas as being under the de facto control of the two rival cartels.

The carnage of the past year gave credence to a growing segment of the population who believed that the war with the cartels had taken too great of a toll on the Mexican people and might ultimately be unwinnable. In May 2011, tens of thousands of protesters marched in Mexico City demanding an end to Calderón's military strategy. A number of notable crimes in an eight-month period from summer 2010 to spring 2011 demonstrated the war's impact:

- In August 2010 in Tamaulipas, Mexican marines uncovered the corpses of 58 men and 14 women, most of them Central and South American migrants believed to have been kidnapped, extorted and eventually killed by the Zetas. A survivor, who escaped despite a gunshot wound to his neck, led the marines to the crime scene. A study by the National Human Rights Commission estimated at least 11,333 migrants had been kidnapped in Mexico between April 2010 and September 2010.
- Mimicking similar attacks on drug-treatment facilities in Ciudad Juárez, gunmen killed 13 men in October 2010 at a Tijuana rehab centre by executing them at close range with assault rifles. The treatment centres became more frequent targets over the past two years because of a reputation for sheltering those seeking to hide from gangs or the authorities. Less than a week after the Tijuana attack, 15 men were killed at a car wash in the Pacific coastal state of Nayarit. The men were almost all clients of the same drug-treatment centre.
- October 2010 also saw the killings of 13 teenagers gathered for a birthday party in a middle-class Ciudad Juarez neighbourhood. Authorities blamed the attack on Juarez cartel gunmen targeting members of the Sinaloa cartel, although there was no evidence that the adolescents were involved in criminal activity, leading many to the conclusion that the assassins had attacked the wrong house. Seven other people were killed the previous week in a different party attack, also in Ciudad Juárez.
- The decapitated bodies of 13 men and two teenagers were found on a beach walkway in the resort town of Acapulco. Over the course of one weekend in January 2011, Mexican police reported a total of 51 killings. The deaths were attributed to intra-gang turf wars for drug-shipment routes among the Sinaloa, La Familia and Los Zetas cartels.
- On 15 February 2011, US Immigration and Customs Enforcement agent Jaime Zapata was killed and his partner wounded after their armoured vehicle came under fire on a highway near the northern city of San Luis Potosí. Zapata was the first US immigration agent to be killed in Mexico. The US government has since issued a warning to US citizens in the states of Tamaulipas, Nuevo León and San Luis Potosí that they could become deliberate targets of drug gangs.

Mexican authorities tried new methods to gain the upper hand against the cartels. The Mexican government confirmed in March 2011 that it was allowing US drone flights over Mexican territory to monitor drug trafficking and gathering intelligence on the cartels. The flights allegedly occurred only along the US–Mexican border.

The United States and Mexico had been close allies; since 2008, the US Congress has appropriated $1.5bn to combat the drug war under the auspices of the Merida Initiative, and Calderón was honoured with a lavish state dinner on a trip to Washington in May 2010. Relations became rockier in the past year as tension grew over a number of bilateral issues, including the obstacles to Mexican truck access on US highways, anger over an Arizona law designed to crack down on illegal immigrant residents of the state, concern over the flow of weapons from US border states to cartels in Mexico, and US complaints about the efforts of the Mexican security forces.

Cables published by the WikiLeaks website dismissive of the security forces, signed by US Ambassador to Mexico Carlos Pascual, ignited fury in Mexico, leading to Pascual's abrupt resignation in March 2011. In the cables from the US embassy in Mexico City, Pascual and other US officials relayed concerns about Mexico's 'insular military establishment that resists modernization' and 'weak federal structure that frustrates cooperation between local, state and federal authorities'. One of the cables also complained that Calderón's 'security strategy lacks an effective intelligence apparatus to produce high quality information and targeted operations ... intelligence entities would rather do nothing than do something wrong'. Calderón criticised Pascual in the Mexican press, saying he was 'ignorant' of the situation and that American diplomats had 'done a lot of harm [to Mexico–US relations] with the stories they tell and that, in all honesty, they distort so as to impress their own bosses'.

The Mexican authorities pointed to successful operations against major cartel figures as evidence that the sustained fight was achieving its objectives. Among the most prominent such successes in the year to June 2011, Mexican authorities captured Edgar 'La Barbie' Valdez Villarreal and Sergio Villarreal Barragan (of the Beltran Leyva cartel) in September 2010 and killed Antonio Ezequiel Cardenas Guillen (from the Gulf Cartel) in November 2010, Nazario 'El Más Loco' Moreno (La Familia cartel) in December 2010 and Louis Humberto Peralta Hernandez (Juarez cartel) in February 2011.

Some analysts suggested that fragmentation within the cartels caused by the arrests and killings of their high-level leaders and deputies in fact increased violence, as more actors vied for control of the organisations and attempted to assert power via expansion to new routes and targeting of rivals. The inability to contain the spread of violence also reflected negatively on the Calderón administration, with polls showing that many perceived Calderón's strategy as ineffective: a November 2010 survey by Mexico's *Milenio* newspaper found that only 21.2% of Mexicans thought that the government was winning the war while 83.8% judged the country's security situation to be worse than the previous year. Nevertheless, over 70% of respondents approved of the decision to challenge the cartels and, according to the polling firm Buendia & Laredo, Calderón's personal approval rating held relatively steady, at 54% in May 2011.

Calderón stated publicly that the current anti-drug strategy would stay in place for the rest of his term, at which point the direction Mexico might take is uncertain. A new president was to be elected in July 2012. Enrique Peña Nieto, governor of the state of Mexico and member of the Partido Revolucionario Institucional (PRI), leads most initial polls. Many in Mexico believed that the PRI, which was in power for 71 years until 2000, tacitly allowed drug cartels to operate in certain areas, thereby maintaining a sort of truce since broken by Calderón. PRI leaders countered that they were simply better at fighting crime. The records of Calderón, his National Action Party (PAN) and the PRI in fighting the drug traffickers and their policy proposals for the next stage of Mexico's drug war, looked to be the key issue in the lead-up to the 2012 race.

Central America: Critical Security Challenges

Despite registering notable economic, political and social gains since the signing of the final Central American peace accord in 1996, the region has become the newest staging ground for the war on drugs, and host to the sort of accompanying violence, corruption and instability already plaguing Mexico. And while Mexico dominated headlines because of the country's pervasive and brutal criminality, Central American nations, particularly the 'Northern Triangle' of El Salvador, Guatemala and Honduras, found themselves caught up in this seemingly intractable fight.

On 19 December 2010, Guatemalan President Alvaro Colom declared a state of siege in Alta Verapaz, a province close to southern Mexico, prompting speculation that large parts of the area had been taken over by Mexican drug traffickers. A reporter for the Associated Press observed gangs roaming the streets 'with assault rifles and armored vehicles, attacking whomever they pleased and engaging in often indiscriminate shootouts'. The state of siege permitted the armed forces to detain suspects and conduct searches without warrants, prevent public gatherings and control the local news media. When the state of siege was lifted two months later, Guatemalan authorities claimed crime had dropped 50%, yet Colom wearily told the local press that Guatemala was 'facing a permanent invasion' of drug traffickers and illicit activity.

The extreme measures practised in Alta Verapaz exemplified both the extent of the problem facing Central America and the absence of an overarching strategy among the region's countries for preventing drug-fuelled violence and maintaining stability. Precarious political institutions, endemic poverty (exacerbated by a drop in remittance flows from the United States) and high levels of inequality rendered the challenge of fighting the effects of drug trafficking all the more daunting.

Guatemala's trajectory over the year to June 2011 especially alarmed observers, and strategies for restoring law and order were expected to be a key theme of the September 2011 presidential, congressional and mayoral elections. Organised crime saw a rapid surge throughout Guatemala, compounding a number of weaknesses and casting doubt on the country's stability. Judicial and police institutions were riddled with corruption, and clandestine criminal networks controlled parallel political structures that operated with nearly assured impunity. The perception of massive corruption was reinforced by the filing of criminal charges against a number of high government officials, including former President Alfonso Portillo (2000–2004), who was arrested in January 2010 on charges of embezzling $15m from Guatemala's Ministry of Defence. Following a series of delays, Portillo and two members of his cabinet went on trial in January 2011.

The International Commission against Impunity in Guatemala (CICIG), a special judicial body assembled in cooperation with the United Nations, played a key role in the lead-up to Portillo's arrest and was involved in many other high-profile prosecutions. In August 2010, the CICIG presented evidence leading to arrest warrants for 19 officials from the Óscar Berger administration (2004–2008) on accusations of murder, drug trafficking and extortion. Among those eventually arrested were the former director of the Guatemalan prison system and Berger's former interior minister. The commission also contributed to the arrest in March 2010 of a former national police chief, Baltazar Gómez, for involvement in drug trafficking and blocking an investigation of corrupt police officers.

Despite what many consider the successes of the CICIG since its mandate began in 2008, the commission was itself beset by controversy in 2010 following a series of convoluted accusations and resignations. Carlos Castresana resigned as head of the CICIG in June 2010 after accusing the Guatemalan government of ignoring the commission's recommendations. He alleged an active campaign to discredit the CICIG among Guatemalan groups with an entrenched interest in continued impunity. Castresana's resignation was most directly provoked by Colom's appointment of Conrado Reyes as attorney general, even after the CICIG had identified Reyes as having ties to drug trafficking and illegal adoption rings. The resignation created a political firestorm, and the country's Constitutional Court ultimately rejected Reyes's appointment on the grounds that the selection process may have been influenced by organised crime. Costa Rican Attorney General Francisco Dall'Anese, a renowned advocate against organised crime, was appointed by UN Secretary General Ban Ki-moon to succeed Castresana in July 2010. CICIG's mandate was scheduled to expire in September 2011.

Guatemala lacked the strong institutions and extensive resources needed to fight organised crime. It was profoundly affected by the brutal and bloody cartel battles waged in Mexico, which caused a southward shift of operations into northern Guatemala and beyond. Members of Los Zetas and the Sinaloa drug cartel came to routinely attack local law-enforcement officials and to control substantial swathes of territory in parts of Guatemala, according to a US State Department report. As a result, Guatemala's homicide rate in 2010 was four times that of Mexico's.

Citizen security diminished as cartels proliferated. In January 2011, a bomb attack on a bus in Guatemala City claimed seven lives. According to Guatemalan police, in 2010 alone, bus drivers paid out over $1.5 million in extortion money to gangs, while local rights groups report that 119 of the country's bus drivers and 51 other transport workers were murdered. Amnesty International chastised the Colom administration in March 2011 after it reported that 685 Guatemalan women were killed in 2010, saying that 'women in Guatemala are dying as a consequence of the state's failure to protect them'.

The country's political outlook was uncertain. Colom's party held barely a fifth of the seats in the legislature, reflecting the fractured nature of Guatemala's political system. Colom's wife, Sandra Torres, announced in March 2011 that she would try to succeed him as president by running as the candidate from his National Unity for Hope. Among the other likely candidates was Otto Pérez Molina of the right-wing Patriot Party, a former general who lost to Colom in the 2007 election.

The legality of Torres's candidacy was questioned, because Article 186 of the Guatemalan constitution bans close relatives of the president from running for office. In an attempt to bypass this provision, the Coloms announced in March 2011 that they would divorce, but in April a Guatemalan court suspended the proceedings after hearing a petition that called the move an unjust circumvention of the law. A decision from the Constitutional Court was potentially necessary to determine the status of Torres's bid for office prior to the September 2011 election.

Guatemala's neighbour Honduras presented a similarly troubled picture. With a population of 7.5m, Honduras averaged 15–16 murders a day in 2010. This was the fastest-growing murder rate in Central America, and one of the highest in the world, attributable to a toxic combination of criminal and political violence unrivalled in the region. The country had become one of the main gateways for cocaine en route to Mexico. The United Nations World Drug Report 2010 labelled Honduras one of the countries most affected by drug trafficking, while charging that 'intense drug-related violence has posed a serious challenge to governance'. With dense jungle territories and a long Caribbean coastline, Honduras was well positioned as a middle point for trade routes from South America to Mexico and the United States. The country's first full-scale cocaine laboratory was discovered near the capital Tegucigalpa in March 2011, heightening concerns that Mexican cartels had penetrated Honduras.

Human-rights organisations alleged an increase in violence and intimidation since the inauguration of President Porfirio Lobo in January 2010. Ten journalists were killed in 2010, leading the non-governmental organisation Reporters Without Borders to call Honduras one of the 'most violent … and most risky' countries in the hemisphere for the press. Some of the journalists had reported on organised crime, and none of the killings had been solved. Human Rights Watch also documented allegations of politically motivated targeting and intimidation, including a 15 September tear-gas attack on the opposition radio station Radio Uno in San Pedro Sula that coincided with marches commemorating Honduran Independence Day. In March 2011 the Inter-American Human Rights Commission of the Organisation of American States (OAS) held hearings on systematic human-rights abuses and the Lobo administration's response.

The unsettling security situation was exacerbated by a political crisis that undermined governance and, in turn, tended to benefit drug trafficking organisations and criminal gangs. Since the 28 June 2009 coup that dislodged the constitutionally elected government of Manuel Zelaya (and exiled him to the Dominican Republic), the country was polarised between Zelaya supporters and supporters of the Lobo administration. The Lobo government struggled to navigate and overcome the country's sharp divisions, including those between restive members of Honduras's left and right wings, since taking office in January 2010. Distrust and bitterness on both sides compounded the difficulties of addressing the country's daunting policy agenda, which included not just expanding criminality but also high levels of unemployment and deepening social and economic distress.

Even though the Honduran economy grew 2.5% in 2010, 44% of the population remained unemployed or underemployed at the start of 2011. Harsh tropical storms also led to soaring food prices, causing the National Congress to freeze the cost of beans, rice, dairy products, eggs and other staples of the Honduran diet in November 2010. The price of beans, for example, had tripled prior to the freeze and afterwards remained 75% higher than during the first half of 2010. Despite complaints from the farm industry, the Congress extended the measure until mid-February 2011.

Honduras remained a significant source of discord in inter-American relations. The OAS expelled Honduras as a result of the coup, only the second time (after Cuba in 1962) that such action had been taken. Despite substantial pressure from the United States and all but one – Nicaragua – of Honduras's Central American neighbours to recognise the Lobo government, key players in regional political affairs, including Venezuela, Brazil, Argentina, Bolivia and Ecuador, still deemed the government illegitimate. Their intransigent position on the Lobo administration's legitimacy led Honduras to begin closing its embassies in these countries in March 2011.

However, Venezuelan President Hugo Chávez and Colombian President Juan Manuel Santos met unannounced with Lobo during a visit to Colombia in April 2011, where the three heads of state discussed Honduras's return to the OAS. The country's continued ostracism from Latin America's major regional body made it difficult for Lobo to remove remaining questions of legitimacy from his government.

The mistrust surrounding the coup and its aftermath persisted as well. A May 2011 court decision voided the fraud and corruption charges against Zelaya, making it possible for the former president to return to the country without facing arrest. Later in the month, Lobo returned to Colombia and met with Zelaya, and the two signed an agreement officially allowing Zelaya to return to the country and his supporters to re-form a party to participate in elections. Zelaya's followers pushed him to re-enter electoral politics in time for the 2013 presidential elections, although Zelaya did not indicate that he would do so. As a result of the accord between Lobo and Zelaya, the OAS voted to restore Honduras's membership at its General Assembly meeting in June 2011.

In El Salvador, President Mauricio Funes, elected in 2009, had governed largely as a moderate pragmatist, modelling his administration after that of Brazil's Lula. Operating within significant constraints, including rising fiscal deficits and a sluggish growth rate in 2010, Funes accorded more emphasis to poverty-alleviation strategies than his predecessors. In September 2010 he announced an overhaul of the country's public-health infrastructure with the creation of the National Integrated Health System, an attempt to provide comprehensive health coverage and medicine to poor citizens and rural, underserved areas. With $110m in additional funds for the Ministry of Public Health's 2011 budget, the reform began in El Salvador's 74 poorest municipalities and was set to expand nationwide by 2014.

Funes also pursued education reform, directing $75m towards initiatives that provide free early childhood and primary education, as well as uniforms, shoes and school supplies to over 1m students. This pragmatic, centrist approach was part of a broader effort by the Funes administration to align the government's available resources with desperately needed social services. In 2011, funds for the Ministry of Public Works, the Ministry of Justice and Public Security, disaster response and temporary assistance to children and single mothers in poor regions were all significantly increased. These reforms greatly contributed to Funes's 72% public-approval rating, the highest for any Central American president in 2011.

Funes's foreign policy was notably pragmatic. His administration was supportive of Honduran President Lobo, strongly urging other Latin American governments to recognise the government and joining with Guatemalan President Colom to advocate the restoration of Honduras's membership of the OAS and Central American Integration System (SICA). Funes re-established ties with Cuba upon taking office and met with President Raúl Castro in Havana in October 2010, becoming the first Salvadoran head of state in 50 years to visit the island.

Funes also received President Obama during his March 2011 Latin America trip. In his first visit to Central America, Obama pledged $200m to improve citizen security in the region, touted the US commitment to economic cooperation with Central America, and praised Funes for his 'courageous work to overcome old divisions in Salvadoran society'.

Despite Funes's even-handed approach, El Salvador was unable to staunch the violence and drug-related corruption that has infiltrated the entire Central American region. El Salvador's upsurge in gang violence, which followed the 1992 peace agreement that ended the country's bloody civil war, fed the more recent drug-related violence. There were an estimated 30,000 gang members in a country of just over 6m, resulting in a toxic mix when combined with the proliferation of firearms, enduring socioeconomic woes, contacts with US-based gangs, and the legacy of armed conflict.

In September 2010 Funes signed a law criminalising gang member-ship with penalties of up to ten years in prison. The gangs responded by threatening transport workers with violence, in effect shutting down nation-wide public transportation for a 72-hour strike and bringing the capital San Salvador to a standstill. The law, however, was not used to great effect. No arrests were made in the months after its passage, most likely because of uncertainty over the legal processes that needed to be undertaken to prove gang membership (as opposed to 'association').

Most worrisome were reports that Los Zetas had begun to make inroads in the country. Salvadorian Defense Minister General David Munguía said in December 2010 that El Salvador's border with Guatemala could allow for infiltration by the group, and by February 2011 he admitted publicly that Los Zetas and the Gulf Cartel were operating within the country, forming relationships with local gangs and actively 'trying to recruit military and police personnel' to assist in trafficking. As a result, the attorney generals of El Salvador and Mexico entered into a formal information-sharing agree-ment in early 2011 in order to facilitate better monitoring and prosecution of the Mexican-based cartels.

Funes also faced a number of challenges from factions within his Farabundo Martí National Liberation Front (FMLN) party, which was upset over his centrist agenda, and from the opposition Arena party that ruled El Salvador for the previous two decades. Funes's legislative majority was a tenuous combination of FMLN members pushing for a more radical agenda, and Arena defectors who split with their party after Funes's victory. Although this unlikely alliance benefited Funes, upcoming congressional elections in 2012 were being targeted by the Arena as an opportunity to reas-sert political power in the country.

Nicaragua, with 14 murders per 100,000 citizens, was not close to approaching the levels of violence seen in Guatemala, Honduras and El Salvador. Part of the explanation was the country's more consistently professional police force, which had been maintained since the transition from Sandinista revolutionary rule to democratic, elected government in 1990. In contrast to its Northern Triangle neighbours, the greatest threat to Nicaragua's stability was the political manoeuvring of President Daniel Ortega to bypass the country's constitution and run for re-election.

Ortega, who led the Frente Sandinista de Liberación (FSLN) from 1979 and was president of Nicaragua from 1985 until his defeat at the polls in 1990, was elected president again in 2006. Despite a constitutional ban that barred consecutive re-election and two-term presidents from serving additional time in office, Ortega carefully positioned himself to run in the 6 November 2011 elections, in part by successfully manipulating the country's judicial system: Ortega issued a decree of questionable legality in January 2010 that extended the expired terms of various officials, including loyalist judges on the Supreme Court.

Given that Ortega would have needed some support from opposition lawmakers to appoint new (and presumably less partisan) judges, the move was interpreted as a blatant power grab. Ortega further inflamed tensions when he surreptitiously had Nicaragua's constitution reprinted to allow the reinsertion of an old clause from 1987 stating that Supreme Court judges and other public officials could remain in office beyond their term limits until new officials were appointed. This aspect of the law was absent from the most recent version of the constitution approved after political reforms in 1995, so many Nicaraguan legal analysts argued that it had expired when the 1995 constitution took effect.

In 2010, Nicaragua's Sandinista-dominated Supreme Court upheld a lower court's ruling that called the re-election ban 'inapplicable' in Ortega's case because it would violate the president's right to equal treatment under the law. Ortega had made much of the same case himself, arguing previously that the 'right to re-election should be for all ... the people should decide whom to award and whom to punish'.

A January 2011 Cid–Gallup poll showed Ortega as the frontrunner, with 36% of the vote, followed by former President Arnoldo Aleman (1997–2002) of the Partido Liberal Constitucionalista with 23% and 80-year-old radio personality Fabio Gadea of the newly created Unidad Nicaragüense por la Esperanza with 17%. Ortega officially announced his candidacy for president on 18 March 2011, completing a two-year process in which he successfully outmanoeuvred the opposition. Only 35% of the vote is needed to win outright and avoid a second round.

Legal motions against Ortega's candidacy were filed with the Supreme Electoral Council (CSE) by a number of opposition parties and civil-society organisations in March 2011, but Ortega's candidacy was upheld. The president of the CSE, Ortega associate Roberto Rivas, was one of the government officials reappointed by Ortega's decree despite the expiration of his term in 2010. Meanwhile, Supreme Court magistrate and Ortega ally Rafael Solís, another official who remained in his post by decree, implied that challenging the legality of Ortega's candidacy was disrespectful of the court's legitimacy and could lead to jail time.

Ortega's actions met with little response from elsewhere in the region. Within Nicaragua, Ortega's government retained a great deal of support and credibility due to successful social-welfare programmes and government subsidies. Ortega was able to maintain these policies due in great measure to the largesse of Venezuelan President Chávez, who had provided $1.6bn in total aid to Nicaragua since Ortega's election in 2007. According to a 2011 report from Nicaragua's Central Bank, Venezuelan aid reached $511m in 2010. The funds were managed by Ortega and his political allies without oversight.

Ortega, perhaps seeking to preserve relations in advance of potential electoral unrest, also accommodated international financial institutions and even parts of Nicaragua's private sector. And, occasionally harsh rhetoric notwithstanding, he was open to dealing with the United States, even fully honouring the 2005 Central American Free Trade Agreement. At the same time, Ortega was one of the few heads of state to publicly support embattled Libyan strongman Muammar Gadhafi. Ortega announced in February 2011 that he had called Gadhafi to express his solidarity, saying the Libyan leader was 'waging a great battle' to defend his country's sovereignty.

In a move few regard as unrelated to Ortega's quest to remain in power, the president sent some 50 Nicaraguan troops to a disputed zone on the country's border with Costa Rica in October 2010, to help dredge the San Juan River. That led Costa Rica to mobilise some of its police force (Costa Rica abolished its military in 1948), resulting in a tense stand-off as Nicaraguan troops occupied Isla Calero, the disputed parcel of land located between the two countries. Despite the adoption of several resolutions, the OAS was unable to get Ortega to withdraw the soldiers. The dispute over an area of approximately $3km^2$ aroused nationalist sentiment in both countries, and boosted Ortega's domestic political standing. Further intervention from the International Court of Justice in March 2011 allowed both sides to save face with a ruling that demanded Nicaragua and Costa Rica refrain from further aggravating the conflict, asking that neither country send military or official government delegations into the disputed area, with the exception of Costa Rican environmental workers and Nicaraguans working on the dredging project. Government officials from each country met to discuss the dispute face-to-face for the first time in April 2011. Although the dispute remained unresolved, tensions subsequently subsided.

Brazil: New President, Similar Agenda

Dilma Rousseff was inaugurated as Brazil's first female president on 1 January 2011, taking the reins of a country that had moved beyond its status as Latin America's leading regional power to become an important player in global affairs. The country's remarkable progress under Lula da Silva set high expectations for Rousseff, who was expected to continue Lula's policies while ensuring that the country maintained its economic prowess and international influence.

Lula left office after two terms with a personal approval rating of 87% and a government approval rating of 80%. Since his election in 2002, the Brazilian real had more than doubled in value against the US dollar, inflation had shrunk from 17% to close to 6.5%, and both poverty and inequality in the country of nearly 200m people had declined sharply. According to government statistics, 24m Brazilians overcame absolute poverty under Lula, while 31m entered the middle class. Brazil overtook Italy in 2010 to become the world's seventh largest economy, and was predicted to become the fifth largest within a decade.

Rousseff nevertheless inherited a country that was still fighting pervasive poverty, widespread political corruption, rampant crime and violence, high levels of social injustice, a troubled education system and deficient domestic infrastructure. Concerns about violence and infrastructure became especially prominent as the country prepared to host the FIFA World Cup in 2014 and the Summer Olympics in 2016. Although Brazil's economy was strong enough to weather the global financial crisis with relative ease, the budget deficit doubled as a result and it was unclear how Rousseff could finance initiatives to address many of these pending issues.

Rousseff began her term with the great confidence of the Brazilian people, although there were clear differences between the more reserved Rousseff and the gregarious, outgoing Lula. Rousseff, who served as Lula's chief of staff and energy minister, has been called 'the Iron Lady' for her demeanour and demanding style. A former leftist guerrilla imprisoned and tortured for three years under Brazil's military dictatorship, she had never run for elected office before the 2010 presidential campaign.

Rousseff's candidacy was marred slightly by a scandal involving Erenice Guerra, a close associate who succeeded her as Lula's chief of staff. Guerra was accused of taking kickbacks from Brazilian businesses in exchange for state contracts and bank loans. Guerra denied the charges but resigned her post, and the scandals did little to permanently harm Rousseff's image. Rousseff ultimately won the 3 October 2010 run-off, beating São Paulo state Governor José Serra 56%–44%. The ten-party alliance supporting Rousseff's bid, led by her Worker's Party (PT), secured majorities in both the Senate and Chamber of Deputies.

After taking office, Rousseff made few major changes to domestic policy. She reappointed Guido Mantega as finance minister, a decision viewed as important in Brazil because it indicated continuity with some of Lula's economic policies. Mantega faced a new set of challenges, including a 6.4% inflation rate in 2011 that 'immensely worried' Rousseff. Mantega was also expected to play a key role in debates over currency values and the extensive budget cuts promised during the campaign. He revealed that the administration planned to cut the budget by over BRL20bn ($12bn) in 2011, signalling that Rousseff would in fact depart from the levels of expansionary spending seen under Lula.

Foreign policy also saw subtle but noticeable shifts. For example, Lula had prominently argued for diplomacy and against sanctions for Iran's nuclear programme, and along with Turkish Prime Minister Recep Tayyip Erdogan he had devised a fuel-swap compromise intended to help Tehran avoid sanctions sought by the United States at the UN Security Council. Lula's advocacy for the fuel-swap agreement created distance between Washington and Brasilia, as did Brazil's vote against sanctions when the compromise ultimately was rejected. Many foreign-policy analysts expected the Rousseff administration to take a more critical stance on Iran, and in January 2011 Antonio Patriota, her foreign minister, announced that Brazil would refrain from new attempts to mediate between the Iranians and the West over Tehran's nuclear programme. This changed stance raised expectations that the Rousseff administration would take a harder line with Iran on issues such as free elections, human rights and the treatment of women. Rousseff told the *Washington Post* in the weeks before her inauguration that 'I do not agree with practices that have medieval characteristics [when it comes] to women. There is no nuance; I will not make any concessions on that matter.' Rousseff adviser Marco Aurélio confirmed the policy changes in an April 2011 interview, saying that the new president 'wants to emphasise human rights issues' in part due to her past as a political prisoner.

Brazil's posture towards Iran had been a major irritant in the relationship with the United States under Lula, and Rousseff indicated that she would make establishing closer ties a high priority. Obama visited Brazil on the first stop of his Latin America tour in March 2011, and the two presidents discussed a wide range of issues, including cooperation on bilateral trade and removing non-tariff barriers; US help on building infrastructure and developing security for the World Cup and Olympics; the formation of a 'Green Economy Partnership' to develop and finance biofuels; climate-change strategy; and the peaceful use of outer space.

Rousseff directed some criticism towards the United States during Obama's visit, saying that if America desired a 'deeper relationship' with Brazil, it 'has to be a construct amongst equals' and not composed of past 'empty rhetoric'. Alluding to the policy differences between the two countries, Rousseff said it would be necessary to 'deal with our contradictions' and stronger ties would be predicated upon Washington eschewing economic protectionism when it came to Brazilian products such as ethanol and cotton.

Although Obama did not endorse Brazil's quest for a permanent seat on the UN Security Council – a major goal of Brazil's foreign-policy agenda – he did recognise the country as a 'global leader' and acknowledged an 'appreciation for Brazil's aspiration' to gain the seat. Brazil, a temporary member of the Security Council, abstained from voting to authorise force against Libyan president Muammar Gadhafi just days before Obama arrived in Brasilia. Although Obama's failure to endorse the aspiration for a permanent seat was not thought to be related to Brazil's stance on Libya, the timing brought the two countries' divergent postures on these critical issues into sharp relief.

Rousseff also sought to change the terms of Brazil's relationship with China, to which it is tied through the BRICs group of emerging nations. The two countries had seen a rapid expansion in trade, which tripled over five years to \$62.6bn. Despite these numbers, Rousseff saw the relationship as lopsided, because Brazil had been flooded with imported Chinese goods while China had restricted access to its own markets for Brazilian goods.

The Brazilian president met Chinese President Hu Jintao and Prime Minister Wen Jiabao during an April 2011 visit to Beijing, where she signed 20 agreements to improve bilateral trade, but also pushed the Chinese to allow a major influx of Brazilian exports. In addition, the Chinese announced an order worth up to \$1.5bn for aircraft from Brazilian aerospace company Embraer, while Brazil agreed to allow Chinese companies to bid for a high-speed rail project that was to be built for the World Cup and Olympics.

In December 2010, weeks before Rousseff took office, Brazil formally recognised Palestine as an independent state. Neighbours Argentina, Bolivia, Ecuador and Uruguay all announced their recognition of Palestine in December as well. Lacking Lula's international stature and ambitions, however, Rouseff stepped back from this debate and was also relatively silent on the uprisings in the Arab world.

Brazil continued to be the main motor behind the Union of South American Nations (UNASUR), the regional body it founded in 2008. Lula had successfully used the union as a framework for Brazil to establish itself as a regional leader, although member governments were generally reluctant to cede too much power on sensitive issues such as combating transnational crime or controlling arms purchases. Other South American powers such as Chile, Colombia and Peru privately expressed some concern about Brazil's growing influence and sought alternate poles of power by forging deeper ties amongst themselves.

Security remained a central challenge over the past year throughout Rio, where the government made extra efforts to impose order as the city prepared for an influx of attention and visitors beginning in 2014. The World Bank estimated that the de facto control of poor neighbourhoods (*favelas*) by criminal gangs cost Brazil as much as $100bn a year in security expenses, lost investment and diminished productivity. A study published in 2010 by a Rio state agency claimed that Rio's drug-trafficking apparatus alone provided work for more than 16,000 people.

Although security officials repeatedly insisted that the resulting violent crime was mostly confined to certain *favelas*, their close proximity to other areas of the city added extra motivation for the state and federal governments as they attempted to assert order. Following an August 2010 shoot-out with police in a slum near Rio's affluent São Conrado neighbourhood, ten suspected drug-gang members escaped into the luxury Intercontinental Hotel, where they took 30 people hostage. The hostages were eventually released unharmed, although a bystander was killed and two police were wounded by gunfire.

On 25 November 2010 Brazilian authorities staged their most aggressive effort yet against gang operations, when they began a week-long military-style invasion of the Complexo do Alemão, a cluster of a dozen *favelas* in northern Rio home to 400,000 people. The area had been one of the city's most violent, notorious as a centre of illicit activity and haven for drug traffickers. The operation was launched after police outposts surrounding the neighbourhood came under fire from gang members, and escalated after more than 800 Brazilian Army troops joined 1,800 riot police, federal police and marines in an attempt to pacify and control what had essentially been a lawless region of the city.

Using helicopters and armoured vehicles, the authorities arrested over a hundred people and seized large quantities of drugs and weapons. Fifty people, including three police officers and many bystanders, were killed. Once the fighting had subsided, the government announced that the army would remain for at least six months to help the authorities maintain order. Alemão was not the only *favela* to see an expanded government presence; 'Pacifying Police Units' (UPP) manned by Rio's state police had been established in ten locations since 2008, covering an estimated 200,000 people. The UPPs were intended to appeal to their communities, which have rarely received much attention from the state; the establishment of units often came with extras such as free Internet access or public soccer fields. Rio announced that another 27 were expected to be in place by the 2014 World Cup.

A seemingly unprovoked deadly shooting at a Rio school in April 2011 shocked the country, perhaps even more than the violent battle of Alemão. A 24-year-old man who had attended the Tasso da Silveira school in Realengo as a child killed 12 students between the ages of 12 and 15 before he was shot in the legs by police and then took his own life. Brazilian law allows certain citizens to own guns if they are over 25, provide a reason for the purchase and pass psychological tests. The gunman, however, had purchased his arms illegally. As Brazil had not previously experienced the devastation of a major school shooting, the incident prompted a wave of outrage and reflection about violence in Brazilian society. It revived a political debate about guns, with Senate leaders quickly preparing a bill that would call a referendum on whether to impose a ban their sale. A similar proposal had been rejected by voters by a wide margin in 2005.

The country also weathered one of its worst-ever natural disasters, when flooding and mud slides killed over 800 people in Rio de Janeiro state in January 2011. Responding to the first crisis of her presidency, Rousseff committed the government to building 8,000 new homes free of charge for Brazilians who had been forced into government-run shelters. Federal and state governments would finance 6,000 of the planned houses, while 2,000 would be donated by construction companies.

The government announced a major oil discovery in September 2010, revealing that the offshore Tupi and Libra oil fields held up 8bn and 15bn barrels of oil respectively. If the estimates proved accurate, Libra would be the second-largest crude discovery in a decade. The government also moved ahead with work on the massive $17bn Belo Monte hydroelectric dam in the northern Amazon state of Para. The dam became a target for environmental and indigenous-rights groups, who charged that its construction could displace tens of thousands of people and damage rainforest wildlife. Despite a request by the Inter-American Commission on Human Rights in April 2011 to suspend work until the concerns of local residents were incorporated into the plans, the Rousseff administration insisted that worries about the project's impact were unfounded.

Venezuela: Approaching the 2012 Presidential Poll

Venezuela's presidential elections were not due until 2012, but the country was already caught up in a tense and unpredictable political process that would have a major impact on President Hugo Chávez's Bolivarian Revolution. Chávez's United Socialist Party of Venezuela (PSUV) lost its two-thirds supermajority in the National Assembly following September 2010 legislative elections, opening the door for greater influence from the previously marginalised opposition. By mid-2011, the political outlook was thrown further into question by the poor health of Chávez, who had an operation in Cuba to remove a cancerous tumour.

The Assembly elections were seen as a crucial test by both Chávez and the opposition, which combined under the umbrella Table for Democratic Unity (MUD) party. After a series of domestic crises in 2009 and 2010 seemed to expose vulnerabilities in Chávez's agenda, the president identified the National Assembly elections as an important first step towards reconnecting with his supporters in advance of the 2012 race. The opposition – which boycotted the last Assembly elections in 2005 and had therefore been rendered legislatively powerless – hoped to translate discontent over high levels of crime, a stagnant economy and woeful public infrastructure into an effective presence at the national level.

All 165 seats were contested in the September election. The PSUV retained its majority, winning 98 seats, while the MUD won 65, over a third of the legislature. The left-wing Patria Para Todos party picked up the remaining two seats. Although the PSUV's total constituted a substantial majority, the MUD's gains were significant, ending the PSUV's previous two-thirds supermajority, so that Chávez's laws and appointments could no longer pass through Congress without debate and compromise.

The results confirmed polls showing growing dissatisfaction with the Chávez administration. The PSUV's loss of its supermajority was a setback for Chávez himself, who had campaigned energetically with the stated goal of maintaining two-thirds control. The president had instructed supporters to 'demolish' the political opposition. Nevertheless, the PSUV's wins demonstrated that he remained Venezuela's most popular and effective politician, at least in terms of campaigning ability. Without his dedicated efforts the opposition's gains would probably have been much greater.

In the weeks following the election, Chávez pursued initiatives aimed at furthering his agenda in spite of his reduced majority. In October, his administration advanced the pace of nationalisations, taking over agricultural-supplies firm Agroislena; the large fertiliser plant Fertinitro; motor lubricants company Venoco; and the Venezuelan subsidiary of Owens-Illinois, a US-based glass-container manufacturer.

In December, one month before the newly elected Congress was due to start, the National Assembly approved a controversial set of laws granting Chávez the power to rule by decree for 18 months; prohibiting elected legislators from switching political parties; and imposing penalties on television, radio or Internet outlets that 'incited' the citizenry or disrupted public order. The 'Enabling Law' ceded to Chávez direct authority to make decisions on congressional issues such as economics, security, housing and agriculture. This was the third time that he had ruled by decree since taking office in 1999.

The president said the decree powers would allow him to quickly address national emergencies like flooding, which had left 130,000 Venezuelans homeless by the beginning of December. The opposition was outraged, seeing his move as a direct usurpation of their power and accusing Chávez of exploiting the natural disaster to bypass parliament. However, he insisted on its necessity; his first use of the decree powers was to create a $2.3bn reconstruction fund to assist flood victims. After declaring a state of emergency in Caracas and three states, Chávez announced that people who had lost their homes in the floods would be housed in the Presidential Palace and ministry buildings, and on army bases.

This was not all. The lame-duck National Assembly instituted procedural restrictions, shortening the time lawmakers could speak about bills and restricting broadcasts of debate to state television. It passed a law prohibiting Venezuelan non-governmental organisations and political parties from receiving foreign money. It also approved changes to the higher-education system, leading to days of violent student protests. Opponents objected to provisions that could be interpreted as a pretext for silencing opposition to Chávez's policies. The bill also created national 'transformation councils' for developing education policy, and gave students and university workers, including administrative staff, a say in electing rectors. Chávez ultimately vetoed his own law in January 2011, in an apparent attempt to calm tensions on campuses where students had faced off with riot police.

Venezuelans continued to suffer from government corruption, violence and inflation. Venezuela was listed as the most corrupt country in the Western Hemisphere in Transparency International's annual Corruption Perceptions Index, ranked at 164 out of 178 countries worldwide. Especially noteworthy reports of corruption implicated the banking and public works sectors, while the state oil company Petróleos de Venezuela (PDVSA) and the government-run food distribution network Mercados de Alimentos (Mercal) also came under extensive scrutiny for dubious practices. In March 2011, allegations emerged that the PDVSA's pension fund was used to finance a Ponzi scheme run by a former company adviser.

Caracas is one of the world's most dangerous cities, with a murder rate as high as 118 per 100,000. The country's homicide rate is estimated to be almost three times higher than when Chávez took office, and more than 90% of murders go unsolved. Inflation and other economic woes have persisted: Venezuela was the only country in the Americas apart from Haiti whose economy contracted in 2010. Inflation, which was nearing 30%, showed signs of slowing in early 2011, although at 27% it was still among the highest in the world. Venezuela devalued the bolivar and announced raised price caps on some basic food items. The Minister of Planning and Finances predicted economic growth throughout 2011, spurred by the construction of 150,000 new homes under a government-financed housing programme and other public spending. Officials from the Central Bank of Venezuela also forecast economic growth of up to 4%, although these predictions were threatened by blackouts and electricity rationing that reduced productivity. The International Monetary Fund forecast that inflation could exceed 30% before the end of 2011, while economic growth would reach 1.8%.

As always, Chávez pursued an ambitious foreign policy agenda. Relations with neighbouring Colombia deteriorated in July 2010, after Colombia made a presentation to the OAS charging that 1,500 FARC rebels were hiding in the Venezuelan jungle, where Venezuela's National Guard allegedly allowed them to commit crimes and plan attacks against Colombia. Chávez denied the accusations and cut ties with Colombia, accusing the country of laying the groundwork for an attempted invasion of Venezuela and calling outgoing Colombian president Alvaro Uribe 'crazed'.

An emergency UNASUR meeting attended by the South American foreign ministers in Quito ended without a final resolution, deepening the animosity and creating an uncertain situation for incoming Colombian President Juan Manuel Santos. Santos and Chávez had publicly reached out to each other in the weeks before the diplomatic row, fuelling expectations that relations between the two countries could improve after years of disputes between Chávez and Uribe. Of specific concern for both countries was bilateral trade; Venezuela was once Colombia's second-biggest export market, but this robust relationship fell apart amid the frequent bilateral tensions of 2010.

Upon taking office in August 2010, however, Santos met Chávez in Colombia and following a four-hour meeting they announced the restoration of diplomatic relations. The relationship continued to progress: Chávez and Santos both stated in November 2010 that they were each other's 'new best friend'. This was surprising, given that Santos served as Uribe's defense minister from 2006 to 2009, when many of the decisions that so enraged Chávez (such as extending US military access to Colombian bases and a raid on a FARC camp in Ecuadorean territory) had been taken.

Outward relations remained positive, although there was little movement on the important trade issues. Venezuelan companies had accrued over $700m in debt to Colombian exporters during the frequent halts in commercial ties, and hundreds of millions of dollars had yet to be repaid. There were also questions about how Chávez would treat Colombia once the 2012 election season was officially under way; in the past, he had frequently used bellicose threats against Colombia to rally his base. Santos surprised many in Colombia when he stated in April 2011 that his administration was 'satisfied that the [FARC] camps that we had previously located' in Venezuelan territory 'are no longer there', although he partially backed off that statement after it received extensive scrutiny in the Colombian press.

Relations with the United States, a favourite Chávez target, hit a major stumbling block over the appointment of a new US ambassador to Caracas. Cooperation between the two countries appeared to be slowly progressing in July 2010, when Venezuela extradited three major drug-trafficking suspects, including an alleged leader of the Colombian Norte del Valle cartel, to the United States. In August 2010, however, Obama's nominee for Ambassador to Venezuela Larry Palmer asserted (in what he believed to be a confidential

The FARC Files

In May 2011 the IISS published *The FARC Files: Venezuela, Ecuador and the Secret Archive of 'Raúl Reyes'*, a Strategic Dossier on the Colombian guerrilla group's activities in Venezuela and Ecuador, using the archive of the group's international chief 'Raúl Reyes'. The Colombian government had invited the IISS to perform an independent study of the archive after seizing it and killing Reyes in a 2008 raid in Ecuador and obtaining confirmation from INTERPOL of the material's authenticity.

The Colombian government had released some of Reyes's information soon after the 2008 raid. However, the dossier was unique in not only including all of the archive material relevant to Venezuela and Ecuador, the vast majority previously unpublished, but also cross-matching it with all other relevant information in the public domain.

The study found that FARC was only interested in peace negotiations as part of a strategy of total war; that they actively sought to obtain international resources; that the Venezuelan government, while failing to supply game-changing material assistance, had provided FARC with territorial, political and logistical support over the past decade; and that although Ecuadorean President Rafael Correa used FARC funds in his 2006 election campaign, this did not lead to a policy of state support.

The publication of the dossier received extensive prime-time TV and print coverage in the Andean region and elicited comment in most countries in the Americas and Western Europe. Although some feared that the dossier would harm regional relations in a reprise of the diplomatic crisis caused by the March 2008 raid, the Colombian government abstained from comment and its Venezuelan and Ecuadorean counterparts merely issued denials.

The dossier intensified Colombian debates over Bogotá's rapprochement with its neighbours, renewed scrutiny of Venezuela by Washington and other Western stakeholders, and prompted the Ecuadorean Public Prosecutor's Office to reopen investigations into Correa's 2006 campaign finances. It may also have played a role in provoking a moderate shift in Venezuelan policy towards FARC, with the government detaining two relatively high-ranking operatives in the weeks just before and immediately after its publication.

Congressional questionnaire) that there were 'clear ties' between the Chávez administration and Colombian guerrillas, morale was low in Venezuela's military and Cuba's influence over the military was potentially worrisome.

Chávez reacted angrily to the disclosure of Palmer's opinions, accusing him of meddling in internal Venezuelan affairs and stating that he would refuse to certify the appointment. The Obama administration insisted that Palmer would be the US nominee, setting off recriminations that ended with Obama revoking the visa of Venezuelan Ambassador to the US Bernardo Alvarez Herrera in December 2010.

The Chávez administration also came into conflict with Spain, after a Spanish court released sealed testimony in October 2010 in which two alleged members of the Basque terrorist group ETA asserted they had taken a weapons-training course in Venezuela. ETA, whose goal is an independent

Basque homeland in northern Spain, was alleged to have sent the two men in 2008 to a training course taught with the help of Arturo Cubillas Montan, a member of Venezuela's Ministry of Agriculture. Cubillas was accused in a separate court case of being ETA's leader in Venezuela. Venezuela denied the charges, with Chávez calling them 'absurd' and referring to the persistent accusations that foreign militant groups operated in Venezuela as 'a permanent international conspiracy'.

Chávez and Iranian President Mahmoud Ahmadinejad remained close allies, and Chávez visited Tehran in October 2010. United by a common ideology of challenging US and Western influence in foreign affairs, the two presidents spoke of establishing 'a new world order based on humanity and justice'. The presidents also entered into a number of agreements meant to encourage cooperation in areas such as trade and public works. Among the most significant was a joint shipping venture between PDVSA and Iran to facilitate the transfer of Venezuelan oil to Iran, Europe and Asia. Prior to the visit, Chávez revealed at the September 2010 UN General Assembly meeting that his government was studying how to implement a nuclear-energy programme in Venezuela and defended the Iranian nuclear programme from accusations that it was intended to produce illicit weapons.

Venezuela also fostered strong ties with Russia and China. On a visit to Moscow in October 2010, Chávez signed a formal agreement for Russia to build a nuclear power plant and research reactor in Venezuela and met President Dmitry Medvedev and Prime Minister Vladimir Putin. During his visit, Chávez received a $4bn credit for further purchases that were said to include tanks, short-range missiles, and an anti-aircraft weapons system. Under Chávez, Venezuela has already spent at least $4bn on Russian arms. China lent $28bn in financing to the Chávez administration between August 2010 and May 2011, directing the money into a bilateral development fund in exchange for Venezuelan oil. China also gave Venezuela a separate $20bn credit line to finance infrastructure projects, principally in energy, housing and agriculture.

Chávez's focus was expected to turn increasingly towards the presidential election to be held in December 2012. Civil unrest rose noticeably, with hunger strikes and work stoppages becoming more common. On 13 April 2011, Chávez marked the anniversary of the failed 2002 coup attempt against him with an appearance at a rally featuring thousands of supporters and his civilian militia. Speaking to the crowd, Chávez alluded to the upcoming election, saying of the opposition, 'We're going to sweep them away'. However, his later illness seemd to cast doubt over this and all other predictions.

Colombia: Santos's New Direction

Colombian President Juan Manuel Santos's popularity soared as he pushed an ambitious agenda of social reforms and a redirection of the country's foreign policy. Santos defeated former Bogotá Mayor Antanas Mockus in a landslide in a June 2010 run-off election, which gave the former defence minister a considerable mandate upon taking office in August 2010. In office, Santos pursued an agenda that mixed continuity of security policies with major structural reform, while deliberately diverging from the polarising political style of his popular predecessor Uribe.

Uribe and his brand of aggressive, ideological politics dominated Colombia's political sphere during his eight years in office, but Santos used his first year to move his administration towards the ideological centre. This more inclusive approach paid dividends: Santos's approval rating held consistently above 70% for much of 2011. As a result, Santos was able to move three major pieces of social legislation towards congressional approval: reparations to victims of Colombia's armed conflict, restoration of land to farmers displaced over the course of the conflict, and the redistribution of natural-resource royalties.

Legislation compensating victims of the armed conflict, originally proposed by Colombia's Liberal Party, had died in the Congress during Uribe's time in office. As president, Santos made a personal appeal before the Congress that emphasised his administration's recognition of the wide range of abuses committed during the fighting. Santos pointedly included victims of paramilitaries, guerrillas and government forces in his version of the bill – a 2009 version of the law approved during Uribe's final year in office had controversially excluded victims of state agents from receiving compensation. With a projected cost of $23m over ten years, the law would provide restitution, debt relief, health care and education assistance to victims, as well as designating funds for future assistance in the case of new acts of violence. Colombian authorities admitted in January 2011 that the whereabouts of over 5,000 demobilised United Self-Defence Forces of Colombia (AUC) paramilitary fighters were unknown, with many feared to have joined the growing crop of criminal gangs.

Another of Santos's key initiatives was the return of land to millions of displaced Colombians, many of whom had been forced by rebel groups and paramilitaries to sell or abandon their property. The Colombian government claimed that 20 years of armed conflict had forced families off 25,000 square miles of land. Over two-thirds of Colombia's 3.3m registered displaced people said they were victims of illegal land seizures. Navigating the land-restoration process proved exceedingly tricky; many who claimed to have lost land did not have (or never possessed) an official title, while many of those inhabiting or working land that had been claimed were loath to give it up. The tensions surrounding who was the 'proper' owner of land raised concerns over possible unrest should the bill pass and land claims increase. Three land-reform campaigners were killed by gunmen in 2011, while at least 11 vocal supporters of land restoration were thought to have been assassinated since the beginning of 2010.

Santos maintained steadfast support for his bill, which would put the burden of proof of ownership on current landowners by making them show how they had acquired the land. His administration said it had returned upwards of 500 square miles of stolen farmland, with Santos claiming that successful land reform 'would be the most profound social revolution in Colombia in its history'.

Santos also sought to redirect Colombia's foreign policy, with an eye towards engaging with emerging world economic powers, repairing bilateral relations with neighbouring Venezuela (see above, pages 180–85) and Ecuador, and lessening the country's sometimes dependent relationship on the United States. After taking office, Santos pursued what Foreign Minister Maria Angela Holguin described as a 'geographic and thematic diversification of the foreign policy agenda'. Most notably, the Santos administration focused on developing deeper ties with China. Trade with China was integral to Colombia's economy, totalling over $5bn in 2010, second only to the United States in volume (although this high figure obscured what had become an increasing trade deficit between Colombia and China).

In September 2010, one month after taking office, Santos accepted a $1m donation from the Chinese government towards the purchase of Chinese military materiel, and the countries' militaries took initial steps towards establishing joint training courses in China. While the small donation was essentially symbolic, it represented the opening of a new relationship and showed that China saw itself as a future supplier of arms to Colombia. The bilateral relationship attracted further attention in February 2011, with the revelation that the two governments were in advanced negotiations for China to help build a rail connection between Colombia's Caribbean and Pacific coasts to facilitate the import of Chinese goods and export of Colombian raw materials.

Santos renewed lobbying for Colombia to join the Asia-Pacific Economic Cooperation (APEC). Peru, Chile and Mexico were already members of this forum that promotes free trade and economic cooperation in the Asia-Pacific region. Colombia also formally applied for membership of the Organisation for Economic Cooperation and Development (OECD). If approved, Colombia would become the third Latin American country (after Chile and Mexico) to join.

Improvements to Colombia's outdated transportation infrastructure were identified by the Santos administration as key to taking advantage of new Asian markets for exports such as coal and coffee. As a result, Santos paid particular attention to building relations with countries like France and Spain, which (along with China) were expected to help finance tens of billions in infrastructure improvements over the course of the next decade. Santos also pursued greater economic links within the Latin American region: Colombia agreed to create the Integrated Latin American Market by joining its stock market with those of Chile and Peru. It constituted Latin America's second-largest exchange behind Brazil's and listed over 560 companies, the highest number in Latin America. The three countries and Mexico also signed a wide-ranging economic pact in April 2011 to form a 'deep integration area' to encourage greater movement of goods and capital between the countries and enhanced competitiveness with Asian markets.

Santos maintained close relations with the United States, although tensions in the relationship appeared more frequently in 2010 and 2011. After more than three years in legislative limbo, a free-trade agreement between the countries moved closer to approval in the US Congress after Santos and Obama met at the White House in April 2011 to discuss outstanding issues surrounding the agreement. With Obama pledging to move the agreement to Congress, where it has support from a coalition of pro-business Republicans and moderate Democrats, Santos promised to work on domestic measures aimed at preventing violence against trade-union leaders and strengthening Colombia's justice system so it could better prosecute crimes against these leaders. The agreement was formalised in an April 2011 'Action Plan Related to Labor Rights', which satisfied the Obama administration's requirements for advancing the pact in Congress.

The United States' lack of progress on the free-trade agreement (which Colombia had ratified in 2007) had been a point of contention between the Santos and Obama administrations, and had contributed to a feeling in Bogotá that Washington was not managing the bilateral relationship with proper care. Even though Colombia was one of the top recipients of US foreign assistance in the world, and a close ally in South America, Obama did not visit the country during his March 2011 regional trip. Santos, in turn, showed a willingness to deemphasise the 'special relationship' between the two countries that prevailed during the tenures of Uribe and former US president George W. Bush. Santos did not challenge the August 2010 decision from Colombia's Constitutional Court that the US–Colombia Defense Cooperation Agreement, which granted the United States access over ten years to seven Colombian bases, was invalid and would have to be submitted for congressional approval to be considered constitutionally sound. News of the agreement in August 2009 had caused uproar in the region, reviving suspicions about US military motives in South America.

The Santos administration also chose to extradite suspected drug lord Walid Makled to Venezuela, despite pressure from the Obama administration to send the Venezuelan national for trial in the United States. Washington officials had lobbied for Makled to be sent to the United States because of his potential as a source of information about links between the Chávez administration and drug-trafficking cartels. In post-arrest interviews, Makled had implicated high-ranking Venezuelan generals in cocaine trafficking and many US anti-drug officials believed he could provide crucial information about the growing role of Venezuela as a cocaine transit point. The Santos administration explained its decision by noting that Venezuela had requested Makled's extradition before the United States had, and that the charges against Makled in Venezuela (which included homicide) were of greater seriousness than those brought by US prosecutors.

Crime and violence related to drug trafficking and Colombia's internal insurgency remained a key concern throughout the past year. A car bomb thought to have been planted by FARC exploded at the offices of national news channel Caracol Radio in Bogotá on 12 August 2010, just days after Santos's inauguration. Santos called the bombing a 'cowardly terrorist act' and vowed that his administration would continue to aggressively fight Colombia's insurgents. The next month, the Santos administration scored two major victories against FARC: on 19 September 2010, Domingo Biojo, the commander and political leader of FARC's 48th Front, was killed along with 22 other alleged guerrillas in a Colombian army operation near the Ecuadoran border. On 22 September 2010, the Colombian army killed Jorge Briceño, also known as Mono Jojoy, in a bombing raid in the Macarena region of southern Colombia. Jojoy, head of FARC's Eastern Bloc and a member of its ruling Secretariat, had been a target of the Colombian government for years and was called 'the symbol of terror in Colombia' by Santos after his death. Oliver Solarte, a FARC leader accused of being the group's main contact with Mexican drug cartels, was killed by Colombian forces in March 2011.

Nevertheless, the group remained a potent force in the international drug trade and a threat to Colombian forces. According to figures collected by the Colombian NGO Corporación Nuevo Arco Iris, FARC killed 2,052 members of Colombia's security forces and injured 488 in 2010. Criminal gangs made up of former paramilitaries also began to be recognised by the Santos administration as a significant threat to stability. With names such as Los Urabeños, Los Rastrojos, Renacer (Rebirth) and Nueva Generacion (New Generation), these gangs had become major players in illicit activity in the majority of Colombia's provinces where they took part in murder, extortion, kidnapping and drug trafficking. Estimates put the total number of members at between 4,000 and 10,000. Most of these criminal gangs were thought to be run by former mid-level leaders from the right-wing militias, although the newer groups appeared not to follow any specific political ideology.

The prospect of peace talks between FARC and the Colombian government was held out multiple times from the beginning of Santos's term, although the political risks associated with talks and FARC's weakened stature made it unlikely that Santos would seriously pursue any agreements in the short term. Santos rejected any negotiations with FARC unless the group ceased attacks and took steps to disarm, while FARC insisted that an end to attacks could only part of a final peace agreement. Santos also demanded the release of all hostages held by FARC.

Haiti: Making a Difference?

The popular singer Michel Martelly was inaugurated as Haiti's president on 14 May 2011 at a critical juncture for the country's rebuilding. Following the January 2010 earthquake, an estimated one million people were homeless or without permanent housing, most of them in Port-au-Prince, while an additional 1.2m lived in temporary dwellings in the ruins of their homes or in tent camps; more than half the population was unemployed; and aid money for recovery projects had to be directed, distributed and supervised in a country that remained the poorest in the hemisphere. Reconstruction efforts were notably slow, despite the large amounts pledged. The United Nations Office of the Special Envoy for Haiti estimated that since the 31 March 2010 international donors conference, $1.7bn had been disbursed of the approximately $4.6bn committed to the Haitian government.

Martelly ran a disciplined and hope-filled campaign, in which he promised to expand access to free education, speed up the country's slow reconstruction efforts, revamp a diminished agriculture industry, attack unemployment and encourage development so that Haitians from rural areas did not have to immigrate to the capital city. In spite of the earthquake's devastation of Port-au-Prince, the capital and its surroundings still contained 23% of Haiti's total population.

The president-elect, however, was notably vague on the specifics of how he would implement his agenda. Governance would be especially tricky because Haiti's parliament, which would have to approve any Martelly legislation and had the power to veto his choice for prime minister, was controlled by former president René Préval's Inite party. And, despite Martelly's wide margin of victory in the 20 March 2011 run-off election, the country's election commission said that only 23% of voters had turned out (the OAS estimate was closer to 30%), putting into question the extent of the mandate Martelly could claim.

The March run-off, coming 15 months after the earthquake, ended an electoral process fraught with delays and claims of voter fraud. The first round was postponed from February to November 2010 following the quake, and was then marred by disagreement over which two of the three frontrunners would go on to the run-off. Former First Lady Mirlande Manigat and President René Préval's preferred successor Jude Célestin were initially declared the top vote-getters, but allegations that Martelly had in fact received more votes than Célestin set off days of political unrest. Observers associated with the OAS issued a report naming Manigat and Martelly as the finalists, which pressured Célestin to concede and appeased pro-Martelly protesters.

The campaign unfolded against a tense and unpredictable political backdrop, as former presidents Jean-Claude 'Baby Doc' Duvalier and Jean-Bertrand Aristide both returned from exile before the run-off. Duvalier returned to Haiti in January 2011, 25 years after he had been forced into exile in France, proclaiming 'I came to help my country'. The former dictator's return sparked fears that he would attempt to influence the election, potentially renewing the unrest that had occurred after the results of the first round in November 2010 were disputed. Two days after his return, Duvalier was charged with corruption, embezzlement and wrongful association. He was arrested and briefly held, then released and ordered to remain in the country. Sixteen individual cases were filed against Duvalier, with Haitian prosecutors signalling they would focus on the alleged human-rights abuses that occurred during his presidency.

In March 2011, less than two days before the run-off, Aristide returned from exile in South Africa. He was received rapturously by thousands of supporters as he made his way through Port-au-Prince to his home. Aristide had become Haiti's first democratically elected leader in 1991, only to be overthrown in a coup and then restored to power with the backing of the United States. Although he was re-elected in 2001, his administration was accused of corruption and authoritarianism, leading to a second coup in 2004.

Aristide maintained a fervent following in Haiti, especially among the country's poor, and his return drew a contrast between the right-leaning politics of Martelly and Manigat and the grassroots, popular movements of which Aristide had long been a figurehead. Although Aristide did not ultimately seek to influence the voting, upon his return he did criticise election officials for barring his Fanmi Lavalas party from participating. Fanmi Lavalas was Haiti's most popular political party, so its exclusion from fielding candidates was something of a surprise. The decision by the Provisional Electoral Council was one of many that changed the course of the election but lacked appropriate transparency. Some Aristide-aligned candidates for the Congress were able to run under different party labels, but other prospective candidates were simply unable to participate. Musician Wyclef Jean, a front-runner in the presidential race, was disqualified by the Council in August 2010 for not meeting the requirement of residency in Haiti for five years before the election, as was Haitian Ambassador to the US Raymond Joseph.

Martelly had gone on record backing the two coups against Aristide, and in his campaign he called for the restoration of the Haitian army, which Aristide disbanded in 1995. The presence of the 14,000-person United Nations Stabilisation Mission in Haiti (MINUSTAH), which functions as the country's military, became increasingly controversial amongst Haitians over the past year. The UN peacekeepers were blamed for outbreaks of cholera, prompting fighting between the soldiers and Haitian protesters in late 2010. Two people were killed in the northern city of Cap Haitien during street protests in the weeks before the first-round elections on 28 November. The unrest closed schools, banks and the airport.

The protests diminished before the election, but wariness about the UN's role remained. In his last address to the UN Security Council as Haiti's president, Preval questioned the effectiveness of the UN mission, saying 'eleven years of military presence in a country that has no war' shows MINUSTAH has not adequately evolved from a peacekeeping force to a development operation.

The cholera outbreak that prompted the initial unrest began in late October 2010, when the disease was detected in the department of Artibonite. Efforts to prevent an epidemic were disrupted by Hurricane Tomas, which hit western Haiti on 5 November 2010 and caused the death of six people and the evacuation of 10,000 due to extensive flooding.

In part due to the dispersal of residents from the area of the outbreak and lack of access to clean water, cholera spread rapidly throughout the country. In Port-au-Prince, the number of reported cases rose from 350 in the week of the hurricane to 2,250 cases in the week ending 14 November. Overall, according to the Haitian Ministry of Public Health and Population, approximately 270,991 people were infected between November 2010 and April 2011, with 4,766 people eventually dying from the disease. Although the mortality rate dropped, the epidemic was not contained and researchers have warned that over 400,000 people could ultimately be affected. Haitians in rural areas, which often lack access to basic medical services, were seen as especially at risk.

The origins of the outbreak remained unclear, but the fact that Haiti had not experienced a cholera epidemic in over 100 years prior to the earthquake convinced many Haitians that foreigners were responsible. The UN denied that any members of its mission carried the infection, but the organisation did ultimately conclude that bad sanitation practices at a peacekeeping camp were the most likely source of the epidemic.

Cuba: Real Reform?

Cuba's ruling Communist Party convened in April 2011 for the first time in 14 years to choose new leadership and propose economic and political reforms. The Sixth Party Congress lasted four days and ended with unanimous approval of over 300 proposals, including a measure to legalise the purchase and sale of private property. In addition, President Raúl Castro proposed limiting senior government officials (including himself) to two consecutive five-year terms, proclaiming a 'need to rejuvenate the revolution'.

Although few details were released about the measures approved by the congress, Raúl Castro's speeches and the selection of new high-level leaders were expected to provide some hints about the orientation of Cuba's opaque political leadership. Castro announced in 2010 that the government would remove more than one million workers from the state payroll (500,000 of them by March 2011) and would begin issuing official licences for entrepreneurs to open small businesses, raising expectations that Cuba would institute greater economic reforms during the congress.

Castro criticised certain aspects of Cuba's economy at the Congress, but ultimately called for an 'updating' of the country's socialist model. Saying that the system of ration cards had become 'an unbearable burden for the economy and a disincentive to work', Castro criticised the subsidies as based on unsustainable calculations in which two plus two 'equals six or eight'. The majority of the new economic proposals were most likely engineered to create incentives for Cubans to move into the newly recognised private sector, reducing dependence on the state and absorbing those whose government jobs are eventually cut.

Despite implicitly endorsing an expanded role for the market, Castro told delegates that the economic changes should proceed at a deliberate pace and would be implemented over the course of years. The difficulty of transitioning so many state employees to the private market, for example, caused the administration to indefinitely delay dismissal plans for the 500,000 state workers set to be laid off in the weeks prior to the congress.

The other significant action taken during the congress was the election of party leaders. Although Castro lamented that Cuba lacked 'a reserve of well-trained replacements with sufficient experience and maturity' to assume top leadership positions, prominent younger Communist Party members were passed over in favour of Cuba's old guard. Two long-time Raúl Castro allies, 80-year-old José Ramon Machado and 78-year-old Ramiro Valdés, were selected as second and third secretaries to the 79-year old Castro. The official in charge of overseeing the economic reforms, 50-year-old Marino Murillo, was elevated to the 15-member ruling committee, as was 46-year-old Havana party head Lázara Mercedes López Acea.

A surprise visit by Raul's brother Fidel prompted an emotional standing ovation from the 1,000 gathered delegates; it was his first public appearance with Raúl in five years. The appearance came on the heels of a column published by Fidel prior to the congress in which he formally revealed that he would no longer be the head of Cuba's Communist Party, a position to which Raúl was then officially elected.

In perhaps the most significant political reform under Raúl Castro's leadership, Havana released 115 political prisoners over the course of nine months beginning in July 2010. The release encompassed all of the dissidents designated by Amnesty International as prisoners of conscience, and was mediated by the Catholic Church with the backing of Spain. The decision to release the prisoners came in the wake of the intense international scrutiny that followed the February 2010 death of imprisoned dissident Orlando Zapata Tamayo after an 85-day hunger strike designed to draw attention to the prisoners.

The Spanish government, which granted asylum to the prisoners and received the majority of them, announced in April 2011 that the agreement between Cuba and the Catholic Church had been satisfied. Spain ultimately received close to 1,000 prisoners and their immediate family members. The releases drew praise for the Castro government, although the prominent opposition group Ladies in White warned that at least 50 more political prisoners unknown to outside groups and governments likely still remained behind bars.

Relations with the United States, which continued to maintain its long-standing commercial embargo on Cuba, improved slightly but there appeared to be little prospect for full rapprochement in advance of the 2012 US presidential election. The Obama administration restored licenses for 'people-to-people' exchanges that had been suspended by the George W. Bush administration in 2004. This was Obama's second change to the rules on travel by US citizens to Cuba, which had been amended in 2009 to allow Cuban Americans unlimited travel to the island.

Although the new guidelines did not permit unrestricted travel to Cuba, they did allow US groups to organise trips for citizens under a variety of auspices (such as language programmes). The changes also expanded the number of airports that could offer flights to Cuba, and permitted journalists, students and recognised religious groups to visit for conferences or other educational activities.

Relations were, however, complicated by the arrest, conviction and sentencing to 15 years in prison of US contractor Alan Gross for distributing communications equipment to Cuban Jewish groups. Gross was arrested in December 2009 and convicted in April 2011 of 'acts against the independence or territorial integrity' of Cuba. Gross had pleaded not guilty to charges of espionage in the course of his work for Development Alternatives, a Washington-area company with a US government contract to promote democracy in Cuba. Gross's work centred on helping Cuba's Jewish community access the Internet. The US government called for Gross's release on humanitarian grounds.

Former US President Jimmy Carter visited Cuba in March 2011, where he called for Gross's release as well as an end to the US embargo. During the three-day visit, Carter met with Raúl and Fidel Castro, as well as with Gross, a range of dissidents and representatives of the Catholic Church. Despite a warm welcome from the Castros, Carter was unable to secure an agreement for Gross's release.

In a move closely watched by the United States, Cuba announced plans to drill five deep-water oil wells in the Gulf of Mexico between 2011 and 2013. Cuba depends on Venezuela for the majority of its oil (receiving approximately 100,000 barrels a day), although it produced 21m barrels domestically in 2010. Studies have estimated that there could be 5–9bn barrels in Cuba's gulf waters. Among the companies expected to finance the new wells are Repsol (Spain), Statoil (Norway), Gazprom (Russia) and PDVSA (Venezuela).

Conclusion

Latin America's growing economy and deepening global connections have been reflected in the region's enhanced confidence and political stability. Recent public-opinion surveys point to higher levels of support for democracy. Policy and electoral choices have narrowed. More consensual, centrist politics have increasingly taken hold, and widening global links have resulted in the growth of the middle class and an increased engagement in global affairs. This has strengthened many countries' ambitions for a seat at the table in global forums and to create distance in their relations with Washington. The United States, in turn, has seen its influence diminish in many countries where it was once the key focus of foreign policy.

The continued influence of the United States has remained a galvanising issue both for countries allied with Washington and those that, despite Obama's attempts to reset relations, remained sceptical of US intentions. US Ambassador to Mexico Carlos Pascual was not the only casualty of the tension that followed WikiLeaks release of cables containing candid assessments of the region by US officials. In addition, US Ambassador to Ecuador Heather Hodges was expelled from Quito in April 2011 after a cable was made public in which she made allegations about high-level police corruption in Ecuador. Mistrust about US motives also prevented the placement of ambassadors in Bolivia and Venezuela.

The United States continued to maintain partnerships with most of the Latin America's governments, but the desire among these countries to independently chart their own economic and political courses has become increasingly clear. Yet the precarious security situation of countries such as El Salvador, Guatemala, Honduras and Mexico means that a declaration of region-wide success would be premature. Levels of inequality, long Latin America's Achilles heel, also remain high, although they have dropped in a number of countries in part as a result of more effective and targeted social programmes. The political implications of such transformations are generally positive: social inclusion and democratic strengthening are mutually reinforcing.

Strategic Geography 2011

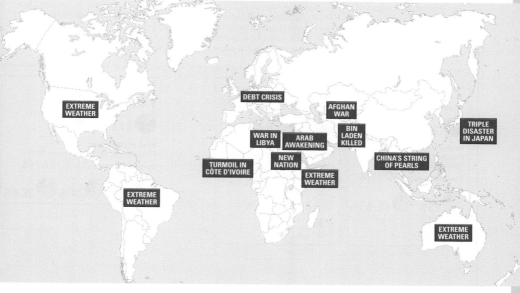

TURBULENT TIMES

Even in their wildest dreams, few in the middle of 2010 could have imagined the shape of the world 12 months later. It was a year of unexpected 'black-swan' events, with uprisings across the Arab world, a new war in Libya and a nuclear crisis in Japan. Arriving on top of a longer-term geopolitical transition of power from West to East, such events left the impression of a world in the midst of an historic shift.

Conditions before the Arab uprisings

The protests that began to sweep across the Arab world in December 2010 took most people by surprise, but academics and other analysts had long pointed to social and economic conditions that made the region ripe for upheaval. Rising food prices have been cited as one catalyst – and social networks as an accelerator – of the Arab Awakening. However, high levels of corruption and long-entrenched autocratic regimes meant that the region's young, educated populations not only wanted more jobs and better economic prospects; they also yearned for greater democracy and openness.

Algeria

34.9m   **Median age:** 30.2 years

73%   46%

Head of state:
President Abdelaziz Bouteflika (since 1999)

Corruption ranking: 105/178

23%   43–53%

5.6%

Tunisia

10.6m   **Median age:** 21.9 years

74.3%   27%

Former head of state:
President Zine El Abidine Ben Ali (in power 1987–2011)

Corruption ranking: 59/178

3.8%   36%

22.2%

Lebanon

4.1m   **Median age:** 29.8 years

87.4%   21%

Head of government:
Prime Minister Najib Mikati (since 2011)

Corruption ranking: Joint 127/178

28%   34%   26.4%

Morocco

32m   **Median age:** 26.9 years

52.3%   16%

Head of state:
King Mohammed VI (since 1999)

Corruption ranking: 85/178

15%   40–53%

10%

TUNISIA

MOROCCO

ALGERIA

LIBYA

EGY

Libya

6.6m   **Median age:** 24.5 years

83%   27%

Head of state:
Muammar Gadhafi (since 1969)

Corruption ranking: Joint 146/178

n/a   37%   1.1%

Egypt

82.1m   **Median age:** 24.3 years

71.4%   26%

Former head of state:
President Hosni Mubarak (in power 1981–2011)

Corruption ranking: 98/178

20%   48.1%   8%

Jordan

6.5m   **Median age:** 22.1 years

89.9%   39%

Head of state:
King Abdullah II (since 1999)

Corruption ranking: Joint 50/178

14.2%   40%

21.5%

Sources: CIA World Factbook, UNDP Arab Human Development Report 2009, USDA. Nomura Food Vulnerability Index, Government of Iraq, International Civil Service Commission, BBC, Ameinfo, Business Insider, Transparency International Corruptions Perception Index. Facebook numbers from Internet World Statistics (March 2011)

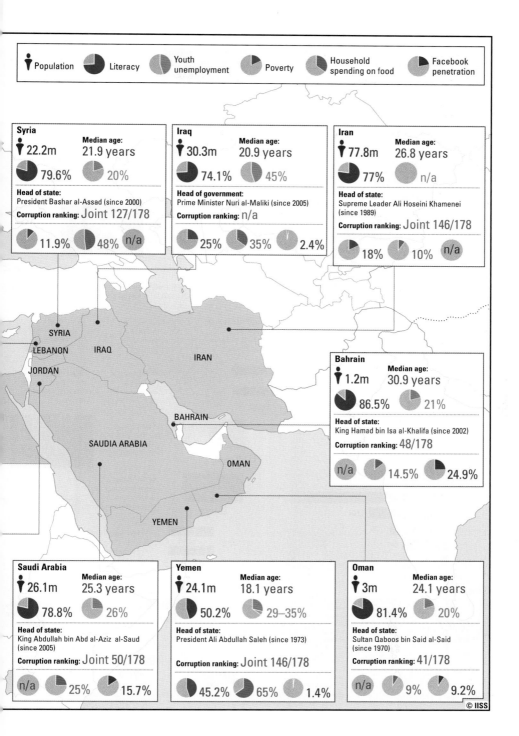

Population   Literacy   Youth unemployment   Poverty   Household spending on food   Facebook penetration

Syria
22.2m   Median age: 21.9 years
79.6%   20%
Head of state:
President Bashar al-Assad (since 2000)
Corruption ranking: Joint 127/178
11.9%   48%   n/a

Iraq
30.3m   Median age: 20.9 years
74.1%   45%
Head of government:
Prime Minister Nuri al-Maliki (since 2005)
Corruption ranking: n/a
25%   35%   2.4%

Iran
77.8m   Median age: 26.8 years
77%   n/a
Head of state:
Supreme Leader Ali Hoseini Khamenei (since 1989)
Corruption ranking: Joint 146/178
18%   10%   n/a

SYRIA
LEBANON   IRAQ   IRAN
JORDAN
BAHRAIN
SAUDIA ARABIA
OMAN
YEMEN

Bahrain
1.2m   Median age: 30.9 years
86.5%   21%
Head of state:
King Hamad bin Isa al-Khalifa (since 2002)
Corruption ranking: 48/178
n/a   14.5%   24.9%

Saudi Arabia
26.1m   Median age: 25.3 years
78.8%   26%
Head of state:
King Abdullah bin Abd al-Aziz al-Saud (since 2005)
Corruption ranking: Joint 50/178
n/a   25%   15.7%

Yemen
24.1m   Median age: 18.1 years
50.2%   29–35%
Head of state:
President Ali Abdullah Saleh (since 1973)
Corruption ranking: Joint 146/178
45.2%   65%   1.4%

Oman
3m   Median age: 24.1 years
81.4%   20%
Head of state:
Sultan Qaboos bin Said al-Said (since 1970)
Corruption ranking: 41/178
n/a   9%   9.2%

© IISS

A snapshot of the Arab Awakening

Tunisia
17 Dec: Fruit seller Mohamed Bouazizi sets himself on fire. Riots begin

14 Jan: President Ben Ali flees. New interim government appointed

27 Feb: Interim PM Ghannouchi steps down amid more protests

3 Mar: New Caid el Sebsi government sets 23 July elections

Algeria
6 Jan: Protests erupt over food prices and high unemployment

13 Jan: A jobless young man burns himself to death in a copycat suicide

12 Feb: Some 2,000 protesters heading for central Algiers are blocked by police

Morocco
12 Jan: Unemployed young graduates demonstrate in Rabat over jobs, cost of living

31 Jan: Protests outside Egyptian embassy to show solidarity with Cairo

20 Feb: Riots break out during protests for reform; 5 killed in a bank blaze

Jordan
14 Jan: 5,000 protest fuel, food prices and demand the PM's departure

1 Feb: King sacks government and requests formation of new cabinet

A selection of events from six months of unrest

Yemen
22 Jan: Thousands at Sana'a University call on President Saleh to go

2 Feb: Saleh vows not to seek re-election when his term ends in 2013

16 Feb: Protests turn deadly as government begins crackdown

2 Mar: Saleh vows to depart in a year; protesters insist he leave immediately

Red text indicates a leader resigning or leaving the country

Egypt
25 Jan: Protests erupt across Egypt, thousands gather in Cairo's Tahrir Sq.

11 Feb: President Mubarak cedes power to the army and leaves Cairo

3 Mar: PM Ahmed Shafiq resigns to be replaced by Essam Sharaf

Iran
14 Feb: Thousands join the largest protests since 2009 disputed election

1 Mar: Major protests erupt after the arrest of two opposition leaders

Bahrain
15 Feb: 24 hours after 'Day of rage', protesters occupy Pearl roundabout

Number of deaths

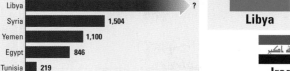

Libya
16 Feb: Rebellion starts in Benghazi; Gadhafi soon threatens revenge

Libya	?
Syria	1,504
Yemen	1,100
Egypt	846
Tunisia	219
Iraq	36
Bahrain	31
Iran	18
Algeria	9
Morocco	5
Oman	3
Jordan	1

Iraq
17 Feb: Crowds call for political reforms in self-governing Kurdistan region

Figures for Libya, Syria and Yemen are estimates, based on news reports. Numbers of deaths in Libya are particularly difficult to estimate, but seem likely to have been at least several thousand; one Obama official suggested in late April that tens of thousands had died in government crackdowns. The Morocco figure comprises five who died inside a bank and may have not been protesting.

Oman
20 Feb: Protest in Muscat demands political reform and better pay

5 Mar: Sultan Qaboos sacks three top officials as protest widens

Syria
Jan–Feb: President claims Syria 'immune' from unrest, but small protests emerge

Sources: Agence France Presse/Getty Images, Al-Arabiya, Al-Jazeera, Associated Press, Bahrain Centre for Human Rights, BBC, Bloomberg, Christian Science Monitor, CNN, Financial Times, Guardian, Haaretz, Muscat Daily, Radio Free Europe/Radio Liberty, Reuters, New York Times, Wall Street Journal, Washington Post.

9 Mar: A court ruling dissolves the party of the former president, Ben Ali

19 Apr: Official is cleared of provoking Mohamed Bouazizi's suicide

3 May: Swiss banks put a freeze on the assets of ex-president Ben Ali

3 Jun: Government further delays elections until October

7 Mar: Thousands of auxiliary police launch protest for better pay

25 Mar: Political rally in Algiers repeats demands for regime change

11 Apr: Security-forces personnel stage sit-in to call for pay and working conditions

2 May: Students protesting for change clash with riot police in Algiers

20 Mar: Thousands march after king fails to implement promised reforms

20 Apr: More protests are held to agitate for constitutional reform and end to corruption

22 May: Protesters come out in Rabat defying a ban, and are beaten by police

7 Mar: $650m more in social-security measures included in draft 2011 budget

24 Mar: Facebook activists set up protest camp in Amman

31 Mar: Facebook activists clash with pro-government rally in Amman

11 Jun: King says cabinet will reflect parliamentary majority in future

18 Mar: Despite new state of emergency, 100,000 protest in Sana'a

22 May: For the third time, Saleh refuses to sign a transition deal

2 Jun: Saleh hurt in mosque attack, later flown abroad for treatment

20 Mar: In national referendum, 77% say 'yes' to reform of the constitution

27 Mar: June parliamentary elections now set for September

13 Apr: Mubarak and sons arrested for 15 days pending corruption probe

8 May: 12 die in sectarian clashes that cast cloud over transition

5 Jun: Egypt agrees $3bn stabilisation loan from IMF (which it will drop three weeks later)

8 Mar: Ex-president Rafsanjani replaced by hardliner on key state body

21 Mar: Supreme Leader Khamenei hails Arab revolts as new 'Islamic' movement

17 Apr: In feud with Khamenei, President Ahmadinejad sacks ally of Supreme Leader

11 Jun: Protests on second anniversary of president's disputed re-election

4 Mar: With seven protesters dead, 100,000 flood into capital, Manama

14 Mar: Saudi Arabia sends troops to assist Sunni minority government

21 Apr: At least 32 medical personnel arrested for treating Shiite protesters

5 May: 47 medical staff charged with treason (and later convicted)

1 Jun: State of emergency imposed in March is lifted

7 Mar: UN Security Council members begin drafting Libya resolution

17 Mar: UN passes resolution 1973 authorising no-fly zone over Libya

For more, see War in Libya, overleaf ⟶

4 Mar: Protests in Baghdad as Iraqis rally for the second Friday in a row

19 Mar: Iraqi Shiites in Baghdad's Sadr City protest about events unfolding in Bahrain

22 Apr: More protests in Baghdad show solidarity with Bahraini opposition

14 Apr: Oman announces $2.6bn extra for job creation and state aid

12 May: The army breaks up a sit-in that began in Salalah city in late February

18 Mar: Syrian police kill at least 5 protesters in city of Deraa

25 Mar: Protests spread to Homs, Hama and Latakia after Friday prayers

25 Apr: Tanks roll into Deraa, beginning a two-week siege

31 May: Images emerge of the body of a 13-year-old tortured by police

3–6 Jun: Security personnel reportedly killed in town of Jisr al-Shughour

otos: AFP/Getty Images, IISS, President of Iran, US Navy/Petty Officer 3rd Class Jonathan Sunderman

War in Libya

After exhausting wars in Iraq and Afghanistan, the West seemed unlikely to undertake further military action in Libya. But an unusual degree of international backing for humanitarian intervention saw the United Nations Security Council authorise the use of 'all necessary measures' to protect Libyan civilians. It was 17 March and Libyan leader Muammar Gadhafi was threatening to 'crush' Benghazi, Misrata and Zawiyah in a crackdown on a month-old uprising. NATO's establishment of a no-fly zone, and airstrikes on regime positions, managed to protect an independent enclave around Benghazi and helped rebels retake Misrata. But the operation has been accused of going beyond its remit and has not decisively changed the balance on the ground – where a relatively weak Libyan army and rebel military inexperience have led to a series of back-and-forth battles.

The campaign in numbers

1973 – the UN Security Council resolution authorising a no-fly zone and other measures to protect Libyan civilians

18 – nations in the NATO-led coalition

10,000 – NATO air sorties flown by the start of June

700 – ammunition stores destroyed

500 – government tanks, armoured personnel carriers and rocket launchers neutralised

100 – command-and-control centres hit

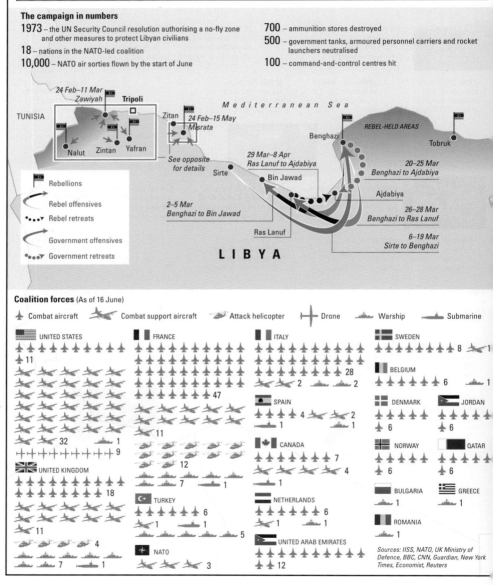

Coalition forces (As of 16 June)

Combat aircraft · Combat support aircraft · Attack helicopter · Drone · Warship · Submarine

UNITED STATES 11, 32, 1, 9
UNITED KINGDOM 18, 11, 4, 7, 1
FRANCE 47, 11, 12, 7, 1
TURKEY 6, 1, 1, 5
NATO 3
ITALY 28, 2, 2
SPAIN 4, 2, 1, 1
CANADA 7, 4, 1
NETHERLANDS 6, 1, 1
UNITED ARAB EMIRATES 12
SWEDEN 8, 1
BELGIUM 6, 1
DENMARK 6
NORWAY 6
BULGARIA 1
ROMANIA 1
JORDAN 6
QATAR 6
GREECE 1

Sources: IISS, NATO, UK Ministry of Defence, BBC, CNN, Guardian, New York Times, Economist, Reuters

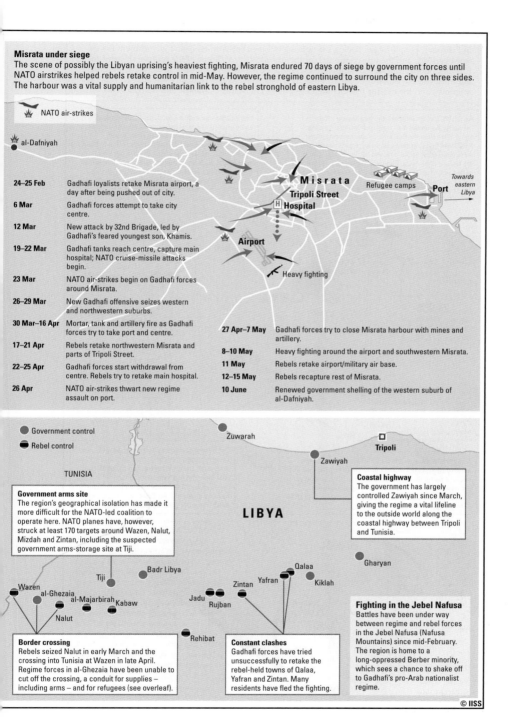

Misrata under siege

The scene of possibly the Libyan uprising's heaviest fighting, Misrata endured 70 days of siege by government forces until NATO airstrikes helped rebels retake control in mid-May. However, the regime continued to surround the city on three sides. The harbour was a vital supply and humanitarian link to the rebel stronghold of eastern Libya.

NATO air-strikes

al-Dafniyah

Misrata
Tripoli Street
H Hospital
Airport

Refugee camps
Port

Towards eastern Libya

Heavy fighting

24–25 Feb	Gadhafi loyalists retake Misrata airport, a day after being pushed out of city.
6 Mar	Gadhafi forces attempt to take city centre.
12 Mar	New attack by 32nd Brigade, led by Gadhafi's feared youngest son, Khamis.
19–22 Mar	Gadhafi tanks reach centre, capture main hospital; NATO cruise-missile attacks begin.
23 Mar	NATO air-strikes begin on Gadhafi forces around Misrata.
26–29 Mar	New Gadhafi offensive seizes western and northwestern suburbs.
30 Mar–16 Apr	Mortar, tank and artillery fire as Gadhafi forces try to take port and centre.
17–21 Apr	Rebels retake northwestern Misrata and parts of Tripoli Street.
22–25 Apr	Gadhafi forces start withdrawal from centre. Rebels try to retake main hospital.
26 Apr	NATO air-strikes thwart new regime assault on port.

27 Apr–7 May	Gadhafi forces try to close Misrata harbour with mines and artillery.
8–10 May	Heavy fighting around the airport and southwestern Misrata.
11 May	Rebels retake airport/military air base.
12–15 May	Rebels recapture rest of Misrata.
10 June	Renewed government shelling of the western suburb of al-Dafniyah.

Government control

Rebel control

Zuwarah

Tripoli

Zawiyah

TUNISIA

Government arms site
The region's geographical isolation has made it more difficult for the NATO-led coalition to operate here. NATO planes have, however, struck at least 170 targets around Wazen, Nalut, Mizdah and Zintan, including the suspected government arms-storage site at Tiji.

Coastal highway
The government has largely controlled Zawiyah since March, giving the regime a vital lifeline to the outside world along the coastal highway between Tripoli and Tunisia.

LIBYA

Tiji   Badr Libya   Qalaa   Gharyan
                    Zintan Yafran
Wazen   Jadu   Kiklah
al-Ghezaia al-Majarbirah Kabaw   Rujban
        Nalut

Rehibat

Fighting in the Jebel Nafusa
Battles have been under way between regime and rebel forces in the Jebel Nafusa (Nafusa Mountains) since mid-February. The region is home to a long-oppressed Berber minority, which sees a chance to shake off to Gadhafi's pro-Arab nationalist regime.

Border crossing
Rebels seized Nalut in early March and the crossing into Tunisia at Wazen in late April. Regime forces in al-Ghezaia have been unable to cut off the crossing, a conduit for supplies – including arms – and for refugees (see overleaf).

Constant clashes
Gadhafi forces have tried unsuccessfully to retake the rebel-held towns of Qalaa, Yafran and Zintan. Many residents have fled the fighting.

© IISS

North African migration crisis

In February, people began fleeing the fighting in Libya between rebel and government forces (see overleaf), and the tide continued for months afterwards. Some of the refugees headed for Europe, joining Tunisians disappointed with their own country's recent 'Jasmine Revolution', but most went in other directions. Before the crisis, Libya was host to an estimated 2.5 million migrants, and the exodus has included Egyptians, Pakistanis, Sudanese and Bangladeshis.

As 135,000 foreign workers fled into Tunisia in late February, the United Nations built the Choucha camp about 12km from the Ras Adjir border crossing. Other Red Cross/Red Crescent camps were built nearby, and more were established near the Dehiba border post in the Nafusa Mountains. Choucha housed up to 16,000 in early April; at least 4,000 refugees remained in Tunisian border camps in late June.

Many of the one million Egyptians in Libya rushed home after forces loyal to leader Muammar Gadhafi began a brutal crackdown on pro-democracy demonstrations. However, thousands of other nationals attempting to escape the chaos in Libya became stranded at the Saloum transit point. Some languished there for weeks, in deteriorating conditions, before humanitarian organisations could repatriate them.

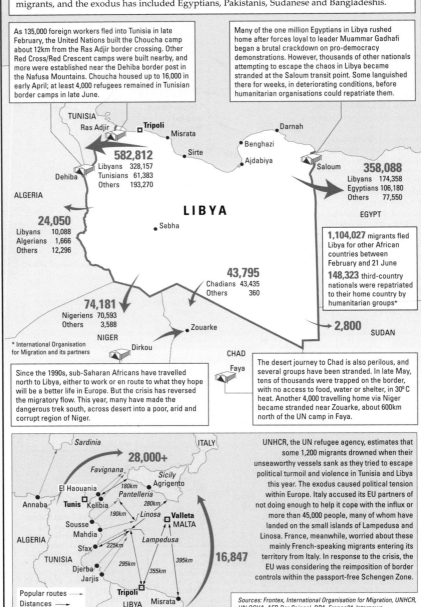

582,812

Libyans	328,157
Tunisians	61,383
Others	193,270

358,088

Libyans	174,358
Egyptians	106,180
Others	77,550

24,050

Libyans	10,088
Algerians	1,666
Others	12,296

1,104,027 migrants fled Libya for other African countries between February and 21 June

148,323 third-country nationals were repatriated to their home country by humanitarian groups*

43,795

| Chadians | 43,435 |
| Others | 360 |

74,181

| Nigeriens | 70,593 |
| Others | 3,588 |

2,800

* International Organisation for Migration and its partners

Since the 1990s, sub-Saharan Africans have travelled north to Libya, either to work or en route to what they hope will be a better life in Europe. But the crisis has reversed the migratory flow. This year, many have made the dangerous trek south, across desert into a poor, arid and corrupt region of Niger.

The desert journey to Chad is also perilous, and several groups have been stranded. In late May, tens of thousands were trapped on the border, with no access to food, water or shelter, in 30°C heat. Another 4,000 travelling home via Niger became stranded near Zouarke, about 600km north of the UN camp in Faya.

28,000+

16,847

UNHCR, the UN refugee agency, estimates that some 1,200 migrants drowned when their unseaworthy vessels sank as they tried to escape political turmoil and violence in Tunisia and Libya this year. The exodus caused political tension within Europe. Italy accused its EU partners of not doing enough to help it cope with the influx or more than 45,000 people, many of whom have landed on the small islands of Lampedusa and Linosa. France, meanwhile, worried about these mainly French-speaking migrants entering its territory from Italy. In response to the crisis, the EU was considering the reimposition of border controls within the passport-free Schengen Zone.

Popular routes ------
Distances ⟶

Sources: Frontex, International Organisation for Migration, UNHCR, UN OCHA, AFP, Der Spiegel, DPA, France24, Internews

© IISS

An election turns violent in Côte d'Ivoire

Around 3,000 Ivorians died and 900,000 fled in the violent aftermath of a contested presidential poll in late 2010. The much-delayed election was meant to finally unite Côte d'Ivoire, which was split into a rebel-run north and government-controlled south by a civil war in 2002–03. Instead, the poll threatened to push the country back into war, when the southern-backed incumbent, Laurent Gbagbo, refused to cede defeat to his northern rival, Alassane Ouattara, the internationally recognised winner. Months of clashes and political stalemate ended with Gbagbo's capture in April and Ouattara's May inauguration. But reported massacres during the unrest and human-rights abuses by both sides are new obstacles on the path to reconciliation.

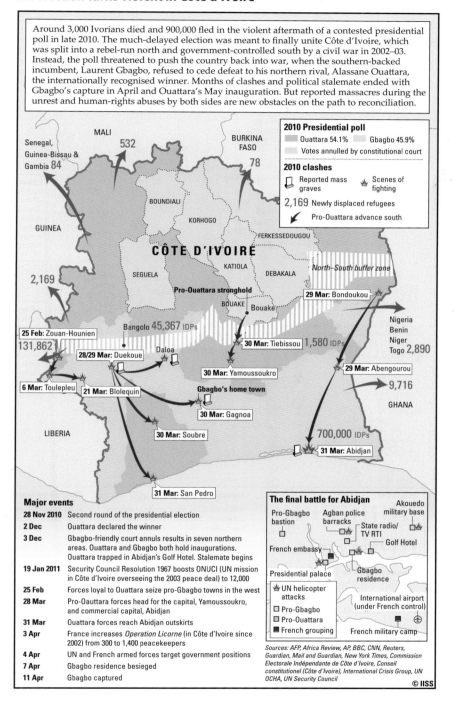

2010 Presidential poll
Ouattara 54.1%   Gbagbo 45.9%
Votes annulled by constitutional court

2010 clashes
Reported mass graves   Scenes of fighting
2,169 Newly displaced refugees
Pro-Ouattara advance south

MALI
Senegal, Guinea-Bissau & Gambia 84
532
BURKINA FASO
78
BOUNDIALI
KORHOGO
GUINEA
FERKESSEDOUGOU
CÔTE D'IVOIRE
2,169
KATIOLA
SEGUELA
DEBAKALA
North–South buffer zone
Pro-Ouattara stronghold
29 Mar: Bondoukou
BOUAKE
Bouaké
Nigeria Benin Niger Togo 2,890
Bangolo 45,367 IDPs
25 Feb: Zouan-Hounien
131,862
28/29 Mar: Duekoue
Daloa
30 Mar: Tiebissou 1,580 IDPs
29 Mar: Abengourou
30 Mar: Yamoussoukro
9,716
6 Mar: Touleupleu 21 Mar: Blolequin
Gbagbo's home town
GHANA
30 Mar: Gagnoa
LIBERIA
30 Mar: Soubre
700,000 IDPs
31 Mar: Abidjan
31 Mar: San Pedro

Major events

28 Nov 2010	Second round of the presidential election
2 Dec	Ouattara declared the winner
3 Dec	Gbagbo-friendly court annuls results in seven northern areas. Ouattara and Gbagbo both hold inaugurations. Ouattara trapped in Abidjan's Golf Hotel. Stalemate begins
19 Jan 2011	Security Council Resolution 1967 boosts ONUCI (UN mission in Côte d'Ivoire overseeing the 2003 peace deal) to 12,000
25 Feb	Forces loyal to Ouattara seize pro-Gbagbo towns in the west
28 Mar	Pro-Ouattara forces head for the capital, Yamoussoukro, and commercial capital, Abidjan
31 Mar	Ouattara forces reach Abidjan outskirts
3 Apr	France increases *Operation Licorne* (in Côte d'Ivoire since 2002) from 300 to 1,400 peacekeepers
4 Apr	UN and French armed forces target government positions
7 Apr	Gbagbo residence besieged
11 Apr	Gbagbo captured

The final battle for Abidjan

Akouedo military base
Pro-Gbagbo bastion   Agban police barracks
State radio/TV RTI
French embassy   Golf Hotel
Presidential palace   Gbagbo residence
UN helicopter attacks
International airport (under French control)
Pro-Gbagbo
Pro-Ouattara
French grouping   French military camp

Sources: AFP, Africa Review, AP, BBC, CNN, Reuters, Guardian, Mail and Guardian, New York Times, Commission Electorale Indépendante de Côte d'Ivoire, Conseil constitutionel (Côte d'Ivoire), International Crisis Group, UN OCHA, UN Security Council

© IISS

Japan's triple disaster

Disaster struck Japan on 11 March 2011, when an unprecedented earthquake precipitated a huge tsunami, triggering the world's worst nuclear accident for 25 years. The tsunami raced through the country's seawalls to leave a trail of destruction as far as 10km inland. After the earthquake had knocked out external power to the No. 1 nuclear power plant at Fukushima, the giant wave also destroyed the back-up generators, leading to a nuclear meltdown. The tsunami killed thousands and rendered half a million homeless, while the nuclear accident sent shock waves around the world. Germany has since cancelled its nuclear programme and other countries have announced reactor safety reviews.

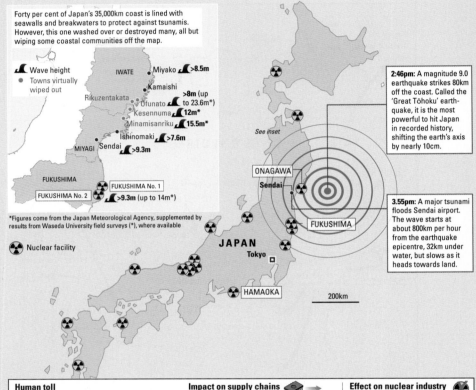

Forty per cent of Japan's 35,000km coast is lined with seawalls and breakwaters to protect against tsunamis. However, this one washed over or destroyed many, all but wiping some coastal communities off the map.

Wave height
● Towns virtually wiped out

IWATE
Miyako >8.5m
Kamaishi
Rikuzentakata
Ofunato >8m (up to 23.6m*)
Kesennuma 12m*
Minamisanriku 15.5m*
Ishinomaki >7.6m
MIYAGI Sendai >9.3m

FUKUSHIMA
FUKUSHIMA No. 1
FUKUSHIMA No. 2 >9.3m (up to 14m*)

*Figures come from the Japan Meteorological Agency, supplemented by results from Waseda University field surveys (*), where available

Nuclear facility

See inset

ONAGAWA
Sendai

FUKUSHIMA

JAPAN
Tokyo

HAMAOKA

200km

2:46pm: A magnitude 9.0 earthquake strikes 80km off the coast. Called the 'Great Tōhoku' earthquake, it is the most powerful to hit Japan in recorded history, shifting the earth's axis by nearly 10cm.

3.55pm: A major tsunami floods Sendai airport. The wave starts at about 800km per hour from the earthquake epicentre, 32km under water, but slows as it heads towards land.

Human toll

15,500 killed

7,200 missing

Estimated economic cost $$$
$185bn–$309bn: post-earthquake/tsunami reconstruction

$71bn–$250bn: Fukushima meltdown

Blackouts
Nuclear provides 30% of Japan's power, and rolling outages have followed the Fukushima disaster.

Impact on supply chains

With Japan a key manufacturer of high-tech components, there were strains on global supply chains after factories were damaged. Japan produces 90% of the world's aluminium capacitors, 45% of its lithium-ion batteries and many car parts. For example:

90% of a resin used in smartphone microchips is made by Mitsubishi Gas Chemical and Hitachi Chemical

70% of a polymer used in iPod batteries is produced by Kureha

20% of the world's silicon wafers (used in computer chips) are made by Shin-Etsu. All of these companies' factories were hit.

Effect on nuclear industry

In Japan, the Hamaoka reactor, which sits on a seismic fault, was temporarily closed in May amid safety concerns after Fukushima and radiation leaks at Onagawa. The country also abandoned plans to expand its nuclear industry. China delayed 77 new nuclear plants; the US, India and several European countries announced safety reviews. In a U-turn, German Chancellor Angela Merkel said Germany would completely phase out nuclear power by 2022. In a June referendum, Italians rejected a return to nuclear power.

Sources: BBC, Bloomberg, CNN, Economist, Financial Times, IAEA, IISS, Foreign Policy, Guardian, Japan Times, Japan Center for Economic Research, Japan Meteorological Agency, Japanese National Police Agency, LA Times, New York Times, NHK, Nuclear and Industrial Safety Agency of Japan, Reuters, Science, Spiegel, TEPCO, Wall Street Journal, Waseda University, World Nuclear Agency, Yomiuri Shimbun

Fukushima's No. 1 nuclear plant

Reactors No. 4, 5 and 6 were offline for routine maintenance when the earthquake and tsunami struck. The three working reactors automatically shut down, but their highly radioactive cores continued to produce heat. Without power, water in the reactors' inner pressure vessels could not be replenished. Steam pressure increased as water evaporated, while the heated zirconium fuel casing reacted with the water and steam to create a build-up of hydrogen. Falling water levels exposed the reactor cores and some spent fuel to the air, leading to several meltdowns.

Reactor 2
Fuel rods are exposed, causing suspected meltdown on 14 March. The next day, the reactor's outer cover is destroyed by a hydrogen explosion. A crack in the reactor's concrete pit is found leaking highly radioactive water into the sea – levels of 1,000 mSv per hour are detected. The leak is plugged on 6 April.

Reactor 1
Building damaged by hydrogen explosion on 12 March. A suspected full core meltdown 16 hours after the tsunami is revealed in May. Seawater is injected; two months later, water is discovered leaking from the reactor vessel.

Reactor 3
After water levels drop, exposing fuel rods, an explosion holes the building on 14 March. Smoke rises. Water later dropped by helicopter into the reactor.

Reactor 4
A fire breaks out on 15 March in reactor's spent-fuel pool, which is then partly refilled.

Reactors No 5 and 6
Temperatures rise in the spent-fuel pools of these shut-down reactors, before power is reconnected and cooling restored.

Excess water
The reactors were doused in seawater and freshwater to cool them, but this now-contaminated water has become a hazard itself. Some 110,000 tonnes of water have built up – enough to fill 40 Olympic-sized swimming pools – and new storage facilities are needed.

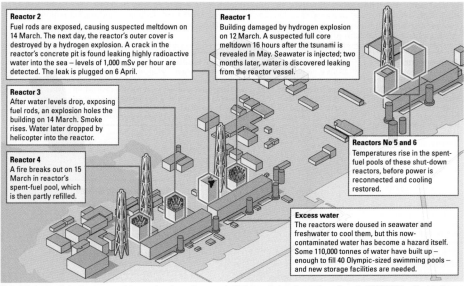

High radiation levels, leaking water and damaged equipment hampered efforts to restart cooling systems. Operator TEPCO (Tokyo Electric Power Company) brought the situation under control in early May, but does not expect to bring the plant to a 'cold shutdown' until 2012.

Several towns outside the 20km mandatory zone were evacuated when radiation levels seemed likely to exceed the 20 mSv per year evacuation limit. Residents 20–30km away were recommended to stay indoors or leave; the US suggested an 80km radius. Radiation hotspots have since been found up to 200km from Fukushima.

○ Locations where residents have been told to leave

● — Sendai (pop. 1.1m)

JAPAN

80km US recommended evacuation zone

20km Evacuation zone

Iitate (pop. 6,850)

Kawamata (pop. 17,250)

Minamisoma (pop. 71,300)

Namie (pop. 21,000)

Katsurao (pop. 1,650)

Fukushima

Naraha (pop. 8,200)

20–30km Voluntary evacuation zone

Tomioka (pop. 48,300)

Tokyo (pop. 13m) 160km

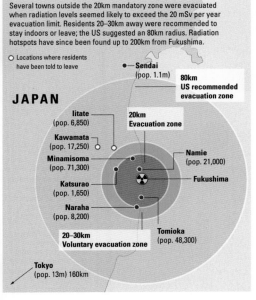

Rating radiation exposure

Fukushima was the second-worst nuclear accident in history, after the 1986 explosion at Chernobyl. Both were assigned the highest level, seven, on the International Nuclear Event Scale, but less radiation was released at Fukushima – an estimated 770,000 terabecquerels (a unit of radiation) compared to 5.2m at Chernobyl. Doses of radiation received by people are measured in millisieverts (mSv).

Fatal within a few weeks	10,000 mSv
50% of those exposed to a single dose would die within a month	5,000 mSv
Single dose causes radiation sickness, but not death	1,000 mSv
Radiation emitted per hour at Fukushima on 14 March	400 mSv
Exposure of Chernobyl residents who were relocated	350 mSv
Allowable short-term dose for clean-up nuclear workers at Fukushima	250 mSv
Lowest annual dose with demonstrable health effects	100 mSv
Full-body CT scan	10 mSv
Annual exposure for airline crew flying New York–Tokyo polar route	9 mSv
Average background dose everyone gets, each year	2 mSv
Chest x-ray	0.1 mSv

© IISS

Extreme global weather

The year 2010 was both the wettest and the second warmest on record, according to the National Oceanic and Atmospheric Administration, and extreme weather has continued to harm food and human security in 2011. Twelve months' weather says little about long-term climate change, and many people say the El Niño-Southern Oscillation – which transitioned from a warm El Niño to a cold La Niña in July 2010 – lay behind many recent anomalies. However, insurers Munich Re did venture after 2010 that: 'The high number of weather-related natural catastrophes and record temperatures both globally and in different regions … provide further indications of advancing climate change.' These two pages give a snapshot of some such catastrophes and records from July 2010 to June 2011.

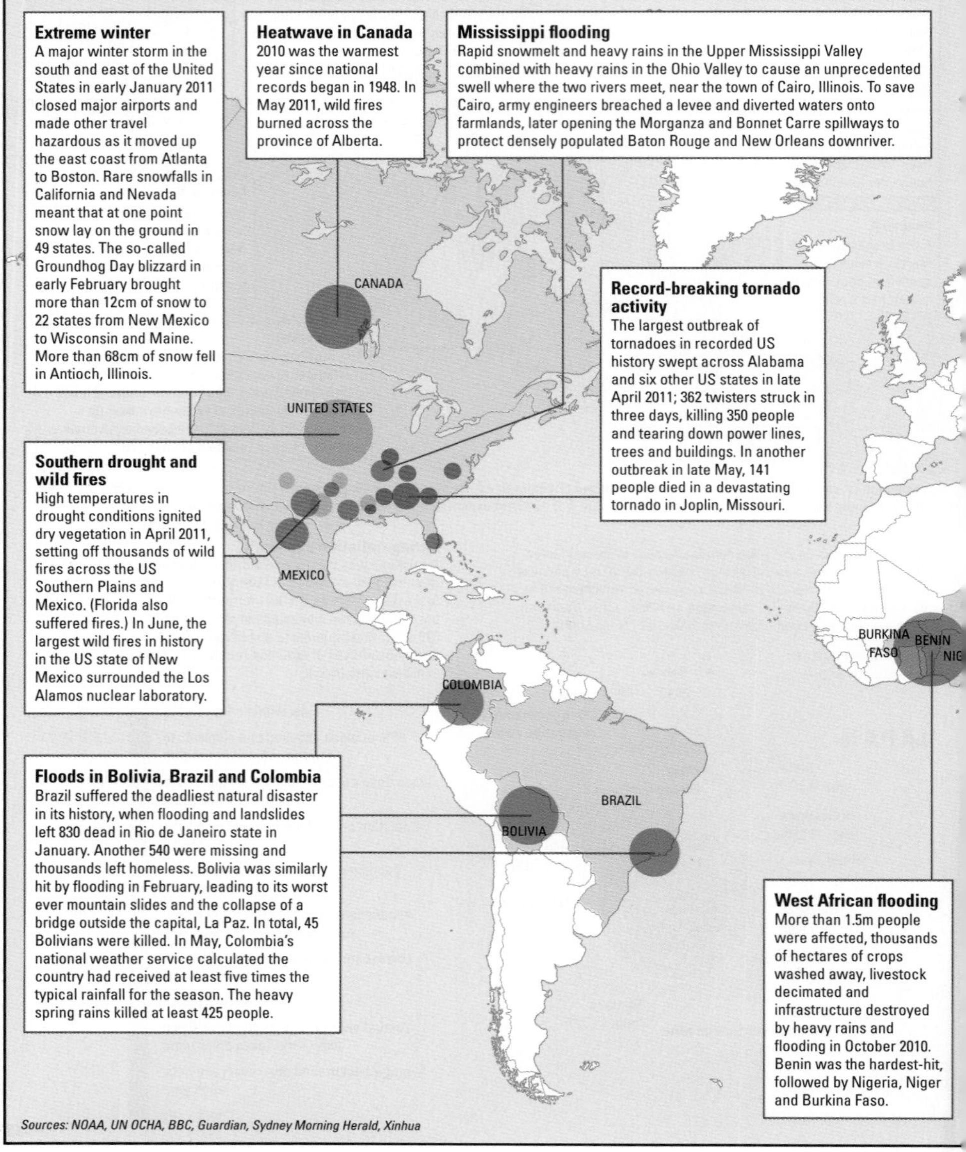

Extreme winter
A major winter storm in the south and east of the United States in early January 2011 closed major airports and made other travel hazardous as it moved up the east coast from Atlanta to Boston. Rare snowfalls in California and Nevada meant that at one point snow lay on the ground in 49 states. The so-called Groundhog Day blizzard in early February brought more than 12cm of snow to 22 states from New Mexico to Wisconsin and Maine. More than 68cm of snow fell in Antioch, Illinois.

Heatwave in Canada
2010 was the warmest year since national records began in 1948. In May 2011, wild fires burned across the province of Alberta.

Mississippi flooding
Rapid snowmelt and heavy rains in the Upper Mississippi Valley combined with heavy rains in the Ohio Valley to cause an unprecedented swell where the two rivers meet, near the town of Cairo, Illinois. To save Cairo, army engineers breached a levee and diverted waters onto farmlands, later opening the Morganza and Bonnet Carre spillways to protect densely populated Baton Rouge and New Orleans downriver.

Record-breaking tornado activity
The largest outbreak of tornadoes in recorded US history swept across Alabama and six other US states in late April 2011; 362 twisters struck in three days, killing 350 people and tearing down power lines, trees and buildings. In another outbreak in late May, 141 people died in a devastating tornado in Joplin, Missouri.

Southern drought and wild fires
High temperatures in drought conditions ignited dry vegetation in April 2011, setting off thousands of wild fires across the US Southern Plains and Mexico. (Florida also suffered fires.) In June, the largest wild fires in history in the US state of New Mexico surrounded the Los Alamos nuclear laboratory.

Floods in Bolivia, Brazil and Colombia
Brazil suffered the deadliest natural disaster in its history, when flooding and landslides left 830 dead in Rio de Janeiro state in January. Another 540 were missing and thousands left homeless. Bolivia was similarly hit by flooding in February, leading to its worst ever mountain slides and the collapse of a bridge outside the capital, La Paz. In total, 45 Bolivians were killed. In May, Colombia's national weather service calculated the country had received at least five times the typical rainfall for the season. The heavy spring rains killed at least 425 people.

West African flooding
More than 1.5m people were affected, thousands of hectares of crops washed away, livestock decimated and infrastructure destroyed by heavy rains and flooding in October 2010. Benin was the hardest-hit, followed by Nigeria, Niger and Burkina Faso.

Map labels: CANADA, UNITED STATES, MEXICO, COLOMBIA, BOLIVIA, BRAZIL, BURKINA FASO, BENIN, NIG

Sources: NOAA, UN OCHA, BBC, Guardian, Sydney Morning Herald, Xinhua

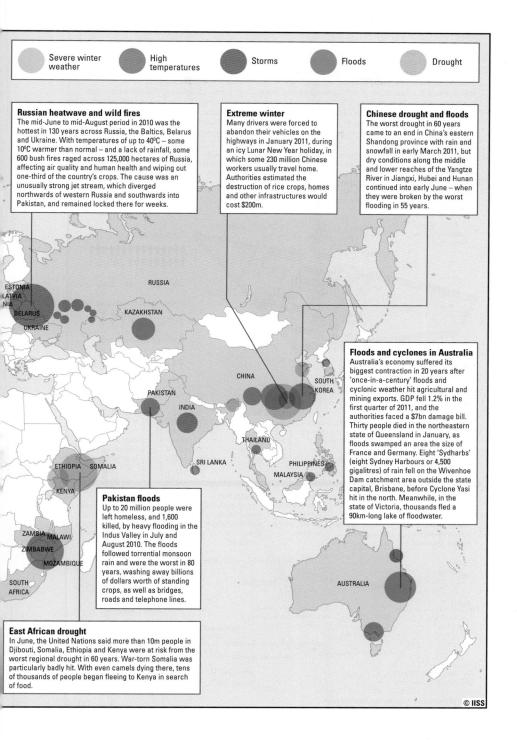

Severe winter weather **High temperatures** **Storms** **Floods** **Drought**

Russian heatwave and wild fires
The mid-June to mid-August period in 2010 was the hottest in 130 years across Russia, the Baltics, Belarus and Ukraine. With temperatures of up to 40ºC – some 10ºC warmer than normal – and a lack of rainfall, some 600 bush fires raged across 125,000 hectares of Russia, affecting air quality and human health and wiping out one-third of the country's crops. The cause was an unusually strong jet stream, which diverged northwards of western Russia and southwards into Pakistan, and remained locked there for weeks.

Extreme winter
Many drivers were forced to abandon their vehicles on the highways in January 2011, during an icy Lunar New Year holiday, in which some 230 million Chinese workers usually travel home. Authorities estimated the destruction of rice crops, homes and other infrastructures would cost $200m.

Chinese drought and floods
The worst drought in 60 years came to an end in China's eastern Shandong province with rain and snowfall in early March 2011, but dry conditions along the middle and lower reaches of the Yangtze River in Jiangxi, Hubei and Hunan continued into early June – when they were broken by the worst flooding in 55 years.

Floods and cyclones in Australia
Australia's economy suffered its biggest contraction in 20 years after 'once-in-a-century' floods and cyclonic weather hit agricultural and mining exports. GDP fell 1.2% in the first quarter of 2011, and the authorities faced a $7bn damage bill. Thirty people died in the northeastern state of Queensland in January, as floods swamped an area the size of France and Germany. Eight 'Sydharbs' (eight Sydney Harbours or 4,500 gigalitres) of rain fell on the Wivenhoe Dam catchment area outside the state capital, Brisbane, before Cyclone Yasi hit in the north. Meanwhile, in the state of Victoria, thousands fled a 90km-long lake of floodwater.

Pakistan floods
Up to 20 million people were left homeless, and 1,600 killed, by heavy flooding in the Indus Valley in July and August 2010. The floods followed torrential monsoon rain and were the worst in 80 years, washing away billions of dollars worth of standing crops, as well as bridges, roads and telephone lines.

East African drought
In June, the United Nations said more than 10m people in Djibouti, Somalia, Ethiopia and Kenya were at risk from the worst regional drought in 60 years. War-torn Somalia was particularly badly hit. With even camels dying there, tens of thousands of people began fleeing to Kenya in search of food.

© IISS

The sudden death of Osama bin Laden

US President Barack Obama interrupted regular television programming around 10pm EST on 1 May 2011 to announce the death of Osama bin Laden. The president reported 'to the American people and to the world', that the al-Qaeda leader had been killed in a US Special Forces operation in Abbottabad, Pakistan. After years in which the trail had gone cold, US intelligence tracked down the 9/11 mastermind through a courier, following the testimonies of captured al-Qaeda members. US–Pakistan relations worsened after the bin Laden raid, which went ahead without Pakistan's knowledge and raised the question of how the world's most-wanted man came to be in a garrison town near the top Pakistani military school.

Operation Neptune Spear

The raid was carried out by Navy SEALs from the Naval Special Warfare Development Group (DEVGRU). They were transported by two stealth-modified Sikorsky UH-60 *Black Hawk* helicopters, one of which crashed on landing and was subsequently destroyed. A back-up team of another two dozen SEALS waited outside Abbottabad in three *Chinook* helicopters. Bin Laden, his son, his courier, his courier's brother and a woman died in the raid, which also yielded substantial intelligence on computer hard disks and USB drives.

The strike team

🮲🮲🮲🮲🮲🮲🮲🮲🮲🮲🮲🮲🮲🮲
🮲🮲🮲🮲🮲🮲🮲🮲🮲🮲 **24** Navy SEALs

🚁 🚁 **2** helicopters

🐕 **1?** dog (reportedly)

The back-up team

🮲🮲🮲🮲🮲🮲🮲🮲🮲🮲🮲🮲🮲🮲
🮲🮲🮲🮲🮲🮲🮲🮲🮲🮲 **24** Navy SEALs

🚁 🚁 🚁 **3** helicopters

Residents in the compound

🮲🮲🮲🮲🮲🮲🮲🮲🮲
9 adults (5 killed including bin Laden)

🮲🮲🮲🮲🮲🮲🮲🮲🮲🮲🮲🮲🮲
13 children

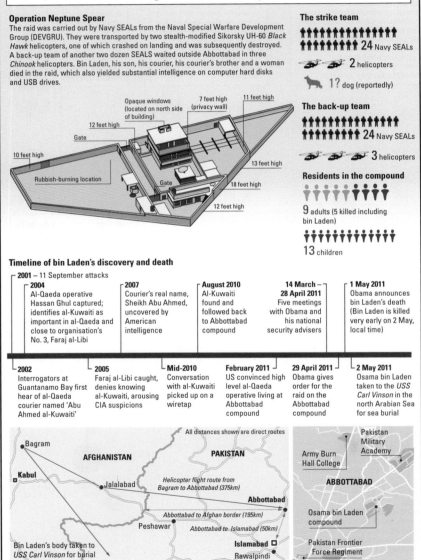

Timeline of bin Laden's discovery and death

2001 – 11 September attacks

2004
Al-Qaeda operative Hassan Ghul captured; identifies al-Kuwaiti as important in al-Qaeda and close to organisation's No. 3, Faraj al-Libi

2002
Interrogators at Guantanamo Bay first hear of al-Qaeda courier named 'Abu Ahmed al-Kuwaiti'

2007
Courier's real name, Sheikh Abu Ahmed, uncovered by American intelligence

2005
Faraj al-Libi caught, denies knowing al-Kuwaiti, arousing CIA suspicions

August 2010
Al-Kuwaiti found and followed back to Abbottabad compound

Mid-2010
Conversation with al-Kuwaiti picked up on a wiretap

14 March – 28 April 2011
Five meetings with Obama and his national security advisers

February 2011
US convinced high level al-Qaeda operative living at Abbottabad compound

1 May 2011
Obama announces bin Laden's death (Bin Laden is killed very early on 2 May, local time)

29 April 2011
Obama gives order for the raid on the Abbottabad compound

2 May 2011
Osama bin Laden taken to the *USS Carl Vinson* in the north Arabian Sea for sea burial

Sources: CIA, Associated Press, Guardian, New York Times

© IISS

South Sudan: a nation is born

After citizens overwhelmingly said 'yes' to partition in a January 2011 referendum, South Sudan became the world's newest nation on 9 July. But it was always possible the country would be born in conflict, because the 2005 peace agreement that ended 21 years of civil war between northern and southern Sudan never fully resolved long-standing border disputes. Just two months before secession, Khartoum sent troops into disputed Abyei and violence subsequently erupted in South Kordofan. Although rival forces were withdrawn and peacekeepers deployed, the control of major oilfields and farmlands, and the rights of border communities, remain heated issues. The proliferation of small arms renders the region extremely volatile.

South Kordofan
This state produced 80% of the united Sudan's oil and will be the north's only oil producer. But many who live here have links to the southern Sudan People's Liberation Army/Movement. After Khartoum launched a full-scale invasion of Abyei on 20 May (reacting to an ambush) fighting erupted in Kadugli in early June.

Other border disputes
1 **Kafia Kinji**: Over copper, uranium and gold deposits
2 **Safaha**: Grazing rights between Misseriya, Dinka and other tribes
3 **Jordah–Winthou**: Rich farmlands near this heavily militarised border crossing
4 **Gulli**: Rich lands between Blue Nile and Upper Nile
5 **Chali al-Fil**: Line disputed by pro-south Blue Nile tribes

Abyei
Although the borders redrawn by The Hague in 2009 left only one major oilfield within Abyei, the region remains disputed. A separate referendum on whether it joins South Sudan has been delayed over questions of whether pro-north Arab Misseriya tribes should be eligible to vote in it. The tribes herd cattle through Abyei during the dry season and farm further northwards in the wet, and despite government assurances fear their migration routes may be disrupted if Abyei joins the South. The Ngok Dinka people who inhabit Abyei have close southern ties.

Nuba Mountains
Many Nuba fought for the south during the civil war and feel like outsiders in Muslim Arab-dominated north Sudan. Southern forces still controlled much of the Nuba Mountains in May, when the north launched ground and air offensives that worried human-rights campaigners.

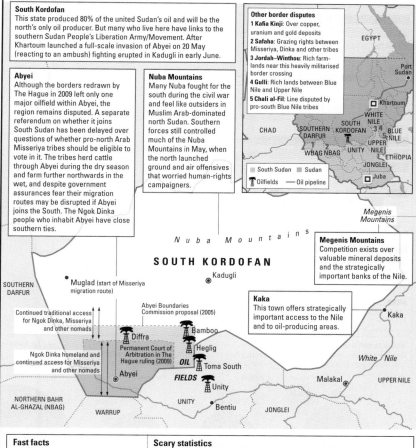

Megenis Mountains
Competition exists over valuable mineral deposits and the strategically important banks of the Nile.

Kaka
This town offers strategically important access to the Nile and to oil-producing areas.

Fast facts

98.83% 'yes' vote for independence

No. 193 or 195? South Sudan is the 193rd UN member, but country No. 195 according to the US Department of State, which counts Vatican City and Kosovo

8.26m? The southern population according to a 2008 census, which local politicians call an underestimate

Scary statistics

South Sudan's road to prosperity will be long, as the figures below show. Its infrastructure was left in tatters by the civil war, and although it has significant oil, most is piped and exported through north Sudan (see inset map) where President Omar al-Bashir has already threatened to block the pipeline. South Sudan will rely on oil for 98% of its revenue.

$1,200 GDP per capita
92% of women illiterate

75.6% live below the poverty line
1.9% of children finish primary school

4.3m requiring food assistance in 2010
102 infant mortalities per 1,000 births

Sources: : IISS, Africa Confidential, BBC, Concordis International, Helomagazine.org, Overseas Development Institute, Thomson Reuters, United Nations Mission in Sudan, UN Sudan Information Gateway

Europe's debt crisis

Europe's sovereign-debt crisis has been unfolding for more than two years, but its political consequences have not always been predictable. With clear gaps between the bloc's strongest economies and the weaker so-called PIIGS (Portugal, Ireland, Italy, Greece and Spain) on the periphery, the multi-billion euro bailouts of Greece, Ireland and Portugal in 2010 and 2011 were long anticipated. However, few international analysts forecast the scale of public hostility to the economic remedies. In June 2011, Greek 'indignants' and other protesters on the country's streets forced a rethink of the austerity measures demanded by Brussels and Berlin – putting the Eurozone and its single currency under further strain.

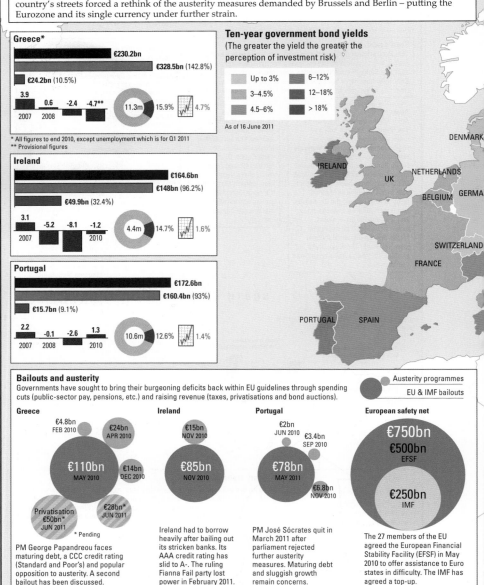

Greece*

€230.2bn
€328.5bn (142.8%)
€24.2bn (10.5%)

3.9 0.6 -2.4 -4.7**
2007 2008

11.3m 15.9% 4.7%

* All figures to end 2010, except unemployment which is for Q1 2011
** Provisional figures

Ireland

€164.6bn
€148bn (96.2%)
€49.9bn (32.4%)

3.1 -5.2 -8.1 -1.2
2007 2010

4.4m 14.7% 1.6%

Portugal

€172.6bn
€160.4bn (93%)
€15.7bn (9.1%)

2.2 -0.1 -2.6 1.3
2007 2008 2010

10.6m 12.6% 1.4%

Ten-year government bond yields
(The greater the yield the greater the perception of investment risk)

- Up to 3%
- 3–4.5%
- 4.5–6%
- 6–12%
- 12–18%
- > 18%

As of 16 June 2011

DENMARK
IRELAND
UK
NETHERLANDS
BELGIUM GERMA
SWITZERLAND
FRANCE
PORTUGAL SPAIN

Bailouts and austerity

Governments have sought to bring their burgeoning deficits back within EU guidelines through spending cuts (public-sector pay, pensions, etc.) and raising revenue (taxes, privatisations and bond auctions).

- Austerity programmes
- EU & IMF bailouts

Greece

€4.8bn
FEB 2010
€24bn
APR 2010
€110bn
MAY 2010
€14bn
DEC 2010
Privatisation
€50bn*
JUN 2011
€28bn*
JUN 2011

* Pending

PM George Papandreou faces maturing debt, a CCC credit rating (Standard and Poor's) and popular opposition to austerity. A second bailout has been discussed.

Ireland

€15bn
NOV 2010
€85bn
NOV 2010

Ireland had to borrow heavily after bailing out its stricken banks. Its AAA credit rating has slid to A-. The ruling Fianna Fail party lost power in February 2011.

Portugal

€2bn
JUN 2010
€3.4bn
SEP 2010
€78bn
MAY 2011
€6.8bn
NOV 2010

PM José Sócrates quit in March 2011 after parliament rejected further austerity measures. Maturing debt and sluggish growth remain concerns.

European safety net

€750bn
€500bn
EFSF
€250bn
IMF

The 27 members of the EU agreed the European Financial Stability Facility (EFSF) in May 2010 to offer assistance to Euro states in difficulty. The IMF has agreed a top-up.

Sources: Bank for International Settlements, Eurostat, Helstat, Central Statistics Office (Republic of Ireland), Statistics Portugal, BBC, Bloomberg, European Commission

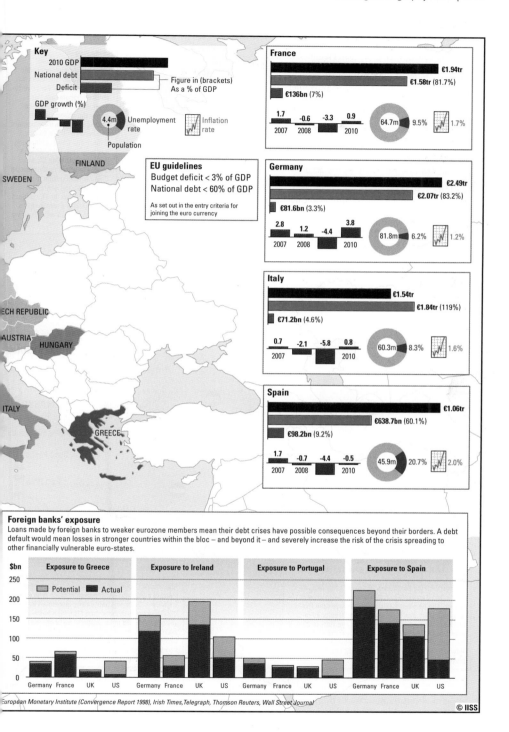

Key

2010 GDP
National debt ——— Figure in (brackets)
Deficit As a % of GDP

GDP growth (%)

4.4m Unemployment rate
Population Inflation rate

FINLAND
SWEDEN

EU guidelines
Budget deficit < 3% of GDP
National debt < 60% of GDP

As set out in the entry criteria for joining the euro currency

ECH REPUBLIC
AUSTRIA
HUNGARY

ITALY
GREECE

France
€1.94tr
€1.58tr (81.7%)
€136bn (7%)
1.7 | -0.6 | -3.3 | 0.9
2007 | 2008 | | 2010
64.7m | 9.5% | 1.7%

Germany
€2.49tr
€2.07tr (83.2%)
€81.6bn (3.3%)
2.8 | 1.2 | -4.4 | 3.8
2007 | 2008 | | 2010
81.8m | 6.2% | 1.2%

Italy
€1.54tr
€1.84tr (119%)
€71.2bn (4.6%)
0.7 | -2.1 | -5.8 | 0.8
2007 | | | 2010
60.3m | 8.3% | 1.6%

Spain
€1.06tr
€638.7bn (60.1%)
€98.2bn (9.2%)
1.7 | -0.7 | -4.4 | -0.5
2007 | 2008 | | 2010
45.9m | 20.7% | 2.0%

Foreign banks' exposure
Loans made by foreign banks to weaker eurozone members mean their debt crises have possible consequences beyond their borders. A debt default would mean losses in stronger countries within the bloc – and beyond it – and severely increase the risk of the crisis spreading to other financially vulnerable euro-states.

$bn
Exposure to Greece | **Exposure to Ireland** | **Exposure to Portugal** | **Exposure to Spain**
Potential | Actual

250
200
150
100
50
0

Germany France UK US | Germany France UK US | Germany France UK US | Germany France UK US

European Monetary Institute (Convergence Report 1998), Irish Times, Telegraph, Thomson Reuters, Wall Street Journal

© IISS

China's string of pearls

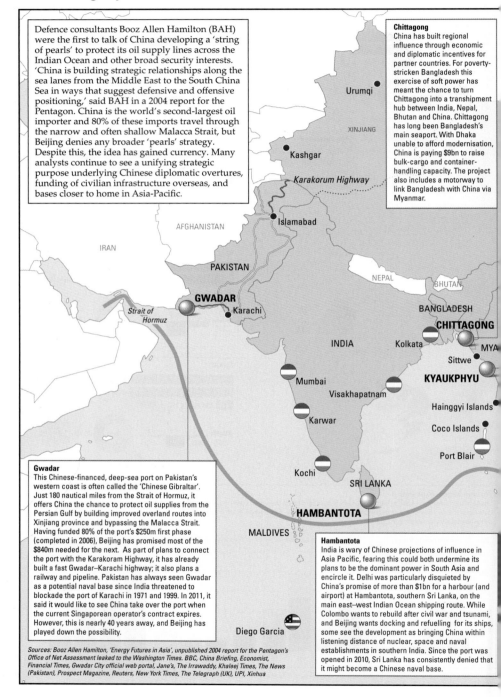

Defence consultants Booz Allen Hamilton (BAH) were the first to talk of China developing a 'string of pearls' to protect its oil supply lines across the Indian Ocean and other broad security interests. 'China is building strategic relationships along the sea lanes from the Middle East to the South China Sea in ways that suggest defensive and offensive positioning,' said BAH in a 2004 report for the Pentagon. China is the world's second-largest oil importer and 80% of these imports travel through the narrow and often shallow Malacca Strait, but Beijing denies any broader 'pearls' strategy. Despite this, the idea has gained currency. Many analysts continue to see a unifying strategic purpose underlying Chinese diplomatic overtures, funding of civilian infrastructure overseas, and bases closer to home in Asia-Pacific.

Chittagong
China has built regional influence through economic and diplomatic incentives for partner countries. For poverty-stricken Bangladesh this exercise of soft power has meant the chance to turn Chittagong into a transhipment hub between India, Nepal, Bhutan and China. Chittagong has long been Bangladesh's main seaport. With Dhaka unable to afford modernisation, China is paying $9bn to raise bulk-cargo and container-handling capacity. The project also includes a motorway to link Bangladesh with China via Myanmar.

Gwadar
This Chinese-financed, deep-sea port on Pakistan's western coast is often called the 'Chinese Gibraltar'. Just 180 nautical miles from the Strait of Hormuz, it offers China the chance to protect oil supplies from the Persian Gulf by building improved overland routes into Xinjiang province and bypassing the Malacca Strait. Having funded 80% of the port's $250m first phase (completed in 2006), Beijing has promised most of the $840m needed for the next. As part of plans to connect the port with the Karakoram Highway, it has already built a fast Gwadar–Karachi highway; it also plans a railway and pipeline. Pakistan has always seen Gwadar as a potential naval base since India threatened to blockade the port of Karachi in 1971 and 1999. In 2011, it said it would like to see China take over the port when the current Singaporean operator's contract expires. However, this is nearly 40 years away, and Beijing has played down the possibility.

Hambantota
India is wary of Chinese projections of influence in Asia Pacific, fearing this could both undermine its plans to be the dominant power in South Asia and encircle it. Delhi was particularly disquieted by China's promise of more than $1bn for a harbour (and airport) at Hambantota, southern Sri Lanka, on the main east–west Indian Ocean shipping route. While Colombo wants to rebuild after civil war and tsunami, and Beijing wants docking and refuelling for its ships, some see the development as bringing China within listening distance of nuclear, space and naval establishments in southern India. Since the port was opened in 2010, Sri Lanka has consistently denied that it might become a Chinese naval base.

Sources: Booz Allen Hamilton, 'Energy Futures in Asia', unpublished 2004 report for the Pentagon's Office of Net Assessment leaked to the Washington Times. BBC, China Briefing, Economist, Financial Times, Gwadar City official web portal, Jane's, The Irrawaddy, Khaleej Times, The News (Pakistan), Prospect Magazine, Reuters, New York Times, The Telegraph (UK), UPI, Xinhua

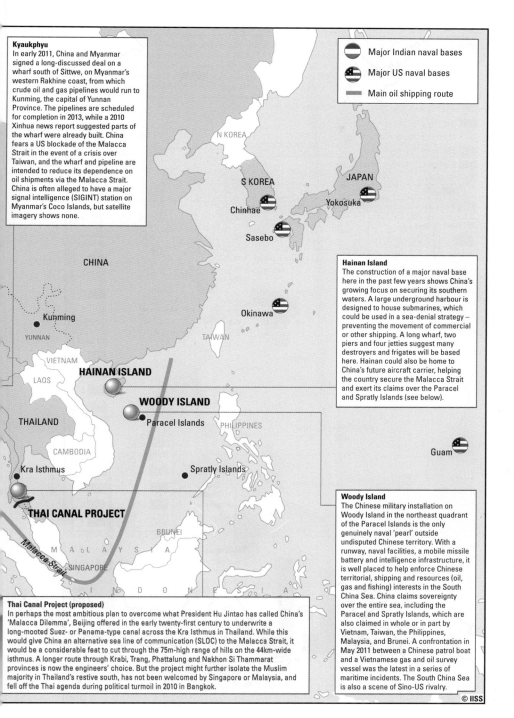

Kyaukphyu
In early 2011, China and Myanmar signed a long-discussed deal on a wharf south of Sittwe, on Myanmar's western Rakhine coast, from which crude oil and gas pipelines would run to Kunming, the capital of Yunnan Province. The pipelines are scheduled for completion in 2013, while a 2010 Xinhua news report suggested parts of the wharf were already built. China fears a US blockade of the Malacca Strait in the event of a crisis over Taiwan, and the wharf and pipeline are intended to reduce its dependence on oil shipments via the Malacca Strait. China is often alleged to have a major signal intelligence (SIGINT) station on Myanmar's Coco Islands, but satellite imagery shows none.

Major Indian naval bases

Major US naval bases

Main oil shipping route

N KOREA

S KOREA

JAPAN

Chinhae

Yokosuka

Sasebo

CHINA

Kunming

YUNNAN

VIETNAM

LAOS

HAINAN ISLAND

WOODY ISLAND

Paracel Islands

PHILIPPINES

THAILAND

CAMBODIA

Kra Isthmus

Spratly Islands

THAI CANAL PROJECT

BRUNEI

Malacca Strait

M A L A Y S I A

SINGAPORE

I N D O N E S I A

Okinawa

TAIWAN

Guam

Hainan Island
The construction of a major naval base here in the past few years shows China's growing focus on securing its southern waters. A large underground harbour is designed to house submarines, which could be used in a sea-denial strategy – preventing the movement of commercial or other shipping. A long wharf, two piers and four jetties suggest many destroyers and frigates will be based here. Hainan could also be home to China's future aircraft carrier, helping the country secure the Malacca Strait and exert its claims over the Paracel and Spratly Islands (see below).

Woody Island
The Chinese military installation on Woody Island in the northeast quadrant of the Paracel Islands is the only genuinely naval 'pearl' outside undisputed Chinese territory. With a runway, naval facilities, a mobile missile battery and intelligence infrastructure, it is well placed to help enforce Chinese territorial, shipping and resources (oil, gas and fishing) interests in the South China Sea. China claims sovereignty over the entire sea, including the Paracel and Spratly Islands, which are also claimed in whole or in part by Vietnam, Taiwan, the Philippines, Malaysia, and Brunei. A confrontation in May 2011 between a Chinese patrol boat and a Vietnamese gas and oil survey vessel was the latest in a series of maritime incidents. The South China Sea is also a scene of Sino-US rivalry.

Thai Canal Project (proposed)
In perhaps the most ambitious plan to overcome what President Hu Jintao has called China's 'Malacca Dilemma', Beijing offered in the early twenty-first century to underwrite a long-mooted Suez- or Panama-type canal across the Kra Isthmus in Thailand. While this would give China an alternative sea line of communication (SLOC) to the Malacca Strait, it would be a considerable feat to cut through the 75m-high range of hills on the 44km-wide isthmus. A longer route through Krabi, Trang, Phattalung and Nakhon Si Thammarat provinces is now the engineers' choice. But the project might further isolate the Muslim majority in Thailand's restive south, has not been welcomed by Singapore or Malaysia, and fell off the Thai agenda during political turmoil in 2010 in Bangkok.

© IISS

Changing the guard in Afghanistan

Building effective local forces in Afghanistan is fundamental to the eventual departure of international combat troops by the stated goal of end-2014. In July 2011, the transition to local security control began in Bamiyan, with another six areas earmarked to follow soon afterwards. Yet despite increased efforts to recruit and train personnel since 2009, many question whether Afghan security forces can meet an ambitious deadline to step into NATO's role.

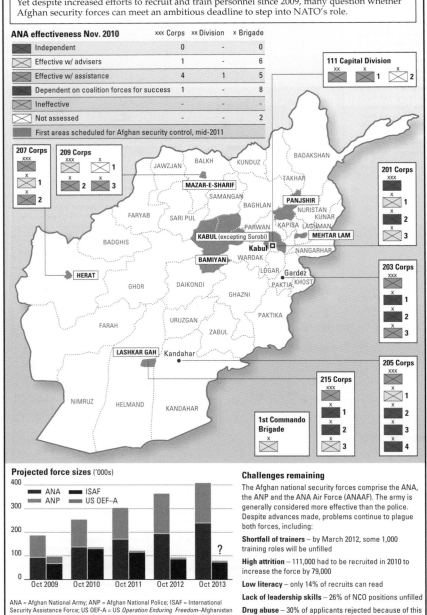

ANA effectiveness Nov. 2010   xxx Corps   xx Division   x Brigade

		xxx Corps	xx Division	x Brigade
	Independent	0	-	0
	Effective w/ advisers	1	-	6
	Effective w/ assistance	4	1	5
	Dependent on coalition forces for success	1	-	8
	Ineffective	-	-	-
	Not assessed	-	-	2
	First areas scheduled for Afghan security control, mid-2011			

111 Capital Division

207 Corps

209 Corps

201 Corps

203 Corps

205 Corps

215 Corps

1st Commando Brigade

Projected force sizes ('000s)

- ANA
- ISAF
- ANP
- US OEF-A

(Chart: 400, 300, 200, 100, 0 — Oct 2009, Oct 2010, Oct 2011, Oct 2012, Oct 2013)

ANA = Afghan National Army; ANP = Afghan National Police; ISAF = International Security Assistance Force; US OEF-A = US Operation Enduring Freedom–Afghanistan

Sources: CENTCOM, CSIS, IISS, ISAF/NATO, UK MoD, Reuters, SIGAR

Challenges remaining

The Afghan national security forces comprise the ANA, the ANP and the ANA Air Force (ANAAF). The army is generally considered more effective than the police. Despite advances made, problems continue to plague both forces, including:

Shortfall of trainers – by March 2012, some 1,000 training roles will be unfilled

High attrition – 111,000 had to be recruited in 2010 to increase the force by 79,000

Low literacy – only 14% of recruits can read

Lack of leadership skills – 26% of NCO positions unfilled

Drug abuse – 30% of applicants rejected because of this

© IISS

Chapter 5

Europe

For Western Europe, the year was dominated by the sovereign-debt crisis. Financial rescue packages were organised for Ireland and Portugal, and at mid-2011 efforts were under way to arrange a second bailout for Greece, the first having proved insufficient. The austerity measures that governments had to impose on their electorates to meet the terms of the emergency loans increasingly seemed politically unsustainable. Governments fell in Ireland and Portugal. Therefore, there was a growing acceptance of the inevitability that at least some debtor nations would have to find ways to reduce their debt burdens, and thereby default. The priority was to ensure that this could occur in an orderly manner, avoiding another panic in the banking system similar to that of 2008. Since losses would have to be taken, the argument was increasingly about how to share them between public and private sectors. (See Strategic Geography, pages XVI–XVII).

Behind these attempts to ensure an orderly outcome were two overriding needs: firstly, to prevent the contagion from spreading to larger countries with larger debts, most immediately Spain and Italy. The long-drawn-out arguments about Greece, featuring an absence of concerted leadership from Europe's major capitals, were hardly helpful in preventing the spread of the crisis. Secondly, governments were seeking to preserve the integrity of the euro, the common currency of 17 European countries. It was feared that the departure of one country, such as Greece, could cause the eventual dismantling of the currency, perhaps triggering the beginning of a reversal of the massive efforts towards European unity that have taken place over the past half-century. But if this was the political priority, Germany – the

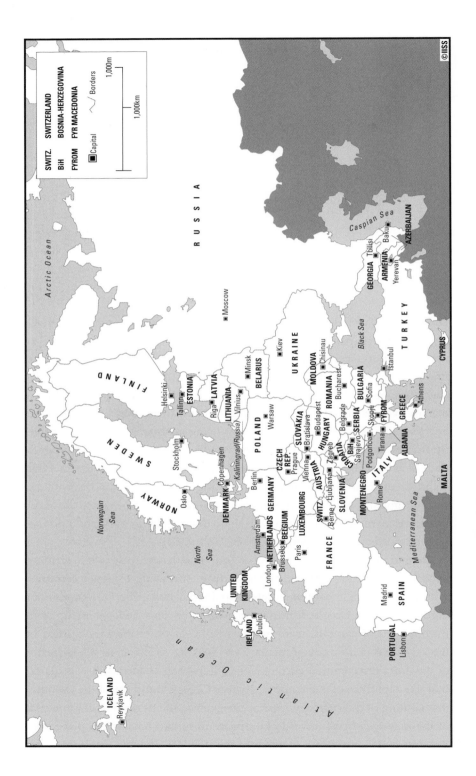

fulcrum of the currency – was determined that the euro should be preserved on its terms, through the adoption by other countries of the same degree of fiscal discipline as its own. This seemed unrealistic. The impatience of some European taxpayers with bailouts of troubled debtors in order to preserve the euro was seen, for example, in the strong electoral performance of Finland's True Finns party.

With the financial system in a precarious state, all European governments were fervently hoping that the spending cuts they were making to reduce their deficits and debts would not stall or reverse slow economic recoveries. If this were to happen, they would face longer periods with high unemployment and resulting political pressures. In addition, they would not be able to improve their fiscal positions, thus adding to the risk of a more general financial crisis engulfing Europe, potentially condemning it to a 1930s-style depression. As of mid-2011, all of these issues remained in the balance, with no clear outcome predictable.

Finance and economics were not the only causes of squabbles in Europe. France and the United Kingdom led a NATO effort to help rebels in Libya, with some other European countries in support. But Germany and other countries did not take part – though this decision prompted criticism and introspection in Berlin. In Germany, a reshaping of the party-political loyalties seemed to be under way, while in France and Russia there was great uncertainty about the likely outcome of the presidential elections in 2012. Turkey was being forced to reassess its foreign policy in light of the upheavals in the Arab world.

Germany: Economically Strong, Politically Adrift?

The solid growth of the German economy, which continued to recover relatively quickly from the economic crisis of 2008–09, underlined its importance as a driving force in Europe. With growth forecast at about 3% for 2011 and about 2% in 2012, the budget deficit was expected to fall to 2% of GDP in 2011 and to 1.2% in 2012, well below the level of most European countries. A significant drop in unemployment, which stood at 7.3% in April 2011 compared to 8.1% a year earlier, completed the picture of robust economic performance in the year to June.

However, the government was determined not to allow the strong tax receipts that derived from a growing economy to dilute its plans to reduce spending so as to restrict the budget deficit. It insisted that a provision inserted into the German constitution in 2009 limiting structural deficit spending to 0.35% of GDP by 2016 left little room for any relaxation. Thus, there was continuing pressure on the budgets of government ministries, including defence. Plans for cuts in defence personnel therefore moved ahead.

On the political side, however, the situation became more confused as voters shook up the balance of power between political parties by basing their voting intentions to a greater extent on short-term perceptions of competence and less on long-term party allegiances. Preoccupation with these party-political power shifts contributed to a leadership gap on important foreign-policy questions, causing consternation among key allies.

Political realignment

With the next federal election due in 2013, electoral contests at the state level served as a bellwether of the political mood. Seven state elections were scheduled in 2011 alone, and were expected to have an impact on the federal level as well, in particular since the trends of the year to mid-2011 pointed to a further fragmentation of the political system and a structural majority for left-of-centre parties.

Political support was moving away from the coalition government led by Chancellor Angela Merkel. Polling data from May 2011 put the partnership between her Christian Democratic Union (CDU) and the Christian Social Union (CSU) at 31–35%, compared to its 33.8% in the 2009 federal elections. Merkel, seen as having failed to define and implement a clear leadership position on the eurozone crisis and related bail outs, was unable to convert positive economic news into political capital. However, this grouping's coalition partner, the Free Democratic Party (FDP) was the biggest loser in the political realignment that seemed to be under way. Its support dropped to 4–5% in 2011 from 14.6% in 2009; a key factor was that the tax breaks promised by the FDP during the election campaign were blocked by Merkel because of the overall economic situation. The biggest winners were the Greens, polling at 22–26% compared to 10.7% in the 2009 elections, gaining especially from their positions on energy policy. In May 2011 their candidate became governor of the state of Baden-Württemberg as head of the first Green-led coalition at state level. With the Social Democratic Party (SPD) unable to recover from its poor showing of 23% in 2009, hovering between 22% and 28% in the polls, it was clear that Germany was no longer dominated by the two-party system, in which smaller parties such as the FDP or the Greens only served to help the larger CDU/CSU or SPD to form governments. The days when voter allegiances remained stable over time were over, and the hierarchy among the political parties was unclear.

These developments contributed to some surprising policy choices, including a 180-degree turn in nuclear policy following the Fukushima accident in Japan. The government had earlier attracted strong criticism from the Green party when it reversed a decision by a previous government to gradually phase out nuclear energy. With Merkel acutely conscious of the political sensitiveness of the nuclear issue and the rise of the Greens, the events in Japan produced yet another turn-around. In spring 2011 she argued that the Fukushima accident had underlined that the residual risks of nuclear energy had to be taken seriously, even in societies as advanced as Japan and Germany. Parties in her coalition then agreed to close all 17 of Germany's nuclear plants by 2022 – a decision that some elements of Merkel's own party found less than credible. One of her cabinet ministers reportedly told a gathering of German business leaders that the turn-around was not a rational decision but rather was heavily influenced by electoral politics. Nonetheless, after elections in the small state of Bremen on 22 May saw a weak showing for the CDU, which came in third behind the SPD and the Greens, Merkel again homed in on energy policy as the key to recovering domestic support.

Abstention on Libya

On the international level, Germany caused a stir when, having just been elected to the UN Security Council as a temporary member, it abstained in the 17 March vote on Resolution 1973 authorising military action to protect civilians in Libya. According to media reports in Germany, Foreign Minister Guido Westerwelle of the FDP, influenced by concerns that a new military engagement would be unpopular domestically and would offer only limited chances for success, even considered voting against the resolution. After further consultations between Westerwelle, Merkel and Defence Minister Thomas de Maizière, the government settled on abstention.

This decision unleashed a barrage of criticism from both international and domestic observers, who argued Germany had proved to be an unreliable partner, particularly to its allies France, Portugal, Britain and the United States who had voted for the resolution. In abstaining, Germany found itself in the company of Russia and of rising powers Brazil, China and India. The vote caused much soul-searching among Germany's foreign- and security-policy establishment and irritation among NATO partners. Former Foreign Minister Joschka Fischer (Greens) called it a 'scandalous mistake' and former Defence Minister Volker Rühe (CDU) said it was 'plain wrong'. Both saw the abstention as an unwarranted break with German foreign-policy traditions, which had always placed a premium on reliability and being a dependable ally. In the future, Fischer and Rühe implied, who would agree to tie their fate to a Germany capable of such unpredictable behaviour? Other observers added that, even allowing for the well-understood and deeply ingrained German reluctance to use military force, the decision to abstain was worrying. If the use of force, based on broad international support (including that of actors in the region) to protect civilians against a murderous regime was not acceptable, some asked, when would Germany ever make a contribution to international peace and security in the future?

The government tried to counter the impression that it was isolated by compensating on other fronts. Whereas Germany had earlier refused to allow its personnel to serve on NATO AWACS planes deployed to Afghanistan on the grounds that this was not covered by the mandate agreed with parliament, it indicated that it would do so in the future to support the sustainability of the AWACS deployment. Merkel furthermore said that the abstention did not imply Germany would be neutral with regard to the situation in Libya. Once the resolution had passed, she said, 'it became our resolution as well'.

Despite such attempts to regain the initiative, the decision was still seen by critics as having been taken with little regard for or understanding of its wider international repercussions. Westerwelle's reported comments that in future Germany might regularly choose its partners based on specific issues did nothing to dispel this impression. On the contrary: it seemed to ignore the importance that multilateral frameworks have had for German security policy in recent decades.

While some commentators in Germany expressed the view that the subsequent difficulties experienced by the NATO-led coalition, and the persistence of the Gadhafi regime in Libya, justified the abstention in retrospect, the episode looked unlikely to provide a guide to German foreign policy in the future. The strong domestic and international backlash reinforced the view that Germany could only implement an effective foreign and security policy as a predictable and reliable partner to its long-standing allies and partners, working through international institutions, first and foremost NATO and the EU. Rather than representing the beginning of a re-orientation of German security policy, the abstention looked likely to be an aberration.

Reform reloaded – new beginnings for the Bundeswehr?

One area where re-orientation was intended was the armed forces, with the Bundeswehr set to undergo wide-ranging change in coming years. While the political leadership at the top of the Ministry of Defence changed in March 2011 when the highly popular Karl-Theodor zu Guttenberg had to step down over embarrassing revelations that he had plagiarised large parts of his PhD thesis, the basic reform parameters remained fairly stable. New minister Thomas de Maizière, however, a long-time confidant of Merkel and a former interior minister, ushered in a new policymaking style. The son of former Chief of Defence General Ulrich de Maizière, his attention to detail and focus on process contrasted markedly with the extrovert zu Guttenberg, who had promoted big ideas without worrying too much about follow-through.

As in many other European countries, budgetary pressures, persistent capability gaps and operational demands had already led to efforts at defence reform. In spring 2010, the Finance Ministry had called for cuts in defence expenditure, and in June the cabinet decided that some €8.3bn should be cut between 2011 and 2014, almost half from personnel costs. A Ministry of Defence task force reviewing procurement projects reported on 25 June 2010, identifying possible cuts totalling approximately €9.4bn ($11.0bn). In September Chief of Defence General Volker Wieker reported on the implications of a cut of 40,000 in the number of active forces for Germany's defence policy, operations, procurement, force posture, conscription and ability to fulfil its alliance obligations.

The key purpose of the report was to analyse whether different force structures might help make the Bundeswehr a more effective, flexible and deployable force (see *The Military Balance 2011*, pages 82–3). A previous restructuring of the armed forces into force categories with different capabilities had not yielded the envisioned increases in force-projection capacity. Wieker argued that crisis response and stabilisation were part of a continuum, not separate phases, and it was therefore not possible to maintain separate force categories. The level of ambition for the Bundeswehr, he suggested, should be a sustainable deployment of 10,000 troops across several simultaneous operations, compared to the previous, unobtainable target of 14,000.

A core assumption was that savings targets could only be met by reducing numbers of both military and civilian personnel. Wieker, in line with zu Guttenberg's preferences, recommended a level of 156,000 professional soldiers augmented by 7,500 so-called voluntary conscripts (or short-term volunteers), a posture seen in the Ministry of Defence as the absolute minimum Germany needed to fulfil its national and alliance obligations. Under the plans proposed by zu Guttenberg, compulsory conscription was to be abolished, since the budget crunch demanded structural reform and contemporary security challenges had further undermined the rationale behind maintaining large contingents of conscripts who could not be used on modern operations. This was highly controversial, but after a short, heated political debate, in January 2011 the last cohort of conscripts began their six-month service.

De Maizière thus inherited the parameters of cost reduction and a smaller but more capable Bundeswehr without conscription when he took over as defence minister in March 2011. In May, he published Defence Policy Guidelines, replacing a previous version from 2003.

The guidelines revealed important tensions. On the one hand, they argued that the Bundeswehr needed the resources to play a role corresponding to Germany's political weight. On the other hand, they stressed that the defence budget would have to contribute to the government's overall budget consolidation course. The expectations created by Germany's international role looked likely to be used as grounds to reduce the savings targets agreed in 2010. Finance Minister Wolfgang Schäuble agreed to extend by one year, to 2015, the period within which the defence cuts had to be achieved. Unconfirmed media reports in May speculated that de Maizière had, moreover, succeeded in reducing the savings target to between €4.5–6.5bn.

Another tension lay in the shift of priority away from international crisis-management operations towards territorial defence, even though international crisis prevention and crisis management were seen as likely to impose the greatest operational demands on the Bundeswehr. It was unclear how the tension between what was judged most likely and what was judged most important would be resolved, in particular since de Maizière declared to the Bundestag that in the future some overseas deployments would be driven by international obligations even if a distinct German national interest was absent. The assumption of the guidelines appeared to be that most capabilities needed for territorial and alliance defence would also be relevant for international crisis-management missions.

Finally, the guidelines flagged up the question of recruitment. With the discontinuation of conscription, the Bundeswehr lost a major recruitment tool; a proportion of conscripts had always signed up to become professional soldiers. Demographic trends in Germany added to the worry: the overall talent pool will be smaller in future, setting up fierce competition between employers. Plans to make service in the armed forces more attractive were still under development in May, with the last batch of conscripts ending their service at the end of June. Initially there had been some difficulty recruiting voluntary conscripts, but the Ministry of Defence reported some 9,400 were recruited in the first five months of 2011.

Several other decisions were announced by de Maizière in May 2011. He explained that reform plans would be implemented within a 6–8 year time frame. The Bundeswehr would have a total strength of 170,000 professional soldiers plus 5,000–15,000 voluntary conscripts, compared to its existing strength of 220,000 including some 188,000 professionals. Civilian staff was to be cut from some 75,000 to 55,000. Staff at the ministry would be reduced from 3,500 to 2,000, although most of this would be achieved by removing the service chiefs and their staffs from the ministry rather than elimination of jobs. The number of departments in the ministry would be reduced from 17 to nine. All services were asked to streamline their command structures by eliminating one level of hierarchy, and the distinction into three different tiers with different levels of capability was to be abandoned. The army would be reduced to three divisions and the number of brigades from 11 to eight.

Further announcements were expected for summer 2011 after a July cabinet meeting which was to set the ultimate financial parameters, and de Maizière was expected to announce key decisions on basing in the autumn. He indicated that he was against concentrating the armed forces in a number of large bases, saying that basing decisions would be driven by a mix of factors including functions, cost, attractiveness and maintaining a geographical balance throughout Germany.

When he resigned, zu Guttenberg claimed that the ground was well prepared for his successor to implement wide-ranging reforms. Although the media reported sources within the ministry suggesting that in fact there were still many loose ends, even after de Maizière's May policy initiative, the reforms in fact appeared to be following rather closely the path zu Guttenberg had established. At mid-2011 it remained to be seen whether Bundeswehr reform, which, as the experience of many European partners has shown, would cost money before it could save money, would be adequately resourced. The European debt crisis and the fundamental shift in German energy policy would continue to have significant financial implications in the years to come. There was pressure on the governing coalition to turn at least one of these three big agenda items into a success if it wanted to break free of the domestic constraints that had become all too apparent.

France: Sarkozy's Electoral Challenge

France, under President Nicolas Sarkozy, yet again played a hyper-active role on the European and world stage over the past year. But despite a number of leadership initiatives and policy successes, Sarkozy's popularity continued to fall, reaching 30% in spring 2011, an all-time low in the history of the Fifth Republic. Some pollsters even predicted that, assuming the president stands for re-election in 2012, he could be nudged into third place in the first round of voting by Marine Le Pen, the new leader of the right-wing National Front. In spring 2011, France was consumed by speculation about the 2012 presidential race which, although still a year away, was already moving into high gear. A political tsunami was unleashed on 14 May when Dominique Strauss-Kahn, managing director of the International Monetary Fund, who in most polls was the clear favourite to win the French presidency in 2012, was arrested in New York and charged with attempted rape of a hotel chambermaid. This made predictions about the political future somewhat hazardous.

Domestic politics: reshuffling the pack

In January 2011, Marine Le Pen, the 42-year-old lawyer and daughter of the National Front's founding figurehead, Jean-Marie Le Pen, fought off several internal challenges to win the presidency of the party, with over 67% of the votes cast. Transcending her father's narrow nationalism, and his anti-semitic and anti-immigrant obsessions, she astutely positioned the party as the defender of the traditional working classes against the predations of the elite Parisian political class. By virtue of the fact that she is a woman, a party that had been associated with virility and the cult of leadership became instantly more mainstream. While appealing to the younger generation of dissatisfied French voters, she also struck a chord with growing numbers of French men and women by comparing Muslim prayers in the street (outside over-packed mosques) with the German occupation. Her new brand of populist nationalism was no longer seen in France as an embarrassment. The growth and electoral success of similar populist parties in Austria, Finland, Hungary, Italy, the Netherlands and Sweden has made this form of politics appear less extreme. Growing numbers of voters no longer feel ashamed to admit their affiliation with the party.

Le Pen has attracted high-profile support from across the political spectrum and has gradually distanced the party from the politics of extremism. Unlike her father, who considered the Holocaust to be a historical 'footnote', she has denounced Nazi concentration camps as 'the height of barbarity' and forbidden the use of the Nazi salute at party rallies. In short, she has introduced a new equation into French politics by combining populism, state-enhanced capitalism with Gaullist and even Colbertist echoes, markedly left-wing social policies, secularism and women's rights. Voters disillusioned with either Sarkozy's right-of-centre Union pour un Mouvement Populaire (UMP) party or the left-of-centre Socialist Party now have much less difficulty in switching to Le Pen's National Front. Several polls have suggested that, in the first round of voting in the 2012 presidential elections, she would actually receive more votes than either of the two mainstream parties, thus ensuring a place in the second round run-off. French politics is undergoing a serious shake-up.

Within the UMP itself, Sarkozy's authoritarian style of government has alienated many from the centre-right and there have been constant rumours of a split, in which a new, more moderate right-wing party might be formed to contest the 2012 presidential election around a candidate such as popular former Environment Minister Jean-Louis Borloo. In June 2010, former Prime Minister Dominique de Villepin – a bitter Sarkozy rival – formed his own political movement, République Solidaire, as a centre-right alternative to the UMP. However, a multiplication of right-wing candidates in the first round of voting would merely increase Le Pen's chances of making it to the second round. It remains to be seen whether the UMP establishment can persuade potential dissenters to rally round the increasingly disliked president in order to block Le Pen. The UMP has also been hit by scandal; two ministers, Alain Joyandet and Christian Blanc, were forced to resign in June 2010 over improper use of public funds and Michèle Alliot-Marie, the high-profile foreign minister, was forced out in February 2011 because of her controversial connections with the former Tunisian leader Zine el-Abidine Ben Ali. Eric Woerth, minister of labour, was also eased out of office in November 2010 as a result of scandals involving his wife's financial dealings with Liliane Bettencourt, France's richest woman, and the sale of a racetrack in Compiègne, currently under investigation by judicial authorities. Le Monde accused Sarkozy of using the French intelligence services to spy on the journalist who broke these stories. In late May, a junior minister and close associate of Sarkozy, Georges Tron, was also fired after accusations by several women of sexual harassment. Sarkozy, whose extravagant lifestyle is heavily criticised, was himself not immune from accusations. When it became clear in spring 2011 that his wife Carla Bruni was expecting a baby, some took their dislike for the president so far as to suggest that the pregnancy had been planned to coincide with the presidential campaign. Both the National Front and the Socialist Party intended to score political points by attacking Sarkozy's lifestyle. That course was subsequently denied to the Socialists by the Strauss-Kahn scandal, handing Le Pen a monopoly of the moral electoral high ground.

In characteristic style, Sarkozy attempted to staunch the haemorrhage of right-wing supporters flowing towards the National Front by launching an attack on Roma immigrants and by making tough noises about crime. In July 2010, Interior Minister Brice Hortefeux announced plans to close down around 300 Roma encampments across the country by force, following violence in which police shot dead a male traveller. Hundreds of Roma were repatriated to Bulgaria and Romania. Of 400,000 Roma in France, around 95% are French citizens, but the government aimed to make maximum political capital out of the expulsion of non-French travellers who had made their way across Europe in the wake of Bulgarian and Romanian accession to the EU in 2004. The campaign was part of a government offensive which linked immigration, crime and citizenship. Declaring a 'war on crime', Sarkozy threatened to strip any naturalised French person of their citizenship if they were found guilty of committing a crime against 'an agent of public authority'. Two days later, Hortefeux announced a similar measure against naturalised citizens of foreign birth who engaged in polygamy, female circumcision, trafficking or other serious crimes. Associated measures were announced to make immigration and the granting of French citizenship more difficult. In August, Industry Minister and Mayor of Nice Christian Estrosi went one step further, proposing that mayors who failed to crack down on immigrant crime should be fined. The explicit linkage between immigration and crime (for which there is no direct statistical evidence) was a blatant political ploy, roundly denounced by jurists and human-rights groups not only because it violated Article 1 of the French Constitution which proclaims the 'equality of all citizens before the law, without distinction of origin, race or religion', but also because it revived memories of the Vichy regime's withdrawal of citizenship from Jews during the Second World War. It also appeared to breach the 1961 UN Convention on the Reduction of Statelessness and the 1997 Council of Europe Convention on Nationality. In late September, the European Commission, in the context of an attempt to generate a trans-European policy on the Roma, whose population is estimated at some 12m, initiated proceedings against France for non-compliance with EU legislation on the free movement of people. Commission Vice President Viviane Reding, whose brief covers justice, human rights and citizenship, called the new French policies 'a disgrace'. There was no evidence that this 'war on crime' won back voters seduced by Le Pen. In the first round of voting for cantonal elections on 20 March 2011, the National Front won 15% of the vote (its highest ever) against only 20% for the UMP. Generalised disaffection with politics translated into a 55% abstention rate.

Another instance of the government's concern about the rise of the National Front was the enactment on 11 April 2011 of a law banning the wearing of the burqa or niqab in public places. Interior Minister Claude Guéant insisted that the law, which imposes an automatic fine of €150 on any woman wearing these coverings in public, would be applied systematically. Police unions, however, insisted that it would be impossible to enforce. It is believed there are no more than several hundred women in the whole of France who wear the burqa. By May, the government was claiming that some 30 women had been stopped, required to uncover their face, and fined. But human-rights organisations and constitutional lawyers claimed that the law was not being applied in part because the police were unwilling to intervene. A lobby group, Touche Pas à Ma Constitution (Hands off my Constitution), organised by a French-Algerian businessman, Rachid Nekkaz, raised over €1m to pay any fines levied. However, as of mid-2011 the group insisted that not a single woman had yet been charged with an offence. There were several instances (including one in front of Notre Dame cathedral in Paris the day the law came into force) of burqa-clad women challenging the police to arrest them – without success. The law appeared to have had no real effect.

History will judge Sarkozy on his stewardship of the economy, and in particular the success of his election promises to transform the state and its finances by cutting public-sector jobs and balancing the budget. During the crucial 12 month run-up to the 2012 election, France faced a potential vicious circle of public-spending cuts, rising unemployment and inadequate growth against the backdrop of a cross-party consensus on the need to reduce both the government debt (rising from 84% of GDP in 2010 to 89% in 2011) and the budget deficit (7.7% of GDP in 2010, with a government promise to reduce it to 6% by the end of 2011 and to 3%, the eurozone's common target, by 2013). The 2011 budget, setting out these targets and presented to parliament on 29 September 2010, was predicated on a growth forecast of 2%. This was questioned immediately by the European Commission, which predicted a growth rate of only 1.5%, and by the OECD in November, with a forecast of 1.6%. Domestically, controversy centred around the speed at which the deficit and the debt could be reduced without damaging the overall health of the public finances. In February 2011, Sarkozy aligned himself with German

Chancellor Angela Merkel in embracing a fast-track reduction schedule, which they insisted should be matched by all EU member states. France introduced legislation to make a 'debt-brake' a constitutional requirement aimed at balancing the budget, a measure adopted by Germany in 2009. In March 2011, Sarkozy and Merkel together drove proposals for harsh discipline on euro-area economic governance through the European Council as the price member states should be required to pay for German acquiescence in maintaining the European Financial Stability Facility agreed in May 2010 to help eurozone countries facing debt problems.

However, the challenge of pulling off this precarious balancing act in France was exacerbated by predictions of growing unemployment (10.5% in 2011) and by Sarkozy's reluctance to increase taxes. His abandonment in spring 2011 of the controversial 'fiscal shield' that had protected those with high incomes, while politically unavoidable, was not expected significantly to affect tax receipts. The last time France succeeded in balancing the budget was in the 1970s, and the last example of the scale of fiscal consolidation being attempted by Sarkozy dates from the 1960s. Economists remained sceptical that he would meet his own ambitious objectives. Meanwhile, the 2007 promise to replace only one out of every two retiring public-sector workers had proved virtually impossible to implement. Of the 2.5m civil-servant positions on the state payroll, approximately 200,000 were expected to disappear by 2013, mainly in the education and research fields. Plans were hastily drawn up in late 2010 to cut another 100,000 positions by 2014.

However, the government's determination in taking on the trade unions over pension reform (see *Strategic Survey 2010*) paid off handsomely when the reform bill was enacted in November 2010, raising the minimum age for pension entitlement from 60 to 62, and the age for a full pension from 65 to 67. The passage of this central reform through the National Assembly and the Senate was accompanied by mass demonstrations and strikes (particularly of workers at oil refineries, which closed down 25% of petrol stations in October). The 'days of protest' continued from late September until early November, but merely demonstrated the ineffectiveness of France's labour unions, with membership rates below 10% of the workforce and falling credibility. By the end of the protests, public opinion, facing the inevitability of the reform, was abandoning the unions, without moving towards political support for Sarkozy. Finance Minister Christine Lagarde hailed the measures as concrete proof of France's ability to put its budgetary house in order, but the reform represented little more than a stop-gap measure which would only help offset the cost of public-sector pensions, estimated at 1.7% of GDP, until 2018. Estimates suggested that, without a new pension reform bill in 2018, France would face a pensions deficit of €100bn by 2050.

Foreign and security policy

Overseas, France played a visible and active role in several major theatres. The signature of the Franco-British Defence and Security Cooperation Treaty in November 2010 was a step towards recognition, by both parties, that their mutual national ambition to play a major role on the international stage was being squeezed by budgetary realities and that the only way to retain international influence in this field was through cooperation. Several key areas were highlighted: a combined joint expeditionary force, an integrated aircraft-carrier strike group, a common support plan for A400M transport aircraft, joint development of equipment and technologies for the next generation of nuclear submarines, military satellite communications, unmanned air surveillance and eventually combat systems. These assets go to the heart of both countries' military ambitions and the treaty represented further recognition of their shared strategic interests. While both countries stressed that they had 'a shared vision as to the future of the NATO alliance', the reality was that the UK was one of the NATO member states most favourable towards expeditionary operations of the Afghan type, whereas France was much more dubious about NATO becoming a global alliance. More significantly, however, France had always promoted an autonomous form of European security and defence cooperation (the Common Security and Defence Policy, CSDP), whereas the UK had stressed synergies between NATO and CSDP. The question most analysts were asking after the signature of the treaty was whether it would function as a complement to CSDP or as an alternative. Would those member states less keen to play a military role through CSDP or NATO see the Franco-British lead as encouragement to follow suit, or would they see it as an opportunity to continue free-riding? Some answers appeared to come during the Libyan operation in spring 2011 (see below).

Alongside the Franco-British initiative, which reflected the Atlanticist dimension of France's strategic posture, were two other dimensions, continental and Mediterranean, which Paris had always sought to keep in balance. The continental dimension, over and above the permanence of Franco-German cooperation on economic and monetary matters, was reflected in France's continuing support for CSDP, actively promoted during the French presidency of the EU in 2008, and which in 2011 found expression through 'Weimar Triangle' discussions between France, Germany and Poland. In particular, a series of high-level meetings in spring 2011 saw Poland (which had increasingly re-calibrated its enthusiasm for NATO in favour of CSDP) embrace the Franco-German dynamic behind an autonomous EU operational planning facility. The three countries also made common cause in sending a joint letter to EU High Representative Catherine Ashton enjoining her to devote more energy to CSDP, an invitation which seemingly fell on deaf ears.

The results for the Mediterranean dimension of France's strategic posture were decidedly mixed. The much-hyped 2007 launch of the Union for the Mediterranean proved in 2011 to be a damp squib as the organisation demonstrated its irrelevance during the Arab Awakening. Paris was caught off guard by events in Tunisia, a former colony, and Egypt. In the former case, the embarrassing December 2010 offer to the Ben Ali regime of French tear gas and riot police, made by then Foreign Minister Alliot-Marie, who was at the time enjoying the hospitality of the Tunisian president, was only marginally compensated for when Sarkozy refused Ben Ali and his family access to French air space during their precipitate flight from Tunis on 14 January. France was hardly more imaginative when Egypt also erupted and the government found itself, like its counterparts in other Western capitals, faced with deciding how to react to the likely downfall of a long-time ally, President Hosni Mubarak. On 10 February, Sarkozy came out in support of democracy in Egypt and gambled on the eventual fall of Mubarak, but then immediately warned that the West could not afford to connive in the rise to power in Egypt of the Muslim Brotherhood, suggesting that such a develop- ment would be worse than the status quo. This was hardly bold diplomacy, considering that US President Barack Obama had called for the departure of Mubarak a week earlier.

Sarkozy tried hard to correct for France's embarrassing or inadequate reactions to momentous events in Europe's southern neighbours through his policy towards Libya. In a prime-time television address on 27 February, the president announced his determination to 'accompany, support and assist people who have chosen to be free'. He immediately engaged both London and Washington over possible military action, was the first to call for Gadhafi to step down, energetically co-sponsored UNSCR 1973 on the imposition of a no-fly zone, and was the first, on 10 March, to formally recog- nise the Benghazi-based Transitional National Council. In all of this he was far ahead of his foreign minister, Alain Juppé, who counselled against most of these actions. France was also the first country to engage Gadhafi's forces militarily, on 19 March, in an effort to prevent a bloodbath in Benghazi, even before the UN-backed coalition had been formally created. Faced with

Obama's reluctance to lead the anti-Gadhafi coalition, Sarkozy attempted to persuade British Prime Minister David Cameron to operationalise the Franco-British Treaty by creating a European command centre, but encountered resistance from both London (which preferred to involve NATO) and Ankara (which was determined to prevent France from exercising too much influence). Resigning itself to accepting a NATO lead, France nevertheless became, along with the UK, the lead nation in *Operation Unified Protector*, flying between 30 and 40 sorties per day, using *Rafale* (air and naval versions), *Mirage* 2000D, *Mirage* 2000-5, *Mirage* F-1CR and *Super Etendard* strike aircraft, C-135 refuelling aircraft, E3F & E2C *Hawkeye* AWACS aircraft. The air campaign was supported by the deployment of a carrier group around the *Charles de Gaulle,* comprising a refuelling tanker, four frigates, a nuclear attack submarine and a full complement of helicopters. The air assets were deployed from a variety of bases in France and Crete. France was responsible for 20% of all NATO sorties and 30% of all ground attack missions, as of the beginning of June. Ironically, Sarkozy was reported to have engaged in sharp exchanges with Obama, protesting the US president's decision to take a back seat in the Libyan mission. In the absence of American ground-attack aircraft, France (along with Britain) began, in late May, to deploy attack helicopters in an attempt to engage Gadhafi's light assets in an urban environment. Sarkozy thus used the Libyan mission as a demonstration of France's capacity for power projection in Europe's near abroad.

Libya was not the only operation in the past year in which French military forces were engaged. In the protracted stand-off in Côte d'Ivoire between outgoing president Laurent Gbagbo and the universally recognised winner of the November 2010 presidential election, Alassane Ouattara, France played a decisive role. As the conflict degenerated into a civil war which the 9,000 UN peacekeepers were unable to control, a Security Council resolution on 4 April 2011 authorised French and UN forces to intervene in support of Ouattara. After four days of action against Gbagbo's presidential residence in Abidjan, defended by 1,000 loyalists, French forces were able to create the conditions under which Ouattara's troops could arrest the former president, bringing the increasingly deadly civil war to an end. Sarkozy capitalised on this success by attending Ouattara's inauguration ceremony in Abidjan on 21 May, putting an end to over a decade of French decline in its former colony. Sarkozy's personal friendship with Ouattara and his French wife Dominique was a factor in his decision to reverse a plan, outlined in the 2008 Defence White Paper, to abandon the French military presence in Côte d'Ivoire and reduce France's pre-positioned forces in Africa to just two bases: Libreville (Gabon) and Djibouti. The 43rd marine infantry battalion, based in Abidjan, was therefore to remain, albeit in slimmed-down form. Sarkozy's 2008 announcement in Cape Town that France 'will not maintain forces in Africa indefinitely' appeared to have been put on hold.

France thus demonstrated in 2011 that it was capable of deploying significant forces in three missions simultaneously (Libya, Côte d'Ivoire and Afghanistan), and the French media did not hesitate to contrast this with Germany's diffidence about power projection. Moreover, France also launched a Sahel Plan to offer military assistance to the governments of Algeria, Mali, Mauritania and Niger, which were facing increasing incursions from al-Qaeda in the Islamic Maghreb, a group also responsible for the kidnapping and murder of several French citizens. None of this, however, succeeded in reassuring the many sectors of France's military which faced massive cuts and restructuring as a result of the 2008 White Paper. Twenty regiments and battalions, 11 air bases and one naval air base were scheduled for closure by 2016, and 54,000 jobs were to be lost.

In November 2010, France assumed the presidencies of the G8 and the G20, for which Sarkozy proposed ambitious agendas. The G8 meeting in Deauville in May 2011 was devoted in part to an examination of the role in global affairs of the Internet, which Sarkozy characterised as the third globalising event in human history (after the voyages of discovery and the industrial revolution). However, the summit, which was widely seen as an attempt on the part of the West to retain its leadership in international affairs, failed to generate any new policy with respect to global governance or the Arab Awakening. It was through the G20 that France held out the greatest hope of reforming global governance. An initial meeting of G20 finance ministers in February 2011 opened the three main chapters of the French agenda: international monetary reform; the need to correct the volatility of commodity prices (see essay, pages 109–18); and the reform of global governance. On monetary reform, the French desire to supplement the dollar as the world's single reserve currency involved a proposal to include the renmimbi in the mix of currencies that form the basis of IMF special drawing rights. The United States opposed such a move. A proposal to create a Joint Agricultural Data Initiative, based on the G8's Joint Oil Data Initiative, gathered support but faced an obstacle in the divergent interests within the G20 between agricultural exporters and importers. Proposals on reform of the UN, greater integration between the G20 and the IMF, and creation of a permanent G20 secretariat proved difficult to move beyond the conceptual stage. The French agenda, which also included proposals on strengthening the social dimension of globalisation, financial regulation, supporting global employment and accelerating development, was widely seen as overly ambitious. The test of Sarkozy's persuasiveness was to be the Cannes summit, set for November 2011.

The legendary energy of France's mercurial president continued, in 2010–11, to make headlines. His political successes appeared to have outnumbered his setbacks. Yet the polls continued to reveal a man who was simply disliked by his countrymen as well as by many of his political colleagues. With the prospect of a Strauss-Kahn candidacy in the crucial 2012 elections, pundits had more or less written off Sarkozy as a one-term president. But after Strauss-Kahn's arrest in New York, Sarkozy seemed to have been granted a reprieve.

United Kingdom: Spending Cuts Cause Strains

The uncertain election result of May 2010 had a remarkable outcome. The coalition it produced, Britain's first since the 1930s, might have been thought to be built on shaky foundations – and in the end, this may still prove to be the case. But the Conservative Party, which came first in the election, and the Liberal Democrats, who came third, combined to produce a government with reformist zeal. Though it inherited wrecked finances and an economy that was barely afloat, its ambitions went far beyond righting the ship. Rather, it embarked on a far-reaching reform programme of which the central theme was to reduce the might of central government after 13 years of interventionist Labour Party rule.

Among the areas for which the government produced proposals for substantial change were the state-funded health-care system, welfare benefits, universities, schools, local government and immigration. The plans far exceeded promises that either party had made in their election manifestos. What made them particularly challenging in political terms was the fact that the coalition was at the same time pressing ahead with steep reductions in government spending to reduce the budget deficit – cuts that, if fully enacted, would eliminate hundreds of thousands of public-sector jobs. Although the electorate seemed to accept that austerity measures were necessary, these had yet to take full effect. Political storms looked likely in coming years.

Most of the government's programme was pursued with a surprising degree of unity by the coalition partners. But by mid-2011, strains were visible. Voting reform, a centrepiece of the Liberal Democrat programme,

was easily defeated in a referendum, putting pressure on a party leadership that had already had to swallow a sharp rise in students' university
tuition fees, which the party membership and many MPs strongly opposed.
Deputy Prime Minister Nick Clegg, leader of the Liberal Democrats, also
faced difficulties from party members over perceived threats to the principle of state-provided health care. He was under pressure to maintain the
party's separate identity and not to align it too closely to the Conservatives.
Coalition was proving to be a bruising experience for him.

The first year of the new government also brought important developments in defence. Prime Minister David Cameron quickly set a deadline of
the end of 2014 for the withdrawal of British combat troops from Afghanistan
– a goal later agreed by other NATO countries. He oversaw a rapid, cost-
cutting defence review that reduced personnel numbers and scrapped
several equipment programmes, provoking predictable complaints from the
military community. But Cameron, whose priorities were clearly in domestic
rather than foreign affairs, then became the latest British prime minister to
be attracted to a military adventure. With French President Nicolas Sarkozy,
he took a leading role in advocating and executing the UN-backed intervention in Libya – a mission that, at mid-2011, was threatening to become a
long-term undertaking.

Politics tempers wave of reforms

Both partners in the coalition came into government following disap-
pointing performances in the election. The Conservatives failed to win a
parliamentary majority in spite of the financial and economic mess and even
though Gordon Brown's leadership as prime minister was widely seen as
poor. Cameron faced criticism from within his party, especially from the
right wing, for failing to define Tory policies clearly enough. He was handi-
capped, however, by the weak state of the nation's finances and perhaps by
a sense that the electorate still broadly supported the large resources being
poured by the previous Labour government into public services: he promised, for example, not to cut funding for health care.

The Liberal Democrats, the latest incarnation of what had been the
third party in British politics since the Liberals fell from prominence in
the 1920s, only marginally improved their vote share and in fact lost seats
in parliament, even though the previously little-known Clegg had shot to
fame during Britain's first live televised electoral debates between party
leaders. A hung parliament had been widely forecast, but if a coalition was
to emerge, it had been thought likely to be between Labour and the Liberal

Democrats. They held talks, but could not muster a majority, which would have required a wider coalition with several minor parties with competing agendas. In any case, Clegg had said the party with the largest number of seats – the Conservatives, in the event – should have the opportunity to govern. Cameron's move on the day after the election to make a 'big, open and comprehensive offer' to the Liberal Democrats proved decisive.

The parties found a surprising amount of common ground, in spite of the right-wing elements of Conservative doctrine and the more left-wing aspects of Liberal Democrat policies (for example, favouring the abolition of Britain's nuclear deterrent). They agreed on devolving power away from the centre so as to boost the role of local communities, on cutting bureaucracy and on promoting civil liberties following a period of greater state intrusion into the private lives of citizens. They also agreed on the need to go further than Labour in cutting the budget deficit so as to maintain the UK's triple-A credit rating in the bond markets, and that this would be done with a concept of fairness 'so that all those most in need are protected'. The two leaders said, however, that they wanted to do more than tackle the deficit: they set out a plan for 'era-changing, convention-challenging, radical reform', and acknowledged that they 'could never have predicted' the joint programme that they had produced.

Cameron and Clegg, both 43 on entering office, educated at top private schools and then respectively at Oxford and Cambridge universities, proceeded to develop a relationship that seemed professional and political rather than personally warm or close. They were, after all, the leaders of parties that wanted to remain separate.

The most radical reform proposed was to the National Health Service (NHS), which employs more people in Britain – 1.4 million – than any other organisation. In terms of improved experience for patients, this had been a success story of the Labour years, though the cost had risen sharply. Conservative Health Minister Andrew Lansley revealed plans to give family doctors (known as general practitioners) the power to commission hospital care for their patients, and so to be responsible for allocating much of the state's funding. They would form consortia, and these would have the freedom to choose private providers rather than state-run hospitals, thus introducing far more competition. More than 150 local bodies that currently manage commissioning of care would be abolished. Health care would remain free to the recipient, and in practice many NHS functions were already being carried out by private-sector providers. However, the changes posed both political problems (as fears were expressed about the 'privatisation' of health care) and practical challenges (as bodies representing all sectors of the NHS, including family doctors, raised objections). Cameron was forced in April to call a pause for a 'listening exercise', and in June he proposed to slow down the reforms and to include hospital doctors and nurses in commissioning care. Even after this rethink, he was still facing the possibility of an embarrassing reversal of course.

This was not the only area where enthusiasm for reform was tempered by political realities. A plan to sell off state-owned forests was dropped, and there were other concessions following protests. This suggested that political compromises might also have to be found in the much larger battles ahead over the effects of public spending cuts. Most departments faced reductions of about a quarter over four years. Because Cameron had promised an immediate defence review, the first since 1998, the Ministry of Defence was the first in which levels of future spending had to be hammered out in real detail, and the outcome was an 8% budget cut in real terms over four years, far less than the reduction of up to 20% that the government had targeted.

Defence cut as operations continue

Since the Balkan wars of the 1990s, the British armed forces, like those of other European countries, have had to cope with the tension between funding constraints and a high level of operational commitments. They were not helped by the fact that defence funding had become increasingly murky: while the 1998 defence review had struck a good match between foreign-policy aims and military capabilities, lax ministerial management later allowed policy to drift, to the extent that the coalition in 2010 faced some £38bn of unfunded commitments to equipment programmes. On top of this came the need to cut government spending: rapid and difficult decisions were needed on where to cut capabilities.

The Strategic Defence and Security Review (SDSR) did not boast the elaborate policy processes of 1998. It was, in the words of officials involved, 'quick and dirty'. And it could only do a partial job, because of the continuing commitment of 10,000 UK troops to Afghanistan. Although Cameron made clear that he wanted an end to the combat presence as soon as possible, the review had to accommodate the deployment. Hence, some cuts were taken immediately while others had to await the end of the Afghan mission, not least because of the political risk of being seen to undermine the forces while in the midst of a tough campaign.

This meant that the Royal Air Force and the Royal Navy took the brunt of the cuts. The £3.6bn *Nimrod* MRA4 airborne reconnaissance programme was axed, and the aircraft were immediately dismantled – before coming into service – so as to forestall second thoughts. *Sentinel* surveillance aircraft were to be withdrawn as soon as they have finished service in Afghanistan. The fast jet fleet was to be trimmed by a cut in *Tornado* aircraft and the end of the *Harrier*. The aircraft carrier *Ark Royal* was decommissioned and immediately put up for sale. The review's most controversial decision was to go without a carrier for 10 years until a new ship comes into service, operating a smaller number of US-made F-35 Joint Strike Fighters than had been previously planned. A second carrier was to continue to be built, so as to retain work for Scottish shipyards, but was to be mothballed. Several other naval ships are being decommissioned. There were also modest cuts in land forces.

The overall effect was to scale down the UK's expeditionary capacity while still retaining a broad range of capabilities so as to be flexible in uncertain times. Military personnel were to be reduced by 17,000 to 158,000 by 2015, and the number of defence civil servants by 25,000 to 60,000. Taken together with planned base closures, and redundancies in industry as a result of cancelled programmes, the impact on employment of cuts in just one department, the Ministry of Defence, was therefore high – and much larger spending cuts were planned in most other departments.

However, Britain remains a significant defence power, with a nuclear deterrent – to help the Liberal Democrats and delay spending, a final decision to replace *Vanguard*-class submarines carrying *Trident* nuclear missiles was put off until the next Parliament. Moreover, the review, which was overseen by a new National Security Council rather than by the Ministry of Defence, added new spending on cyber security, protected intelligence agencies and foresaw new investment in unmanned aircraft.

The aim to remain flexible because of global uncertainties was quickly shown to be appropriate by the sudden upheaval in the Arab world. UK service chiefs, as they engaged in a dogfight over whose assets would be eliminated, could hardly have expected that within months they would be undertaking military action against Libya while still fully engaged in Afghanistan. Still less could they have thought that Cameron, who wanted to end the combat presence in Afghanistan, would be at the forefront of international action. Yet on 28 February, as rebel forces in eastern Libya battled the forces of Muammar Gadhafi, Cameron became the first leader to suggest a no-fly zone, announcing that he had directed defence chiefs to draw up plans. After UN Security Council Resolution 1973 was passed on 17 March, mandating action to protect civilians, British aircraft and ships were prominent in the NATO-led military action, and continued to be so in the following months as questions were increasingly raised about the purpose of the operation and the difficulty of dislodging Gadhafi.

French forces also took a prominent role. Although Britain baulked at France's desire for a joint French–UK-led operation rather than a NATO command, a move towards Anglo-French cooperation was another surprising element of defence policy under the Conservative-led government. Previous Conservative governments, under pressure from their own anti-European members of parliament, had been allergic to European defence cooperation outside the NATO framework and especially about sharing military assets with France. However, in November Cameron and Sarkozy signed a defence cooperation treaty under which aircraft would fly from each other's carriers, a joint expeditionary force would be formed, and research would be carried out jointly on nuclear warheads, unmanned aircraft, missiles and cyber security. The agreement between Europe's two largest defence powers was not only a practical response to financial stringencies but also was likely to drive further intra-European cooperation moves. But it would have to overcome long-standing cultural barriers within the two defence establishments.

Economic gamble

In opting for radical surgery to the public sector, Cameron and George Osborne, the finance minister, were taking a calculated risk. Watching the fate of Greece, Ireland and Portugal, they judged such action to be vital to maintain Britain's creditworthiness through slashing the budget deficit, which was among the largest in Europe as a proportion of GDP. Spending cuts risked sending a fragile economy back into recession, in which case there would be no prospect of replacing the many jobs they were axing. The view of some economists was that there was still a need for the government to provide more stimulus for economic growth, since banks were holding back new credit. They feared a long period of anaemic or no growth. Quarterly economic figures provided no clear picture of which side of the argument was correct. But the stage was set for political brawls to come. The government's initial plans for spending cuts, and especially the sharp rise in university fees, had already provoked large public protests, some of which turned violent.

Cameron, whose ability to hold the reins of office with natural ease was as evident as had been Gordon Brown's inability to do so, seemed well suited to the struggle, determined to press ahead but with the ability to adjust and to withstand setbacks. The Libyan mission notwithstanding, he had not yet carved out a place on the world stage, or forged a distinctive foreign policy; the exigencies of the public finances, the domestic reform agenda and the coalition experiment were pressing enough. The qualities of his chief opponent were yet to be seen, since the Labour Party surprisingly elected as its leader Ed Miliband, the former energy minister, who narrowly defeated his better-known elder brother David Miliband, the former foreign minister. Labour entered a period of policy review, its new leader reportedly saying that he was starting with a 'blank piece of paper'. This seemed likely to be prolonged, especially since the coalition partners had pledged that they would stay together for a full five-year Parliament, until 2015. However, it remained to be seen whether Clegg and other Liberal Democrat leaders could maintain their party's allegiance to an arrangement with which its members could become increasingly uncomfortable.

Russia: Leaders Foster Uncertainty

The year to mid-2011 was marked by public differences between President Dmitry Medvedev and Prime Minister Vladimir Putin, as both leaders presented themselves as possible candidates for the 2012 presidential elections. The two men clashed on a wide spectrum of issues, especially on the role of the state in the economy, decentralisation of state power, freedom of expression and political pluralism. The import of this apparent discord was not clear, however, since only one of them seemed likely to stand as the candidate of the ruling elite.

Observing these rhetorical battles, Russian and Western experts were unclear about their significance in the context of the country's Byzantine power politics, transparent only to a small inner circle of players – perhaps only to Putin and Medvedev themselves. One group of observers saw the disagreements as genuine, a sign that Medvedev was becoming sufficiently confident to challenge his political patron. Some even inferred that Medvedev might have begun to free himself from his role as Putin's loyal subject, and to assert his independence. Others, however, dismissed the differences as political theatre designed to create the impression of pluralism where none really existed and to give a veneer of legitimacy to Putin's system of governance, which remained in essence one-man authoritarian rule. In this view, Putin took all the key decisions and would be the one who would decide whether to return to the Kremlin in 2012 or allow Medvedev to run again.

Beyond the political smoke and mirrors, pressures were building within Russia's system of state-led capitalism. While the economy showed good growth, driven mostly by rising energy and commodity prices, there remained an urgent need for Russia to diversify away from dependence on oil and gas exports. High oil prices were discouraging the government from taking necessary steps, particularly as the election year approached. A sharp rise in manufacturing growth was an encouraging feature of the 2010 performance, but a rise in inflation was worrying, as was a continuing high level of capital outflow. While Putin said fighting inflation was the number one economic priority, Medvedev insisted that no lasting progress could be made without modernisation and investment. In an attempt to attract foreign investors, the government announced plans to spend $500bn on infrastructure over the next three years. It also launched a new privatisation programme, including a 10% stake in VTB, the country's second-largest bank, and 7.6% of the country's top lender, Sberbank. But Medvedev's talk of modernisation had produced so few practical results that it was in danger of becoming a devalued concept. Russia's growing wealth – with Moscow boasting the largest number of billionaires of any city in the world – contrasted awkwardly with the accelerating brain drain among university-educated people and entrepreneurs. Some 40% of 18–24-year-olds wanted to emigrate.

More broadly, there was a widening gap between Russia's perception of itself as a major power in a multipolar world and the actual role it was playing in global and regional affairs. Two security problems in Eurasia – inter-ethnic clashes in Kyrgyzstan and the threat of escalation of the Armenian–Azerbaijani conflict over Nagorno-Karabakh – demonstrated the limits of Russia's power to prevent and resolve conflicts on its periphery. Meanwhile, the situation in the troubled North Caucasus deteriorated further, with violence spreading into central and even western areas. In January 2011 a suicide bomber from the North Caucasus region killed 35 people and injured over 100 in the arrivals hall of Moscow's major international airport.

Political uncertainty

The election season began with local polls in March 2011, due to be followed by parliamentary elections in December 2011 and the presidential vote in March 2012. While the political system is far from genuinely democratic or pluralistic, uncertainties surrounded the elections, of which the biggest was over the presidential race.

Both Putin and Medvedev hinted that they might stand for the next six-year presidential term (increased from four years by a constitutional amendment), but indicated they would not compete with each other and would agree between themselves on who should be the candidate. There seemed three possible scenarios: Putin could come back for a third term as president, with Medvedev taking another role; Putin could allow Medvedev to remain president while retaining de facto supreme power, perhaps by continuing as prime minister; or Putin could retain effective power but could select a different candidate for the presidency.

The natural reaction of the bureaucracy was to wait until the uncertainty was resolved – an announcement was expected in autumn 2011. This led to paralysis in decision-making and ineffective policy implementation. Many initiatives launched by Medvedev as part of his drive to modernise Russia, to fight corruption and to reform institutions such as the police were not followed by practical steps. For example, his call for a new recertification process for police officers was sabotaged, with only a small fraction undergoing the procedure in the allocated time frame. Another important move by Medvedev was to remove government officials from the boards of major state companies, to reduce the scope for corruption and state interference. This was nominally implemented, but in fact a system of state directives preserved the government's power over state-controlled companies. These half measures reinforced perceptions of Medvedev as weak, and discredited the modernisation agenda.

Meanwhile, popular resentment towards the political elite grew, as a result of corruption, lack of accountability and indifference to the problems faced by citizens, particularly the expanding middle class. Many people, suffering from a deteriorating social-security system and a widening gap between rich and poor, increasingly saw the ruling elite as part of the problem. According to opinion polls, 52% of Russians believed officials were now more corrupt than in the lawless 1990s. Over 90% believed officials were hiding money abroad. The popularity rating of Medvedev fell from 62% to 46% and of Putin from 69% to 53%, his lowest since he became president in 2000.

This popular dissatisfaction was evident in the outcome of the regional elections which took place across the country in March 2011. Votes for the United Russia party – chaired by Putin, and consisting of state officials and loyal beneficiaries of the state-capitalist system – fell by as much as 20% compared to the 2007 parliamentary elections, and the Communist Party, Just Russia and Liberal Democrats all improved their positions in many regions. This was a wake-up call for the elite, which had long taken its dominance for granted.

In response, Putin adopted a new strategy for the parliamentary elections due to be held in December. Distancing himself from United Russia, he established the All-Russia People's Front, a looser political movement. He invited potential supporters of opposition parties to join, promising them places in parliament or in government in exchange for their backing. The movement established coordination councils in all parts of Russia. Putin himself began to campaign for the Front and called for the development of a joint programme between it and United Russia for the Duma elections. Although many organisations joined the Front – including veterans' bodies, businessmen and even state companies such as the railway monopoly – it was too early to tell whether its public-relations campaign could reverse the popular sense of delegitimisation of the political system. Moreover, the effect was to undermine a developing institution, the United Russia party, in favour of yet another structure based on personal loyalty to Putin himself. His move to set up the Front was taken as a sign that he was considering a return to the Kremlin – if he stood, there was little doubt that he would win.

Competing visions

While Medvedev and Putin were keen to emphasise that they were part of a single political team, the visions of Russia's future they expressed increasingly diverged.

In 2011 Medvedev presented a more detailed vision for Russia's modernisation, building on his original 'four I's' – institutions, infrastructure, investment and innovation – from his Krasnoyarsk speech delivered at the start of his presidency in 2008. At a meeting of his Commission for Modernisation in Magnitogorsk, he listed ten ways to improve the investment climate. 'Russia needs technologies and it needs finances adequate to its size', he said. 'Investments will enable us to develop a new economy and provide properly paid jobs for the people … They will strengthen security and guarantee democratic development.' He called for measures to incentivise business and reduce corruption, for a reduced role for the state in running and owning businesses, and easier access for foreign investors in the energy sector. He forecast that, 'until we make our country attractive for business and private initiative, we will not achieve our main goal of improving the quality of life for our people'.

The picture he painted contrasted markedly with that presented soon afterwards by Putin. Addressing the Duma, the prime minister expressed pride at the state of the economy: 'I think it is our common achievement that Russia successfully avoided serious shocks that could have weakened the country, undermined its economic and human potential'. He mentioned multiple examples of state intervention and subsidies. The father of state corporations and of renationalisation, he made no mention of privatisation, suggesting instead that public–private partnerships could be an 'efficient model' – differing sharply with Medvedev's advocacy of privatisation.

The argument continued when Medvedev, addressing the St Petersburg International Economic Forum in June 2011, said: 'I want to announce very clearly: we are not building state capitalism. This is not my choice. My choice is different. The Russian economy should be dominated by private enterprise and private investors. The state should protect property and the choice of those who knowingly risk their money and reputation.' Medvedev said an increased state role in the economy had been important in stabilising the situation after the chaos of the 1990s. 'But now the potential of this path has been exhausted.'

The two men differed in their attitudes to corruption and to links between state bureaucracy and business. Under Putin's state capitalism, officials received benefits as members of the boards of state-controlled enterprises operating in the very sectors they are charged to oversee. Medvedev, who ordered the removal of officials from company boards, viewed corruption as the key obstacle to successful modernisation of Russia and a prime reason for capital flight. In 2011, Russia slid to its lowest rating on Transparency International's corruption index, at 154 out of 178 countries.

One focus of the president's anti-corruption campaign was on police reform, which was pushed forward by a new law. This introduced a three-stage qualification test and ordered a 20% reduction in police numbers to 1.1m by the end of 2011. Serving officers were to be recertified to weed out incompetence and dishonesty. More money was to be spent on pay, equipment and training. During 2011, 87 of the Interior Ministry's 427 generals lost their jobs as part of the plan. However, the overall impact was limited.

In spite of Medvedev's efforts at modernisation, there was widespread scepticism over the extent to which he could change the system. The fact that he was unable to state clearly whether he was planning to run again in 2012 left the impression that the choice ultimately lay with Putin. His failure to implement the reforms he championed could be explained partly by the fact that he had failed to bring in his own political team. Most top decision-makers owed their allegiance to Putin, who appointed them and allowed them to earn significant profits through the system of state capitalism. Putin's allies also continued to control the key television channels.

Foreign policy: progress with US

In the realm of foreign policy, Medvedev was able to leave a more significant footprint. His modernisation agenda found a more supportive audience in the West than it did at home. He sought to improve relations with the United States, Europe, and ex-Soviet neighbours. Opinion polls showed that Medvedev's efforts to improve relations with the West were viewed well by citizens. Business and the military were also in favour. But progress was limited by Russia's strongly expressed disapproval of the NATO campaign in Libya, which Moscow felt went far beyond the mandate of the UN Security Council resolution, on which it had abstained.

The president saw foreign policy as an instrument of domestic modernisation. Instead of presenting the West as a threat or as a competitor to Russia, as had Putin, Medvedev called on Russian diplomats to find common ground on key issues with European countries and the United States. He favoured stepping up Russia's engagement with the Asia-Pacific region. Although he spoke of post-Soviet countries as Russia's 'sphere of privileged interests', he indicated to the *Financial Times* that he meant this 'not in the sense that there is a country that cannot be touched without our approval', but rather in the sense that Russia had had close relations with those countries for a long time.

The past year brought significant progress in relations with Washington, helped by a personal rapport between the two presidents. Their approach was pragmatic and transactional. After the United States changed its George W. Bush-era plans for a missile-defence system in Europe, which Russia viewed as a threat, and downgraded its engagement in the Caucasus, Moscow reciprocated by voting in June 2010 to back tougher UN sanctions on Iran. Medvedev then banned Russian sales of S-300 air-defence systems and other arms to Iran. Russia also facilitated transit of more US equipment and personnel through its territory and airspace to Afghanistan. The two countries conducted a joint counter-narcotics operation in Afghanistan and expanded cooperation on tracking illegal finances of drug traffickers. Russia supplied equipment including helicopters and small arms to the Afghan National Army.

In addition, the New START arms-control treaty was ratified, and bilateral talks were held on how to develop cooperation on European missile defence. A visit to the United States by Russian Defence Minister Anatoly Serdyukov, followed by a visit to Moscow by US Defense Secretary Robert Gates, heralded the relaunch of military cooperation, which had been suspended in the latter years of the G.W. Bush administration. Other areas of cooperation included the Armenian–Azerbaijani conflict over Nagorno-Karabakh, with US President Barack Obama strongly supporting Medvedev in taking the lead on the talks with each of the parties. Medvedev ensured that his numerous meetings with the protagonists were fully transparent to the United States and France, the other co-chairs of the Minsk Process. However, there were heightened concerns that the conflict could escalate, with frequent violations of the ceasefire and belligerent rhetoric on both sides.

In spite of warming relations since the 'reset' called for by the Obama administration, difficult issues remained. One was missile defence. Russia wanted legally binding guarantees that the US system in Europe would not be directed against Russia. Obama could not agree to any such limitations because of strong opposition in Congress.

Missile-defence talks

Medvedev, who had failed to win international support for his proposal for a European security treaty, seemed to have abandoned this ambitious idea. Russia instead refocused on developing pragmatic partnerships with NATO and the EU.

In November 2010 Medvedev took part in a NATO–Russia summit in Lisbon, a day after NATO adopted its new strategic concept. Moscow had been reluctant to commit to the meeting due to uncertainty over whether the new concept would identify Russia as a threat or as a subject of NATO's Article V commitments to mutual defence. In the event, the meeting passed in a friendly and constructive atmosphere, marking a shift away from frosty relations after the 2008 Russia–Georgia War. The summit agreed on an ambitious programme of cooperation between NATO and Russia and reaffirmed a commitment to building trust and overcoming the legacies of the Cold War. Afterwards, Medvedev refused to rule out future Russian membership in NATO, though he said this seemed unlikely in the near future.

Cooperation on missile defence emerged as a key issue for NATO–Russia relations. NATO agreed that missile defence in Europe would be the business of the alliance rather than a bilateral issue for Washington – even though in practice the technology and funding would come almost entirely from the United States. Medvedev proposed that cooperation should be based on a 'sectoral approach', with Moscow responsible for defending its own territory and that of northeastern Europe, including the Baltic states (which are NATO members). This was opposed by NATO, and by March 2011 the Russians seemed to drop this approach and to insist instead that NATO – meaning the

United States – should provide legally binding guarantees that future land-based interceptors aimed at intercontinental missiles would not be geared to intercept Russian weapons. They asserted there was no evidence that Iran could develop intercontinental missiles in the foreseeable future and that the only actor with such missiles in the region was Russia. The United States offered a counter-proposal to start practical cooperation on earlier, shorter-range phases of the missile-defence system, and use these to establish trust.

Russia also made an effort to deepen security relations with the EU. While Medvedev agreed with German Chancellor Angela Merkel on a proposal for an EU–Russia security committee, Merkel suggested that Russia should first demonstrate its commitment to resolving the conflict in Moldova's break-away region of Transdniestr. While Russia did host a meeting on the subject, it remained unclear whether any serious progress could be achieved soon. Indeed, the conflicts remaining on Russia's periphery continued to loom as Russia entered an important election period.

The Balkans: Rocky Road to Europe

European Union (EU) officials like to talk of the 'regatta' principle: once a western Balkan yacht has completed the course necessary to win EU accession and crosses the finishing line, it will become a member. In fact, the seven western Balkan states are more like old cars than elegant yachts. At times they chug forward, but they often break down, and sometimes they reverse gear. At mid-2011 Croatia, Serbia and Montenegro were moving forward, while Albania, Macedonia, Kosovo and Bosnia were all stalled or in reverse.

Croatia was given a provisional green light to join the EU, and Serbia took a big step towards membership with the arrest of the fugitive Ratko Mladic, the former Bosnian Serb army general who had been under indictment by the UN's International Criminal Tribunal for the Former Yugoslavia (ICTY) since 1995 for war crimes.

The EU-led force in Bosnia was reduced from some 2,000 troops to approximately 1,600, and its UN Security Council mandate was extended to November 2011. In Kosovo, the NATO-led force KFOR, whose numbers had stood at some 10,000 at the end of 2009, was reduced to 5,927 by June 2011, with Germany, Italy, Turkey and the United States providing the largest contingents. The EU's police and justice mission in Kosovo, known as EULEX, consisted of some 1,700 foreigners and 1,200 local staff.

Serbia: Mladic arrested

Mladic's evasion of capture for almost 16 years was the biggest obstacle to Serbia's integration into European institutions. He was indicted for war crimes, including genocide, for his role in the July 1995 massacre of some 8,000 Bosniak (Bosnian Muslim) men and boys at Srebrenica, as well as in ethnic-cleansing campaigns and attacks on civilians from 1992 to 1995. He was arrested at his uncle's house in the Serbian village of Lazarevo on 26 May 2011, the same day Catherine Ashton (the EU foreign-policy chief), Stefan Fule (the EU enlargement commissioner) and Miroslav Lajcak (in charge of the Balkans for the EU's new External Action Service) were in Belgrade. This led many to speculate that the authorities had known Mladic's location for some time, and decided to arrest him at a moment that served their desire to gain EU candidate status.

But this was unlikely to have been the case. From his indictment until the fall of Serbian leader Slobodan Milosevic in 2000, Mladic had lived more or less openly. From then until 2008, when the party of Serbian President Boris Tadic gained full control of the Serbian intelligence services, he was protected by formal or informal military-cum-intelligence networks. The government of Zoran Djindjic, the first post-Milosevic prime minister, shied away from tackling the issue. Following Djindjic's assassination in 2003, his successor Vojislav Kostunica may well have helped protect Mladic until 2008. However, after the 2008 arrest of Radovan Karadzic, the wartime Bosnian Serb president, there seemed no reason for the Serbian authorities not to arrest Mladic if he could be found. Tired and in need of medical and dental attention and with his family under constant pressure and deprived of his pension, which was restored after his arrest, it is possible that Mladic simply gave up the struggle and stopped running, waiting at his uncle's house to be found. He was rapidly flown to The Hague to face the charges of genocide, crimes against humanity and war crimes, to which he declined to enter a plea. Following the arrest, the Serbian government hoped not only to gain EU candidacy status during 2011, but also to skip a stage in the integration process and immediately be given a date for the opening of accession talks.

Meanwhile, there were political tensions in Serbia's predominantly Bosniak Sandzak region among Bosniaks, and between the Serbian authorities and Muamer Zukorlic, leader of one of Serbia's two Islamic communities. Money, local power and Bosniak nationalism were the core issues, rather than matters of Islamic doctrine and its application, although these also played a role. Zukorlic demanded autonomy for Sandzak, promising its people that once this was attained, they would attain the living standards of Monaco. The idea of autonomy was rejected by Serbian leaders, not only because Bosniaks were only a slight majority in the whole of Sandzak but because, in light of the Yugoslav experience, autonomy was feared to be the beginning of a slippery slope to secession.

A notable feature of Serbia's economy over the past year was the growth of its arms industry, which was expanding beyond its traditional base in producing ammunition. Defence sales accounted for some 4% of Serbian exports and provided jobs for 10,000 people. In 2010 Serbia earned $250m from arms exports, and signed a $400m contract to build three arms factories in Algeria. It was on the point of a signing a $500m agreement to build a military hospital in Libya, but the deal fell through as Libya collapsed into chaos.

Kosovo: corruption and crime overshadow independence

A key factor in Serbia's progress towards the EU was the way it dealt with Kosovo, which declared independence from it in 2008. In July 2010, the International Court of Justice (ICJ) in The Hague delivered its advisory opinion in answer to Serbia's question of whether Kosovo's declaration had violated international law.

Almost all concerned had expected the court's opinion to be ambiguous. It was not: it stated clearly that the declaration was legal. Since Serbia had posed a very specific question, the opinion did not discuss the legality of Kosovo's secession per se, but addressed only the declaration. Nevertheless, it was interpreted as a vindication of Kosovo's independence, both by ethnic Albanians and countries such as the United States and United Kingdom which had backed Kosovo's independence. However, the court's judgment did not bring the wave of international recognition for which Kosovo's leaders had hoped. Before the opinion, Kosovo was recognised by 69 countries, including 22 of the 27 EU states. By June 2011 it was recognised by 76, but of the additional seven none carried much weight. Two were Pacific island microstates, and another was Andorra.

At the insistence of the EU, Serbia and Kosovo began a dialogue in Brussels in March 2011 on so-called technical matters. The idea was that this should reduce tensions, make life easier for ordinary people and eventually serve as the beginning of talks which, one day, would lead to a final resolution of the Kosovo issue. By mid-2011 there had been several rounds of talks, held in a good atmosphere, but no agreements. Serbia's main aim was to be seen as cooperative so as to achieve EU candidate status.

Meanwhile, Kosovo's own standing suffered several setbacks. In July 2010 EULEX arrested Hashim Rexhepi, the head of the central bank, on suspicion of accepting bribes, tax evasion and money laundering. Two days earlier Ramush Haradinaj, leader of Kosovo's main opposition party and a former prime minister, was arrested and sent for a retrial at the ICTY at The Hague. He had been acquitted in 2008, but the appeals chamber expressed concerns about witness intimidation. Corruption and organised crime remained a major concern. Ethnic Albanian gangs were prominent in heroin distribution in Europe. The UK's Serious Organised Crime Agency noted that long sentences handed down to Albanians involved in pimping and brothels appeared to be having a deterrent effect, but that many of those involved were moving into narcotics.

A general election on 13 December was marred by what one diplomat dubbed 'industrial-scale' fraud. The cheating was most notable in the central Skenderaj region and was committed mostly by members of the party of Prime Minister Hashim Thaci. Although reruns were held, the election delivered a huge blow to his credibility. Kosovo was becoming increasingly isolated. In December 2010, Albania and Bosnia gained the right to visa-free travel for their citizens to Europe's 25-member Schengen zone. This left Kosovars as the only people in the Balkans who still needed visas to travel to the Schengen area.

Two days after the election, a draft report written for the Council of Europe accused Thaci of being a mafia 'boss' connected to an organised-crime ring which, just after the Kosovo war in 1999, had kidnapped Serbs and others and murdered them for their organs. The report's author, Dick Marty, a Swiss politician and former prosecutor, claimed to have corroborated well-known stories which had previously been dismissed for lack of solid evidence. He alleged that Thaci and his group of former guerrilla commanders from the central region of Drenica were connected with men responsible for the murder, in Albania, of prisoners from Kosovo, for their organs in 1999. The report also said that at least five foreign agencies combatting the drugs trade had named Thaci as having exerted violent control over the region's heroin trade. All this had been tolerated by the United States and Kosovo's foreign friends, Marty argued, because they wanted peace and stability at any cost. The report, angrily denounced by Kosovo's authorities as a litany of slander, was adopted by the Council of Europe's parliamentary assembly, and EULEX appointed a working group to investigate the allegations.

Meanwhile, Kosovo remained generally peaceful. Serbian enclaves south of the Ibar river gradually became more integrated into the state, with more Serbs voting in the Kosovo general election than in previous polls. However the Serbian-inhabited area north of the river remained mostly beyond the control of the Kosovar authorities. East of the border, ethnic Albanian-populated areas of south Serbia remained calm, although some leaders were excited by speculation that Serbia might eventually agree to recognise Kosovo, so long as Kosovo gave up the Serbian-controlled north. In this case, the region's Albanian leaders said they would demand their annexation to Kosovo.

Mixed progress elsewhere

The political paralysis which had plagued Bosnia and Herzegovina since 2006 continued. In October 2010's elections, a significant change was that Haris Silajdzic, the Bosniak representative on the tripartite presidency, was replaced by Bakir Izetbegovic, son of Bosnia's wartime president. It was widely hoped that Izetbegovic's more moderate positions would lead to agreements with Milorad Dodik, president of Republika Srpska (RS), the Serb part of Bosnia, on much-needed constitutional and other changes. However, none was forthcoming by mid-2011.

In a major challenge, in April 2011, the RS national assembly voted in favour of a referendum which, if successful, would have undermined Bosnia's state court and prosecutor's office. This was widely seen as a dress rehearsal for a referendum on independence. However, the poll was set aside after last-minute intervention by Ashton. Her agreement, on a visit to Banja Luka, the RS capital, to hold a 'structured dialogue' on Bosnia's judicial institutions as a step to Bosnia's EU accession caused irritation in Washington, where it was seen as undermining the Bosnian state.

In Bosnia's other political entity, the Bosniak–Croat Federation, Croatian leaders complained that they were being marginalised by Bosniaks. The result of the complex political wrangling was that more than eight months after the election there was still no new central government in Bosnia, though there were governments for the Federation and the RS. Integration into Europe remained stalled.

Croatia, by contrast, made progress. In June 2011 the European Commission announced that talks on its accession were complete and it was recommending to the EU's Council of Ministers that the country should join the EU in 2013 – though progress on corruption and judicial reform would be monitored. This followed the December arrest, in Austria on a Croatian warrant, of former Prime Minister Ivo Sanader. The arrest was seen as a major breakthrough in the country's anti-corruption drive. In March the head of INA, Croatia's largest company, was also arrested on suspicion of soliciting bribes. In April 2011 there were demonstrations by people angry that the ICTY had jailed Ante Gotovina, a former Croatian army general, for war crimes committed in the wake of the Croatian reconquest of the Serbian-held Krajina region in 1995. The government feared that since the arrest of Gotovina had been a key EU demand, this might prejudice people against the EU in a country already marked by a deep eurosceptic vein.

A state of political paralysis persisted in Albania since June 2009 when Edi Rama, leader of the opposition Socialist Party and mayor of Tirana, accused the Democratic Party of Prime Minister Sali Berisha of stealing elections. Waves of Socialist-led protests followed. In January 2011 Ilir Meta, deputy prime minister from a breakaway socialist party, resigned after a video secretly filmed in March 2010 appeared to show him putting pressure on another minister to intervene to secure a deal over a hydroelectric plant which would have seen them both benefit financially. On 21 January, as thousands gathered to protest, violence broke out and four demonstrators were shot dead on the street by members of the Republican Guard, who allegedly fired from the government building. Berisha claimed that the Socialists had been plotting a *coup d'état* with guns disguised as umbrellas and pens.

As the threat of further violence abated under international pressure, attention focused on local elections held on 8 May. It was widely hoped that a clear vote for one side or the other would trigger early general elections which would end the political stalemate. This was a forlorn hope. In Tirana, the capital, Rama declared himself the victor as mayor when he held a margin of 10 votes out of a quarter million cast. The Democratic Party claimed that, if votes cast in the wrong boxes were counted, its candidate Lulzim Basha was the winner by 81. Albania's Electoral College at first accepted the Democrats' argument, but then demanded a recount. In mid-June it was still not known who the mayor was and the political stalemate was not over. EU officials took the view that if Albania, a NATO member, was not able to hold local elections in which the results were accepted by all, it was in no position to move forward towards EU membership.

EU integration was also halted in neighbouring Macedonia. In the wake of Greece's effective veto of Macedonian NATO membership in 2008, Skopje began proceedings against Greece at the ICJ and hearings began in March. Since Macedonian independence in 1991, Athens had objected to its choice of name, arguing that it implied territorial ambitions towards that part of historic Macedonia which is now Greek territory. From 2008, the dispute prevented progress towards EU accession.

An early general election in June 2011 saw the party of populist Prime Minister Nikola Gruevski returned to power. Earlier, there were ethnic tensions between Albanians (who make up 25% of the population) and Macedonians over the erection of what the authorities claimed was a museum in the shape of a church. Macedonians in turn complained about the building of scores of new mosques in recent years, some of which fly Saudi Arabian flags from their minarets, indicating the source of their funding. Meanwhile, Macedonia's government was accused by the opposition of trying to shut down A1 television, which had positioned itself against Gruevski. Its bank accounts were frozen. While the opposition said the government was trying to close down the country's last bastion of free speech, government supporters claimed that this was simply part of a clampdown on corporate tax evasion.

In Montenegro Milo Djukanovic, who had run the country, from different posts, for more than 20 years, stepped down as prime minister in December 2010. Igor Luksic, the former deputy prime minister and minister of finance, took over following the arrest on corruption charges of the deputy mayor of Budva, the brother of one of Djukanovic and Luksic's political foes. This was taken to mean that Djukanovic would continue to exercise power from his position as head of the ruling Democratic Party of Socialists. The 34-year-old Luksic denied that Djukanovic still called the shots but indicated he would seek to gain more power as time permitted.

With Serbian–Montenegrin organised-crime groups emerging as a major threat in the worldwide trafficking of cocaine, Montenegrin merchant sailors were being recruited to move drugs across the Atlantic. Some arrests were made in Montenegro, but intelligence sources indicated that powerful figures in the business still appeared to enjoy immunity. Nevertheless, Montenegro achieved EU candidate status in December 2010 and was given a list of seven priority areas to work on. In the EU 'regatta', however, it was probably still some way from port, though the opening of accession talks in 2012 was a realistic aim.

Turkey's Diminished Role

In the general election of 12 June 2011, the ruling Justice and Development Party (AKP) became the first Turkish political party in more than half a century to secure a third successive term in power. Buoyed by a booming economy, the AKP won 49.9% of the popular vote, giving it 327 seats in the country's 550-member unicameral parliament. But the consolidation of the

AKP's grip on government came amidst signs of deepening fissures in the nation that it governed, with opposition parties bitterly accusing the AKP of abusing its political dominance to stifle free speech, prosecute and imprison its critics and enrich its supporters. Nowhere was the alienation deeper than in the predominantly Kurdish southeast of the country, where the AKP's abandonment of a strategy of engagement and conciliation in favour of a return to the confrontational policies of its predecessors had triggered a campaign of civil disobedience by Kurdish nationalists and another rise in violence in the long-running insurgency by the Kurdistan Workers' Party (PKK). Nevertheless, the AKP's fresh electoral mandate at least provided it with a solid platform on which to confront the growing domestic tensions.

In international affairs, however, the foundation on which the AKP had built Turkey's newly assertive foreign policy appeared to be crumbling due to the unrest that was sweeping the Arab world. Starting in 2009, the AKP had increasingly sought to pursue a foreign policy independent of Turkey's traditional Western allies. Its ultimate aim was to establish Turkey as a regional power in its own right, based on its growing wealth and its stature as the only functioning democracy in the Middle East other than Israel – attributes which, claimed AKP officials, made it a natural leader and an inspiration to the Muslim masses throughout what they were fond of describing as the 'former Ottoman hinterland'.

The main architect and advocate of Turkey's ambitious strategy was Foreign Minister Ahmet Davutoglu, who energetically cultivated closer ties with other Muslim governments in the region. In media interviews and contacts with his Western counterparts, Davutoglu repeatedly trumpeted Turkey's growing influence. History, he assured his interlocutors, was resuming its natural flow; nothing could now occur in the Middle East without Turkey's active involvement. But when regimes across the broader Middle East began to falter under pressure from a succession of pro-democracy public protests, the government was caught unprepared. Not only did it play no role in the momentous changes sweeping the region, but Turkey's ambivalent attitude towards the protests – and what sometimes appeared to be implicit encouragement to the beleaguered authoritarian regimes – set it in opposition to both its Western allies and the Muslim masses who were supposed to support its regional leadership.

From leadership to prevarication

At first blush, the so-called 'Arab Awakening' should have been the AKP's finest hour. Government officials had long boasted of their popularity in the

Arab world. Turkey's bilateral trade with the Middle East was growing faster than that with any other region in the world. Prime Minister Recep Tayyip Erdogan's outspoken defence of Palestinian rights and excoriating attacks on Israel had made him a folk hero to many Muslims. Glitzy Turkish soap operas dubbed into Arabic helped fuel a rapid rise in the number of Arab tourists visiting Turkey, which was, AKP officials claimed, a democratic and increasingly affluent Muslim country to which others in the region aspired. There were even conservative opposition parties in Arab countries that explicitly modelled themselves on the AKP, such as the Parti de la Justice et du Développement (PJD) in Morocco.

Yet the AKP's populist rhetoric – whether in attacks on Israel or defiant assertions of Turkey's independence from the West – ran parallel to a policy of forging close political and economic ties with the ruling elites in many Muslim countries in the Middle East. Egypt was an exception, in substantial part because Ankara regarded Cairo's traditional role as the political leader of the Arab world as a threat to Turkey's own regional status. The AKP was also ideologically closer to the opposition Muslim Brotherhood than to the secular regime of Hosni Mubarak, and had aggravated Mubarak with sympathy for Hamas and opposition to Mubarak's support for the Israeli blockade of Gaza. Thus, after cautiously endorsing the Tunisian Revolution of January 2011, the AKP was considerably less circumspect when the wave of popular unrest spread to Egypt. On 1 February 2011, Erdogan became the first world leader to publicly call on Mubarak to resign. 'No government can survive against the will of its people', he declared.

Erdogan's attitude changed when the unrest spread to Libya, where Turkish firms had signed $15bn worth of construction contracts with the regime of Muammar Gadhafi, with whom the AKP had long enjoyed close ties. On 29 November 2010, Erdogan had even travelled to Tripoli to receive the Al-Gadhafi International Prize for Human Rights. On 1 March 2011, amidst speculation that NATO would intervene in Libya to support rebels seeking to overthrow Gadhafi, Erdogan publicly vowed that Turkey would use its membership of the Alliance to forestall intervention and pledged his support for the Gadhafi regime. On 18 March 2011, the day after the UN Security Council approved Resolution 1973 imposing a no-fly zone over Libya, Erdogan announced that Turkey would respect the motion but opposed any military action against what he described as 'brotherly, friendly Libya'. As international pressure began to mount, the AKP gradually modified its position, and on 27 March joined its NATO allies in approving a plan under which the Alliance would assume command of all air operations against Libya. To justify his about-face to the domestic public, Erdogan announced that NATO had agreed to transfer control of Benghazi port and airport to Turkey and make Turkey responsible for coordinating the international humanitarian aid effort to Libya. In fact, there was no such agreement. Erdogan subsequently issued several unsuccessful calls for Gadhafi to agree a ceasefire with the rebels. Eventually, on 3 May, Erdogan publicly called on Gadhafi to step down and leave Libya.

The growing pro-democracy protests in Syria in February and March 2011 presented Turkey with an even greater challenge. In recent years, despite Syria's international isolation, the AKP had forged even closer political and personal ties with the regime of Bashar al-Assad than with Gadhafi's regime. In 2009, to fuel cross-border trade and boost the local economy in chronically underdeveloped southeast Turkey, the two countries had mutually abolished visa requirements, causing concern among Ankara's Western allies that terrorists' movements would become harder to track. On 21 December 2010, at the meeting of the Turkey–Syria High Level Strategic Cooperation Council, involving 26 ministers from the two countries, Davutoglu described Turkish–Syrian cooperation as a model for other countries to follow, with the potential to transform the entire region. When Syrians took to the streets in March 2011 to press for political reform, the government refused to condemn the Assad regime's brutal suppression of the protests. Instead, AKP officials gently encouraged their Syrian interlocutors to implement reforms while reaffirming their support for Assad's retention of power. As the death toll continued to rise, individual AKP officials privately expressed their frustration at his intransigence. But Erdogan still studiously avoided calling for Assad to step down.

The Arab unrest also strained the AKP's previously warm relations with Iran. Although the two countries have remained historical rivals, a shared distrust of the West and each government's desire to boost domestic and regional support have led to increased cooperation between Ankara and Tehran. For example, in June 2010, Turkey, as a non-permanent member of the UN Security Council, unsuccessfully attempted to block additional UN sanctions against Iran over its nuclear programme. When pro-democracy demonstrations erupted in Bahrain in February 2011, however, Turkish officials suspected that Tehran was fomenting unrest amongst Bahrain's Shia Muslim majority in an attempt to extend Iranian influence into the Gulf states. As a result, Turkey not only sided with the Sunni ruling elite in Bahrain but also supported its decision to invite Saudi Arabian troops in to help suppress the demonstrations. Turkey applied the additional UN sanctions against Iran it had attempted to block in June 2010, in March 2011 twice forcing Iranian cargo planes transiting Turkish airspace to land following intelligence reports that they were carrying illicit materials. The Turkish warplanes' first interception revealed nothing suspicious, but the second yielded a cargo of arms and ammunition suspected of being destined for Lebanon. The Turkish authorities impounded the weapons but allowed the plane and crew to return to Iran.

Relations between Israel and Turkey were effectively frozen when an Israeli commando raid on a Turkish-led aid flotilla to Gaza on 31 May 2010 resulted in the deaths of nine ethnic Turks. On 3 December 2010, however, Turkey did dispatch two CL-125 fire-fighting planes to Israel to help contain the forest fires that were ravaging the hills around Haifa. A few days later, Turkish and Israeli officials held confidential talks in Geneva to try to resolve their differences, but these failed to produce a breakthrough. On 10 December 2010, the Turkish Ministry for Foreign Affairs issued a statement declaring that a restoration of normal ties remained dependent on Israel's publicly apologising and paying compensation for the flotilla raid. Israel has resolutely refused to do so. As of mid-2011, Turkey's relations with Israel had not thawed.

Discomfort with the West

Although the forced landing of the Iranian planes in March 2011 demonstrated Turkey's willingness to apply UN sanctions, Ankara was less amenable to US pressure to take tougher measures against Iran. Through late 2010 and the first half of 2011, the government consistently rejected US requests to clamp down on the activities of Iranian financial institutions in Turkey – particularly the Iranian Bank Mellat, which had first opened a branch in Istanbul in 1982 and which US officials believed was being used to procure items related to Tehran's nuclear programme. In mid-2011, the standoff was straining the AKP's relationship with Turkish banks, many of which were reluctant to sever their ties with Iranian financial institutions without an explicit instruction from the Turkish government but feared that maintaining them would draw US sanctions.

Through early November 2010, AKP officials continued to insist that Turkey veto the deployment of elements of NATO's proposed missile-defence system on Turkish soil on the grounds that it would primarily target Iran. The government backed down at the NATO summit in Lisbon on 19–20 November 2010, joining other alliance members in approving plans to develop the missile-defence system in return for the exclusion of any explicit reference to Iran as a threat. But NATO members were already questioning the depth of Turkey's commitment to the alliance. On 7 October 2010, Turkish officials announced that China and Turkey had held joint air exercises over the Turkish Konya air base in central Anatolia from 20 September to 4 October as part of the annual international *Anatolian Eagle* exercises. Since their inception in 2001, these exercises had included NATO members and Turkey's regional partners, such as Israel and Jordan, but never China. Ankara had not announced Chinese participation in advance and officially confirmed it only after the Turkish media reported sightings of Chinese warplanes in Turkish airspace. Turkish officials denied rumours that Turkey's advanced US-made F-16 *Fighting Falcons* had participated in the exercises alongside Chinese Sukhoi-27 *Flankers*, which had raised fears that sensitive NATO technology could have fallen into Chinese hands. They insisted that they had deliberately used older F-4E *Phantoms*. Nevertheless, it was the first time that China had ever held joint military exercises in a NATO member country. Starting on 8 November 2010, the Turkish military and the Chinese People's Liberation Army held a week of joint land exercises in Anatolia, focusing on counter-insurgency drills in mountainous terrain.

Reinforcing concerns that Turkey was drifting away from the West was the ongoing lack of progress in Ankara's negotiations for EU accession. At their summit meeting in Brussels on 16–17 December 2010, EU leaders decided to extend for another year the suspension of eight chapters of the accession process pending Turkey's implementation of the Ankara Protocol of 30 June 2005, under which it had pledged to open the country's ports and airports to ships and planes from the Republic of Cyprus. Such a move has now effectively become dependent on a successful conclusion to the UN-sponsored negotiations to reunite the divided island. Although the Greek Cypriot and Turkish Cypriot leaders continued to hold regular meetings, in mid-2011 there was still no sign that they were any closer to an agreement.

There were also rising indications that the AKP had lost interest in EU membership. Although the EU's suspension of eight chapters, and the freezing of another nine by France and Cyprus, had restricted Turkey's room for manoeuvre, in mid-2010 there were still three chapters that Turkey could have opened had the AKP pushed the required legislation through parliament. But Belgium's six-month EU presidency ended in December 2010 without Turkey having opened any new chapters – the first cycle in which it had failed to do so since accession negotiations were launched in October 2005. Nor were any new chapters opened during the Hungarian EU presidency in the first half of 2011. Tellingly, the AKP's 156-page manifesto for the general election of June 2011 contained just one page on the EU, and that was devoted mainly to attacking EU member states that had expressed reservations about Turkish accession rather than detailing plans to implement the reforms it required.

Increasing AKP control, rising domestic tensions

The year to mid-2011 saw the AKP tighten its control over the apparatus of state as opposition parties and human-rights activists claimed that it was politicising the judicial system and persecuting its critics. On 22 March 2010, the AKP announced a package of amendments to the Turkish constitution, which had been promulgated in 1982 under military rule and still included many authoritarian provisions. Most of the proposed changes were, as the AKP maintained, liberalising. They included creating a legal framework for the establishment of an ombudsman, removing obstacles to positive gender discrimination, allowing civil servants to join trade unions, and restricting the jurisdiction of military courts. But critics pointed out that other proposed amendments appeared to reduce judicial impartiality by increasing political control over the appointment of judges and prosecutors. They also noted that the reform package made no attempt to overhaul clauses in the 1982 constitution that effectively discriminated against Turkey's ethnic and religious minorities, such as the Kurds and the large heterodox Alevi religious community.

On 7 May 2010, 336 deputies approved the package. Under Turkish law, changes to the constitution require the support of 367 of the 550 members of parliament in order to be enacted automatically. If at least 330 deputies vote in favour, however, the president can choose to put the amendments to a referendum, which President Abdullah Gul subsequently did. The referendum was scheduled for 12 September 2010, and the associated campaign dominated Turkish politics through summer 2010. The AKP favoured the amendments, while the main opposition Republican People's Party (CHP) and Nationalist Action Party (MHP) opposed them. On 13 August 2010, the PKK had declared a temporary unilateral ceasefire after Erdogan announced that state officials had initiated negotiations with the organisation's founder Abdullah Ocalan, who has been imprisoned on the island of Imrali since 1999. Many Kurdish nationalists suspected that the talks were merely a ploy by the AKP to win Kurdish support in the run-up to constitutional referendum. Their suspicions intensified when, during his weekly meetings with his lawyers, Ocalan complained that his interlocutors consistently avoided discussing anything of substance. In the event, the pro-Kurdish Peace and

Democracy Party (BDP) called on its supporters simply to boycott the vote owing to the absence of any minority rights provisions. On 12 September 2010, the electorate approved the package by a margin of 57.9% to 42.1%. The weeks following the referendum witnessed wide-ranging personnel changes in the judiciary, with political appointees dominating the higher echelons. None of the other constitutional changes approved in the referendum had been implemented by mid-2011.

Through late 2010 and early 2011, an expansion of the controversial investigation into Ergenekon – an alleged clandestine organisation with roots in the Turkish military dedicated to overthrowing the AKP – resulted in the detention of a police chief, left-wing journalists and even Islamic theologians who had criticised the government (including the influential Islamist preacher Fethullah Gulen, long one of the AKP's main supporters). By mid-2011, almost 300 people had been formally charged with membership of Ergenekon, although prosecutors had yet to produce convincing evidence that the organisation even existed. In January 2010, prosecutors initiated a second investigation, codenamed *Sledgehammer*, of a supposed military plot to stage a coup in 2003. Despite highly flawed evidence, by mid-2011, 196 serving and retired Turkish military officers, including more than 10% of Turkey's serving generals and admirals, had been imprisoned on charges related to the alleged plot.

Even so, concerns about the rule of law and freedom of speech in Turkey had little impact on the AKP's electoral popularity. One of the main reasons appeared to be the government's impressive economic record. In 2010, Turkey's GDP grew by 8.9%. By early 2011, there were indications that the Turkish economy was overheating, fuelled by an overvalued currency and unsustainable increases in the country's foreign trade and current account deficits. But despite unprecedented levels of personal debt, the economic slowdown had yet to arrive when Turks went to the polls for the general election in June. Perhaps equally importantly, if a growing number of voters were having problems keeping pace with the rising cost of living, few had any confidence that either the CHP or the MHP was better qualified than the AKP to manage the economy.

In the election of 12 June 2011, the AKP was returned to power with 49.9% of the vote and 327 seats in parliament, ahead of the CHP's 25.9% and 135 seats and the MHP's 13.0% and 53 seats. The remaining 35 seats went to independents, all of them members of a bloc created by the BDP who had stood as independents to overcome the 10% national threshold for political parties seeking representation in parliament. It was the post-election period that appeared likely to pose the greatest challenge to the AKP, particularly Erdogan. The AKP's election manifesto called for the drafting of an entirely new constitution. Under Turkish law, the government needs the support of at least 367 deputies to push a new constitution through parliament, although the votes of 330 deputies are enough for a draft to be put to public approval in a referendum. Through the first half of 2011, Erdogan had repeatedly declared that he believed the new constitution should include a transition from a parliamentary system to a presidential one, after which he was expected to run for president for two successive five-year terms. Opposition parties accused Erdogan of seeking to concentrate even more power in his own hands. Privately, Gul also opposed the plan. He had offered to step down to allow Erdogan to become president, but only under the existing system, in which the prime minister – an office Gul planned to seek – wielded the real political power. In mid-2011, it was unclear how the impasse could be resolved. One possibility was that Erdogan would abandon his presidential ambitions, hold negotiations with the other parties and promulgate a compromise constitution in 2012. However, a more likely scenario was that he would bide his time and try to persuade individual members of the opposition to defect to the AKP in order to give the government the 330 seats it needed to draft its own constitution.

Fresh insurgent threats

Turkey also faced the threat of renewed Kurdish insurgency. Through late 2010 and early 2011, Turkish authorities detained hundreds of Kurdish nationalists on charges of belonging to the PKK, including many known for their opposition to the organisation and its use of violence. The BDP responded with civil disobedience, such as regular mass protests in town squares across southeast Turkey. On 28 February 2011, the PKK announced that it was abrogating its unilateral ceasefire, although it pledged that its units would stage only limited attacks against military targets in the run-up to the general election in June. During the first half of 2011, both the BDP and the PKK made it clear that they regarded the promised new constitution as an urgent opportunity for the Turkish state to meet their demands for greater political and cultural rights for the country's Kurds.

Since it first launched its insurgency in 1984, the PKK has dominated the Kurdish nationalist movement. The BDP's civil-disobedience campaign in early 2011 came amidst growing signs that the movement was becoming more variegated and less inclined towards violence. Through May 2011, however, the PKK also threatened to step up its campaign of political violence if the government did not offer substantive concessions to their demands in the immediate aftermath of the general election. But it appeared highly unlikely that the government would, for example, submit to requiring Kurdish-language courses in state schools in a new constitution. And no Turkish government could implement the most extreme demand – political autonomy for southeast Turkey – without risking a violent Turkish nationalist backlash. A seemingly unbridgeable gap between Kurdish demands and the Turkish government's ability to meet them suggested that tensions were set to rise, with the possibility of a commensurate escalation in PKK violence.

Neither east nor west?

Domestic concerns such as the Kurdish questions, the drafting of a new constitution and the AKP's growing authoritarianism appear likely to dominate Turkish politics for the foreseeable future. Confusion and uncertainty hobbled the country's international stature and influence. The AKP's drive to establish Turkey as a neo-Ottoman regional power has been largely based on demonstrating its ability to pursue its own foreign policy independent of – and often in opposition to – its traditional Western allies. The government has simultaneously formed closer ties with other Muslim regimes in the Middle East and cultivated popular support by implicitly highlighting the shortcomings of those regimes that Turkey did not suffer – for example, their failure to embrace democratic values, inability to deliver prosperity and unwillingness to confront Israel. Underpinning the AKP's strategy was the erroneous belief in a centripetal Ottoman nostalgia, in which the Muslims of the Middle East still looked to Turkey as the natural centre and leader of the region.

Even if the respective protest movements sweeping the Arab world drew inspiration from one another, each of them was marked by a desire to determine its own destiny. While as of June 2011 it was still unclear whether the unrest would lead to genuine democratisation, it was plain that Arab populations were not looking to a hegemonic regional power for leadership. Furthermore, the AKP's deteriorating domestic record and its equivocation in supporting pro-democracy demonstrations in Libya, Bahrain and Syria seriously undermined its credentials as a force for Middle East democratisation. As a result, in mid-2011, far from being able to exchange its traditional close alliance with the West for a new role as the pre-eminent regional power, there was a danger that Turkey would be left with neither.

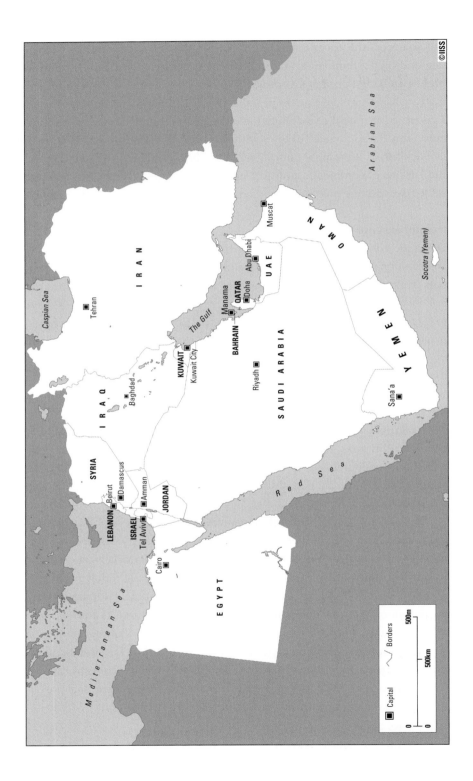

©IISS

Arabian Sea

Socotra (Yemen)

Caspian Sea

I R A N

Tehran

The Gulf

Muscat

O M A N

Abu Dhabi

U A E

Doha

QATAR

Manama

BAHRAIN

KUWAIT

Kuwait City

Baghdad

I R A Q

Riyadh

S A U D I   A R A B I A

Sana'a

Y E M E N

Red Sea

SYRIA

Damascus

Beirut

Amman

LEBANON

JORDAN

ISRAEL

Tel Aviv

Cairo

E G Y P T

Mediterranean Sea

Borders

Capital

500m

500km

0

0

Chapter 6
Middle East/Gulf

This chapter contains analysis of political and diplomatic developments in Iran, Iraq, Israel and Palestine. The events of the Arab Awakening are covered in a special chapter (pages 43–96).

Iran: Domestic Struggle Dims Hope of Nuclear Deal

Defying tough sanctions imposed by the UN Security Council and tougher measures adopted by the United States and its allies, Iran further expanded its controversial nuclear programme. Computer malware reportedly launched by Israel and the United States destroyed a portion of the Islamic Republic's uranium-enrichment centrifuges, while trade controls limited its ability to produce more advanced centrifuge models. Such limitations contributed to the formation of less alarmist judgements about how soon Iran could produce nuclear weapons. The IISS itself assessed the timeline to be a minimum of about two years. Yet Iran's stockpile of low-enriched uranium – enough for two weapons if further enriched – grew at an accelerated pace and Iran boasted of plans for new enrichment facilities. Meanwhile European Union-led efforts to re-start negotiations with Iran went nowhere. Even more sanctions were thus in store.

Seeing time and history as on their side, Iran's leaders improbably claimed that the wave of unrest sweeping the Arab world was inspired by their own 1979 revolution. Notwithstanding the problems posed by protests in Syria,

Iran emerged as a winner from the fall of Egyptian President Hosni Mubarak and the turmoil in Bahrain. The Arab protests were a potential double-edged sword for Iran, if such examples were to rejuvenate Iran's own spent reformist groups, but the Green Movement which had led protests in 2009 showed few signs of revival. Instead, Iranian politics were wracked by splits among the conservatives. President Mahmoud Ahmadinejad expanded his power, firing ministers and encroaching on clerical authority, but in spring 2011 he stepped across a line by provoking a fight with Supreme Leader Ayatollah Ali Khamenei that he seemed destined to lose. Whatever the outcome, the internal divisions further darkened the prospects for any negotiated settlement to the nuclear crisis.

Nuclear programme expands despite sabotage

Over the year to mid-2011, Iran's nuclear programme continued to expand in several ways. In contravention of Security Council demands that it suspend enrichment activities, Iran announced in August 2010 that it would build ten more enrichment plants, starting in April 2011. In retaliation for earlier sanctions, Iran continued to refuse to provide the International Atomic Energy Agency (IAEA) with advance design information about new nuclear facilities, as required by IAEA safeguards. In December 2010, Iran declared that it had produced its first batch of milled uranium, called yellowcake, from a mine at Gchine and that the nation was stepping up exploration of uranium ore elsewhere. Iran had been using imported yellowcake that was running low.

Despite technical problems with its enrichment equipment, Iran increased both its stockpile of enriched uranium and its rate of production. As of mid-May 2011, Iran's underground uranium-enrichment plant at Natanz had produced over 4,100kg of 3.5% low-enriched uranium (LEU), the level needed for nuclear power plants. If this amount were further enriched, it would be enough for at least two implosion-type nuclear weapons. Approximately 6,000 centrifuges were being used to produce the enriched uranium, and the stockpile was growing at a rate of about 140kg a month. By way of contrast, a year earlier, about 4,000 centrifuges were operating, producing a little less than 120kg of LEU a month.

In a separate facility at Natanz, Iran was enriching smaller quantities to 20% U-235 content. This was particularly worrisome because it is a short step from enrichment to this level to production of weapons-usable highly enriched uranium (HEU). Iran had been producing at 20% since January 2010, on the grounds that it was necessary to produce replacement fuel for the ageing Tehran Research Reactor. If Iran had a capability to fabricate fuel from enriched uranium – which as of mid-2011 it lacked – the 60kg of 20%-enriched uranium produced by June 2011 would be enough to run the research reactor for several years. To justify continued production at the higher level, Iran in April announced that it would build four or five new research reactors. In June, Iran announced that enrichment at the 20% level would move to a previously clandestine facility at Fordow, near the holy city of Qom, and that the output would triple. These moves were expected to shorten the time Iran would need to produce HEU.

After many years' delay and technical troubles, the Russian-built nuclear power plant at Bushehr started operations in May 2011, although additional glitches put off electricity generation until August at the earliest. Bushehr, the first nuclear power plant in the Middle East, does not pose the kind of proliferation risk attached to the enrichment programme. The reactor-grade plutonium that Bushehr will produce as a by-product of power generation is not well-suited to weapons use and Russia is obliged to take back the spent fuel when it is cool enough to do so. Yet Iran's Gulf neighbours feared that the reactor could present a safety risk. Sensitised by the nuclear accident at Fukushima in Japan, some of Iran's own citizens raised concerns about Bushehr; such safety issues appeared to be the only grounds allowed for questioning the nuclear programme. The government offered reassurances that Bushehr was perfectly safe. Indeed, although it is in an earthquake zone, the reactor was built to withstand tremors of at least up to magnitude 8. However, the various technical troubles that delayed the opening of the plant by more than half a year, after a premature fuel-loading ceremony in August 2010, left lingering concerns about how safely it would be operated. Iran's impatience over the delays and its refusal to accede to the Nuclear Safety Convention (the only country to operate a nuclear power plant not to do so) also raised questions about whether safety would be the highest priority.

The technical troubles at Bushehr were not caused by the mysterious Stuxnet computer virus that attacked Iran's enrichment programme in 2009. The malware apparently was the reason why 1,000 centrifuges were taken off line in December that year, although the worm was not discovered until the following summer. In November 2010, Iran acknowledged that its uranium-enrichment programme had been targeted by a cyber attack. That month, Iran suspended enrichment for a week, after which it announced that 'limited' damage caused by the worm had been repaired. The *New York Times* later reported that Stuxnet was developed by Israel in collaboration with the United States. Although some computer and nuclear experts claimed that the Stuxnet attack had been a 'huge success' in retarding Iran's progress at Natanz, this was difficult to substantiate. As noted above, at mid-2011 Natanz was producing more enriched uranium each month than before the Stuxnet attack.

In addition to industrial sabotage, there was evidence that a continuing 'decapitation' strategy was being employed against Iran's nuclear programme. In January 2010, a nuclear scientist died in a bomb blast outside his house, and in November, motorcyclists attacked two scientists working at the nuclear-engineering department of Shahid Beheshti University in Tehran, killing one and injuring the other. The scientist who survived, Fereydoon Abbasi, had been named in UN sanctions for links to proscribed nuclear activities. The following February, he was appointed to head the Atomic Energy Organisation of Iran (AEOI). The decapitation strategy also employed recruitment efforts. In July 2010, a nuclear scientist who reportedly had been working at the Fordow enrichment facility returned to Iran after having been lured by the CIA to defect a year earlier. Upon his return, at which he was treated as a hero, he claimed to have been kidnapped. However homesick he had become in the United States, however, a worse fate awaited him during interrogations by security agents in Iran; he was reportedly imprisoned and tortured, and could be convicted of treason.

International concerns about Iran's nuclear programme were heightened by additional information about what the IAEA cautiously called nuclear activities of a 'possible military dimension'. A May 2011 IAEA report said the agency sought Iranian answers about seven kinds of activities relating to 'possible past or current undisclosed' weapons work, including experiments with nuclear bomb triggers. IAEA Director General Yukiya Amano told reporters in June that these activities seemed to have 'continued until quite recently'.

In February 2011, the US intelligence community reportedly produced an updated National Intelligence Estimate (NIE) on Iran's nuclear programme. This was the first update since an NIE in November 2007 which concluded, to great consternation in conservative circles, that Iran in 2003 had explicitly suspended work on nuclear-weapons development. The 2011 NIE was not made public, so it was not possible to judge the accuracy of some media speculation that it had reversed the key conclusion of the 2007 NIE to judge that Iran had now restarted nuclear-weapons design work. Attributing its information to unnamed officials, the *Wall Street Journal* reported that the new NIE 'adjusts but does not contradict' the 2007 finding.

Notwithstanding the additional reasons for concern, talk about a military option to stop Iran's nuclear programme died down during the course of the year to mid-2011. In July 2010, an article in *Atlantic* magazine by Jeffrey Goldberg claimed that a hawkish mood in Israel made it a better than 50% likelihood that Israel would launch a strike in the following 12 months, unless Israeli leaders were persuaded that US President Barack Obama himself would order an attack. US Republican Senator Lindsey Graham called for bombing Iran, not just to neutralise its nuclear programme but also to 'neuter' the regime. Yet within Israel a debate raged about the imminence of the perceived existential threat that would be posed by a nuclear-armed Iran. In January 2011, outgoing Mossad director Meir Dagan told parliamentarians that because of domestic ferment in Iran, the bite of international sanctions, and technical setbacks from sabotage efforts, 'Iran will not achieve a nuclear bomb before 2015, if that'. Israeli Prime Minister Benjamin Netanyahu disagreed, and Israel's military intelligence chief later that month said Iran could produce a weapon within a year or two of making a decision. But officials in Washington also voiced optimism that technical problems had set back Iran's nuclear programme. 'We've got more time than we thought', said General Michael Hayden, former CIA director. Hayden said he now thought the 'key decision point' for possible military action against Iran had been postponed until the next US presidential term. The CIA timeline tallied with an IISS assessment that it would take at least two years to produce a single weapon using the facilities Iran was known to have in 2010.

Sanctions tighten

Adoption of tough sanctions by the Security Council in June 2010 and even tougher follow-on measures by the European Union and several other Western states contributed to the mood that a military option need not be considered for the time being. Intelligence agencies concluded that the punitive measures were seriously impeding Iran's alleged nuclear-weapons work. In May, the UN Panel of Experts formed to assess the implementation of sanctions similarly concluded that sanctions were preventing Iran from obtaining items that were critical for more advanced centrifuges. The sanctions were also impacting the Iranian economy and its conventional military capabilities. The EU sanctions adopted in July 2010 banned technical assistance to Iran's oil and gas industry, among other measures. Even Russia went further than required under the UN sanctions resolution. To Western delight and Iranian consternation, President Dmitry Medvedev banned the sale of S-300 air-defence systems that Tehran had contracted to buy several years earlier. In January 2011, the Reserve Bank of India declared that oil payments to Iran could no longer be settled using the Asian Clearing Union mechanism because such transactions lacked transparency. Under pressure from the US Treasury, banks in the United Arab Emirates ended their role as a conduit of funds to Iran. This squeezed Iran's dwindling foreign-exchange reserves and sparked a sharp fall in the value of the Iranian currency. In May 2011, the EU expanded its own sanctions against Iran by banning 100 more individuals and entities, including the Hamburg-based European–Iranian Trade Bank, Iran's main avenue of access to European financial markets, from doing business in the EU.

Washington also ratcheted up its pressure. In July 2010, a new law expanded sanctions on companies that invest more than $20m in Iran's energy sector and on the sale of refined petroleum products to Iran. In December, the United States barred the state-owned shipping company the Islamic Republic of Iran Shipping Line (IRISL) and four other entities from using the US financial system. This forced global firms to pull their insurance from IRISL, leading to bank foreclosure on mortgaged vessels and a temporary seizure of three of its ships in Singapore harbour. Two IRISL vessels were also seized in Hong Kong and Malta. In May, the United States sanctioned seven foreign companies, including Venezuela's state-owned oil company and an Israeli firm, for providing Iran with refined petroleum in violation of US extraterritorial sanctions. Meanwhile, several members of Congress introduced legislation to penalise foreign firms that bought petroleum from Iran Revolutionary Guard Corps (IRGC) companies. Iranian human-rights violators were also targeted.

Although the sanctions did not generate any apparent shift in Iranian policies, Western officials claimed that the tougher steps had sparked a debate among the Iranian elite. In July 2010, opposition leader Mir Hossein Mousavi lashed out at Ahmadinejad for dismissing the UN sanctions and urged the government to brief people about their impact, claiming they would decrease GDP, increase unemployment and create more hardships for the people. The same day, the head of the AEOI acknowledged that the sanctions could pose difficulties for the uranium-enrichment work. According to some critics, however, sanctions do not really damage the political elite because they reinforce the black-market advantages held by the IRGC, which has the cash and connections to circumvent sanctions. The relatively pro-Western private sector is hurt more by a squeeze on finance, export opportunities and imports of spare parts. Although the IRGC was specifically targeted by both UN and other sanctions, it had been able to form new aliases and front companies faster than its antagonists could add the new firms to sanctions lists. To lessen the impact of a cut-off of refined petroleum by several major global firms, Iran boosted domestic production and lowered domestic demand. Iran was also able to find partners willing to buck the US-led pressure. According to various reports, Chinese firms continued to supply Iran's missile and nuclear programmes with dual-use goods.

Deadlocked talks

In response to the sanctions measures, Iran's parliament, the Majlis, passed a bill obliging the government to continue 20% enrichment and to limit cooperation with the IAEA. In August 2010, Ahmadinejad indicated a willingness to resume talks with the E3+3, (the five permanent members of the UN Security Council plus Germany), but he delayed agreeing to a date for several months so as not to appear to be conceding to pressure.

When the parties met in Geneva on 5–6 December, neither side showed any hint of compromise and Iran declined to meet separately with the United States. The negotiators agreed only to meet again in late January in Turkey. But the subsequent meeting in Istanbul proved even less fruitful. The E3+3 tabled a reformulation of the US fuel-swap proposal that Ahmadinejad had tentatively accepted in October 2009 but was then forced by political rivals to reject. As first proposed, the fuel swap would have provided replacement fuel for the Tehran Research Reactor in exchange for Iran first exporting 1,200kg of LEU to Russia. In October 2009, the 1,200kg that was proposed to be exported would have constituted 75% of Iran's LEU stockpile, leaving less than the amount needed for a weapon (when further enriched to weapons grade). When Turkey and Brazil brokered a revived fuel-swap proposal in May 2010, 1,200kg amounted to less than half of Iran's growing stockpile. The January 2011 E3+3 plan based the swap details not on how much LEU Iran would export, but on how much it would retain: less than a weapon's worth. The smaller amount of 20%-enriched product would also have to be removed. But Iran refused to consider the proposal, or to enter into any discussion of its nuclear programme unless economic sanctions were first lifted and Iran's 'right' to enrich uranium was acknowledged. Iran also again refused a tête-à-tête with the United States. With no agreement to even meet again, the EU-led negotiating team left Istanbul discouraged about prospects for diplomacy.

In Tehran, the post-Istanbul mood was more upbeat. Ahmadinejad said the two meetings laid the ground for an agreement, 'if the other side is committed to justice and respect'. In May 2011, Iranian negotiator Saeed Jalili sent a letter to EU High Representative Catherine Ashton suggesting further talks on a range of issues, including the root causes of terrorism, drug trafficking, piracy in the high seas, energy security, global nuclear disarmament and non-proliferation and cooperation for peaceful uses of nuclear energy. The letter was not received with much enthusiasm in Brussels or other Western capitals, especially after Ahmadinejad repeated that 'Iran's nuclear train has no brake and no reverse gear'.

One of those capitals, London, had long been viewed by Iran as its bête noire – the 'Little Satan' supposedly pulling the springs behind international intrigue directed against the Islamic Republic. Angered by the British ambassador's criticism of Iran's human-rights record, the Majlis repeatedly threatened to cut or downgrade diplomatic relations with the UK. As of June 2011, the UK continued to maintain an embassy in Tehran, but its work was severely hampered by Iranian restrictions and harassment. Unrelated US legislation to restrict New-York-based Iranian diplomats to within 25 miles of the city may have been seen in similar light by Iran.

Iran added fuel to US reasons for antipathy in autumn 2010 when it released several senior members of al-Qaeda who had been under house arrest since entering Iran from Afghanistan in 2002. The move was in exchange for the release of an Iranian diplomat kidnapped in Peshawar in 2008. Al-Qaeda leaders set free included leading military expert Saif al-Adel and Suleiman abu Ghaith, a former spokesman for the organisation. As part of the deal, Iran also reportedly supplied anti-aircraft weapons to the Haqqani network in Pakistan.

Impact of the Arab Awakening

Closer to home, Iran's ties with most of its Gulf neighbours soured over spying accusations and the impact of the Arab Awakening. In March 2011, a Kuwaiti court pronounced a death sentence on two Iranians and a Kuwaiti who had been arrested the previous year spying for Iran by passing information on Kuwaiti military installations. Two other Arabs were given life prison sentences and Kuwait temporarily expelled Iran's ambassador.

A deeper rift erupted with Bahrain, and by extension Saudi Arabia, over the popular protests that spread to the island country from February 2011. Although the street protests were non-sectarian in nature, the protesters were predominantly from Bahrain's majority Shia population and the al-Khalifa ruling family saw them as under the influence of Tehran. When the government cracked down and welcomed the protection of a 1,000-

person Saudi force under the banner of a Gulf Cooperation Council (GCC) operation, the Iranian Majlis issued a statement warning Saudi Arabia and calling for its troops to pull out. Some commentators hyperbolically termed the situation a 'proxy war' between Iran and Saudi Arabia. With Iranian public outrage over the Bahraini crackdown spanning the political spectrum, the Majlis also called for the overthrow of the Bahrain government. Several weeks of tit-for-tat name-calling ensued, with GCC countries complaining to the UN Security Council about Iranian interference in their internal affairs and Tehran condemning the 'baseless accusations and hostility'. The commander of the Basij paramilitary forces in Iran even suggested publicly that Iran should become 'directly involved' in the Bahrain situation, though calmer heads prevailed. They realised that Iran could continue to exploit sectarian tensions in Bahrain without sending either troops or money.

Well before this increase in tensions across the Gulf, Saudi Arabia was upping its guard against Iran's growing missile and nuclear capabilities. In October 2010, the US administration notified Congress of a proposed new $60 billion arms sale to Saudi Arabia. Sales would include fighter aircraft, attack helicopters, upgrades to existing fighter aircraft, and technical assistance with the new equipment. The sale was also intended to increase the relative power of Saudi Arabia with respect to Iran and to reassure the kingdom of US support lest the Saudis seek to emulate Iran by acquiring an independent nuclear capability of their own.

Revelations in November by the WikiLeaks website of US embassy reporting in the region the previous year demonstrated the depth of concern felt by several Gulf states towards Iran. The king of Bahrain insisted that Iran's nuclear programme had to be stopped: 'The danger of letting it go on is greater than the danger of stopping it'. The deputy supreme commander of the United Arab Emirates Armed Forces described Ahmadinejad as Hitler and counselled against appeasement. The king of Saudi Arabia said the United States should not just strike against Iran's nuclear facilities but also 'cut off the head of the snake', and the emir of Qatar offered his territory as a base from which to strike Iran.

In light of the antipathy of unelected Arab leaders towards Tehran, Iran unsurprisingly saw itself the winner of the wave of protests that engulfed the Arab world in spring 2011. Iran's claim that the protests were inspired by its own 1979 Islamic revolution was clearly false. But the initial events of the Arab Awakening did seem to support Iran's view that it was on the ascendancy and America on the decline. Iran had reason to be pleased by the removal of Egypt's Mubarak, who was seen as overly compliant towards the United States, overly willing to maintain peace with Israel, and decidedly anti-Iranian. Tehran took immediate advantage of the new situation by sending two warships through the Suez Canal, the first since before the shah fell in 1979. Commercial flights between the two capitals resumed and Tehran pronounced itself ready to resume diplomatic relations that had been broken for many years. It anticipated that any new government in Cairo would be more antagonistic towards Israel and less beholden to the United States. More generally, Iran saw increased instability in the region as a way to deflect international attention directed against itself.

Even before the Arab Awakening, Iran was boasting that it was on a roll. Claims that Iran was becoming isolated in the region were contradicted by opinion polls of Arab citizens, who seemed to increasingly side with Iran in its nuclear dispute with the West. Polling in summer 2010 in Egypt, Jordan, Lebanon, Morocco, Saudi Arabia and the UAE found that 77% believed Iran had a right to pursue its nuclear programme (up from 53% in 2009) and 57% believed that Iran's acquisition of nuclear weapons would be a positive outcome for the region. In October 2010, Ahmadinejad made his first visit to Lebanon, speaking to adoring crowds and touring villages along the Israeli border. Later, Iran's Hizbullah clients gained the ascendancy in the Lebanese government. Tehran also continued to work its influence in Iraq.

Iran's public narrative about the Islamic, anti-American origins of the Arab Awakening was contradicted by events in Syria, its only state ally. Worried about unsettling comparisons with Iran's own protest movement and the regime's suppression of it, Iranian state media networks were initially reluctant to publicise the protests in Syria. When they became impossible to ignore, Iran's media sought to avoid the hypocrisy of supporting Arab protests elsewhere by labelling the Syrian protesters as criminal gangs and claiming that they were fomented by the United States. As if in mirrored reply, Washington charged Iran with aiding Syrian security forces. Lending credence to this charge, a May 2011 report by the UN Panel of Experts on implementation of Iran sanctions cited nine violations of the UN ban on arms exports from Iran since 2007. Six of them were illicit transfers to Syria; the others were to non-state actors in Afghanistan, Egypt and Gambia. (The latter shipment, discovered in Nigeria, led 20 African countries to downgrade relations with Iran.) The panel concluded that the arms transfers were not intended to generate revenue, but rather to increase Iran's influence in developing regions of the world.

Divided leaders

Boasts by Tehran's leaders of their gains from the Arab Awakening seemed to ignore the danger of protest contagion striking Iran itself. In February, Green Movement leaders Mousavi and Mehdi Karroubi, who were already under a kind of house arrest, were imprisoned lest they find a way to ride the wave of demonstrations in the Middle East. Throughout the first half of 2011, government suppression prevented reformists from re-marshalling the spirit and the crowds that captivated world attention after the disputed 2009 presidential election. But political fissures of another sort rocked Tehran in spring 2011 as Ahmadinejad fell foul of Khamenei. The only connection to the Arab Awakening was that regime loyalists sought to capitalise on public anger at the events in Bahrain as a means to distract attention from the unprecedented political infighting.

At the beginning of 2011, Ahmadinejad had appeared to be growing ever more powerful. The stock market was booming and he had overseen a largely successful economic reform in December. The government ended a decades-long subsidy programme for basic foodstuffs, heating oil and gasoline, saving $60bn, and replaced it with direct payments of about $40 per month per individual. The move hurt the middle and upper classes but its redistributive character pleased the more populous and poorer strata of society. Although it led to a temporary inflation hike, it also rationalised energy use. It led to a 20% fall in demand for gasoline and helped the government weather sanctions directed at its import of refined petroleum. A report by the International Monetary Fund praised the subsidy-reform programme and also noted real GDP growth in 2009/10 of 3.5%. While the reported growth was based solely on government figures, and thus disputed by some critics, it belied claims that sanctions were crippling the economy.

On the political front, Ahmadinejad placed an increasing number of loyalists in key positions and saw the downfall of his most powerful rivals. In March, former president Ayatollah Akbar Hashemi Rafsanjani was forced to step down as head of the Assembly of Experts, one of the government's most powerful bodies. His removal was engineered by Khamenei, who was unhappy with Rafsanjani's support for the Green Movement. Rafsanjani and his family had been the targets of a concerted campaign by Ahmadinejad, who had bested Rafsanjani in the 2005 presidential election and had been feuding with him ever since. Rafsanjani remained the head of the Expediency Council, but this position was to expire in 2012, and he appeared to be running out of options. His marginalisation marked a significant shift in the political balance of power.

Not long after Rafsanjani was ousted, the president found himself on the wrong side of a dispute with the supreme leader. Trouble had been brewing since August 2010, when Ahmadinejad unilaterally appointed his own foreign-policy envoys, without seeking the approval of Foreign Minister Manouchehr Mottaki or of Khamenei, who was in charge of foreign policy. One of the envoys was Ahmadinejad's highly controversial chief of staff, Esfandiar Rahim Mashaei, who wore many hats. In December, Ahmadinejad ungracefully fired Mottaki while the foreign minister was on an official trip to Africa, replacing him with AEOI head Ali Akbar Salehi. The main reason appeared to have been Mottaki's closeness to speaker of the parliament Ali Larijani and to other rivals of the president.

In April 2011, Ahmadinejad dismissed Intelligence Minister Heidar Moslehi on grounds of having bugged the offices of Mashaei. Putting his own man at the head of the ministry would allow the president to control the intelligence vetting of candidates for the 2012 parliamentary elections. When Khamenei overturned this plan by invoking his absolute authority and ordering Moslehi reinstated, a sulking Ahmadinejad refused to attend cabinet meetings for ten days. In May, Ahmadinejad escalated his public rift with Khamenei by firing three additional cabinet ministers without Majlis approval and seeking to take over the Oil Ministry himself, a move that was partially blocked by Khamenei supporters. Meanwhile several Ahmadinejad-related websites were blocked and a number of his associates were arrested.

This extraordinary struggle between Ahmadinejad and Khamenei was over power, not policy. They represent different factions of conservatives. Neither brooks any compromise over the nuclear issue or with Iran's trod-upon reformists. It was Khamenei, after all, who settled the 2009 election dispute by weighing in heavily in Ahmadinejad's favour at considerable damage to his own moral authority. Now, however, there was a larger matter at stake: in the short run, the battle was over who would control ministries. In the longer run, the struggle was over the soul of the regime.

Ahmadinejad and Mashaei, his closest adviser and reputed political heir, have increasingly promoted nationalism at the expense of religion, and speak of an 'Iranian Islam' and the glory of pre-Islamic Iranian civilisation. They want to secularise the Iranian polity. Websites run by Mashaei even criticised the theory of *velayat-e faqih* (guardianship of the jurist) that gives the clerics their political supremacy. For his part, Khamenei naturally seeks to retain the religious nature of the regime. His supporters have characterised Mashaei as a 'deviant', lumping him together with the Green Movement as threatening the very nature of the Islamic Republic. In what was termed an irrevocable break, most observers predicted ultimate victory by the mullahs. But the unprecedented infighting looked like it might well continue until Ahmadinejad's term ends in June 2013 – if he lasted that long. In the meantime, the struggle looked to make it impossible for the president to make any kind of compromise on the nuclear issue. Ahmadinejad might not have been inclined to do so anyway. However, Mashaei was known to have sought contacts with Washington – a move that raised the extraordinary possibility that the United States could be a beneficiary if Ahmadinejad's faction were to prevail in the domestic struggle.

Iraq: Surviving the US Withdrawal

Iraqi politics was dominated by jockeying for power among four multi-party coalitions in the wake of the third set of national elections since Saddam Hussein was toppled by the US-led invasion in 2003. During the run-up to that election, held on 7 March 2010, incumbent Prime Minister Nuri al-Maliki assembled the State of Law Alliance, which was run by Hizb Dawa, his Shia Islamist party. Maliki hoped to utilise the popularity he had garnered across the south and centre of the country based upon his claim to have been responsible for the drop in inter-communal violence since 2007. After prolonged negotiations, Maliki refused to join any overtly religious coalition seeking to maximise the Shia vote. This left the two other strong Shia Islamist parties, the Islamic Supreme Council of Iraq (ISCI), and the Free Independent Party (al-Ahrar) run by the radical Shia cleric Moqtada al-Sadr, to form the Iraqi National Alliance. The State of Law Alliance and the Iraqi National Alliance then fought each other for the support of the Shia population, splitting the vote. The two leading Kurdish parties, the Kurdistan Democratic Party (KDP) and the Patriotic Union of Kurdistan (PUK), re-established the Kurdistan Alliance in hopes of maximising the Kurdish vote in northern Iraq to preserve the substantial autonomy won by the Kurdish Regional Government (KRG) between 2005 and 2007, when the government in Baghdad was in disarray. In turn, the former interim prime minister, Iyad Allawi, built a coalition, the Iraqi National Movement or Iraqiyya, that sought to mobilise not only the Sunni community but also secular and nationalist voters across the south and central Arab parts of Iraq. This coalition proved to be Maliki's most potent rival during the election campaign.

Maliki's arduous victory

The elections delivered a fractured result. The new Iraqi parliament consists of 325 members; thus, the government would need a working majority of 163 to rule effectively. No one party or coalition came near this number, necessitating a set of time-consuming and complex negotiations to build another multi-party government of national unity. During the elections, Allawi's Iraqiyya group proved adept at mobilising the previously marginalised Sunni population, which had provided the support base for Iraq's insurgency, across northwest Iraq. In addition, it picked up a small but consistent cross-sectarian vote in the south. As a result, Iraqiyya won 2,851,823 votes and 91 seats. With the Shia vote split, Maliki's State of Law Alliance was a close second with 2,797,624 votes (89 seats), the Iraqi National Alliance third with 2,095,354 votes (70 seats), and the Kurdistan Alliance fourth with 1,686,344 votes (43 seats). The turnout in 2010 was 62.4% compared with 76% in 2005, reflecting widespread disillusionment with the ruling elite.

The election was run on a semi-open-list system that allowed voters to endorse parties and specific candidates within each coalition. Maliki, running in Baghdad, demonstrated his personal popularity by winning 622,961 votes, the highest tally for an individual candidate. However, Moqtada al-Sadr's Free Independent Party ran the most tactically astute campaign, turning its vote into 39 seats. This made al-Sadr's party the single largest party-level bloc in the new parliament. Maliki's Dawa Party was second with 35 seats, followed by Allawi's party with 31 seats. ISCI, previously one of the dominant parties and a key interlocutor with both Iran and the United States, was fifth, with 20 seats.

Due to the deep legacy of bitterness and mistrust over the de-Ba'athification process (which banned mainly Sunni candidates during the campaign), legal wrangling over the vote count and who had the right to form the government, the highly factionalised nature of the voting, and the reduced leverage of the American and British governments over the political process, it took 249 days to build a government of national unity (compared to 156 days in 2005). Two opposing fears deadlocked coalition negotiations. On the one hand, the majority of politicians were worried that Maliki's growing power could lead to dictatorship. On the other, incumbents feared that the success of Allawi's coalition in mobilising the Sunni vote could enable a radical transformation of Iraqi politics and undermine the political settlement that allowed Kurdish and Shia parties to run the government since the invasion. In particular, the Shia Islamist parties – Dawa, the Sadrists and ISCI – perceived a dominant role for Sunni parties in government as a direct threat.

Allawi's campaign success pivoted on his appeal to Sunnis living between Baghdad and the Kurdish north. While this gained him the largest number of seats, it also hampered his chances of becoming prime minister, since the Kurdistan Alliance – Iraqiyya's main potential coalition partner – is in direct competition with the Sunni Arab parties in Allawi's coalition for control over border areas abutting the KRG's territory. Thus, Maliki's State of Law Alliance opened negotiations with the other main Shia grouping, the Iraqi National Alliance, and in May 2010 the two announced a coalition pact. The new group had 159 seats in parliament, four short of a majority. Maliki, in turn, negotiated a deal with the Kurdistan Alliance whereby his party would support incumbent Iraqi President Jalal Talabani of the PUK for re-election by parliament, and Talabani would nominate Maliki as the next prime minister. On 11 November 2010, these moves were duly made.

Masoud Barazani, the head of the Kurdistan Democratic Party and president of the KRG, had chaired three days of negotiations to bring Allawi and Iraqiyya into the government. Key members of Allawi's Iraqiyya coalition, Saleh al-Mutlaq and Osama al-Najafi, also opened up separate negotiations with Maliki. After securing positions for themselves in government – deputy prime minister and speaker of the parliament, respectively – they strong-armed Allawi into accepting a formal deal by threatening to split Iraqiyya if he rejected it. The breakthrough deal, later named the 'Irbil Agreement', focused on Maliki's signing a 15-point agreement designed specifically to limit the power of the prime minister. Concessions included his handing over control of counter-terrorism forces to the Ministry of Defence and building more robust chains of command over the army and police force. At the centre of the agreement was the formation of a National Council on Strategic Policy that Iyad Allawi would chair. All major policy decisions would be sent to this council for approval before they were enacted by parliament.

According to the Iraqi constitution, Maliki, once nominated on 11 November by Talabani to be prime minister, had 30 days to submit his new cabinet for parliamentary approval. In the event, Maliki did not make his submission until 21 December, and then filled only 31 of the 42 positions. But additional cabinet positions were announced in the middle of February 2011, and parliament agreed to three vice-presidents in the second week of May. A new government had finally coalesced, and it constituted a political triumph for Maliki. In spite of coming second in the elections he retained the premiership, skilfully escaped attempts to constrain his power and managed to appoint a number of loyalists to important cabinet positions. He consistently outmanoeuvred Allawi and Iraqiyya, which failed to secure the prime ministership, the presidency and, as of July 2011, top positions in any of the three security ministries – interior, defence or national security – which Maliki deferred appointing on grounds of political sensitivity. Allawi's possible chairmanship of the National Council on Strategic Policy would have been small consolation, as Maliki stated in December 2010 that the council would have no oversight or executive role, whereupon Allawi publicly declared that he would not chair it.

The upshot was that in July 2011, the Irbil Agreement had not been implemented and no meaningful constraints on Maliki's grip on power were in place. He had not relinquished control of Iraq's anti-terrorism forces, the National Council on Strategic Policy had not met and the KRG had not seen 19 demands that Maliki had promised to meet as part of the coalition package delivered. By waiting out his adversaries, dividing the parties that opposed him and bribing individual politicians with jobs they coveted, Maliki had, if anything, tightened his control of the Iraqi state and its security forces.

Legitimacy undermined

The prolonged struggle surrounding government formation did a great deal of damage to the legitimacy of Iraq's politicians, exacerbating popular dismay over the government's chronic inability to reduce unemployment or deliver sufficient electricity. Indicating the extent of the people's anger towards the Iraqi government – especially on the part of the young urban population – and a degree of inspiration from the Arab Awakening, some 1,000 people forced their way into local government offices in the southern provincial capital of Diwaniya in February 2011. The next day, Maliki attempted to stem the rising tide of protest by announcing that he would cut his own salary by half. A day later one of his advisers went so far as to suggest that he might not seek a third term in office, although this statement was quickly diluted by a number of caveats. In any case, these attempts at placation were unsuccessful, as demonstrations against the government spread across Iraq. Protesters seeking to emulate the demonstrators in Cairo set up a tented encampment in Baghdad's own Tahrir Square, only to see it broken up by non-uniformed government supporters wielding clubs and knives.

The government then adopted a dual strategy to defuse popular resentment. At the end of February, Maliki announced that he had given his cabinet 100 days to improve the performance of their ministries. He also tried to devolve blame for the failure to deliver services on the provincial governments and called for new local elections only two years after the previous ones. He re-allocated $1bn that had been earmarked for the purchase of US fighter jets to increase government ration payments and promised to create 280,000 new jobs. But while publicly striking these conciliatory notes, Maliki's government used state power to crush the demonstrations. On 25 February, Iraq's 'Day of Rage', the government banned all cars from Baghdad, forcing protesters to walk to Tahrir Square. Then, in the aftermath of the demonstrations, 300 intellectuals were arrested and two parties were banned and evicted from their headquarters. Finally, in mid-March, Maliki denounced the demonstrators, claiming they were out of touch with the popular will, small in number and deliberately trying to sow the seeds of discord.

The KRG, too, faced popular protest in the northern cities of Irbil and Sulaimaniya. The demonstrators denounced the KRG as corrupt and dominated by the two main Kurdish parties, the KDP and PUK. When protesters threw rocks at party buildings, guards responded with deadly gunfire. Like the Iraqi national government, the KRG employed state-sponsored violence in the central square of Sulaimaniya to break up demonstrations and arrest their organisers.

The US withdrawal

The Status of Forces Agreement (SOFA) negotiated between the Iraqi and American governments in 2008 at the end of the George W. Bush administration was the main factor in shaping the security environment during 2010–11. In June 2009, under the auspices of the SOFA, the US military withdrew its forces from all of Iraq's towns and cities. On 31 August 2010, the US military ceased combat missions in Iraq, leaving primary responsibility for maintaining order to Iraq's indigenous security forces. Under the SOFA, all US forces were to leave the country by 31 December 2011.

The end of combat operations in August 2010 transformed the American role in the country from a kinetic operation to a training mission. The three separate military commands – Multi-National Force-Iraq, Multi-National Corps-Iraq and Multi-National Security Transition Command-Iraq – were merged into one organisation, the Iraq Training and Advisory Mission (ITAM). US troop numbers, which at their peak had numbered 176,000, had as of July 2011 been reduced to 45,000. From August 2010 onwards, the working assumption of American ground commanders was that the US deployment would be reduced to the 'tens or low hundreds' as the final SOFA deadline of 31 December 2011 approached. ITAM's goal was to train and mentor the Iraqi security forces in the hope that they could reach what the US government termed the 'minimum essential capability' standards needed to replace all US forces by then.

By April 2011, it was clear that the US government was keen to renegotiate the SOFA to allow between 10,000 and 20,000 American troops to remain past the deadline. Both Secretary of Defense Robert Gates and Chairman of the Joint Chiefs of Staff Admiral Mike Mullen visited Baghdad in an attempt to gain permission from the Iraqi government to allow the troops to stay, and to secure legal protection for them and approval from the Iraqi parliament. In late May, Gates estimated that the United States would need a minimum of 8,000 soldiers in the country to meet its ongoing commitments to train Iraqi forces.

The Iraqi government and wider Iraqi public opinion was not receptive to US requests for a renegotiation of the SOFA. In private, key Iraqi politicians acknowledged that the Iraqi armed forces, particularly the Iraqi air force, were still heavily dependent on US support for key functions. In public, however, Iraqi opinion was vociferously opposed to any renegotiation. Moqtada al-Sadr's party mobilised popular sentiment against a continuing US presence, staging a number of large demonstrations and promising to use violence if necessary to drive the remaining American troops from Iraq. In his public statements, Maliki attempted to balance the needs of the Iraqi military with the political reality of Iraqi opinion. In an interview with the *Wall Street Journal* in December 2010, he appeared to leave little room for revision, stating: 'I do not care about what's being said. I care about what's on paper and what has been agreed to. The withdrawal of forces agreement expires on December 31, 2011. The last American soldier will leave Iraq.' Yet he also left open the possibility of a new agreement if the Iraqi parliament accepted it. Given that the Sadrists were the largest party in parliament and only the KDP and PUK were expressly backing a new agreement, however, enacting any such legislation before the deadline seemed highly unlikely.

In 2012, then, the US State Department will have to shoulder substantial responsibility for protecting its diplomats and training the Iraqi security forces. The American Embassy was planning to hire 5,000 private security contractors to meet these needs. It will also take over a substantial proportion of the base adjacent to Baghdad International Airport and open consulates in both the north and south of the country. The Embassy will house an Office of Security Cooperation to manage the US government's relations with Iraq's armed forces.

Iraqi security capacity and capabilities

The Iraqi forces responsible for ensuring the stability of the country from 2012 forward are split between the Ministry of Defence, with 250,000 personnel, and the Ministry of Interior, with 410,000. A broad set of problems continued to plague the Iraqi army and needed to be addressed for it to fulfil its new responsibilities. The first involved weaknesses in management, logistics and strategic planning. The inflexible unwillingness of senior military officials to delegate continued to stifle innovation and independent decision-making down the chain of command. Furthermore, there remained a problem of loyalty to the state insofar as the influence of sectarian and ethnically based political parties persisted at all levels of the army. The Ministry of Defence challenged bias by, for example, repeatedly moving locally raised forces and breaking their links with political parties, but doubts remained about the overall loyalty of the army to the central government.

The Ministry of Interior, with larger force numbers, had acquired responsibility not only for day-to-day law and order but also for paramilitary counter-insurgency. The risks involved in this expansion of its role were evident in Iraq's recent history. Between 2005 and 2006, Ministry of Interior forces were a major factor in driving Iraq into civil war. The Ministry's Special Police Commandos (later renamed the Federal Police), acted as a sectarian death squad, frequently resorting to extra-judicial execution and torture. After 2007, the Federal Police were purged of their most egregious sectarian elements when 60,000 officers were dismissed and the force was greatly expanded and further restructured. But despite extensive vetting, restructuring and sustained expansion, the force is still plagued by corruption and sectarianism.

The politicisation of Iraq's security forces was most evident in the Iraqi National Counter Terrorism Force. The force had over 6,000 men in its ranks, was organised into two brigades and was considered to be one of the best trained in the Middle East. It operated its own detention centres and intelligence-gathering operations and had surveillance cells in every governorate. Its politicisation began in April 2007, when managerial responsibility was transferred from the US special forces, which established the force, to the Iraqi government. Maliki set up a ministerial body, the Counter-Terrorism Bureau, to control it, effectively removing the force from the oversight of parliament or the control of either the Ministry of Interior or Ministry of Defence. The force subsequently became known as the Fedayeen al-Maliki, a reference to its reputation as the prime minister's tool for covert action against his rivals as well as an ironic comparison to Saddam Hussein's militia. Iraq's intelligence services were similarly politicised. Maliki's personal control over them directly hampered their ability to collect and analyse intelligence professionally and objectively without close US supervision.

The politicisation of the military extended well beyond the national police and intelligence services. From 2006 onwards, Maliki used a number of tactics to tighten his personal grip over Iraq's armed forces. First he used the Office of the Commander in Chief to control overall security policy, undermining the independent chains of command within both the Ministries of Interior and Defence. Maliki then forced technocratic senior commanders aside, appointing those close to him into positions of influence in both ministries. These appointments were labelled 'temporary' to avoid parliamentary oversight. Finally, Maliki set up nine joint operation commands. Each of them consolidated, under one commanding officer, the management of all the security services operating in each of the nine provinces (out of 18 in total) considered unstable. These officers, in turn, were appointed and managed from a central office in Baghdad under Maliki's control. Through the use of the joint operation commands, Maliki bypassed the security ministers and their senior commanders, securing control over Iraq's armed forces at the operational level. While this arrangement made a military coup in Iraq highly unlikely, it also lent incoherence to the chain of command, allowed the promotion of political cronies over talented commanders and detracted from the military's *esprit de corps*.

Shaky outlook

Overall, in spite of ongoing inefficiencies and politicisation, Iraq's security forces looked able to impose rough order on the country from 2012 onwards. But politically motivated violence remained a major problem across south and central Iraq. Sectarian violence peaked in October 2006 when 3,709 people were murdered in a single month. From then until 2009, due in part to the US-led 'surge', violence steadily decreased. From January 2009 onwards, politically motivated violence remained fairly constant, with an average of 200 deaths a month. The majority of those were murdered in mass-casualty attacks or random bombings and shootings.

A sizeable minority, however, were specifically targeted for assassination. There were 14 such political murders in Baghdad in February 2011, 31 in March and 44 in April. Most of the victims were government employees, usually in the police or intelligence services. The assailants used either silenced weapons or small 'sticky bombs' placed under the target's car. They often utilised accurate real-time intelligence that could only have been supplied by those working within government service. These features indicated that violence in Iraq had moved from the wholesale slaughter associated with the religious cleansing of Baghdad at the peak of the civil war in 2006, to the targeted assassination of senior members of the security services by groups with substantial political cover and government access.

It was al-Qaeda in Mesopotamia (AQM) and the Shia militias associated with Moqtada al-Sadr and funded by Iran that drove Iraq into civil war in 2005 and 2006. The ability of these organisations to employ violence on a mass scale has been greatly reduced: the Iraqi armed forces have the capability to keep the activities of AQM and the Shia militias at their current levels. However, the rising trend of assassinations of senior civil servants and security personnel clearly indicates that political murder remains a favoured tool of Iraq's political elite in the ongoing struggle to control the state. This is likely to remain the case at least over the next several years, and the incidence of assassination may well increase once US forces have left Iraq. Such a development, especially if accompanied by continued poor civic performance by the government and corresponding protests, would significantly increase the likelihood that violence and political instability could escalate close to the level of civil war again. This would push the Iraqi armed forces near the limit of their capacity.

Israel and Palestine: Turbulence on All Fronts

Though the United States attempted to get Israeli–Palestinian negotiations back on track, regional developments as well as Palestinian and Israeli domestic politics made genuine progress impossible. Iran's commitment to its nuclear agenda and the swift collapse of the Mubarak regime in Egypt diverted Israel's attention from a quiescent West Bank, while the eruption of mass demonstrations across the Arab world against corrupt, authoritarian governments had a chilling effect on the Palestinian Authority (PA) leadership. Domestically, conservative elements constrained ruling coalitions on both sides from making concessions to advance peace talks. Yet despite these forbidding circumstances, the Obama administration was persisting at mid-2011 with its labours to obtain an agreement.

The impetus was the PA's push for recognition of Palestine as a sovereign state by the UN General Assembly at its September 2011 meeting – an initiative described by former US official Aaron David Miller in the *Washington*

Post as an idea that 'takes dumb to a new level'. His point was that the PA's nominal success, if achieved, would in fact precipitate stiffer American and Israeli resistance, potentially setting back the two-state effort for a genera-tion. Nevertheless, the very unpredictability of the move's consequences for all the parties, including Washington, re-energised the peace process. It remained to be seen whether enough could be achieved for the Palestinian leadership to be able to walk safely away from a unilateral declaration of statehood that they belatedly realised could result in an irretrievable loss of credibility.

From an Israeli perspective, if there was one other dominant theme in this period, it was 'delegitimation'. This term was adopted to describe the perceived acceleration of a long-term trend, particularly in Western Europe, to privilege the Palestinian narrative over the Israeli one and embrace more open opposition to Israel's occupation of the West Bank and blockade of Gaza. The fear of Israelis was that a UN General Assembly vote would impart new momentum to this shift in opinion and result in diplomatic isolation.

The settlements issue

A new cycle in Israeli–Palestinian relations began on 1 May 2010, as Arab League foreign ministers met in Cairo at the Palestinians' request to re-endorse plans to begin proximity talks, with the proviso that the Palestinians would not move to direct negotiations until Israel stopped all construction of settlements beyond the 1967 borders. The Obama administration had demonstrated its commitment to the peace process in 2009 by demanding that Israel halt settlement construction. But years of tangled bilateral diplo-macy on the issue had produced unintended consequences. In particular, the settler movement had evolved into a powerful voting bloc as the Israeli Jewish population on the Palestinian side of the Green Line mushroomed to nearly half a million. The political leverage that the settlers could wield outweighed the Obama administration's influence on an Israeli government that faced no real pressure from the left. PA President Mahmoud Abbas was boxed in. He could not plausibly appear to be less concerned with settle-ments than his American counterpart, and thus was forced to embrace the administration's emphasis on them even though he was aware of the politi-cal futility of doing so.

In the wake of the Arab League ministerial meeting, US special envoy George Mitchell arrived in the region for another in a series of visits to secure formal PA–Israeli agreement to proximity talks. The PA demanded that Israel halt all new settlement construction and evictions of Palestinians during the four months of negotiations, while Israel demanded that the PA cease all incitement of protest, which, from Israel's standpoint, included the Palestinian boycott of settlement-made goods. As a gesture of good will, the Israel Defense Forces (IDF) destroyed several structures in the Shavei Shomron settlement that had been built in violation of the ten-month settlement freeze.

Demands and counter-demands ricocheted for five days before Mitchell, Israel and the Palestine Liberation Organisation (PLO) Executive Committee formally agreed on 9 May to launch the talks, the first since December 2008. Although the talks were apparently unproductive, Israel did take some conciliatory steps that Washington had wanted, including a relaxation of some restrictions on West Bank movement and access. Promised measures included removing 60 roadblocks (around 10% of the total) across the West Bank, moves to improve Palestinian tourism and trade, and lifting some restrictions on Israeli Arabs' access to the West Bank.

The *Mavi Marmara* crisis

Whatever progress there might have been was forestalled by the crisis that erupted between Turkey and Israel over the Israeli interception of a six-vessel humanitarian flotilla that had set out from a Turkish port despite Israel's 27 May warning that it would not allow the boats to reach Gaza, their declared destination. The flotilla had been organised by the Free Gaza Movement (FGM) and a Turkish organisation, Humanitarian Relief Fund (IHH), to defy Israel's 'siege' of Gaza and deliver 10,000 tonnes of humanitarian aid. On 30 May, three Israeli Navy missile ships intercepted the flotilla in international waters. Israeli commandos in boats and helicopters commandeered five small boats without incident, but soldiers rappelling from a helicopter on to the main vessel, the *Mavi Marmara*, opened fire, killing nine Turkish activists (one with dual US citizenship); another 53 passengers were wounded and seven Israeli commandos were stabbed or shot.

The IDF claimed its troops acted in self-defence against a premeditated attack by passengers; the FGM and IHH said the passengers were unarmed and non-violent and at most acted in self-defence. As the facts unfolded, it appeared that some of the activists had prepared to assault the boarding team. In light of the incident, the United States cancelled a meeting between President Barack Obama and Israeli Prime Minister Benjamin Netanyahu scheduled for 1 June, saying that the United States was 'deeply concerned by the suffering of civilians in Gaza' and 'will continue to engage the Israelis on a daily basis to expand the scope and type of goods allowed into Gaza'.

The fight on the *Mavi Marmara* marked a turning point in perceptions of Israel, especially in Europe. The speed with which Israeli–Turkish relations deteriorated as a result of the incident also seemed to suggest a steeper decline in Israel's regional position than had previously been perceived. The White House summoned Israeli Ambassador Michael Oren and National Security Advisor Uzi Arad to a four-hour meeting to discuss how to contain the effects of the flotilla raid and to find ways for Israel to ease the siege of Gaza without degrading Israeli security. Egypt then announced that it would open its border with Gaza for unlimited travel for humanitarian purposes, though the importation of goods would remain restricted in accordance with Israeli security requirements. Cairo proceeded to open its side of the Rafah border in both directions to Palestinian medical patients, students, other humanitarian cases with proper travel documents, and foreign passport holders. Although Egypt ended up denying entry to a significant number of Palestinians approved for exit by Hamas, thousands of Gazans streamed to the border crossing in hopes of reaching stores in Egyptian Rafah, and the crossing remained open until the end of September.

Damage control

As the aftershocks of the flotilla episode rippled through the region, Obama proposed that Israel move from a wholesale ban on imports to Gaza with few exemptions to a regime that allowed most imports except for a narrow list of prohibited items. After two days of heated debate, Netanyahu's security cabinet, under heavy international pressure, agreed to increase the quantity of goods already allowed for import (including building materials for construction overseen by credible third parties, such as the UN) and to add some new items to the exemption list (which would now include all foodstuffs). The strict naval blockade, however, would remain in place. A few days later, Mitchell travelled to the Kerem Shalom crossing to monitor Israel's easing of restrictions on imports to Gaza, including the transfer of the first tranche of goods from the FGM–IHH flotilla. Gaza's electricity plant received a load of industrial fuel as well, allowing it to resume operations after a four-day outage, the longest since the beginning of 2010.

None of these concessions seemed to buttress Abbas's political position – a central concern in Washington. Hours before the Palestinian Central Elections Commission's deadline to submit electoral lists for municipal elections slated to begin on 17 July, the PA postponed the elections indefinitely, claiming that they would derail national unity talks with Hamas. Most observers, however, attributed the decision to the inability of Fatah, the leading secular Palestinian party, to agree on its own slate of candidates, and to pre-election polls indicating that non-Fatah independent candidates were poised to win key races.

As Obama and Netanyahu agreed to meet in early July, Mitchell reported that Palestinian and Israeli negotiators were ready to consider renewing proximity talks. However, Israel's Jerusalem Planning Commission then granted preliminary approval for the re-zoning and demolition of 22 Palestinian homes in the Silwan neighbourhood in order to build an archaeological park, a 1,000-unit Jewish residential area, and a tourist zone. The re-zoning measure also retroactively approved Jewish settlers' Beit Yonatan construction, which had been judged illegal by Israel's Jerusalem District Court in May.

Netanyahu's arrival at the White House signalled another Obama administration push to get the parties to resume direct negotiations. Netanyahu urged Obama to press Abbas to begin talks before Israel's ten-month settlement freeze expired on 29 September; he pledged that Israel would take 'concrete steps'. PA negotiations adviser Saeb Erekat rejected this gambit, saying that the onus was on Israel to halt settlement construction and to agree to begin talks from the point they had reached in late 2008. Obama encouraged Abbas to moderate these terms, but the PA leader instead demanded a comprehensive settlement freeze including East Jerusalem and assurances that all final status issues would be discussed. At this point, the White House enlisted the help of Mohammed bin Zayed Al Nahyan, crown prince of Abu Dhabi, and Egyptian President Hosni Mubarak to cajole Abbas. They and Mitchell were evidently successful: Abbas agreed to direct talks and, by the end of July, Arab League foreign ministers had met to provide him with pan-Arab diplomatic support.

In August, the administration sensed that the situation on the ground had stabilised sufficiently to warrant a sustained presidential push for an agreement. US Secretary of State Hillary Clinton therefore announced that the United States would host Abbas and Netanyahu on 2 September for their first face-to-face negotiations since late 2008, with the United States declaring that a final-status deal could be reached within a year. The Quartet – the United States, the United Nations, the European Union and Russia – simultaneously issued a statement reiterating its endorsement of direct talks towards a final agreement that 'ends the occupation which began in 1967' and would result in the creation of a Palestinian state, as well as calling on 'both sides to observe calm and restraint, and to refrain from provocative actions and inflammatory rhetoric'. Netanyahu's office welcomed the proposal. Not unexpectedly, Hamas's military wing, the Izzeddin al-Qassam Brigades, lashed out, killing four Jewish settlers, marking the deadliest West Bank attack on Israelis in more than two years and the first staged by Hamas since before the 2006 Palestinian elections. Abbas and Netanyahu agreed that the attack should not derail peace talks. Nor did it.

Frustrated diplomacy and its fallout

The pace of diplomacy throughout the fall was frenetic. Direct Israeli–Palestinian negotiations were re-launched in Washington, accompanied by a joint Abbas and Netanyahu pledge to meet again ten days later in Egypt and then every two weeks thereafter to 'keep momentum going'. Clinton, Abbas, Netanyahu and Mitchell then met, and a private Abbas–Netanyahu encounter followed. Mitchell announced that the leaders had decided to work towards a framework agreement within a year that would outline compromises to be made by each side to achieve peace, as an initial step before attempting to reach a comprehensive treaty. A second round of direct talks opened in the Egyptian resort of Sharm el-Sheikh, where Mubarak hosted Abbas, Netanyahu and Clinton for the first day of meetings with talks set to continue in Jerusalem and Ramallah later in the month, and thereafter alternating between Jerusalem and Jericho. For all the dynamism on display, however, the United States failed to secure Israeli–Palestinian agreement on the agenda.

To keep up the pressure, Clinton widened the circle of players, briefing Jordan's King Abdullah on the Sharm el-Sheikh talks. Mitchell briefed Syrian President Bashar al-Assad, saying that the United States intended to push for renewed Israeli–Syrian peace talks parallel to Israeli–Palestinian talks. He assured Lebanese officials that Washington would urge a comprehensive Israeli–Arab peace to include Lebanon and Syria. At the same time, Clinton tried to narrow the agenda to maximise chances for concrete results. She and Mubarak recommended that Israel agree to a short extension to the settlement freeze, during which the parties would focus on border issues with an eye to determining which settlements would stay or go under an eventual final status agreement. The impending 26 September expiration of the freeze concentrated minds: no one knew whether Netanyahu would extend it at the eleventh hour, or whether Abbas would stay in the game if Israel let it expire.

Against this tense backdrop, Israeli Defence Minister Ehud Barak arrived in Washington with a back-channel proposal for Israel to extend the freeze for a short period in exchange for a large package of advanced aircraft and other forms of military assistance. When the details were released, the vast gap between the meagre Israeli concession and the substantial reward led to public stupefaction, with denials on both sides that the purported quid pro quo had even been broached. There was also a surreal quality to Netanyahu's bid to secure the backing of right-wing coalition partners for a short extension of the settlement freeze in return for US guarantees: he proposed legislation that would require those becoming Israeli citizens to pledge a loyalty oath to 'the State of Israel as a Jewish and democratic state', as opposed to simply 'the State of Israel' as it is now worded.

In the event, Netanyahu let the freeze expire. Efforts to keep Abbas at the table were unavailing. On 2 October, after convening the PLO Executive Committee along with the Fatah Central Committee in Ramallah, he issued a statement to the effect that the Palestinian leadership was in agreement that direct negotiations should not resume without a halt to Israeli settlement construction. Hamas welcomed the statement. Abbas then left for Jordan and Egypt to win Arab backing for the Palestinian position, which Arab League foreign ministers, meeting in Libya, strongly endorsed.

Two unexpected events added to the complexity of the peace process. Firstly, Netanyahu publicly declared his acceptance of the idea of a demilitarised Palestinian state. This raised once again questions that had surrounded him since his first spell as prime minister in the 1990s, in particular whether he was an ideologue or a pragmatist. Israeli observers seemed to be as divided on this as outside analysts. In any case, the prime minister was now on record as favouring a two-state solution to the conflict.

The second, related event was the publication by the Qatari-based news organisation al-Jazeera in January 2011 of the 'Palestine Papers', so called by analogy to the fabled Pentagon Papers composed in the late 1960s, which when leaked and published by the *New York Times* and *Washington Post* in 1971 disclosed internal government deliberations about Vietnam at odds with what Washington had stated to the public about the progress of the war. The Palestine Papers reflected the Palestinian interpretation of a lengthy negotiation between Abbas and former Israeli Prime Minister Ehud Olmert, in which both sides made far-reaching concessions on the core issues of refugee resettlement, borders and the status of Jerusalem. Both Abbas and Olmert confirmed the authenticity of the narrative presented by the Palestine Papers, and Olmert gave the Israeli side of the story in his autobiography. Among Palestinians, the papers' revelations produced vituperative criticism of Abbas and made a serious dent in his public standing and political viability. This suggested that Palestinians, certainly on the

West Bank, were ill-prepared for the compromises that a successful peace deal would entail.

The papers also strongly suggested that the relatively determined American push over the course of 2010 for direct talks never achieved traction, despite Clinton's expressed intention to obtain an agreement within the year, primarily because the insertion of a settlement freeze as a precondition politically hobbled both sides.

The peace process and the Arab Awakening

From early 2011, the diplomatic paralysis of the peace process was rendered acute by the wave of unrest that swept the Arab world, combined with continuing preoccupation with Iran's nuclear agenda. Israeli attention became focused on at least five potential problems connected to the Arab uprisings: a crisis in Egyptian–Israeli relations; large-scale unrest in Syria; from a planning perspective, the prospect of a multi-front war; a youth revolt among Palestinians on the West Bank; and increased tension in Israel's special relationship with the United States.

Israel's bilateral relationship with Egypt had for years benefited Israel in the Palestinian context as well as that of regional security. The Mubarak government suppressed the Muslim Brotherhood, viewing the organisation as a profound threat to the existing political order. Since Hamas is an offshoot of the Brotherhood and embraces its ideology, Egypt viewed assistance to Israel in containing Hamas as being in its own interest. From the standpoint of the Mubarak regime, any success achieved by Hamas in managing Gaza while thumbing its nose at Israel would only burnish the Brotherhood's credentials. Thus, Israel had a ready partner in restricting the smuggling of weapons and ammunition into Gaza. This, in turn, facilitated Israeli control of the territory. As was feared by Israel, the removal of Mubarak led to a relaxation of Egyptian vigilance on the Gaza border and increased flow of men and materiel to Hamas. To the extent that the Hamas leadership is emboldened by this reversal of diplomatic and operational fortune, Israel will expect increased provocations from Hamas, probably in the form of missile attacks, which will in turn make renewed Israeli shelling and possibly incursions into Gaza more likely.

The peace treaty reached in 1979 between Israel and Egypt had been a bulwark of Israeli security strategy ever since. Under the treaty, the state of war between the two countries ended and they recognised each other. Israel withdrew its forces from the Sinai Peninsula and Egypt agreed to keep most of it demilitarised. As of mid-2011, the interim government in Cairo had been assiduous in reassuring Israel that the treaty was not in jeopardy. Public sentiment did not look to be a major problem, at least in the near term. An April 2011 Egyptian poll cited by the *Wall Street Journal* indicated that 60% of respondents supported the peace treaty. The Muslim Brotherhood's position was that the treaty should be 'reviewed' and its advantages or disadvantages for Egypt publicly assessed. However, the Egyptian military seemed likely to judge the treaty to be essential to its – and the country's – interests. Adherence to the treaty wins a minimum of $1 billion per year in security assistance from the United States and greatly reduces Egypt's strategic exposure, much as it does Israel's. Yet pessimistic Israelis remained worried that Egypt's revolution might only have begun and that, at some point, either religious extremists or extreme nationalists would dominate the country, leading to a replay of the Six-Day War of June 1967.

Israelis were also apprehensive about the swelling demonstrations against Assad's regime in Syria and his increasingly lethal repressive crackdown. With protesters unable to dislodge the regime and Assad vaguely offering a national dialogue and the possibility of a multi-party government and a new constitution in a 20 June speech, Israeli analysts were still inclined at mid-2011 to believe that he would quell the revolt and hold on to power. But they could not be sure, as protests, mass displacement and lethal state repression continued, and opposition figures remained sceptical of the genuineness of Assad's nod to reform. From an Israeli strategic vantage point, the Assad dynasty had functioned somewhat like a loyal opposition. Prior to the accession of Hafiz al-Assad in 1970, instability on Israel's border with Syria was chronic. From Israel's perspective, the Assad regime, though not well disposed towards it, was at least stable and the relationship was, for the most part, non-violent – though there were exceptions such as the 1982 Lebanon war and Israel's 2007 destruction of a Syrian nuclear facility. In Lebanon, there had at times been tacit cooperation. Hence the dismay of Israeli analysts over UN Security Council Resolution 1559, adopted in September 2004, which mandated Syria's withdrawal from Lebanon. Israel, which withdrew its forces unilaterally from southern Lebanon in May 2000, relied on Syrian authority to ensure that Hizbullah would not exploit the redeployment by attacking northern Israeli towns. The departure of Syrian troops presaged a round of miscalculations that led ultimately to the summer war of 2006. The subsequent slow reassertion of Syrian influence in Lebanon was welcomed by some Israelis, who believed that Assad-style discipline was the best hope for keeping the situation on the border on an even keel.

Other Israeli analysts, however, were focusing on the potential advantages of a new Sunni regime in Syria that could replace Assad's Alawite Shia one. Foremost among these would be reduced Iranian influence. This reasoning presupposed that no Sunni regime would tolerate – let alone invite – the sort of Iranian influence over Syria that Tehran was enjoying. This, in turn, would eliminate Iran's land link to Lebanon and weaken its effective presence (by its proxy, Hizbullah) on the Israel–Lebanon border. The result, in the view of these analysts, would be a more stable border and renewed possibility of a peace agreement with Damascus. But whether a new regime would be disposed to cooperate with Israel was an open question. Pessimists suggested that the shattered remnant of Islamist opposition in Syria could be reinvigorated in a transition, or that another leader could emerge to take control of revolutionary passions and channel them toward a nationalist agenda that could entail confrontation with Israel. Whatever the future holds, Israel's confidence in stability on its border with Syria, and by extension with Lebanon, can no longer be taken for granted.

The developments in Egypt and Syria, then, shook Israeli security doctrine. Israeli planners had long presupposed a secure southern flank. The Israel–Egyptian peace treaty, combined with the extensive warning afforded by the wide no-man's-land that it mandated, sharply reduced the threat of Egyptian attack while increasing the stability of existing arrangements in a serious crisis. A collateral effect was the freedom it accorded Israeli planners to allocate forces to other fronts and missions. Furthermore, the historical record suggested that to the north, Syria would not strike without a simultaneous Egyptian attack. Since that was no longer possible, neither was a major conflagration involving entire armies. The treaty therefore signalled a sea change in Israel's strategic position and, in the view of many Israelis, effectively foreclosed the possibility of another major land war. Now, however, this plank in Israel's security doctrine could no longer be considered a sure thing. Nor could Egypt's anti-Iranian stance.

Palestine in the balance

The upheaval in the Arab world had a further effect on the Israel–Palestine confrontation in that it added a new element to domestic Palestinian politics. Although the PLO had long ago abandoned revolutionary rhetoric, Israelis feared that a revolutionary mood could re-emerge in Palestine in protest against the same transgressions by the elite that motivated demonstrators in neighbouring countries: corruption, cronyism, incompetence and subordination to outsiders. The target of such protests would be Palestinian president Mahmoud Abbas. Protests did break out in Palestine, but focused mainly on the agreement between Hamas and Fatah, signed on 4 May, to form a unity government. This development made restarting peace talks all the more difficult, as Israeli officials repeated their long-held refusal to talk to Hamas unless it renounced its vow to extinguish the state of Israel. Mitchell, perhaps sensing futility, resigned on 13 May 2011.

Both the United States and Israel hoped that Abbas would return to negotiations on a solution to the Israel–Palestine dispute. However, the eruption of large-scale demonstrations against a backdrop of plunging poll ratings would probably deter him from re-entering a process that would entail unpopular compromises, which the Palestinian Papers episode suggested would be difficult to sustain politically. To make matters worse, Abbas's main backer in the Arab world, Mubarak, was no longer available as a diplomatic ally.

As of June 2011, Abbas's political position remained tenuously viable. A strong US push on the peace process, initiated by Obama's 19 May speech on the Middle East and North Africa at the State Department during Netanyahu's visit to Washington, was intended to strengthen Abbas, to spur both sides to resume talks and to encourage European opposition to the PA's quest for UN recognition. The administration had been split between those who felt that the United States had to remain in close consultation and coordination with Israel and proceed cautiously, and those favouring a bolder approach whereby Washington laid out a specific framework for peace addressing divisive issues such as the status of Jerusalem, Palestinians' right of return and settlements. Obama effectively split the difference, avoiding pronouncements on those matters but, in affirming US support for a two-state solution and a demilitarised Palestinian state, put forth one explicit territorial principle: that 'the borders of Israel and Palestine should be based on the 1967 lines with mutually agreed swaps, so that secure and recognized borders are established for both states'. This formula did not reflect any major substantive change in US thinking in the larger context of the 2000–2001 Camp David/Taba process and subsequent Bush administration initiatives. But in a press statement following a meeting between Obama and Netanyahu at the White House the next day, the Israeli prime minister defiantly asserted that Israel's pre-1967 borders were 'indefensible', and that Israel could not return to them – pointedly ignoring Obama's 'mutually agreed swaps' qualification.

In subsequent conferences with American Jewish leaders, the administration tried to impart to Israel a sense of urgency in suggesting that re-engaging with the Palestinians would help head off the PA's push for UN recognition in September, but some American critics read this linkage as an administration attempt to 'bully Israel' into talking with Hamas. France's 7 June proposal of a July international conference in Paris on the Israeli–Palestinian conflict met with a cool US reception, and in any case did not appear likely to bear fruit. As of June 2011, the worry was that if the US initiative failed to gather critical momentum, or was seen to be stymied by Israel, the push could galvanise rather than diminish Palestinian anger. If, in addition, a UN General Assembly vote formally established a Palestinian state and peace flotillas converged on Gaza, serious Palestinian unrest could arise. If Hamas provocations and harsh Israeli reactions ensued, US–Israeli relations could rupture. They would then require arduous resetting. These eventualities would make actual peace on the ground an even more distant prospect than it had been during the year to mid 2011.

Chapter 7
Africa

Emerging from the global economic downturn, Africa averaged 3% economic growth in 2010 on the back of higher commodity output and exports from petroleum-centred economies such as Nigeria and Angola, and resurgent mineral exports and manufacturing investment from South Africa. China and, increasingly, India remain major trade and development partners for Africa, as do the European Union and the United States. African diasporas have become major investment partners for the continent, and there has been a shift in emphasis from mere remittances to direct investment. For a number of countries such as Ethiopia and South Africa, however, impressive economic figures belied a trend of 'jobless growth'. Furthermore, the last quarter of 2010 saw slower growth in a number of African economies as higher global food prices hindered progress.

The year to mid-2011 was a busy one for politics, with national elections in many countries. In general, ruling parties and incumbents won, but there were wide divergences in the quality and results of the elections. Overall, it was not the electoral process so much as the immediate post-election environment, particularly where there were run-off elections, that was problematic. A case in point was the bloody four-month battle in Côte d'Ivoire between the internationally recognised victor Alassane Ouattara and incumbent Laurent Gbagbo following the December 2010 presidential run-off. Moreover, intimidation and fraud continued to affect the integrity of elections, although the indictment of Kenyan politicians by the International Criminal Court (ICC) following the post-election violence in Kenya in 2007–08 underlined a trend towards international accountability.

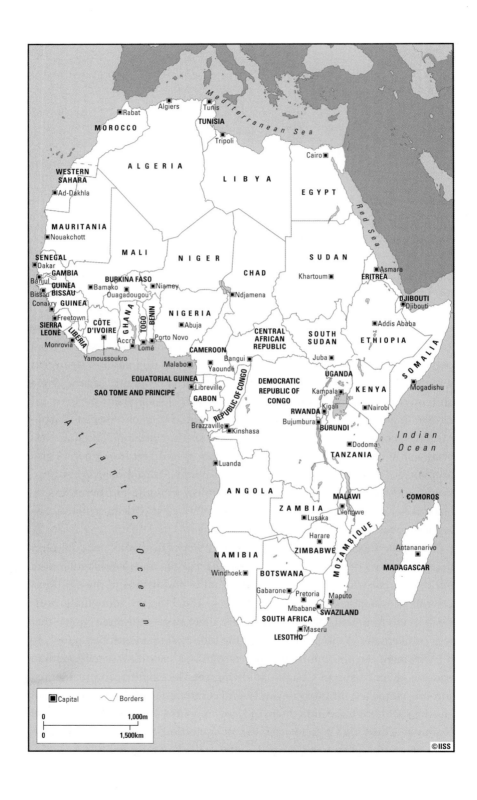

The UN and French interventions in Côte d'Ivoire, as well as the US and NATO intervention in Libya, crystallised an unusually firm global consensus on the legitimacy of the use of force to protect civilians. But the interventions also raised questions about whether Africa was being forced to sub-contract its conflict resolution to the West due to its lack of capacity. As of June 2011, African Union (AU) attempts to broker a political solution to the conflict in Libya had been futile.

Africa and the Arab Awakening

The so-called Arab Awakening, which began with the self-immolation of Tunisian street vendor Mohamed Bouazizi on 17 December 2010, challenged entrenched notions that North Africa and the Middle East were not ready for democracy. Protesters in Tunisia, Egypt, Libya, Yemen, Syria and Bahrain confronted, and in some cases ousted, established autocracies. But unique political and social circumstances also drove each uprising, and they had not spread to sub-Saharan Africa as of mid-2011. This was in substantial part because the region was still progressively adjusting to the new era of multi-party government that began in the early 1990s as the Cold War ended. The advent of constitutionalism and an abundance of elections over the past five years acted as a 'safety valve' for anti-government sentiment. In addition, many of Africa's most autocratic leaders, such as Rwandan President Paul Kagame and Ugandan President Yoweri Museveni, were credited with engendering national cohesion, stability and economic growth.

Even so, the Arab Awakening made many rulers nervous, and pushed regions to take democracy and justice more seriously. The Libya intervention was also a wake-up call for the AU: the Benghazi-based rebels spurned AU mediation mainly because – with some justification, given Libyan leader Muammar Gadhafi's central role in forming the AU – they saw AU leaders as Gadhafi sympathisers. The Arab Awakening, alongside the ICC's push for post-conflict justice, also strengthened civil-society movements. Thus, although it looked unlikely that sub-Saharan Africa would experience the kind of spectacular revolts seen in the Arab world, Africa could see a slower, second-wave 'African summer' of popular protest, particularly if economic growth were to slip. If the Arab Awakening relied on Facebook, an African movement would likely rely on the ubiquitous mobile phone.

The Arab upheavals also highlighted a dilemma for the West, which prior to 2011 had made stability a priority over democracy. With the Arab protests prompting a new Western emphasis on democracy and governance, there was increasing pressure on Western powers to urge autocratic African partners to enact political reforms. This had the potential to lead to a greater degree of foreign-aid conditionality.

Sudan: Separation Marred by Violence

In January 2011 Sudan faced its most significant event since independence in 1954. A referendum on independence for the south passed overwhelmingly, and South Sudan duly became an independent state on 9 July. Ahead of the separation, relations between the Sudanese government and South Sudan over the border area of Abyei descended into violence. Meanwhile, the situation in the troubled region of Darfur remained challenging. The Darfur peace agreement reduced but did not end the conflict, and fractious negotiations between the ruling National Congress Party (NCP) and various Darfuri opposition and insurgent groups had yet to yield a definitive peace.

Independence for the south

The war between north and south Sudan, which raged intermittently from Sudan's independence until the signing of the Comprehensive Peace Agreement (CPA) of 2005, was estimated to have cost nearly 2m lives, and displaced and traumatised millions more. A key provision of the CPA was a referendum to be held within six years. In mid-2010, relations between Juba (the southern capital) and Khartoum became increasingly fraught, as the south accused the north of trying to delay or cancel the vote. From August to November 2010, increasingly urgent diplomacy by the United States and the AU led Khartoum to agree that the referendum, scheduled for 9 January 2011, would be held on time. In the interim, an estimated 500,000 southerners who had been living in the north emigrated back to the south to vote. Though an estimated 30,000 northerners living in the south also returned north, most northerners opted to remain. In four days of voting, nearly 4m people – almost half of the south's total population – cast ballots. The stark choice was between unity with the north (represented by a drawing of two clasped hands) or independence (represented by a single open hand). An emphatic 98% voted for independence.

Crafting a constitution for the new country led to considerable factionalism. Pursuant to a 'road map' formulated at the All Southern Sudanese Political Parties Conference ('the Juba Conference') in October 2010, the

Political Parties Leadership Forum (PPLF) was established, headed by Salva Kiir Mayardit, president of the Government of South Sudan (GOSS) established under the 2005 interim constitution and chairman of the ruling Sudan People's Liberation Army/Movement (SPLA/M). Riek Machar, vice-president of GOSS, was named rapporteur. On 7 February 2011, GOSS appointed a 24-member Constitutional Review Committee to assess the 2005 constitution, but 23 were from the SPLM. The Alliance of South Sudan Political Parties (SSPP), comprising most of the non-SPLM opposition parties, objected that the committee's composition contravened the resolutions of the Juba Conference. Further disputes concerning the make-up of the committee charged with drafting a new constitution led to the withdrawal of the SSPP. The SSPP's substantive objections were that the draft constitution made no provision for multi-party power-sharing; that the stipulated transitional period of four years from 9 July 2011 was too long and should be reduced to two years or less; and that too much power was concentrated in the presidency.

Besides the political wrangling over the constitution, there was also an alarming degree of violence after the referendum. From January to May 2011, nearly 1,000 civilians were killed in attacks by militias and renegade former southern soldiers in Jonglei, Unity State and Western Equatoria. In March 2011, Malakal, the second-largest town in the south, became a battleground between militias loyal to Lam Akol, a former commander in the SPLA, and GOSS forces, leading to the deaths of nearly 400 civilians. During the same period, southern government clashes with a rebel group led by General George Athor Deng in Jonglei state killed nearly 3,000 and forced thousands more to flee. The international community, however, had taken a major interest in the development of South Sudan, pouring in billions of dollars in aid and investment since March 2010. Furthermore, despite infighting, GOSS held together remarkably well, and the national army remained a cohesive force.

Abyei: violence and peace deals

The CPA had provided for a referendum on independence for the region of Abyei, to be run concurrently with the South Sudan referendum, but disagreements between north and south over voter eligibility and the referendum process postponed it indefinitely. Abyei, with its strategic location on the border and wealth of oil fields, had as expected become a flashpoint between north and south, with both sides laying claim to the territory (see Strategic Geography, page XV). Embedded in the geostrategic dispute were local rivalries between the pro-southern Dinka and pro-northern Misseriya nomadic communities over land and grazing rights.

In 2011, the build-up toward conflict continued. In March, the Satellite Sentinel Project (SSP) – launched in 2010 by American actor George Clooney to provide real-time, high-resolution satellite photo analysis of people, buildings and equipment in conflict situations – reported a massing of northern tanks, helicopter gunships and fixed-wing aircraft on the southern border. Later that month, clashes between Misseriya and Abyei police left 20 dead. The violence escalated, and in mid-April, SSP imaging showed burnt-out settlements in the towns of el Feid and Um Barmbita in South Kordofan state, which contains part of Abyei.

On 23 May 2011, a United Nations Mission in Sudan (UNMIS) patrol escorting a detachment of the Sudan Armed Forces was fired on by unknown forces, although Khartoum blamed the SPLA, and accused Juba of violating the CPA. Within days, northern troops attacked and occupied the town of Abyei, leading to a counter-protest from GOSS. But with preparations under way for independence, Juba was not prepared to go to war over Abyei, and Kiir issued a statement to that effect on 25 May. The crisis, however, remained unresolved. More than 30,000 civilians were displaced and the joint north–south administration and joint security patrols that had been established to maintain security and stability ceased.

Khartoum's military and administrators dominated Abyei town, and the war of words between Khartoum and Juba continued. However, behind the scenes, mediation from the UN and AU paid off when the SPLM and NCP signed the Agreement for the Administration and Security of the Area of Abyei on 20 June 2011 in Addis Ababa. The agreement stipulated the withdrawal from Juba of national forces from both the north and the south; they were to be replaced by a 4,000-strong UN Interim Security Force for Abyei (UNISFA). The force, which will comprise mainly Ethiopian personnel, was to bolster the 1,000-strong UN peacekeeping force (comprising Zambian, Namibian and Pakistani soldiers) which had been in Abyei since 2009. UNISFA's mandate was to protect civilians and create an enabling environment for the provision of humanitarian assistance; but there were doubts as to whether it would have the capabilities to monitor, intercept and prevent border incursions by northern or South Sudan forces or their proxies. The Addis Ababa Agreement also called for assistance to allow residents of Abyei town who had fled the fighting to return, and for the establishment of a civilian government acceptable to both north and south. It was thus a major step forward in attempts to resolve the perennial conflict over Abyei. But it remained to be seen whether the fragile accord would hold, and whether UNISFA forces would have the wherewithal to cope with the inevitable challenges they would face.

South Sudan was to host the UN Mission in South Sudan (UNMISS), initially expected to number 7,000 with a one-year mandate covering peacekeeping, stabilisation and humanitarian operations in the new republic. Meanwhile, Khartoum refused to allow the renewal of the UNMIS mission in the north, despite UN requests for an extension to the mandate when it expires in August. It was thus likely that the UNMISS force would largely consist of UNMIS personnel transferred from north to south.

Abyei was not the only disputed area; the first half of 2011 saw increased fighting in the Nuba mountains of South Kordofan between northern forces and the SPLA/M forces. There was a surge in violence following the controversial victory of incumbent governor Ahmed Haroun in the gubernatorial elections of May 2011. Haroun, the NCP incumbent wanted by the ICC on charges of crimes against humanity allegedly committed by his forces in Darfur, defeated SPLM candidate Abdel Aziz al Hilu in elections which opposition parties in South Kordofan alleged were rigged in Haroun's favour. Within weeks of the 16 May announcement of Haroun's victory by the Khartoum-based Electoral Commission, there was a spate of skirmishes between rival northern and southern forces and their local proxies in the towns of Umm Durein, Angaruthu and Kadugli. The Addis Ababa Agreement included a subsidiary deal on South Kordofan and the Blue Nile; as with the Abyei Agreement, it stipulated a ceasefire in South Kordofan. The deal also posited the creation of a north–south power-sharing arrangement through a joint political and security committee. The committee was tasked with paving the way for a more comprehensive agreement on the future of South Kordofan.

Bashir under pressure

The March 2010 elections had confirmed NCP dominance in the Republic of Sudan. President Omar al-Bashir was re-elected and the NCP won 92% of the National Assembly seats. But internal factionalism within the NCP over future north–south relations, and an implicit 'who lost the south' narrative of recrimination, arose. There were also disputes over appointments to local government positions. State and federal government posts in south Darfur and White Nile states were particularly hotly contested amid complaints that the nomination process had bypassed the traditional shura (council of elders) mechanism. These grievances undermined the NCP's alliance with smaller parties, many of which felt marginalised when the new governors of those states appointed relatives to key posts.

There was also friction over cabinet posts. In April 2010, Bashir established a committee led by Ali Osman Taha, vice-president of the National Unity Government, to nominate new cabinet members. Taha's preference for appointing a cabinet of hawks was endorsed by Bashir, who knew he needed cabinet and military support for the likely fallout over southern independence. In turn, Bashir's alliance with Nafie Ali Nafie, NCP vice-president for organisational affairs – who competed with Taha for Bashir's favour – reduced the power and relevance of the shura, the party's influential consultative council. That body, however, was not completely disempowered. During its annual meeting on 2 December 2010, Bashir tried to nudge the shura towards endorsing a proposal for the north to declare war on the SPLM on the pretext of southern support for Darfuri rebels and southern 'intransigence' over Abyei. The shura refused to do so. He then changed tack, authorising state governors to expel foreign organisations or individuals who 'disrespected Sudan's sovereignty'. This proposal also met resistance from the shura. Bashir's position as head of government and party thus looked tenuous during the run-up to the referendum and immediately thereafter, particularly when Arab Awakening-style student protests racked Khartoum in March 2011.

The 2009 ICC indictments of Bashir for war crimes did not greatly affect his freedom to travel across most of Africa. Overall, his political alliance with military and party hardliners reduced the likelihood of a putsch to remove him from power. On 26 April 2011, in a show of power, Bashir sacked the outspoken Salah Gosh, his security adviser, from the national security committee for 'talking with opposition groups'.

Darfur problems persist

Darfur continued to be a vexing problem both domestically and internationally. Direct talks between the Sudanese government and the Justice and Equality Movement (JEM) rebel groups stalled in 2010. The 2006 peace agreement between Khartoum and Sudan Liberation Movement (SLM) rebel leader Minni Minnawi also broke down when the SLM withdrew from the agreement in December 2010 and Minnawi fled to southern Sudan. He was dismissed from his posts as senior assistant to Bashir and head of the Transitional Darfur Regional Authority, which the NCP had established as an inclusive local government for Darfur. Ten SLM representatives were dismissed from the authority by the new chairman. JEM and the SLM formed an informal alliance and presented proposals – rejected by Khartoum – for a more unitary Darfur state. On 9 March 2011, the government announced that two more states were to be established in central and eastern Darfur. The Darfur insurgent groups protested, insisting that this was another attempt at divide and rule by Khartoum.

Since February 2009, there had been talks in Doha (hosted by the Qatar government) between Khartoum and various Darfuri opposition groups, particularly JEM. But these discussions also stuttered in 2010. With JEM and Khartoum accusing each other of negotiating in bad faith, Qatari and AU mediators found little common ground between the two groups. Both Qatar and the AU endorsed the inclusive, popular and consultative Darfur Political Process (DPP) as the best way forward. In January 2011, a UN-sponsored summit meeting on Darfur was held in Khartoum. Representatives from the AU, United States and the African Union/United Nations Hybrid Operation in Darfur (UNAMID) agreed to support the DPP and proposed an all-stakeholder Darfur conference in mid-2011. But as of June 2011, it was unclear whether the mistrust among the rebel groups, and between the groups and the NCP, would abort this conference. Khartoum turned its energies to nego-tiating a peace deal with other Darfuri rebel groups such as the Liberation and Justice Movement (LJM) by June 2011. Abdel Wahid al Nur and Minni Minnawi, heading separate factions of the SLM, signed a pact on 13 May 2011, pledging to 'build a democratic regime in Darfur and Sudan' and to over-throw the NCP in Darfur. Khartoum alleged that Juba was sponsoring Darfuri rebel groups, particularly JEM and the SLM. Although peace talks on Darfur appeared likely to continue throughout 2011 in some fashion, it was clear that only a deal that included JEM and the SLM would yield durable peace.

More positive was an attempt by Chad and Sudan to begin a rapproche-ment to end the simmering animosity that had risen over the six years from 2003, during which period each government sponsored and hosted proxy rebel groups against the other. Khartoum in particular was in need of friends, as it faced increasing isolation because of the ICC arrest warrants issued for Bashir and other NCP leaders for alleged atrocities commit-ted in Darfur. Southern independence also threatened to tilt the national and regional balance of power away from Khartoum. Following visits by Chadian President Idriss Deby to Khartoum and Bashir to N'djamena, in the latter part of 2010 Sudan expelled nearly 2,000 Chadian rebels from its territory and Chad expelled over 500 Chad-based Sudanese rebels. While a number of militia groups from both countries remained active, the Chad–Sudan border area became less violent.

The independence of South Sudan, fraught as it was with risks of internal and north–south strife and also brightened by hopes of mutual prosperity and co-existence, was a watershed moment in contemporary African history. While there was no doubt that regional and international stakeholders played a major role in mediating north–south differences, it was the Sudanese themselves who led the drive towards self-determination for South Sudan.

West Africa: Democracy and Conflict

The year to mid-2011 in West Africa was dominated by an abundance of elections, with polls occurring in Côte d'Ivoire, Guinea, Niger and Nigeria. In Côte d'Ivoire and Nigeria the elections were triggers for national violence; in Niger and Guinea, they were catalysts for nation-building. Although great progress was made in embedding constitutionalism in West African politics, ensuring peaceful post-electoral transitions remained a challenge. During the Côte d'Ivoire crisis, the Economic Community of West African States (ECOWAS) and the AU also revealed their strength and weaknesses; regional economic and diplomatic sanctions were vital in weakening Laurent Gbagbo's legitimacy and hold on power. But regional and AU military weakness meant that it was a coalition of rebel groups loosely allied with UN and French forces that brought about Gbagbo's downfall. This raised the question of whether Africa really could protect its people from violence, or whether the continent would have to outsource its security to foreign forces.

Nigeria: Jonathan's victory

For Nigeria, the key political dynamic following the death of President Umaru Yar'Adua in May 2010 was preparation for the April 2011 presidential election. The 2007 elections that brought Yar'Adua to power had been tainted by fraud, violence and intimidation. Yar'Adua was keen to promote constitutional and economic reforms, particularly in the banking sector, but ill health and the resulting decentralisation of executive power took much of the impetus out of the reform agenda. As Yar'Adua, a Muslim, became increasingly incapacitated, the behind-the-scenes struggles for power within the ruling party intensified. Vice President Goodluck Jonathan, a Christian southerner and former governor of Bayelsa state, became acting president in February 2010, and formally became president on the death of Yar'Adua.

Jonathan was therefore in a strong position to contest the 2011 elections as his party's nominee, and he proceeded to strengthen it further. Jonathan retained 13 of Yar'Adua's ministers to continue the reformist agenda of the new government, and to avoid alienating the Muslim wing of the ruling party. Prior to Yar'Adua's death, there had been talk that the tradition of rotating the People's Democratic Party (PDP) leadership between northerners and southerners every two terms would lead to a bitter intra-party disputes over who would contest the elections. But Jonathan's rising presidential gravitas kept such discussions from becoming too divisive. Following intense negotiations, he was chosen as the PDP candidate for the national elections scheduled for April 2011.

A credible election was essential to national development, international stature and foreign investment. In 2010, the National Electoral Commission (NEC) had received new equipment, including technology that used photographic imaging to match voters' faces and fingerprints to names, and better training. Substantial efforts were made to tidy the national, provincial and district voter rolls. These measures increased electoral transparency and public confidence in the voting process.

Elections for the National Assembly, in which 360 House of Representatives seats and 109 Senate seats were contested, were held on 9 April 2011. There was a relatively low voter turnout in Lagos state, but a high turnout in the north. After early losses, the PDP rallied to win the bulk of seats in both houses. Other parties made significant inroads, with the Action Congress of Nigeria (ACN) gaining in the southwest, especially around Lagos, and the Congress for Progressive Change (CPC) in the north. The All Nigeria Peoples Party also took seats from the PDP. High-profile PDP casualties included Speaker of the House Dimeji Bankole. Voting preferences followed a regional pattern, with northern-based parties such as the ACN winning in the north and southern-based parties winning in the south, despite efforts by all the parties to adopt non-regionalist platforms and to campaign nationally.

After the NEC delayed the vote by a week to remedy logistical problems including missing party logos and occasionally defective software, the presidential election was held on 16 April 2011. The three contenders were Jonathan (PDP), Mallam Nuhu Ribadu (ACN) and former President Muhammadu Buhari (CPC). On 18 April 2011, the commission declared Jonathan the winner with 22.4m votes against Muhammadu Buhari's 12m and Ribadu's 3m. Jonathan avoided a run-off by winning at least a quarter of the vote in at least 24 states.

Even before the full results were in, however, the election triggered a wave of violence. Early results showing Jonathan in the lead led to rioting in the mainly Muslim north. In Kaduna state, Vice-President Namadi Sambo's house was burned, and in Kano state clashes between soldiers and supporters of Buhari killed 79. On 20 April, a failed bomb plot in Kaduna City killed two would-be perpetrators. Clashes between Muslims and Christians and between PDP and CPC supporters followed, leaving hundreds dead. There was post-election violence nationwide, with Kano, Kaduna, Adamawa, Niger and Katsina states hardest hit. On Easter Sunday, bomb blasts – allegedly set off by remnants of the Islamist Boko Haram group that had fought the military in 2010 – rocked the north-central state of Maiduguru. By the end of April, the Civil Rights Congress of Nigeria estimated that over 600 had died and over 60,000 civilians had been displaced in post-election violence, mainly in the north. In June, bomb blasts in Abuja and further bomb attacks in Maiduguru heightened concerns about security in Nigeria; the timing of the attacks and the fact that they occurred in disparate parts of the country, with different groups claiming or being accused of responsibility, also led to fears that the attacks might presage a new informal coalition of armed anti-government forces. Jonathan also faced political challenges; Buhari rejected the presidential election results, claiming that they were rigged on the NEC computers. He launched a legal challenge, but this seemed unlikely to succeed or to materially distract Jonathan. Nevertheless, and particularly with regard to choosing his new cabinet, Jonathan faced a stiff challenge in placating mainly Muslim northerners who opposed him.

Jonathan continued the banking reform that Yar'Adua had initiated. In 2009, Lamido Sanusi, governor of the Central Bank of Nigeria, established new rules that tightened fiscal accountability, and removed a number of bank directors for corruption and incompetence. The sweeping reform became known as 'Sanusi's tsunami'. In 2010, he imposed further regulations requiring all banks to divest from non-banking activities by 14 May 2012, and concentrate on core banking activities. As part of this process, the National Insurance Commission established an advisory committee on the divestment of banks from insurance institutions in Nigeria.

In his inaugural address, Jonathan announced his priorities for the next five years. They included strengthening relations with the international community, increasing budgetary support for education, remedying inadequate and irregular power supplies, and lowering unemployment. Most of these pledges echoed those of his predecessors. But Jonathan differed in his enlistment of professional technocrats rather than party apparatchiks to implement his policies. In response, international investment in key sectors rose. For instance, the government's privatisation and greater regulation of the power sector to increase efficiency and accountability prompted investors to sink more than $20bn into the country's power sector. These distinguishing features of Jonathan's government and approach justified guarded optimism about Nigerian governance.

Côte d'Ivoire: election leads to conflict

The disputed result of the December 2010 presidential election between incumbent Laurent Gbagbo and his challenger Alassane Ouattara, the former prime minister, led to a deadly and very personal struggle between the two men and their supporters that drew in other regional countries, the AU, the EU and the UN. Ultimately, the international community, showing extraordinary unity of purpose, forced Gbagbo, who had lost the election, out of office following large loss of life in a nationwide conflict between the two men's forces. The nation, however, remained divided. (See Strategic Geography, page IX.)

Preparations for the presidential poll had taken five years. The election was originally scheduled for 2005, but was postponed six times over issues including security, the electoral roll, the eligibility of voters and candidates, and identification and registration standards and procedures. These issues were finally resolved, and the first round was held on 31 October 2010. Gbagbo was the official winner with 38.3% of the votes, against Alassane Ouattara's 32.1%; another contender, Henri Konan Bedie, was credited with 25.2%. Despite claims from supporters of Ouattara and Bedie that the tally was fraudulent and that Ouattara had in fact scored a narrow victory, the Constitutional Council was quick to endorse the official result. In any case, the slimness of Gbagbo's declared margin of victory required a run-off election, which was held on 28 November as a joint United Nations Operation in Côte d'Ivoire (UNOCI)/Independent Electoral Commission (CEI) effort.

Gbagbo supporters criticised the conduct of elections in northern Côte d'Ivoire, alleging that fraud, violence and intimidation there had prevented Gbagbo supporters from exercising their right to vote. On 2 December, Youssouf Bakayoko, president of the CEI, announced that Ouattara was the winner with 51.1% of the vote, while Gbagbo had received 45.9%. Turnout was 81%. Bakayoko made his announcement at the Golf Hotel in Abidjan, which was heavily guarded by UN forces. Paul Yao N'Dre, president of the Constitutional Council, then announced that the CEI had no authority to announce the results, having already missed several deadlines, and insisted that the tally in the seven northern regions was invalid because of claimed irregularities. According to the Constitutional Council, Gbagbo had beaten Ouattara by 51.4% to 48.5%. However, on 3 December, the UN and the CEI swore in Ouattara as the new president at the Golf Hotel, while Gbagbo's inauguration in the State House was broadcast on national television. Côte d'Ivoire now had two presidents and a full-blown crisis.

Forces loyal to Gbagbo closed the borders and imposed a national curfew. On 3 December, the African Union expressed 'deep concern', and on 5 December former South African President Thabo Mbeki arrived in Abidjan to try, unsuccessfully, to broker a resolution. On 25 December ECOWAS, with UN and EU backing, recognised Ouattara as the winner and urged Gbagbo to step down, threatening military force if he did not do so. Gbagbo demanded that UN peacekeepers leave the country; the UN instead extended the UNOCI mission to 30 June 2011.

Gbagbo's refusal to step down and both men's rejection of any power-sharing deal moved each side to resort to force. Violence increased in Abidjan as government forces attacked civilians, and there were daily battles between supporters of the two men. Meanwhile, ECOWAS and the EU imposed sanctions on Gbagbo and his retinue. With ECOWAS's help, Ouattara also gained control of the Reserve Bank, which made it difficult for Gbagbo to pay civil service and military wages.

Pro-Ouattara Republican Forces of Côte d'Ivoire (RFCI) insurgents – formerly known as the New Forces, and representing Muslim northerners who felt that they were discriminated against by Gbagbo's politically domi-nant and mostly Christian southern constituency – launched campaigns in western and central parts of the country. Beginning in February, they captured town after town, in late March taking control of Yamoussoukro, the country's administrative capital, in the west and capturing the key cocoa-growing and port city of San Pedro. ECOWAS called on the UN to take 'immediate measures' to resolve the crisis. On 30 March, UN Security Council Resolution 1975 recognised Ouattara as president and authorised the use of 'all necessary measures' to protect civilians under imminent threat of attack.

By 31 March, RFCI forces had encircled Abidjan from various direc-tions. UN forces seized Abidjan airport, and patrols of UN and French forces deployed in the city. With the morale of Gbagbo's forces declining, on 1 April Army Chief of Staff General Phillippe Mangou took refuge in the South African ambassador's house. Military Police Chief Thiape Kassarate defected to Ouattara on 3 April. A spate of defections among Gbagbo's senior commanders followed, and within days his military support was reduced from a force of 40,000 to a loyalist core of about 2,000, consisting of the Republican Guard, gendarmerie and militia units, which fought to control the suburb of Cocody, the Presidential Palace in Abidjan, and the Trenchville district. For a few days it appeared that Gbagbo's forces might retake Abidjan, but UN air-strikes and French special-forces attacks repelled them. On 11 April 2011, following a joint assault on his Abidjan residence by pro-Ouattara, UN and French forces, Gbagbo, his wife and children, and ten other supporters were taken into custody.

Ouattara's chief challenge was to ensure human security. An estimated 1,000 people were killed in the conflict and more than 900,000 were displaced. The RFCI continued to support Ouattara, but it is unclear to what extent he controlled them. Ouattara did not have a military background, yet one of his primary governance tasks was to build a truly national military that somehow merged – or at least neutralised – the RFCI, former pro-Gbagbo forces and various militias. Ouattara said justice and the rule of law would be key features of his administration. During the post-election conflict, forces loyal to both Ouattara and Gbagbo were accused of committing atrocities in which dozens of men, women and children were shot or knifed to death. Ouattara acknowledged the need for an impartial investigation, and to bring perpetrators to justice. He promised a Truth and Reconciliation Commission to examine evidence dating back to the 1999 coup.

Niger: elections after coup

Presidential elections were held in Niger following the February 2010 military coup which toppled Mamadou Tandja, who had been president since 1999. He was replaced initially by a junta, the Supreme Council for the Restoration of Democracy (CSRD). Under pressure from ECOWAS and the international community, the CSRD established a transitional government and announced a one-year timetable for elections. The first round of the presidential election was held on 31 January 2011, with ten candidates certified. The Electoral Commission announced that Mahamadou Issifou of the Party for Democracy and Socialism of Niger (PNDS) and Seyni Oumarou of the National Movement for the Development of Society (MNSD) were the two highest-polling candidates, with 36% and 23% of the vote respectively. Issifou had been the key opposition leader throughout Tandja's presidency, while Oumarou was seen as a Tandja loyalist. Both had campaigned on platforms of job creation and poverty alleviation.

The close result required a run-off, which was held on 12 March. After generally peaceful polls, the Electoral Commission announced that Issifou had won with 58% of the vote, against Oumarou's 42%. Turnout was estimated at just under 50% for both rounds. Oumarou graciously accepted the results, indicating his desire to avoid 'a new spiral of endless difficulties' and his preference 'to work for national reconciliation'. In legislative elections in January, the PNDS had won 78 out of 127 seats in parliament, giving Issifou a strong mandate.

Terrorism and banditry remained major challenges in Niger. Over the previous decade, groups such as al-Qaeda in the Islamic Maghreb (AQIM) had exploited the porous desert borders of Mali, Niger, Mauritania and Algeria to ambush government troops and attack or kidnap foreign tourists and aid workers. Although in 2010 a regional joint military headquarters was established in the southern Algerian border town of Tamanrasset, there was little progress in coordinating regional security largely because of disputes between Algeria and its neighbours. In January 2011, suspected AQIM militants kidnapped two Frenchmen – Antoine de Leocour and Vincent Delory – in Niamey, Niger's capital. In a joint Nigerien–French rescue attempt on the Niger–Mali border, the two Frenchmen were killed along with three AQIM militants and two Nigerien soldiers. The abduction of the two Frenchmen in the capital rather than the desert, as with previous incidents, was a possible signal of more aggressive and ambitious operations on the part of AQIM. Such a development would pose a stiffer challenge to Niger's security forces.

Guinea: reform after turmoil

Political progress was made following the upheaval that followed the death in December 2008 of long-standing president Lansana Conté. After Moussa Camara came to power as head of a military junta, the junta's forces in September 2009 massacred hundreds of civilians who were protesting Camara's attempts to revise the constitution to allow him to be installed as president. Camara was shot by an aide and forced into exile in Morocco to recuperate. At a January 2010 meeting in Ouagadougou, Burkina Faso President Blaise Campaoré brokered an agreement between Camara and Acting President Sékouba Konaté establishing a 'twelve principles' road map to return Guinea to civilian rule. Under regional and international pressure, on 21 January 2010 the junta appointed Jean-Marie Doré, a civilian, as interim prime minister in a transitional government pending national elections.

The first round of the presidential elections were held on 27 June 2010, with former Prime Minister Cellou Diallo and fellow opposition leader Alpha Condé advancing to the second-round run-off vote, which Condé won in November. Condé came into office promising to reform the military and the mining sector, against a backdrop of disputes with global mining partners such as Rio Tinto, Vale and RUSAL over state participation and black empowerment. Little military reform was accomplished, but the Mining Code of Guinea was rewritten and joint-venture deals were explored. New regulations increased transparency, and the minimum required state share in joint partnerships was increased to 35%. There were also tougher standards for mining concessions. The government's assertive policies on mining partnerships won Condé a good deal of populist support but also produced greater investor uncertainty.

Southern Africa: Pretoria's Growing Influence

Overall, southern Africa's economies, driven by South Africa's emergence from recession and Angola's commodities boom, registered growth of 4–6% in the year to mid-2011. Peaceful and generally free and fair elections in Mozambique in 2010 and South Africa in 2011 were also good news. But the continued political crises in Madagascar and Zimbabwe, and the growing political fault lines in the kingdom of Swaziland, inhibited investor confidence.

In South Africa, President Jacob Zuma consolidated power within the African National Congress (ANC) but there were still questions about the often fractious Tripartite Alliance – the ANC, the Congress of South African Trade Unions (COSATU) and the South African Communist Party (SACP) – which helped bring the ANC to power. In Africa's largest economy, there were debates over service delivery, economic inequality and jobs. While South Africa remained the chief mediator in Zimbabwe's ongoing political crisis, its relations with Rwanda nosedived over the attempted murder of exiled Rwandan General Faustin Kayumba Nyamwasa in Johannesburg.

The first half of 2010 brought a boost for South Africa's economy, mainly due to a tourism windfall and a huge investment in urban infrastructure arising from hosting the FIFA World Cup football finals. A surge in mining and fruit exports also stimulated the economy, which grew by just under 3% in 2010, buoyed by a resurgent mining sector and strong consumer spending. Threats of nationalisation and expropriation by populists such as Julius Malema, head of the ANC Youth League, remained merely rhetorical.

But nearly five million South Africans remained unemployed, and the number appeared to be growing. In addition, while the Black Economic Empowerment process had created a genuine black middle class and promoted entrepreneurship, it had also extended the gap between the black upper class and a growing underclass and widened income and wealth disparities. A wave of strikes in August–September 2010 by teachers, health staff, train drivers and others necessitated military crisis assistance for hospitals and schools. After weeks of tense negotiations, the government agreed to pay increases of 8–10% for public-sector employees.

In political developments, the September 2010 ANC National General Council Meeting, key forum for the political power brokers, proved a triumph for Zuma. In particular, Malema was forced to acknowledge his 'errors' and face a disciplinary hearing in which he was required to undergo counselling and political re-education. Many had expected Malema, whose utterances had often embarrassed the ANC, to be expelled from the party. But he was still popular with the Youth League, which in turn won vital grassroots support for the party. Differences among the Tripartite Alliance partners were also papered over. COSATU had insisted on strategic nationalisation of key industries and businesses to deal with poverty, while the ANC's antidote was labour-driven economic growth. The two parties privately negotiated a working agreement whereby COSATU would not contest the ANC's economic plan at the meeting in exchange for greater COSATU and SACP representation within the government.

Local government elections were held on 18 May 2011. 13.6 million South Africans voted, the highest turnout since the inaugural municipal election in 2000. The ANC won 61.7% of the vote, while the opposition Democratic Alliance (DA) won 25.6%, improving on its 16.6% showing in the general election of 2009. The ANC won overall in the provinces of the Eastern Cape, Free State, Gauteng, KwaZulu-Natal, Limpopo, Mpumalanga, North West and the Northern Cape. The DA won the Western Cape outright. Whilst this was a good result for the ruling party, the fact that the ANC's municipal majority was reduced in every province laid bare voter discontent with the party. The 2011 vote also reflected the consolidation of support for DA opposition leader Helen Zille in Cape Town, the Cape Province and parts of Natal. Although the DA lost to the ANC in Johannesburg and Pretoria, it increased its voting percentage in these ANC strongholds. This increase in support was attributable to South Africans' displeasure with the local government record on service delivery, salaries and corruption. Overall, the elections solidified the DA's position as a national opposition party, and the fact that the DA received most of its votes from blacks showed that Zille's party was no longer perceived in racial terms, as a party for whites. The results also meant that there would be increased power-sharing between the ANC and the DA in local government.

South Africa's role on the world stage continued to expand. It continued to be the continent's leading proponent of African internationalism, wielding rising influence in global trade talks and post-Copenhagen climate-change discussions. South Africa was also a main contender for Africa's first permanent seat on the UN Security Council, and a major advocate of UN reform. The EU–South Africa partnership continued to deepen, and the October 2010 EU–South Africa summit was a clear recognition of South Africa's role as a continental anchor state.

Within the region, Pretoria remained the dominant voice within the Southern African Development Community (SADC) and the foremost trading partner for other SADC countries. South Africa also remained the linchpin of the regional security architecture, particularly in terms of airlift capacity and logistics for the fledgling SADC Standby Brigade, mandated to perform regional stabilisation functions as a component of the Africa Standby Force. Further, 2011 saw a more concerted effort by South Africa, as chief mediator, to get Zimbabwe's fractious governing coalition partners to agree on a road map to free and fair elections. In particular, Zuma took a harder line with Robert Mugabe's Zimbabwe African National Union–Patriotic Front (ZANU-PF), and blocked the early elections that Mugabe had pushed for tactical reasons.

Relations turned chilly between South Africa and Rwanda. In June 2010, exiled Rwandan General Faustin Nyamwasa was wounded in Johannesburg in a failed assassination attempt. Five of the seven suspects arrested in Johannesburg were Rwandan, and South African media speculation that Nyamwasa was the victim of a Rwandan 'hit squad' prompted furious denials from Kigali. Rwanda, where Nyamwasa faces terrorism charges, and Spain, where he has been indicted for human-rights abuses, then demanded that a recuperating Nyamwasa be extradited to Kigali or to the ICC's jurisdiction. South Africa refused. A war of words ensued, and Pretoria briefly recalled its ambassador from Kigali in July 2010. The two countries subsequently patched up their differences to some extent, but Rwanda remained concerned that South Africa could become a staging area for exiled Rwandese opposition and militant groups.

Zimbabwe: political manoeuvres

The continued survival of Zimbabwe's Government of National Unity (GNU), formed in February 2009, confounded many who had predicted its early collapse. The economy grew by 7%, there was increased investment and trade with regional partners, as well as China and India, and an estimated 20,000 diaspora Zimbabweans returned part-time or permanently. But Zimbabwe's future still hinged on four political factors: the constitutional outreach/referendum process; dynamics within the coalition parties; the health of 87-year-old President Robert Mugabe; and the timing of the next presidential election.

In May 2010, a national Constitutional Select Committee was established to implement the public consultation/outreach process intended to help forge a new constitution. Seventy outreach teams were dispatched across the country in a process that lasted until January 2011. Violence marred the process from the outset, with supporters of Mugabe's ZANU-PF attacking the constitutional facilitation teams and their audiences at meetings in Harare, Bulawayo, Masvingo and Mashonaland West province. The decade-old ZANU-PF practice of harassing civil-society groups also continued. For example, on 20 September 2010, 83 women from the group Women of Zimbabwe Arise were arrested and detained at Harare's Central Police Station for three days for protesting against the lack of professionalism of the Zimbabwe Republic Police. Despite such intimidation, more than one million Zimbabweans expressed their views on a new constitution through the outreach exercise. Parliament will probably prepare a draft constitution that takes into account public viewpoints and put the draft to a referendum in late 2011.

Between December 2010 and May 2011 each major party held its congress. The ZANU-PF congress endorsed Mugabe as its leader and candidate for the next election and insisted it be held in 2011. At the Movement for Democratic Change (MDC)-Tsvangirai congress, Prime Minister Morgan Tsvangirai and Tendai Biti retained their posts as party president and secretary-general respectively, but many party veterans and Tsvangirai loyalists were voted out. Nelson Chamisa, former co-minister of telecommunications, became national organising secretary. Popular with the grassroots, he was seen as a rival to Biti.

Within the MDC-Mutambara party, Deputy Prime Minister Arthur Mutambara was supplanted as party leader by the party's founder, Welshman Ncube. Their rivalry proved highly divisive and toxic for the party. Ncube demanded that Mutambara, who is seen as a Mugabe ally, step down as deputy prime minister and that the other signatories to the

Global Political Agreement (GPA), which created the unity government, recognise Ncube as Mutambara's successor in that position. By June 2011 this had not happened and Ncube was seeking judicial intervention. In May 2011, he appealed to South African President Jacob Zuma (his father-in-law) to recognise him as the new deputy prime minister, but the ANC declined to get involved in the controversy. Meanwhile, the revived Zimbabwe African People's Union (ZAPU), ZANU-PF's partner during the 1967–79 liberation war and in government from 1987 until 2008, chose former home affairs minister and war hero Dumiso Dabengwa as party president for five years. Traditionally, ZAPU is seen as an ethnic Ndebele party; it remained to be seen whether it could position itself as a truly national force.

SADC kept up its efforts at political mediation, begun after the last presidential election in 2008 resulted in deadlock between Mugabe and Tsvangirai. Throughout 2010, ZANU-PF and both MDC wings continued to vie for SADC support. Although ZANU-PF managed for a time to contain SADC impatience with its failure to carry out agreed reforms, in April 2011 SADC leaders openly criticised Mugabe in his presence and demanded that he introduce reforms and implement the road map to elections to be held in 2012. At the SADC Heads of State and Government meeting in Johannesburg on 12 June, Zuma presented a report detailing his concerns about failures by all parties to implement the GPA. He was particularly critical of ZANU-PF's failures to abide by the agreement and castigated Mugabe's party for promoting a climate of violence. Zuma made recommendations for a clear road map and timeline towards elections in Zimbabwe, insisting that the constitutional referendum and new constitution had to precede elections. He also recommended an enhanced SADC mediation/facilitation team on Zimbabwe. After the Johannesburg meeting, both ZANU-PF and the MDC claimed a tactical victory; it was clear that SADC was hardening its stance against Mugabe and ZANU-PF and that Mugabe's insistence on early elections prior to a new constitution had not been accepted by SADC.

Zimbabwe sought in vain to have international sanctions lifted. Its relations with the EU remained fraught. On the one hand, the EU was Zimbabwe's largest humanitarian aid donor. On the other, the EU and the United States had imposed sanctions including asset freezes, arms embargoes and travel bans on ZANU-PF and the Zimbabwean military since 2003. In 2010, the government and the SADC called for the sanctions to be lifted, but the EU merely exempted the wives of 30 ZANU-PF officials, citing ZANU-PF's sustained political violence against its rivals, particularly since December 2010. In response, ZANU-PF began a campaign to get a million signatures for an anti-sanctions petition. Tsvangirai's party also came under pressure as diplomatic cables released by the WikiLeaks website showed that the party had advocated retention of sanctions on ZANU-PF even after the unity government was formed. ZANU-PF used this revelation to portray the party as a tool of the West.

ZANU-PF's drive for early elections was fuelled by Mugabe's failing health. He frequently travelled to Singapore for treatment – officially for his eyes, but many suspected also for cancer. At the August 2010 SADC summit in Windhoek, pictures of an aged Mugabe moving short distances in a golf cart increased speculation. On 15 May 2011, he reportedly collapsed at home and had to receive emergency treatment. It remained unclear who would succeed him as ZANU-PF party leader. Deputy President Joice Mujuru and Defence Minister Emmerson Mnangagwa were regarded as Mugabe's most likely successors, but military chiefs were also keen to secure the party presidency for themselves or a close ally. In June, there were rumours that a hardline cabal within the military and ZANU-PF were planning to install Army Chief General Constantine Chiwenga as national president in the event of Mugabe's demise. June also saw a ratcheting up of the perennial war of words between the military and the MDC. That month, and follow-ing rumours of a planned military takeover in the event of Mugabe's death, Tsvangirai called on soldiers to resign from the military if they wanted to enter politics. This in turn provoked a furious outburst from Brigadier-General Douglas Nyikayaramba, who said that the military would 'die for Mugabe to ensure that he stays in power'. Thus, at mid-2011, the increas-ingly vicious in-fighting between the GNU parties and between the MDC and the military, and doubts about Mugabe's health and his control over the party and the military, heightened speculation that unless SADC and the international community took decisive steps, Zimbabwe could be plunged back to the chaos of 2008.

Mozambique and Madagascar

Mozambique continued to be politically stable but economically compro-mised. In September 2010, there were food riots in Maputo that quickly spread across the country in response to government cuts in the wheat-flour subsidy that substantially increased the price of bread. After 11 deaths and dozens of injuries in battles between rioters and the police, the government restored the higher subsidy, following up with price cuts in water and elec-tricity and continuation of price controls on food through the first half of 2011. But no clear strategy emerged for dealing with the linked problems of rising unemployment (estimated at 30%) and a high crime rate, which negatively affected Mozambique's status as a prime tourist destination.

Madagascar's political crisis continued unabated. On 18 March 2009, former disc jockey Andry Rajoelina had illegally seized power from then-President Marc Ravalomanana, who went into exile. Since then, Rajoelina had refused to commit to political reforms or to a road map for free and fair elections, despite the AU/SADC stick of sanctions and the carrot of political recognition. The impasse created a political vacuum and with it instability. In November 2010, as Madagascar voted on a new draft constitution, a group of rebel soldiers led by Colonel Charles Andrianasoavina attempted a coup. Though it was quickly quelled by loyal troops, the coup attempt and persistent rumours of others produced a climate of fear and uncertainty. In February 2011, Ravalomanana announced that he would return to Madagascar, despite threats of arrest. Rajoelina, for his part, embarked on a diplomatic offensive to woo regional leaders and end Madagascar's isolation. As of spring 2011, any efforts falling short of AU/SADC demands seemed unlikely to yield him legitimacy.

East Africa and Great Lakes: Elections Boost Existing Rulers

Eastern Africa saw a series of elections that tended to increase the authority of existing rulers. In Kenya, governance was dominated by the aftermath of the last election and efforts to prevent a recurrence of the tribal violence that broke out afterwards. Indictments handed down by the ICC provided a salutary reminder of international accountability.

Kenya: continued aftermath of political crisis
Kenya's Government of National Unity remained fragile. However, the new constitution, promulgated on 27 August 2010 following a national referendum, was a major achievement that set a positive tone for the 2012 general election. Nevertheless, the violence that had followed the last elections in December 2007 continued to hang over the country, and the ICC in The Hague handed down indictments.

Kenya had operated under a much-amended version of the 1963 Independence Constitution, and it became clear that a new constitution, based on popular consultation, was key to avoiding a rerun of the post-election troubles. The process of drafting was lengthy and occasionally acrimonious, but eventually bore fruit. The initial draft of the Harmonised Constitution, written by an appointed Committee of Experts, was released in November 2009 and then discussed – often heatedly – between a Parliamentary Select Committee and the Committee of Experts. Amidst debate over whether the draft should incorporate hundreds of proposed last-minute amendments, and under public pressure for a final draft, parliament unanimously approved the proposed constitution without amendments. In the referendum, 67% voted in favour.

Key changes were designed to enforce the separation of powers among the executive, legislature and judiciary. There was to be an upper house, the Senate. More stringent qualifications were to be required for judicial office; devolution was to increase, with greater autonomy for county administrations and more equitable sharing of resources. The document explicitly recognised the freedom of the media and the independence of the judiciary. There were not to be both a president and a prime minister – an interim arrangement adopted to ameliorate the 2007–8 crisis; the president was to remain head of state and head of government, but would require approval from the National Assembly and Cabinet to declare war or a state of emergency. Presidents were to be limited to two terms.

With Kenya under international pressure to investigate the 2007–08 election violence, and also to tackle political corruption, Chief Public Prosecutor Keriako Tubiko announced in April 2011 that over 1,000 cases of election violence had been investigated, more than 700 people tried and 320 sentenced. But this followed action by the ICC after the Kenyan parliament failed to set up a special tribunal into the 2007–08 violence. In December 2010, ICC prosecutor Luis Moreno-Ocampo indicted Deputy Prime Minister Uhuru Kenyatta, Cabinet Secretary Francis Muthaura, former Police Commissioner Mohammed Hussein Ali, Minister of Industrialisation Henry Kosgey, Joshua arap Sang, a radio presenter, and William Ruto, the education minister who had been suspended over corruption allegations. The 'Ocampo Six' indictments for involvement in the violence and pending trials led to increased tensions within the coalition, and also looked likely to affect the 2012 election. In an attempt to regain some control, the Kenyan government made a fresh bid in April 2011 to have the Ocampo Six trials transferred to Kenya, asserting that the Kenyan judiciary was willing and able to render justice.

Internationally, despite disagreements over the pace of political reform and corruption, Kenya continued to maintain fairly good relations with the West, and to cultivate closer relations with China and India. Yet the Mau Mau insurgency of the 1950s continued to cast a pall over Kenya's relations with the United Kingdom. The UK government had refused financial compensation to survivors of British concentration camps in the colonial era. In 2011, documents were released detailing British abuses during that time, prompting an outcry in Kenya that had the potential to sour bilateral relations.

The Kenya–Ethiopia border was a source of tension. In May 2011, border clashes between the Kenyan Turkana community and Ethiopian Merille militias led to 23 deaths, and a bomb explosion in Kajiado killed five school children. President Mwai Kibaki said Kenya had to be ready to defend itself from 'foreign aggression'. General Jeremiah Mutinda Kianga, chief of the Kenyan General Staff, said that the Kenyan armed forces were 'awaiting orders' to attack militias from neighbouring countries that targeted Kenya or used Kenya as a rear base. These were clear references to the Ethiopian militias as well as to Harakat al-Shabaab al-Mujahideen (the Somali al-Qaeda affiliate generally known simply as al-Shabaab) and other Somali militias. But many saw the sabre-rattling as aimed more at thwarting international pressure for security-sector reform, and as a tacit show of loyalty to Kibaki over Prime Minister Raila Odinga, who had a far more tenuous relationship with the military.

There were also increased tensions between Kenya and Uganda, centring on Migingo and Ugingo Islands in Lake Victoria, which both countries claim and which Uganda occupied with a naval and civilian force in 2004. On 18 May 2011, Kenya formally requested that Uganda immediately withdraw its personnel from the islands on the grounds that colonial records proved the legality of its claim. Uganda refused. The competing claims serve as proxies for broader geopolitical rivalry: Kenya is the dominant economy of the Great Lakes region, but Uganda and Rwanda have the strongest militaries and have increased their economic power.

Rwanda: growing authoritarianism

Concern about the increasing authoritarianism of President Paul Kagame's government emerged during the August 2010 presidential election. In the run-up to the election, scores of opposition activists were arrested. They included Victoire Ingabire, chair of the Unified Democratic Forces coalition opposition group, who had returned from exile to run for president. Shortly after her arrival in January 2010, during a visit to the Genocide Memorial Centre in Kigali, she stated that Hutus were as much victims of the 1994 genocide as Tutsis and that all the perpetrators should face justice, later insisting that tribal differences in Rwanda were a reality. Ingabire was subsequently arrested for genocide denial, a crime in Rwanda, and for promoting ethnic divisions. She was released from jail but kept under house arrest and barred from contesting the election.

Opposition leaders were also attacked. On 30 July 2010, the headless body of André Rwisereka, vice-president of the Democratic Green Party, was found in Kigali. Prominent journalist Jean-Léonard Rugambage was shot dead on 24 June. Exiled General Faustin Nyamwasa was shot in South Africa, allegedly by a Rwandan 'hit team'. By election time, Kagame's main opposition in the election consisted of former health minister Jean Ntawukuriryayo, Vice President of the Senate Prosper Higiro, and Senator Alvera Mukabaramba, all of whom were widely considered 'token' candidates. The election was held on 9 August 2010, and Kagame won 93% of the vote. The opposition maintained that the election was not credible due to intimidation. Hours after the official results were announced on 11 August, a grenade attack in Kigali suggested that anti-Kagame sentiment remained a problematic issue for Rwanda.

Uganda: new pressures
Concerns about increasing political repression in Uganda arose both before and after the presidential election, held in February 2011. Uganda's controversial troop contribution to the AU Mission in Somalia (AMISOM), which protects Somalia's Transitional Federal Government, also made for a climate of uncertainty.

On 15 July 2010, separate bomb attacks at a restaurant and rugby club in Kampala killed 74 people watching the World Cup football final on television. Al-Shabaab militants in Somalia, who had declared that they would target Uganda and Burundi on account of their AMISOM deployments, claimed responsibility. Following the bombings, Ugandan President Yoweri Museveni insisted that Ugandan forces would not only remain in Somalia, but could be increased to 20,000. He also appealed for greater international support for AMISOM. By January 2011, the Ugandan contingent in AMISOM had increased from 5,000 to 7,000, with public opinion generally in support of the intervention.

The presidential election boiled down to a direct contest between Museveni and veteran opposition leader Kizza Besigye. Uganda's Electoral Commission announced that Museveni had won with 68% of the vote to Besigye's 26%. The opposition claimed fraud, but its own divisiveness was probably the main reason for Museveni's easy victory. The security forces then cracked down on journalists and citizens who declined to use personal or public transportation in popular 'walk to work' protests against rising food and fuel prices, beating and arresting many of them. Besigye was roughed up and detained several times. While the protests appeared to constitute a nascent social movement, it was unlikely that Museveni would allow them to become a full-blooded people's revolution that could threaten state power. But the fact remained that Museveni, who had been in office for 25 years, was facing growing domestic challenges from a new generation.

As national debt rose, the International Monetary Fund gave the Ugandan government until June 2011 to carry out key economic reforms. It was unclear whether the government would implement the changes.

Other Elections

The overriding political factor in the Democratic Republic of the Congo (DRC) was the presidential election scheduled for November 2011. In 2010, there had been debate over whether the election should be conducted over one round or two. President Joseph Kabila's government proposed the former, citing post-run-off violence after the 2006 election. The opposition countered that a one-round election would increase the likelihood of fraud and violence. Jean-Pierre Bemba, a principal opponent of Kabila's in 2006, was not competing as he was on trial in The Hague for war crimes. Kabila's challengers were likely to include veteran opposition leaders Etienne Tshisekedi and Vital Kamerhe, but it was unclear whether they would be able to set aside their personal differences to form an effective coalition. Campaigning separately, they would probably split the vote and weaken each other's chances, as occurred in 2006.

Security during the elections looked likely to remain a major issue, following the dispatch of an EU force to supplement UN peacekeepers during the 2006 elections. Kabila called for a reduced UN Mission in the DRC (MONUC) peacekeeping presence, and the size of that force and the duration of its mandate were under review as of June 2011. Should the UN force be significantly downsized, insecurity in the eastern Congo, which has the world's highest recorded incidence of rape, and during the 2011 election looked to prove difficult to contain.

In Burundi, violence followed the ultimately uncontested June 2010 presidential election, during which members of the ruling National Council for the Defence of Democracy–Forces for the Defence of Democracy and the opposition Front for Democracy had clashed violently. The five opposition candidates, including front-runner Agathon Rwasa, had withdrawn from the election, citing incumbent President Pierre Nkurunziza's fraud and intimidation. There were grenade attacks in Bujumbura, the capital, and in Kanyosha in the west.

In the self-declared but internationally unrecognised state of Somaliland, President Ahmed Silanyo, who took office after June 2010 elections, engaged in a vigorous outreach campaign to win wider political recognition of and investment in the polity. He emphasised its relative stability, especially compared with neighbouring Somalia. Shifting away from the traditional 'one Somalia' regional position, nearby Djibouti, Ethiopia and Kenya indicated that they would accept international recognition. But Somaliland still had major territorial, security and ethnic disputes with Somalia in general and the bordering semi-autonomous Puntland state in Somalia in particular. Both rejected Somaliland's independence and sovereignty. Nevertheless, it seemed increasingly likely that Somaliland would achieve a higher degree of international recognition over the next decade.

Somali Piracy: Persistent and Evolving

For years, Somali piracy has imperilled commercial shipping and posed a potentially significant threat to international security. The shipping corridor off the coast of Somalia is strategically and economically significant, as 7% of the world's oil supply travels through the Gulf of Aden. Somali piracy has also proven a major economic nuisance. Several shipping companies have diverted ships around the Cape of Good Hope to avoid the Gulf of Aden altogether. The increase in the cost of specialty maritime risk insurance for ships travelling through the region has been estimated at $400m annually. And the problem has been on the rise. According to the International Maritime Bureau (IMB), there were 97 Somali pirate attacks in the first quarter of 2011, up from 35 during the same period in the previous year. Somali piracy is not yet a truly strategic problem, but it could become one if nascent trends of tactical cooperation with jihadists gather momentum.

The business of Somali piracy
Up to 5,000 Somali men, divided into five large groups, work as pirates. Somali piracy is a low-technology enterprise with a simple business model.

Pirates in small speedboats, armed with AK-47s and rocket-propelled grenade launchers, capture a larger dhow or fishing vessel, then use it as a mothership to patrol ocean waters for unguarded, lightly manned, slow-moving cargo ships. The use of motherships, which sustain smaller vessels operating at some distance from shore, connected by satellite phones and GPS, has extended the radius of operations well beyond Somalia's coastal waters and enabled the pirates to move unnoticed in the shipping lanes. Hijacked ships are anchored in territorial waters near pirate strongholds in the villages of Eyl, Hobyo and Gharardeere, on the Horn, until ransom negotiations are concluded. Somali harbours cannot accommodate a modern tanker or bulk carrier or any commercial infrastructure that would allow pirates to move cargo off the ships to sell it in regional markets, and it is not feasible for pirates to disguise a stolen ship and sell it.

Somali piracy is therefore a hijack and ransom business. As of 31 March 2011, Somali pirates were holding 596 crew members captive aboard 28 ships. The absence of post-hijacking commercial options explains the low ransoms relative to the value of the cargo. But ransoms too are on the rise. Somali pirates gleaned roughly $40m in 2008, nearly $75m in 2009, and about $85m in 2010; the average ransom came to roughly $5m, which translates to $35,000 to $50,000 per individual pirate. The premium on ransoms explains the relative non-violence of Somali piracy compared to, say, that in the Strait of Malacca through the 1990s, in which the culprits typically killed the crew and sold the ships and their cargos. In 2009, Somali pirates took 867 hostages, wounding ten crew members and killing four, mostly by accident. Detention and prosecution are legally problematic – Kenya had begun to detain and try Somali pirates, but ceased doing so due to the legal complexities – and the financial rewards make recruitment and 'reload' relatively easy.

The international response
As of spring 2011, three multinational naval operations, all backed by UN Security Council resolutions, were working to control piracy off the coast of Somalia. The EU launched its first joint naval operation, *Operation Atalanta*, in November 2008 to protect shipping in the region and ensure that World Food Programme (WFP) vessels were able to deliver aid to Somalia. NATO's *Operation Allied Protector* began in October 2008 and was replaced with *Operation Allied Provider* in March 2009. NATO operations initially aimed to protect WFP aid and expanded to include general counter-piracy. Under the authority of the Combined Maritime Forces, based with the US Fifth Fleet in Bahrain, Combined Task Force-151 (CTF-151), a multinational coun-

ter-piracy force that includes assets from Australia, Denmark, France, the Netherlands and Turkey as well as the United States, was set up in January 2009 to deter, disrupt and criminally prosecute those involved in piracy. In addition, a number of navies, such as those of Russia, India and China, patrol the area to protect their own cargos and ships.

These international efforts have contained the Somali piracy problem, and have certainly facilitated the delivery of aid. They have also resulted in some spectacular takedowns, such as the one in spring 2009 in which US Navy SEALs shot three pirates dead, and the April 2011 operation in which Dutch marines killed two pirates. However, while a collaborative international effort by Indonesia, Malaysia and Singapore did thwart piracy in the Strait of Malacca, even well-equipped modern navies, using state-of-the-art technology such as *Reaper* drones as the United States has done, cannot identify and target all of the small pirate vessels operating in the vaster expanses of the Indian Ocean. Thus, the deterrent effect of international counter-piracy efforts there has been minimal. Indeed, to some extent it has motivated the pirates to raise their game, reinvesting their profits in better kit – including cell phones, satellite phones, GPS, outboard motors and upgraded weaponry. And their financial sophistication has grown: according to the US Navy, pirate syndicates now sell shares in the proceeds of planned attacks to raise capital.

Since 2009, they have also been more inclined to attack and seize ships farther off shore, well into the Indian Ocean – as far south as Madagascar and almost as far east as the Maldives (see map, IISS *Military Balance 2011*, page 403). Britain's Royal Navy has noted the use of larger and better-equipped motherships that allow smaller vessels to loiter near known shipping routes, sometimes for days, to attack vessels. Establishment by the 60-nation Contact Group on Piracy off the Coast of Somalia of best management practices – including 24-hour lookouts, passive sonar, charging fire hydrants and evasive manoeuvres – has helped counter some attacks. So have on-board armed security officers now employed by some shipping lines. But pirate attacks have also become better planned – for instance, in employing preliminary probes to determine the crew's capability to resist. While the IMB reported 50 attacks abandoned at the arrival of naval ships and helicopters from January 2008 to June 2009, there were 251 attacks during this period and 72 resulted in successful hijackings.

More ominous leanings?

In 2010, Somali pirates appeared to become more non-lethally violent towards their captives. The presumed explanation was that they wanted to hasten the payment of ransoms, which roughly doubled over the course of the year. But Somali pirates' killing of four American hostages in February 2011 was more starkly inconsistent with the business imperative of keeping hostages alive to command high ransoms. The pirates' apparently rising inclination to seek out and do violence to Americans and Europeans suggested that they might be seeking revenge against lethal counter-piracy operations, and more broadly pushing back against the US Navy-led international anti-piracy effort. Even more troublingly, acute hostility towards Westerners could imply a rising tendency among the pirates to collaborate (at least on a tactical, non-ideological level) with Somali jihadists.

Of special concern is the increasingly ambitious al-Shabaab, which has recruited from the Somali diaspora in the United States, Canada and Europe, executed its first out-of-area operation in Uganda in July 2010, and proclaimed its allegiance to al-Qaeda. Pirates constitute a lucrative financing source for al-Shabaab, having reportedly paid the group between 10% and 50% of their ransom take in 'taxes'. Pirates are also believed to be smuggling weapons for al-Shabaab into Somalia from Yemen and Central Asia for a fee, as well as helping the terrorist group stand up a maritime capability for transporting jihadists into and out of Somalia. Al-Shabaab, unlike the Islamic Courts Union, its more moderate predecessor, has not forbidden piracy, and has occasionally allowed pirates safe harbour in port towns that it controls.

Such indirect alliances of convenience are mutual force multipliers, and as their benefits increase could evolve into more kinetic and lethal forms of cooperation, which in turn might lead to some pirates' jihadisation. Given Somali pirates' improvements in technical capabilities, as well as better planning, they could furnish al-Qaeda affiliates with a robust maritime terrorism capability. While they have survived without one, the Tamil Tigers in Sri Lanka demonstrated the operational and political value of such a capability, and supporting maritime operations were critical to Pakistani jihadists' execution of the devastating Mumbai attack in late 2008.

Although al-Qaeda's strategic direction remained uncertain in the wake of Osama bin Laden's death on 2 May 2011, the Somali pirates' modus operandi is adaptable to transnational terrorism. It could rekindle al-Qaeda's interest in sea-based attacks, which peaked with the highly effective bombing of the USS *Cole* in October 2000 but remained dormant after the attack on the French oil tanker *Limburg* in 2002. There has been speculation that in October 2010, al-Shabaab attempted to use a ship hijacked and supplied to the group by pirates to attack a vessel carrying supplies for AMISOM that was being escorted by a Spanish warship detailed to the EU Naval Force

Somalia's anti-piracy operations. In April 2011, General Carter Ham, head of US Africa Command, stated in Senate testimony that al-Qaeda's links to al-Shabaab suggested that it was only a matter of time before al-Qaeda forged connections to pirates as well.

Management versus victory

The conventional wisdom is that any maritime military response to Somali piracy is inherently inadequate, and that Somalia's ground-based govern-ance problems need to be addressed before piracy can be substantially eliminated. But the country's internationally recognised Transitional Federal Government remains dysfunctional – unable to collect taxes, provide effec-tive social services, enforce the rule of law or make collective decisions for the populace – and challenged by Somalia's Islamist militias (mainly al-Shabaab) and self-declared states.

Somalia's internal problems may be too profound to be materially addressable in the near or medium term. Deeper solutions, such as revitalis-ing Somalia's fishing industry to provide an economic alternative to piracy, would require a level of government control unlikely to exist for years. Establishing a basic coast guard without an effective central government is a comparably daunting proposition. While some Somali entities (particularly Somaliland) do have maritime-security capabilities and the will to arrest, convict and imprison pirates, their resources and capacity are woefully inad-equate. The UN and the United States frown on their retention of private military companies to augment security capabilities, fearing that this will ultimately be more destabilising. In Puntland, where most Somali pirates are based and most instances of passive cooperation between pirates and jihadists have arisen, clan-based groups appear to have fashioned a security milieu just reliable enough to afford the pirates a comfortable safe haven.

As criminal mercenaries, pirates are a manageable if vexing scourge. As active terrorist collaborators, they would graduate to a bona fide strategic threat. To forestall this development, the challenge for international secu-rity policy may be to resist the urge to use lethal force against pirates. The SEAL takedown and other applications of lethal force have energised the anti-piracy push. But in the longer term they could have the perverse effect of antagonising pirates into escalating. The use of lethal force will some-times be necessary. But a non-kinetic focus on preventing piracy could be less likely to drive pirates towards jihadists. One measure along these lines is to target pirate leaders in transnational law-enforcement operations, as the FBI did in arresting Mohammed Saaili Shibin – alleged head of the group that killed the four Americans – in Somalia with Somali cooperation in April 2011. Another is to rigorously enforce the use of designated shipping lanes so as to shrink the pirates' effective area of operations and render it easier to deny them opportunities to seize ships. Such calibrated measures may not defeat Somali piracy, but they could keep it manageable.

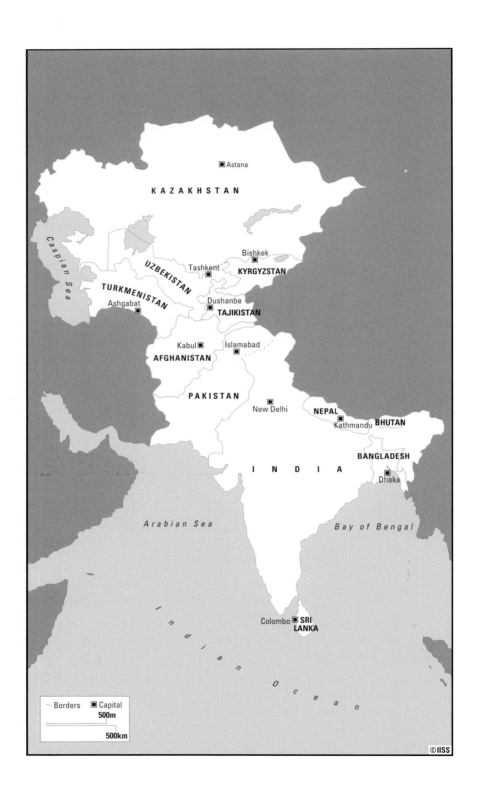

Chapter 8

South and Central Asia

Afghanistan: Goal Set for Troop Drawdown

Afghanistan and the international community are engaged in an attempt to neutralise the Taliban insurgency and develop the capacity of the Afghan state and its armed forces ahead of the end-2014 deadline that NATO leaders have set for handing responsibility for the country's security to President Hamid Karzai's government.

The first milestone on the route towards that deadline was in July 2011, when the United States was to begin withdrawing combat troops from the country under the timetable set in 2009 by President Barack Obama.

The commitment to pull out NATO-led combat forces by the end of 2014 was made in November 2010 at the Alliance's Lisbon summit. It was couched in careful language: the leaders affirmed their 'support for Karzai's objective for the Afghan National Security Forces to lead and conduct security operations in all provinces by the end of 2014'. It was expected that military trainers would remain to support Afghan forces, and that special forces would stay to conduct anti-terrorism operations. Anders Fogh Rasmussen, the NATO secretary-general, offered assurances that 'we will not transition until our Afghan partners are ready. We will stay after transition in a supporting role.' However, there was no mistaking the desire of the US administration and the UK government, as well as other troop contributors, to conclude the combat element of what will be, by then, a 13-year deployment.

The number of casualties caused by the conflict continued to rise. According to the United Nations, 2010 was the worst year for civilian deaths since the operation began, with more than 2,700 fatalities. The UN blamed the insurgents for a 15% increase in civilian deaths, and said the number killed by foreign forces fell by 16% following an effort by NATO to limit the use of artillery, missiles and air-strikes. In 2010, 711 non-Afghan troops were killed, the highest annual total in the decade-old campaign. Several countries, including Canada, Denmark and the Netherlands, announced plans to end or reduce their military deployments.

NATO leaders insisted that they would remain committed to Afghanistan's development even after the planned troop withdrawal. The year to mid-2011 saw a new focus on building stronger local government structures whilst still attempting to reform central institutions in Kabul. The tripling of US forces stationed in Afghanistan that had taken place after Barack Obama became president was supposed to be accompanied by a 'civilian surge', a redoubled attempt to dramatically increase the non-military capacity of the Afghan state. However, this had not produced the resources or the progress that had been hoped for. Overall, the planned transition to Afghan responsibility continued to face huge challenges from ineffective government, pervasive corruption and underdeveloped security forces.

The past year also saw a developing consensus across Afghanistan and internationally that sustainable stability could not be achieved without successful negotiations with the Taliban. These would aim to reintegrate at least some of militants' senior commanders into the political process in return for a disavowal of violence.

Military campaign

The international military operation reached a peak in terms of numbers by the end of 2010, when 132,000 troops were deployed by a total of 48 countries. This followed a 'surge' ordered by Obama in December 2009, when he committed 30,000 more US troops to the mission but set July 2011 as the date when these additional forces would start to be withdrawn. Vice President Joseph Biden unambiguously declared: 'In July of 2011, you're going to see a whole lot of people moving out – bet on it'.

This and previous decisions by Obama to increase the number of troops, in the view of the military commanders involved, for the first time gave them the resources they needed to tackle the Taliban insurgency. Between 2006 and 2009, the NATO-led International Security Assistance Force (ISAF) and the Afghan National Security Forces (ANSF) had been able to clear insurgent-dominated areas, but did not have sufficient forces to keep control of them. The result was that many areas were ceded back to the Taliban, with dire consequences for Afghans who had cooperated with foreign forces.

Since then the approach was to clear only areas that could subsequently be held, to focus on the more heavily populated districts, and to support the introduction of Afghan government structures into those areas. This strategy was drawn up by US Army General Stanley McChrystal and led by him until he was dismissed by Obama in 2010 after indiscreet remarks were made to *Rolling Stone* magazine. It was continued by General David Petraeus, who replaced him – and was also the author of the US Army's counter-insurgency doctrine.

From early 2010, ISAF's main effort was in southern Afghanistan. Most US reinforcements were deployed there, as well as increasing numbers of Afghan forces. ISAF's understanding of the complex Afghan environment had greatly improved since 2006, through human intelligence and improved surveillance. Large numbers of unmanned aerial vehicles and other surveillance assets were redeployed by the United States from Iraq to Afghanistan.

ISAF sought to extend Afghan government control over populous areas in Helmand and Kandahar provinces. The drive began with *Operation Moshtarak* in Helmand province. Launched in February 2010, the operation eventually led to significant improvement of security in central Helmand around the provincial capital of Lashkar Gah. Clearance of the insurgent stronghold of Marjah proceeded more slowly, but by January 2011 the bazaar there was thriving. In June 2010, *Operation Hamkari* was launched to clear the city of Kandahar and surrounding districts. Heavy fighting between the Taliban and US, Canadian and Afghan troops resulted in ISAF claiming that the districts of Panjawi, Zhari and Arghandab had been both cleared and held.

However, in April 2011 the Taliban managed to tunnel into Kandahar prison, allowing several hundred prisoners to escape. This highlighted the fact that, despite improvements in Afghan police capability, there was much to be done to improve the rule of law. A subsequent effort to stage a spectacular attack with gunmen and suicide bombers in Kandahar was successfully countered by the ANSF. At mid-2011, ISAF was planning to clear further areas in Kandahar and Helmand provinces, as well as to shift resources into eastern Afghanistan to counter the Haqqani network, a militant group linked to but separate from the Taliban.

A separate thrust of ISAF's campaign was to increase 'night raids' conducted by special forces against insurgent leaders. In 2010, a tripling in the number of raids resulted in the killing of more than 1,200 people, including some 300 thought to hold leadership roles, according to ISAF. Captured militants indicate that this had eroded insurgents' capability, leadership and morale.

At mid-2011 the framework for the military campaign was the planned transition to Afghan control. Congressional testimony by Petraeus and other officials indicated that offensive operations in the south had improved security, and that attacks had caused considerable losses of experienced Taliban commanders. There was cautious optimism that improvements in security would endure in the fighting season that began in spring 2011. In March, Karzai announced that responsibility for security in several areas would be transferred to Afghan forces from July: Kabul province (except Surobi), Panjshir and Bamiyan provinces, and the four provincial capitals of Herat (Herat province), Lashkar Gah (Helmand), Mazar-e-Sharif (Balkh) and Mehtar Lam (Laghman). These areas cover 20% of the Afghan population. Some ISAF forces deployed in these areas were expected to be moved to other districts to bolster security or into training roles, though governments were likely to be keen to bring troops home.

Political challenges

Since all parties – including military commanders – agreed that there was no purely military solution to Afghanistan's problems, the sustainability of international policy towards Afghanistan was hugely dependent on Karzai and his cabinet. The system of government set up in the aftermath of regime change in 2001 placed a great deal of executive authority in the office of the president. Karzai was not only responsible for appointing his cabinet, but also 34 provincial governors, 400 district sub-governors and all government officials down to the level of district administrator. Doubts about Karzai's ability to handle this level of authority became widespread in 2010–11.

These worries were fuelled by leaked diplomatic cables from the US Embassy in Kabul and its ambassador Karl Eikenberry. A report from the embassy to Secretary of Defense Robert Gates placed Karzai 'at the centre of the governance challenge'. It stated that he struggled to strike 'the correct balance between institutional and traditional (i.e. tribal) governance'. Eikenberry was blunter, doubting that Karzai would ever lose the habit of blaming the United States for everything that went wrong in Afghanistan. He wrote that Karzai was unable 'to grasp the most rudimentary principles of state-building' and had two competing personalities, one 'paranoid and weak' the other 'an ever-shrewd politician'.

On the political front, Karzai continued to try to build support among the dominant Pashtun community. In June 2010 two of the most highly respected members of his government abruptly resigned. The departure of Chief of Intelligence Amrullah Saleh and Interior Minister Hanif Atmar was initially explained as a result of their failure to stop the Taliban shelling a three-day 'peace jirga' held in Kabul. However, it soon became apparent that both had resigned because of long running tensions with Karzai, who claimed he had lost trust in both men.

The sackings may have been caused by the shifting basis of the president's political coalition. Saleh, one of the longest-serving members of the government, had come to prominence because of his links to the anti-Taliban commander Ahmad Shah Massoud, who was murdered in September 2001. The Northern Alliance, the grouping which Massoud founded and which seized Kabul from the Taliban in November 2001, later became a key pillar of Karzai's ruling coalition. However, since 2007 Karzai had attempted to reduce the influence of Northern Alliance leaders within government as he sought to build support among the Pashtun population which dominates southern and eastern Afghanistan. In 2009 this triggered the presidential campaign of a prominent politician from the Northern Alliance, Abdullah Abdullah.

Saleh's departure may therefore have been related to Karzai's long-running attempt to reduce the influence of the Northern Alliance within his government. However, both Atmar and Saleh were seen to be among the most effective members of the government. Their removal had a clear detrimental effect on the coherence of Afghanistan's security forces, as well as indicating the depth of Karzai's long-held suspicion of the forces, whom he perceived as disloyal.

Karzai was meanwhile trying to rebuild domestic political legitimacy, which had been damaged by the electoral fraud that surrounded his re-election for a second five-year term in August 2009. Central to this attempt were elections to the lower house of parliament, the Wolesi Jirga, in September 2010.

The Wolesi Jirga has the power to accept or reject Karzai's choice of cabinet ministers. In 2010 it rejected 17 of the 24 people proposed for ministerial appointments, and then tried to reject ten of the new list. However, the parliament's power has severe limitations. Firstly, members are not organised along party lines, so their ability to act collectively is minimal. Secondly, there have been persistent rumours that parliamentary votes on key issues are influenced by widespread bribery. Finally, Karzai has circumvented parliamentary votes against him through the use of presidential decrees announced when parliament is not sitting, as well as through votes in the appointed upper house and judgments from the Supreme Court. For example, the ten people rejected by parliament for cabinet posts still took up their positions, with the president labelling their appointments 'temporary'.

For all its shortcomings, elections to the Wolesi Jirga on 18 September 2010 were seen as a vehicle to prove that the country had moved beyond the controversy that dominated the 2009 elections. But this was not to happen. To begin with, competition for the 249 seats appeared fierce, with 2,545 candidates registering. In the capital, because of its comparative security, 662 people competed for 33 seats. However, the election campaign was disorganised because political parties were not strongly represented. A law passed in 2009 required Afghanistan's 110 parties to re-register if they wished to compete in the elections. Only 25 managed to do so by the deadline, and government inefficiency led to just five of these actually being licensed in time for the elections. These were the only parties permitted to have their candidate's affiliations mentioned on the ballot paper. Meanwhile, intimidation and insecurity limited the ability of candidates to campaign outside Kabul. When researcher Tina Blohm visited the southeastern province of Paktika, she found that only six of the 22 registered candidates were present in the province and only two were actually campaigning.

Fraud and violence undermined the election's outcome. Instability led to the reduction of the number of polling centres from 6,300 to 5,900, raising fears that Pashtun areas where violence was greatest could be disenfranchised. On the day of the election a further 461 centres were closed because of security issues, and 63 polling stations were attacked. ISAF recorded a total of 380 attacks, a hundred more than on the day of the presidential election the previous year.

Even greater damage to the electoral process was caused by widespread and systematic voter fraud. The Independent Electoral Commission rejected 1.3 million of 5.6m ballots cast and disqualified 21 of 249 successful candidates. The exclusion of a number of Pashtun candidates triggered Karzai's intervention and his attempt to use an investigation by the attorney general to overturn the commission's judgment. However, after muscular diplomatic negotiations, the election result and the exclusions were not challenged and the parliament opened on 26 January 2011. Much attention focused on the dramatic reduction of Pashtun parliamentarians in the new Wolesi Jirga. However, a greater concern was arguably the electoral turnout. With no reliable voter-registration tally, the total size of the electorate is hard to judge, with estimates ranging from 10.5 to 12.5m. In the 2010 elections 3.6m ballots were cast compared to 6.4m in the previous parliamentary poll in

2005. This dramatic decrease had also occurred in the presidential elections, with 4.8m votes cast in 2009 compared with 7.4m in 2004. Given the widespread corruption amongst the political elite and their continuing inability to deliver government services, it was hardly surprising that the population of Afghanistan was losing its appetite for voting.

Poor governance

The diminished legitimacy of government did not bode well for the success of the counter-insurgency campaign and its ability to win the confidence of ordinary Afghans in the government. The field of governance also provided few encouraging developments.

Corruption continued to affect every level of the state's interaction with Afghan society. At the lowest level, policemen on the streets of Kabul demanded money from drivers to let their cars through the numerous checkpoints that had been set up across the capital. Karzai used presidential largesse to bribe parliamentarians and made sure that prominent allies were given land in the now-affluent Sherpur district of Kabul on which to build grand houses. In a survey carried out in 2010, Integrity Watch Afghanistan found the everyday bribery of government officials had doubled since 2007, with ordinary Afghans having to pay an average of $156 in bribes each year to access government services. Overall, the US government reported in September 2010 that 80.6% of Afghans polled believed corruption affected their daily life.

Although Karzai acknowledged that corruption was a serious and destructive problem, very little was done to limit its corrosive effects. Attorney General Mohammed Ishaq Aloko was repeatedly accused of delaying, obstructing or stopping criminal investigations into senior government officials charged with corruption. A hostile attitude to the investigation of corruption was revealed following a raid on the New Ansari Hawala Money Exchange in Kabul in January 2010. The police raid showed the company to be responsible for shipping government officials' private resources, as well as drug smugglers' and Taliban funds, to Dubai. Afghan and US investigators using phone taps recorded Mohammad Zia Salehi, head of administration of the Afghan National Security Council, offering to stop the investigation if those connected to the New Ansari Hawala would give his son a new Toyota car. Salehi was arrested in July 2010, but newspaper reports suggested that he telephoned Karzai from his prison cell. He was then driven away from the jail in a car sent from the presidential palace. The Anti-Corruption Unit, which led the investigation and arrested Salehi, was closed down on the orders of the attorney general. The prosecutor responsible for the case, Fazel Ahmed Faqiryar, was forced into retirement and then charged with libelling members of Karzai's cabinet.

With such a poor Afghan government record in tackling corruption, NATO set up its own organisation to tackle the problem. Shafafiyat or 'Transparency', which became operational in October 2010, aimed to coordinate between the international community and the Afghan government to better tackle corruption. This involved ensuring ISAF's own approach to contracting did not exacerbate the situation whilst deploying enhanced NATO resources and personnel to bolster and support Afghan anti-corruption campaigns. The importance that NATO attached to this initiative was indicated by the appointment of one of its most respected generals, H.R. McMaster of the US Army, to head Shafafiyat.

However, Karzai's own approach to governance was indicated in August 2010 when it was revealed that the presidential palace had amassed a fund estimated at $10–50m. Each year Karzai used this money to buy loyalty from Afghanistan's politicians. It came not only from Afghan businesses eager to curry favour with the president, but also from the country's allies and neighbours. In October 2010, Karzai admitted that his chief of staff, Umar Daudzai, received cash payments from Iran of as much as €700,000 'once or twice every year'.

Afghan security forces

The building of effective security forces was also expected to be key to a successful transition. The international resources devoted to this effort grew considerably – some $20 billion in 2010 and 2011 combined, equal to the total of the previous eight years. The quality of training improved, and investment was made in training bases. The average level of capability and performance improved, but progress continued to be patchy.

The Afghan National Army (ANA) reached a strength of 134,000 in August 2010 and was on track to reach its target of 171,600 by October 2011. It was playing an increasing role in military operations, including *Moshtarak* and *Hamkari*. The better ANA units and formations proved themselves capable of taking the lead in operations against the insurgents. For example, the third phase of *Moshtarak* saw an Afghan corps headquarters take the lead in a substantial operation and later phases of *Hamkari* were initiated with set-piece orders by Afghan rather than NATO commanders.

The effort to build the Afghan National Police (ANP) was lagging behind that of the Army. Its strength stood at 109,000 as of January 2011, with

NATO confident that the target of 134,000 could be reached by late 2011. In 2009 it had seemed that the ANP was almost as much a part of the security problem as of the solution, with low-level corruption and predatory extortion at checkpoints a particular concern. Efforts to train the ANP were then bolstered, supported by initiatives such as a British-led Helmand Police Training Centre. However, there were still significant signs of weakness, including corruption. Many of these resulted from less international effort having been applied to the ANP than the ANA.

There were also incidents in which Afghan police and servicemen turned their weapons on their ISAF mentors. Some 25 NATO personnel had been killed in this fashion by June 2011. The ANSF were attempting to counter this in a number of ways, including increased vetting and intelligence and banning the sale of uniforms.

While teaching was carried out mostly by NATO personnel, the aim was that ANSF experts would lead the training by 2013. Efforts to combat illiteracy, which was a significant brake on the development of the ANSF, acted as a strong recruiting draw.

A separate ISAF-sponsored programme was the development of local self-defence forces in villages that had opted to resist the Taliban in areas with little ISAF or ANSF presence. This exploited successful revolts against the Taliban by some villages, for example in Gizab district in Uruzgan province. Described by Petraeus as a 'community watch with AK47s', the aim was to have such forces in 70 districts, 27 of which were operational by March 2011.

Talking with the Taliban

Moves towards a negotiated settlement with the Taliban gathered pace during 2010-11. However, although a series of public initiatives were announced and high level meetings between the government in Kabul, the United Nations, NATO and Taliban commanders were held, there was little evidence so far to suggest that these moves would result in substantive reconciliation or the basis of a sustainable peace deal.

New momentum towards talks with the Taliban was heralded in January 2010 with Karzai's announcement at an international conference in London of a major push for negotiations. This involved plans for a 'peace jirga' in Kabul and additional funding to drive reconciliation forward by demobilising and reintegrating low-level Taliban fighters. Karzai also backed an amnesty law and encouraged the UN to remove five senior Taliban leaders from a 'watch list' of 137 of the movement's current and former leaders. At first this initiative was greeted with scepticism by the United States, as the results of the troop surge were still unfolding across Afghanistan. However, by July 2010 it was evident that the United States had moderated its previous reluctance to engage in negotiations with the Taliban and was now actively facilitating them.

In June 2010, Karzai attempted to solidify support for the Afghan government's approach to peace talks with the Taliban by holding a three-day 'peace jirga' in Kabul. Some 1,600 hand-picked delegates were assembled in the capital to give their blessing to the president's policy. After heavy lobbying from the government, the jirga elected the former president Burhanudin Rabbani as its chair. However, key members of the country's governing elite expressed their opposition, with Abdullah Abdullah, the former presidential candidate, pulling out of the jirga along with 60–70 senators and members of parliament.

Undeterred by this opposition, Karzai attempted in September to build on the momentum surrounding plans for peace talks by announcing the 'Process of Peace, Reconciliation and Reintegration'. This set up a high peace council under Rabbani to lead the government's negotiations with the Taliban.

In March 2011, veteran diplomats Lakhdar Brahimi and Thomas Pickering gave their backing to peace talks in a report calling for confidence-building measures that would lead to the establishment of formal negotiations. The report suggested that if the United States suspended the assassination of senior Taliban leaders then the Taliban might in return be persuaded to stop the use of roadside bombs and the killing of government officials.

Behind these public initiatives it was clear that all sides were engaged in confidential and limited discussions to see if substantive peace talks were possible. In April 2010, reports began to circulate that both Karzai himself and the then UN special representative in Kabul, Kai Eide, had opened negotiations with the senior Taliban commander, Mullah Baradar, and representatives of the Taliban's leadership in exile, the Quetta Shura. In September, Petraeus confirmed that senior members of the Taliban had indeed approached the Afghan government about the possibility of peace talks. In October he said NATO had 'facilitated' negotiations between the government and the Taliban. Far less formal but much more public talks were held in the Maldives in November, attended by 47 members of various Afghan factions, including the Taliban, the Haqqani group and Hezb-e-Islami, as well as representatives of senior politicians. Although the Afghan government refused to send a delegation, the country's two vice-presidents sent personal representatives. Then, in February 2011, *New Yorker* magazine reported that the US government itself had conducted direct talks with senior Taliban leaders. These talks were unofficially confirmed, with US government sources saying they were carried out to ascertain if the Taliban was serious about a peace deal with the Karzai government.

In spite of these important Afghan and international initiatives, there were few indications that the proposals and talks would lead to either an immediate breakthrough or a sustained and structured dialogue. Numerous informal talks about talks were held, but the Taliban insisted that formal talks would be dependent upon acceptance of its central non-negotiable demands: a timetable for the withdrawal of all US forces and the release of all Taliban prisoners held by both the US and Afghan governments. There appeared to be little incentive for the militant groups to take part in substantive reconciliation talks, particularly in view of the general lack of confidence in the Afghan government to deliver prosperity and security. A Pentagon report to Congress in November 2010 stated: 'The Taliban is not a popular movement, but it exploits a population frustrated by weak governance. The Taliban's strength lies in the Afghan population's perception that coalition forces will soon leave, giving credence to the belief that a Taliban victory is inevitable.'

Pakistan: Shock at bin Laden Raid

The Pakistani establishment suffered a major shock when US special forces launched a raid in the early hours of 2 May 2011 (local time) and killed Osama bin Laden, the al-Qaeda leader who was living in a house close to Pakistan's main military academy (see Box, pages 34–5; Strategic Geography, page XIV).

The attack was a severe embarrassment for the beleaguered government and the military, who were facing a growing threat from Islamist militants and had an increasingly testy relationship with the United States. The incursion by American helicopters was apparently not detected. The government had for years denied that bin Laden was hiding in Pakistan, when in fact he was residing quietly in pleasant Abbottabad, 50km from Islamabad. Immediately, questions were raised in the United States about whether anyone in the Pakistani establishment had known of his presence.

In the daring assault, which was based on intelligence that had been developed over a long period but was still imprecise, US Navy SEALs entered the high-walled compound, meeting surprisingly little resistance. After killing bin Laden and four other people, they took his body and personal computer files, destroyed a helicopter that had malfunctioned, and left Pakistani airspace before they could be challenged by the late scramble of two Pakistani F-16 aircraft. Bin Laden was quickly buried at sea from a US aircraft carrier sailing in the north Arabian Sea. US President Barack Obama said that the death of bin Laden marked the most significant achievement to date in the US effort to defeat al-Qaeda. Washington, he said, had made it clear that it would take action within Pakistan if it discovered bin Laden's location. It was essential that Pakistan continue to join the United States in the fight against al-Qaeda and its affiliates, Obama said.

Pakistan's reactions were all bluster and confusion. Though welcoming bin Laden's death, high officials protested against the US violation of Pakistani sovereignty, and blamed other countries for the intelligence failure to locate bin Laden.

US attention focused on whether the Pakistani military and intelligence establishment had in any way been involved in bin Laden's efforts to hide – he had been living in Abbottabad for about five years – or whether they had simply been unable to locate him. Army chief General Pervez Kayani had visited the Pakistan Military Academy, a kilometre from bin Laden's hideout, a week before the raid. Although public opinion in the United States was angered by what was widely considered to be official Pakistani complicity, Obama and senior US officials consistently stopped short of directly blaming Pakistan's civilian and military leadership for harbouring the al-Qaeda leader. National Security Adviser Tom Donilon said there was 'no information indicating foreknowledge by the political, military or intelligence leadership in Pakistan'. However, Obama said, bin Laden had 'some sort of support network inside Pakistan'. On her first visit to Pakistan after 2 May, Secretary of State Hillary Clinton stated that senior Pakistani officials had said 'that somebody, somewhere was providing some kind of support'. Pakistani irritation at such comments was compounded by the fact that US officials had not briefed their Pakistani counterparts before the operation for fear of a leak by extremist sympathisers within the armed forces and the intelligence establishment.

The Pakistani military was humiliated by its inability to prevent a violation of Pakistani sovereignty and respond to a US military raid deep inside the country. This led to unprecedented public criticism of the army in the local media and on the streets, with questions raised about the army's priorities and preparedness. There was increasing pressure on Kayani, who was already attempting to quell growing anti-American sentiment within the military. The raid thus raised the prospect that the military's influence would decrease at a time the civilian leadership, elected after the end of military rule by President Pervez Musharraf in 2008, remained weak. As a result, there was increased concern that Islamist militant groups would gain greater sway in parts of the country.

The government sought to salve Pakistani dignity and put the country's embarrassment behind it. Prime Minister Yousuf Raza Gilani, addressing the National Assembly and the Senate, said: 'Pakistan alone cannot be held to account for flawed policies and blunders of others'. He elaborated on the number of Pakistani victims of terrorism and Pakistan's role in capturing and killing top al-Qaeda members. 'It is disingenuous for anyone to blame Pakistan or state institutions of Pakistan including the ISI [Inter-Services Intelligence] and the armed forces for being in cahoots with al-Qaeda.' Parliament passed a unanimous, if weak and largely non-binding, resolution, condemning the US raid on grounds of sovereignty and threatening to close NATO land supply lines into Afghanistan unless strikes by American unmanned aircraft in Pakistan were stopped. It called on the government to 're-visit and review its terms of engagement with the United States'. Meanwhile, the army's influential Corps Commanders' Conference recognised 'shortcomings' in intelligence and announced an investigation 'into the circumstances that led to this situation'. On the degree of cooperation Pakistan had extended in the run up to the operation, it added that the 'CIA developed intelligence based on initial information provided by ISI'.

US relations at new low

Pakistan's defiance further angered the US Congress, and some members threatened to cut off aid. This was resisted by the Obama administration on the basis that it was essential that Islamabad and Washington continue to fight together against al-Qaeda and its affiliates in Pakistan. Nevertheless, it was obvious that US–Pakistan relations had reached a nadir.

Within Pakistan, regular CIA drone strikes on extremist targets in Waziristan, which had increased in frequency under Obama, continued to arouse public resentment. Although leaks of US diplomatic cables showed Gilani's tacit approval of the strikes, the government's public posture was consistently to denounce them. There were 117 such attacks in 2010 compared with 53 in 2009.

Even before the death of bin Laden, the United States and Pakistan had been at loggerheads over the case of Raymond Davis, an American employee of a private security firm, who shot dead two men in the street in Lahore. There was long-standing resentment of the increased presence of US private contractors, who were suspected of being undercover CIA operatives – as indeed Davis proved to be. After having been held for six weeks, Davis was released in exchange for compensation payments, but the settlement failed to extinguish public anger against the United States. The trust deficit between the two countries widened, and during a meeting in April, ISI chief Lieutenant-General Ahmed Shuja Pasha and CIA Director Leon Panetta failed to agree terms of an accord that would formalise the presence of US forces and other security personnel in Pakistan. The Pakistani government subsequently ensured the removal of a number of US counter-intelligence staff and trainers for its Frontier Corps, which was battling the Pakistani Taliban in the tribal areas. Joint intelligence cooperation cells were closed. For the second time in less than six months, the name of the CIA's station chief in Islamabad was leaked and the agent had to be replaced.

There were yet further issues between the two countries. Pakistani authorities were angered by a US civil court order summoning Pasha, along with two Lashkar-e-Tayiba (LeT) militant leaders, in connection with the 2008 Mumbai terror attacks. Meanwhile, Washington reportedly agreed to reimburse only a third of Pakistan's $3.2 billion claim for its contribution to fighting militants between January 2009 and June 2010. It alleged that the military was deceitful in its expenses claims.

Nevertheless, it was clear that neither Pakistan nor the United States could afford a significant further worsening of relations that would jeopardise the long-standing interests of each side. Pakistan relied on US support to finance its economy and its counter-terrorism operations. In addition to $12bn in overt security-related disbursements made to Pakistan since 2001, Washington also followed up on its pledge to devote $1.5bn a year for five years to non-military development assistance under the Kerry–Lugar–Berman Act of 2009. The threat to Pakistan from Islamist militants was underlined by many terrorist incidents, including a suicide-bomb attack that killed over 80 paramilitary personnel in reprisal for the bin Laden raid. Pakistani Taliban fedayeen also staged a brazen attack on a naval base at Mehran, near Karachi. They held off the security forces for 16 hours after destroying two P-3C *Orion* surveillance aircraft. The arrest of a disgruntled former naval officer in connection with the attack raised concerns over the threat from insiders in parts of the military establishment.

For its part, the United States needed Pakistan to contain the rise of extremist violence, and to play a role in facilitating a political end-game in

Afghanistan, given its long-standing links with the Afghan Taliban leadership resident in Pakistan. It was also concerned to ensure the security of Pakistan's nuclear arsenal. US Senator John Kerry, travelling to Pakistan soon after the Abbottabad raid, said this was a 'make or break moment' for the US Congress with regard to its economic aid to Pakistan. He called on both countries to make 'fundamental choices' about their relationship, delivered a list of 'specific demands' to Pakistan and called for pressing the 'reset button' in their bilateral relations. A clear test of relations would be the level of intelligence provided by the ISI to support continued drone strikes, as well as the assurance of logistical supplies to NATO forces in Afghanistan.

The floods

In addition to chronic violence, Pakistan was afflicted by a severe natural disaster in the year to mid-2011. The 2010 monsoon was the heaviest in the region for about 80 years. Running down the Indus river basin, floods affected Pakistan-administered Kashmir and all four provinces, destroying property, livelihoods, infrastructure and crops such as wheat, cotton and sugar cane which provided both domestic food supplies and export earnings. Disease was widespread as a result of contaminated drinking water. Some 5.3 million jobs were lost, out of the country's total workforce of 55m, and 1.7m households were destroyed. The World Bank put the cost to the economy at $9.7bn, while Pakistan said the damage amounted to a quarter of its GDP. Gilani said 20m people had been made homeless.

The nation's response reflected the flawed character of its institutions. The government was heavily criticised for its slow and ineffective reaction. Few politicians visited the affected areas, perhaps conscious that they would become the focus of demonstrations. President Asif Ali Zardari continued with pre-planned visits to the UK and France, where a helicopter trip from a family chateau attracted much unfavourable publicity. In the absence of adequate civilian leadership, the security forces redeployed tens of thousands of personnel from anti-insurgency operations in the tribal areas adjoining Afghanistan. But even that was insufficient and militant groups such as LeT gained credit for filling gaps, as they had at the time of the earthquake in Kashmir in 2005.

Politics and security

At mid-2011, Pakistan was midway through its five-year electoral cycle, with elections due in early 2013. A constitutional amendment in 2010 had relieved Zardari of most of the key executive powers accumulated by his military predecessor, General Musharraf. Operational duties now fell more upon Prime Minister Gilani. But Zardari, widower of former Prime Minister Benazir Bhutto, remained deeply unpopular, with only a 20% approval rating as a result of his perceived ineffectiveness and accusations of corruption.

The opposition, however, failed to capitalise fully on the weaknesses of the government, a coalition led by the Pakistan Peoples Party (PPP). Nawaz Sharif, former prime minister and leader of the main opposition party, the Pakistan Muslim League-Nawaz (PML-N), was in no hurry to assume the reins of government. His brother Shahbaz Sharif, chief minister of Punjab, meanwhile ensured continued dominance over the party's traditional heartland ahead of the elections. Opposition parties did, however, seek to profit from the PPP's weakness. In January, the Muttahida Quami Movement (MQM) withdrew from the coalition for a few days before rejoining after winning concessions from the government on fuel-price increases and tax reform. Weeks later the cabinet was reduced from 54 to 22 members as an austerity measure but also to improve the PPP's positioning before the 2013 elections. Foreign Minister Shah Mahmood Qureshi was removed and Hina Rabbani Khar, a 34-year-old US-educated businesswoman, carried out this role as a minister of state.

Pakistan's political and military establishment seemed increasingly under threat from growing Islamist radicalisation and violent extremism. The country continued to be rocked by terrorist attacks, affecting civilians and security forces alike. On 4 January 2011 the governor of Punjab province, Salmaan Taseer, was assassinated in Islamabad by one of his bodyguards, 24-year-old Mumtaz Qadri, who objected to Taseer's campaigning for repeal of Pakistan's blasphemy laws. Taseer had publicly championed the cause of Asia Bibi, a Christian woman who had been sentenced to death in late 2010. Both mainstream Islamic religious movements, the relatively moderate Barelvis and the more hardline Deobandis , immediately praised Qadri's action. Thousands took to the street in support and lawyers showered Qadri with rose petals when he came before the courts. While the liberal elite were horrified by such reactions, the response of the main political parties and the army was cautious and muted. This might have reflected a wish not to provoke the street power of conservative and militant religious forces, and to avoid alienating the Barelvis, whom the government was trying to induce to take action against Pakistani neo-Taliban groups. On 2 March, Minister for Minorities Shahbaz Bhatti, a Christian who had previously received death threats, was assassinated in Islamabad for supporting repeal of the blasphemy laws. Bhatti was the only government minister from the Christian community, which makes up 1.5% of Pakistan's population. The government announced that it did not intend to repeal the laws concerned. These laws had not led to any recent executions.

Although statistics showed a somewhat lower level of violence in 2010 than in 2009, violence and killings were nonetheless extensive. In 2010 there were 68 recorded suicide bombings, which had hardly ever occurred before 2005, compared with 87 in 2009. As extreme or indiscriminate violence increasingly permeated its social fabric, the country faced multiple challenges including domestic militancy, the war in Afghanistan and poor relations with the United States. At the same time, the country's political and military establishment was under siege.

Central Asia: Authoritarian Rule, Regional Tension

Central Asia was characterised by the consolidation of authoritarian regimes in the region's more resource-rich states and growing insecurity and inter-ethnic violence in its poorer countries. It remained peripheral for the major powers, although Kazakhstan did host the annual summit of the Organisation for Security and Cooperation in Europe (OSCE) in Astana in December 2010 and several regional states increased their supporting roles for NATO-led operations in Afghanistan. Russia and China, both of which have their eyes on Central Asia's energy resources, have been increasingly reluctant to intervene to address security challenges.

These included the ethnic violence which engulfed southern Kyrgyzstan in June 2010 (see *Strategic Survey 2010*, pages 316–19) and posed a major security challenge for Kyrgyzstan's neighbours, especially Uzbekistan and Kazakhstan. There were increasing tensions between Uzbekistan and Tajikistan over energy issues such as the Roghun Dam, and between Kyrgyzstan, Uzbekistan and Tajikistan over borders. Moscow's influence in the region lessened with the effective end of its monopoly on gas purchases, while Beijing's increased, especially in the area of natural-gas production. Turkmenistan continued to expand its links with China, especially in the field of energy, and to engage with US efforts in Afghanistan.

Kyrgyzstan: aftermath of violence
Despite the ethnic violence and increased tensions that rocked the country in June 2010, Kyrgyzstan's interim government went ahead with a referen-

dum on a new constitution. The referendum confirmed interim President Roza Otunbayeva in office – she was sworn in on 3 July – but she would not be eligible to run in the presidential election set for December 2011. It also established rules for elections to a new parliament which would devolve power from the president to the prime minister. Seats were to be distributed proportionately to parties winning at least 5% of eligible voters nationwide and at least 0.5% in each of Kyrgyzstan's administrative regions and two key cities.

The parliamentary election, held on 10 October 2010, saw a turnout of only 55% of eligible voters and failed to produce a clear winner. The Ata-Zhurt (Fatherland) Party, drawing its support from ethnic Kyrgyz in the south and led by former officials of the government ousted in April 2010, garnered 16.1% of the vote but only 8.69% of eligible voters. The Social Democratic Party (SDPK), one of the architects of the new constitution, came in second with 8.13%. Only five parties reached the 5% threshold for representation in the 120-seat parliament. In late November three of them – Social Democratic Party, Respublika and Ata-Meken – agreed to form a coalition, which collapsed a month later when parliament failed to agree on a speaker. On 15 December, however, Respublika announced that it had successfully negotiated the creation of a coalition government with SDPK and Ata-Zhurt. SDPK's Almazbek Atambayev became prime minister with 92 votes, Ata-Zhurt's Akhmatbek Keldibekov was chosen as speaker with a 101–14 vote and Respublika's Omurbek Babanov became deputy prime minister.

Kyrgyz politics continued to be haunted by the legacy of the June 2010 clashes. In May 2011, the independent Kyrgyzstan Inquiry Commission (KIC), mandated by Otunbayeva and chaired by Kimmo Kiljunen, a Finnish politician and OSCE representative, reported that Kyrgyz security forces may have been complicit in the violence. The commission said about 470 people had been killed: 74% Uzbek, 25% Kyrgyz and 1% other ethnicities or nationalities. The violence did not amount to war crimes or genocide, but certain attacks on Uzbek neighbourhoods in Osh in June 2010, if proven in a court of law, would amount to 'crimes against humanity'. The government rejected the report as unacceptable and one-sided, saying it displayed an 'overwhelming tendency that only one ethnic group has committed crimes, ignoring the victims and deaths of this very group'.

Kyrgyz authorities claimed that in 2010 there had been two dozen skirmishes on the Kyrgyz–Uzbek border, closed by Uzbekistan after Kyrgyz President Kurmanbek Bakiyev was ousted in June of that year. Otunbayeva announced in March 2011 that negotiations on border delimitation and demarcation remained suspended. There was also tension on the Kyrgyzstan–Tajikistan border. Kyrgyz officials claimed that several former high-ranking officials, including Bakiyev's security-chief brother Janysh, had escaped to Tajikistan following the April 2010 uprising. Kyrgyz security officials, fearing that the June events would be exploited by groups such as the ethnic Uzbek Islamic Movement of Uzbekistan (IMU), accuse Dushanbe of ignoring the threat of Islamic militancy.

Tajikistan: security concerns

Events underlined the fragility of Tajikistan's internal security and the continuing legacy of the country's 1992–97 civil war.

The security services were embarrassed in August 2010 when 25 inmates – including Tajik, Russian and Afghan citizens – escaped from a remand centre in Dushanbe, killing four guards in the process. The escapees were alleged to have been former loyalists of Lieutenant-General Mirzo Ziyoev, a military commander during the civil war. The escape prompted President Emomalii Rahmon to dismiss Colonel-General Khairidin Abdurakhimov as head of the State National Security Committee (SNSC). This was followed by intense fighting in the Rasht valley, a region long dominated by warlords. A military convoy was ambushed and 25 soldiers were killed. Tajik government troops searched houses in the valley belonging to former members of the United Tajik Opposition (UTO), the leading opposition front during the civil war. They uncovered a large weapons cache consisting of six machine guns, three grenades, ten mines, 6,000 rounds of ammunition and 20kg of TNT. Officials said the explosives were going to be used in terrorist attacks in the capital. The intensity of confrontations between government forces and suspected rebels increased after the ambush. The government's main target, Mullo Abdullo, top commander during the civil war and suspected of being one of the main leaders responsible for the recent violence, was killed during an operation in April 2011 after a seven-month hunt.

The agreement that ended the civil war had provided for coalition government, bringing some leaders of the UTO into Rahmon's cabinet. However, the spirit of reconciliation and unity did not last, with many former UTO commanders remaining outside the political process.

Kazakhstan: Astana summit and elections

For Kazakhstan, the year was dominated by its chairmanship of the OSCE and its hosting of the first OSCE summit since 1999, held in December 2010 in Astana. The fact that the summit took place was a success for Kazakhstan, the first post-Soviet state to hold the chairmanship. Many member states did not see any purpose in holding it, given their disagreements on regional issues. Others argued that a meeting was necessary to revitalise the OSCE amidst growing perceptions of its ineffectiveness and marginalisation.

The only declaration to emerge from the summit went little further than reaffirming commitments to the founding documents of the OSCE, such as the Helsinki Final Act and the Charter of Paris. Moreover, the meeting served to focus attention on Kazakhstan's poor human-rights record.

Questions about governance were highlighted in June 2010 when a law was passed awarding President Nursultan Nazarbayev the title 'leader of the nation' and giving him immunity from criminal prosecution. A constitutional amendment was then proposed that would have allowed him to further extend his term until 2020 – he has ruled since 1990 – by standing in the next two elections. It was to be put to a referendum, but was rejected by the Constitutional Council. Rather than pressing ahead with the referendum, Nazarbayev opted to drop it and to call elections for 2011, a year early. In the elections on 3 April, he won 95.5% of the vote, an increase from 2005 when he won 91.2%.

Underlining China's challenge to Russian dominance of Central Asian economies in general, and energy resources in particular, the Kazakh–China oil pipeline reached full capacity, carrying 10m tonnes of crude oil per year from western Kazakhstan 3,000km to the Dushanzi refinery in China's Xinjiang province. China's state oil company said it planned to increase the pipeline's annual capacity to 20m tonnes by 2013. Chinese companies were also seeking to compete with American and European companies operating Kazakhstan's largest oil projects; subsidiaries of China National Petroleum Corporation now produce about one-fifth of Kazakhstan's oil.

India: Scandals Overshadow Economic Advance

The past year was an *annus horribilis* on the political front for the second Manmohan Singh government, which marked two years in office in May 2011. The Congress Party-led government was caught up in swirls of scandal and there was growing doubt about its will to get things done, and reason to worry about an eroding mandate. Nevertheless, there was no real challenge from opposition parties to the government's stability, despite strains within the ruling coalition, styled the United Progressive Alliance.

Singh's seven-year tenure was already the third-longest among all prime ministers in the country's 64-year post-independence history. He said he intended to complete his second five-year term, which runs until 2014, but there was speculation about whether he would be able to achieve this. The Congress Party's heir apparent was 40-year-old Rahul Gandhi; but most people saw him as yet to earn his spurs.

Undisturbed by turbulent politics, the economy continued to do well, recording 8.6% GDP growth in the year to March 2011, up from 8.0% and 6.8% in the previous two years. Growth forecasts for 2011/12 dropped from initial estimates of 9% to 8%, as the Reserve Bank raised interest rates to fight inflation, which was running at 9%, but the five-year growth target for 2012–17 was set at an ambitious 9–9.5% per year.

The internal security situation was reasonably quiet after a stormy 2010 summer in the Kashmir valley that saw 102 deaths and the arrests of 5,000 people for stone-throwing (in imitation of tactics employed during the Palestinian intifada). The other main internal security challenges did not boil over in the same way. There was a slight increase in left-wing extremist activity, but no spectacular attacks on trains, jails or police of the kind seen in recent years. The ethnic and separatist conflicts in the often troubled northeast manifested themselves in a sustained road blockade of the state of Manipur by neighbouring Nagaland, which would like to claim Naga-occupied parts of Manipur; the government had to fly essential goods into the Manipur capital of Imphal. The demand for a new state of Telengana, to be carved out of Andhra Pradesh in the south, found expression in an occasional outburst by students or activists, but remained well short of causing a political crisis. The government used the lull to improve police coordination across states, and to build fortified police stations in areas facing a Maoist challenge.

Meanwhile, the defence forces were busy with an ambitious rearmament programme that recognised the challenges flowing from growing Chinese military ascendancy and Pakistan's advances in relative capability.

Political scandals

From late summer 2010, the headlines were dominated by one scandal after another. Acting under sustained public pressure, and nudged by the Supreme Court, a reluctant government finally began taking action towards the end of the year. The telecommunications minister, Andimuthu Raja, and a handful of senior officials landed in jail, facing corruption charges over the allotment of mobile-phone licences and spectrum. They were kept company by senior officials of the body that organised the 2010 Commonwealth Games, including chairman Suresh Kalmadi, following charges that contracts for games equipment and facilities had been rigged. Also in jail were half a dozen owners and executives of telecom companies, accused of making large-scale payoffs relating to the telecom scandal, with some of the money going to a television company owned by the wife and daughter of M. Karunanidhi, chief minister of the southern state of Tamil Nadu and head of the regional party, the Dravida Munnetra Kazhagam (DMK), an important member of the Congress-led alliance in New Delhi.

The scandal involved allegations that officials hand-picked companies to whom mobile telecom licences were given, and then granted them spectrum at a fraction of the going price. Some of the companies quickly cashed the gift of under-priced spectrum by off-loading equity to international investors, the share price reflecting the full value of the spectrum. Estimates of the loss to the government varied widely. The largest figure of Rs1.76 trillion (about $39bn) came from the comptroller and auditor-general and sparked a firestorm of criticism that led eventually to the arrests and pressing of formal charges.

That there was substance to the charges of large-scale corruption became evident in a series of audit and enquiry reports – by the comptroller and auditor-general, by an enquiry committee that looked at Commonwealth Games contracts, and by a parliamentary committee whose 'draft' report itself became the subject of controversy. Another parliamentary committee was still investigating the telecom issue as of June 2011, while the Central Bureau of Investigation had filed two charge-sheets and promised a third, which was expected to cast the net wider and to implicate even more telecom companies.

This was the first time in 25 years (since the Bofors pay-off scandal that engulfed Rajiv Gandhi's government) that a government had become entangled in such a web of corruption charges. The fact that Singh was universally recognised as a scrupulously honest man did not prevent the perception from growing that his coalition had no shortage of corrupt ministers. The winter session of parliament failed to conduct any business, as the opposition demanded a parliamentary enquiry into the telecom scandal – a demand the government finally conceded in order to salvage the subsequent session.

Before that, preparation for the Commonwealth Games of October 2010 was marked by incompetence and the allegations of corruption. There were also signs, such as leaked recordings of conversations with a corporate lobbyist, of business influence on the formation of the cabinet after the May 2009 elections, and sundry smaller embarrassments such as a 28-storey building on defence land in downtown Mumbai built in violation of several laws. The backlash against these and other cases of corruption took the form of a movement for a sweeping law to create a government ombudsman. In a mini-variant of Egypt's Tahrir Square, civil-society groups and much of the media mobilised behind Anna Hazare, a 71-year-old campaigner who adopted the Gandhian tactic of a 'fast unto death' in New Delhi, demanding an effective ombudsman. His fast ended after four days when the government agreed to draft a revised bill and to involve activists in the process.

Political fallout from the scandals manifested in early summer 2011 when the DMK–Congress alliance was routed in elections to the Tamil Nadu state legislature. In West Bengal, however, the Left Front coalition was ousted after 34 years in power. The Congress Party also defeated the Left Democratic Front in Kerala and won a third term in Assam. While the results were a mixed bag for the Congress Party, the big winners were two state parties, both led by women: J. Jayalalithaa of the All India Anna Dravida Munnetra Kazhagam in Tamil Nadu and Mamata Banerjee of the Trinamool Congress in West Bengal. The big loser, other than the regional DMK, was the left, which lost two states that it controlled, on top of its sharply reduced numbers in parliament following the 2009 general elections. The principal national opposition party, the Bharatiya Janata Party, had little presence in the east and south, and was not a factor in the elections, which were a reminder that state parties in India are as important as national ones.

Economic worries

In contrast to the political bedlam, in which the opposition underperformed even more than the government, the economy continued to be buoyant. In the financial year ending in March 2011, agriculture recovered with a good harvest, consumer confidence remained high and found reflection in car sales and house purchases, and exports grew by a record 37%. But there were signs of a slowdown: although business confidence remained high, by April 2011 it had dipped about 10% from its October peak, reflected in a slowdown in the capital-goods sector. The stock market was rocky, surging until October before beating a retreat. In May 2011, the main market indices had gained about 7% on the previous year, but growth in corporate earnings had begun to slow. The rupee remained strong against the dollar, and was at the same level as a decade earlier, despite higher inflation in India; however, it fell by 30–40% against the euro and yen.

The two big economic worries were a slowdown in industrial growth (under 3% in the four months to March) and stubborn inflation which, at 9%, was proving the Reserve Bank of India's 5% forecast embarrassingly wrong. The central bank responded with a series of interest-rate hikes beginning in early 2010, but these had little effect on inflation. Worried by the risks, a government that had tended to overspend presented parliament in February with a budget that promised tight control on expenditure and a sharp fiscal correction. Sceptics thought the ambitious targets unattainable: if the economy were to slow, the tax-revenue targets would be missed.

There were no major pronouncements on economic policy during the year. Long-awaited decisions that would allow more foreign investment in sectors such as retailing and insurance, and reduce restrictions on the activities of foreign banks, remained in limbo. A decision seemed likely on removing the bar on issuing banking licences to big industrial houses, but in an atmosphere thick with accusations of crony capitalism, the government moved slowly and cautiously. An important announcement on the introduction of an integrated goods and services tax (akin to a value-added tax) still awaited final approval from state governments, which would have to give up some of their taxation rights. And the roll-out of an ambitious identity scheme that incorporated biometrics, to facilitate targeted cash transfers or other programmes for the poor, made slow progress. It was launched in September 2010, but by March only 4 million identity numbers had been issued. The finance minister promised a million new numbers a day from September 2011 as the government began a tentative – and controversial – shift from providing subsidised goods to the poor to making cash transfers instead.

Land and forestry rights became issues of contention because of the displacement of people to make way for projects such as new dams and bauxite mining. The Environment Ministry halted a number of projects (for example, in steel making, township development and coal mining), citing forestry, displacement and other issues, but by early 2011 Environment Minister Jairam Ramesh was under intense pressure from his ministerial colleagues to be more flexible when it came to giving clearances. He did become more accommodating, declaring that pressure from other parts of the government was forcing him to condone violations of the law.

There was, nevertheless, a fear was that the country would suffer a growing energy shortage if more coal mining approvals did not come through. A cabinet committee examined areas in which coal mining was and was not allowed, and eventually reduced the 'no-go' areas to about two-thirds of their initial size. The government also prepared legislation on the auctioning of mining rights and on more generous relief and rehabilitation for people displaced by industrial, mining and dam projects, but dissension from coalition partners prevented them from being passed.

These issues had a bearing on internal security, since Maoist groups had traditionally recruited mainly from displaced or otherwise marginalised populations, especially in forested areas that were the focus of mining companies. The fairness of the Indian development model was questioned by a growing band of civil-society activists. However, the latest data showed that those below the government's poverty line (roughly equivalent to the World Bank's $1.25 a day definition, using purchasing power parity) had continued to fall by one percentage point per year, down to 16% of the population in 2009/10 from 22% in 2004/05 and 26% in 1999/2000. Meanwhile, the government adopted a more comprehensive definition of poverty, taking into account not just a basic calorific intake but also the consumption of a range of other essential goods and services. According to this metric, the proportion of poor people dropped from 37% in 2004/05 to 32% in 2009/10.

Pressures on defence

Concerns about inclusive growth were reflected in a slow shift in government spending priorities towards social sectors such as health and education and investment in a perennially insufficient physical infrastructure. One result was a squeezing of the $36bn defence budget, from about 3% of GDP at the turn of the century to no more than 2% in the latest budget. Within the defence budget, however, there was greater stress on hardware, which grew from about a third of defence spending to over 40%. India became the world's top importer of defence hardware, athough its defence budget was only the tenth largest, reflecting its failure to develop a sufficient domestic defence-industrial base. China, in contrast, had a $92bn defence budget but imported far less.

India was in the midst of an ambitious weapons-upgrade programme that looked likely to cost much more than the $100bn over ten years that had been forecast. Much existing defence hardware was out of date, and defence planners admitted that the country was 10–15 years behind where it should be in its modernisation programme. The largest fleet (about 11 squadrons) in the air force comprised the ancient MiG-21, which had been upgraded but had suffered scores of crashes over the years. In addition, there were seven squadrons of Su-30MK1s (with more on order), and handfuls of *Jaguars* (first ordered in 1978), Mirage-2000s, and MiG variants (MiG-23s, MiG-27s and Mig-29s). Almost all these had gone through upgrades but would have to be phased out in the next few years. In total, there were only about 30 combat squadrons against a stated requirement of 42 (of 18 aircraft each). The army was in a similar situation; the last major acquisition of artillery was the Bofors howitzer in 1986. And the navy had about as many hulls in 2011 as it did 25 years earlier.

The slow and unsure business of assessing defence requirements and placing orders for new equipment began some years ago. After hiccups caused by bribery scandals, changes in specifications and other disruptions, not to mention bureaucratic delays, weapons acquisition finally gathered momentum. Future air force strike squadrons began to take shape: some 15 squadrons of Su-30s, up to 11 squadrons of either the French *Rafale* or the Eurofighter *Typhoon* (most to be made or assembled in India under licence), a combination of the indigenously built *Tejas* light combat aircraft and a medium combat aircraft still under development, some leftovers from the existing fleet and a handful of fifth-generation stealth fighters under joint development with Russia. A fresh lot of 57 *Hawk* jet trainers, which can be used in combat, was ordered in July 2010 for $2bn.

The air force also ordered six C-130J *Hercules* transport planes for special-operations forces from Lockheed Martin (with options on another six), while negotiations were under way for ten heavy-lift C-17 *Globemasters* from Boeing (an order said to be worth $4.1bn), with a possible further six to be ordered later. Options for several hundred helicopters in utility, attack and transport modes, to replace an ageing, largely Russian fleet, were also being evaluated. Possibilities included the US *Apache* and Russian aircraft, while some orders were to go to Hindustan Aeronautics for its *Dhruv* light combat helicopter. These were complemented by six *Phalcon* AWACs from Israel, mounted on Ilyushin aircraft, and a range of missile systems, including a $3.1bn order with Bharat Dynamics for *Akash* surface-to-air missiles and a longer-range Israeli *Barak*.

The navy – at 165,000 tonnes combined displacement, only slightly bigger than Taiwan's – remained more ambitious than the air force. Its extended procurement and production cycle was scheduled to see 32 ships added over the next decade. Of these, 27 were being built in India's four domestic defence shipyards, three in Russia (including the $2.9bn refit of the aircraft carrier *Gorshkov*), and two in Italy. Mazagon Docks was building six French-designed conventional *Scorpène* submarines, while bidding started for another six. Mazagon and Garden Reach Shipbuilders were to turn out four stealth destroyers (on top of an earlier order for three) and 12 stealth frigates. An indigenous aircraft carrier was being built at Cochin Shipyard (though delays beyond its original delivery date of 2012–13 were expected) and Hindustan Shipyard at Vishakhapatnam was working on the *Arihant* nuclear submarine. Russia was to lease one or two nuclear submarines to the navy. Boeing was to supply 12 P8i *Poseidon* long-range maritime patrol aircraft, and the primary anti-ship weapon was to be the long-range *BrahMos* cruise missile, jointly developed with Russia. The challenge for India's shipyards was to meet the tight delivery schedules. The *Gorshkov* was already four years behind schedule – the MiG-29s intended for it were delivered in 2009. There were fears that the *Scorpène* submarines might be similarly delayed.

Ambitious plans on the drawing boards included one or two bigger (65,000-tonne) aircraft carriers to be built at Cochin, and nuclear-powered submarines at Vishakhapatnam. The stated aim was to create a blue-water navy that could patrol the Indian Ocean all the way from the east coast of Africa to Australia – a distant prospect, and one to be viewed in the context of an expanding Chinese navy that is well ahead of India's. There were signs of emerging competition: Chinese ships were deployed off the East African coast to deal with pirates from Somalia, while Indian ships took part in joint exercises in the Pacific with the US and Japan. Joint naval exercises with South Korea were to become an annual affair.

The army's modernisation programme, in contrast, remained patchy. There were continued weaknesses in air defence, there was a shortage of field artillery (the last gun was ordered in 1986), and the deployment of heavier tanks suffered from long delays. A contract for light howitzers that can be airlifted to the front (useful in particular in the mountainous terrain along the border with China) suffered yet another setback, with the lead bidder opting out. The army's helicopters were for the most part obsolete, and the generals could not make up their minds on a choice of tanks. Both the indigenously developed *Arjun* and the Russian T-90 main battle tanks were, however, being locally produced in large numbers.

On paper, the plan was to modernise the infantry, equipping soldiers with a variety of contemporary equipment, including bullet-proof vehicles, anti-material rifles, surveillance radar and night-vision goggles. Battlefield-management systems that put front-line soldier in contact with command headquarters were also to be ordered, and an unmanned vehicle programme was also under way. But the army's efforts remained less focused than those of the other services, which were working to clearly enunciated long-term plans.

Defence production in India was traditionally an almost exclusively government affair, but the private-sector has been slowly cranking up, with the industrial houses of Tata, Mahindra and Godrej responding to government initiatives to broaden the scope for indigenous procurement, and waking up to opportunities stemming from the defence-offsets policy. Private companies had mixed experiences with government orders: Tata and Larsen & Toubro (L&T) provided multi-barrel rocket launchers, Mahindra planned to turn out personnel carriers and the *Tejas* aircraft-development programme involved dozens of private-sector component suppliers. But L&T complained that it had not been given orders despite its fully equipped shipyard. Meanwhile, the government more or less went back on its promise that selected private-sector manufacturers would be treated as equals with public-sector defence production units and given the same incentives, including publicly funded budgets for research and development.

The push to modernise defence forces followed belated recognition of changes in the security balance with China and Pakistan. India's plans, if successful, looked likely to give it forces in ten years more convincing and more in consonance with its rising position in the global economy.

Security concerns

India's status as a rising regional power, and its potential to play a bigger role on the world stage, was underlined by separate visits to New Delhi by the heads of government of all five permanent members of the UN Security Council within the space of a few months, and by the Indian prime minister's annual calendar of meetings with his Russian and Chinese counterparts. More broadly, Indian diplomats were seeking friends everywhere: among the smaller East Asian countries that would welcome a counterpoint to China; in countries such as Japan and Australia, also wary of China's new assertiveness; in the Gulf countries (host to five million Indian workers); and in eastern and southern Africa.

Within South Asia, the main positive development was a new level of cooperation with Bangladesh, while continued political uncertainty in Nepal was troubling. Further afield, there were worries that an early US withdrawal from Afghanistan could reduce India's leverage in the country. Singh visited Kabul in May. India's engagement with Afghanistan was largely civilian, with an aid programme that had spent $1.5bn on highways, hospitals and electricity networks. Singh promised a further $500m during his visit. New Delhi had opposed any rapprochement with the Taliban, refusing to make the distinction between 'good' and 'bad' Taliban, but Singh's comments in Kabul, welcoming reconciliation, pointed to a shift in position and perhaps recognition of the emerging reality.

Fresh dialogue with Pakistan began tentatively: the two prime ministers met during a high-voltage cricket World Cup semi-final between the two nations at Mohali, outside Chandigarh. Although Pakistan continued to drag its feet on punishing those who organised the attack on Mumbai in November 2008, Singh believed that the diplomatic stand-off of more than two years was no longer paying any dividends, and that it was time to talk again. In trade talks that followed the cricket diplomacy, Pakistan surprised Indian officials by their openness to discussions on extending most-favoured nation status to India, an issue that had frustrated Indian businessmen for years. Even after the killing of Osama bin Laden in Pakistan by US special forces, the Indian government made clear that it wanted to keep talking.

Rising tensions with a more assertive China seemed to abate after Singh's meeting with President Hu Jintao during a summit of the BRIC countries (Brazil, Russia, India and China) on Hainan Island in April 2011. China signalled a mini-thaw by rescinding its recent practice of stapling visas into Indian passports of people from Jammu & Kashmir (which had signalled that Beijing did not recognise the state's accession to India in 1947). Meanwhile, relations with the United States gained a fillip after President Barack Obama's visit in November 2010, when he extended carefully worded support to India's claim to a permanent seat in an expanded UN Security Council. Slow progress on nuclear, trade and environment issues in both bilateral and multilateral contexts, and the rejection of two American contenders for a $10bn order for combat aircraft, however, exposed the frustrations felt on both sides in a relationship that continued to hold enormous promise.

The rejection of the F/A-18 and the F-16 in an impartial technical assessment that gave higher marks to European aircraft caused diplomatic ripples. Washington had been expecting a pay-off for the civil nuclear deal of 2008, and the $10bn order was a big prize. The US ambassador to New Delhi, Timothy Roemer, expressed deep disappointment and announced his resignation on the day the exclusion of the US aircraft was announced. Boeing and Lockheed Martin, the US manufacturers, subsequently sought to know why their aircraft were rejected, and a legal challenge was not out of the question; but both companies stood to gain from other Indian defence orders and were reluctant to sour relations with New Delhi.

Approaching the mid-point of 2011, India's democracy was beset by concerns about corruption, but there were signs of movement towards correcting its excesses. The pursuit of a substantial weapons-acquisition programme indicated that long-term external security challenges were finally being faced up to, while the internal security situation remained no worse than in most years. This was an environment that allowed the economy to continue to grow rapidly, critically influencing regional dynamics.

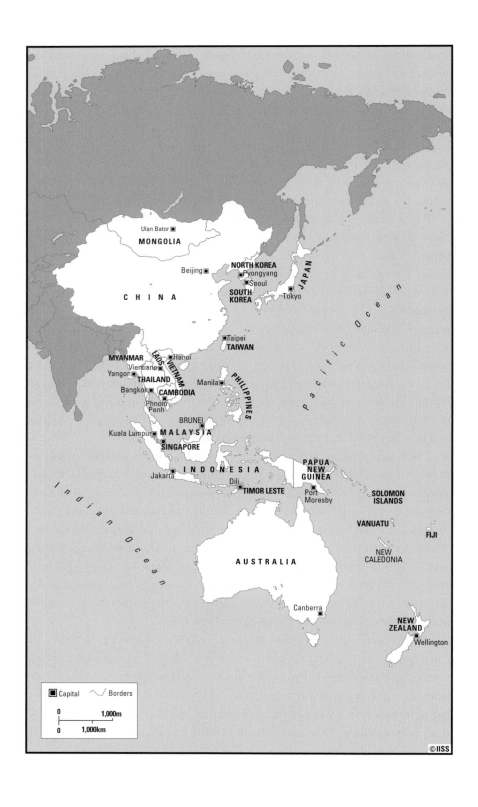

Chapter 9

Asia-Pacific

Japan: Disaster Overshadows Political Wrangles

Japan has endured its most calamitous year in recent memory. On 11 March 2011 it suffered three interlinked disasters – the 9.0 magnitude Great Tohoku Earthquake, the tsunami it triggered, and the reactor meltdowns and release of radiation at the Fukushima No. 1 nuclear power plant. The earthquake and tsunami claimed at least 15,000 lives and displaced up to half a million people in the Tohoku region north of Tokyo. The stoicism of the Japanese people in the face of these disasters evoked an outpouring of respect and support, as the government battled to restore services, deal with the nuclear accident and return to normality.

Intensive rescue efforts were undertaken involving Japan's Self Defense Forces (JSDF), the US military, and domestic and foreign civilian resources, but the tsunami also required a massive clean-up operation. The economic impact of the disasters was very great, with disruption to port and fishing facilities, steel and chemical plants, and especially automobile supplier and assembly factories. Many companies around the world reported disruptions to their supply chains. Japan's GDP was expected to contract by around 3% in the wake of the disasters, and to resume growth only at the end of 2011. Tokyo Electric Power Company (TEPCO), the operator of Fukushima, looked to incur massive losses as it shut down and cleaned up the plant. The Japanese government was estimated to face a total reconstruction bill of approximately ¥25 trillion ($310bn).

A Three-fold Disaster

Japan was struck by a 9.0 magnitude earthquake on Friday, 11 March 2011. The quake was the largest ever recorded in Japan, the largest globally for 50 years and the fourth largest since records began in 1900. The epicentre of the earthquake was on the Pacific Ocean side of northeast Japan, or the Tohoku region, and was termed by the government the 'Great Tohoku Earthquake'. The population centre closest to the epicentre was Sendai City in Miyagi Prefecture, but the seismic impact was strongly felt in Tokyo close to 400km to the south. Japan experienced around 900 aftershocks in the following weeks.

Although the earthquake wrought significant damage, the truly cataclysmic destruction was inflicted by the 5–14m tsunami which struck a 180km stretch of the Tohoku coastline. The tsunami and earthquake combined were estimated by the National Police Agency in June 2011 to have claimed over 15,000 lives, with a further 8,000 people missing. Another 5,000 were injured in the disasters, which also accounted for the loss of around 125,000 buildings and left up to half a million people temporarily displaced or homeless.

The country's misery was compounded when the tsunami triggered the failure of the cooling systems of the three operating reactors at Fukushima No.1 nuclear power plant. The reactors experienced meltdown and spent fuel rods were exposed in cooling ponds of two of them, as well as one of the three additional reactors that had been shut down for maintenance at the time of the accident. Radiation levels rose to 1,000 times greater than normal inside the plant and eight times greater in the 20km zone around it, from which around 200,000 residents were evacuated. Radiation was later found to be leaking directly into the sea. TEPCO was not able to bring the plant under reasonable control until early May. On 12 April, the Japanese authorities raised the severity of the accident to the highest level – seven – on the international measurement scale, ranking it with the explosion and fire at Chernobyl, Ukraine in 1986.

(See Map, Strategic Geography, pages X–XI.)

The disaster zone was expected to eventually recover economically, with special reconstruction budgets providing a useful stimulus. Moreover, the quake offered an opportunity to start afresh and strengthen the industrial base of the predominantly rural regions concerned. Nevertheless, the reconstruction efforts were expected to add to the fiscal woes of the government, and inflicted a blow to the confidence of Japanese industry and the population more widely.

Meanwhile, domestic politics, after the promise of dynamism the previous year in the transition to the Democratic Party of Japan (DPJ)-led government, slumped back into a pattern of gridlock and leadership instability. Foreign policy fared little better, with stasis in US–Japan attempts to realign American military bases, deep Sino-Japanese tensions over territorial and maritime security issues, and even renewed friction with Russia over the disputed Northern Territories/Kuril Islands.

Domestic politics: Kan can't?

Prime Minister Naoto Kan assumed office on 4 June 2010, following the resignation of his DPJ predecessor Yukio Hatoyama over the failure to resolve the Okinawa base issue, and with the DPJ still entertaining hopes of maintaining momentum after its crushing victory over the Liberal Democratic Party (LDP) the previous year. Kan, mindful of impending elections for the National Diet's Upper House, attempted to tackle some of the intra-party issues which had clouded the political agenda under Hatoyama. He first distanced himself from Ichiro Ozawa – leader of the DPJ's largest internal grouping, whose implication in political funding scandals had damaged Hatoyama – by promoting figures closer to himself, including his ally Yoshito Sengoku, who was appointed chief cabinet secretary, to key party posts and the cabinet. Secondly, Kan sought to adjust economic strategy. While keeping his party's emphasis on moving away from the LDP's 'pork barrel' special interests and towards more consumer- and welfare-oriented policies, he veered towards a tougher fiscal stance in light of the parlous state of government finances – for example, by raising the possibility of increasing the consumption tax above its 5% level.

However, Kan's interest in fiscal restraint fared well neither with the electorate nor within his own party. The DPJ and its coalition partners, the People's New Party and New Party Nippon, saw their number of seats fall in the July 2010 elections, leaving the DPJ short of a majority in the Upper House and weakening its ability to use its majority in the Lower House to pass legislation. Kan was then challenged by Ozawa in September for the leadership of the DPJ. Ozawa accused Kan of retreating on the DPJ's economic and welfare agenda, while Kan focused on Ozawa's record of shady political financing. Kan was returned by a strong margin of 721 to 491 votes within the party, and once again began attempting to sideline Ozawa's influence, totally excluding his followers from the cabinet and moving the neutral figure of Foreign Minister Katsuya Okada into the position of DPJ secretary general. Okada was replaced as foreign minister by former DPJ leader Seiji Maehara.

Nevertheless, Kan's leadership continued to be hampered by battles with Ozawa. Despite his criminal indictment in January over alleged improprieties in political fund-raising, Ozawa appeared confident he would defeat the charges, sought to push out Sengoku and continued to agitate against Kan's policies. This undermined public confidence in the DPJ and Kan's leadership, and the prime minister's credibility was further damaged by his perceived weakness in response to Sino-Japanese disputes over the Senkaku/Diaoyu islands, and by Japan's generally poor economic performance, with recovery from recession especially hampered by the high yen. Kan's previously high opinion-poll ratings of around 60% at the time of his appointment slipped to around 20% by the end of 2010.

Kan reshuffled his cabinet in January in an attempt to regain control of the political agenda, discarding Sengoku in favour of another ally, Yukio Edano, as chief cabinet secretary, and appointing the former LDP finance minister and fiscal conservative Kaoru Yasano as minister for economic and fiscal policy to demonstrate his government's resolve to tackle the public finances. Nevertheless, Kan found it hard to make headway in subsequent months.

Kan's leadership in the aftermath of the March disasters attracted severe criticism. Although public-opinion polls showed a measure of satisfaction with the initial response, the government appeared to lack measures to control the nuclear crisis and longer-term plans to deal with reconstruction of the afflicted areas. Kan was criticised personally for his lack of visibility during the crisis, when Edano served as the apparent coordinator of government policy. His public support dipped to levels that had proved the undoing of many LDP predecessors. The DPJ's lack of coalition partners and a majority in the Upper House hampered legislation, although the DPJ did eventually pass a record ¥96tr ($1.2tr) budget in April 2011. The LDP continued to block DPJ legislation and threatened to slow down passage of a supplementary disaster-recovery budget unless the DPJ reduced spending in other areas. Kan was further hit with poor local election results in April 2011, and Ozawa continued to snipe at the prime minister's crisis-management and economic policies.

By mid-2011 Kan's political survival was becoming increasingly uncertain. A tough political operator, he appeared determined to tackle the aftermath of the nuclear accident and the growing fiscal crisis. In his favour at that time was the fact that that he had few serious rivals for the premiership, and that the bulk of the DPJ would prefer not to precipitate an election.

US–Japan ties: under control?

Kan's awareness that Hatoyama's downfall was largely triggered by failure to manage the US–Japan alliance meant that he moved particularly carefully to, if not resolve, at least keep under wraps the highly sensitive issue of US military bases. Hatoyama had sought to establish a measure of Japanese autonomy from the United States which the DPJ felt had been sacrificed under LDP administrations and through Japan's support for US military actions in Afghanistan and Iraq. He had sought to renegotiate the agreement made under LDP governments to relocate the US Marine Corps Air Station from Futenma to Camp Schwab in the north of Okinawa Prefecture, arguing that, rather than relieving the disproportionate burden on the prefecture, the new facility would consolidate the US presence for the long term, and would actually exacerbate local tensions and weaken the alliance. Hatoyama's campaign to seek relocation to other parts of Japan foundered in the face of stiff domestic and US opposition, and he left office committing the Japanese government to maintain the existing agreement.

Kan's administration worked assiduously to reassure Washington it was committed to the alliance and to the Futenma relocation agreement, even if it showed little dynamism in trying to implement it. The US–Japan Security Consultative Committee (SCC) pledged to maintain the existing relocation agreements, and a bilateral Futenma Replacement Facility study was completed in August 2010 which compared the feasibility of the original plan for a 'V-shaped' double runway at Camp Schwab against the Japanese plan for an 'I-shaped' single runway. However, the report made no specific recommendations for which plan to pursue, and the Japanese government made it clear that it would await the results of the Okinawa Prefecture gubernatorial election before moving forward. The election was won by the incumbent Hirokazu Nakaima, who, despite being a past supporter of the relocation of Futenma within Okinawa, now argued that the facility should be moved elsewhere in Japan or outside Japan altogether. Consequently, even though the US and Japanese governments insisted that Okinawa could eventually be persuaded to accept the relocation, this appeared politically unrealistic, and no resolution was in sight. At the very least, though, Kan's government had managed to establish a degree of political control over the issue. It was hoping that the United States would not push hard on this in the near future, and indeed at the SCC meeting in mid-June the two sides agreed that the projected 2014 date for relocation would now have to be pushed back.

Meanwhile, the government was obliged to backtrack on other aspects of Hatoyama's alliance policy and move back closer to Washington. In the wake of a clash with China over the Senkaku/Diaoyu islands (see below), the Japanese government immediately looked for high-level alliance reassurances from the United States. Foreign Minister Maehara, on the sidelines of the UN General Assembly, extracted a commitment from US Secretary of State Hillary Clinton that Article 5 of the US–Japan security treaty did extend to include the islands; and this pledge was repeated publicly the same day by US Secretary of Defense Robert Gates. These pledges reassured Japanese policymakers, although the United States was not offering anything new. They also enabled a quick compromise in talks on the level of host nation support for US bases. The DPJ had sought to reduce this, while Washington was seeking an increase. The two sides agreed to maintain the same level of ¥188 billion ($2.33 billion) annually for 2011–15.

The utility of the US–Japan alliance was reinforced for Tokyo after the March disasters. The United States launched *Operation Tomodachi* ('Friend') using its full panoply of military assets in Japan and the Pacific. The aircraft carrier USS *Ronald Reagan* provided refuelling and logistic support for the disaster-relief operations of the Japan Self Defence Forces (JSDF); the US Air Force assisted in transport of key supplies; and US Marine Corps units transported displaced persons and helped restore infrastructure. The fact that many of the UMSC units were dispatched from Okinawa looked to have some impact on the debate over military bases in the prefecture, and the JSDF and US military also enhanced their capabilities for joint military operations.

Japan–China relations: trawlers, lies and videotapes

On taking power, the DPJ had consciously sought to distinguish itself from the LDP by portraying itself as the party of engagement with China. The DPJ argued that the LDP had disastrously mismanaged ties with Japan's most important neighbour, especially over issues of colonial history during the premiership of Junichiro Koizumi, and that Japan should shift towards closer relations. However, despite China's courting of the DPJ in the early part of its administration, bilateral relations began rapidly to deteriorate in 2010 over a range of security issues familiar from the period of LDP rule.

Japanese policymakers had long expressed anxieties over the lack of transparency in China's military expenditure and build-up, and in particular about its aspirations to project maritime power around Japan's territorial waters and the implications for bilateral territorial disputes. The DPJ government had already anxiously watched the Chinese navy's dispatch of a large flotilla around Okinawa Prefecture and the southernmost Japanese atoll, Okinotorishima, in April 2010, and then in May protested China's pursuit of a Japanese research ship operating near the median line of the two countries' disputed overlapping Exclusive Economic Zones.

Tensions drastically intensified over the disputed Senkaku/Diaoyu islands. On 7 September, the Japan Coast Guard (JCG) detained the captain and crew of a Chinese trawler which had attempted to ram two of its patrol ships after they had warned the vessel away from entering waters around the islands. Japan's detention of the captain was carried out under domestic law, sending an infuriating signal to China that Tokyo was not acknowledging any territorial dispute between the two countries. China argued that the crew had been illegally detained in Chinese territory. The incident was captured in a JCG video, which the Japanese government refused to release, but was later leaked by a JCG officer for distribution on YouTube. The video showed that the trawler had repeatedly attempted to ram the JCG vessels, contrary to Chinese claims that the JCG had taken aggressive action against the trawler.

China reacted to the incident with intimidation, exerting intense diplomatic and economic pressure on Japan. It suspended all high-level contacts and working-level talks, including negotiations on gas fields in the East China Sea, and was especially offended by Japan's appeals to the US for security guarantees covering the disputed islands. China also flexed its economic muscles by suspending exports of vital rare-earth minerals to Japanese industry. The Japanese government partly buckled under Chinese pressure, first allowing the release of the trawler crew, then intervening behind the scenes in the judicial process to ensure the release of the trawler captain. Kan's desperate efforts to arrange bilateral meetings at various summits resulted in a supposedly impromptu, although in fact prearranged, 'corridor summit' with Chinese Premier Wen Jiabao outside a meeting room at the Asia–Europe meeting in Brussels in October. Kan managed only a 10-minute informal meeting with Wen at the East Asia Summit in Hanoi at the end of the month, and then talks with President Hu Jintao at the APEC summit in Yokohama in November, arranged at a late stage even though Kan was the summit host.

Meaningful diplomatic contacts were not restored until the end of 2010, after which relations were cordial if frosty. Japanese policymakers drew some comfort from the fact that China, with its aggressive diplomacy towards Japan and Southeast Asian countries over territorial disputes, appeared to have damaged its regional image. Nevertheless, the DPJ government was berated by the LDP and the general public for its apparent failure to deal with China's assertiveness, and found itself deviating from its preferred policy of engagement and slipping instead into Sino-Japanese wrangling. The DPJ's response was not to retreat from attempts to engage China, but to continue to hedge militarily against its neighbour's rise.

Korean Peninsula, East Asia and Russia

Japan's contacts with the Korean peninsula, as opposed to the situation on the peninsula itself, were relatively quiet in year to mid-2011. Earlier years had seen direct missile provocations from North Korea and the gradual ratcheting up of nuclear tensions. In the past year, there was continuing nuclear stalemate, the Six-Party Talks were in abeyance and there was continued deadlock in Tokyo's normalisation talks with Pyongyang. Japan's principal strategic engagement with the Korean peninsula was to pledge diplomatic unity with the United States and South Korea in response to the shelling of Yeonpyeong Island by the North. Nevertheless, Japan did show signs of greater initiative in relation to North Korea. Maritime Self Defense Force officers for the first time were observers at US–South Korea military exercises in July 2010 as a demonstration of trilateral unity in the wake of the sinking of the Korean corvette *Cheonan*. South Korea Navy officers likewise participated as observers for the first time in large-scale US–Japan military exercises in December, following the Yeonpyeong incident. Japan and South Korea in early 2011 were also considering an Acquisition and Cross Servicing Agreement (ACSA) along the lines of Japan's existing ACSAs with the US and Australia, under which militaries share logistical supplies.

Japan's foreign policy elsewhere in East Asia failed to show the dynamism first espoused by the DPJ upon taking power. Hatoyama had advocated the establishment of an East Asian Community (EAC), driven by Sino-Japanese cooperation and involving ASEAN members, Australia, New Zealand and India. However, US concern that this would reduce Washington's regional influence, coupled with China's perceived overbearing behaviour, dampened the DPJ's enthusiasm for the idea. Instead, Kan became more preoccupied with hosting the APEC summit in November. The DPJ found itself divided on a US proposal for a Trans-Pacific Partnership (TPP), a high-end free-trade agreement involving East Asian and other Asia-Pacific states. Kan favoured the TPP as a means to induce liberalisation and reform in the Japanese economy, but other elements opposed it because of the potentially damaging effect of agricultural liberalisation on Japanese farmers. The debate indicated that the DPJ had gradually begun to move away from its earlier vision of leading a more East Asia-centred region.

The government's other plans for reinvigorating Japan's foreign policy and lessening dependence on the United States also ran into a brick wall. LDP and DPJ policymakers had hoped to boost ties with Russia to counterbalance China's rise, and particular hopes were expressed for ties under Hatoyama given that his grandfather, Prime Minister Ichiro Hatoyama, had normalised diplomatic ties with the USSR in 1956. Hatoyama, though, devoted little attention to Russia and simply repeated the LDP's previous line that Japan demanded the return of all four of the disputed Northern

Territories (called the Kuril Islands by Russia). Russia, apparently sensing Japanese weakness in the face of Chinese territorial provocations, reacted by pressing its claims. On 1 November President Dmitry Medvedev visited the island of Kunashiri, occupied by Russia but claimed by Japan, strongly demonstrating Russia's determination to retain control. The move further shook Japan's confidence in the relationship and in its ability to develop alternative diplomatic options to deal with China.

Japanese defence-policy developments

The government made important changes in defence policy in December 2010 when it published revised National Defence Programme Guidelines (NDPG), alongside a new Mid-Term Defence Programme (MTDP) for 2011–2015. The NDPG set out Japan's defence doctrine and the force structure necessary to achieve it, and the MTDP indicated procurement plans.

The policy changes were significant, even though the diplomatic setbacks during the year dictated that the guidelines also involved striking continuities with the previous government's policy, including a focus on regional security challenges and the US–Japan alliance. The DPJ had originally intended to place a heavier emphasis on multilateral cooperation via UN peacekeeping operations to redress the perceived overemphasis in recent years on US–Japan military ties.

The NDPG expressed a shift in threat perceptions. While North Korea was predictably identified as a major source of instability, the language about China changed significantly from that of the previous NDPG in 2004, which had stated obliquely that Japan should remain 'attentive' to China's military modernisation. The 2010 guidelines stated more boldly that China now posed 'concerns' for regional and global security. The most striking innovation was the abandonment of the concept of the 'basic defence force' in favour of a new 'dynamic defence' force. The previous concept was a holdover from the Cold War period, when Japan maintained the minimum capabilities deemed sufficient to defend its territory. In contrast, under the dynamic defence force concept the JSDF will closely calibrate its capabilities to counter specific sources of threat and contingencies. Under the new guidelines, Japan thus plans to overturn its passive military doctrine of the past and to deal more actively, possibly outside its own territory, with regional and global threats.

The force structures and procurement priorities of the Ground Self Defense Force (GSDF) continued to be slimmed down from the Cold War structure of heavy tanks and artillery concentrated in Hokkaido, designed to counter a Soviet threat, in favour of a lighter force for more rapid deployment. The GSDF also began to shift its resources southwards, with plans to garrison, for the first time, some of Japan's smaller islands in Okinawa Prefecture to ward off Chinese incursions. The Air Self Defense Force (ASDF) was to continue to improve its airlift capacity and also move to acquire a stronger fighter aircraft force. The Ministry of Defence finally announced in April a long-expected Request for Proposals for its F-X fighter, with the Lockheed Martin F-35, Eurofighter *Typhoon* and Boeing F/A-18 as the competing candidates. Reflecting concerns about China's growing maritime power, the Maritime Self Defense Force (MSDF) was perhaps the greatest beneficiary of the defence review. In addition to a continuing programme of light helicopter carriers and maintaining a fleet of 48 destroyers, the MSDF's submarine fleet was to increase from 16 to 22 boats by 2013. The MSDF would also complete the fitting out of six of its destroyers for a ballistic-missile defence (BMD) capability.

However, the NDPG shied away from challenging one of the main taboos on Japanese defence policy. There had been speculation that the government might lift bans imposed in 1967 and 1976 on the export of military technology, and instead introduce partial exemptions to allow joint development of weapons systems with other industrialised states. This measure was thought essential to preserve a measure of indigenous defence production, given the climbing costs of developing systems nationally, without economies of scale. However, Kan prevented a lifting of the export ban, fearing that it might jeopardise a hoped-for coalition with the dovish Social Democratic Party of Japan. The issue seemed likely to be revived.

Japan's outlook: domestic troubles and foreign-policy encirclement?

At mid-2011, Japan's domestic political outlook remained highly fluid. Kan's position as prime minister became increasingly precarious, with sinking opinion-poll ratings, and demands from the LDP and his own party to resign. Kan only survived a no-confidence vote in the National Diet in early June by promising that he would eventually resign once the reconstruction efforts were fully underway, but without specifying a date. Hence, Kan was able to last over one year as premier, a feat that his four immediate predecessors had failed to achieve. But his refusal to indicate exactly when he would resign had begun to deprive him of political allies, and there was speculation that he would be isolated and would step down. Exactly who could replace Kan was unclear; credible candidates were lacking. Maehara was forced to resign as foreign minister in March for a comparatively small political funding impropriety. While Ozawa continued to harass Kan, his embroilment in funding scandals ruled out a leadership role. Other possible candidates included Edano and Okada, but their ambitions were unclear. Another favoured candidate was Finance Minister Yoshihiko Noda, who was seen as able to unite the different wings of the party. Another scenario discussed in Japan was the creation of a DPJ–LDP 'grand coalition' to forge national unity to deal with the March 2011 disasters. The LDP, however, was clearly reluctant to join the DPJ in government. Political instability seemed likely to persist.

Meanwhile, the DPJ looked to have lost dynamism and direction in foreign affairs. Japanese policymakers felt encircled, confronted by an increasingly assertive China and by a Russia unwilling to fully engage. Once again, the country was obliged to fall back on the US-Japan alliance as its only safe haven.

China: Assertiveness Raises Regional Concern

China's more assertive stance in 2010 raised concerns that the world's most populous country, which was also now the second-largest economy, was becoming a fundamentally revisionist power. Chinese challenges to international norms became commonplace; they included coercive diplomacy to wrest free the captain of a Chinese fishing trawler who had been detained by Japan, intimidating actions to enforce maritime territorial claims in the South China Sea, and warnings to the United States and South Korea against conducting naval exercises in international waters near China. It seemed that China had abandoned its previous strategy, established in the 1990s, of a 'peaceful rise', which aimed to reassure the nations of Asia, as well as the United States, that its rapid economic rise and expansion of military capabilities would not pose a threat to peace and stability, and that other nations would benefit from China's growing power and influence.

After successive incidents in which China demonstrated truculence, and in some cases even belligerence, signs emerged in late 2010 and the first half of 2011 that Beijing recognised that its increased assertiveness had created consequences that were contrary to Chinese national interests. It began to recalibrate its strategy. Efforts were made to restore China's amicable relations with its neighbours and return its relationship with the United States to a more cooperative footing. It remained to be seen, however, whether the change in Chinese behaviour was temporary and tactical or enduring and strategic.

Sino-US relations: visible thaw

Tensions between the United States and China were triggered in early 2010 by US arms sales to Taiwan, US President Barack Obama's meeting with the Dalai Lama, a spat over alleged hacking by Chinese of the servers of the US Internet company Google, and diverging responses to North Korea's sinking of the South Korean naval vessel, the *Cheonan*. By the end of August, however, both countries played down their differences and created a positive narrative for the relationship as they began to prepare for the state visit of President Hu Jintao to the United States the following January. The visit was a success from the perspective of both sides and served to stabilise the bilateral relationship. It was followed by further efforts at cooperation, including a fruitful round of the Strategic and Economic Dialogue in May. That a rupture of ties was avoided despite intense friction on numerous issues was a testament to the resiliency of the Sino-US bilateral relationship.

Diplomatic confrontations over the Yellow Sea and the South China Sea erupted in July. As Washington and Seoul consulted on steps to take to deter further North Korean provocations and enhance South Korea's anti-submarine-warfare capabilities, reports surfaced that the two allies were preparing to conduct joint military exercises in the Yellow Sea that would include the carrier USS *George Washington*. Despite disavowals of a concrete plan by the Pentagon, China's Foreign Ministry spokesman declared that China 'firmly oppose(s) foreign warships and military aircraft carrying out activities in the Yellow Sea and other Chinese coastal waters that affect China's security interests'. Beijing likely had two concerns. Firstly, a show of force in the waters where the *Cheonan* had sunk in March 2010 risked provoking a violent North Korean response that could escalate to military conflict. Second, strong opposition among Chinese Internet users to the deployment of a carrier close to China's coast presented the danger that the Chinese leadership could be vulnerable to charges of failing to adequately defend China's core interests. To reinforce China's message of resolve, its navy conducted exercises in nearby waters.

Concerned about further inflaming bilateral tensions, the Obama administration agreed to conduct joint US–South Korea military drills west of the Korean Peninsula in September, but postponed deployment of the *George Washington*. The Pentagon's spokesman stressed that the exercises were not intended to antagonise China; they were aimed at sending a warning to

Pyongyang. Nevertheless, American officials were determined to dispatch the carrier eventually since failing to do so risked an assessment by China and other regional nations that the United States was weak and had caved to Chinese pressure. The deployment took place in late November, after North Korea shelled Yeonpyeong, a South Korean island, killing two marines and two civilians. China's official response was comparatively restrained: the Foreign Ministry spokesman asserted that an unnamed country was 'brandishing swords and spears'.

The South China Sea fracas burst into the open in mid-July at the 11th ASEAN Regional Forum meeting in Hanoi. Spurred on by complaints from China's neighbours about increasing actions by Beijing that were destabilising, intimidating and inconsistent with the 2002 ASEAN–China Declaration on the Conduct of Parties in the South China Sea, Washington orchestrated the meeting to highlight concerns about peace and stability in those waters. US Secretary of State Hillary Clinton joined representatives of 11 other countries in addressing the issue. She maintained that the United States had a 'national interest in freedom of navigation, open access to Asia's maritime commons, and respect for international law in the South China Sea'. Clinton offered assistance 'to facilitate initiatives and confidence building measures consistent with the declaration', but did not alter the United States' long-standing neutral position on territorial disputes in the region. Caught unawares, Chinese Foreign Minister Yang Jiechi lashed back with sharp rhetoric, warning against internationalising the South China Sea territorial disputes.

According to various reports, high-ranking Chinese officials had told US counterparts in closed-door meetings that the South China Sea was one of China's 'core interests', suggesting that the issue was non-negotiable. However, no such statement was ever made publicly by a Chinese official. Within weeks of the ASEAN Regional Forum meeting, civilian and military officials were insisting to their American counterparts that China had never claimed the South China Sea was a core interest. Once again, China backed down, recognising that a confrontation with the United States did not serve its interests.

Friction over economic issues served to exacerbate the already tense relationship between Beijing and Washington. Complaints by American corporations about unfair Chinese trading practices resulted in three cases against China being filed with the World Trade Organisation between September and December. Frustration also grew over the glacial rate of appreciation of China's currency, seen by many as substantially undervalued. But the Obama administration refrained from officially citing China as a currency manipulator and Congress failed to pass legislation permitting the US Department of Commerce to treat undervalued currencies as illegal export subsidies. In response to US pressure, Chinese officials asserted that the valuation of the renminbi was not to blame for the broader economic troubles of the United States, but acknowledged that 'gradual' appreciation was necessary. After the US mid-term elections in November, US–Chinese economic tensions eased significantly. To smooth the way for a successful presidential visit to Washington, Beijing agreed to address several US concerns at a meeting of the US–China Joint Commission on Commerce and Trade. The most notable was to eliminate indigenous innovation policies that favour domestic companies at the expense of their foreign counterparts. Appreciation of the renminbi accelerated in spring 2011 as Beijing used the exchange rate to dampen inflation, which surged to 5.4% in March, the highest level in 32 months. On April 29, the renminbi reached 6.49 against the US dollar, a record high since Beijing undertook exchange rate reforms in 2005.

A slow thaw also began in the military sphere nine months after China froze military-to-military exchanges with the United States in response to the Obama administration's decision to sell a weapons package worth $6.4 billion to Taiwan. In October 2010, US Defense Secretary Robert Gates and Chinese Minister of National Defense Liang Guanglie met on the sidelines of the 'ASEAN plus Eight' defence chiefs gathering in Hanoi. A few days later, senior officials from the US Pacific Command and China's Ministry of National Defence held a two-day plenary session under the US–China Military Maritime Consultative Agreement (MMCA) in Honolulu to discuss maritime-safety issues. In December, the 11th round of the Defense Consultative Talks were held in Washington DC after a hiatus of 18 months. According to the chair of the US delegation, Undersecretary of Defense for Policy Michele Flournoy, the two sides discussed how to develop a more durable framework to put the military-to-military relationship on 'a more sustained and reliable and continuous footing'. General Ma Xiaotian, deputy chief of the People's Liberation Army (PLA) General Staff, who headed the Chinese delegation, insisted that that the United States and China need to 'respect each other's core interests and major concerns'. He cited the main obstacles in the relationship as US arms sales to China's Taiwan province, Congress's restrictions on military exchanges between the two countries, and US air and sea military surveillance operations in China's exclusive economic zones.

More progress was made in January 2011, when Gates travelled to China just over a week before Hu departed for his state visit to the United States. The most significant achievement was an agreement to establish a working group to develop guiding principles and a new framework for improving ties between the US and Chinese military establishments. The two sides also agreed to convene a Military Maritime Consultative Group (MMCA) working-group meeting to discuss future operational safety and to expand cooperation in the maritime domain. Gates proposed launching a joint civilian–military strategic security dialogue on nuclear, missile defence, space and cyber issues. His counterpart, General Liang, said the Chinese side would consider the proposal. To further promote the bilateral military relationship, the two defence leaders agreed that Chief of the PLA General Staff General Chen Bingde would visit the United States – and that visit took place the following May.

What attracted the most attention during Gates' visit, however, was the unexpected test flight of the PLA's new stealth jet fighter, the J-20. When Gates queried Hu about the test, the president at first seemed to know nothing about it, but later acknowledged the test and maintained that it had been planned well in advance of Gates's visit. Foreign observers were divided over whether the incident was a purposeful move to signal China's growing power and resolve or was a result of lack of coordination between the Chinese military and its civilian leaders. It was widely agreed, however, that the new fighter was just one of an array of capabilities that the PLA was developing as part of an anti-access, area-denial strategy that would increase the risk of US intervention in any conflict near China's periphery.

The shared desire for a successful state visit to the United States in early January 2011 provided an incentive to both the US and China to play down their differences. The visit marked the eighth face-to-face meeting between the two presidents in two years. Beijing's priority for the summit was securing all the ceremonial trappings of a state visit that had been denied Hu by the George W. Bush administration when he last visited the United States in April 2006. The Obama administration provided the requisite symbols of respect for China's leader: a welcoming ceremony on the South Lawn of the White House that included a 21-gun salute and an honour guard, and an opulent state dinner. Washington attached priority to concrete achievements that demonstrated the value of the US–China relationship to its domestic audience. Key deliverables included Chinese purchases of $45bn of American goods that would support approximately 235,000 jobs for American workers, and pledges by Hu to end discrimination against

American companies when they compete for Chinese government procurement contracts and to strengthen protection of intellectual property. The two countries also launched a US–China Governors Forum and agreed to increase exchanges of American and Chinese students.

The Joint Statement negotiated between the two countries was a carefully worded compromise that also reflected their differing priorities. Beijing attached greatest importance to the language used to describe the US–Chinese relationship and successfully persuaded Washington to include wording that committed the two countries to 'work together to build a cooperative partnership based on mutual respect and mutual benefit in order to promote the common interests of both countries to address the 21st century's opportunities and challenges'. The Obama administration convinced China to agree to express concern about North Korea's uranium-enrichment programme and to voice opposition to 'all activities inconsistent with the 2005 Joint Statement and relevant international obligations and commitments'. The document also highlighted shared approaches to Iran and Sudan, issues on which the United States and China had found overlapping interests and were cooperating relatively effectively. Notably absent was any mention of 'respecting each other's core interests' which had been included in the Joint Statement that was signed when Obama travelled to China in November 2009.

The third round of the Strategic and Economic Dialogue was held in Washington DC in May. It further stabilised US–China ties and expanded bilateral cooperation, as shown by a list of 48 'Outcomes of the Strategic Track' that specified new and ongoing areas of tangible cooperation. Joint civilian–military discussions were launched that focused on cyber and maritime security and it was agreed that new consultations would soon be initiated on the Asia-Pacific region to complement existing talks on other regions of the world, including the Middle East, Latin America, Africa and Central Asia. The countries also signed a US–China Comprehensive Framework Document to promote strong, sustainable and balanced economic growth and economic cooperation.

Nuclear proliferation: China's conflicting interests

Growing international concern about the nuclear programmes in Iran and North Korea posed dilemmas for China as it sought to balance its national interests with its desire to be seen as a responsible global player. Its track record was mixed. Beijing stepped up its cooperation with the other members of the P5+1 – the permanent members of the UN Security Council plus Germany – to penalise Tehran for failing to suspend its uranium-enrichment programme, but Chinese willingness to put pressure on Pyongyang diminished.

After much cajoling, Beijing voted for UN Security Council Resolution 1929 in June 2010, which imposed a fourth set of sanctions against Iran, though China insisted on excluding sanctions targeting Iran's oil and gas industry. After Australia, Canada, the European Union, Japan, Norway, South Korea and the United States implemented stringent unilateral sanctions, including measures that targeted Iran's energy sector, the United States and the EU pressed Beijing to ensure that Chinese companies did not fill the void. Based on available evidence, Beijing not only did not take advantage of business opportunities created by companies leaving Iran, but also stopped new investments in Iran's energy sector and improved controls over weapons-technology exports to Iran. Ongoing deals between China and Iran to develop gas fields continued, but China generally maintained unity with the P5+1 process.

China's increased cooperation on Iran was probably partly due to the fact that the Obama administration put the issue at the top of the agenda of the US–China relationship. Faced with mounting frictions in relations with Washington in 2010, Beijing was careful not to run afoul of the United States in its dealings with Iran. A common approach to Iran was displayed in the January 2011 US–China Joint Statement, in which the two countries reiterated a shared 'commitment to seeking a comprehensive and long-term solution that would restore international confidence in the exclusively peaceful nature of Iran's nuclear program'. Both sides also agreed that Iran had the right to the peaceful use of nuclear energy under the Non-Proliferation Treaty and that Tehran should fulfil its international obligations under that treaty.

Even as Beijing worked with the international community to pressure Tehran, China's interest in preserving good relations with Iran remained high. Bilateral trade between China and Iran reached $30bn in 2010 and was expected to increase to $50bn by 2015. Iran was China's third-largest supplier of crude oil, providing China with roughly 11.5% of its total annual oil consumption. China was the only major foreign country still active in Iran's oil exploration and its role in the international effort to forestall Iran from acquiring a nuclear capability remained critical.

Meanwhile, Beijing's refusal to censure North Korea for acts of violence further complicated efforts to resume six-party negotiations aimed at achieving denuclearisation of the Korean Peninsula. In July 2010, the UN Security

Council issued a presidential statement on the sinking of the *Cheonan*. Compromise language condemned the 'attack', but did not assign blame to North Korea, due to opposition from both China and Russia. Two months later, when the final report of an international inquiry into the sinking was issued, confirming that a North Korean torpedo was responsible, China remained silent. Then, in November, Pyongyang shelled Yeonpyeong. In sharp contrast to the immediate condemnations of North Korea issued by Moscow, Tokyo and Washington, Beijing avoided blaming either side and called for 'maximum restraint'.

China did work assiduously behind the scenes to restart the nuclear negotiations, but made no headway due to US and South Korean insistence that an improvement in North–South relations was a prerequisite for forward movement on the talks. Even the revelation by Pyongyang of a uranium-enrichment facility that was operating in clear violation of UN resolutions did not prompt Chinese criticism. Instead, China blocked a UN committee from adopting a report on the enrichment programme, citing a lack of concrete evidence and possible adverse impact on early resumption of the six-party talks. The inclusion of a sentence in the US–China January 2011 Joint Statement expressing concern about North Korea's uranium-enrichment activities was agreed upon at the eleventh hour, after Hu's arrival in Washington, only after it was clear that the United States would not view the summit as successful if the issue was left unaddressed. Even after that significant achievement, China continued to oppose discussion at the UN, insisting that the Six-Party Talks were the sole appropriate venue for broaching the issue.

Tensions with Asian neighbours

China's relationship with many Asian countries worsened, as its more aggressive policy stance and actions in the seas between China and Pacific Rim countries created concerns. Friction with Southeast Asian neighbours increased over disputed territories in the South China Sea. In response to increased activity by other claimants that Beijing perceived as posing a challenge to its sovereignty, China more assertively defended its claims. It reconfigured military ships for use in enforcing unilateral fishing bans, and conducted the largest joint military drills yet undertaken by the Chinese military in the South China Sea in July 2010. In August, Vietnam accused China of violating its sovereignty by carrying out seismic exploration near the Paracel Islands, which Vietnam claims but China occupies. A spat between Beijing and Manila occurred in March 2011 when the PLA entered the territorial waters of the Philippines and ordered an oil exploration vessel to leave the area. Chinese officials insisted that Beijing had 'indisputable sovereignty' over the South China Sea and opposed outside – by which they meant American – interference in the disputes, calling instead for problems to be handled by the nations directly involved. The frequent conduct of large-scale PLA military exercises as well as stepped-up surface ship and submarine patrols in the South China Sea caused unease in many Southeast Asian capitals, prompting those countries to seek closer ties with the United States as a hedge against a more intimidating China.

Recognising the risk of a major setback in its relations with ASEAN and individual Southeast Asian countries, Beijing re-emphasised a message of good neighbourliness and cooperation, even as confrontations continued in disputed waters. At the 13th summit between China and ASEAN in Hanoi in October 2010, Premier Wen Jiabao and his ASEAN counterparts adopted a bilateral agreement on sustainable development and a plan of action to accelerate cooperation in security, trade and politics during the next five years. Consultations between China and ASEAN representatives on implementing and advancing the 2002 Declaration on the Conduct of Parties between China and ASEAN Regarding Disputed Territory in the South China Sea resumed at a working group meeting in Kunming, China in December 2010 and were held again in Indonesia in March 2011.

Despite tensions over conflicting territorial claims between China and some Southeast Asian nations, trade between China and ASEAN flourished. In 2010 China became ASEAN's leading foreign trading partner and ASEAN enjoyed a trade surplus with China of over $7bn compared to a $15bn trade deficit in 2009. Since the China–ASEAN free trade agreement came into effect in January 2010, trade had increased dramatically, reaching $292.8bn by March 2011, a 37.5% increase year-on-year. China also pursued various infrastructure projects with Southeast Asian neighbours, including plans to link current railways to create a route that would connect its Yunnan province with Bangkok via Thailand and Laos by 2014, and construct oil and gas pipelines with Myanmar.

China's relations with Japan took on a positive tone after Naoto Kan, who became Japanese prime minister in June 2010, emphasised efforts to strengthen economic ties with China. Bilateral talks were convened on joint development of the Shirakaba/Chunxiao gas field in the East China Sea. However, tensions quickly resurfaced. A Chinese fishing trawler operating near the Senkaku/Diaoyu Islands rammed two Japan Coast Guard ships in September and its captain was detained by Japan for more than two weeks, setting off a diplomatic row. When Japan deviated from past practice and detained the captain and crew, Chinese protesters took to the streets. The intensity of the demonstrations escalated in October, with attacks on Japanese shops and clashes with police in several Chinese cities. Beijing postponed senior-level meetings with Japanese officials, cancelled scheduled consultations on the East China Sea gas fields, dispatched patrol vessels to the disputed area, called off Japanese students' visits to the Shanghai Expo, and halted exports of rare-earth minerals to Japan. Even after the ship's captain was released, China's foreign ministry demanded an apology and compensation, insisting that Japan's actions were unlawful, infringed China's sovereignty and violated the human rights of the Chinese people.

China's frequent dispatch of fisheries patrol boats to waters near the disputed islands and the expansion of Chinese naval activities to areas distant from its coastal waters, from the East China Sea to the Pacific Ocean, sparked Japanese concerns. In December Japan adopted new National Defense Programme Guidelines. In contrast to the previous guidelines, which cautioned Japan to 'remain attentive' to China's actions, the 2010 document cast China's military build-up and increasing maritime activities as 'matters of regional and international concern'. Beijing insisted that its defence policies were strictly defensive in nature and charged that 'some countries take it upon themselves to represent international society and without cause irresponsibly complain about China's development'.

The massive earthquake and tsunami that devastated northeast Japan on 11 March 2011 provided an opportunity to mend the bilateral relationship, which Beijing duly seized. China swiftly offered $4.5m in aid, sent an international rescue team to assist recovery efforts, and later provided gasoline, fuel and relief supplies. Hu took the highly unusual step of visiting the Japanese Embassy to express China's condolences over the tragedy. Nevertheless, Sino-Japanese relations remained uneasy.

China's ties with North Korea strengthened over the past year, while its relations with South Korea frayed. North Korea's leader Kim Jong-il travelled to China with unusual frequency – three times in a little over 12 months, an indication of the North's growing dependence on its neighbour. In May 2010, Kim met with every member of China's Standing Committee of the Politburo in Beijing. His second trip took place in August, where he met Hu in the city of Changchun in China's northeast Jilin province. On his third visit in May 2011, Kim travelled to Changchun, Yangzhou, Nanjing and Beijing, where he met Hu and other senior Chinese leaders. During each of these visits, China attempted to encourage North Korea to implement economic reforms and return to denuclearisation talks. In addition to Kim's travels to China, a flurry of high-level party and military exchanges were conducted between China and North Korea during the past year, including visits to Pyongyang in October by Zhou Yongkang, secretary of the Chinese Communist Party's Political and Legislative Affairs Committee and one of nine top party leaders on the Politburo Standing Committee, and by Guo Boxiong, vice chairman of the Central Military Commission, to celebrate the 60th anniversary of the entry of the Chinese People's Volunteers into the Korean War. According to Korea International Trade Association statistics, North Korea's trade with China jumped 32% in 2010 to $3.47bn. Chinese investment in North Korea increased, but continued to lag behind that in other neighbouring states, including Thailand, Vietnam and Myanmar. Amid the overall trend of closer China–North Korea ties, however, there were signs of tension. During Kim's May 2011 visit, for example, Wen rebuffed Kim's appeal to involve the Chinese central government in bilateral economic projects, instead stressing that economic cooperation should be achieved through 'normal business processes'.

China–South Korea relations remained strained by Beijing's refusal to condemn North Korea for the sinking of the *Cheonan* and were challenged further by China's muted responses to North Korea's shelling of Yeonpyeong Island and its unveiling of the uranium-enrichment facility. Differences over how to deal with North Korea continued in the first half of 2011 as Beijing pressed for resumption of the Six-Party Talks while Seoul called for an apology by the North for its attacks, international condemnation of the North at the UN for its violations of Security Council resolutions, and political steps by Pyongyang to improve North–South relations. Beijing–Seoul tensions also increased over disputed exclusive economic zones (EEZs) when violent clashes occurred in December in the Yellow Sea between the South Korean Coast Guard and a Chinese boat suspected of illegally operating in South Korea's zone. Economic ties nevertheless remained strong, with bilateral trade during 2010 amounting to $171bn according to official South Korean figures, a 21% increase from $141bn in 2009.

Cross-strait relations

Since the inauguration of Ma Ying-jeou from the Kuomintang party as Taiwan's president in May 2008, cross-strait relations have been on a steady upward climb. Taiwan entered into 15 agreements with the mainland, the most significant being the Economic Cooperation Framework Agreement (ECFA) signed in June 2010 and brought into effect in September.

Implementation was under the guidance of the newly established Cross-Strait Economic Cooperation Committee. In addition to anticipated benefits for both side's economies, the ECFA opened the door for Taiwan to pursue bilateral free-trade agreements with countries other than China. In August, Taiwan and Singapore announced that the two would conduct a feasibility study on an economic cooperation agreement and in December they declared formal negotiations would begin in 2011. Beijing's reaction was subdued, stating simply that it believed Singapore would hold to the one-China policy and handle relations with Taiwan accordingly.

While the ECFA attracted much of the limelight in cross-strait relations, other interactions were noteworthy. Business and educational exchanges expanded, and the number of tourists from the mainland visiting the island grew by 67% to 1.63m in 2010. Beijing attached a high priority to cultural exchanges, and while Taipei was willing to pursue such exchanges, it resisted signing a cultural agreement.

Taiwan's strengthened economic ties to the mainland have already borne fruit. Its economy grew by 10.8% in 2010, the fastest pace since 1986. Taiwan's exports in 2010 were up 34.8% at $274.6bn, with over 40% going to China and Hong Kong. Confidence-building measures – though not explicitly referred to as such – also paved the way for closer relations. The largest joint search-and-rescue drill carried out by the two coast guards, for example, took place in September between Kinmen and Xiamen. Taiwan's Straits Exchange Foundation and mainland China's Association of Relations Across the Taiwan Strait continued to be vital as the primary means by which the two sides interacted on a semi-official level. Taiwan also made limited progress in improving its diplomatic position. After gaining observer status at the World Health Assembly, the executive arm of the World Health Organisation, in 2009, it joined several additional, albeit less important, international bodies, including the South Pacific Regional Fisheries Management Organisation and the Inter-American Tropical Tuna Commission, and the Civil Air Navigation Services Organisation. With this momentum, Taipei set its sights on the UN Framework Convention on Climate Change and the International Civil Aviation Organization, but made little progress toward observer status in either due to opposition from Beijing.

Despite substantial improvement in cross-strait ties, several issues still plague the relationship and are likely to continue to do so. The PLA continues its military build-up opposite the island in an effort to ensure that – despite warming relations – Taiwan will not grow so bold as to pursue independence. Now that the ECFA has entered into force, Beijing has been subtly urging Taipei to hold discussions on more sensitive political and security issues. As a stepping stone, mainland China has supported Track Two dialogues to explore such topics, some of which have included uniformed military officers from the mainland and retired military officers from Taiwan. However, due to the complex domestic political situation in Taiwan, the Ma administration rejected discussing anything beyond economic issues. The Democratic Progressive Party (DPP) strongly criticised Ma's cross-strait policy, rejecting the '1992 Consensus' that provided the basis for resumption of dialogue and charging that the ECFA widened the gap between rich and poor in Taiwan. In the November 2010 special municipality elections, the DPP showed some strength, winning the popular vote by more than 400,000 votes over the KMT even though it secured only two out of five seats. In the run-up to the January 2012 presidential election in Taiwan and the leadership change on the mainland, both sides appeared to have less room for manoeuvre, which could stifle further progress.

China–Europe relations

In September 2010, China and the European Union held the bilateral Strategic Dialogue, co-chaired by Chinese State Councilor Dai Bingguo and Catherine Ashton, EU high representative for foreign affairs and security policy. This elevation of the dialogue, previously held at the vice-foreign-minister level, signalled a mutual sense of the growing importance of the China–EU relationship. The second round of the dialogue took place in Hungary in May 2011. Dai described it as 'comprehensive, productive and candid'. Ashton went so far as to say it was 'an essential part of the post-Lisbon relationship' between the two countries. Bilateral trade relations were on an upswing. In 2010, bilateral trade volume reached $395bn – a 32% increase from 2009. This was not a new trend: China had been the EU's second–largest trading partner and the EU China's number-one trading partner since 2004, and they had been each other's largest export market since 2009. In the past year, China sought to alleviate the European sovereign-debt crisis by purchasing treasury bonds of various countries, including heavily indebted Spain, Portugal and Greece. Foreign Minister Yang Jiechi portrayed this policy as 'cooperation through mutual help'.

EU–China diplomatic relations were not always congenial, however. A period of frustration, for example, followed the October 2010 EU–China Summit, which served as a reminder of persistent problems. For Beijing, failure to gain traction on several of its key objectives, including persuading the EU to lift its arms embargo and grant China market-economy status, were key sources of contention. Meanwhile, Europeans grew frustrated as they made little headway in gaining greater market access, stronger intellectual property right enforcement, and respect for the rule of law and human rights. The tendency of EU member states to pursue their own interests with Beijing directly perpetuated a disjointed approach to Europe's relations with China, undercutting its potential leverage.

The year 2011 presented new opportunities, beginning with Vice Premier Li Keqiang's successful January visit to Spain, Germany and the United Kingdom. Several exchanges and high-level visits between China and EU member states took place in the first half of 2011, including the EU–China Year of Youth which began in January; the second phase of the EU–China Trade Project, which was launched in March; the first bilateral minister-level strategic dialogue between China and Germany in April; and the visit by European Council President Herman Van Rompuy to China in May. The launching of the EU's 2020 Strategy and China's 12th Five-Year Plan in 2011 also boded well for further strengthening ties. The two plans converged in some areas – such as environmental protection, innovation and technology – and appeared to present significant opportunities for collaboration. China's plan also emphasised increasing the country's domestic demand, which had the potential to benefit European exports.

Against the background of France's G20 leadership in 2011, relations between France and China, which had been chilly in the past few years, improved somewhat. President Nicolas Sarkozy set ambitious goals for reform of the international monetary system, for which he needed China's support. Beijing, eager to be portrayed as a responsible global player, emphasised cooperation. Chinese media downplayed past tensions in the run-up to Hu's November 2010 visit to Paris, which produced a dozen business deals worth $22.8bn, including a $14bn deal with Airbus for about 100 aircraft and a $3.5bn agreement on long-term supply and sale of uranium.

Despite positive developments, China's relationship with Europe still faced several stumbling blocks. The EU had long been at odds with China over many human-rights issues, ranging from limitations on freedom of expression and religious freedom to the persecution of political activists. When Chinese dissident Liu Xiaobo was awarded the Nobel Peace Prize in 2010, Beijing indefinitely postponed bilateral trade talks on a China–Norway free-trade agreement and warned countries not to send official representatives to the award ceremony. Aspects of China's burgeoning economic development and military modernisation were also contentious. In March 2011, a Globescan/PIPA poll on public perceptions of China among the EU's

27 member states found that negative views in Europe of China's economic and military growth had increased since 2005. A significant increase in negative perceptions was recorded in France, Germany, Italy and the UK.

Domestic scene: keeping control

Despite the efforts of the ruling Chinese Communist Party (CCP) to maintain one voice in policymaking, pressures from an increasingly pluralistic society continued to grow. China's one-party system is ill-equipped to handle the emergence of many competing voices, and this becomes especially apparent when unforeseen crises or volatile international disputes arise.

A diverse cast of characters lobbied for the leadership's attention and sought to influence decision-making with varying degrees of success. Business executives, bank directors, local government officials and leading media representatives all became more vocal and jockeyed for influence. Public opinion as expressed on Internet bulletin boards cannot be ignored by Chinese leaders. The military also sought to have greater sway in national-security policymaking and had some success, exploiting opportunities presented by the increased salience of traditional and non-traditional security concerns, and by a continuing rise in defence spending.

As they sought to manage these pressures and retain control, Chinese leaders remained concerned that development was not sufficiently balanced, coordinated or sustainable. After experiencing a GDP growth rate of 10.3% and surpassing Japan as the world's second largest economy in 2010, China began to shift its focus away from growth of the aggregate economy in favour of a growth pattern that emphasised balance and sustainability. At the 4th Plenary Session of the 11th National People's Congress (NPC) in March 2011, it set target growth rates of about 8% for 2011 and about 7% over the next five years. These goals, modest compared to the prior five-year plan, suggested the government was seeking to dampen domestic expectations for continued double-digit growth as it addressed problems such as resource depletion and pollution and managed its exchange, interest and inflation rates to achieve sustainable economic growth.

Per capita income in purchasing power parity terms, at approximately $7,400, was significantly below the world average of $11,200, and the widening income gap between China's rich and poor posed a risk of social instability. Other concerns included an imbalance between investment and consumption, persistent weakness in the agricultural sector, insufficient scientific and technological innovation, uneven development between urban and rural areas, and resource and environmental constraints that hinder economic growth. Mounting local government debt resulting from economic stimulus policies created new challenges, which the Ministry of Finance acknowledged could not be overlooked. In addition, housing prices continued to rise – up 6.4% in some cities. Following the NPC, Wen affirmed Beijing would hold local governments responsible for regulating housing prices, stating that this was of the 'utmost importance'. Worries about inflation mounted. In March, Wen said inflation in 2010 had been held to 3.3% and that the government planned to restrict it to about 4% in 2011. However, in both January and February, it stood at 4.9% and reached 5.4% and 5.3% in March and April respectively, suggesting that this target may be unattainable.

Maintaining social stability remained a top priority for the Communist Party in the face of domestic complaints about rising food and real-estate prices. Sensitivity was heightened by the upheaval that swept through the Arab world in early 2011, which was followed by anonymous online calls for a 'Chinese Jasmine Revolution'. In February Hu stressed the need for the country's leaders to recognise and understand the shifting internal dynamics of civil society, and called for a 'social management' system to resolve problems that could threaten social harmony and stability. Strengthening public security, implementing social management and addressing sources of discontent were also prominent elements of Wen's report at the NPC. The 12th Five-Year Plan (2011–2015) allocated 624.4 billion yuan (about $95bn) for mechanisms to improve social management, including plans to build a national response system for addressing emergency incidents (a euphemism for demonstrations and protests that often become violent), recruit volunteers to help monitor local incidents, and increase government surveillance of non-governmental organisations.

Although conjecture about political reform spread, there were no official declarations indicating moves in this direction. Expectations mounted following Wen's August 2010 visit to Shenzhen, during which he emphasised the need for both economic and political reform. Hu's failure to echo the premier's sentiment during a subsequent visit to Shenzhen then prompted speculation about a possible debate within the CCP leadership. At the NPC, however, it became clear that the CCP would not embark on new political reforms when Wu Bangguo, chairman and party secretary of the NPC's Standing Committee, stated that China would eschew adopting a 'system of multiple parties holding office in rotation, a system with the separation of the three powers, or a bi-cameral system'. He warned that chaos would follow should China stray from 'the correct political orientation'. In his report to the NPC, a document that is a product of compromise, Wen pledged only to 'actively yet prudently advance political restructuring'.

Meanwhile, China continued to emphasise developing as a military power. In February 2011, Beijing announced a 12.7% increase in military expenditures, a return to double-digit growth after the prior year's 7.5% increase, bringing China's total defence spending to 601bn yuan (about $91.5bn). Officials described the increase as reasonable, as defence spending now accounted for 1.4% of China's GDP – well below that of the United States – and roughly 6% of its total budget. Nevertheless, foreign experts believed that China's actual expenditures were considerably higher. Concerns about Beijing's lack of transparency about its expanding military capabilities and intentions were not assuaged by the contents of a Chinese Defence White Paper released in April 2010 (see essay, pages 126–37).

Assertiveness tempered

In addition to complicating the decision-making process, greater pluralism has spawned heightened nationalism. Fuelled by rapid economic growth and perceived international pressure to constrain China's rise, national pride and the victimisation narrative endemic in China's educational system coalesced to cause sudden flare-ups of hyper-nationalism. The most note-worthy instance was the dispute over Japan's detention of the Chinese trawler captain. The fact that Chinese protesters took to the streets gave the dispute a domestic context which likely contributed to the harshness of the measures taken by the government against Japan.

The episode highlighted the new assertiveness in Chinese foreign policy that was on display in 2010. It was by turns confrontational, aggressive, threatening or overbearing. A confluence of factors explained this behaviour. Firstly, after the onset of the global financial crisis, Beijing perceived that the global balance of power was shifting in China's favour and providing it with greater potential leverage to employ in advancing its interests. It incor-rectly predicted that a United States in relative decline and distracted by conflicts in Afghanistan and Iraq would pay less attention to developments in Asia. Secondly, China wrongly understood the Obama administration's desire for greater cooperation on issues such as climate change and global economic rebalancing as weakness and attempted to pressure Washington to forego taking steps that Beijing viewed as harmful to its interests, such as selling weapons to Taiwan and welcoming the Dalai Lama at the White House. Thirdly, an increasingly pluralistic society with strongly national-istic tendencies and pent-up frustration over perceived long-term Chinese submission to foreign pressure exerted growing influence on a leadership that was insecure and paranoid about potential social instability. Fourthly, succession politics in the run-up to the leadership transition expected in 2012 may have advantaged harder-line views, though there was insufficient evidence to prove that this influenced policy.

By the end of 2010, Beijing seemed to have realised that its overbearing behaviour had alienated its neighbours and threatened to reverse three decades of successful diplomacy. Signs emerged that Chinese leaders had recalibrated policy as they renewed emphasis on reassuring other nations that China's rise would bring benefits rather than harm. Efforts at fence-mending were apparent in both rhetoric and action. These accelerated in 2011 and were notably manifest in relations with major powers such as the United States and the EU, with neighbours such as ASEAN and India, and to a lesser extent in ties with South Korea and Japan.

China's assertiveness, however, was limited to issues pertaining to sovereignty or domestic stability, and there was thus no basis to predict, based on the pattern of 2010, that China's overall foreign policy was likely to become more assertive or aggressive in the longer term. It was also premature to conclude that recent signs of a more conciliatory approach meant that there had been a lasting return to China's traditional policy of keeping a low profile and reassuring the world that its rise would be peaceful and benign.

Korean Peninsula: Risk of Escalation

Tensions on the Korean Peninsula reached new heights following North Korea's shelling of Yeonpyeong Island near the disputed Northern Limit Line (NLL) in November 2010. Coming after the sinking of the South Korean corvette *Cheonan* earlier in the year and new revelations about North Korea's nuclear activities, the shelling incident briefly raised the prospect of all-out war and ensured that the Six-Party Talks, established in 2003 to denuclearise North Korea, remained dormant. North Korea's provocations were, in a familiar pattern, followed by conciliatory language in 2011, but by summer the diplomatic rhetoric had soured once more. The deterioration of inter-Korean ties highlighted the significance for both North and South Korea of their relationships with their great-power protectors, respectively China and the United States.

North Korea's provocations came in the context of preparations for a leadership transition from Kim Jong-il to his youngest son, Kim Jong-un, who made his first public appearance and was given the rank of general in September 2010 at the age of about 27. Meanwhile, reports describing the large numbers of North Koreans who were approaching starvation and the many others condemned to the gulag confirmed the brutality and backwardness of the regime he was due to lead. By contrast, South Korea continued to enjoy a steady recovery from the global economic crisis. The North's behaviour gave President Lee Myung-bak a popular mandate for a tougher diplomatic and military policy towards Pyongyang. But Lee also faced political difficulties in the run-up to the election of his successor in late 2012.

Fallout from the *Cheonan*

South Korea had avoided a reflexive military response following the sinking of its corvette *Cheonan* on 26 March 2010, with the loss of 46 of the 104-man crew. Instead, the government commissioned an international investigation into the sinking, which in May concluded that 'there was no other plausible explanation' than that the *Cheonan* had been sunk by a North Korean submarine. Seoul announced that inter-Korean trade would cease and threatened to revive propaganda directed against the Kim regime. In a sign of its reluctance to see the issue escalate, Seoul's suspension of inter-Korean trade excluded the joint-venture Kaesong Industrial Zone (located just over the border in North Korea and the focus of the majority of such trade), and the threat to restart propaganda loudspeaker broadcasts at the Demilitarised Zone (DMZ) was not carried out. By June, South Korea had referred the sinking to the UN Security Council. North Korea threatened that any UN condemnation could lead to war. China's protection of North Korea ensured that it escaped direct blame for its actions, leading US President Barack Obama to argue that China was guilty of 'wilful blindness'. On 9 July, the UN Security Council issued a 'Presidential Statement' condemning the attack that led to the destruction of the *Cheonan* and expressing 'deep concern' over the findings of the investigation. But it also took 'note of [North Korea's] response denying responsibility for the sinking'. The North Korean permanent representative to the UN announced that the statement was a 'great diplomatic victory' for his country.

South Korea sought to bolster its deterrence through a series of military exercises throughout the summer, including joint naval exercises with the United States. Beijing had reacted strongly to suggestions that *Operation*

Invincible Spirit be held in the Yellow Sea, with some Chinese commentators referring to this area as Chinese 'coastal waters'. The decision to hold the exercises to the east of the peninsula was widely perceived as a concession to the Chinese. In early August, however, South Korea did hold exercises in the Yellow Sea, near to the NLL (where the *Cheonan* had been sunk). Washington, as well as demonstrating its military commitment to its ally through joint exercises and a joint visit by Secretary of State Hillary Clinton and Defense Secretary Robert Gates to South Korea in July, imposed new sanctions against North Korea in July and August. Not unrelated to this, Seoul also imposed sanctions against Iran in September 2010, despite the commercial pain this would bring to South Korean business and its heavy reliance on Iranian oil.

South Korea had announced that it would not return to the Six-Party Talks until it had received an apology for the sinking and a sign that North Korea was sincere about denuclearisation, as opposed to merely seeking further economic concessions. No apology was forthcoming, although there were some minor improvements in inter-Korean relations. Following floods in North Korea, the South Korean Red Cross pledged to dispatch a small aid package northwards. Seoul and Pyongyang agreed to hold reunions of families divided by the Korean War, with the meetings taking place at the beginning of November at Mount Kumgang. But these gestures produced no diplomatic breakthrough, and prospects for denuclearisation were dealt a grievous blow in November by new information concerning North Korea's nuclear activities.

An ominous revelation

The United States and other countries had long suspected that North Korea had a clandestine uranium-enrichment programme, but the extent of its technical success was unclear. Most analysts assumed that North Korea might have developed a small, pilot-scale enrichment capability, but that export controls and engineering challenges would limit the pace of its growth.

In early November 2010 North Korea showed groups of US academics construction work in the Yongbyon nuclear complex that was said to be the early stages of a small prototype light-water reactor (LWR). On 12 November, three US experts (including Siegfried Hecker, on his fourth visit to Yongbyon) were also shown a new centrifuge plant that was surprisingly large and technically advanced. Although it was not possible to confirm the operational status of the plant, Hecker estimated that it contained approximately 2,000 centrifuges. He was told that the centrifuges would produce low-enriched uranium (LEU) fuel for the future LWRs. However, Hecker calculated that, if configured to produce highly enriched uranium (HEU), they could produce about 30–40kg a year, enough for at least one nuclear weapon. If the Yongbyon site were used to produce a stockpile of LEU, even relatively small enrichment plants elsewhere could use this as a feedstock and thus produce HEU at a faster rate.

From a diplomatic perspective, the news of the centrifuge facility was highly significant. It is much easier to conceal a uranium-enrichment pro-gramme compared to one based on extracting plutonium from spent reactor fuel, the process on which North Korea's existing weapons programme was based. The fact that a 2,000-machine facility was established 'in plain sight' at Yongbyon, which was under continual overhead surveillance, highlighted the difficulty of detecting centrifuge facilities in the absence of reliable human intelligence. North Korea's ability to establish such capa-bilities means that any eventual denuclearisation would be much harder to verify.

North Korea claimed that the facility was constructed using indige-nous materials, but it seemed likely that a sizeable amount of the relevant technology was procured from abroad. Pyongyang's ability to import sufficient technology for a facility of this size raised alarming questions about the effective enforcement of export controls, interdiction efforts and international sanctions, and the ability of the international community to 'contain' its nuclear ambitions. In addition to technology from abroad, the technical training provided to North Korea by Pakistan in the 1990s would have been very helpful in building up its own base of engineering expertise. North Korea is probably now able to produce most of this inde-pendently, and most likely now has an indigenous centrifuge-production capacity.

North Korean officials claimed that construction of the enrichment facility had begun in April 2009 and was completed in November 2010. However, it was more likely that the centrifuges and related equipment had been assem-bled in another location, and then transferred to Yongbyon. Given the speed with which the centrifuges at the Yongbyon plant were installed, combined with the industrial-scale procurement efforts detected during the early part of the 2000s, it seemed probable that North Korea had already established at least one other enrichment plant of a similar size to the one at Yongbyon. This raised the prospect of North Korea's production of HEU for weapons purposes, whether at the declared site at Yongbyon or at clandestine facili-ties that surely exist.

These revelations shattered the credibility of Pyongyang's denials, vehemently maintained from 2002 to 2009, of American accusations of an enrichment programme. They strongly suggested that North Korea had never been truly willing to relinquish its nuclear capabilities, let alone its nuclear weapons. In January 2011, former US Assistant Secretary of State for East Asia Christopher Hill, now retired but previously the leader of the US Six-Party Talks delegation, argued at a public lecture that in light of North Korea's lies about its enrichment programme, there was 'absolutely no value' in restarting the Six-Party Talks. As well as perhaps permanently destroying any remaining North Korean diplomatic credibility, the existence of an enrichment programme made any potential denuclearisation agreement vulnerable to the charge that compliance by North Korea could never be adequately verified.

International reaction was relatively restrained in the immediate aftermath of the publication on 20 November of Hecker's report on the Yongbyon visit. Yet only three days later, North Korea would dramatically escalate tensions.

Pyongyang raises the stakes

On 23 November North Korean artillery bombarded Yeonpyeong Island, located near the NLL in the Yellow Sea. Pyongyang claimed to be acting in response to South Korean military provocations. South Korean forces had indeed been conducting regular training exercises in the area, but any live fire was directed to the southwest, in the opposite direction from North Korea. Preparations for a leadership transition in Pyongyang (see below) almost certainly were the main factor behind the attack. The documented visit of Kim Jong-il and his son to the coastal region housing the attacking artillery shortly before the bombardment was unlikely to have been a coincidence, and suggested the attack was premeditated. Generating a crisis of this kind and maintaining a war footing were both an attempt to force Washington and Seoul to return to negotiations (and the political and economic concessions that Pyongyang had learned to expect) and a useful method of securing support within North Korea itself for the regime and the young heir.

Two South Korean civilians and two marines were killed. South Korean forces returned fire, but no other form of retaliation, such as air strikes, was used. The bombardment was the first time that Northern artillery had landed in Southern territory since the Korean War, and the death of civilians in an attack watched avidly across the country on live television ensured that the provocation could not be ignored.

With South Korean public opinion much more bellicose than after the sinking of the *Cheonan*, Seoul felt it had to respond more forcefully than it had done earlier in the year. Lee initially warned that his country would respond with 'enormous retaliation' to further attacks. Humanitarian transfers were cancelled. The United States held joint naval exercises with South Korea in the Yellow Sea within a week of the attacks, no doubt to persuade Pyongyang of their ability to respond forcefully to any further provocations. On 3 December, new South Korean Defence Minister Kim Kwan-jin stated that Seoul would respond to future provocations with air strikes, marking a significant shift in the rules of engagement.

China's first response to the Yeonpyeong crisis was to call for an emergency meeting of the Six-Party Talks. In UN Security Council meetings, as it had done with the *Cheonan* earlier in the year, China vetoed language condemning North Korea. Once again, as with the *Cheonan*, it urged 'both sides' to exercise restraint. Moreover, in late 2010 and early 2011 China also blocked discussion of the North Korean enrichment programme at the Security Council. While China may have calculated that its interests were best served by shielding North Korea and thus dampening down regional tensions, its actions fuelled a growing belief in Seoul that China's behaviour in fact enabled and encouraged North Korean aggression, and that it could not be viewed as an 'honest broker' in negotiations.

China's role in the peninsula's dynamics was the subject of renewed American efforts in the following months. In early December 2010 Obama telephoned Chinese President Hu Jintao and, according to the White House, 'urged China to work with us and others to send a clear message to North Korea that its provocations are unacceptable'. Press reports noted an increasing closeness between the United States, South Korea and Japan in their coordination against the North Korean threat and, implicitly, China. Washington announced that military and diplomatic teams would be sent to both countries to coordinate deterrence policies. Following the 20 December live-fire exercises conducted by South Korea, US officials suggested to American newspapers that China had intervened to temper North Korea's response, although no evidence for this intervention was presented.

There were some signs over the following weeks that diplomatic progress had been made. In December Lee said South Korea remained amenable to dialogue, as long as North Korea committed itself to denuclearisation. From the beginning of 2011, a variety of North Korean newspapers and entities promoted the idea of inter-Korean dialogue, albeit mixed with residual venom towards Seoul. South Korea suggested bilateral talks to discuss the

Cheonan and Yeonpyeong incidents, and accepted a North Korean proposal to hold military discussions. Obama administration officials said China had applied pressure to North Korea, and that Beijing's more helpful position was a result of Washington's warning that it would respond to an unconstrained North Korea by redeploying its forces in Asia. At the US–China summit in Washington on 19 January, China for the first time publicly joined the United States in expressing 'concern' at Pyongyang's 'claimed enrichment programme'.

These superficially positive developments were short-lived. Although the Koreas did go on to hold colonel-level talks on 8 February at Panmunjom that were intended to set the agenda for further meetings, North Korea walked out on the second day after South Korea warned that higher-level talks could not take place until Pyongyang took responsibility for the *Cheonan* and Yeonpyeong Island attacks. China continued to thwart South Korea's efforts to bring the North Korean enrichment programme to the UN Security Council. It reportedly blocked the publication of a report by a UN Panel of Experts on North Korean violations of sanctions in February, and in May went on to block a similar report on North Korean transfers of ballistic-missile technology to Iran.

Diplomacy remains bogged down

In April Wu Dawei, China's special representative for the Korean Peninsula, announced a three-stage plan aimed at restarting the Six-Party Talks, similar to one proposed in 2009. Sequential North Korean bilateral discussions would be held with Seoul and Washington about the nuclear programme before the full resumption of the Six-Party process. In this way, the enrichment programme would remain in China's favoured forum of the Six-Party Talks, rather than moving to the Security Council.

North Korea apparently accepted this proposal, but South Korea was less enthusiastic. The suggested bilateral talks did not get under way, mainly because of Pyongyang's refusal to apologise for its attacks on South Korea in 2010, and mixed messages from Seoul and Washington about how necessary this would be for dialogue to resume.

In addition to difficulties with preliminary discussions, South Korea and the United States remained fundamentally distrustful of the North's motivations, seeking some demonstration that it was actually committed to relinquishing its nuclear capabilities. After travelling to China in May (his third visit within a year, after May and August 2010), Kim Jong-il reportedly signalled his desire to ease tensions on the peninsula and restart the

Six-Party Talks. However, Western scholars involved in Track II dialogue with senior North Korean officials warned that North Korea considered itself a nuclear power and that 'denuclearisation' in its terms meant the removal of the US nuclear umbrella from South Korea and Japan, coupled with intrusive inspections to ensure that US tactical nuclear weapons no longer remained in South Korea. According to them, Pyongyang would only seek further political and economic concessions at future Six-Party Talks. It was notable that, while Chinese state media in May referred to Kim's wish to restart the talks, North Korean media only said that the two leaders agreed that denuclearisation should occur 'on the whole Korean Peninsula'.

Within a week of Kim's visit to Beijing, Pyongyang's more emollient approach of the first months of 2011 had reverted to its usual confrontational stance, blaming Seoul for propaganda dispatched into North Korea by private organisations (though South Korea had not resumed official propaganda operations). The National Defence Commission (NDC), echoing statements of a year before, said it would never again deal with the 'traitor Lee Myung-bak and his clan'. In an attempt to discredit Lee, North Korea claimed in June that during meetings in Beijing in May the South had 'begged' for an inter-Korean summit, and promised financial aid in return. Seoul argued that these meetings had in fact been arranged to extract an apology from Pyongyang for the 2010 attacks.

The NDC also threatened to close a military hotline with its southern neighbour. South Korean officials appeared relaxed in response to this threat, arguing that multiple alternative channels of communication remained open. Several South Korean military accidents over the past year (including the firing of a howitzer at Yeonpyeong Island on 28 November, the discharge of a machine gun at the DMZ on 15 April and South Korean Marines mistakenly firing on a civilian airliner in June 2011) highlighted the importance of being able to communicate with the North in an emergency, so as to prevent the consequences of a low-level military miscalculation or accident from escalating. Gates warned at the 2011 IISS Shangri-La Dialogue that tensions on the peninsula were in 'danger of unpredictable escalation in the event of another provocation'. By raising the spectre of more serious disorder on the peninsula, North Korea appeared to be hoping that the United States and South Korea would relax their policy of 'strategic patience', and see dialogue and concessions, even if based on the unlikely premise that North Korea would ultimately dispense with its nuclear weapons, as the lesser evil.

South Korea: seeking credible deterrence

The events of 2010 highlighted the military threat posed to South Korea by its northern neighbour and its dependence on the strong military relationship with its American ally. In response to the *Cheonan* sinking, Lee and Obama agreed to postpone the transfer of wartime operational control from Washington to Seoul from its intended date of 2012 to 2015. South Korea also formed a presidential commission to review national defence reform. It recommended streamlining the armed forces, but in the wake of the Yeonpyeong Island incident it also suggested restoring the two-year period of compulsory military service and doubling the size of the South Korean marine force to protect the western islands more effectively.

Since 2010, South Korea had announced at various points a new stance of 'proactive deterrence', although the specifics of such a policy remained vague. In June 2011 Kim Kwan-jin explained that 'proactive deterrence means that if there is a provocation, we will respond very strongly'. This rhetoric reflected the public mood. A survey conducted shortly after the Yeonpyeong incident revealed that 65.7% disapproved of their government's reaction to the shelling, and 80.3% of respondents believed that the government should have led a stronger military response. Approval ratings for Lee had dropped to 45% from a high of 60% reached immediately after hosting the G20 summit earlier in November. However, only 33% of respondents were willing to risk a war with North Korea to deliver a military response to the attack.

Seoul's statement that further attacks would be answered by air strikes demonstrated a clear desire to establish deterrence against new provocations. But it raised the question of whether, in such a scenario, Seoul would be able to maintain 'escalation dominance'. For instance, if the South Korean air force were to launch air strikes, and North Korea retaliated by shooting down a civilian airliner near Incheon Airport, it was doubtful whether Seoul could respond with sufficient harshness without provoking an all-out conflict that would devastate the peninsula.

There were also unsubstantiated suggestions that South Korea could revise its policies on nuclear weapons. Immediately after the disclosure of North Korea's uranium-enrichment facility, then-Defence Minister Kim Tae-young hinted that US nuclear weapons could once again be deployed in South Korea. The Lee government quickly emphasised that the minister was asserting his personal view and that government policy was unchanged (Kim's outspokenness contributed to his departure from office after the Yeonpyeong attack). However, conservative politicians continued to argue for such a redeployment. In June 2011 the outgoing commander of US Forces in Korea underlined Washington's stance that the defence of South Korea, and the credibility of the US nuclear umbrella, did not require the physical presence of nuclear weapons on South Korean soil. South Korea has not stated any official intention to change this policy, and certainly has no plans to acquire nuclear weapons of its own.

However, North Korean challenges to its conventional deterrence, along with the stagnation of disarmament diplomacy, underlined the potential significance of the South's push to acquire a pyroprocessing capability. Seoul has been developing this form of reprocessing since 1997, and presents it as a proliferation-resistant method of reducing the pressing problem of spent nuclear fuel storage that will become even more acute as the South Korean nuclear-power sector expands. Although plutonium is not separated from other elements in spent fuel as part of pyroprocessing, further chemical separation would be fairly simple to perform. Both the 1974 nuclear-cooperation agreement with the US and the 1992 Joint Declaration on Denuclearisation of the Korean Peninsula prevent South Korea from reprocessing spent fuel. Washington has expressed strong reservations about pyroprocessing in its discussions with South Korea on the re-negotiation of their cooperation agreement, due to expire in 2014. To put off the issue, both countries in January 2011 agreed to launch a ten-year joint study on the technique.

Economics and politics

A much more publicised area of contention with the United States was the long-running delay over the implementation of the bilateral free-trade agreement (FTA) signed in 2007, but unratified by either the American or South Korean legislature since then. Despite the public urging of some prominent US politicians earlier in 2010, the FTA was not ratified in time for South Korea's hosting of the G20 summit in November. But on 3 December the two countries finalised the FTA when South Korea agreed to change elements of the deal. US Democrats had been fighting for amendments to open the Korean market to American car makers, although they were unsuccessful in their attempts to remove the Korean ban on US beef. Seoul did not officially acknowledge that its flexibility was due to Washington's robust support following the Yeonpyeong incident some two weeks earlier, although opposition politicians accused Lee of sacrificing Korean interests. The finalising of the agreement could not help but improve bilateral relations, and highlighted the economic ties binding the United States and South Korea as well as the security ones. Despite this, as of summer 2011 the agreement remained unratified by both countries due to domestic politics.

South Korea meanwhile continued its strong recovery from the 2008 global financial crisis. Economic growth in 2010 reached 6.1%, the highest level for eight years. Yet positive economic trends did not shield Lee and his Grand National Party (GNP) from electoral difficulties and internal fighting. Although for much of the year the opposition Democratic Party failed to make ground against the GNP, by April 2011 the tide appeared to be turning. The GNP fared poorly in elections for three parliamentary seats and one governorship, losing the Bundang seat to Sohn Hak-kyu, the likely leader of the Democratic Party in the 2012 elections. Lee's approval ratings sank further to 31.8% in 2011, while levels of support for the Democratic Party (21.4%) edged nearer to those of the GNP (25.1%). Part of the Democratic Party's growing support may have been due to its perceived advantage over the GNP in wealth redistribution, an increasingly important issue, particularly amongst the young.

Lee also faced opposition from within his own party. On 29 June 2010 a rebellious faction in the GNP (supporters of Park Geun-hye, the daughter of a former president and Lee's defeated rival in the 2007 campaign for the GNP nomination) helped thwart the president's plans to scale back a grandiose scheme put in place by the previous administration to relocate much of the government out of Seoul. As a result, Prime Minister Chung Un-chan resigned in July 2010. South Korean presidents are limited to one term in office, and Lee risked being seen as a lame duck in the run-up to presidential elections at the end of 2012.

North Korea: future leader makes debut

North Korea's preparations for leadership transition, a key issue since Kim Jong-il's stroke in 2008, took shape over the course of 2010–11. Throughout 2010 there had been various allusions in internal media to the coming new generation. Yet the name of Kim Jong-un, Kim Jong-il's youngest son, was never mentioned officially until 27 September 2010, when he was named as a senior general. The next day the young man, born on 8 January 1982 or 1983 (or possibly 1984), made his public debut at the first Workers' Party of Korea (WPK) delegates' conference for decades and was given several party positions. Changes were made to the party's charter that not only strengthened the WPK's role, but facilitated Kim Jong-un's future accession, including by making the general secretary automatically chairman of the Central Military Commission and by giving that body supervision over all military affairs. A five-year interval rule for the party convention was eliminated, thereby allowing Kim Jong-un to be named general secretary quickly in the event of Kim Jong-il's death.

These were only first steps, however. Although the succession is now firmly in place, Kim Jong-un was not officially named as successor. There was speculation that a meeting in early April 2011 of the pliable Supreme People's Assembly (SPA) would elect Kim Jong-un as first vice-chairman of the NDC (a position vacant since November 2010) and thereby make *de jure* his de facto status as the second most powerful figure in the country. Appointment to this position would have repeated a key step in Kim Jong-il's own rise to power. However, for whatever reason, the election did not take place in April.

Since his stroke, Kim Jong-il seemed to have reached the conclusion that the only people around him that he could trust were his family. Kim Jong-un, Kim Kyong-hui (Kim Jong-il's younger sister), and Jang Song-thaek (her husband), emerged as key figures in North Korean politics. It was widely believed that Jang Song-thaek would play the role of regent to Kim Jong-un. Jang, who as recently as 2003–05 was mysteriously purged and disappeared from public view for more than two years, was appointed to the NDC in 2009. In June 2010 he became one of its vice-chairmen at an abruptly convened session of the SPA. Jang is also director of the Party Central Committee's Administration Department and a member of its Central Military Commission (CMC). He thus had power in both the party and the military. To the surprise of outside observers, however, he failed to assume any further influential positions during the September 2010 party conference, being named only as an alternate member of the party Politburo.

Kim Kyong-hui, on the other hand, was named a regular member of the Politburo. She was also made a four-star military general just before the September party convention. Kim Jong-il thus showed that he was determined to rely on his sister and brother-in-law to protect Kim Jong-un. However, he also tried to prevent his brother-in-law Jang from acquiring a predominant political status, applying a balance-of-power principle even to his own family members. This demonstrated the cunning of an able politician, and suggested that more changes were likely to follow. It was likely that the September reshuffle was designed to forge a vanguard group to bolster Kim Jong-un's succession. When his father dies, Kim Jong-un will need the support of the state security apparatus and the military, as well as of China. But this support will probably impose constraints on his strategic and policy choices. The power transition thus has wider strategic implications. Despite the party's efforts to control the military, the generals will remain influential in domestic politics, foreign relations and national defence. In the short run, policy changes on any front are unlikely, as maintaining the status quo will remain the leadership priority during and for some period after the power succession.

Despite his father's all-out support, plus implicit recognition of the succession by Beijing, Kim Jong-un has had no time, nor any apparent opportunity, to acquire political skills, nor to demonstrate leadership ability. It was not known whether the youngest son's hasty elevation created resentment among older members of the elite or disrespect among the public at large. But the foundations of Kim Jong-un's power appeared fragile, in comparison with those of his grandfather and father. Coupled with this disadvantage, he confronted a multitude of challenges in the domestic and the international domains that presented hurdles on the path to power succession. Given his dearth of experience and preparation, his political autonomy was likely to be even more constrained by the political influence of the military. A personality cult was being created for him, with various fabricated stories casting him as a man of genius. He accompanied his father on a series of 'field guidance' visits around the country, demonstrating to the people his status as heir apparent. Significantly, in the month after the September party meeting the two Kims twice visited the State Security Department, an autonomous agency in charge of surveillance and control over the North Korean people.

The younger Kim's prime focus on the security apparatus implied that he – and his accession to power – would rely more on physical power, political surveillance, punishment and enforcement than on the voluntary support of the North Korean people. That said, he would inherit a system already remarkable for the level of control and brutality inflicted upon its people. In May 2011 Amnesty International reported that North Korea's prison-camp system contained around 200,000 people, out of a total population of about 24 million.

The accession process was also reliant on Chinese support. Soon after the September 2010 party meeting, China issued a statement in the name of President Hu welcoming the new leadership line-up in Pyongyang and promising China's continued cooperation. China's implicit endorsement of the power transfer to Kim Jong-un fortified his position as successor. China had long been North Korea's main source of foreign investment and trade, but this was magnified by international sanctions, North Korea's diminishing trade with South Korea, and an increase in Chinese investment. According to the Korea Trade–Investment Promotion Agency, China accounted for 83% of North Korea's international commerce in 2010. North Korea's growing economic dependence on Beijing reinforced

Pyongyang's political dependence. This dual dependency was apparent in Kim Jong-il's three visits to China in May and August 2010 and May 2011. The purpose of the first and third visits seemed to be to win economic assistance, while the second appeared to be political, to confirm Chinese support of the succession. China and North Korea were also strengthening their military relationship by exchanging visits of high-level military officers.

Economic woes

In March 2011 the UN's World Food Programme (WFP) reported that a quarter of North Korea's population was starving. However, a long-standing concern of potential food donors is that food supplies would be diverted to the military or held in reserve for later distribution to celebrate the 2012 centenary of Kim Il-sung's birth. On 19 May the WFP called for urgent assistance and noted that North Korea had granted new monitoring powers to build confidence about the ultimate destination of supplies. The following week, a US team arrived in North Korea in an attempt to gauge the true situation. By late June, Clinton said the United States still had concerns about diversion, and that it had made 'no decision about providing food aid to North Korea at this time'. Reports from aid workers in North Korea suggested that Pyongyang had cut public food distribution, in some areas to as little as 150 grams of food a day, and that people had resorted to eating grass. Given the ability of the regime to survive mass famine in the 1990s, it was unlikely that the suffering of its people would prompt it to make any domestic or diplomatic concessions.

Over recent years, China had promoted the notion that its economic metamorphosis could provide a model for future North Korean reform. Premier Wen Jiabao emphasised this point to Lee in Tokyo in late May 2011. Indeed, Lee himself argued in October 2010 that North Korea should emulate China, in the hope that this would allow for eventual reunification (in August 2010 he had proposed a tax to help pay for future reunification costs). But Pyongyang has steadfastly refused to open up, believing that this could create intolerable pressures on its regime. In the context of a potentially insecure leadership transition, it seemed unlikely that Kim Jong-un would risk liberalising North Korea's economy and exposing its society to additional outside influences. Instead, reports suggested that Pyongyang had created a special riot squad and imported significant quantities of anti-riot equipment from China, and dispatched students to manual labour until 2012. This was apparently in the hope of preparing for any unrest inspired by economic deprivation or news of the wave of revolutions in the Arab world. Despite ample reason for protest, however, as of July 2011 there was no visible sign of popular discontent in North Korea.

Southeast Asia: Domestic Challenges, Regional Incoherence

There were significant domestic political developments in several Southeast Asian states over the course of the year to mid-2011. In Thailand, superficial normality returned to political life in the aftermath of the deadly clashes in April–May 2010 between Red Shirt protesters and security forces in Bangkok, but unease returned in advance of fiercely contested elections in July 2011 that brought to power proxies of populist former Prime Minister Thaksin Shinawatra. In Myanmar, the parliamentary elections in November 2010 – the first since 1990 – were controversial and resulted in an overwhelming victory for a party backed by the country's military junta and the installation of a government representing the military's interests. Nevertheless, the elections did represent a limited political opening, and led to the release of the country's veteran pro-democracy advocate, Aung San Suu Kyi. In Singapore, a watershed general election in May 2011, against a background of considerable popular discontent over the People's Action Party government's domestic policies, resulted in opposition politicians securing more than token parliamentary representation for the first time since the city-state's independence in 1965.

On the security front, long-running insurgencies continued to challenge government control in areas of Myanmar (where clashes between government and ethnic-minority forces escalated significantly after the elections), Thailand and the Philippines, although in the latter case there were signs of progress towards peace settlements with rebel groups. In Indonesia, new forms of extremist violence challenged the government's counter-terrorist strategy. The outbreak of open conflict over disputed territory on the Thai–Cambodian border further undermined the credibility of the Association of Southeast Asian Nations (ASEAN), a long-established sub-regional institution which seeks to establish a 'Southeast Asian Community', including an important political-security element, by 2015. Meanwhile, China's growing assertiveness over its claims in the South China Sea increasingly challenged the security interests of Southeast Asian claimants, notably the Philippines and Vietnam, and contributed to escalating unease over the evolving regional order and particularly about China's place in that order.

Thailand: election vindicates the Red Shirts

Following the army's resolution through force in May 2010 of the anti-establishment urban uprising in Bangkok led by the United Front for Democracy Against Dictatorship (UDD) or Red Shirts, a surface calm temporarily prevailed in Thai political life. Millions still supported the UDD, which had grown out of the political frustration of many poorer Thais (particularly in the north, northeast and Bangkok) after governments led by Thaksin Shinawatra were removed by military coup in 2006 and by a judicial decision in 2008. However, following the deaths of 92 people during the Bangkok disturbances, the government detained key UDD leaders and activists, and charged 15 of them with terrorism, an offence carrying the death sentence. It also imposed a draconian state of emergency on 24 provinces – roughly one-third of the country. In these circumstances, the Red Shirts lost momentum during the second half of 2010. There was some concern in the government that the UDD might resort to more widespread violence. Red Shirts operating on a freelance basis were apparently responsible for several bomb explosions between June 2010 and January 2011, and there were reports that the Red Shirts were organising weapons training in neighbouring Cambodia. However, there was no clear evidence that the UDD leadership had decided to develop an armed wing.

At the height of the Bangkok uprising in early May 2010, Prime Minister Abhisit Vejjajiva's government proposed a road map towards national reconciliation, including an election within five months. After the army crackdown in Bangkok, the government retracted the offer of an early election (which still, however, needed to be held by November 2011). The rest of the proposal remained, though, leading to the establishment of bodies charged with investigating the April–May 2010 violence, and with looking into possible constitutional amendments, socio-economic reform, and media reform with the aim of reducing the tensions that had contributed to Thailand's drawn-out political crisis. However, the security forces' patchy cooperation compromised the Truth for Reconciliation Commission of Thailand's fact-finding in relation to the violence. The constitutional-amendment committee proposed changes to the electoral system, including an increase in the number of 'party-list' (non-constituency) members of parliament (MPs) and a change from multi-MP to single-MP constituencies; parliament approved these amendments in February 2011. Overall, though, these changes probably favoured the ruling Democrat Party. And while the government charged two committees, one of which attempted to engage civil society, with looking into socio-economic reforms – 14 key areas were identifed, including land reform, social welfare, education, decentralisation, the justice system, health care and water management – little progress was made except for the suggestion of a progressive taxation system to advance land reform.

Critics of the government pointed to the suppression of media aligned with the Red Shirts, and the uneven application of the law (notably the slowness to prosecute the pro-establishment Yellow Shirt activists who seized two airports and a TV station in 2008, and the increasing use of lese-majesty provisions of the Criminal Code against Red Shirt activists) as obstacles to genuine national reconciliation. Nevertheless, in an effort to win support from at least some of those who backed Thaksin and the Red Shirts, in January 2011 Abhisit's government instituted a nine-point populist policy aimed at meeting the poor's basic needs, including expansion of the social-security scheme, low-interest loans and the provision of free electricity.

Abhisit's coalition government, led by his Democrat Party, had been helped to power in 2008 by the protracted Yellow Shirt demonstrations organised by the conservative, ultra-nationalist and ultra-monarchical People's Alliance for Democracy (PAD). However, by early 2011 there were signs that the close links between Abhisit's administration and the Yellow Shirts were fraying. In December 2010 Cambodian security forces in a disputed border area arrested seven Thais, including Veera Somkhwamkid, the leader of the Thai Patriots Network (a Yellow Shirt group), and a Democrat Party MP. In mid-January 2011, the Cambodian government released five of those it had arrested, but Veera and his assistant Ratree Phiphatthanaphaibul were convicted of illegal entry, trespassing and espionage and sentenced to lengthy prison terms. In late January, against the background of growing tensions on the border, the Yellow Shirts had begun a major new demonstration in Bangkok, calling for the government to adopt tougher policy positions on the border dispute. After the sentencing of Veera and Ratree, the PAD attacked Abhisit's leadership directly, charging that his government was corrupt and calling for a new and 'virtuous' leader. There was much speculation that the Yellow Shirts – concerned over not only Abhisit's supposed weakness, but more importantly the prospect of a government backed by Red Shirts gaining power – favoured another military intervention. However, as the PAD's position became more extreme, it seemed that their once large-scale support was diminishing, a fact reflected in the relatively small size of their demonstrations in front of Government House during early 2011.

Following a plan revealed two months earlier, in early May Abhisit announced the dissolution of parliament; soon afterwards the general election date was set for 3 July. While many Thais' voting preferences were already clear, a significant proportion (perhaps 20% nationwide) was undecided when the election campaign started. Bangkok emerged as a key locus of contention, with more than 50% of voters undecided according to some surveys. Elsewhere, the Democrats were strongest in the south, while the Pheu Thai Party – political heir to Thaksin's earlier Thai Rak Thai and People Power Party (PPP) – had its strongholds in exactly the same areas of north and northeast Thailand as its two earlier incarnations. In the northeast, though, Pheu Thai faced a major challenge from the Bhumjaithai Party, led by Newin Chidchob, whose political faction had been aligned with Thaksin before switching to support the Democrats during the 2008 political crisis, thereby giving Abhisit the parliamentary numbers necessary to form a government.

It quickly became clear from polling as well as anecdotal evidence that there was a good chance Pheu Thai could win the election. Apart from the grassroots strength of the party in the Red Shirt movement, where sentiment against *Amathayathipatai* (rule of the traditional elites) had grown in the context of perceived injustice following the 2010 Bangkok uprising, economic circumstances weighed against the Democrats and their allies. While Thailand's GDP expansion of 8% in 2010 made it the fastest growing economy in Southeast Asia despite its serious political problems, inflation – particularly in food prices – was a serious and mounting problem that preoccupied millions of poorer Thais in a country where income distribution remained markedly skewed in favour of the wealthiest 10% of the population. With Thaksin in self-imposed exile in Abu Dhabi because of his wish to avoid a Thai prison term (for favouring his wife in a business deal while he was prime minister), and many other former Thai Rak Thai and PPP leaders legally disqualified from politics, Pheu Thai had lacked a strong or charismatic leader since it was established in 2008. However, the announcement in May 2011 that Thaksin's youngest sister, the engaging and telegenic (if politically inexperienced) Yingluck Shinawatra, would lead the party into the July election neatly resolved this problem. The electorate understood that Yingluck was effectively Thaksin's creature, and she proved to be a great draw on the campaign trail during May and June. At the same time, Pheu Thai's programmatic emphasis on poverty alleviation, with a promise to double the daily minimum wage to 300 baht (approximately $10) – and to raise it to 1,000 baht by 2020 – continued to have wide appeal.

Its supporters and opponents alike assumed that, if Pheu Thai was able to form a government after the election, it planned to bring Thaksin back to Thailand as soon as possible with the implicit intent of restoring him as prime minister, perhaps by way of amnesty legislation or a government-appointed panel for 'victims of injustice'. The prospect of a Pheu Thai victory and Thaksin's possible return did not, however, suggest any imminent reversion to political stability. It was by no means clear that the country's traditional elites would easily relinquish power again to the Red Shirts, particularly in light of their continuing concern to ensure a royal succession that would protect establishment interests. The 83-year-old King Bhumibol Adulyadej remained seriously ill and in hospital, where he had been since September 2009, and the succession to the monarchy remained uncertain. In mid-June, during the election campaign, army commander-in-chief General Prayuth Chan-ocha reminded Thais, in a TV broadcast, of the 'burning of Bangkok' during the Red Shirt protests; claimed the existence of an illegal movement intending to overthrow the monarchy; and called on voters to elect 'good people and good parties'. Many observers saw Prayuth's remarks as indicative of the army leadership's continuing political partiality and the continuing potential for direct military intervention in the event of voters selecting Pheu Thai to lead the next government. Alternatively, if Pheu Thai suffered a defeat, new and possibly widespread Red Shirt unrest seemed entirely possible.

In the event, the election result was resoundingly clear-cut. Notwithstanding some nervous Western foreign ministries' travel advisories warning of election-related violence, election day was overwhelmingly peaceful, with a record voter turnout almost reaching 75%, just above the previous high of 74% in 2007. While informed observers had forecast that Pheu Thai might be able to form a government with other parties' assistance, the Red Shirt party surprised even many of its own supporters by gaining an absolute majority, with 262 out of 500 seats in the lower house. The credibility of the Pheu Thai triumph as a measure of the popular will provided considerable assurance against political instability, including a military coup, at least in the short term. Crucially, after speaking to the military's leaders, Minister of Defence General Prawit Wongsuwon said that the armed forces accepted the election result and would 'not get involved'. Yingluck was statesmanlike in victory, and moved quickly to reinforce further the legitimacy of her government-in-waiting by joining with four smaller parties to form a coalition with 299 seats, though this number might be reduced if the Electoral Commission disqualified MPs because of electoral fraud, or if they defected. Thaksin's strong influence or even control over Yingluck doubtless continued. However, with national reconciliation ranking alongside economic development as a declared priority for the new government, in the election's immediate aftermath Thaksin played down the idea that he might return to Thailand imminently, let alone aspire to become prime minister again: it was widely understood that such developments could provoke new unrest and strengthen his opponents.

Meanwhile, Thailand's three southernmost provinces of Pattani, Yala and Narathiwat remained locked in a cycle of violence that began in 2004 and had resulted in more than 4,400 deaths by June 2011. The perceived political injustice suffered by ethnic Malays in the region, including the lack of progress towards prosecutions over previous serious human-rights abuses by the security forces (such as the Tak Bai incident in 2004, and the 2009 Al-Furqan mosque attack), continued to provide the context and justification for the regional lawlessness that has become known in Thai as *fai tai* ('southern fire'). However, criminal violence linked to trafficking in small arms, narcotics and sex-workers, combined with personal rivalries and retribution, probably accounted for a significant proportion of the deaths and injuries often attributed to what the international media has often portrayed as a 'Muslim insurgency'. Distracted more than ever by politics at the centre, Thailand's government appeared to lack an effective strategy for resolving the conflict. Despite Abhisit's promise on coming to power to consider lifting the emergency decree in the three provinces, which gives draconian powers to the army and police, it continued to be renewed every three months, apparently due to military resistance. One positive development was the passage of legislation in November 2010 to strengthen the authority of the Southern Border Provinces Administrative Centre, allowing it to report directly to the prime minister and to operate independently of the army-controlled Internal Security Operations Command. However, efforts to devise a political solution – which would necessarily involve dialogue between the government and groups representing ethnic Malay interests, and a more fundamental reform of governance perhaps involving some form of political devolution – seemed a distant prospect. Although Yingluck promised during her campaign that a Pheu Thai government would 'transform the three southernmost provinces into a special administrative area', the resentment of many ethnic Malays over the serious abuses that occurred in the south under Thaksin in 2004–05, combined with likely continuing resistance from the army to significant political changes, meant that the advent of the new administration in July 2011 did not promise to bring a thoroughgoing settlement any closer.

Myanmar: the emperor's new clothes

In late March 2011, the swearing in of a nominally civilian government in Myanmar and the simultaneous disbandment of the State Peace and Development Council (SPDC) junta which had ruled the country since 1988 represented the culmination of the former military regime's 'roadmap to democracy', other key elements of which were a constitutional referendum in 2008 and national elections in early November 2010. Many in Myanmar and abroad, including veteran pro-democracy activist Aung San Suu Kyi, whose National League for Democracy (NLD) boycotted the polls, condemned the elections – from which foreign observers and media were barred – as unfair and fraudulent. The new parliament, which convened for the first time in early February, clearly did not reflect the political views of Myanmar's people: one-quarter of the seats in both the upper and lower houses were reserved for the armed forces, and the military-backed Union Solidarity and Development Party held almost 80% of the remainder. Ethnic minority parties that had reached accommodations with the government were quite well represented, but opposition representation was essentially limited to a relatively small number of seats held by the National Democratic Force, a faction of the NLD. The new government was similarly still dominated by the armed forces, despite its superficially civilian appearance: the cabinet overwhelmingly comprised retired military officers, half of whom had been ministers under the former, military regime.

One significant result of the November 2010 election was that, within days of the polls, the military regime released Aung San Suu Kyi from house arrest after more than seven years, a gesture apparently designed in part to appease the country's international critics. While the government claimed that her political platform was no longer relevant, approximately 5,000 supporters greeted Aung San Suu Kyi's reappearance in public on 13 November. However, there were no other significant indications of improvement in the country's human- and civil-rights policies. In January 2011, Myanmar's Supreme Court declined to hear an appeal by Aung San Suu Kyi which sought to overturn the government's dissolution of the NLD following its failure to re-register in order to participate in the 2010 elections. More than 2,000 political prisoners remained behind bars, an important factor in the United States' decision in May 2011 to renew economic sanctions against Myanmar, in spite of the elections, Aung San Suu Kyi's release and the subsequent end to the SPDC regime. According to US President Barack Obama, the new government was responsible for 'large-scale repression of the democratic opposition'. During a subsequent visit to Myanmar, also in May, senior

US diplomat Joseph Yun called for 'concrete steps toward democratic governance, respect for human rights and the release of all political prisoners' as pre-conditions for improved relations with Washington. Yun also mentioned US concerns over fresh reports of arms shipments to Myanmar from North Korea, possibly including missiles and nuclear technology. American policy towards Myanmar thus continued to contrast with that of China, which in May welcomed President Thein Sein (who was formerly the SPDC's prime minister) to Beijing on a state visit. The two countries signed nine agreements on economic cooperation, and agreed to establish a comprehensive strategic partnership, signalling a further tightening of their relationship. Meanwhile, Myanmar's relations with the rest of ASEAN remained uncomfortable: in early May, the association's members had made their approval for the semi-pariah state's assumption of the grouping's rotating presidency in 2014 dependent on further political reforms.

Though the NLD officially no longer existed as a political party, in late May 2011 Aung San Suu Kyi announced that she planned shortly to test her freedoms with a tour of the country. Her previous nationwide tour, in May 2003, had highlighted both the continuing massive popularity of the NLD and her own special status as Myanmar's leader-in-waiting. However, that tour had ended with an attack on Aung San Suu Kyi's convoy in the town of Depayin in Sagaing region by an estimated 800 government-sponsored thugs, who killed at least 70 NLD supporters. A common assessment of the incident was that it represented an assassination attempt against Aung San Suu Kyi, who was injured during the attack and subsequently imprisoned again. Her planned new tour of the country in 2011 opened up the possibility not only of political mobilisation in support of the NLD, but also serious risks for herself and her supporters.

One important result of the Myanmar regime's attempt to consolidate its power through new political mechanisms was the intensification of its conflict with ethnic-minority insurgent groups. In the November election, the government claimed that the troubled areas of Kachin, Kayah, Kayin, Mon and Shan states and the Wa division were too dangerous for voting to proceed, and that many candidates proposed by ethnic-minority groups did not meet the electoral commission's requirements. On top of this effective electoral disenfranchisement, it was clear that the new government would continue to force ethnic-minority insurgent groups that had entered into ceasefire agreements to incorporate with the army-controlled paramilitary Border Guard Force (BGF). Indeed, on 8 November, the day after the election, clashes between government troops and the Democratic Karen

Buddhist Army (DKBA) caused more than 20,000 Karen civilians to seek refuge across the Thai border.

Responding to renewed offensives by Myanmar's army after the election, ethnic-minority insurgents opposed to the government intensified their efforts to forge greater unity. In January 2011, it was reported that the combined forces of the DKBA, the Karen National Liberation Army (the armed wing of the largely Christian Karen National Union (KNU)) and the All Burma Students' Democratic Front were fighting six government battalions close to the border. Later the same month, the Mon National Defence Army rejoined its parent organisation, the New Mon State Army (NMSA), whose truce with Myanmar's government had broken down the previous September. By early February, Myanmar's media was for the first time since 1995 describing the NMSA as 'insurgents'. Only days later, the Kachin Independence Organisation (KIO) clashed with Myanmar's army for the first time in 13 years, forcing four army battalions to leave Kachin territory. The United Wa State Army (UWSA), the largest group to reject the government's BGF plan, expressed support for the KIO. Aware of the threat that increasing cooperation between armed rebel groups posed to the government's control of the country's periphery, in February 2011 Myanmar's army deployed an estimated ten battalions supported by armoured vehicles into the eastern part of Shan state along the border with Thailand to break up an emerging alliance between the Shan State Army-North (SSA-North), the Shan State Army-South (SSA-South) and the UWSA. Also in February, representatives of the KIO, NMSA and SSA-North (all previously in ceasefire with Myanmar's government) met with the KNU and Chin and Karenni groups for a five-day conference, resulting in the United Nationalities Federal Council (UNFC). The UNFC's stated aim was to establish a 'genuine federal union' with Myanmar, with equal rights for all ethnic groups. By mid-March, a merger between the UNFC and a parallel grouping, the Ethnic Minorities Council, seemed possible.

Fighting between government and ethnic-minority forces intensified during the second quarter of 2011, stimulating further cooperation between rebel armies. In late April, as the government continued its offensive in Shan state, the KIO (whose Kachin Independence Army had, before its ceasefire in 1994, constituted the most serious armed threat to Myanmar's government) warned that it was ready to go to war at any time should Myanmar's army attempted to enter its territory in pursuit of SSA-North forces. There were clashes following the expiry of the KIO's 25 May deadline for the army to withdraw its troops. In mid-June, amidst continued fighting, the KIO declared that 'civil war' had resumed and soon afterwards destroyed bridges in western Kachin state to cut the Myanmar army's lines of communication. The KIO refused a dialogue with the government, saying negotiations needed to involve the UNFC and could only be held in a third-party country with foreign mediators. While this implied that China might broker a ceasefire, Beijing's main concern – as China's Prime Minister Wen Jiabao reportedly told Myanmar's President Thein Sein when the latter visited Beijing in late May – was apparently that Myanmar should protect joint infrastructural development projects, including oil and gas pipelines, hydroelectric power plants and roads in Kachin state. The revival of widespread and intense conflict with the government had severe repercussions for large numbers of ethnic-minority people. Even before the upsurge in fighting during 2011, the UN Refugee Agency reported that approximately 150,000 refugees from Myanmar were living in camps on the Thai side of the border. Moreover, there were numerous reports of Myanmar government troops committing serious human-rights abuses, including using civilians as human shields, arbitrary arrest and torture, forced labour in support of military operations, and sexual violence. In the absence of major political change at the centre, there seemed little prospect of an amelioration of the conflict.

Singapore: signs of change

In the general election of May 2011, Singapore's electorate provided the People's Action Party (PAP) administration, which had governed the city-state since 1959, with its biggest political shock for decades. Against a background of increasingly intense and uninhibited use of the electronic media for political discussion, and of widespread popular frustration with a government that was perceived to be 'out of touch', particularly in relation to housing costs, inadequate public transport, failure to control inflation, and the negative impact of an influx of immigrants and foreign workers on ordinary Singaporeans' interests, a new generation of voters (more than one million of whom had not voted previously) gave the PAP its lowest share of the vote since independence in 1965, electing the largest cohort of opposition members of parliament since 1963.

The main beneficiary of the shift in Singapore voters' sentiment away from the PAP was the long-established Workers' Party (WP), which gained a Group Representation Constituency (GRC) comprising five parliamentary seats, as well as a single-ward constituency. The WP gained an additional two seats for non-constituency members of parliament (NCMPs), under a scheme originally instituted when the opposition was weaker in order to provide token parliamentary representation. The Singapore People's Party also secured an NCMP seat. Among those government MPs who were defeated, George Yeo, minister for foreign affairs and ironically a would-be reformer and one of the PAP's more popular ministers, stood out as a major loss for the government. Three days after the election, Yeo claimed that 'as the campaign went on we heard the growing cry from the heart'. Reiterating his earlier call for the PAP to transform itself, he went on to argue that 'we are entering a new phase in Singapore's political development. How we respond ... will decide Singapore's destiny.' But while Yeo spoke of continuing to contribute to public life and it was rumoured that he might stand for election as Singapore's president (in succession to S.R. Nathan, whose term was set to in August 2011), he soon made it clear that he did not see this as an option.

Though the opposition gains were not as great as some informed observers had expected, the 2011 election nevertheless constituted a watershed in Singapore's politics. While the PAP, with 81 seats, still held a clear majority it was widely expected that the new, much stronger opposition would challenge the government on the full range of issues of popular concern once parliament reconvened, probably in September or October 2011.

Indonesia: problems beneath the surface

By many measures, Indonesia has appeared increasingly successful under the leadership of President Susilo Bambang Yudhoyono since 2004, particularly when compared with its apparent political, social and economic disarray during the early years following the overthrow of long-term authoritarian leader President Suharto in 1998. After relatively slow economic expansion in 2009, in 2010 GDP growth returned to the 6% level of 2007–08. Foreign investment rose 52% during 2010, and in 2011–12 the economy was expected to grow even faster. The country's membership of the G20 grouping recognises its overall economic success, and by 2010–11 it was sometimes referred to as an honorary member of the BRICs category of large, fast-growing states. However, Indonesia's economic success clearly derived mainly from the prevailing boom in energy and commodity prices, and many economists argued that it needed to attract much greater investment in labour-intensive sectors including transport, food and manufacturing if high growth rates were to be sustained. Other serious challenges for the economy included widespread corruption, bureaucratic inefficiency and an infrastructure strained by economic expansion.

Indonesia has also registered successes in the political sphere, including institutionalising democratic elections and an accountable government, thoroughgoing withdrawal of the armed forces from government, and the resolution of the separatist war in Aceh and large-scale communal violence in eastern Indonesia. In addition, there has been a large-scale process of administrative and fiscal devolution to sub-provincial entities which has undermined secessionist impulses around the country's periphery, though this process has reputedly also spread money politics, waste and inefficiency. A further important element of Indonesia's overall success has involved its counter-terrorism campaign, which has received substantial support from Australia, the United States and other countries concerned since the 2002 Bali bombings over its potential as an incubator of violent Islamic extremism. By 2010, more than 560 terrorist suspects had been brought to trial and most had been sentenced. However, reports suggested that extremist ideology justifying violence still fermented among convicted terrorists held in Indonesian jails, and that many of the approximately 250 who had been released were unreformed.

The lethal simultaneous terrorist attacks on two hotels in central Jakarta in July 2009 gave new impetus to the Indonesian security forces' counter-terrorist activities and led to the arrest of hundreds of suspected militants. In February 2010, counter-terrorist police closed down a terrorist training camp in Aceh, and subsequently arrested more than 120 suspects linked to the camp, as participants in training or as financial supporters, the latter including cleric Abu Bakar Bashir, who was widely believed to have been the 'spiritual leader' of the former regional terrorist network, Jemaah Islamiah, and who had been imprisoned between 2002 and 2006. Re-arrested in August 2010, and initially charged with leading fundraising efforts for the Acehnese camp, in June 2011 Bashir was sentenced by a court in Jakarta to 15 years in prison on a charge of inciting terrorism.

Following a major bank robbery in Medan by militants linked to the camp in Aceh, in September 2010 paramilitary police mounted multiple raids across North Sumatra and Lampung provinces, in the process killing three terrorist suspects, capturing another 15, and seizing weapons and explosives. Three days later, gunmen struck back, killing three policemen. Following these shootings, National Police Chief General Bambang Hendarso Danuri claimed that Indonesian militants were seeking help from the Middle East in order to start 'urban warfare'. In response, the police-led but inter-departmental National Counterterrorism Agency (Badan Nasional Penanggulangan Terrorisme or BNPT), established in August 2010, for the first time in almost a decade involved military-intelligence and special-forces personnel in operations against suspected terrorists.

Among the alleged terrorists hunted by the Indonesian authorities was Umar Patek, thought to have been a leading figure in the 2002 Bali bombings and believed as late as November 2010 to be hiding in the Sulu archipelago in the southern Philippines. However, on 25 January Pakistani security forces apprehended Umar in the town of Abbottabad and captured him alive. Given the US military action that killed Osama bin Laden in the same town on 2 May, Umar's earlier capture there raised interesting questions. While some reports suggested that Umar and bin Laden had intended jointly to plan spectacular terrorist attacks to mark the tenth anniversary of the 9/11 attacks, such speculation probably exaggerated and dramatised the danger Umar had posed. In reality, Umar was probably in dire straits by the time he was captured. Shortly after the US raid, Indonesian Defence Minister Purnomo Yusgiantoro did claim that Umar had been planning to meet bin Laden. But, more specifically, Indonesian officials said that Umar and his wife were seeking bin Laden's 'support and protection'. This seemed to fit with reports that an innocent local man had taken Umar and his Filipina wife into his home after finding them begging for food on the street. In July 2011, Umar remained in Pakistani custody. He apparently confessed under interrogation by Pakistani intelligence to involvement in the Bali bombings, and supplied information on attacks planned against Australia and other countries. But while Indonesian officials also interrogated Umar, Jakarta showed little enthusiasm for bringing him to trial at home. According to retired General Ansyaad Mbai, head of the BNPT, a trial for Umar in Indonesia would be 'like fresh air for remnants of the terrorism network'. It seemed that Umar might remain in legal limbo in Pakistan indefinitely.

With many major terrorist figures linked to the once-powerful Jemaah Islamiah network either killed or captured, it became clear during 2011 that terrorism in Indonesia was assuming a new form. Lax law-enforcement since the end of the Suharto era, combined with widespread poverty and unemployment, have encouraged the emergence of fundamentalist groups that have, with substantial impunity, used vigilante tactics as part of their push for Indonesia's transformation into an Islamic state. As well as conducting 'sweeps' against what they see as manifestations of immorality such as karaoke bars, vigilantes have victimised religious minorities, and notably the Ahmadiyyah community since the Indonesian Ulema Council condemned it as an 'heretical sect' in 2005, a development on which the government remained silent. In 2008, a mob of Islamic zealots in Jakarta attacked a peaceful demonstration in support of Ahmadiyyah, while police stood by. In October 2010, a 200-strong mob looted homes and burned down a school and a mosque belonging to Ahmadiyyah in Bogor. In early February 2011, this combination of bigotry and official indifference climaxed with the beating to death of three Ahmadiyyah adherents in Banten, West Java, in front of several hundred bystanders, some of whom used their mobile phones to film the violence, a graphic video later being posted on the Internet. Again, the police made no serious effort to protect the victims, and leaders of the Prosperous Justice Party – the country's leading Islamist party and a member of the ruling coalition – claimed that acts of 'blasphemy' had provoked the attackers. When 12 men were brought to trial for the killings in April, a 2,000-strong crowd prayed and chanted Koranic verses outside the court in a display of solidarity. Extremists – often citing their concern over 'Christianisation' as justification for their actions – also targeted Indonesia's sizeable Christian minority, particularly in West Java, where they attacked numerous churches. In September and October 2010, there were serious clashes between Muslims and Christians in the working-class Jakarta suburb Bekasi, raising fears of wider conflict between the communities. In April 2011, a 1,000-strong crowd, demanding the death sentence for a Christian accused of blaspheming Islam, attacked a courthouse and churches in Central Java.

This apparently widening atmosphere of lawlessness, in which it seemed possible for extremists to use violence with relative impunity, may have contributed to a new outbreak of Islamist terrorism, perpetrated by small groups whose members belonged to legitimate, if extreme, 'above-ground' militant bodies such as Abu Bakar Bashir's Jamaah Anshorut Tauhid and were not linked to known terrorist organisations. In mid-April, a suicide bomber exploded himself at a police mosque, injuring 30 people. Subsequently, police arrested 25 people connected to the bomber and revealed that they were looking for another 15 suicide-vest bombs. Later in April, just before Easter, an investigation into a letter-bombing campaign the previous month led the Detachment 88 police counter-terrorism unit to uncover a major bomb plot targeted at a 3,000-capacity church in Serpong, West Java, 20km from Jakarta. The would-be terrorists had allegedly planned to film and broadcast the attack, which was intended to include explosion of an underground gas supply near the church. The discovery led to a massive deployment of police (20,000 in the capital alone) to protect churches across the archipelago over the Easter weekend. However, it was ever more apparent that managing internal security effectively would probably require Indonesia's government to contain the vigilantism and lawlessness that provided the breeding ground for the new-style terrorism that emerged in early 2011.

The Philippines: political drive needed

Many Filipinos had high hopes for the presidency of Benigno Aquino III, who took office for a six-year term in June 2010. Much of Aquino's popularity derived from his family background: after security forces acting on the orders of then-dictator Ferdinand Marcos murdered his father, opposition leader Benigno Aquino, Jr, on his return to the Philippines in 1983, his late mother, Corazon Aquino, led the 1986 People Power revolution and was president from 1986 until 1992. He also benefited from the unpopularity of his immediate predecessor, Gloria Macapagal Arroyo. However, the new president's first year in office turned out to be less than inspiring, with the new leader apparently focused overly on pursuing corruption allegations against Arroyo and insufficiently on delivering substantive policy changes deriving from his reform agenda, which notably included strengthening the country's economy. Despite encouraging GDP and export growth figures, the economy continued to trail those of other Southeast Asian countries by many indices: unemployment and poverty remained rife. By May 2011, apart from the annual budget, no major new legislation had been passed and Aquino was facing criticism for his reputedly relaxed work ethic.

Less than 4% of foreign direct investment in Southeast Asia was directed to the Philippines between 2007 and 2010, and the country's poor internal security contributed to the lack of investor confidence. While an incident in August 2010, when eight tourists from Hong Kong taken hostage by a former policeman died during a botched rescue attempt, highlighted the shortcomings of the security forces, the country's three major long-running insurgencies continued to pose the most serious internal security problems. However, in view of the economic as well as human costs of the four-decade long conflict involving the New People's Army (NPA) which had not only resulted in an estimated 40,000 deaths but also impeded investment in resource-rich areas, a significant early initiative by Aquino was to revive peace talks with the left-wing rebels after a six-year interval. Following a confidence-building Christmas truce, in February 2011 teams from the Philippine government and the National Democratic Front (the political umbrella organisation of the NPA) met in Oslo and agreed to complete their peace negotiations within 18 months. Specifically, they agreed to complete and sign Comprehensive Agreements on social and economic reforms in September 2011, on political and constitutional reforms in February 2012, and on the ending of hostilities and the disposition of forces in June 2012. However, mutual distrust evidently remained between the two sides, and armed clashes continued in numerous provinces between government forces and the NPA, which retained an armed strength of around 4,000 guerrillas, during the first half of 2011. Elements within both the Armed Forces of the Philippines and the NPA remained uncommitted to the peace process, and ensuring that ceasefire violations did not derail efforts to achieve a settlement would clearly be a major task as negotiations progressed.

Aquino's administration also restarted peace talks with the Moro Islamic Liberation Front (MILF), which has sought political autonomy for the Muslim population of the southern Philippines. In February 2011, government and MILF representatives convened in Kuala Lumpur for their first negotiations since the last round collapsed in 2008. The two sides agreed to extend the mandate of the International Monitoring Team (IMT), which supervises the ceasefire between government and MILF forces and is sponsored by the Organisation of the Islamic Conference. The Malaysian army provides leadership and military observers for the IMT, but it also includes military and civilian personnel from Brunei, the European Union, Japan and Libya (it was agreed in March 2011 that the five-strong Libyan army contingent would remain with the IMT despite the conflict in Libya). Suggesting that Jakarta saw the new talks as holding substantial potential, in March Indonesia indicated its interest in joining the IMT.

At the February meeting, MILF submitted a 'comprehensive draft', and there was agreement to meet again in late March, although in the event the next round was delayed until the end of April. MILF emphasised that, apparently at least in part due to pressure from Malaysia, it had abandoned its bid for an independent state, and would be content with autonomy in Mindanao, allowing Manila to retain control over defence, foreign affairs, currency and postal services. By early May, MILF frustration with Manila's slow response to its proposal was apparent, the front's chief negotiator warning that his organisation would abandon the talks unless the government quickly submitted its own proposal for a settlement. Despite a commitment to do so at the next round of talks in late June, the government failed to produce its counter-proposal, choosing to delay this until the next meeting, planned for early August. This delay indicated doubts on the government's part about MILF's reliability as a negotiating partner in light of apparently serious splits within the organisation. Shortly before the February talks, MILF leader al-Haj Murad admitted that Ameril Ombra Kato, who had led a revolt against the MILF leadership in 2008, had now left MILF with more than 1,000 armed personnel to form the Bangsamoro Islamic Freedom Fighters (BIFF). Subsequently, Manila emphasised – and perhaps exaggerated – the threat that this renegade group posed to the peace process. A further complication was the defection of some MILF units to the Moro National Liberation Front (MNLF), from which MILF had split in 1977 and which had agreed a peace settlement with Manila in 1996. These defections took place in the context of clashes in early 2011 between elements of MILF and the MNLF, and various local militias and private armies over land disputes and other local problems. For its part, MILF played down the significance of the defections from its ranks, but it did provide elements on the government side opposed to the peace process with a justification for foot-dragging.

Meanwhile, there was no sign of abatement in the lethal campaign waged by the Abu Sayyaf Group (ASG) in Basilan and Sulu in the country's far south, despite Manila's continuing major commitment of troops, supported by the United States' *Operation Enduring Freedom – Philippines*, which has involved the deployment since 2002 of US special-operations troops to advise and train the Armed Forces of the Philippines (AFP) in the region. While the AFP managed to kill or capture several alleged ASG leaders during the course of its offensives (which displaced large numbers of civilians, including 100,000 people in Basilan in January–February 2011), Abu Sayyaf continued to mount improvised-explosive-device attacks and targeted kidnappings. The ASG, reputed to number less than 400 members, was linked to the bombing of a bus in Makati, Metro Manila, which killed five people in January 2011 (remarkably, the day before three ASG members were convicted of an almost identical attack in the same area five years previously), and the bombing of a church on Jolo on Christmas Day. It seemed clear that the military campaign against ASG was doing little more than containing the terrorist group's activities. However, the new talks between Manila and MILF promised change in the southern Philippines' social, economic and political environment on a scale that might help significantly to undermine the conditions in which the ASG survived.

Regional cooperation stymied by a border conflict

Since 1967, when the grouping was established, relations among ASEAN member states have always featured elements of tension and conflict in various forms, as well as cooperation. However, while certain members may have figured in the worst-case military planning of others, and there have been armed clashes resulting in fatalities in the past (notably the Battle of Border Post 9631 between Myanmar and Thailand in March 1992), the deterioration of relations in 2010–11 between Cambodia and Thailand over a territorial dispute on their border was unprecedented in its intensity and duration.

There had been tensions on the Thai–Cambodian border since 2008, deriving essentially from Thai activists' reaction to Cambodia's success in July 2008 in securing the designation of the 1,100-year old Preah Vihear temple as a World Heritage site. In the view of some Thai nationalists, this development effectively compromised Thai claims to sovereignty over land adjacent to the temple. As a result, both sides deployed additional military units to the border area, and there were armed clashes in October 2008, April 2009 and January 2010, by which time five Cambodian and four Thai troops had been killed. The Cambodian government's appointment in November 2009 of deposed Thai Prime Minister Thaksin Shinawatra as an economic adviser further damaged bilateral relations: both countries withdrew their ambassadors. Full diplomatic relations were restored in August 2010 and in December Cambodian Prime Minister Hun Sen said relations with Thailand were 'normal' after a series of meetings with Thai Prime Minister Abhisit. However, the arrest of seven Thai activists on Cambodian territory in late December soured bilateral relations anew, complicating efforts to manage the territorial dispute, particularly in the sense of increasing the pressure on Thailand's army to adopt a tough posture on the border. In early February 2011, there was fighting on the border for several consecutive days, leaving eight Cambodian and two Thai troops dead, and more than 90 soldiers and civilians wounded on both sides. UN Secretary General Ban Ki-moon called for 'maximum restraint'.

Alarmed by this conflict between two member states, Indonesia – then chair of ASEAN – offered to mediate. The UN Security Council urged a permanent ceasefire and backed ASEAN's mediation efforts. While Cambodia described itself as 'at war' with Thailand and asked for UN peacekeepers, Bangkok responded that third-party involvement was unnecessary. However, at an emergency meeting of ASEAN foreign ministers in Jakarta on 22 February which followed a ceasefire, the Thai and Cambodian ministers both agreed to the deployment of 30–40 Indonesian military and civilian monitors on the border. It soon became clear, though, that the Thai army had no intention of allowing Indonesian monitors into the border area; moreover, the army refused to attend meetings of the Thai–Cambodian General Border Committee in early April. There were further serious clashes on the border in late April, this time for four days running at Ta Krabey temple, 200km west of Preah Vihear, resulting in more soldiers killed on each side; Cambodia claimed that Thailand had used cluster bombs and chemical weapons in the fighting, which the Thai armed forces denied. There was also more fighting near Preah Vihear, and then in late April and early May again at Ta Krabey and nearby Ta Moan.

Probably as a result of pressure from other ASEAN member states, the two sides reached a tentative truce in advance of the ASEAN summit meeting in Jakarta from 7–8 May. The border conflict overshadowed the summit, but while the two countries' prime ministers met on the sidelines there was no breakthrough beyond agreement on a 'package of solutions'. Phnom Penh's submission on 28 April of a petition to the International Court of Justice (ICJ), asking for elaboration of the ruling in 1962 under which it awarded sovereignty over Preah Vihear to Cambodia, promised to complicate matters further. The ICJ was due to give its verdict on 15 July, and seemed likely to place one side or the other in a difficult position. Thai Minister of Defence General Prawit Wongsuwon's statement on the sidelines of the IISS Shangri-La Dialogue in early June that the ICJ would have no authority to order Thai troops to withdraw, and that Thailand would not comply with any such order, brought a swift rebuke from Phnom Penh. Ultimately, however, the change of government in Bangkok as a result of the 3 July elections, which brought to power a party better disposed to accommodation with Cambodia, probably held the key to achieving a more peaceable modus vivendi.

Peaceful relations among ASEAN member states were clearly desirable if the association was to be able credibly to meet its objective of becoming an 'integrated community' by 2015. Against the background of not just the Thai–Cambodian dispute, but also persistent problems in implementing agreements on economic integration, ASEAN Secretary-General Surin Pitsuwan attempted in June 2011 to manage expectations regarding the ASEAN Community. In his assessment, 2015 'will not be an absolute cut-off date … it is going to be a work-in-progress … not an end-date. A lot of work needs to be done.'

The evolving regional order and the challenges it posed to the security of Southeast Asian states was one important reason for ASEAN to strive for greater cohesion and unity. China's assertiveness in relation to its territorial claims in the South China Sea showed no signs of abating, and formed part of a wider pattern of behaviour that also affected the East China Sea, where it drew protests from Japan. In March 2011, the Philippines complained about alleged Chinese harassment of an oil-exploration team. In May, and again in June, Hanoi claimed that Chinese vessels interfered with exploration vessels inside Vietnam's Exclusive Economic Zone. These incidents prompted concern in Washington, and in June a US Senate resolution deplored China's use of force in the sea. While Chinese civilian auxiliary vessels (though possibly acting under naval direction) were responsible for the controversial incidents, and in June China's Maritime Surveillance Force deployed its largest patrol ship in the South China Sea, the People's Liberation Army Navy also flexed its muscles there, for example with major exercises – described by Beijing as 'routine' – in April and June 2011. But other states also staged naval exercises in the South China Sea – for example, India and Singapore in March 2011, the Philippines and the United States in June, and Australia, Japan and the US in July – exacerbating concerns in the region and beyond about the possibility of conflict arising out of accidental maritime confrontation in the absence of agreements on avoiding incidents and other maritime confidence-building measures.

Australia, New Zealand and the Southwest Pacific

Australia: political and strategic balances

Prime Minister Julia Gillard, who replaced the ousted Kevin Rudd in June 2010, survived an exceptionally close election two months later. The Labor Party lost its outright majority in parliament, but Gillard was able to form a minority government with the support of three independents and a Green party representative.

Gillard struggled to consolidate her position, despite an efficient response to weather-related natural disasters in early 2011, including a cyclone hitting the Queensland coast and flooding in the three main eastern states. Erratic policy on carbon pricing to tackle climate change and evidence of wasteful spending in fiscal stimulus programmes to keep the economy growing through the 2008–09 global financial crisis caused a loss of public faith in the Labor government's overall competence. Towards mid-2011, opinion polls showed Tony Abbott, leader of the conservative opposition coalition, in a position to win if a collapse of support for the government in parliament were to force an election. From July 2011, Gillard's dependence on the Greens was due to increase when their swelled numbers in the Senate (the upper house) gave them a swing position on legislation.

Among the issues confronting Gillard's government was a growing debate about Australia's strategic position amidst changes in the balance of power in the Pacific region. The prospect that American power in the Western Pacific is headed towards a relative decline was put sharply by Hugh White, Professor of Strategic Studies at Australian National University (ANU) and a former senior defence official. In a provocative study for the

Melbourne periodical *Quarterly Essay* in September 2010, White wrote that China could already challenge American sea control 'where it matters most' – in waters close to China. 'A peaceful new order in Asia to accommodate China's growing power can only be built if America is willing to allow China some political and strategic space,' he wrote. 'Such concessions do not often happen. History offers few examples of a rising power finding its place in the international order without a war with the dominant power.'

White saw a choice between an American retreat, a deal to share power with China as equals, or a deepening competition for primacy. The emerging power balance in the Asia-Pacific was more multipolar than the US–Soviet contest during the Cold War. 'The best outcome for Australia would be for America to relinquish primacy and share power with China and the other major powers in a Concert of Asia,' White argued. He said Canberra should use its influence in Washington towards this end, including urging the United States to adopt an overt policy in favour of Taiwan's 'eventual, peaceful and consensual' reunification with the mainland.

Carrying on this theme, a February 2011 assessment by the Australian Strategic Policy Institute, a Canberra think tank, said the global financial crisis had 'compressed' changes that had already started, 'accelerating the long-running shift in power away from the Western world and towards developing nations'. Asia was moving towards a 'multipolar, balance-of-power strategic environment', away from US regional primacy, though the United States would hardly disappear from the scene. China would struggle to replace America's regional leadership, especially as its recent assertive actions in the South China Sea and around the disputed Senkaku/Diaoyu islands looked 'opportunistic rather than visionary'. India and Japan would emerge as major regional factors – with Japan looking 'more like an Asian actor and less like a Western ally' – while a second tier of powers including South Korea, Indonesia and Australia would be increasingly active, in various partnerships.

The response from the Australian and New Zealand governments to such strategic forecasts has been to try to apply the brakes to regional shifts, encouraging the United States to return to more active regional engagement. The annual meeting of US and Australian foreign and defence ministers in November 2010 produced a pledge to collaborate further on regional security, as well as agreement on a partnership to address the 'increasingly interdependent, congested, and contested nature of outer space'. In practice, this will see a new space tracking facility at the joint very-low-frequency radio station at Exmouth, Western Australia, which allows communication with submerged submarines. Aside from an innocuous role in tracking space junk, it will have a particular focus on covering the 'southern trajectory' of potential ballistic missiles from North Korea.

The US and Australia also agreed that American forces could store equipment and supplies in Australian cities such as Darwin and Townsville, to help with faster responses to natural disasters and ease logistical demands for joint exercises. They agreed on more frequent US patrols and port calls at Australian bases by US Navy ships, and more exercises with Australian and other regional forces, including those of Indonesia and Singapore.

A tighter embrace of America had strong political attraction for Gillard, who needed to shake off a reputation as a left-winger lacking familiarity with foreign policy. Addressing a joint session of the US Congress in March 2011, she declared that 'we are with you' in a time of strategic and economic uncertainty. On her first major trip within Asia, she pointedly went to Japan and South Korea before visiting China. In Tokyo, she focused on greater defence and intelligence collaboration, opening the possibility of Japanese forces joining exercises in Australia. In Seoul, she announced new annual bilateral meetings of defence and foreign ministers similar to those held with Japan and the United States.

A tougher stance towards China seemed to resonate with the Australian public, despite the knowledge that China was buying a quarter of Australia's exports, generating some $10,000 per Australian household in 2009–10, and was the source of Australia's largest cohort of foreign students and the fastest growing tourist numbers.

An April 2011 survey by the Lowy Institute, a think tank, found 52% of respondents saying they would support sending Australian troops to join the defence of South Korea in the event of an attack by the North, increasing to 56% in case of intervention by Beijing on the side of Pyongyang. The Institute detected concern among Australians about China's assertive behaviour. While three-quarters of those polled thought China's growth was good for Australia, 44% thought it likely China would become a military threat within 20 years, but principally because they saw Australia becoming drawn into a conflict between China and the United States.

Such worries have been tempered by Canberra's public refusal to see conflict as inevitable, thus avoiding the need to choose sides. Cooperation with the United States in Iraq and Afghanistan has allowed Canberra to keep its alliance credentials burnished, while positioning itself as an honest broker between Washington and Beijing (to the extent it has the ear of either).

For its part, the Chinese leadership overlooked annoyances such as visits to Australia by the Dalai Lama and the exiled Uighur leader Rebiya Kadeer, and focused on the economic relationship. Beijing has maintained annual visits by at least one member of the Politburo Standing Committee, including rising stars Xi Jinping and Li Keqiang. Canberra's approach, as shown in a speech by Gillard in Beijing in April 2011, has been to draw a link between Chinese's new prosperity and the implicit regional security underpinnings provided by the United States and its alliances, but to say that these arrangements are open to Chinese participation – though the steps towards this are left vague. 'China, now more than ever, is an active participant in global and regional architecture, helping shape it and in turn being influenced by it', Gillard said. 'As China's role in the world grows, so its role in supporting the international system will grow.'

With annual consultations already taking place between Chinese and Australian defence chiefs, Gillard also suggested raising the tempo of bilateral naval exercises and giving them a more combat-related focus, including live-firing drills. But her agenda for jointly pursuing mutual interests focused on North Korea and on getting Beijing to use its influence to persuade Pyongyang to scrap its nuclear-weapons programme.

Gillard meanwhile quietly dropped the proposal by Kevin Rudd, her predecessor, for a new Asia-Pacific security organisation, which had gained little traction in regional capitals. She noted that, with the inclusion of the United States and Russia from 2011, the East Asia Summit (EAS) would comprise all the region's key countries. From the politically safe area of natural-disaster response, she suggested, the EAS could move on to 'other regional challenges, such as maritime security'.

New Zealand: in from the cold

A visit to Wellington by Hillary Clinton in November 2010 marked what New Zealand Foreign Minister Murray McCully called 'turning a new page' after 25 years spent in the wilderness due to the country's ban on entry by nuclear-powered or nuclear-armed vessels and Washington's resulting suspension of obligations under the ANZUS Treaty.

Although the two foreign ministers' 'Wellington Declaration' on a new strategic partnership did not mark a return to the close three-way alliance established by the treaty, and relations looked to remain a level below those between the United States and Australia, it meant that joint training, exercises and intelligence sharing would be restored, along with annual political-military talks. New Zealand did not look to set to obtain a free-trade agreement with the United States but was to be included in the yet-to-be-negotiated Trans-Pacific Partnership, a trade arrangement with several Asian countries.

The Clinton–McCully meeting was preceded by release of Wellington's first Defence White Paper for a decade, with an emphasis on strengthening capabilities to deploy forces around the South Pacific and contributing modestly to coalition operations further afield, while maintaining protection of New Zealand's own territory and exclusive economic zone. While this would not mean restoration of abandoned capabilities such as fighter/strike aircraft, it would see continuing investment in two frigates to maintain interoperability with US and Australian forces, an increase in the army's highly-regarded special forces, and new long-range transport aircraft and air surveillance platforms.

New Zealand's White Paper also saw the international order as more uncertain over the next 25 years, with a shift in economic power, emergence of new military technologies and growing terrorism and proliferation threats. 'The United States is likely to remain the pre-eminent military power for the next 25 years', the paper observed. 'But its relative technological and military edge will diminish.'

The document saw New Zealand and its territories as unlikely to face any threat, but likely to feel growing pressure on its maritime resources. Illegal migration was likely to grow, amidst greater fragility of South Pacific island states. The resilience of those countries and the effectiveness of regional institutions looked to remain under pressure. Likely tasks in and around New Zealand and the South Pacific would form the basis for choosing military capabilities, but with new configurations that would allow defence forces to deploy more troops on overseas operations for longer, 'add weight' to Australian operations, and contribute to regional and international obligations.

In February 2011, New Zealand was struck by disaster when an earthquake devasted the centre of Christchurch, the second largest city, killing 181 people.

Southwest Pacific: China's growing presence

The Pacific island nations, ranging in size from Papua New Guinea's 6.6 million people to Niue's 1,400, have increasingly become an arena for diplomatic competition, despite a tacit agreement between Beijing and Taipei to end their attempts to buy recognition. The advent of new economic powers, especially China, is weakening the influence traditionally wielded by former colonial powers or trustees such as Australia, New Zealand, the United

States and France. China's trade with the region jumped 50% to $3.66 billion in 2010, according to its ambassador in Fiji, augmented by donation of conspicuous public buildings in regional capitals and supply of uniforms and other low-level military kit. In September 2010 a two-ship training squadron of the Chinese navy visited Papua New Guinea, Vanuatu, Fiji and Tonga as well as Australia and New Zealand, the first such calls in the island states.

In Papua New Guinea, Chinese corporations have moved into nickel and other resource projects, and Chinese demand has boosted prices of tree crops, contributing to five straight years in which economic growth has outpaced population growth. The anticipated revenue stream from ExxonMobil's $16 billion liquefied natural gas project, due to come on stream later in the decade, has begun to overshadow the importance of Australia's A$450 million a year foreign-aid programme. As the ANU's *Pacific Economic Bulletin* points out, foreign aid, which represented 12% of Papua New Guinea's gross national product in the early years after independence in 1975, is now about 4% and dwindling. A joint Australian–Papuan review of Canberra's aid programme in 2010 found 'a perceived lack of impact and failure to obtain value for money', with too much recycled back to Australia via well-paid 'experts' who were unable to prevent 'large-scale corruption'.

Australian banks and the national carrier Qantas have been reducing investments in the South Pacific, while an influx of Chinese traders (many of them illegal immigrants) are taking over retail sectors once dominated by Australian trading firms. There has been some backlash at street level – riots trashed Chinese shops across towns in Papua New Guinea in 2009 after a clash between Chinese and local workers at the Ramu nickel project near Madang, run by a Chinese state-owned company. Riots in the Solomon Islands capital Honiara in 2006 torched businesses run by new Chinese investors and shopkeepers. But the new sources of investment and aid have been welcomed by political elites tired of lectures about better governance.

None have been more grateful than Papua New Guinea's Michael Somare and Fiji's Commodore Frank Bainimarama. The latter has been moderately successful in using post-colonial resentments and Chinese aid to undermine the sanctions applied against his military regime, installed by coup in December 2006. The sanctions were imposed by the 16-nation regional grouping, the Pacific Islands Forum, with strong encouragement from Canberra and Wellington. The forum expelled Fiji in 2009 over its failure to hold promised elections, but Somare and Bainimarama have been drivers of the Melanesian Spearhead Group, an alternative sub-regional alignment whose headquarters building in Vanuatu was built by China.

Chapter 10

Prospectives

The assertion of people power across the Arab world and its possible spread to other regions was a defining feature of the year to mid-2011. For the coming year, the defining question will be what sets of personalities stay in power and who assumes, and for how long, the mantle of power in affected countries.

In a time so consumed by the collective popular desire for change and democratic representation that characterised the Arab Awakening, what is remarkable is the persistent importance of personalities in shaping international relationships. Analysts ask how relations are between one leader and another – Obama, Medvedev, Karzai, Zardari, Hu, Sarkozy, Cameron, Assad, Khamenei, Netanyahu, Abdullah, Singh, Lee, Lula, Merkel, Mugabe, Chávez, Santos – the names seem to stand so often as synonyms for their countries even in this age of mass communication and institutionalised negotiations. This is so because personal relationships remain a central barometer of the quality of international diplomacy and of regional exchanges.

There is a natural tendency, even a need, to collude with the arrangements that throw up one leader as opposed to another. Yet the preferment that a foreign country bestows upon a particular leader always risks causing problems when change occurs; less so between democracies, which move easily between and through electoral cycles, but certainly between them and other countries whose political systems respond to more unpredictable rhythms. Politicians, whether of democratic or autocratic stripe, grow accustomed to the foreign leaders with whom they deal. But when personal relations between leaders become the totality of the foreign-policy exchange, there are problems when one quits the scene. Similarly, when countries rely too long on one powerful or charismatic leader, the leader's departure can expose the institutional vacuity and weakness of a fragile or a badly governed state.

Just before Europe began experiencing the movement of its own geostrategic tectonic plates, Margaret Thatcher, then the British prime minister, famously said of the leader of the Soviet Union, Mikhail Gorbachev: 'We can do business together'. There was an instinctive sense that a person could make a difference; and that the business that could be done might lead to change that was positive, even if its scope was at the time not foreseen.

Doing business with leaders in countries who sit atop unhappy or repressed populations has always been, and remains, a necessary expedient of international diplomacy. Some in the West found this convenient when the leader was sympathetic to a Western point of view and the populations were judged to be less so. Where the situation was reversed and the leader was unsympathetic to Western attitudes, diplomats comforted themselves with the thought that perhaps the populations, released from the shackles of state control, would become 'pro-Western'. These thoughts were less frequently in the minds of non-Western states as they dealt with each other. For them, the public diplomacy favoured by Western diplomats was just intervention by other means; dealing with the centres of power and seeing in them the entirety of a state's external expression was natural for leaders who ran only partially democratic states, or who were plainly autocratic.

Hence the dramatic shock to the Western encounter with the Arab Middle East when presidents began to fall in 2011. The ease with which, as it was perceived, US President Barack Obama let Hosni Mubarak fall after 30 years as Egypt's ruler was a special affront to leaders, especially in the Gulf, for whom personal diplomacy and state interaction are near-perfect synonyms. For them, the fact that the United States felt the need to move with the flow of peacefully expressed popular will, and that in backing a transition it was supporting the Egyptian military, with whom it had been as much in cahoots as with Mubarak himself, were mere debating points. The judgement was that the United States had abandoned a friend. It had acted unreliably. Foreign policy towards the United States became, for a moment, reduced to a loyalty test: the pledge of internal allegiance that was asked of the domestic population would now be asked of Washington itself.

There were complex motivations for the dispatch of the Saudi-led Peninsula Shield Force into Bahrain once it appeared that the government in Manama had lost control of the streets, but one important intent was to show the United States that kingdoms would not be so easily challenged as republics. This demonstration was felt necessary, despite the fact that Washington had no strategic incentive to see anything other than a happier accommodation between the ruling family in Bahrain and its youthful, mixed-faith population. Still, recent history had shown the Arabs that the United States could give Iraq, a majority Shia state, over to Iran – as they saw the outcome of the 2003 US-led invasion. This meant that any reform championed by Washington was perceived as signalling an intention also to hand Bahrain over to the Islamic Republic, given that any political modernisation would translate into greater empowerment of the Shia population. Ultimately, there will need to be a Bahraini solution to a Bahraini problem, even if that solution has to find its place within a larger Gulf framework. The tragedy is that the initial protests in Bahrain were not uniquely sectarian, but were inspired by the wider trend in the region to seek faster general political reform.

In fact the gap between ruler and ruled in the Middle East lay exposed by the different interpretations that leaders and the people on the street had, not just of the nature of the changes called for, but of the mood that protesters wanted to capture. While for years Arab leaders had paid tribute to the idea of the 'Arab nation', they had an overriding interest in distinguishing their own state from others in the region. Conversely, as much as citizens saw themselves as belonging to a particular state, they also felt a common bond with Arabs elsewhere. The state was not always seen as the most important tie for them personally. So once the Tunisian regime began to topple, Arab leaders argued that their own countries were not like Tunisia, but their citizens thought: if Arabs in other countries could do this, why not us? While leaders thought themselves exceptions from a rule, their people wanted to help create and benefit from modernisation and change.

Six months after the start of the Arab Awakening, every state had again become exceptional, and no general rule could be relied on. Tunisia had overthrown its president, but not yet gained a new system; Egypt was similarly caught between the past and an uncharted future; Bahrain, Libya, Syria and Yemen were each individual cases. The wider geopolitical impact of these incomplete revolts and counter-revolutions will take time fully to be felt. But the presumption that the Middle East has changed definitively, and has a chance to change further, is the only safe strategic bet. The region's geopolitics are still in flux, but those both within and outside the region who will navigate them best are those able to show strategic flexibility, and who can develop options for themselves.

Saudi Arabia was angered by the US stance during the Arab Awakening, yet announced that prospective purchases of American arms would reach $90bn from the previously agreed $60bn. Defence is still in effect a US monopoly, despite the desire of most Gulf countries to diversify their strategic connections and deepen them with the rising powers of Asia. The Arab Gulf countries have a 'look East' policy in mind as they seek to strengthen interactions with India, South Korea, China, Japan and Australia. South Korea, through its sale of nuclear power-plant technology to the United Arab Emirates, has become a strategic actor in the region; India's defence cooperation agreement with Qatar equally demonstrates an interest to become more directly involved in the security of a region that contains so many of its own nationals. China's substantial economic interests in the region will inevitably lead it to take strategic decisions, or at least be subject to strategic pressures from countries that are competing with each other – Saudi Arabia and Iran – in the Gulf. The souring of US–Gulf relations does not yet put in question the primacy of the US regional security role, but it does strengthen the magnetic attractions of Asians as alternative partners. The next year will see an attempt by the Gulf states to find more ways to engage with Asia, where they will find sympathetic, and non-interfering, potential allies.

While the Arab Awakening upset the domestic and regional certainties on which so much of Arab politics had been based, the fear emerged that Islamist parties would gain greater hold on the political systems that emerged from the rebellions. Tunisia and Egypt, and others too, might become subject to the organisational power and emotional pulls of Islamic groups that were better able than others to organise politically. Iran's hand was seen behind the events in Bahrain, even though domestic dissent needed no assistance to take shape or express itself. Perhaps Iran might seek to exploit the situation but it, too, has vulnerabilities that limit its capacity to take strategic advantage of the meltdown of regional regimes.

The appeal of Iran is in fact eroding. While the Islamic Republic traverses the dangerous fault lines of Middle East politics with cunning tactical efficiency, it is not in itself a trend-setter and can, as much as other states, be caught by surprise when definitive strategic shifts take place. Certainly the costs to Iran of pursuing an aggressive strategy during the Arab Awakening and its aftermath are high, given both its own occasional vulnerability to popular protest and the fractious nature of relations within the Iranian leadership. Iran's non-state allies have also now to hedge their positions if they are to keep up with popular trends.

In Palestine, Hamas appears to be shifting its political affections from both Syria and Iran and getting closer to Egypt. In Lebanon, Hizbullah needs to ensure that it poses not just as a resistance force but also as a supporter of positive change: if the group is too linked to the repressive stance of Syria, supported by Iran, it loses a measure of its purchase on the Lebanese psyche and is left only representing a sectarian point of view. Set against this is a contrast: while Iran often proves itself to be risk averse, Hizbullah has more risk-taking tendencies and might provoke a crisis. In general, these trends mean that the Israeli–Lebanese–Syrian balance is very much in play and that the risks of conflict in the Levant are high. Even were Hizbullah to lose its Iranian patron, a war with Israel remains possible if the group were to feel the need to assert its special resistance role.

In these times, then, it is hard to see which of the region's great powers will emerge able to shape strategic outcomes. Iran is hobbled by internal leadership disputes and by its unsatisfactory hold on a young population. Its nuclear programme continues to make strides and serves as a signal source of pride as well as an ever-present fuse for potential war. Missile testing, increasing stocks of enriched uranium and suspicions of a possible resumption of design work on a nuclear weapon will push Iran towards a crisis with the international community, which in turn will prefer engaging in the tactics of diplomatic delay rather than military confrontation. But Iran's possible brinkmanship on the nuclear file will not strengthen, and indeed could shrink, its aspiration to play a genuinely influential regional role. Saudi Arabia's ageing leadership takes initiatives on regional issues, but its ability to sustain diplomatic action and drive towards decisive and satisfactory outcomes is in doubt. Saudi strategies in Iraq and Yemen have not yet delivered results in line with declared interests or in a manner that strengthens Riyadh's regional role. Continued courtship of Pakistan assures Saudi Arabia of a potentially important military ally, but that association alone, given Pakistan's diminished status, hardly burnishes its regional crown. Meanwhile, there are expectations that after the 2011 elections there will be a renaissance in Egypt's power and influence regionally, especially if a genuinely new government is able to operate internationally with the full-blooded support of its newly enfranchised large population. For that to happen, the election process would need to proceed without major controversy, and a figure with the charismatic authority to represent a newly empowered country would have to emerge. These remain high hurdles. The dynamism and diplomatic athleticism of Qatar can frequently mesmerise; but despite its wealth and imagination it can only fix problems, not set the strategic agenda, unless it teams up with a larger state. Iraq is diminished, and Turkey perhaps too keen to have good links with everyone to shape the region's destiny.

In this milieu, politics and international affairs in the wider Middle East will be buffeted by domestic, regional and international winds; those richer countries with stable systems will be able to withstand the jolts, while poorer nations with unsettled political systems will be in regular search of strategic benefactors.

A United States apparently determined to 'lead from behind' as it did in Libya, committed to withdrawal from Afghanistan, absorbed by domestic economic challenges and facing a presidential election campaign in 2012 will in most strategic theatres be reacting to, rather than shaping, events. Clearly dispirited by the apparently declining capacity in European states to mount expeditionary military operations, Washington did not wish to play the lead role in Libya once the Arab League, the GCC and both the United Kingdom and France declared their willingness to address the problem. Still, even though Obama did not want to intervene, the United States was dragged in as a super-enabler of the no-fly zone. As for Afghanistan, the decision in effect to drop the ambitious counter-insurgency strategy, withdraw forces and prioritise a political solution will be seen as signalling the end of a decade-long US interventionist policy. Along with the choices on Libya, it also indicates the start of a period when regional solutions to regional problems become not just the motto of local powers, but, to a degree, a more central aspiration of US strategic policy.

The tug of US regional involvement is hard to shake, and will perhaps be hardest in the Asia-Pacific. The region is hugely sensitive to the appearance of US strategic prevarication, but top American officials have reasserted regularly the 'resident power' status that Washington wishes to maintain. The Taiwan Strait remains a flashpoint. Delicate cross-strait relations, much improved in recent years, could be shaken in the event of a DPP victory in the next Taiwanese presidential elections. North Korea has made it a recent habit to provoke South Korea. The very reluctance of Seoul to respond so far heightens the likelihood that a further act of military aggression will be met forcefully, as South Korea's doctrine of deterrence and public opinion will demand a forceful answer. The United States could be involved in either of these contingencies. Added to the previously set menu of East Asian crises are the recent challenges surrounding the South China Sea. China appears determined to protect its interpretation of territorial claims, while other claimants, particularly Vietnam, are equally keen not to be bullied into submission. The United States regularly speaks of the freedom of the seas, just as China speaks of the need for non-interference in territorial disputes. There is every possibility that these two devoutly held tenets will in time come into conflict. To avoid unfortunate clashes, the Asia-Pacific would do well to advance more steadily towards a code of conduct on these claims that is comprehensive, universal and has genuine adherents.

This is all the more important as China moves into a period of leadership transition that will not just see two new figures assume the roles of president and premier, but also a generational change in the management of the world's most populous country. On the one hand, the leadership is bound to be more confident about the place that China is taking in the global system and the international respect it can rightly demand in view of its growing economic heft. On the other, it will notice the weakness of its own regional and broader 'alliance system' which does not include a prestigious membership. It could also face domestic difficulties if any elements of the present economic boom were to suffer from a bubble effect, or if needed economic reforms go awry. Close engagement with China will remain a high strategic priority for most outsiders, and the effort to establish a strong personal relationship with the new leaders will be robust. In 2012 and into 2013, assessing the new Chinese leadership and the characters of those it may choose as its trusted internal advisers will be a foreign-affairs priority and a strategic parlour game of some importance.

People will also look to see what changes take place in the Russian duopoly of power. The US–Russian diplomatic 'reset' was much predicated on the person of President Dmitry Medvedev, in whose continued prominence the United States, in particular, has much invested. Were Prime Minister Vladimir Putin to return to the presidency, the reset might be put at risk. Modernising Russians and concerned outsiders might smell the whiff of Brezhnevian stagnation with the return of Putin, and feel diffident about engaging fully. As the drawdown from Afghanistan continues, however, the need to collaborate with Russia in building – with Central Asian states, India, Pakistan and Iran – a stronger regional support system for the still deeply wounded Afghan state is considerable. Diplomatic efforts in many other crises will also turn on the personalities in power in Moscow, and on the relations that others can build with them. Continuing to build the NATO–Russia Council into a partnership of equals will help to institutionalise healthy cooperation that is not dependent on the quality of personal relationships.

US relations with the crucially important intelligence and military institutions in Pakistan were strained and then virtually snapped in the wake of the successful operation that led to the killing of Osama bin Laden in Abbottabad. The task of US–Pakistan cooperation on Afghanistan, on nuclear safety and on counter-terrorism is now very hard to carry out. Within Pakistan, the military has lost a great deal of prestige, while the civilian leadership is not yet in a position to assume effective leadership. The space for militant organisations to operate has expanded and the pockets of liberal political thinking and activity are bound still to shrink. While quiet progress has been made in the back channels of India–Pakistan talks, the precarious domestic position of Prime Minister Manmohan Singh in India and the suspicion that a debilitated Pakistani state cannot deliver make a breakthrough difficult to achieve.

The lesson of 2011 that most leaders got used to repeating to themselves and their supporters was that good governance and economic strength are amongst the most prized strategic assets. The two tend to go together, but good governance cannot just be achieved by managing a country like a good company for healthy profits. The electoral losses that the PAP ruling party in Singapore took on 7 May 2011 were a sharp reminder that, in today's world, delivering fantastic economic growth is not enough; managerial competence is not the only measure by which governments will be tested. The people power expressed in the Middle East had its small reverberations in Asia and leaders were reminded that man does not live by bread alone. The taste for greater democratic freedoms having touched the heartland of the Asian paternalist political culture, the pressure for political modernisation is bound to persist. It remains the case that democratic societies evolve best when civil society is sophisticated and political competition is based on clearly defined platforms. Democracy relies on the floating voter. Political competition that is founded on things hard for a person to change – such as tribe, ethnicity, sect or religion – is just demagoguery by other means.

Weak economic performance in Europe has, despite good governance in other areas, crippled Europe's strategic ambitions. This is not just because defence budgets are dwindling and expeditionary capabilities are being reduced, but also because Europe's political leadership is having to put its financial house together again. So, too, is the United States, where the administration had to do such eccentric battle with its opponents on the small matter of the debt ceiling. Given these preoccupations, the appetite in the West ten years after the 9/11 attacks to engage in active forward and anticipatory self-defence is lower than it has been for generations. The case for liberal interventionism can still be made, but the cry has to be loud and the cause irrefutably perfect for it to be answered positively. Other societies are unlikely to promote it any time soon. For proof one need only look at the votes in the UN Security Council on the Libya operation, where so many of the pretenders to permanent membership of the Council abstained.

Political leadership of the most inspiring kind, moved only for the best of intentions, backed by a real zeal for implementation, and fuelled by genuine, not imagined, capacities, will be hard to come by in 2012, when so many key political transitions, through elections, managed hand-overs or deaths, natural or forced, seem bound to take place. In this transitional phase, the West is suffering from strategic arthritis and resignation, the rising powers of the East from strategic growth pains and indecision. In this context, the room for rogues and mavericks to manoeuvre for their own gain is expanded. Who will come to the rescue if these start doing real damage, and how effectively, is anybody's guess.

Index

Figure acknowledgements

Page 120, Figure 1: Adapted from Peter Good et al., *An Updated Review of Developments in Climate Science Research since the IPCC Fourth Assessment Report* (AVOID Consortium, 2010), p. 18.
Page 121, Figure 2: Adapted from Joel B. Smith et al., 'Assessing Dangerous Climate Change through an Update of the Intergovernmental Panel on Climate Change (IPCC) "Reasons for Concern"', *Proceedings of the National Academy of Sciences*, vol. 106, no. 11, 17 March 2009, pp. 4133–7.